Working Dollars

HERSCHEL HARDIN

Dollars

The VanCity Story

Douglas & McIntyre
Vancouver / Toronto

96 97 98 99   5 4 3 2 1

Douglas & McIntyre Ltd.
1615 Venables Street
Vancouver, British Columbia
V5L 2H1

Canadian Cataloguing in Publication Data

Hardin, Herschel, 1936-
  Working dollars

  ISBN 1-55054-432-2
  1. VanCity Credit Union—History.   2. Credit unions—British Columbia—Vancouver—History.   I. Title.
HC2039.C2H37 1995   334'.22'09711   C95-910540-9

Editing by Brian Scrivener
Front cover photos by B. Clark/Tony Stone Images (top) and
   T. Bruckbauer/Tony Stone Images (bottom)
Jacket design by Peggy Heath
Typeset by Brenda and Neil West, BN Typographics West
Printed and bound in Canada by Friesens
Printed on acid-free paper ∞

The publisher gratefully acknowledges the assistance of the Canada Council and of the British Columbia Ministry of Tourism, Small Business and Culture for its publishing programs.

Contents

Acknowledgements

THIS STORY OF MANY OF VANCITY'S people and of others who were involved is largely based on extended interviews. My thanks to all those I talked to for their time and especially for their frankness. I can't name them all here— virtually everyone who comes up in the story, and is still alive, was interviewed, many over multiple sessions. One person in particular, however, Wayne McKay, deserves special thanks. The interviews with Wayne served as the original reference source for the 1965-1990 period. Wayne, sensing the drama of the VanCity story, was the one who pushed for a history in the first place; this book owes its start to him.

My thanks also to the many VanCity and B.C. Central staffers who helped me put my hands on documents I needed and often directly ferreted out information for me. John Lee and Susan Konopacki in the CEO's office were stalwarts. Editor Brian Scrivener provided crucial assistance, advising me as I cut the manuscript down to size and made the many editorial judgements required along the way. My research assistant, Cherie Summers, as well as my wife, Marguerite, helped with research. Of all those who contributed, I owe most to Gail Smith, my typist, who transcribed the interviews—binder after binder, filling a whole shelf, as it turned out.

Finally, I want to acknowledge the role of the VanCity board in deciding to underwrite this history, and acknowledge, also, the arrangement between the credit union and myself. My contract with VanCity gave me complete freedom, my only obligation being to turn in a final manuscript at the end. It became clear, too, as I went along, especially from the openness of the interviews, that everyone wanted me to tell the real story as I saw it. Consequently, the book I wrote is the book you have in hand. *Working Dollars* is, in that sense, a commissioned history unlike what one might expect; the author was allowed to catch contemporary history unrestrained. The telling of the story, of course, could only benefit.

Herschel Hardin
West Vancouver, B.C.
July 15, 1996

PART ONE

1946-1955

CHAPTER 1

Makovichuk Becomes a Member

IT WAS SIX IN THE MORNING on an overcast October day in Vancouver, 1946. Martha Makovichuk struggled out of bed in the house on Sophia Street in the East End, which her mother owned and had left in her care. Martha was thirty-three years old, a slim brunette. She washed, ate breakfast and did her chores. The skirt she planned to wear that morning had a few creases from the previous day, so Makovichuk, fastidious as ever, pulled out her ironing board and gave the skirt a lick with an iron.

By eight-fifteen she was heading to Main Street, where she caught the number 3 streetcar going north down Main. Tickets were four for a quarter. She was lucky, though. A weekly pass, costing $1.25, came free with her job. The number 3 streetcar always had a lot of passengers. Not too many people whom Makovichuk knew owned cars. Even if they had a regular job, where could they possibly get a loan to buy a car? Certainly not at the banks, least of all at the main branches downtown, with their mammoth columns and sepulchral solemnity.

So the streetcar made progress slowly, ingesting and expelling passengers, through Chinatown, turning left at the majestic Carnegie Library, where it eased around the junction in the rails and proceeded west down Hastings. By the time the streetcar reached Cambie and Hastings, it was almost nine o'clock. Makovichuk hurried into the lobby of the Dominion Bank Building and took the elevator up to the offices of the British Columbia Credit Union League, where she worked. The Dominion Bank Building had a presence of its own. Its pillars in the front—stuck into the small entrance in a half-hearted attempt to add grandeur—looked ridiculous. But its twelve storeys of cut stone had their own, serious geometric beauty, which intimated that business—transactions, documents, downtown savvy, money changing hands—permeated its corridors.

Makovichuk quickly got down to work. First she made up the bank deposit, a duty left over from the previous afternoon. The B.C. Credit Union League was the central organization of the credit union movement in the province. It serviced about 145 small credit unions that had been formed since the first—the Powell River Credit Union—had been chartered in 1939. The fact that the League existed at all seemed a wonder. It now had a supplies department with a printing room that provided deposit slips, loan application pads, notepads and passbooks to its member credit unions. Orders and money came in regularly. The League also published a little magazine called the *B.C. Credit Unionist* and had an addressograph machine to help get the magazine into the mail for each credit union member. No one could deny it was a going concern. Some of its member credit unions actually had assets of over $100,000.

The managing director of the League was Jack Burns, a B.C. Electric Railway Company "motorman," in other words a streetcar driver. Burns had a gruff facade. Makovichuk, who knew that Burns's bark was worse than his bite, thought him a kind man. The night before, Burns had written a couple of letters in longhand and left them for her. Makovichuk typed them out on the old Underwood, a heavy clunker with a long arm protruding from its carriage.

Sometime during the day, a Mr. C. P. Crad walked in the door. He had three $100 bills in his hand, representing his fortune. He was looking for a credit union. He had just arrived from Saskatchewan and knew about such things. He wasn't an employee of a company or a member of a labour union or church that already had a credit union. The only one he was eligible to join, Makovichuk told him, was something called Vancouver City Savings, which was open to anyone resident in Vancouver. It was just starting. The charter hadn't even come back from Victoria yet.

"Where do I deposit my money?" Crad asked.

Makovichuk had no idea. She had never seen $100 bills before; most people hadn't. In fact, she had never seen $50 bills, despite being in her early thirties. Jack Burns was in the office in the middle of a split shift, talking to supplies manager Art Copp in the print shop at the back. Makovichuk hurried over to Burns. "There's a man in the other room with three $100 bills," she explained, "and he wants to join the new credit union."

"Take his money," Burns barked.

"But I'm not a member," Makovichuk protested. "I can't do that."

"Well," Burns replied, "sign yourself up and then sign him up."

So she did, throwing in 50 cents for membership dues and $1 for a fifth of a share. Martha Makovichuk, a secretary, a woman of Ukrainian extraction, of no standing at all in the young but already proud British Columbia credit union movement, became book member number 1. When the charter came back from Victoria and the founding group learned what had happened—that numbers 1 and 2 were gone—they were furious. They drew lots for the numbers that followed. A couple of the charter's signatories, instrumental in putting the organization together, never forgave Makovichuk for the presumption. The more that Vancouver City Savings grew and astonished the city, the more her membership number 1 grated on them. But it was a good way to begin.

The new credit union, open to any resident of the city who walked through the door, was on its way.

CHAPTER 2

The Originals

THE STREET RAILWAYMEN—THE MOTORMEN and conductors who operated the Vancouver streetcar system for B.C. Electric—were a hotbed of credit union activity. Next to the Canadian Pacific Railway, B.C. Electric was the dominant corporate power in British Columbia. Where there was a strong corporate power in the province there was likely to be a strong labour union, too, and the street railwaymen were no exception.

Dick Monrufet was twenty-three years old when it all began in 1939. Monrufet was a conductor. His father, a Great War veteran and something of an activist, had always believed that if there was a job to be done, one got in there and tried to do something about it, and this had rubbed off on the son. Monrufet realized that the Street Railwaymen's Union was important for the motormen and conductors on the line, and he never missed their monthly meetings. At one of those meetings, a dynamic and determined socialist, Dorothy Steeves, the Co-operative Commonwealth Federation (CCF) member of the provincial legislature for North Vancouver, showed up as guest speaker. Steeves, a brilliant political advocate, had twice tried to get a Credit Unions Act through the legislature, as a private members' bill, and had twice been rebuffed. The Liberal government, however, subsequently brought in a bill of its own, in the fall of 1938. Listening to Steeves talk about the concept, Monrufet became more and more excited. "Holy mackerel," he thought, "this is for me. This is the way to go."

He approached Steeves after the meeting. She gave him a copy of the Credit Unions Act and suggested that the street railwaymen hold a study group to discuss how the legislation would work. Monrufet, another conductor named Farley Dickinson, motorman Jack Burns and several others latched on to the idea. After a few meetings, they decided to apply for a charter for a Stry (Street Railwaymen) Credit Union. They ended up with charter number 17, in 1940. Monrufet was Stry's first president—the president of an honest-to-goodness, incorporated, chartered, bona fide financial institution.

The sheer novelty of the idea was exciting—that motormen and conductors, and not just imposing officers of huge companies at the seats of capital like Montreal and Toronto, could establish and operate a bank. The street railwaymen, in fact, were gung-ho for anything new. They took pride in their boldness and militancy, even if it sometimes got them into trouble. The credit union concept was a progressive new idea. Talk about it bubbled through the ranks. Joining the credit union became the thing to do.

Monrufet, himself, was the youngest credit union president in North America—and fifty-five years later still claimed the record. Farley Dickinson was the original treasurer, the person who operated the credit union. He had been a school teacher in the British Columbia interior through the early years of the Great Depression. He then came to Vancouver to attend the University of British Columbia, where he earned a degree in agriculture. He worked nights as a streetcar conductor to help pay his way and stayed on after graduating. Streetcar conductor Dickinson was a go-getter and an intellectual ahead of his time.

He was a detail man and an idea man simultaneously. Dickinson ran the Stry Credit Union with imagination. He carried the entire "front-office" operation—records, membership lists, forms and all—in an old-style, multi-section, brown briefcase, which he took with him on his runs. Other Stry people could check the schedule to see what run Dickinson was on that day and when he would be passing the point most convenient to them. They would hop on the streetcar accordingly and do their business with Dickinson between stops. Since the motorman did the driving up front, isolated from the rest of the streetcar, the conductor at the back had his hands free. It was the original mobile banking service.

The whole idea of a credit union was, of course, to lend money. This was considered something of an adventure. In its initial days, the Stry Credit Union just collected money. Since B.C. Electric employees averaged $110 a month—a fair wage at the time and, best of all, regular—the deposits trickled in. Eventually, however, with money coming in, Stry had to decide whether to make a loan. There was a great debate among the directors about this. Should they make loans or should they not? Dickinson, ever the confident one, lost patience. "If we don't start doing these transactions," he said, "we'll never get into a proper operation. We're supposed to be gathering this money to help our members with provident and productive loans." Nobody had asked for a loan, however. "Let's go out and find somebody who would like one, then," Dickinson countered. One venture-some member finally stepped forward and applied for a loan to buy a small movie camera. A loan for a set of false teeth followed. Another early loan was for the purchase of a cow. You could still keep a cow in your back yard in Vancouver in those days, and a member needed one to help feed his large family. The directors soon got the hang of it. It wasn't long before five directors signed for a $500 loan from the Royal Bank—a large sum in those days—to boost the credit union's capital for lending to members.

Another earth-shattering decision involved the purchase of a hand-operated adding machine. Dickinson was doing all the calculations in longhand, which took a lot of time and was sooner or later open to mistakes. The directors spent a whole meeting arguing about the purchase.

One director, book member number 1, considered it an imprudent waste of members' money. It took forever to bring him around.

Dickinson's briefcase and the Vancouver back-yard cow were a long way from the beginnings of the credit union movement, yet the Stry adventurers knew they weren't just operating a credit union for street railwaymen. They saw themselves as part of a larger movement that already had a long history, which they had talked about in earlier study sessions, and whose drama added to their conviction and provided them with ongoing motivation.

Through a circuitous but clearly marked route, they could trace their origins to the mid-nineteenth century and three people: the British vision-ary Robert Owen and German pioneers Friedrich Raiffeisen and Hermann Schulze-Delitzsch. Owen inspired the weavers of Rochdale, England, to form the first modern-style consumer co-operative in the world, in 1844. The idea of co-operatives spread quickly throughout Europe. This early co-operative work involved the development of some key principles that later came to underpin credit unions: one member, one vote; democratic struc-ture; no discrimination, and member ownership and control.

Almost simultaneously, and independently, Schulze-Delitzsch and Raif-feisen were putting into place the first co-operative banking institutions. Schulze-Delitzsch, a Prussian economist, was jolted into action by the woeful condition of labourers and artisans in his state. He fastened onto the idea of co-operatives. He could not see any other way for small tradespeople to hold their own. He withdrew to his birthplace—Delitzsch, in Prussian Saxony—and devoted himself to organizing co-operatives and *Vorschuss-vereine* (literally, "advance-money societies," or loan societies).

Raiffeisen was mayor of a borough in Rhenish Prussia. A public servant, he was once described as a "kindly, cranky, half-blind, poor and chronically sick philanthropist." He became increasingly distressed by the plight of his impoverished peasant constituents. He attributed their hopeless situation to the absence of credit facilities; capital was being drawn away to the newly industrializing cities. Raiffeisen started the first agricultural co-operative bank in 1864, using the Schulze-Delitzsch model. By the time he had finished his co-operative work, he had developed 425 local banking socie-ties, a federation with an advisory service, a semi-monthly paper, a library and press, a training and organizing capability and an insurance service. *Darlehnskassenvereine*, or "loan bank society," was the official name for these societies. "Raiffeisen banks" is what they came to be called.

By a serendipitous coincidence, about a decade after Raiffeisen died, the work that he and Schulze-Delitzsche had done carried over into Canada. The conjunction of events began on the afternoon of April 6, 1897, in the House of Commons in Ottawa. Michael Quinn, a young, mustachioed opposition member of Parliament from Montreal, was holding forth. He had submitted a private member's bill aimed at relieving borrowers from having to pay exorbi-tant rates of interest. The government side, led by Wilfrid Laurier, wasn't particularly concerned. It had a comfortable majority. Laurier, distinguished in his grey frock coat, high collar, cravat and stick pin, was nevertheless paying close attention. On the floor between them, along with the Clerk of the House and others, was the French-language Hansard reporter, a former journalist from Lévis, Quebec, named Alphonse Desjardins.

"We have had cases throughout the country," Quinn declaimed, "particularly in the city of Montreal, in which a rate of interest equal almost to 3,000 per cent per annum has been collected." Other members in the House, reading their newspapers or signing their mail, suddenly raised their heads. Desjardins jumped in his seat, horrified by what he had just heard. "There was one notable case in Montreal within the last few days," Quinn went on, "in which a man obtained a loan of $150, and was sued for, and was compelled to pay, in interest, the sum of $5,000."

Desjardins was shaken. He had always had a well-developed social conscience. He thought of the workers and farmers in and around his native Lévis. He knew their problems first-hand—grinding poverty, large families with meagre incomes which made impossible demands on women, frustration, despair and often, as a result, drunkenness. He also knew that exorbitant interest rates—usury in short—were becoming an increasing scandal. He decided to do something about it. "For the love of God, let's begin," he mumbled to himself. Fortunately, he had lots of time on his hands. Debates in French were relatively rare in the House. Separated from his family, he was in the habit of spending his evenings studying social problems. He used his spare time now, amid the gothic beauty of the parliamentary library, to research old debates on interest rates and do book searches. He soon discovered the ghosts of Friedrich Raiffeisen and Hermann Schulze-Delitzsch, as if they were waiting for him to come calling.

The Raiffeisen model had spread through Italy and France with the help of the Roman Catholic church, and the Italian example in particular caught the attention of the deeply religious Desjardins. The church connection was useful in Quebec. Catholic church notables in Lévis were quickly brought on board. Desjardins patched together various elements of the European co-operative banks in drafting a working constitution. He got rid of the unlimited personal liability, which was part of the German model and which would impose too much risk on depositors. He called his new version a "caisse populaire"—a people's bank.

Desjardins became obsessed by the concept: one was either for Desjardins's caisse populaire or against it. His stiff chin, piercing eyes and severe mien said as much. The shy and sensitive dreamer, to those who knew him well, metamorphosed into an intense talker who would not accept that the notion of a people's bank was fantasy.

Part of his obsession was doing things right. He was constantly afraid the project might be discredited by mistakes.

He and his growing Lévis group went through eighteen study sessions before Desjardins was convinced that he had the concept and constitutional wording in order. The founding meeting was on a snowy December day in

1900. The operation itself began in Lévis on January 23, 1901, and the first deposit was 10 cents. The caisse operated out of a local workers' society office three nights a week and out of the Desjardins house during the day.

Desjardins moved forward cautiously. In the next four years, only two other caisses were established, both nearby—in Lauzon and Quebec City. Requests for caisses came in from about thirty parishes, but Desjardins wanted to make sure his system was working properly first. He did, however, keep spreading the idea in the poor countryside and city working areas. He also spent time educating potential movement leaders, including several of the clergy in Lévis and Quebec City. All the while, he was spending part of the year in Ottawa as Hansard reporter, which work was his main source of income, and making the 260-mile train journey between Lévis and the country's capital. His wife and family remained in Lévis. He made the trip, like a galley slave, for twenty-five years.

The last preparatory step, for Desjardins, was enabling legislation, to provide a legal footing for the movement. He organized a powerful lobby, including a strong eclesiastical wing. When Laurier and the federal government proved indifferent, he turned, successfully, to the Quebec legislature. With the necessary legislation in place, the movement spread quickly throughout the province.

Desjardins, growing in fame, exhausted himself travelling and organizing. In 1909, he was invited to organize a caisse populaire in New Hampshire. Because U.S. legislation prohibited the terms "co-operative bank" or "people's bank," the words "credit union" were chosen. The term had originally been used in a passing experiment in Belgium in 1848. Desjardins's work in the United States was backed by a millionaire Boston merchant, Edward Filene. Filene ended up hiring a young lawyer, Roy Bergengren, to expand the movement. Bergengren, like Desjardins, had the touch. By 1935, an average of one hundred credit unions were being opened every month in the United States and their Credit Union National Association, or CUNA, as it became known, was going strong.

One day, in those bleak depression years, Filene gave Bergengren a call. A few priests on the faculty of St. Francis Xavier University in Antigonish, Nova Scotia, led by Moses Coady, were organizing co-operatives. They were doing it through their extension department as "adult education." They were interested in credit unions. Coady had grim stories to tell of the plight of fishermen and farmers in his area. Filene thought it would be a good idea if Bergengren went up to Antigonish. Bergengren made the trip and explained the possibilities. Before long, Coady's department had established credit unions throughout the Maritimes. The credit unions were set up on a community basis, in the context of a broad co-operative strategy. This grassroots co-operative organizing became known across the country as the "Antigonish Movement."

Early in the decade, in British Columbia, a few utopian socialists, anguished by the depression, met in South Burnaby and decided to establish a co-operative. They called themselves the Army of the Common Good and their organization the Common Good Co-operative. Their long-term objective was to use co-operative means, province-wide, to settle land and undertake industrial production so that the needs of the vast ranks of the unemployed and their families could be met. They began with self-help work parties and barter, exchanging everything from seed potatoes to scrap leather belting for mending boots.

The Common Good Co-operative had all the appearance of woebegone and desperate futility, but by 1936 it had branches in Burnaby, Vancouver, Point Grey, New Westminster and North Vancouver. Also, the group had study materials from St. Francis Xavier University. It decided to establish a credit union—the first in the province, though it ended up with charter number 3. The original five members did not think it was legal to call their creation a credit union, since there was no legislation in force, so they dubbed it the Common Good Co-operative Association Credit Unit No. 1. It, too, looked pitiful to begin with. After two years, it had only twenty-five members. Total loans outstanding amounted to $115. To be altogether scrupulous in handling funds, the officers dutifully ran their Credit Unit No. 1 through an account in a local branch of the Royal Bank.

By the late 1930s, credit union organizing activity was mounting everywhere. Antigonish sent staff to the West Coast. They were instrumental in organizing the credit union in Powell River (charter number 1) and generated interest elsewhere in fishing communities up the coast. Pacific Stage Lines bus drivers had been running a small illegal credit union of their own in a corner of the bus depot, like a bookie joint, as an adjunct to the bus drivers' credit union in Seattle, and they were putting a credit union together. Postal employees, too, were at it. Fishermen's co-operatives along the coast asked the University of British Columbia's extension department to help them establish credit unions. The department, Antigonish style, sent out educational field workers.

Charting the trail from Prussia to Quebec to the United States to Antigonish to British Columbia was, for Monrufet and the rest of the Stry gang, like a litany. Monrufet never tired of explaining how "Old Alphonse," as he called Desjardins, operated at his own risk out of his kitchen in Lévis. This wasn't casual nostalgia. Monrufet knew that a familiarity with the history of credit unions, particularly with how the caisses populaires in Quebec had started and what they had done, was a key device in getting people to organize.

The Stry Credit Union was only a home base for the Stry people. The task of organizing and building credit unions had no bounds. The Stry organizers had two advantages. The demonstration effect of existing credit unions was powerful. Above all, people didn't need large sums of capital to start an operation. The young British Columbia credit-union movement, consequently, offered a rare open vista for enterprise driven by idealism. This meant, in turn, that a stream of people not enamoured of capitalism, or people stuck by class or happenstance in prosaic jobs, suddenly had the chance to do remarkable things.

For Monrufet and many others the war intervened, but the credit union movement grew nonetheless. By the time the war ended, credit unions were proliferating so fast that the movement was outstripping itself. At one stage, the League had to put a moratorium on the formation of new credit unions. "All of this, all of it, including the treasurers, was volunteer stuff," Monrufet recalled, and most of them didn't have any experience. Yet many were now dealing with serious money. Treasurers, directors, supervisory (audit) committees, credit committees and other volunteers needed educational programs. Credit union "chapters" were organized in various regions of the province to hold monthly meetings on different topics and bring people together. Monrufet became president of the Vancouver chapter. He remembered making sure all the members had a pad and pencil handy so that they wouldn't fail to report back to their individual credit unions on progress in the movement and on how things should be handled. He also made expeditions to help organize new credit unions.

The mushrooming of activity was "like a fairy story ... like somebody blowing up a bubble," he recalled. He was no longer working for B.C. Electric; he and his wife had bought a pet shop. He found himself relentlessly being squeezed between his credit union commitment and his own business.

Meanwhile, Farley Dickinson, the conductor-intellectual with the credit union in a handbag, seemed to be everywhere and doing everything. Dickinson had moved from the back of a streetcar to a job in the general ledger section at B.C. Electric's head office. The real Farley Dickinson, however, like some Phantom of Financial Institutions, would only arise in the after hours, in the dark evenings of the rain forest. Dickinson had turned over the work of Stry Credit Union treasurer to a lanky French Canadian, Joe Chaussé. This left Dickinson free for greater doings. Were some credit union's books in a mess? Dickinson would saunter forth, straighten out the books, give the volunteer treasurer a quick lesson on how to keep things in order henceforth and disappear into the night. Did the League need a treasurer? Dickinson was it. Later he became League president. At a certain point in any meeting he would announce, "I think it's time we had a little break, fellows," and produce a mickey of something strong from his coat pocket. Everybody would take a swig, and he would put the balance back in his coat.

In 1944, only five years had elapsed since the first fledgling credit unions had been chartered but, as Dickinson calculated, if you were going to have credit unions, there was no point in waiting to take the next step. Why stand in awe of the banking system? The League crowd, with Dickinson in the middle, established a central "bank." Its functions were to pool and invest credit union reserves, handle transactions with the chartered banks and redistribute surplus deposits from one credit union to another that needed extra loan capital. They called their new baby B.C. Central Credit Union. Dickinson was its manager for the first year, then took on the presidency for several terms.

The 1940s were glory years for thinking and devising. The idealistic Dickinson had in front of him a tabula rasa upon which he could apply a central idea—membership-owned credit unions. It was a philosopher's paradise, and Dickinson knew how to dream. Bill Ramsell, who was a member of the Dairyland Employees Credit Union and knew Dickinson through the League, remembered that in this developmental stage of the movement, Dickinson could go on without end, elaborating and planning. "He thought it was wonderful," Ramsell recalled. Dickinson was also, however, a diligent organization man. He had a strong grasp of detail and of how to solve problems, to the point where sometimes he could be a pain in the neck. "He was so goddamn busy," one of his friends put it, "that he didn't have time to follow through on all of his good ideas."

The excitement for Dickinson was in looking ahead. Ramsell, a route inspector for Dairyland, sensed that Dickinson was different from other people. He was a "great philosopher type," Ramsell explained, because he was always thinking and writing. Dickinson would telephone Ramsell at some godawful hour in the morning—one or two o'clock, when Ramsell was sound asleep—about some brilliant notion that he wanted feedback on. It never occurred to Dickinson that he should wait until the next day. Ideas, for Dickinson, had their own schedule. He was spending so much time in the League office, working into the late hours of the night, that Ramsell began to suspect he was the victim of an unhappy marriage and was trying to stay away from the house. His marriage was in fact unhappy. It didn't help soften the rumours that Dickinson had the reputation of being a ladies' man. Dick Monrufet, who knew him best, laughed at this image. Dickinson talked a great game, Monrufet said, but that was as far as it went.

Jack Burns, another member of the Stry gang, was spending a lot of time in the League office, too. Burns was the League's field secretary. He had earlier put in a term as president. "Field secretary" was an honorific title for somebody who was enthusiastic enough to do a lot of work and keep things going—volunteer managing director, in short. Burns was no refined ex-schoolteacher like Dickinson. He had worked first as a paperboy in Vancouver. He had been brought up on the streets and had a reputation as a streetfighter. He was aggressive and dynamic. He masterfully followed the politician's credo: "When in trouble, attack." His style intimidated people. He didn't shout much, but controlled meetings anyway. If he set his mind on something, he would rush out and plow through everything in his way to try to make it happen. Burns did not hold grudges, though. For Burns, you argued your case as hard as you could in debate. Since he liked talking, that meant a lot of words passed across the floor, too.

Martha Makovichuk, who worked for Burns in the League office, was struck by his intensity. If he thought of something that should be done, it was going to be done then and there. If he seemed a hard taskmaster, he was also hard on himself. He didn't hesitate to help Makovichuk out with routine tasks, if she had too much work in the office. It didn't bother him at all.

The credit union movement was something Burns could get his teeth into and make move. There were two schools of opinion about the wiry, intent motorman. One was that he was passionately committed to the movement. His enthusiasm and intensity said as much. The other, for exactly the same reason, was that he was out for Jack Burns. Since there was no way to get into the man's mind, it all depended on which way he rubbed individuals at the time.

Burns's reports as field secretary were strong and cogent analyses of weaknesses in the movement and what had to be done to correct them. He wasn't afraid of tough managerial decisions. When someone had lifted some money from an early credit union, Burns recommended prosecution, even though it might produce some bad publicity. Credit union members had to be protected, Burns insisted.

He, himself, was going flat out, a victim of overenthusiasm. He was travelling around the province, making field-work calls and attending individual credit union meetings. He represented the League at the newly organized Canadian Federation of Credit Unions and at CUNA conferences in Wisconsin. He was promotion and publicity manager of the League's magazine, the *B.C. Credit Unionist.* He also spent time on B.C. Central Credit Union, the Co-operative Union of Canada locally, and his own Stry Co-op, as well as on League committee meetings. By 1946, he was averaging four nights a week at meetings (about two hundred meetings a year) and often took in three meetings in a day—all the while working as a motorman, for which he had to get up at four-thirty in the morning. The League commitment, taking time from his streetcar shifts, was cutting dangerously into his earnings. He had almost no home life, although he was married and had three children.

Burns was not the only person travelling. New credit unions had been springing up so quickly that the inspector of credit unions, who had added the job to other duties, needed help and a superintendent was appointed. The position went to a burly, bespectacled, outgoing character, Tom Switzer, who a few years later became the inspector proper. Switzer was an old-fashioned father figure. He patrolled his territory in a sober, albeit rumpled, three-piece suit and a hat to match. Once, to make a surprise inspection in the Kootenays, he had to row across a lake. He wore the suit and vest. He did the same at picnics.

Switzer was enthusiastic, almost evangelical. He became so caught up in what the credit unions were doing that he began organizing them as well as inspecting them. He ended up as midwife to about eighty-five credit unions.

The League had another iron in the fire: co-operative medical and hospital insurance for credit union and co-op members. Public medical care did not exist in those days. Unplanned hospital and doctors' bills could destroy a family's finances. A committee had been struck in late 1944 to look into the insurance possibilities. It was chaired by a prairie native, John Hunter. Hunter was very quiet, but this was one case, as a friend said, where still waters did run deep. He thoroughly believed in co-operatives—a legacy of his prairie days. He was a bargeman, working the coast. Nothing would happen for hours on these trips, which gave Hunter plenty of time to read, reflect and jot down notes. By the time the League got together for its annual convention in the spring of 1946, eighteen months after the committee was formed, Hunter's health insurance plan was ready to go.

The 1946 convention, held at Powell River, was charged with electricity and all the more exotic because the only access to Powell River was by steamship. There was a sense of history in the air: Powell River was the home of charter number 1. There was also a sense that the participants were succeeding in doing something quite extraordinary. "The expectations!" Monrufet recalled of the movement's first days, beginning in 1939. "We used to dream great big dreams. We figured that one day we'd see the movement flourishing in the province, with 10,000 members and a million dollars in assets. We could see it in the far future, that if we were fortunate, we might be able to achieve it." Now, just seven years later, they already had 19,000 members and $1.7 million in assets.

Things were happening so fast that organizing credit unions had become something of a game. Gordie Allen, a teacher at Vancouver's Templeton High School, who became VanCity's nineteenth member, remembered joining as many credit unions as he could. It was what one did. It boosted the membership numbers and added a few extra dollars of share capital to start-ups. Allen's original membership was at the Kitsilano Credit Union, later absorbed by VanCity. After a while, accumulating memberships took on the appearance of a contest. Allen managed to get six memberships before he decided to rest on his laurels. Those who joined early enough received a founder's pin; this was a gimmick that came from the movement in the United States. Bill Ramsell had five founder's pins. If somebody didn't have a founder's pin, a newly organized credit union was found for the purpose. This exuberance meant that credit unions were sometimes formed before members were ready to manage them. As a result, they occasionally got into trouble, but the bonding seemed to protect them. Nobody lost any money.

There was much more to talk about in Powell River, however, than all the new credit unions. Umpteen committees, including several educational committees, reported and made recommendations. A lot of work had gone into the reports, so the delegates, well-informed, went through business item after item with competent dispatch. Vote followed vote. There was a growing feeling of being in charge. Even the announcement of the number of delegates, alternates and guests (125 in all) was greeted with applause. Jack Fortnum, the comptroller of the CUNA Mutual Insurance Society in

Madison, Wisconsin, was feature speaker. He was greeted with applause. Most important was the health insurance report, in which Hunter and his committee had developed detailed alternative insurance schemes, ready for the members' choosing.

The resolutions to adopt the plan and select a favoured scheme were passed in a wave of fervour. The delegates called it CU&C Health Services (for Credit Union and Co-operative Health Services). There was a problem with the plan, however. People had to be members of a credit union or a co-operative to join. This was all right for the residents of Powell River or Rossland, who had their small community credit unions, but it left most people in larger cities like Vancouver and Victoria out in the cold.

Evan Roberts, one of the conference delegates from Vancouver, was quietly listening to the CU&C debate when the implications of the problem hit him. He had been pushing for an open-bond or "community" credit union for Vancouver, which anybody in the city could join, but nobody had paid much attention to him. It was too unorthodox an idea. He thought he was right, however, and as his wife Nancy recounted, once he believed in something he could not be pushed off track. Now he had an extra argument behind him. If Vancouver had an open-charter credit union, then anyone in the city who wanted to join CU&C for medical insurance could qualify by joining the credit union first. He began discussing it with his gang—Jack Burns, John Hunter, Farley Dickinson and others—and suddenly they were listening. The key man was Burns. Roberts quickly got him on side. "Jack has a good head," he thought.

Roberts was an unlikely prophet. He was very tall, slight, long-faced, innocent-eyed and asthmatic. A touch of frost in November, haziness in August, a dog or a cat, or rich desserts, especially with nuts in them, set his asthma going. In the standard three-piece suit, he looked like a moon-struck choir boy who had grown too tall, too fast. Despite his asthma, he was extremely energetic, always on the go. "Go, go, go," Nancy Roberts described it.

He was an assistant foreman at Dairyland, conscientious and intrigued by the dairy business, particularly by the making of ice cream, which he managed. He liked things to be right. If they weren't right, he would stay as late as necessary to straighten them out. He was a workaholic. His two daughters did not see much of him when they were growing up. He was too interested in what he was doing for his own good—far too trusting and innocent, his family thought. "Honest John," his older daughter came to call him.

It was a mystery where the social commitment behind Roberts's credit union work came from. There was no family, church, political or labour connection. Perhaps, Nancy mused, it was because he had worked hard for everything he had, or because he favoured the underdog. He was a member of the Dairyland Employees Credit Union. He was also business manager of the *B.C. Credit Unionist*. He was always travelling to meetings at night.

"I gotta be at the meeting," he would say to Nancy. He had his heart in it and he liked it. They were good times, and the League crowd were a good bunch. They all worked together. "We had a good meeting," he would invariably report back. Even when the group went bowling or for coffee, they would begin talking and turn the outing into a meeting, impromptu. His own credit union, however, never sat right with him. The Dairyland Employees Credit Union was too limited. Roberts felt credit unions should be for everybody. "We have nothing in Vancouver for our neighbours," he kept saying. Returning home from Powell River, he kept up the argument.

"I'm convincing everybody that I talk to," he told his wife. "They're swinging. They know that what I say is right."

"You really must have given them a pep talk," Nancy replied.

"Oh, yes," Evan said, unassumingly. "I explained everything to them."

With Jack Burns also pushing the idea, enough key people were convinced. Nor did the group have to go through study-club sessions on credit unions. They already knew everything about the subject. It was just a matter of doing it. Doing it, however, was more revolutionary than it seemed.

The original idea of credit unions was that money would be lent on the basis of character rather than of wealth and property, that is, collateral. Character would be the lender's bond. Credit, in this way, would finally be available to those who needed it. The credit committee or the treasurer, by the same token, were expected to know enough about loan applicants—their upbringing, their work habits, their reliability—to make that judgement. This would be the case in, say, a small-town credit union, or even the credit union of a small city, or of a parish or a labour union. Main street, church hall and shop floor brought with them propinquity and familiarity. This was the essence of the idea of the "common bond," which, until then, was at the heart of credit union philosophy. People who knew each other and had ties to each other got together and pooled their savings for their common use.

But how does a treasurer judge the character of somebody walking in off the street, in a city of hundreds of thousands of people, wanting to borrow money? Traditionalists, for whom the "common bond" was the very working principle of credit unions—and the idea of the common bond was truly inspired—said it couldn't be done without the bond. To attempt it was a contradiction in thinking. Roy Bergengren, the famous CUNA man himself, in Wisconsin, had been against the idea of open-charter credit unions. "It may be accurately concluded from much experience," he warned in 1935, "that the open-charter credit union—that is, a credit union to which all residents of a relatively large community may belong—will not work well in practice." The B.C. Credit Union League was an active member of CUNA—it had joined almost from its inception—and the League people were all aware of the CUNA doctrine.

Most of the credit unions in Vancouver itself, moreover, followed the CUNA model and were based on a "closed bond," such as a workplace, like

Stry itself, or an ethnic affiliation, like the Edelweiss Credit Union. Anyone who didn't belong to one of those groups couldn't join. People were expected to get together with friends with whom they shared a bond in common and organize a credit union of their own. There were, at the same time, also a few small neighbourhood credit unions in the city and many community credit unions elsewhere. Credit unions for smaller places might be said to have a common bond based on their location. No matter how one stretched the term, however, one couldn't really say there was a common bond tying together 350,000 people of different backgrounds, religions, jobs and politics, even if they did live in the same city. The caisses populaires in Quebec had geographical common bonds, but they were based on well-defined parish limits.

Roberts and the other advocates of the idea could see Bergengren's reasoning. There were plenty of activists in the British Columbia movement, too, Dick Monrufet among them, who were leery of what was being planned and—given who might get into such a credit union—what it might lead to. The idea of the common bond was so strong that they could not quite grasp the nature of something so different. But what if the idea could be made to work? Well, then, the benefits of credit unionism could be spread much farther and much faster than anybody had ever imagined. Wasn't that worth attempting? Besides, if CU&C were going to get on its feet and do what it was supposed to do, it needed as many members as it could round up.

The decision to go ahead was fed, however, by something much deeper than a disagreement about the common bond. There was a noticeable and growing difference of approach between the Canadian and American credit union movements. American credit unions sprang up largely in the industrial sector of the U.S. economy. They were workplace credit unions whose closed bonds were associated with individual, privately owned companies. The Canadian movement, however, at least in the West, aimed primarily at the community and at broader co-operative doings. It had a good mix of credit unions. The community credit unions in British Columbia might have been located in smaller centres or neighbourhoods, but they were expressions of an open philosophy and a boisterous approach. This was part of the Antigonish co-operative tradition, too, which had fed the B.C. stream. At CUNA meetings, the rambunctious B.C. bunch were considered uncontrollable radicals.

Closed-bond versus open-bond arguments at this stage hardly mattered anyway, for the core group. The Powell River factor—the rush of enthusiasm from the conference—was at work. Jack Burns had been made managing director of the League at the conference and was now receiving a stipend for his time. Burns went to work on the new idea. The doubters, not openly opposing the project but still uneasy, stood back to see what would happen.

The charter for the proposed new credit union was drawn up by the end of September. Those who were around that evening signed, and others came in the next day. The blood lines of the new organization were in the names. Jack Burns, Farley Dickinson and Joe Chaussé were all Stry people. Bargeman John Hunter was the man behind cu&c Health Services. Jack Fortnum, the cuna Mutual Insurance fellow who had spoken to the conference, had struck delegates as a comer and was invited to become the first managing director of cu&c. He needed to join the new credit union in order to become a member of cu&c. His wife, Florence, also added her signature. Gordon Butcher, who worked for the Unemployment Insurance Commission, was League president and later succeeded Fortnum at cu&c.

Lin Brown—Dorothy Lindop Brown was her full name—was a field worker with the ubc extension department and had organized credit unions up the coast, Antigonish style. Bill Ramsell, the Dairyland member, was also, now, second vice-president of the League and the following year would become president. Bill McIntosh, a pipefitter originally from Saskatchewan, was slated to become the credit union's first treasurer. Jim Gaunt, who worked in the post office, was a director of the Vancouver Federal Employees Credit Union (Vanfed), the third-largest credit union in the province and the second to be incorporated, in 1939. Gaunt had been one of the more active delegates at Powell River.

Martha Makovichuk had taken to working overtime, making addressograph plates. The platemaking machine was such a noisy contraption that it was much easier to use after hours. During the day, if she were running the machine, she couldn't hear the telephone. As a result, she happened to be around on occasion when the group got together. She sat in on some of the meetings. She asked Burns now, hesitantly but with an edge of importunity, if she could sign the charter, and Burns said of course she could. The next thing she knew she was writing in her name. The two other signatories were Alfons Bruyneel, a director of the Rosary Credit Union and an accountant, and Stan Scanlon, treasurer of the B.C. Projectionists Credit Union.

Evan Roberts, the one person who could legitimately have claimed to have gotten the whole thing off the ground, missed signing the certificate. He had been called in to fix something, at a start-up ice-cream business he was helping, the night of the final meeting. The next day he was at his regular job at Dairyland. He didn't realize the charter was being signed. Although he would be on the first board of the new credit union as a director, he later was deeply hurt for having been overlooked for the charter signing because his role wasn't recognized with the others'. He wasn't the kind of person, though, to say anything about it at the time.

The group decided to call the new venture Vancouver City Savings Credit Union. Jack Burns put the document in an envelope and mailed it to Victoria.

CHAPTER 3

The Odd Couple

MARTHA MAKOVICHUK WAS A DETERMINED young woman. She had grown up on a farm near Hairy Hill, a hamlet about 110 kilometres east of Edmonton. Her father was a CPR section hand. Her parents' marriage didn't last, and when she was eight she was shipped to the Presbyterian Mission in nearby Vegreville. She missed the independent way of life on the farm. The mission was run regimental style. Chores were assigned, homework was assigned, bedtimes were assigned. You did what you were told.

The young Makovichuk, however, prospered. She was a tomboy. She skated, played softball and basketball and was on a girl's hockey team. After graduating from high school, she went to Normal School (teachers' school) in Edmonton. A $200 government loan covered her room and board for the ten months. She ended up in Golden Spike, a hamlet southwest of Edmonton, which, like other prairie outposts, was trying to survive the Great Depression. Farm children came to Makovichuk's school from several miles away in buggies or cutters, bringing along a sheaf of oats to feed their horses, which they tied up in the school barn. Makovichuk was the senior room teacher in a two-room school, teaching grades 4 to 10 inclusive. She had as many as forty-six pupils at a time. Supervising lunch hour and recess and organizing sports added to her duties. After six years, the workload had taken its toll; Makovichuk was a bundle of nerves. Her doctor told her to take a year off, and she went to Vancouver for a change of scenery.

She remembered her intensely patriotic spirit at the time. The war was raging. She had lost a brother-in-law in the war, in Hong Kong. She found herself a job with Kelly Douglas, the grocery wholesaler. Whenever she had a few extra dollars, she would send them to her two younger brothers or her sister in Alberta to help them make ends meet. But Makovichuk was unhappy. Her immediate boss, another woman, was hard to get along with. Makovichuk had a cousin who was a conductor at B.C. Electric and who knew Jack Burns and Farley Dickinson. A casual encounter on the street led to an interview and her job at the League.

Those were the days. Her pay was $125 a month, $35 more than at Kelly Douglas—a huge difference. It wasn't as good as what men were earning, but Makovichuk used to that. The school board in Golden Spike had paid her less than her male predecessor. "You couldn't argue," she remembered.

"The school boards were pretty well all male." Nellie McClung, she knew, had fought the good fight for women's rights, but it hadn't been enough. Still, $125 meant being truly well paid. It was work that meant something, too. Overtime was routine. "There was no such thing as overtime pay," she recalled, "and I didn't expect it."

She loved old-time dancing. Dancing was also a good way to meet men: in those postwar years, ballroom dancing was in fashion. One night, to escape an unwanted boyfriend, Makovichuk and a girlfriend jumped off the street-car downtown and dashed over to a dance at the Boilermakers Hall. It was the only place nearby they could think of. She met a carpenter's apprentice, a Eugene Mackie, whom she did allow to walk her home. They started going out together and then decided to get married. He happened to be a member of the long-established Vanfed credit union.

VanCity, on the other hand, whose transactions she handled at the League, was just a baby—really just a name and a charter. It consisted of the original organizers and a score of others who had liked the idea and become members. At year-end 1946, after three months of activity, a financial report was produced. Assets were $2,966.75. Loans outstanding were $1,200. Net profit for the three-month year was 83 cents. There were thirty-one members all told, including the fourteen who had signed the charter.

A net profit of 83 cents? Well, it was a profit. As for the assets, reaching the $1,000 mark, earlier on, had been a red-letter day. The volunteer treasurer, Bill McIntosh, had waved the financial statement in the air. Tripling that to $3,000 wasn't bad at all. As they all knew, a community credit union had no other way of starting except to start small. As with the whole movement, it was the future that counted or, more precisely in this case, how this particular idea of a credit union would capture the future. The incorporation form for credit unions in British Columbia required applicants to state how many members they expected to have. Burns, Hunter, Dickinson and the others had cockily estimated two thousand in "prospective membership" and a whopping ten thousand in "potential membership."

VanCity, too, was already doing things that just weren't done. The first loan it made was to a young woman who had stepped off the streetcar and walked into the League offices. She wanted a $100 loan. She wasn't a member; somebody had told her about something called a credit union upstairs in the Dominion Bank Building, where a woman, and not just a man, could get a loan. So there she was. "I dare you to lend me the money," her presence said, in effect. Jack Burns was on VanCity's original credit committee. He happened to be behind the counter when she appeared. Struck by the occasion, he signed her up and took the loan application. It caused a stir. "What the hell," said Burns. "It's only $100." The credit committee gave her the loan. There would be other loans to women in the early years, but very few, because they did not apply. Martha Makovichuk, herself, later took out a small loan.

The first annual meeting was held April 1947 in the Flack Building, just across Cambie from the League office, about six months into the young credit union's existence. Twenty-four people showed up, "half of them directors," Makovichuk quipped. There were just enough new faces, however, to establish the organization in earnest. Six new board members were elected as the original signatories, overcommitted, began to bow out.

Total membership was about one hundred by this time. By the end of the year, it was 333. Assets reached a magnificent $41,000, with $28,000 of that in loans. Word was getting around to just those people the credit union had been formed to serve—working people who would never think of approaching a bank manager for money. That October, the directors were even forced to limit individual loans to $100 because of the heavy demand and shortage of funds, and that $100 was a problem. Twenty members had to come in with an average $5 in savings each to provide funds for a $100 loan, and $5 a week or a month was a hefty saving for working people in those days. Borrowers were taken in turn and were obliged to wait while this deposit money trickled in. New members had to wait for a month regardless.

Makovichuk watched this progress with growing interest. She was VanCity's assistant treasurer and took minutes at board meetings. By this time, the League's days at the Dominion Bank Building were numbered. The landlord complained that the floor couldn't take the weight of the League's printing equipment. In late 1947, the League and B.C. Central Credit Union, and Makovichuk with them, moved holus bolus into a building of their own at the corner of Broadway and Quebec, a former machine shop, proudly renamed the Credit Union Building. For Martha Makovichuk, the credit union movement was now unstoppable.

It happened by magical synergy, or it would have been magical had it not been the outcome of days, months and years of talk and debate by the activists about the possibilities. The League, when it moved to Broadway and Quebec, established a separate credit union services section to act for VanCity and two other small credit unions in the same situation. Burns and McIntosh had put their heads together and worked it out. One of the strategic reasons for forming VanCity was to open the door, for Vancouverites at large, to membership in CU&C Health Services. CU&C and VanCity were now in the same building. People who had heard about CU&C and its non-profit medical insurance and had come in to join, but who weren't qualified, were sent down the hall to take out a membership in VanCity first. For the young credit union, this was a small bonanza—just what it needed to consolidate itself.

Martha Mackie, née Makovichuk, now was working full time for Credit Union Services and, with it, VanCity. Her boss, Bill McIntosh, a hard-drinking Saskatchewan native, was also now on a full-time paid basis. McIntosh was a signatory to the VanCity charter and an initial board member. His official title for each of the credit unions in the group, including VanCity, was "treasurer"—the label provided for anybody, paid or unpaid, who looked after a credit union's business. McIntosh's past was hazy. He had worked in a bank at one time, in Saskatchewan, although nobody was quite sure in what capacity. During the war he had been a pipefitter in Burrard Shipyards in North Vancouver. He was a member of the Plumbers and Steamfitters Credit Union, for which Credit Union Services also acted.

He always wore a tie, either with a suit or a sweater, befitting the dignity and seriousness of the credit-union movement—or at least McIntosh's notion of what a banker should look like. His shoes were polished. He got along with everybody, and with the ladies twice as well. He was especially charming because he was a small man and physically had to look up to most women. He wasn't much more than five feet tall and wore a size five boy's shoe. He had tiny hands, too, but he was wiry and tough. He also kept a bottle in his desk, handy for putting the seal on a particularly meritorious loan or for a snort or two, or three, with his pals from down the hall at the end of the day, or in the middle of the day if one of them dropped by.

For all of his small size, he wouldn't take anything from anybody. He was cocky, blunt, gregarious, moody, often cantankerous and bull-headed, but also kind and good-hearted. He would argue about anything at the drop of a hat. His mood changed according to the number of snorts he had consumed. He had a temper. He didn't take differences of opinion casually. If somebody on one of his boards took exception to the way he did things, McIntosh would reply that if they didn't like it they could find themselves a new treasurer, so they didn't take him on too frequently. He was an ardent credit unionist. He had been a director of the League and, in the early days, had helped out treasurers with their books on his own time.

McIntosh and Mackie made for an odd couple. Mackie's membership number 1 continued to rankle McIntosh, who was member number 4. His name for her was "Lady Kid." He refused to call her Martha. Every once in a while he would mutter aloud, "If Lady Kid here hadn't been so quick to sign herself up ..." or some variation thereof. Mackie, however, outspoken, was not one to be pushed around, either. She was also prim and proper. McIntosh's drinking habit did not bother her, but only as long as it did not interfere with business. She wore simple tailored clothes, preferring suits to dresses. See-through blouses, a growing fashion, were taboo—not that she would have indulged. Dress coats—what one wore on the way to work— were important to her.

She was friendly and quick-witted, and was soon as much of a fixture in the Credit Union Building as the man under the umbrella. The man under the umbrella was a logo, originated by CUNA, showing a smiling little man walking along, protected by his credit union umbrella from the rain of hard times, sickness and financial distress. Almost before she knew it she was explaining to people, who would tell her of their problems and hopes, how their credit union could help. By this time there wasn't too much she didn't know about the mechanics. She loved credit union work.

In one case, a woman had lost her husband as a result of an industrial accident. Their account had a loan outstanding of $324 against shares of $306. The woman had calculated that with another $18 she could at least square the account. One of the advantages of belonging to a B.C. credit union, however, was that its loans and shares were both insured up to $1,000. Mackie explained to the baffled widow that not only did she not have to repay the loan, which was insured, but also that the credit union would match the amount of her shares, because of the insurance. The woman found herself with a bit more than $600 to tide her over, instead of being $18 out of pocket—when even $18 was a lot of money. She could be counted on to tell family, friends and even strangers about her good fortune and how wonderful it was to be a credit union member.

The insurance coverage was provided by CUNA Mutual Insurance in the United States, CUNA's insurance offshoot. The B.C. credit union movement, taking advantage of the possibilities, introduced the Endowment Savings Plan. It was really a clever insurance scheme, where one borrowed, for example, $1,000 (an "endowment loan") and immediately put it in shares ("endowment shares")—a transaction that required neither money nor collateral. Since both the loan and the endowment shares were insured, one magically had $2,000 in insurance. The only requirement was to gradually pay off the loan, in tiny increments over ten years, at the end of which one had an untrammelled $1,000, which was still insured to double in the case of death.

This had been Jack Burns's project. The scheme had marketing punch— what 1940s credit union activists, who didn't believe in marketing, called "educational value." You could sell the idea of built-in insurance coverage (although not free coverage, because the loan repayment arrangement took into account the cost of the premiums). The incremental payback of endowment loans, in the meantime, helped bring a regular flow of money into the credit union's coffers, which could be lent out.

Mackie fought her own private battle with the banks—not that bank managers paid much attention to credit unions, except to snort when the subject came up. Mackie had a friend who worked for the Bank of Montreal in the Hotel Vancouver. The friend's boss was airily dismissive of credit unions. He called them "fly-by-nighters." He pointed to their 12 per cent interest on loans as compared with the bank's rate, which was half that.

What the bank manager hadn't mentioned was that the credit union rate was really 1 per cent a month on the unpaid balance. The interest declined to virtually nothing at the end. The banks, on the other hand, charged 6 per cent based on the opening principal, although *the principal* declined to zero at the end, when the borrower was effectively paying a huge interest rate on the tag end of money owed. The bank also deducted the whole of the interest at source, from the money it actually forwarded. In an alleged loan of $100, for example, the borrower would take away only $94. There were other, tricky administrative arrangements that anted up the bank's take. When one sat down and worked out the terms, the bank rate was higher than the credit union rate, sometimes as high as 15 or 16 per cent. "God," Mackie exclaimed many years later, "I used that argument often enough."

The banks had no compunction about misleading the public. The credit unions, on the other hand, were committed to citing the effective interest rate. The difference required some explaining, but once the explanation sank in, members were all the more enthusiastic. They spread the word, which helped in turn to build up membership numbers. The banks in any case never lent money to ordinary wage-earners who badly needed a loan to see them through a crunch. They had to depend on finance companies, with interest rates starting at 24 per cent.

Instalment buying was the coming thing and was making suckers of people. Stores were as blandly devious in misleading their customers about interest rates as were the banks. Car dealers were effectively charging up to 28 per cent. Mackie turned missionary again. A visit to the Credit Union Services counter was probably the first time, for most members, that they had a chance to learn what others were doing to them and their wage packets.

McIntosh, meanwhile, was interviewing the loan applicants. Although he wasn't a soft touch for a loan, he always tried to help. The major reason for loan applications was the consolidation of debt. The biggest reason for the debt, in turn, was doctors' and hospital bills. People often owed four or five months' wages in medical costs. McIntosh would spend endless hours on the phone haggling with doctors and hospitals for various members. Bill collecting, using full-time collectors, was a major task for doctors and hospitals, so they were willing to deal.

People caught in a jam for other reasons now also had a place to go. A carpenter had his tools stolen. McIntosh gave him the money to replace them in time to save his job. A few car loans and loans for buying homes were made, too, although their real growth wouldn't come until later. VanCity would even lend a member money for a holiday.

McIntosh willy-nilly was doing something that had never been tried before. Unlike the situation in a closed-bond credit union, or one in a small community, he usually didn't know the loan applicant, unless the person was a long-time member or had borrowed before. The credit committee of three members, who approved loans, likely did not know the applicant, either. McIntosh had to interview the applicant and make a recommendation nevertheless. Here, in this simple encounter, was the crux of what VanCity had taken on—operating an open-bond credit union in a large city. The absence of character information was no problem for the banks in big cities. They didn't lend on character. For the other credit unions in McIntosh's stable, like the Plumbers and Steamfitters, the City Hall and

Hospital Employees, or the Vancouver and District Danish, he could easily check out references or tap personal networks, but not for VanCity. One could look at whether a person was working, in what kind of job and with what monthly income, to set up some measurable thresholds. One could ask for co-signers, take note of collateral, make a call to where the applicant worked and get something of a reference. The trick was, having done that, to go one step further and allow at least some margin for the living, breathing, aspiring members themselves.

Ex-pipefitter McIntosh, with a supplicant in front of him—some stranger who had probably joined only in order to apply for the loan—set out to make this new idea work. He didn't go far wrong in most cases. It was a harbinger of things to come—low loan write-offs despite large volume. At the same time, VanCity's assets were leapfrogging. In 1948, they more than doubled, to $98,000. By year-end 1949, they were up to $160,000; by 1950, they were $196,000, and by 1951, a positively majestic $289,000. Membership was 1,600, about the population of a good-sized little town.

A third person, Alice Willson, was taken on for typing and filing. Martha Mackie was doing more than ever. As well as handling the business of five credit unions now served by the common counter, she did VanCity's books. Suspense attended each monthly calculation. Every $10,000 increase was a milestone. Then, every $100,000 increase became the measure. When McIntosh delivered each new figure to the board, they could not contain their wonder. They found it difficult to believe that they were actually working towards $300,000. Even McIntosh, whom everybody knew had worked in a bank, was taken aback.

New membership was another measuring stick. Twenty new members a month was considered a hot pace. This worked out to about one new member each business day. If that one new person a day showed up, the universe was unfolding as it should. For Martha Mackie, dealing with potential new members had its own small agony. She had to quiz them to see if they qualified first for other credit unions. If they did, she would send them along, although it meant one less member for VanCity. She was honour bound not to snatch potential members from other credit unions, which also desperately needed membership. Some of those credit unions, unwilling to trust the situation, kept a hawk eye on the kind of people she was taking in. If, however, somebody who already belonged to another credit union also wanted to join VanCity, they were fair game. VanCity had a dual membership provision in its charter. This was common. Most of the original signatories to the charter, for example, had been members of other credit unions.

Mackie was also conducting the initial loan interviews. Often she would write out the loan application herself, filling in both sides of the blue form. A surprising number of people coming through the door started off by saying, "I'd like to join this here credit union," or at least Mackie began to feel there were a lot of them. The phrase irritated her, and not just because she was a former teacher who had taught grammar. She had noticed that "this here credit union" invariably meant a loan application was on the way. Time after time, it did. It was like a red flag. It never ceased to astonish Mackie how many people had heard of loans that might be available without the impossible qualifications demanded by the banks.

When, on the other hand, the person saying "this here credit union" really wanted to join a credit union, she would mutter to herself, "Thank goodness." She could reasonably expect them to come up with badly needed deposit money. Prairie people, especially from Saskatchewan, were sophisticated credit union joiners. Many of them had been co-op members as well as credit-union members.

Once a woman came storming into the office and pitched into Bill McIntosh. She absolutely forbade him to lend her husband any more money. He had been putting it on a race horse. Mostly, however, borrowing was pathos—men with $5 for membership were trying to borrow $100 or $200. Hardship was part of the atmosphere. Usually applicants had their backs to the wall. They owed money to the hospital, the doctor and sometimes to the corner grocery store. Fortunately for them, poverty was something Mackie and McIntosh understood. A man's face would break into relief, hard to disguise, as the credit union, almost miraculously it seemed, converted an impossible bag of debts into a single loan with manageable payments. VanCity's directors understood, as well. They were all working for a living. Several of them were borrowing too, just like other members.

Members did not have personal cheques and chequing accounts. Credit unions were not allowed to provide chequing for members. Mackie, however, could make out cheques on VanCity's own bank account—and soon on its B.C. Central account—and pay bills for members, given their instructions. She would then debit the members accordingly. This was particularly useful for members who were self-employed. Mackie in effect acted as their bill-paying secretary. It was a service that VanCity offered as a matter of course, and she gave no thought to it.

The cardinal rule for new members was to remember their book number, that is, membership number, because this was the first thing Mackie would ask them for, until she got to know them. Members were identified by this number rather than by name or account, with different kinds of accounts for each person having the same number. Only the original membership card was filed by name, for cross-reference.

This person was book number 384 and that one was 622. As a member walked in, Mackie pegged their names and numbers at the same time, or tried to. It was amazing how many members' numbers one could remember. This could prove embarrassing. When she met members on the street and they began talking to her, she would have to place them in her head by number, and then try to put a name to them. Forty years later, she could still remember some members' book numbers.

Mackie's credit union social life also expanded. Bowling was big in credit union circles—the Street Railwaymen's Union even had its own co-op bowling alley—and Mackie became an avid bowler. She had become acquainted with a young sawmill worker, Bert Gladu, who was book member number 95 and was on VanCity's credit committee. Gladu was a bowler. The Mackies, Gladus and others in their circle were members of the Vancouver Credit Union Bowling League. Mackie wrote "Down the Alley" for the *B.C. Credit Unionist* and eventually became secretary-treasurer of the League, which had forty-eight teams, going strong. She also took an interest in the Vancouver Chapter of Credit Unions, which brought together Vancouver-area credit union activists for educational and social purposes.

Then, one day, McIntosh did something Mackie took exception to, and her world suddenly changed. It was the end of the relationship for the odd couple. The split had been coming for a long time. McIntosh was a bit of a freewheeler in operations. Mackie had noticed that sometimes he approved loans in advance of the credit committee, instead of the other way around, and doled out the money. He did it quite openly. If the application for a loan came in the day after the credit committee met, the applicant might otherwise have to wait another two weeks until it met again. Sometimes that posed difficulties. McIntosh didn't mind cutting a corner to serve a member.

The cheques for the loans needed two signatures, one from a signing officer of the board, but George Payton, VanCity president at the time, obliged. Payton and McIntosh were old credit union buddies. Payton was founder and treasurer of the small Canadian Pacific Railway employees' credit union, CER&S, which had also recently come under the Credit Union Services umbrella.

Once, to make a point, the credit committee unanimously refused to approve a loan that McIntosh had already paid out. The supervisory committee spotted the missing authorization and raised the issue with the board. McIntosh and Payton mumbled an explanation. Why let a goddamned silly rule get in the way of service? The sloppiness with proper procedure, however, bothered Mackie.

To upset her more, McIntosh would sometimes have her, as second signing officer, sign the cheques for loans, rather than doing it himself, for no evident reason. This added to her suspicions and discomfiture, especially when someone on the credit committee asked her about it. She had particular misgivings about a housebuilding loan. She hadn't agreed with it. She had seen the member go into McIntosh's office with a bottle and pour him a drink. Maybe some bankers might consider this business as usual—a bit of sociability in the banking relationship—but Mackie took it as a bribe. She spoke to McIntosh about it. They argued.

"You signed the cheque," McIntosh retorted, referring to the cheque for the loan. This only infuriated Mackie more. Now she openly challenged McIntosh about his deviousness with the signatures. He denied it.

There was another, gnawing point of contention underlying this clash of personalities. McIntosh had originally wanted to take Credit Union Services under his own wing, as a business on a contract basis. Mackie had said something to a couple of directors about it. She opposed the idea, favouring the existing co-operative arrangement. McIntosh learned about this and had never forgotten. Now he reminded her.

"I could have fired you then," he said, "but I still kept you on."

"Only because you knew I could do the work," she shot back. The situation was quickly becoming irretrievable.

"If you don't like it, you know what you can do," McIntosh countered hotly, in typical McIntosh fashion.

"Fine," said Mackie. "I'll be gone at the end of the month."

And so she was. She worked for Vanfed Credit Union for three years and then became treasurer of the Operating Engineers' Credit Union, where she stayed for almost twenty years. She kept active in the Vancouver Chapter of Credit Unions. But in the subsequent years, she greatly begrudged what had happened that day in the old Credit Union Services office. She had ended up leaving in a temper and had lost contact with VanCity, neither of which she wanted to do. "I could have minded my own business," she told herself, by way of solace, "but there was a principle involved." Several years after the event, she read in the financial notices that VanCity had foreclosed the loan she had objected to and seized the house. "Ah, ah," she blurted out. She allowed herself a little smugness, like the cat that licked the cream.

Shortly after the confrontation, McIntosh was gone from VanCity, too. He had taken one liberty too many, extending a $20,000 line of credit to a business over and above the loan amount the board had approved. The board had already been losing patience with him. It held a special meeting and severed VanCity's connection with him and Credit Union Services. Besides, the credit union's assets were soaring. By the end of the year, 1952, they would pass the half-million dollar mark, almost doubling over the previous year. It was time for VanCity to set off on its own, with its own manager.

McIntosh stayed with the remaining credit unions in his stable. He was there for another decade. He developed a rasping cough and a chest problem from his pipe-smoking. His drinking got out of hand and became a major problem. He was blunter and more irascible than ever with members who had a complaint. In the end, he was just in the way. His board called him in for a chat and retired him. A common counter for embryonic credit unions was in any case a fading concept, as existing credit unions grew rapidly and smaller ones merged with them. Eventually, the component credit unions McIntosh had managed themselves decided to amalgamate. The common counter and McIntosh were forgotten.

The pipefitter ex-bank clerk from Saskatchewan and the Lady Kid from Hairy Hill, Alberta, were no longer on the scene.

CHAPTER 4

Trimmer Man Gladu

BERT GLADU WAS THIRTY-FOUR years old and worked in the Robertson and Hacket sawmill on the north side of False Creek, underneath the old Granville Street bridge. He was a trimmer, deciding where to cut each piece of lumber and trimming it to length. It was April 1947. His friend Bill Bradley, a B.C. Electric conductor, bowled in the Credit Union Bowling League, at the Stry Co-op Bowling Alley. Bradley belonged to the Stry Credit Union. His team needed an extra bowler. Gladu went along. He felt like an interloper, however, because unlike the others he wasn't a member of a credit union or co-operative. Then Bradley, who was on the bowling league's executive, tried recruiting him for that as well. He knew Gladu had lots of energy.

"Hell," muttered Gladu. "I can't do that. I don't belong to a credit union. I can't join Stry. I can't join the church groups. I don't belong to any of them."

Bradley replied, "I can fix that for you. Meet me when I get off work, at Cambie and Hastings, and we'll go upstairs in the Dominion Bank Building to the Credit Union League office."

Bradley did fix it. Gladu joined Vancouver City Savings, a credit union open to all Vancouver residents. He was member number 95. Just a few days later, the first annual general meeting took place. Gladu showed up and found himself appointed delegate to the Vancouver Chapter of Credit Unions. Six months later, in the fall, there was a semi-annual membership meeting. Some of the originals, like Jack Burns, who was on the credit committee, wanted out. They had meant to be there only provisionally. They had enough on their hands with their own credit unions and the provincial movement. Gladu, as a result, ended up on the credit committee as well, filling a hole.

It was more than just accident, however, that Gladu became a credit union activist. He had knocked about without much money all his life. He didn't have to give much thought to know why credit unions were needed and what VanCity could do, even if it had only $15,000 in assets. Or, rather, he knew what it could do because it had $15,000 in assets. That was a lot of money. The banks sure weren't going to help people who needed help. As for A. L. Gladu himself—the first initial stood for Albert—he was a cheerful survivor.

Gladu, although born in Winnipeg, belonged to Vancouver, particularly the working-class East End, where he grew up. No matter where he went to get work, he schemed to return to Vancouver. His mother, who was on her own, supported her son and herself by housework until Bert was old enough to quit school and go to work. His first job was at the A. P. Slade jam factory on Water Street, on the top floor of an old Gastown building. He ran a boiler and rolled 100-pound sacks of sugar around—a heavy task for any teenager, and Gladu was small. He started at $12 a week.

His next job was in a butcher shop as delivery boy and general helper. At age eighteen he got married, during the "Hungry Thirties." Then he delivered flyers and neighbourhood newspapers. Next he went to Vancouver Island to work in a sawmill in Sidney. He kept changing jobs, looking for something better. The war began, and he moved his family to Victoria so that he could work in a shipyard, where there was more money. He wasn't happy in Victoria, however. The only way to get back to Vancouver, with wartime labour controls, was to work in another shipyard in North Vancouver. He stayed there until the war ended, helping make Liberty Ships. By this time he had five children. It was so hard to find a house in Vancouver, especially for those who had kids, that at the beginning Gladu had to leave three of his children in Victoria with friends. He settled for some barely livable rooms over some stores on Kingsway. Eventually he succeeded in buying a house in the 1800 block East Pender, on a 25-foot lot, for $100 down and $35 a month. The full price was $2,500. The attic served as a second storey.

There was nothing about getting by with little money that Gladu didn't know. At the sawmill in Sidney, in the depths of the depression, working on a profit-sharing basis, he had earned less than 15 cents an hour. He had never in his life had a bank account; there wasn't enough money left over even to think about it. As for the house in Vancouver, it was bought with an agreement for sale, common in those days. His first account anywhere with a financial institution was the $5 in his VanCity share account, so he could join the bowling league.

Suddenly Gladu found himself not just with an account, but also on the credit committee of something that was a kind of bank. He, Bert Gladu, was a banker, in a manner of speaking. He went to meetings of this committee, reviewed loan applications and creditworthiness, and put his John Henry on the line approving or disapproving loans. They just left him to it. He was impressed with their trust in him, even if he knew it was only because he was an available body that could be dragooned into the job. He reported to the board, so he attended board meetings as well.

The board meetings were interesting, too. At every meeting the directors voted to accept new members in a block, say, numbers 224 to 336. How members paid for their shares was a little complicated. The qualifying share was $5. They could begin with just $1, but they had to pay the rest within thirty days. Without being a fully paid-up member, moreover, one could not

borrow. Then there was something referred to as a "share call." This went
back to the early days of the co-operative movement and was a way of
ensuring there would be enough investment capital for future growth. Each
member had to answer the "call" for extra share capital. As early as 1947,
the call had gone out for payment on a second share, due within twelve
months of becoming a member, or $10 in total. Not everybody paid this
extra share capital on time. That could become a pain in the neck, Gladu
saw. There were also membership dues, of $1 per year. Each member
received a year's subscription to the *B.C. Credit Unionist* for the payment.
That was a good move.

Another thing: VanCity was hardly on its feet and it was already absorbing
other credit unions. When the UBC Employees Credit Union was disbanded
in May 1947, VanCity took over its assets and liabilities. A young forest
laboratory administrator, Rolf Perry, who had been involved in the UBC
credit union, joined VanCity's board. He was a small guy, too, like Gladu.
These acquisitions weren't raids, like the predatory manoeuvres of one
corporation against another. VanCity never then, or in future years, sought
to take over others. It did, however, open the door to smaller credit unions
that, for one reason or another, wanted to fold or whose members saw a
common advantage in belonging to VanCity. The transactions were called
"mergers" or "amalgamations," although those words, suggesting two
equal parties coming together, did not quite capture what was happening.

It was fascinating how money could be moved around from one place to
another, as if it did not matter who actually had their hands on it. And it did
not matter, Gladu realized. VanCity deposited its spare cash at the Bank of
Montreal. Weren't the banks supposed to be the enemy? Reserves, meanwhile, were deposited with B.C. Central. What did B.C. Central do with that
money? Gladu didn't know, but it had to go somewhere. Now, here was
something curious: VanCity needed extra money to meet the overflowing
demand for loans by its members, so CER&S Credit Union deposited $2,000
in its coffers. The president of CER&S, George Payton, was a director, and
soon to be president, of VanCity as well. This was convenient. It was a lot
easier, too, to get the money through that connection than through the
young B.C. Central.

The best part was that, when credit unions needed something, they went
ahead and got it, or did it, using common sense. They weren't intimidated
by the cabalistic mystique of banking. Take the case of people moving to
Vancouver from elsewhere in the province where they belonged to a credit
union, probably one whose office was a card table. Their account could be
moved to VanCity using the mails. The Powell River Credit Union had a
better idea. It deposited $500 with VanCity for the benefit of any of its
members moving to Vancouver who might want to join. This was like
passing on cousins from one part of an extended family to another.

They even did their own audits. VanCity, like its fellow credit unions
in those first years, wouldn't think of paying a chartered accountant to

do an audit. Why spend the money? Co-operatives and credit unions, organized around the principle of member-shareholders looking after their own affairs, had an auditing arrangement built-in. In the case of credit unions, it was a supervisory committee of non-directors whose job was to make sure the books were in order.

Gladu learned fast, as committees reported and items were discussed at board meetings. Being the delegate to the Vancouver Chapter of Credit Unions gave him an additional opportunity to pick up know-how quickly. A lot of learning was done by everybody at chapter meetings, which consisted of a monthly educational meeting and a monthly business meeting. They met in a hall on Main Street. If somebody had an operational problem at their credit union, they would bring it up, hoping that someone else had already been faced with that same problem and solved it. If not, they would reason it through. Talks and seminars were given by credit union activists and others on different operational aspects and on subjects of common interest, like a chequing system or co-operatives. The chapter also prepared a printed treasurer's course—in effect, a manual on how to run a credit union.

Every once in a while, a chapter meeting would be a social. The highlight was the annual international picnic with Washington State credit unionists, at Peace Portal Park, on the Canadian side of the border. It reminded them all how much larger the movement was. Gladu's wife, Flo, by a second marriage, became active in the chapter, too. She was a streetcar conductor and had become a Stry member. They met at credit union bowling games. "You might say bowling got me into the credit union and bowling got me my second wife," he liked to joke.

It was something quite personal, however, not too long after he had taken an active interest, that made Bert Gladu a VanCity partisan for the rest of his life. One of Gladu's sons was badly burned by firecrackers. He was in hospital for several months. The doctor and hospital bills were impossible to pay. There was no point in Gladu going to a bank; he had never had any dealings with them. In other circumstances, he would have tried Household Finance, a personal loan company that did a lot of advertising. Being a member of the credit union, he went to see Bill McIntosh instead. He knew that whatever interest Household Finance charged, the credit union would charge less.

"It's all right, Bert," McIntosh said, when Gladu approached him. "Leave it with me. I'll see what I can do."

The problem was old hat for McIntosh. He had Gladu sign a loan application form and then got on the phone to negotiate the bills. Gladu ended up paying $150, financed by a VanCity loan which he retired at $10 a month. VanCity, as it turned out, received not only the interest on the loan but thirty-three years of free time from Gladu in almost every voluntary capacity possible—twenty-seven of those years on the board.

CHAPTER 5

The Sawmill Worker
Dispenses Credit

BERT GLADU, SAWMILL WORKER BY DAY, banker by evening. The credit committee met afternoons at five o'clock, sometimes once a week, sometimes every two weeks, and dispensed its rough financial justice. At first, Gladu sat and listened. It wasn't too long before he got the hang of it. In a way, deciding on loan applications was easy. The board had laid down certain restrictions, so the treasurer and the credit committee could go only so far. Then one asked for security or for co-signers where possible. If members had taken out a previous loan and made their payments on time, they could be given extra leeway. They had proven themselves and shown character. The committee had what it called its "automatics" or "almost automatics"—loans wholly or partially offset by the members' deposits in their share accounts or by other savings. Members, in fact, were encouraged to borrow against their share capital, rather than withdrawing the share capital itself, because that way they had double insurance coverage.

Sometimes, when the applicant was a bit short on security, the committee would decide to gamble anyway. They called these their "boy scout" loans —doing a good deed every day. "How about this being our boy scout loan?" a committee member would opine, and they would give the lucky applicant the money.

Bill McIntosh was a help, too. He had already interviewed the applicants. If everything was in order and the security lined up, the loan was approved routinely. If, on the other hand, the loan was chancy, McIntosh, while not turning down the loan himself, would speak against it to the committee. Or, at least, he was supposed to. What about people who seemed to be good bets but had little in the way of security? The credit committee didn't know most loan applicants. The committee members simply made a snap judgement on their character.

Then there were members who had landed themselves in just a terrible mess—they had probably become members in the hope of getting a loan to bail themselves out. They had massive debts, in the range of $200 to $300, sometimes as much as $400. For Gladu and the other credit committee members, for whom $50 or $100 was a substantial loan, this was stunning. These people had talked and walked themselves into it, Gladu felt, not a little indignantly. *They* had done it. Nobody else had done it to them. They had fallen for the pitch of a dollar down and a dollar a week—a sewing machine here, something else there—and before they knew it, they didn't have enough dollars to go around. Their creditors began hounding them. For a while they would play one creditor off against another, until it all became too much and they would drag themselves into VanCity like refugees—financially displaced persons. Because such supplicants would put off making the move until they had run out of options, the credit committee could tell, by how recent their membership number was, just how desperate they were. To get a better handle on this, Gladu had the board add a blank for the date of membership to the upper-left-hand corner of the loan application form.

The credit committee insisted that such members come in and be interviewed. Loans like that couldn't be approved on the basis of an interview with the treasurer alone. There was another, equally important reason for the second interview. It allowed the committee to talk to these new members and explain to them what VanCity was trying to do. The talk had a lecturing, moralistic quality to it. There was no other way to do it. "Fine," the explanation went, "you've applied for this loan. But there's one thing you've got to remember. The money doesn't come out of a hole somewhere. It's people's money. It's one of our member's money, some of our members' money. You're a member now, too. We're not loaning out our own money, we're loaning out members' money. So we have to be very cautious about what we do." This would be followed by a stern critical analysis of how the members had landed in their fix—"See here, seems you've been recklessly buying this and that"—and a demand for assurance that they would get their spending down to what they could afford and would make the loan payments on time. In exchange, if the loan was approved, the credit union would get the financial monkey off the loan applicant's back.

If it was a family problem, the man and the woman would both be invited in. Gladu found himself getting an education that he hadn't expected, listening to all these woeful stories of runaway debt. The humorous part, as he realized later, was that he was so young and yet he was telling them what to do. And although the committee was supposed to help people by lending money, they were also supposed to protect the members' money that they were lending. The members had to have at least a reasonable expectation that loans would be repaid. That was a nice twist. You could see what happened when you didn't keep the protection of depositors in mind. In January 1948, VanCity had taken the A.M. & A. Credit Union under wing and done what later would be called a due diligence study. More than half of A.M. & A.'s loan portfolio consisted of bad loans and another big chunk were only fair. VanCity discounted them at 80 per cent and 50 per cent, respectively. A.M. & A.'s members had to take a loss, at least temporarily, until recoveries began to be made. One couldn't run a credit union for long, the way they were going.

The more the credit committee thought about its responsibility to members, the rougher it became with people who had carelessly run up debts.

"Don't forget," Gladu would warn, "once you get this loan, you'll be able to go back to these people [retailers] and start all over again. But if you do, don't ever let us find out about it. It's going to be that much harder the next time around, because what's the use of helping you?"

Gladu, although just on the credit committee, felt at the centre of things. No loan is a financial transaction unto itself; everything is interconnected. Every time the treasurer, or the credit committee, or the directors, wondered how much of a loan they could give to members, they found themselves questioning other parts of the operation and musing about the future of VanCity as a whole.

For example, if somebody needed $300 to ward off collectors and the credit committee approved that loan, three members who needed $100 each, or six members who wanted to borrow $50 each, would have to wait in line. Chattel mortgages—lending money against cars or furniture as collateral—were fine. But house mortgages were out of the question. There just weren't enough deposits to provide for them. Second mortgages were all the credit committee could manage. They were riskier than first mortgages, but VanCity took the gamble. Strangely enough, as Gladu recalled, they never lost on a second mortgage in those early days. Loan losses overall were small—less than half a per cent. They were proud of that.

But that didn't solve the problem of not enough money. Credit unions needed more deposits. The much sought-after expansion was a double-edged sword. Although saving was a basic part of the credit union ethic, new members were likely to bring with them more in the way of loan requests than deposits. Another problem was half-way members. They joined, but they hardly used their account. They probably had money sitting in a bank somewhere. If they would only get into the habit of coming by more often and using the credit union, they would likely leave more of their deposits behind. In the fall of 1948, McIntosh wrote a somewhat plaintive "half-way" letter, meant to be clever, with the right side blank for replies, asking members with dormant accounts what the credit union might be doing wrong.

One thing it wasn't doing wrong, but could do nothing about, was its single location in the Credit Union Building at Broadway and Quebec. That was a long way to go for many people in a big city like Vancouver, especially at the end of a working day, and especially if they didn't have a car. The banks, meanwhile, had branches everywhere. If only VanCity had branches. Well, one could dream, but in the real world the idea of the credit union opening branches was preposterous. Assets at the end of 1948, when the frustration began, were only $98,000. Membership was 580. The credit union didn't even have, or need, an office or employee of its own. Besides, credit unions didn't have branches.

The absence of a chequing system was another impediment. It didn't take a financial genius to realize how much this was holding the credit union back. If people couldn't write cheques against a chequing account at

VanCity, they were likely to keep most of their money elsewhere, and it was people who were used to writing cheques who had extra money to deposit. The problem was the cheque clearing system. The banks—the damnable competitor—controlled it.

B.C. Central was looking after the matter, but it didn't seem to be making much progress. Gladu watched as the VanCity board, as early as December 1947, began getting after Central to hurry things up. A chequing system wasn't all that important for a closed-bond credit union in a factory, where members showed up every day for work and could withdraw whatever cash they needed when the card table was set up. It wasn't that important in a small town, either, where one could saunter over to the credit union and where most local accounts were settled in cash rather than through the mails. There were those credit union purists, too, who were simply against chequing as well. As these adherents saw it, credit unions were places where one saved money for security or borrowed money for the necessities of life, like tools for the job or reroofing the house. Writing cheques was too easy a way of spending money; a cheque itself carried with it the idea of spending. Besides, in this fundamentalist view, a chequing service was not why credit unions existed. They were supposed to provide self-help within a closed common bond. For that, only the most basic services should be provided— a savings account, loans and education—with minimum overhead.

Another problem was regulatory. Did a chequing system qualify as "banking?" If so, it was probably illegal, since credit unions were not part of the federal banking system. Some credit unionists in a hurry—weren't cheques a useful service to members?—went ahead anyway. The Prince Rupert Fishermen's Credit Union began using cash withdrawal and transfer vouchers—in effect, cheques under another name—that could be cleared at the credit union itself. The idea spread to some other small locations. B.C. Central was faced with having to create a framework for a chequing system that was creating itself regardless.

The problem of inadequate deposits to service VanCity's rising loan demand was a symptom of success and growth rather than the contrary, whatever frustration it produced. The small things sometimes gave the best indication. Less than a year after the credit union went into operation, it was advertising. George Payton had brought some lawn bowling scorecards to a board meeting and suggested they produce similar ones in an advertising campaign. The board approved the printing of a thousand cards. A similar idea, for whist cards, was referred to the chapter. Others might laugh, but it was a start. A year later, the chapter sprang for advertisements on the front billboard of streetcars—the first advertising proper by credit unions in the province. Pamphlets and books were used, too, and worked well. You could give people real information in them and proselytize the cause. They could be provided to members over the counter as well as at annual meetings and in mail-outs.

Then there was the hiring of a piano player, to provide entertainment for the annual meeting in the spring of 1948. An organization with actual assets, deposits, operations and margins could put out a few dollars for such things. It was just another small bit of business, but it had a gay, optimistic note about it. It set a pattern for entertainment, refreshments and door prizes later on—something to balance the speaker for the night and the serious credit union talk. The next general meeting, the mid-year session that fall, was moved to the White Rose Ballroom on West Broadway.

The one event that Gladu particularly remembered, though, occurred in 1949: VanCity handed out its first $500 loan. Everything seemed to blossom after that. Deposits strengthened. Soon they were issuing "real estate loans" —in effect, first mortgages, albeit modest ones. At the end of 1949, assets had reached $160,000—not bad, but only a promise of things to come. Three years later, they were up to $567,000, half way to a million dollars. There were 2,500 members. At one annual meeting, held in the Manhattan Ballroom, also on West Broadway, Evelyne Warde of the Evelyne Warde Dancing Academy demonstrated the treasurer's report in tableau with her children's dancing class, decked out variously in shorts and bandannas, majorette sequins and Hollywood flash. Bill McIntosh, not much taller than the children himself, ceremonially gave them all passbooks. The one boy in the group, a ten-year-old in black tie and tails—a veritable Fred Astaire junior—proudly held aloft the credit union umbrella, his face glowing. The tableau idea was corny, but it had emotion.

By this time, the early 1950s, VanCity and several other credit unions had a chequing service, with cheques cleared by B.C. Central, which in turned cleared them through an arrangement with a bank. It wasn't as good as Central's being an integral part of the banks' clearing system itself, but it made chequing possible. The credit union movement also sponsored its own radio program, on station CKNW in Vancouver, every Wednesday evening from 9:05 to 9:30. Radio reached people. Credit unions were also able to offer 3 per cent or more on savings, a favourable rate that propelled growth. Gladu, in 1952, in the spirit of things, ran for the board and was elected. He held on to his credit committee work. He could handle that, too. Then, a couple of years later, he ran for the League board as well, and was elected. Farley Dickinson was amazed at Gladu's electoral success, because Gladu wasn't one to raise hell at meetings and promote himself.

Gladu thought it was because so many people knew him, largely from his work with the Vancouver Chapter, which took in a lot of credit unions. And when he did say something, people seemed to believe him—at least, enough to keep voting for him.

He could have been the little man under the umbrella himself, making his way with a big smile on his face. Something else brought a smile to his face, as 1952 wound down. The board had decided it was time to break away from Credit Union Services, hire an employee or two, and open its own office. It would become a full-fledged credit union that could do things in its own way.

CHAPTER 6

Mr. Swell

TED SEWELL WAS A FRIENDLY GUY, and he was looking for a job. He already had a job, at Grouse Mountain Resorts, but the work had its limitations. It consisted mostly of collecting as much money as possible from the chairlift operation on the weekends so that an outfit doing work on the chairlift could be paid. Sewell also did the books, in an office on the top floor of the old Sun Tower on Pender Street. Even though he was easygoing and didn't have much ambition, he had more ambition than that. Besides, as a forty-eight-year-old man with a family, maybe he could pick up a few more dollars elsewhere and free up his weekends as well.

Enter into his dilemma Fred Graham, an old friend. Graham was a Vancouver chartered accountant. The two had known each other from a Bible class for young adults at St. Mark's Anglican Church in Kitsilano. As they got older, the study group was replaced by the DUO Club—the Do Unto Others Club. They began to put on amateur theatricals, vaudeville style, in St. Mark's and other churches to help the club raise a few dollars. Eventually they rented the old Avenue Theatre near Georgia and Main for two performances in the fall and two others in the spring. Sewell, who had come to Canada from London, England, as a seven-year-old in 1911, liked the old English songs best. Tall, with a moustache—with a hint of David Niven—he would strut across the stage as "the man who broke the bank at Monte Carlo," belting out songs like the best of them on the stages of New York and London, or so he felt.

Graham, diminutive, with a quiet, thoughtful manner, was the more serious one. Through his credit union connections, the firm he worked for had become the auditor of B.C. Central and was about to become the auditor of VanCity. Graham knew that VanCity was looking for a full-time treasurer and sent Sewell over to see one of VanCity's board members, Tom Wiltshire, who was looking after the matter. Wiltshire was the general manager of CU&C. Sewell had some credit union background and considerable bookkeeping experience. He seemed to get along with Wiltshire when they met; seeming to get along was, for Sewell, the standard against which everything else was measured. Wiltshire was enthusiastic. Sewell was hired by the board, and VanCity had its first employee. Alice Willson, who had succeeded Martha Mackie at Credit Union Services, now also went to work full time for VanCity and was eventually joined by another teller who did the bookkeeping. All of a sudden, there were three of them. One of Willson's tasks was to read the obits every day in the paper, so that if a member had died, she could make sure the family collected the insurance on the deceased's share account.

Members loved Ted Sewell. He liked to chat them up, joke with them. Members, for their part, could count on him to listen to their woes and try to help them out. One of them recalled Sewell as a tall man with glasses, holding a document in his hand and laughing. Another remembered him as a polite Englishman, exact with his words and debonair, whom everybody wanted to have serve them.

Sewell's connection to the credit union movement went back almost a decade, before Vancouver City Savings was formed. He had moved to West Vancouver in 1930, a year after getting married. Some time later, the proprietor of the hardware store in Dundarave, one of the old West Vancouver village clusters, got Sewell and several others interested in credit unions. His name was Ted Dinsley. He knew all about the Powell River Credit Union, the first in British Columbia. He described credit unions as a community banking system. He talked about the credit union organization in Quebec that had done so well. Sewell saw it as a new idea and decided it was worth pursuing. Led by Dinsley, the small coterie of West Vancouverites went ahead and established the Hollyburn Credit Union in 1951, with a small part-time office in Ambleside, in the municipality. Sewell's membership number was 13.

So when Sewell went to work for VanCity, he already knew something about credit unions. The office arrangement was somewhat odd. Sewell and the other VanCity employees shared quarters with Credit Union Services and Bill McIntosh—Sewell called him "Mac"—in an old wood-frame tabernacle building adjacent to the former machine shop. Later the two operations were moved to a temporary location half a block west, while a new Credit Union Building was being constructed. McIntosh, the dismissed VanCity treasurer, acted as a mentor to the new one, Sewell. Those who didn't call Sewell by his proper name were welcome to call him "Cookie," his long-time nickname, which he had picked up while working at Dad's Cookies and which he fancied. He even used "Cookie" Sewell for the occasional folksy pieces he did for the *B.C. Credit Unionist.* He always wore a flower in his jacket buttonhole, lifted from his West Vancouver garden.

Member number 452, Bill Haynes, a landscape gardener, recalled getting a $5,000 loan from Sewell—a huge amount in those days. Haynes lived on the wrong side—the eastern side—of Ontario Street, which divided Vancouver into East and West, and took it for granted that he could never get a loan from a bank. He had learned about VanCity from neighbourhood talk. His loan application, secured by a piece of property, was at first turned down by the credit committee. Sewell nevertheless promised him he would put the loan through, although how he did it, Haynes never learned. Haynes paid off the loan early and never forgot Sewell's kindness.

In the end, Sewell's compassion and good cheer got the better of him. He allowed one particular member to overdraw his account instead of putting him through the loan-application process. Before he knew it, the account was overdrawn by $1,000. The board was concerned for another reason as well. Sewell didn't have much push. He was fussy with details. They decided they needed somebody else. Sewell had been on the job for about fifteen months. They didn't want to fire him. He stayed on to look after delinquent accounts and to assist families in settling their affairs after the death of a husband or father—in Sewell parlance, after they had gone to the great lodge above. Because of the mispronunciation of his name, he came to be known as Mr. Swell.

The directors fastened on to a Port Alberni schoolteacher, Ivor Mills, to replace Sewell. Mills was taken up with credit unions. When his first child, a girl, was born, he and his wife were going to call her Cuna, after the Credit Union National Association in the United States. They changed their mind at the last moment, but the sentiment was there.

Mills had grown up in Saskatchewan during the worst of the depression. His father, a widower, was dirt poor, and difficulties compounded themselves. At one point, living in Colonsay, east of Saskatoon, the family survived on a regular diet of biscuits and syrup, potatoes, and onions, with the occasional chunk of meat earned by doing odd jobs for a relative who was a butcher. For a period, they had to go on relief.

Ivor's father, "Hop" Mills, was a strong-minded, eccentric idealist and an avowed Marxist-Leninist. He would say, "Yeah, I'm a communist. If you want to call me something, that's it." He was involved in the Saskatchewan Wheat Pool movement and helped organize the Colonsay Co-op and the Colonsay and District Credit Union. He ran the credit union, as treasurer, from his house for its first two years. Then he moved to Vancouver and was on the board of cu&c for a while. Hop was an enigma in local credit union circles because he was such a political maverick and so likable at the same time. Ivor inherited his father's co-operative idealism.

VanCity was serious business now. The new Credit Union Building at Quebec and Broadway opened to much fanfare—a modern two-storey structure of brick and concrete block, with solid rows of windows, dominating the corner on both sides. Central occupied the Broadway frontage with VanCity immediately behind it. The new space had a long counter with multiple teller stations and plenty of room for member services. Robert Bonner, the province's attorney general in the W. A. C. Bennett Social Credit administration, officiated at the building's opening ceremony. Bonner, in the spirit of bonhomie, joined VanCity and was given the all-important passbook. He was member number 5,134 (because of drop-outs, there were about 3,300 members at the time). He also signed up his small son in the School Savings Club—two hundred children with accumulated savings of $14,000, ostensibly for higher education, or that's how the account was sold. Junior membership accounts were one of Mills's pet projects.

There were times, particularly on Saturday mornings, when the office felt like the busiest financial institution in the world. A picture taken in early 1955 shows long line-ups at the teller wickets and the member services end of the counter fully occupied. Up to as many as ten people a day, on a busy Saturday, were joining. Members, in their inchoate way, seemed to realize something important was happening. The 1955 annual meeting was exuberant, with a large and voluble crowd in the Stry Co-op Hall speaking their minds on every subject they could think of. Assets hadn't quite reached $1 million by the time of the meeting, which meant a moment of drama missed, but everybody knew it was just a matter of time.

The VanCity activists were now also openly talking about the logic of establishing branches. They weren't convinced it was the right moment, and they expressed concern about encroaching on the territory of other community credit unions—"a thing which we desire least of all"—but they wanted the matter discussed. This disclaimer about other people's territory didn't carry far. Scratch another credit unionist and one found a critic of "City." It was growing too fast, the critics said. It was going to weaken other credit unions. Because it didn't have a real common bond, lending would get out of control. Grumblings surfaced in a multi-part series on credit unions in the *Vancouver Sun*, attributed anonymously to "a number of far-sighted credit unionists" and "some credit union officials."

Well, if they wanted to grumble, let them grumble, VanCity's directors shrugged. A little bit of backbiting was not about to dampen their enthusiasm. Something, however, was wrong. The founders of VanCity, from a combination of idealism, shrewdness and hope, had started a venture that now really did have promise—promise that one could read in an actual balance sheet, almost as if touching it. Ivor Mills, however, like Ted Sewell, was not working out. It wasn't that there were operational breakdowns. Mills, the board felt, just didn't have the kind of personality that could motivate people in a business operation. Good-natured Sewell, who had helped Mills learn the ropes, later ascribed it to Mills being a school-teacher. Mills treated the board in the same school-teacherish fashion. He would ignore certain board instructions. When asked why he hadn't done something, he would reply that he didn't think it was necessary. "Well, damn it all, what the hell," Bert Gladu remembered thinking, in frustration.

There was something indefinable missing in the organization. As VanCity continued to grow, that something expanded into a gnawing uneasiness. It was as if the organization, by growing, was creating a limbo around itself as it did so. The venture was no longer just fourteen people throwing 50 cents each into the pot. A million dollars in assets meant almost that much out on the street in loans, and new members and money and borrowers coming through the door every day.

CHAPTER 7

The President
Finds the Man

THE "SOMETHING MISSING" GRATED ON Tom Wiltshire. Wiltshire had been president of VanCity since the 1953 annual meeting. He had played a role in bringing in Ted Sewell and then Ivor Mills as treasurer. He realized now, however, that hiring a person with some credit union background and some office experience wasn't enough. He had the uneasy feeling that, as things were, a bit of the future was being lost each day.

Adding to his discomfiture was Mills himself. "I can see him right here, right now," Wiltshire remembered forty years later. "I can see him sitting behind the desk with his glasses on, and I'm talking to him about something, I don't remember what it was, and I'm thinking to myself, he really isn't one of my favourite people." Wiltshire liked the old man, Hop, even with his communist tendencies. Religion and politics didn't bother Wiltshire. That was an individual's business. The younger Mills's stiffness, though, was something he couldn't get used to.

In one way at least, the son was like the father—or so Wiltshire thought—and that was the bigger problem. Wiltshire speculated that old Hop had so ingrained in Ivor the communistic co-operative ethos, with its accent on membership participation based on a sharing of ideals, that Ivor's inflexibility was beyond cure. Wiltshire wanted Mills to go out of his way to meet people beyond the credit union—to get away from what he considered the very tight guidelines of a co-operative and to promote VanCity in Vancouver at large. This was something that Mills wasn't doing and probably couldn't do—not so much because of doctrine, as Wiltshire imagined, but because of temperament. The fact that Mills was running the shop systematically and conscientiously, and providing detailed reports to the board, did not placate Wiltshire at all.

Mills, himself, felt increasingly ill at ease. After about a year on the job, he returned to teaching. His leaving was one of those cases of unspoken understanding, accomplished without the board having to face up to its dilemma and fire him. Ironically, VanCity's assets had grown an impressive 30 per cent in the year under his tenure. The growth, with its new demands, was Mills's undoing. Now Wiltshire had the chore of finding somebody else, someone with what he could only call "drive."

If anybody on the board understood what was needed, Tom Wiltshire was the one. He was a driven man himself—driven by the sheer opportunity to do things. He had grown up in Meota, a hamlet on Jackfish Lake, near North Battleford, Saskatchewan. He had been an RCAF pilot during the war, attached to the RAF, flying Boulton-Paul Defiants, Hurricanes and Typhoons. After wandering around California for a while, when the war ended, he and an air force buddy started a sawmill on the banks of the upper Fraser River in Tête Jaune Cache, near the Alberta border. Unfortunately, the 1948 flood on the Fraser washed away six million board feet of lumber, the sawmill's dry kiln and all. The banks stepped in. "We went out of business pretty fast," he remembered.

Disappointed but not defeated, Wiltshire and his wife flipped a coin to see which coast they would go to. The West Coast won. Wiltshire, responding to a newspaper ad, ended up as general manager of CU&C Health Services. The insurance co-operative was struggling. The previous manager had lost control of the liabilities. CU&C found itself owing much more to doctors and hospitals than it had collected in premiums. Things got so bad that the volunteer president, Jerry Lundie—an engineer-custodian at Point Grey High School—lost all patience. He set up office at CU&C and, in his off time, often into the small hours of the morning, systematically rebuilt the records and operated the organization. This went on for years, until he had put CU&C on a sound footing. Accountant Fred Graham was called in to see exactly how far in the hole they were, when the crisis came to light. It turned out to be $40,000, a whopping 40 per cent of annual income.

The underlying problem, though, was that CU&C did not have enough members. It was true that people were joining, with many of them joining VanCity at the same time. For an insurance co-operative that needed to spread risk, however, the numbers weren't there. Wiltshire decided that CU&C needed a salesman—a salesman just like Tom Wiltshire. He liked to talk to people. He focussed on labour unions. The Vancouver firefighters were already a group member. If he could convince others to sign up as a group, say as part of their collective agreement, he could bring people into CU&C en bloc. He did, and CU&C never looked back. VanCity, meanwhile, was right next door. Wiltshire joined the VanCity board and then became president, because VanCity was there. He could see it was an organization that could go places. The board was helping build the credit union, and he was a builder, willing to work like hell.

His pipe in hand, a bit of a double chin and weight around the middle, a clipped moustache, hair combed back off a bald temple—a compact bundle of enterprise—Wiltshire leaned on the CU&C counter like a man who knew he had done a lot and knew he was going to do a lot more. "A blustery, outgoing, extroverted salesman," one acquaintance described him. He had a touch of the flamboyant and spontaneous. If he got an idea into his head, he pursued it, to try to make it happen. "Everything I've ever done in my life is push, push, push," he once remarked, "because you don't get anywhere by sitting still."

That still left the problem, at VanCity, of finding a new treasurer. Along the way, Wiltshire had signed up the fishermen's union and fishermen's co-operatives for CU&C. He began hearing about a bright, young comptroller with experience in the movement, Don Bentley. George Viereck, a mutual friend and credit union dynamo who was running the Prince Rupert Fishermen's Credit Union, kept telling Wiltshire that if he needed a good man down in Vancouver, this was the one he should get, that he couldn't go wrong. After meeting Bentley, Wiltshire agreed, but the first time he brought up the VanCity possibility with him, Bentley declined in favour of a trucking company he was interested in. Bentley now was of two minds about the transport venture and was available again.

Wiltshire then introduced Bentley to Harold MacLean, another board member, over lunch at a local Vancouver cafe. Wiltshire was looking for support, because of the salary they would have to pay. MacLean was enamoured with Bentley. Bentley had wonderful ideas about where to take VanCity, and he also had the business background.

Bert Gladu was opposed to the move, although he wanted Bentley. "We can't possibly afford to hire this man at this kind of money," he said. Several other directors were also opposed. The salary was modest, but not something they were used to paying. Wiltshire and MacLean argued that if VanCity was going to go anywhere, they had to have the best possible man they could find. They finally managed to push the idea through the board.

Bentley, at this time, was thirty-five years old. He was quiet but well-liked, and had a reputation in co-operative circles as a problem solver. He was easy to talk to and knew the movement. He had come to British Columbia from the Consumers' Co-operative Refinery in Regina. He had worked, in Vancouver, as comptroller of the Fishermen's Co-operative Federation in a difficult transition phase. He had recommended that the federation move its headquarters to Prince Rupert, to bring it closer to the centre of fishing activity—although, because he wanted to stay in Vancouver, the relocation put him out of a job. The federation had tried for several years to get him to move up the coast, even offering to build him a house on the water if he would come.

Earlier, in 1946, Bentley had briefly looked after the bookkeeping of the Lower Fraser Fishermen's Credit Union, one of the earliest credit unions in the province, with charter number 35 (now the Gulf & Fraser Fishermen's Credit union). Best of all, he had impressive banking experience, as a young man out of high school in Saskatchewan.

VanCity, by corporate standards, wasn't much. On the other hand, it was a credit union—part of the co-operative movement—and its broad charter had possibilities. It already had $1 million in assets. Merely by thinking of it, Bentley began envisioning what might be done. On August 15 he became the new treasurer. Neither Don Bentley nor VanCity would be the same again.

PART TWO

1955-1965

CHAPTER 8

Saskatchewan

THE SASKATCHEWAN THAT DON BENTLEY grew up in was the worst of places and the best of places. Bentley was just nine years old in October 1929, when the New York stock market crashed and plunged the United States, and with it Canada and Europe, into the Great Depression. The repercussions were particularly severe for the farmers of the U.S. Midwest and the Canadian prairies. A city like New York, and central Canadian provinces like Ontario and Quebec, had accumulated wealth, manufacturing plants, and head offices, and even in a depression at least some people still bought things. Saskatchewan, dependent on wheat exports, might as well have been on another planet. It was devastated.

The depression threw King Wheat into the gutter. In 1929, wheat was selling for $1.03 a bushel; by 1932, the price had tumbled to 38 cents. If that weren't enough, farmers in the heart of the wheat bowl, across the south of the Prairie provinces, were hit by a drought that endured seemingly forever—it did not end until 1939. Legend has it that when it finally did rain, small children cowered with fear: they hadn't seen rain before. Malnutrition was widespread. Few in the stricken areas could pay their taxes. Municipalities went bankrupt. Doctors often didn't bother charging their patients. Cases were reported of people living in the most appalling conditions, reduced to rags and shivering in their houses in the bitter prairie winter, with no mattresses and insufficient blankets.

The Bentleys escaped this suffering. Don Bentley was born in Preeceville and grew up there, in Kelvington and in Canora—small towns in the parklands north of Yorkton, towards the Manitoba border. The drought did not extend that far and the mixed farming in the area somewhat offset the devastating drop in the price of wheat. The depression, nevertheless, left vivid memories. Almost daily there were hobos doing yard work for Nora Bentley, Don's mother, and other households. There were hundreds of them on the trains going back and forth on the CNR line through Canora. Once a week, like clockwork, Nora would bake up a storm so that each hobo who came by, and who wanted to do something in exchange for food, could be packed off with several loaves of bread, buns and a jar or two of jam or jelly that she had put up the previous summer.

The dustbowl was only 200 kilometres away. Ruth Bentley, Don's kid sister, recalled how, as a child, she and the others dug vegetables from their garden, put them into sacks, and carried them in a wagon to a train siding, where the sacks were loaded into boxcars for delivery south. The Bentleys thought of people in the south as family. In a way, they were. They had all, in a prior generation, homesteaded the land together, and were all prairie people together against the world.

Don's father, Tom Bentley, was well known in and around Canora. He was a war hero, having served with distinction in the Great War. He worked for the Saskatchewan Wheat Pool as a district representative, or "fieldman." The Pool wasn't just another grain elevator company. It was the product of a long and colourful struggle by Saskatchewan farmers who joined together against the exploitive grain merchants and private elevator companies, not to mention the eastern banks and the railways. It was also one of the country's largest businesses.

The Pool was a co-operative, owned by the farmers who joined it according to the basic co-operative principle of one member, one vote. It was the leading symbol and practical buttress of a growing co-operative movement that included retail stores, a wholesale supplier, bulk fuel outlets and, by the end of the 1930s, an oil refinery and embryonic credit unions. It survived, amid great anguish, near-bankruptcy when the depression hit and prices collapsed. The Pool represented a defiant spirit of self-reliance. These seemingly ordinary farmers had gone about systematically learning the grain business and had decided boldly to go into the business themselves.

Tom Bentley's reputation as a farmers' champion grew. He was a Canora town councillor for a while, looking after hunger relief. He became heavily involved in the CCF—the Co-operative Commonwealth Federation—the socialist party rising up in Saskatchewan. Later he would be elected to the House of Commons and then join the famous Tommy Douglas CCF provincial government, where he was minister of public health, overseeing Saskatchewan's then revolutionary public hospital care plan.

Co-operation was the thing and Tom Bentley was in the middle of it. Increasingly, farmers and townspeople knew the ropes—how to incorporate, hold meetings, take minutes, keep accounts, prepare annual reports, make presentations. If something needed to be done, people could be brought together to do it. Credit unions were a fine co-operative idea, Tom Bentley thought to himself. Why not help get them started while he was on the go? So he did that, too, as the depression ended. To get things moving, he volunteered to sit on the board. Soon he was a director for a string of small community credit unions in his area. He and the other directors would sit on nail kegs—boardroom furniture in rural Saskatchewan—and decide on loans off the cuff. Old co-operative hand though he was, working for the great Saskatchewan Wheat Pool, he was nevertheless excited by the ability of people in and around a town to start their own co-operative bank, beginning with just a few members and virtually no capital.

CHAPTER 9

Growing up Co-operator

CHILDHOOD FOR DON BENTLEY, his sister and his three brothers in small-town rural Saskatchewan was as normal as one could ask for. Their father, Tom Bentley, always earned sufficient income to be a good provider and even manage some extras, depression style. The children had a bicycle—one bicycle for the five of them, but still a bicycle. The family also had a car, an old Buick touring model, needed by Tom Bentley for his Wheat Pool work.

Conditions that might now be regarded as primitive were, for Don Bentley, ordinary middle-class reality. He was a responsible young man, diligently doing his share of the chores. He emptied the five-gallon honey pot for the indoor toilet, used in winter when it was too cold for family members to casually stroll to the outhouse. He toted water from the standpipe on the corner—there was no running water in the house—using two big cream cans and a sled or wagon to carry them, depending on the season. Splitting kindling to light the stove was another chore. In winter, he filled copper-lined tubs with snow to melt down for laundry. Before the family purchased a wringer washing machine, Don helped his mother wash clothes on a scrub board. They had no electricity until they got to Canora. They used kerosene lanterns and coal oil lamps for lighting.

As kid brother Jack remembered, in the way that small brothers look up to big ones, Don was the toast of Canora. He shared his father's mental brilliance and his ability to remember details. He routinely got the best grades in school. He won the provincial governor general's medal for the highest marks in the province for veterans' children when he graduated from high school. He was better known, though, as an athlete. Don and his older brother Wells were powerful swimmers. The Bentley children were taught to swim at the lake when they were three or four years old. Bentley senior, himself a powerful swimmer and athlete, coached his children and worked on their swimming strokes. Every morning and evening—father's orders—they had to swim the half kilometre to the point across the lake and back. One just didn't do something, in the Bentley family, one put one's mind to it. That's what minds were for. Don, later, was also a star baseball pitcher, a fair hockey player and, in his late teens, became a top-notch golfer, shooting in the high 70s.

Canora had about 1,200 people—a fair size, as small-town Saskatchewan went. The population was an ethnic mix, with Anglo-Saxons making up about half. Don's best friend was Ukrainian. Between the two of them, big and burly for their age, and popular, they were on top of things. Notwithstanding his size, Don was gentle, quiet, studious, and never pushy. The gentleness came from his mother. He had the self-assurance, nevertheless, of physical strength. On one occasion, two hefty, trouble-making rowdies came to town for a wedding, went to the local theatre and decided to push their weight around. Don had snagged himself a job as usher at the theatre. He chased them, pushed them out of the theatre and, like a marshall brought into town to restore law and order, told them to go. They did.

He kept his emotions bottled in. He wouldn't offer words of sympathy to anybody, nor ask for them. Keeping things to oneself he took for granted. Mild-tempered as he was, he was deeply loyal to his family and reacted to anything derogatory said about them. He also wasn't used to the mudslinging of politics. The son of a Canora town council candidate running against Tom Bentley once casually slurred the opposition's wife, namely Don's mother. This was too much for Don who, still in his early teens at the time, confronted the man and "beat the crap out of him," as his older brother Wells put it. This made Don's reputation.

Radio had come to Saskatchewan. The Bentleys had an old Atwater Kent radio, the kind shaped like a church window, with filigree where the sound came out. Don and his two older brothers listened to Cab Calloway and his orchestra from Harlem, New York. Don's interest in jazz became a deep and abiding love, particularly for the New Orleans style of music and the blues. "Why we didn't become country and western fans, or something else, I have no idea," Wells Bentley tried to explain later. "We just loved the sound of jazz. Maybe some of the music expressed things that we felt. The boys that rode the rods, we knew of them. The people who went through the depression, we knew of them. We could relate to the problems that the black people had, because their music expressed many of the things that we felt. Maybe we just liked the beat. I don't know the real reason, but part of the love for jazz ... it did express feelings that we had."

The co-operative, CCF influence of Tom Bentley was absorbed osmotically. Even years later, with the benefit of experience, the Bentley children were hard-pressed to describe exactly how this influence came to bear. Their father, they knew, tried to teach them what was right and what was wrong, how to live in society, and how to be a person who had a feeling for other people. He also raised them to think of politics as something for people at large and not just for powerful businessmen. Yet he never preached at them. He simply told them what was going on and what people in the co-operative movement were trying to do about it.

School dances, skating, barn dances in the summer, athletic prowess, popularity, girls, top marks in school, the hot licks of jazz, a father doing important things—halcyon days. Then, all of a sudden, it seemed, Don had finished school and had to decide what to do. There was no money for university in Saskatoon. Even governor general's medals didn't come attached with scholarship money. Except for a chosen few, the assumption was that after you finished high school, you went out and earned a living, whatever that living might be.

Don had wanted to be a doctor but that, obviously, was out. He had a vague interest in business rather than politics. That left him with only one choice in small-town Saskatchewan: the banks. Through a great uncle, whom he never met, with connections to the Bank of Nova Scotia, he landed a job with the bank in Tisdale, northwest of Canora and further into the parklands. Although the chartered banks were anathema to the CCF, his father wasn't concerned. Besides, if the banks were ever going to be nationalized, the expertise would come in handy. The move took Don away from home and gave him the feeling of making his way.

His pay was $40 a month. The prestige that went with being a bank employee was supposed to make up for the feeble salary. People particularly deferred to bank employees in a small town, as if they were a mystic order, because they knew how much money everybody had. They were also sworn to silence; hence they carried themselves with a certain enigmatic reserve when it came to gossip about who had what. Don supplemented his stipend with side bets at the golf course. He was shooting around par and always won. The local professionals—doctor, dentist, lawyer—wanted to play with him because he was so good and they didn't mind losing their spare change.

A year after the move to Tisdale, Canada declared war on Germany. The war hero's son found himself declared 4F because his eyesight was so bad. They said that if his glasses were knocked off, he would shoot his friends. He also had a heart murmur. In Tisdale, in his rooming house, he met a striking young woman, Ethel Davis, who was as bright as he was and actually earning $10 a month more. She was secretary to the manager at the Bank of Montreal. Soon they were going out together and making plans. Even if they weren't as poor as proverbial church mice, marriage at the time was impossible: the bank did not allow its male employees to get married unless they were making a certain income. Banks more or less controlled their employees' lives.

After five years, he was an accountant in a branch in Saskatoon. He had taken some university courses through the bank, by correspondence, and had done well. He had always been interested in the co-operative movement, however, and in the co-operative principle of helping people. Lending somebody $100 if they had $100 in their savings account—the inside joke about banks told by their employees—did not go very far. He wanted to work co-operatively with people and not have to refer to such-and-such a page and item in a manual every time he wanted to turn around. He decided to leave.

The bank was loathe to see him go. They offered him a small branch—an exceptional gesture from a chartered bank to someone who was only twenty-three. It would have made him a manager and was the first step on the way to the top and banking power in Toronto. The offer only reinforced his decision. He turned them down. He did not want to work for an organization that had to be pressured into giving promotions or into changing the way it operated.

Now, a little more than a decade later, starting at VanCity, Don had come to the beginning of another cycle. He and Ethel had married and had a growing family. They had recently bought a house on West 37th Avenue, off Cambie, not a prestigious address but quite pleasant. VanCity, with its one location in the Credit Union Building, could not compare to a main branch or regional headquarters of any of the chartered banks, where he might have been had he stayed with the Bank of Nova Scotia. That thought, however, did not occur to him.

VanCity was a better fit than he knew. He brought something to the credit union the importance of which not even he was aware, because it was so much a part of himself—the psychic imprint of his Saskatchewan youth. In places like British Columbia and Ontario, co-operatives and credit unions were on the margins of economic and financial activity, except for a few producers' co-operatives like Dairyland and the B.C. Fruit Growers Association. In Saskatchewan in the 1930s, on the other hand, especially rural Saskatchewan, co-operators were everywhere and had shown great enterprise. Every town had a Wheat Pool elevator and most towns of any size had a co-op store. The co-operative his father had worked for, the Wheat Pool, was a formidable, dominant force, whose reach extended to its fortress-like terminal at the Lakehead. Co-operatives were mainstream, had presence. They were for everybody, even if many people had an ideological prejudice against them.

VanCity, vaguely in the back of Don Bentley's mind, was also for everybody, although everybody in Vancouver did not know it quite yet.

CHAPTER 10

The Manager
Goes to Work

THERE WAS A LOT TO DO, but for Don Bentley that was the fun and the beauty of it. Auditor Fred Graham had been grumbling to Wiltshire about the need for VanCity to improve the efficiency of processing transactions. He was particularly concerned about record-keeping. Also, somewhere, and sooner rather than later, a branch had to be opened. VanCity had almost four thousand members, all flowing through the one office.

The inconvenience of just one location wasn't the only thing that was holding VanCity back. Bentley was saddled with an antiquated lending procedure, in which all loans, at least technically, had to go through the credit committee and be signed off before they could be issued. This was more than a nuisance. It held up the approval of loans and wasted the time of the volunteer credit committee. The committee had enough on its hands with the job that counted—reviewing applications for large loans. The extra administrative chore also wasted Bentley's time. He streamlined the procedure, to try to eliminate most of the nuisance, but was still stuck with its awkwardness.

The absence of a reserve board or a deposit insurance system also bothered Bentley. The conundrum was the classic one: how to create an atmosphere of financial security in order to attract depositors when the security depended on depositors handing over their money in the first place. At first glance, the conundrum seemed easy enough to solve. One lent a bit less than one took in, leaving a small margin, called a "reserve," for unforeseen circumstances. What would happen though if, say, because of a recession, more loans defaulted than one expected? Or if depositors in large numbers started withdrawing their money? The big chartered banks had huge stores of capital drawn from across the country and were conservative lenders. They could withstand almost any shock. A credit union was in an altogether different position.

Bentley and others in the B.C. credit union movement weren't the first to put their minds to this. The conundrum went back to the moment Hermann Schulze-Delitzsch and his friends opened their original co-operative bank in Germany in the mid-nineteenth century. They struck upon the idea of "unlimited liability," a venerable German tradition. If their new-fangled *Vorschussvereine* got into trouble, not only would their members'

53

deposits stand against defaults, so would all of their other assets, like their homes and their furniture. This exposure wasn't such a bargain. To attract the necessary deposits nevertheless, Schulze-Delitzsch's credit societies offered dividends ranging from 12 to 20 per cent.

This, unfortunately, only created a different problem. With dividend rates that high, one had to charge even higher interest rates for loans. It was true that 20 per cent for a loan was not so bad—it might even be considered a gift—when money was scarce and 50 or 100 per cent were considered "ordinary" rates for a hard-pressed tradesman; one non-people's bank loan was recorded at 730 per cent! It still meant, though, that the *Vorschussvereine* ended up essentially as co-operatives for depositors who made handsome profits at the expense of borrowers. The whole purpose of credit unions, on the other hand, was to help people by providing low-cost loans, with, necessarily, deposit rates to match. VanCity in the 1950s, by comparison to the *Vorschussvereine*, was paying its members a dividend on their share accounts—in effect, annual interest—of just 3.5 per cent.

Alphonse Desjardins had approached the conundrum quite differently. He simply set it aside. He depended, instead, on the members' collective sense of responsibility and on the intimate, parish-based context—in particular, on borrowers conscientiously paying off their loans—to demonstrate that the caisse-populaire principle worked and that depositors' money was secure. One of the earliest boasts of the Caisse populaire de Lévis was that in its first ten years it had made 3,800 loans, without a single loss. VanCity, although accepting members at large in the city and lending money to strangers, was not much different.

Desjardins's solution, however, still was not good enough for Bentley. It was one thing to demonstrate viability for people committed to the concept of a credit union. It was quite another thing, however, to attract significant numbers of members across a large city against bank competition, when the banks had their reputation as conservative, safe monoliths.

Even if Bentley did have a province-wide stabilization fund, he and the movement would be left with another problem. They needed to bring word of the credit union's advantages to more people by going beyond traditional credit union circles. That was the point of fighting for the changes to begin with—at least in the mind of expansionists like Bentley, and almost everybody in the movement was an expansionist.

It was one of those rare circumstances where the manager of an organization finds himself managing and thinking in different ways simultaneously, embodying multiple business cultures like an actor in a one-man stage show who is playing different parts. Equally rare is the actor who can do it spontaneously, with a built-in diversity. Bentley had that diversity. In his office at 96 East Broadway, chatting to members, he was the corner-store operator. Improving procedures and managing staff, he was the bright white-collar manager. Reporting to a board, devising tactics and undertaking major innovations, he was the chief executive officer of a nascent corporate enterprise. As one of the inside players in the B.C. credit union movement, region-wide, with connections across the country and in the United States—replete with both internal politics and outside dealings with legislators—he was an executive in what amounted to a conglomerate, in complication if not in size.

His office was at the front of the premises, so he could step out and see how long the line-ups were and catch any glitches in dealings with members. It was important to Bentley to provide members with the best possible service. Sometimes he helped behind the counter, filling in during busy periods. At the same time, he handled loans, which allowed him to know some of his members better and catch glimpses of the human drama.

It was relationship banking before the phrase was invented, and with a difference: the relationship was with people taking out a small mortgage or who had deposited modest savings, rather than with large corporate borrowers. The biggest difference was that these people owned the credit union and were members, not customers. They took a proprietary attitude. Walking into 96 East Broadway to deposit money wasn't, for many of them, just conducting a banking transaction. It was something of a social rite, where, in handing money across the counter, they were confirming their status as member-shareholders—their being part of an adventurous and knowing band. They were subconsciously monitoring, too, how friendly the service was and, by inference, how wonderful the credit union concept was when put into action.

A prerogative of ownership, and part of the rite for a few retired members with time on their hands, was talking to the manager—that bright young fellow who was doing great things—and asking him how he was getting along. Customers in banks didn't casually say hello to the manager and take up his time, especially when no business was involved. All the greater was the pleasure in doing it here. Besides, he was their manager, in the direct sense that they employed him. Bentley reciprocated. Other than cutting himself off, he didn't have much of a choice, but he also wanted to be accessible, despite the interruptions.

One of the first things Bentley did as manager was to revamp the deposit account, equivalent to the banks' current account. Until then, the teller updated the member's deposit account passbook when the member came into the branch and used the account. This meant fetching the appropriate ledger card and copying into the passbook all the chequing entries. Bentley changed this to issuing a monthly statement and cancelled cheques. It made sense and could hardly have been avoided. The teller no longer had to arduously write in all the entries by hand—and there were an increasing number of them, as cheques became widely used.

To Bentley, the change was an administrative measure. Underneath the surface, however, it was also a major cultural shift. To understand the shift, one had to go back to the philosophical origins of credit unionism. Credit unions functioned by a peculiar, contradictory, but self-balancing yin and yang. The yin was the loan account, either to allow for new possibilities or to rescue people from distress. The yang was savings, symbolized by the share account. The act of saving might even have a shade of credit-union revivalism to it: a process of redemption. The missal of this saving rite was the pass book. The member handed it to the teller, the teller inserted an inscription ordained by the amount of money deposited, and the pass book was handed back, carrying recorded history on it with as definite an authority as a hieroglyphic on a rock. The member walked away clutching the passbook with all the ardour of ownership.

There was a third kind of account, however: the "deposit account," for current deposits and withdrawals. It wasn't part of the yin-yang of loans and savings. At first, this anomaly wasn't apparent and could be overlooked, since chequing wasn't yet part of the account. When chequing was introduced, however, the anomaly could no longer be ignored. Diehard traditionalists denounced chequing as an outrage against the true meaning of credit unionism. Bentley, in issuing monthly statements with cancelled cheques enclosed, was codifying this apostasy. The artifact of the yin and yang—the passbook—was out of place for deposit accounts, so he replaced it. There wasn't just yin and yang anymore. There was a third element: financial services. VanCity's character was changed forever.

Bentley's closeness to the routine work meant noticing small incremental ways of improving how work was done—the beginning of an organizational culture of always thinking of how to do things in a more efficient or attractive way. The administrative guts of a credit union, as of a bank branch, were paper and information. Either during the day or after closing, each transaction had to be recorded and tabulated. This was traditionally done manually on ledger cards, which were kept in large, open files—one set for each type of account, with a card for each member. "Posting," the exercise was called. Cheques that members had issued and that had come in from the clearing system also had to be posted. Then, at the end of the month, the individual balances had to be totalled up—so much in share accounts, so much in deposit accounts, and so on.

A running tally of aggregate totals was also kept in a "general ledger." Tellers would balance their own transactions at the end of the day. Then the deposits and withdrawals for the day, plus the payout for cheques, would be totalled up by kind of account, and new overall balances calculated.

When the balances from the members' ledger cards were added up at month's end, the totals were supposed to correspond to the parallel totals already entered in the general ledger. If not, one had to trace the source of the discrepancy. It could be something simple, like a misplaced ledger card. Otherwise one had to painfully go back into the individual ledger cards and the vouchers (deposit and withdrawal slips).

The final step each month was to add up the general ledger totals—the asset accounts (like loans) and the liability accounts (like deposits). Those two sides should balance. This was the general ledger function, or "trial balancing."

Bentley had organized this work so well that the credit union inspector, going through VanCity's books, was struck by the operation's efficiency. Efficiency, however, is relative. With membership growing 10 to 20 per cent a year compounded in the late 1950s, and assets growing 25 to 30 per cent, the pile of vouchers at the end of each day, that had to be posted, was bigger and more time-consuming than ever. Bentley, with Fred Graham's help, investigated how they could change that. They soon focused on a new bookkeeping machine. One of Bentley's strengths was making decisions, but when it involved something big, he did not like to be rushed. He wanted to be sure the timing was right and he had thought the matter through. A decision on a new machine was postponed from month to month during the spring and summer of 1959. Finally, in November, with board approval, he sprang for a Burroughs F4200 "Sensitronic" machine complete with an automatic reader. The machine cost $20,000, a whopping sum for the credit union, roughly equal to all of the retained earnings the previous year.

No other credit union in western Canada had one of these clunking, heavy weapons of bookkeeping, otherwise known as an electronic accounting machine. It functioned by three magnetic strips on the back of each ledger card which encoded data. The machine was a wonder. For monthly totals when balance day rolled around, the operator just stacked the cards in the reader and flipped a lever; the reader ran the cards through, picking up the last balance on each one. For posting deposit-account (chequing) entries throughout the month, a double card was used, with the same entries being recorded on each half. At the end of the month, one half was sliced off and became the member's statement, handed out with the cancelled cheques. Other manual steps were eliminated and, with them, the possibility of errors.

Bentley brought in somebody who had worked for him in his Fishermen's Co-operative days, Laura Smalley, to operate the machine. It took a year to gradually switch over to the new system. "Electronics at Work in Vancouver City Savings," trumpeted a headline over a proud story in the *B.C. Credit Unionist.* The overtime of several people was eliminated, and additional operators and more old-style bookkeeping machines were avoided. What counted more, however, was the psychological impact of having the machine —the latest in banking technology, and in a member-owned credit union with fewer than fifteen employees. Bentley realized, looking at the Sensitronic, that despite VanCity's small size, the landscape had changed. He had the means, now, to gain a technical advantage. His operation could be as sophisticated as a bank branch—maybe, he reflected, more sophisticated.

Branches were also on the agenda. In a sense they always had been. VanCity's directors had begun talking about opening a second branch as early as 1950, and had been muttering about the need for it ever since. Actually doing it, however, meant crossing an invisible political line—the equivalent, in the B.C. credit union movement, of starting a revolution. By 1955, when Bentley was hired, the directors in their own minds had already crossed that line. They were beyond being cowed by critics in the movement.

A combination of factors finally forced the decision. The growing pains at 96 East Broadway had become truly intolerable. One just had to walk into the office to see how bad it was, Wiltshire recalled. The noise and the crowding were putting extraordinary pressure on staff. Wiltshire and Payton worked on the branch idea for quite a while. They met with a group of members in south Vancouver, where there was considerable membership strength. The members wanted a branch close to home. The new branch, in a rented storefront on East 41st Avenue just off Victoria Drive, opened on August 15, 1957, complete with spot announcements on CKNW, school book covers, and 17,500 leaflets distributed to households in the neighbourhood.

Wiltshire, Bentley and Payton presided at the opening. It was a modest, almost awkward, ceremony, with only a few people present. The three of them had no doubt, though, that what they were doing was historic. Wiltshire and Payton, the founding fathers of the branch, flipped a coin to see which of the two would have the first membership number in the branch.

Even as he was posing for the requisite photograph, Wiltshire knew that VanCity would be attacked for overreaching itself. Opening a branch was giantism, as some people saw it—moving away from intimate democratic control, which was not possible once membership passed a certain number. At the following annual general meeting, the ever-ingenious Wiltshire put a pre-emptive spin on what they had done. Opening a branch was actually a defence against the problems of size, he maintained. "A community-type credit union in a large city like Vancouver," he declared, "is—as it grows up into the big business class—in imminent danger of losing that neighbourliness and personal contact so necessary to credit unions, and becoming something similar to a large and impersonal finance company. Your board, recognizing this danger, last year embarked upon what might be called the beginning of a 'decentralization' program. We opened our first branch office. Not only has its operation been successful financially, but its worth has been proven in the closer and more personal relationship we have been able to maintain through it with our members living in that area."

Nobody could argue against a more personal relationship with members. By the spring of 1958, less than a year after the opening, the branch was already profitable. Instead of solving VanCity's problem, however, it just underlined what the real problem was: VanCity needed more branches. For every two people joining at the main office, one other member was leaving. In the summer of 1959, Bentley had staff try to keep track of the reasons, in a kind of exit poll. The main reason, in close to 40 per cent of the cases, was "leaving the area, or location inconvenient." "The necessity of branch operation as early as possible seems to be imperative," Bentley reported to the board.

Members in the Hastings and Clark Drive area, in lower east Vancouver, had called for a branch at the last general meeting. If the southern side had a branch, why not them? It wasn't until the fall of 1961, however, that Bentley made the decision to go ahead, and not until 1962 that the next branch actually opened. It was in the 2600 block of East Hastings, the thoroughfare running parallel to Burrard Inlet. It was also within hailing distance of the municipality of Burnaby, just a kilometre away. The location was an obvious one. Bentley had marked a map with membership concentrations. There was already a nucleus of members living in the area. The building was constructed double size to allow for expansion (and rental income in the interim). VanCity now had fingers deep into both sides of the working-class East End, anchored in turn by the main office just off the Kingsway-Main Street-Broadway hub in what might be described as Centretown.

Thinking about what they would do from scratch on East Hastings also got Bentley thinking of the importance of premises generally. He realized the quality of the premises themselves could help a boost a branch's growth. In that case, something needed to be done about the earlier branch, which was in happenstance rented quarters. The board committee artfully put it to the board as a matter of equality: If the East Hastings members were going to have modern premises, weren't those members supporting the original branch at 41st and Victoria entitled to the same? A lot was found a block north of the existing location. The upshot: two modern branches built specifically for the purpose.

Bentley kept pushing. He needed more space for the main branch, but there was no place to go, other than expanding the building westward. B.C. Central, which was now the sole owner of the Credit Union Building, dragged its feet, arguing that expansion was beyond its means. Bentley formed a partnership with Central to underwrite the project and get it done. VanCity occupied the whole of the new section on the ground floor, with its frontage on Broadway and stretching back to the alley. Then parking became a problem. Bentley wanted Central to buy the lot next door and use it for parking. Central again waffled and dodged. It said nobody else in the building was concerned, which was true. For Bentley, however, parking was a key ingredient of the future. More and more members had cars. Convenient parking was not just a good idea in itself, but also a way of gaining a march on bank branches in the city, which, having been established long before, generally did not have offstreet parking.

He refused to be held in check. Although he was on the board of Central himself, he began making plans to leave the building, in conjunction with cu&c, and build elsewhere ... whereupon Central decided that VanCity's idea about picking up the property next door made sense after all. "We were prepared to do what we had to do," Bert Gladu remembered.

Bentley hired a Royal Bank accountant, Ron Spooner, to run the first branch at 41st and Victoria. This caused ripples. It had been taken for granted that credit union managers needed to have a credit union or co-operative background, or at least sympathies, like Ted Sewell and Ivor Mills, and Bentley himself. Otherwise, how could they be trusted to protect and amplify the credit union's co-operative principles? Bentley wasn't concerned. He wanted people who knew at least a little bit about the core business. He felt intuitively that the membership-owned principle of credit unions was such a forceful idea, and so built into the organization, that it wouldn't make any difference where he hired people from. They would see that the credit union system was a better alternative. Banks were the natural source of people with experience.

The electronic bookkeeping, the new branches, and the parking were just a part of a systematic effort by Bentley and his board to build up VanCity's strength, with an eye firmly on the chartered banks. Each move by itself might not mean much, but together, reinforcing each other, they translated into muscle and agility. Hours were extended, with closing time moved from 4:30 to 5 P.M. weekday afternoons and from noon to 1 P.M. Saturdays. On Mondays, VanCity was closed down. The banks still shut their doors at 3 P.M. and weren't open Saturdays at all. The beauty of this and any other change, by Bentley and the board, was that they could go ahead and just do it—change hours, change procedures, change anything—without having to work their way up through an extended bureaucracy ending in Montreal or Toronto. The manager of a bank branch in Vancouver would not even bother lobbying for change, since head office was so remote. He would simply follow the manual as if it were handed down by God.

Every month something was added, changed, adjusted, tried. Access was broadened to allow for business accounts, including partnerships and limited companies (corporations) where a member was a major owner. Educational meetings were tried, on subjects like buying a house (taking out a mortgage) or on loans. Personalized cheques were introduced, the first among B.C. credit unions. Modernism was in. Bentley even had the board approve a contract to pipe music into the premises.

Lawyer Bob McMaster was put on retainer, beginning in 1956, for the princely sum of $300 a month. If a new contractual form had to be devised, say an agreement to transfer money from one account to another to cover an overdraft, McMaster looked after it. Employees were encouraged to take courses that could be useful, like a course on interest at UBC, which set VanCity back $8 per employee. Bentley himself attended a few management programs, mostly ones for credit union managers, like a five-day seminar at UBC sponsored by the League. He enjoyed these sessions if they were any good—which, for Bentley, meant if they had workable substance to them.

Rarely with Bentley, but it did happen, the original credit union culture caused a delay in adapting. Term deposits were a case in point. Finance companies and trust companies offered them, and the Bank of Nova Scotia had also aggressively entered the market. Term deposits, however, ran across the grain of credit union culture, with the share account at its centre. The share account summoned up the idea of ownership, whereby members were rewarded in dividends according to how well their co-operative venture had performed the previous year. True, the directors set the dividend rate with an eye on the interest rate that banks were paying on savings accounts, the nearest equivalent. True, also, the dividend rate remained relatively constant, reflecting this "market." The share account, however, still carried its own, credit union mystique. Term deposits, on the other hand, offered up their interest rate from the beginning—a rate that continued for as long as five or six years, however well the enterprise did.

Unfortunately, once people thought of a term deposit, they as likely as not were inclined to shop around for the best rate. It would also be more attractive than their savings accounts (or VanCity's share account). The lower administrative costs of term deposits, which were for relatively large sums and for a long period of time, made the higher rate possible. Credit union members were not supposed to crassly shop around. Theoretically, in joining a credit union, they were actively participating in an enterprise. Bentley knew, however, that—people being people—the interest rate attractiveness of term deposits would be irresistible.

Losing deposits in themselves wasn't his only worry. Such a movement would also pose a threat to VanCity's liquidity—the availability of enough ready money to cover VanCity's obligations. VanCity's loan portfolio was increasingly weighted towards larger and longer-term mortgages, which were locked in and had to be covered. Bentley did a study of the share account which showed that most of its funds were held by just one-quarter of the membership. If those larger shareholders began depleting their accounts, VanCity would be looking at a liquidity crisis. The top 100 of those members alone could withdraw $500,000, or 13 per cent of VanCity's deposit base.

Some credit union treasurers found the idea of having to pay set rates of interest for a long period of time scary. For Bentley, on the other hand, the length of term deposits in a mix was an advantage. The term deposits would more closely match the length of the mortgage mix, improving financial stability, which was exactly the protection he wanted.

There was another hurdle. McMaster wondered whether credit union term deposits were legal. As a fixed-term investment instrument, they could be construed as a specifically "banking" activity and hence fall under federal legislation as being the prerogative of banks and trust companies. This raised the spectre of the banks lobbying government to close off credit unions' freedom of action. Vanfed, the federal employees' credit union, however, put a term deposit agreement into play. Bentley borrowed the plan. VanCity term deposits came on stream in mid-1962. They almost immediately began raising substantial new money. There were no legal repercussions.

Making VanCity larger, more efficient and financially stronger meant that it could make more loans to people who couldn't get them from banks and that borrowers with modest incomes would not have to pay extortionate interest. Where, however, was the credit union purpose beyond that? Credit union treasurers and board members talked about keeping up to date. At one VanCity annual meeting, Bob McMaster, invited as feature speaker, encouraged the audience, and through them, VanCity, to be flexible enough to enter into new activities and discover new ways of being of service to members. What, though, did it all mean?

Bentley didn't need to be told to be flexible, as McMaster knew. Innovation doesn't come from instruction in any case, but from cultural liveliness. VanCity had that liveliness, from its credit union roots and from Bentley's own Saskatchewan-bred feelings. One day in 1959, Bentley was musing about mortgages. If you took out a mortgage from an insurance company, trust company, or mortgage loan company—banks at that time were excluded from most of the residential mortgage market—you were locked into its schedule of payments and the interest owing until the final payment was dutifully submitted—in another century, it seemed. It made no difference how much money you had saved in the meantime and how high the mortgage interest was compared with the interest earned by your savings. You had to continue coughing up that higher interest, or pay such a stiff cancellation penalty that it was hardly worth changing. The mortgage issuers, of course, wanted it that way.

It didn't make credit union sense, however, to stiff a member that way. The faster members paid off their mortgages, moreover, the more money was available to the credit union to write another mortgage and increase membership. Bentley created an "open mortgage," in which members could pay off the balance ahead of time without a cancellation penalty. The rate was slightly higher than otherwise but was well offset by the open terms. It was the first open mortgage in Canada.

Bentley used the openness of credit unions in other ways. Credit unions had long passed on extra benefits to members. Patronage refunds, an old co-operative practice, were an example. Patronage refunds were paid out from surplus, over and above dividends on shares. They were based on the amount of patronage a member brought to the co-operative. In the case of credit unions, this usually meant a refund to borrowers, according to the amount of interest they had paid the previous year. VanCity had two lending rates—a low rate, where property was used as collateral (in effect, a first-mortgage rate), and an appreciably higher rate for unsecured loans and second mortgages. On several occasions VanCity had distributed patronage refunds to members who had borrowed money at the higher rate—those who in principle deserved it the most and who, probably, needed it the most.

VanCity also held back on raising interest rates on loans in the late 1950s, despite the climb in the bank rate. In 1962, Bentley did what for a trust company or a bank would have been unthinkable. Because results were so good, he unilaterally lowered the rate on second mortgages from 12 to 9 per cent, a 25 per cent decrease, although the borrowers contractually had been locked in. He sent an upbeat letter to applicable members announcing the break, explaining that the faster VanCity grew, the less its operatings costs per dollar of interest on loans, and the more benefits and advantages it could offer. It was a powerful advertisement.

VanCity was also the first generally to offer mortgages to owners of homes east of Cambie Street. It had been doing so all the while. Other financial institutions weren't interested. It was the wrong side of town—working class and otherwise lower down the socio-economic scale, with lower property values and lower incomes. Conventional wisdom dictated that east-siders were poor risks. Cambie Street was like a financial wall extending across the city. "Agreements for sale" were used instead, out of necessity, with the seller in effect acting as the mortgager and receiving instalments and interest over a lengthy period. The builder of a new home, meanwhile, had to find money as catch can. VanCity changed all that. Most of its members lived east of Cambie.

Bentley also began to think seriously about doing more about loans to women. Banks asked women to provide a male signature for a loan. A woman's income was deemed to be unstable; her main job was in the home. She might quit work to have children. The man, a man—any half-respectable man who was willing to sign—was required. This was absurd, but the banks had always done it this way. The chance of a woman getting a mortgage loan on her own, from mortgage lenders, was equally remote.

VanCity and other credit unions, on the other hand, lent to women under their own name. Women nevertheless rarely came forward for loans or mortgages, since most did not know about the possibility. There was a cultural divide that stopped them from even thinking of it. As VanCity grew, however, word of the possibility began to circulate. Bentley was intent that the principle would be adhered to. A member-shareholder was a member-shareholder, man or woman. There would be one financial place in the city, called Vancouver City Savings, where women would be treated equally. The equal lending policy was doubly extraordinary because of the times— women weren't accepted as equals, and not just by the banks. The latter-day feminist movement—with its Status of Women organizations—did not yet exist. American writer Betty Friedan's feminist manifesto, *The Feminine Mystique*, was still a few years away. As women made their way with VanCity loans, the word spread. By the mid-1960s, loans or mortgages from VanCity had helped more than a few of them.

Interesting as these developments were, though, nobody had any idea that in the next ten years, 1965-75, this same VanCity disposition would revolutionize retail banking.

CHAPTER 11

The Governors

IT WAS LOVE—BY THE BOARD for Don Bentley—at first order of business. Bentley had hardly gotten his seat warm, in 1955, when the staff announced it planned to unionize. Although the credit union movement had many labour union ties, going back to the 1930s and the Street Railwaymen, and although Bert Gladu, on the board, was an International Woodworkers of America member, the announcement still came as a bit of a shock. The board struck a negotiating committee. Bentley managed the process, put in extra time, and looked after the details. He actually seemed to know how to manage. Board member Rolf Perry, who chaired the negotiating committee, made a point of citing, at the next board meeting, how much credit was owed to Bentley for seeing the negotiations through. He was their man.

For Tom Wiltshire, this was a relief and a godsend. He had always felt that if you hired a man to do a job, you let him do the job. Now he had somebody that he could leave it to. Paradoxically, the directors became more involved in VanCity rather than less. Bentley needed them as a sounding board and to provide a sense of something behind him. He worked hard at making this collective exercise work. This, too, functioned paradoxically. "We got more input from the general manager than we ever did before," Wiltshire recalled, "and the general manager got more leeway from us, the board, than ever before." A collegiality, akin to a family relationship, developed.

Most important decisions were made with and through the board. Someone once suggested to Bentley that he forget about the directors, who were just a bunch of amateurs thrown up by the annual meeting. He should simply go ahead and do things, was the advice. Bentley was taken aback. The directors were elected by the members who owned the credit union, he said. Ignoring them meant ignoring the principle on which the enterprise was based. It wasn't just a dry principle, either. Member-elected directors were a practical advantage. They helped bring members' concerns and ideas forward. They also helped bond members to the enterprise. Moreover, no matter what a director's background, that person lived and worked, and brought an experience to bear. If, on the other hand, Bentley thought of someone who could add strength to the board, he didn't hesitate to urge them to run for election. Bentley also organized board business. Was this the manager managing his board or serving it? The directors, with a growing affection for Bentley, did not think much about it.

They were a mixed bunch. Wiltshire lasted until the end of 1958. He then abruptly left the entire co-operative and credit union movement, out of self-defence against his enthusiasm. He had let his commitments pile up— president of this co-op wing, director of that, VanCity president, manager of cu&c—until literally, in his case, he could not move. He was felled by a severe case of sciatica and spent two months lying immobile in bed, looking out the window. It never stopped raining the whole two months. Wiltshire became so depressed that he decided to leave there and then. His doctor had told him to find a different kind of work in a different climate. He ended up buying a tiny seven-unit motel on Osoyoos Lake. Wiltshire being what he was, this was just the start of another business career. He and his wife expanded the motel to a 48-unit complex with a restaurant and marina, until he had a heart attack and they sold out.

George Payton, the old CER&S (Canadian Pacific Railway employees) credit union hand, took over as president of VanCity again. He had originally been president from 1947 to 1951. Rolf Perry, the credit union enthusiast from UBC, with his signature brush moustache, became vice-president. Payton was already long in the tooth, but a certain polite pattern set in by which it appeared he would stay in the president's chair forever. After every annual meeting, the board met for a few minutes to elect officers. Payton and Perry would be re-elected automatically, unanimously. Everyone was reluctant to run against Payton because he was dedicated and, as they saw him, a great old guy.

He was also an autocrat. Usually he was quiet, not the type to set the world on fire, and a good, solid worker. If somebody didn't share his opinion, however, he became caustic, pointed, opinionated and crusty. "A little czar," a fellow board member described him—Payton was short and stocky. He had been an infantryman in World War I. He had fought in the Battle of the Somme. When he had downed a few drinks, he would talk about life in the trenches, evoking the grim horror of what he and his mates had gone through. As one friend said, he had something to be caustic about. The trick, with Payton, was to persist in arguing with him. He would blow up and get bombastic. Then he would cool down and everything would be fine. Most people liked him. One just had to get used to his gruffness.

Bert Gladu was now a veteran board member. Harold MacLean, a chemist at the federal government's Forest Products Laboratory, where Rolf Perry worked, was another carryover. MacLean had needed an extra $100 to begin work on a house so that he could draw on a mortgage already arranged with an insurance company. He was building the house himself: he had decided that what one fool could do, another could as well. Perry suggested he try VanCity. He did, and got the money from Bill McIntosh.

MacLean was an immediate convert to VanCity. He was a convinced CCF voter. He felt strongly that the CCF would produce "the greatest good for the greatest number," as he liked to put it. The credit union movement's co-operative philosophy fitted this outlook. When he was asked to run for the board, he thought to himself that VanCity had extended the hand of friendship to him, so he should repay it. He was down-to-earth, energetic— not the stereotypical remote, pure scientist. He joked about having no business background of any kind. He was a chemist, he said, a fish out of water. He knew, though, that his feelings about things were the way a co-operative member should feel, and that was just as important. He also had considerable acumen. He was more effective than he let on.

Some new blood joined the board. Bentley in 1957 had asked Geoff Hook, a bright and energetic Englishman, to run for the board. Hook was treasurer and vice-president of finance of B.C. Co-operative Wholesale. The wholesale had a line of credit with B.C. Central, which is where he met Bentley, who was on Central's credit committee and was also, for a time, president. Hook was a certified general accountant and shared Bentley's interest in giving the co-operative movement more professional management. He took to Bentley's self-confident Saskatchewan charm, and they became friends.

Moffat Goepel was another accountant on the board. Goepel was the comptroller at Dairyland. His father had been one of the province's early credit union pioneers. Goepel had the unusual talent of consuming large quantities of alcohol and maintaining a sharp mind all the while. He was clear, concise and a joy for Bentley to work with. He could glance quickly at a page or two of a financial statement and then talk authoritatively about it. He had an exuberance about him; he liked parties. He was always ready to arrange a dinner or a Christmas party for the board.

Stan Parsons, a plumbing and heating supply salesman, also joined the board in this period. In the early 1950s, Parsons and his wife had needed $110 to buy an oil stove for their house. A friend of his with a small trucking business, Doug Forbes, was a VanCity director and suggested Parsons try there for a loan. He got the money. Shortly after, he joined the supervisory committee. Parsons was a super-aggressive salesman. His client list included half a dozen big accounts—large plumbing and heating contractors—and he routinely won the lion's share of their business. If there were competitive bids, he always got the last crack, as if the customer had wanted to buy from him in the first place. Mike Betts, a young protégé who later also became a VanCity board member, considered Parsons the best salesmen he had ever run into.

Parsons lived in the Joyce Road and Kingsway area, almost into South Burnaby—a middle-class neighbourhood, but modest, middle-class plain, a world removed from posh Shaughnessy or Kerrisdale and Vancouver's power brokers. Something about VanCity's membership-shareholder idea attached itself to his feelings. VanCity was open to him. Although just a salesman, albeit a good one, he could actually participate in governing the enterprise. His friend Forbes had told him how, sitting on the board, he had met people from different walks of life, doing different kinds of work, and how the discussions on an intellectual level at board meetings were stimulating and educational. Forbes was also struck by the positive attitude of the staff—an intangible, energizing something one felt when one walked into VanCity's premises. Maybe, Forbes speculated, it was because staff, in their work, were helping people. He had learned a lot from his board sojourn, he told Parsons. He knew Parsons had aspirations to move up in his line of work. He thought VanCity would be good for him, too. He encouraged Parsons to get involved. Parsons did, and became increasingly, devotedly drawn into what VanCity was trying to do until it became as much a part of his life as his own family.

Parsons ran for the board in 1959. The annual meeting was held in the Alpen Auditorium, a kitschy Bavarian-style hall on Victoria Drive. A certain Lloyd Widdifield was nominated from the floor without being on the list of the nominating committee, and he was elected, too, knocking off a long-time incumbent, a carpenter, Norman MacLean, to the dismay of many old-timers. Unlike Parsons, Widdifield had co-operative roots running deep into his youth. He was now manager of the British Columbia office of Co-operative Fire and Casualty, the co-operative general insurance operation headquartered in Regina.

Widdifield was complex, intense, aggressive, argumentative and pushing to do new things. Of all the board members, he was the one most likely to be critical of Bentley and take him on. He thought VanCity was stagnating and had stopped growing, and that some board members were coasting. Assets the prior year had increased 26 per cent and membership 21 per cent. This seemed a long way from stagnation. Widdifield had other things on his mind, however. There were still, at that point, only two VanCity locations in the entire city of 375,000 people. VanCity hardly counted a damn. There were no articulated strategic objectives. The board carried on aimlessly from one meeting to another. It had a limited self-image of VanCity as a small community credit union, which it was comfortable with. It didn't realize VanCity's potential.

Widdifield had spent his childhood years on a farm in depression Saskatchewan—in the decimated drylands in the southeast to which the Bentleys and others in the parklands had sent their relief help. The family survived by growing its own vegetables and raising chickens, pigs and cows. The nearest town, where the family moved when he was twelve, was Creelman, a hamlet of two hundred people, not far from Weyburn. Amid the desolation, the CCF and its agrarian socialist ideas swept over the area like a fresh rainstorm. Widdifield became interested and got caught up in the growing commitment to the co-operative movement. He began his insurance career with Saskatchewan Government Insurance in Regina, the new CCF government's ground-breaking publicly owned insurance company. While there, he joined the Sherwood Credit Union, which, along with the Sherwood Co-operative store, was the flagship of the co-operative movement in the city.

He began the co-operative insurance operation in British Columbia from scratch, with a pencil and a notepad in an empty office, and ultimately built it into the second-largest insurance company in the province.

Soon after arriving in Vancouver, in 1952, Widdifield was plugged into the credit union scene: The co-operative movement in the province was an intimate extended family. He attended VanCity annual meetings as a matter of course. Unlike most members, he was interested in how the organization was being managed. He spent some time on the credit committee, learning about the credit union business first hand. By the time he joined the board, he had already built up a head of impatience.

From the moment Bentley became manager and began putting items on the agenda, the pace of board decision-making increased, although who exactly was making the decisions and how they were being made were different matters. It depended on the eye of the beholder, and even the beholder could have two or three different views.

Tom Wiltshire, while he was president, figured that he, Bentley and Fred Graham made all the decisions, and the board routinely approved them. And, oh yes, there was George Payton, the vice-president, around somewhere. Wiltshire at the same time, however, felt that directors had more power at VanCity than they did in most other organizations because they didn't get a damn nickel for their work and they really believed in what they were doing. The power flowed from commitment. Ethel Bentley and those close to Don at work thought he came up with all the ideas and set the agenda, while skilfully giving board members the impression they were making the decisions, and giving them the credit. Harold MacLean didn't want any credit, even if he deserved it. He liked to describe himself as just a Bentley foot soldier. Lloyd Widdifield, after his own image, saw the board actively engaged. "We always had good boards," he remembered.

Bentley made use of the committee system, with himself as the common connection. All credit unions had a supervisory committee (for auditing), a credit committee (for approving loans), and, for annual meetings, a nominating committee. The credit committee was the workhorse. The key board committee strategically at VanCity, however, was the administration committee. It consisted of Bentley, the president, the vice-president and a third director on a rotating basis. It dealt with core questions about operations, like the opening of a new branch. It met in Bentley's office. Bentley would supply a bottle of rye, and the committee would order in Chinese food. It wasn't just a discussion club; it formally presented recommendations to the board, reporting regularly at almost every meeting, and it did actual work.

Committees could be struck for any purpose. Education and planning committees were established. There were short-lived ad hoc committees to look into such things as delinquent loans and how better to promote the credit union. VanCity began to have a board committee structure approximating that of General Motors.

Bentley also fed off the credit union mafia in the building: Wiltshire from CU&C, B.C. Central manager Rip Robinson, Lloyd Widdifield from Co-op Insurance, and Dick Monrufet, managing director of the League. Monrufet had replaced Jack Burns, who had gone to work for CUNA Mutual's Canadian office, in Hamilton, Ontario. The group met ritually for coffee in the Co-op Coffee Shop every morning. They all had opinions about VanCity and credit union problems. Auditor Fred Graham was in and out of the building. Having them around, each doing future-oriented work, gave Bentley the feeling of being part of a large enterprise already underway. Sometimes he asked Graham to work with him on the VanCity administration committee, on specific issues.

He was interested in developments elsewhere. His executive, despite limited funds, agreed to send him to a CUNA meeting in Milwaukee. He later made other such expeditions. CU&C and B.C. Central were developing new business methods and ways of handling information. Jac Schroeder, director of education for the League, was doing operational seminars. Schroeder was particularly interested in how to get the word about credit unions out to the public. Bentley also was in touch with the larger credit unions in the area, like Vanfed and Richmond Savings, which shared some of his vision.

By the early 1960s, he and the board had established their own collective dynamic. The seemingly exaggerated committee system was proving productive. It meant that the small organization could look at a lot of things and make decisions promptly. It could also look ahead.

Mike Betts, a young colleague of Stan Parsons who joined the board many years later, once characterized it as a family, with all its members pitching in. About once a year, Don and Ethel Bentley entertained the board and committee members and their wives at their home on West 37th Avenue. Bert and Flo Gladu played host one year. Every time VanCity hit another million-dollar mark in assets, it had a big blow-out in some restaurant or hotel, until it was passing million-dollar marks so often, it had to stop doing it. The banquets devolved into an annual Christmas dinner for the board and senior management. Staff, still not very numerous, held parties in their own branches.

Families produce their own quiet tensions. Bentley rarely pushed anything to a vote before he was sure he had the board's support. If the board was having trouble with a proposal, he would pull it back rather than argue it out to a finish, to give himself more time to talk the idea over with them. He never went into a meeting blind. Sometimes he called up board members to sound them out.

At first, he could not get the board to take the time at meetings to go into issues in the depth he wanted—in particular, to explore in a freewheeling way where they were heading as a growing organization. The ambitious ideas of some of the directors, though, when the board changed composition and became more activist, really troubled Bentley. He feared the board would do something precipitate and, worst of all, damage VanCity's financial position, on which everything depended, especially since credit unions did not have the outward respectability of the banks. He would let board members discuss some bright idea one of them had brought up, and then take the opposite side—as a check on something that had not been completely worked out. He liked to argue in this contrarian fashion, as a method of understanding. He had a gentle hand. He wouldn't just dismiss ideas he thought were impractical. When something was happening that he really didn't like, however—that had a pitch of belligerence to it rather than collegiality—he became quieter and quieter, as if he didn't trust himself to speak out for fear of what his words might do. He swallowed tensions.

He would stew around at home after a board meeting, instead—cross, letting off steam, talking to Ethel about the long-run problems in an idea that the board, seeing it only up close, hadn't grasped. He still was contained, however. He didn't let the tension out by shouting and raging. It got to his stomach, and he was often in agony. Ethel was sure he had stomach cancer. He went to see a specialist several times. His pain was ultimately diagnosed as a nervous stomach, like a captive volcano. He kept a jar of Tums on his desk and gobbled them like peppermints. He was hard to read, seemingly relaxed and analytic regardless of what was happening inside.

Bentley's strategy, when an idea worried him, was to drag his feet or otherwise delay. He would talk to some of the board members until he got enough of them thinking about the negative implications. His quiet-spokenness was deceiving. Ethel thought of him as an iron fist in a velvet glove. If he was determined, there was no moving him.

This foot-dragging distracted Widdifield no end. Widdifield liked and admired Bentley, and knew him well—he thought Bentley was a great guy and a great humanitarian—but as for being innovative, Bentley was, in Widdifield's view, the most conservative creature one would ever want to run across. He had to be pushed into everything that happened at VanCity, Widdifield thought. Widdifield saw the board dynamic as a continuing struggle between an innovative board always pushing—at least, a Lloyd Widdifield always pushing—and a conservative manager, always resisting.

For Widdifield, credit unions should be doing whatever they could. When Bob McMaster questioned the legality of credit unions offering term deposits, Widdifield considered the lawyer's misgivings a good reason why VanCity should go ahead and find out. Bentley's long delays over new branches, like the one at East Hastings—five years after Victoria Drive— especially irked Widdifield, all the more so because Bentley agreed new branches were needed. They would have stubborn arguments about it. Gladu was as impatient as Widdifield. Bentley, he was convinced, was holding the strings too tight. VanCity at one point found itself desperately checking that mortgage and loan payments were made on time, not because it was afraid of defaults but because it could not make any more new loans until money from the old loans came in. The way to get additional funds to expand lending was, of course, to open new branches.

Bentley's concern was that VanCity didn't yet have the money for it— there wasn't a large enough contingency fund if necessary to cover initial losses. For him, not the idea of expansion in itself, but timing, was the crucial factor, and timing depended on his reading of the financial data, which he personally pulled together at the end of every month. He liked to do the financial statements, working with the components like a sculptor working with clay, to give himself a more intimate feel of where the organization was. He knew he couldn't compete with the banks unless there was strength there. When Gladu asked him about the delay in opening the next branch, Bentley used his financial statements to pacify him. "But when?" Gladu asked him later. Bentley talked about the uncertain economy. These responses automatically defeated Gladu. He wasn't in a position to turn around and argue the point.

What was on Bentley's mind, though, ran deeper than figures on a page. He was a child of the depression in Saskatchewan, when banks ran up long lists of undischarged debts. If something like that happened to VanCity, it would be devastating. He thought there would eventually be another depression, and he wanted VanCity to be able to ride one out for at least five years. Widdifield, although a child of the depression himself, wasn't mollified. He had come out of the same era with an urge to push the co-operative movement as far as it could go.

The opening of the East Hastings branch in 1962, because of its symbolism of growth, triggered a decision by Gladu, Widdifield and others finally to move Payton out of the president's chair. According to Gladu, Bentley himself had initiated the action, although he liked Payton. Payton was too comfortable with things as they were, they felt. He didn't have the dynamism they wanted and was holding them all back. He had been around too long. Their sensitivity to his feelings could no longer be allowed to get in the way. They devised a plot worthy of Shakespeare. The evening after the subsequent annual general meeting, in March 1963, the board met for a dinner meeting at the Biltmore Hotel at 12th Avenue and Kingsway, a venue with a certain fashionability. Instead of Payton being unanimously elected president, there were, as pre-arranged, four nominations—Payton, Gladu, Perry and Parsons—so there was no identifying a Brutus in the crowd. Perry and Parsons declined. Gladu was elected president. Widdifield was elected vice-president. The board also decided that the term of president be limited to two consecutive years. Payton was deeply hurt at losing the presidency, but that couldn't be helped.

They were now ready to open the throttle.

CHAPTER 12

The Lawyer
and the Accountant

BOB MCMASTER AND FRED GRAHAM. They were Mutt and Jeff, Castor and Pollux. One was a lawyer, the other an accountant. They were the lawyer and auditor respectively for the credit union and co-operative movement, giving even an inexperienced, start-up credit union a touch of professionalism and a sense of assurance. McMaster drafted forms and contracts and advised on procedure. He showed credit unions how they could do new things and how to keep out of trouble as they did them. Graham acted as a de facto management consultant on recordkeeping and accounting, helping credit unions stay up to date and improve their internal operations.

They were even more valuable as drafters of legislation, lobbyists and negotiators. Everything that had to do with the credit union future depended on how skilful and successful they were, since credit unions could only compete and expand as far as legislation would let them. The original 1938 British Columbia legislation was framed with small, quasi-tribal co-operative savings societies in mind. Except for a pro forma Act covering credit union centrals, federal legislation did not include credit unions at all. This meant that credit unions were cut off from the larger world of banking and finance.

Bentley also was involved. It was a natural role for him. VanCity, always pushing on the edge, had the most at stake. It was the province's fifth-largest credit union when Bentley took over, and in 1963 it passed the Prince Rupert Fishermen's Credit Union to become the largest. Bentley, too, was sagacious and intelligent. Geoff Hook, on the board in that period, remembered him mostly in those years as a movement leader, consorting with Graham, McMaster and B.C. Central head Rip Robinson, as if managing VanCity were almost incidental. McMaster and Graham gave something invaluable to Bentley in return. They were soul brothers—professionals, slow to anger, and analytic, but nevertheless deeply committed and enthusiastic about co-operation. Graham was particularly close to Bentley.

McMaster was a child of that rare and glorious strain of social conscience and commitment—the Canadian social gospel, Protestant-church variety. It was a current that included J. S. Woodsworth, the federal leader of the CCF in the 1930s, and Tommy Douglas, who became premier of Saskatchewan, both of whom McMaster knew. Like them, he was a CCFer. He was also a pacifist, believing that war resolved nothing and that negotiation was the way to work out differences.

McMaster grew up in Burnaby but was really a product of the United Church and its flourishing youth groups. At the end of the war, as a partner in a downtown law firm, he acted for the 10,000 Japanese Canadians, interned in settlement camps, whom the federal government was then trying to deport. It was a celebrated case. McMaster also did labour law. He was an institution at Davis & Company, an establishment legal factory he had become part of through a merger; he was the kind of left-wing, odd man out in such a place, who just would have an unusual client like a credit union. McMaster, though, with his characteristic warm smile, his civility and his sense of humour, was hard to dislike, whatever kind of clients he worked for.

McMaster was infamous for his peculiar filing system—multitudinous messy piles upon his desk—and famous for his ability to find the right file amid what appeared to be chaos, after searching and shuffling, and hemming and hawing, back and forth among the piles. If the sought-after document didn't ultimately come to hand, it was ipso facto in his other filing system: his inside suit jacket pocket.

The suit jacket was always rumpled. McMaster was thin to the point of being gaunt and scrawny. He rumpled his clothes simply by putting them on. His pipe in the side jacket pocket added a prominent bulge. The pipe was forever in and out of the pocket and invariably needed to be lit, which meant that McMaster was constantly searching for another box of matches somewhere in his pockets, rumpling his clothes further. Clothes, though, were the last thing on his mind. Nor did he seem to care about his health. Once into an interesting case, he lost sense of time. He had a chronic drinking habit—coffee. He was a teetotaller when it came to alcohol—he even acted for the Woman's Christian Temperance Union—but coffee went down the McMaster gullet at the beginning of every meal and at all hours of the day and night. He was a caffeine junkie.

He was also a junkie of ideas. He would light his pipe while talking at the same time out of the side of his mouth, maybe leaning back in his chair, and expound some theory. Principle was important to him. If he felt something was not the right thing to do, he wouldn't do it and would give up the fee. Conversely, as with the Japanese Canadians, he would represent unpopular clients if he felt a cause was just. He was calm and intense. He could concentrate completely on an assignment. Above all, he loved the law. He was like a monk serving a religious order, with its rites and its constant consideration of moral dilemmas—except that he was having such a good time at it.

Fred Graham was less of an intellectual than McMaster. He was more of an erudite technician, although he could make his way in a philosophical argument if it came down to that. He took the value of credit unions for granted, because they were exercises in self-help. Graham was taken by the fact that so many good people had pitched in to get them off the ground. He found it rewarding to be useful to those people, and best of all to be useful while exercising his profession, to which—like McMaster and the law—he was deeply attached. He was mild-mannered, quiet and thoughtful. After all, he was a chartered accountant. He had the graces that went with the profession. However, if by chance his professional integrity was questioned, as happened at one CU&C meeting, he could be outspoken, loud and intense—he would rise up, with his small stature, like David, and verbally smite the philistine.

Graham had become involved in the credit union movement through B.C. Central manager Rip Robinson, a west-side neighbourhood friend. When, later, Central had accumulated $300,000 in assets, it decided to begin using an auditor. Graham's firm, Frederick Field & Company, was appointed. The $300,000 mark became the magic figure at which individual credit unions also began using an external auditor.

Graham's first client in the movement had been CU&C. He had helped sort out its books in its financial crisis in 1949. This had been a revelation in the power of grassroots co-operation. Meetings were held with credit unionists to see if they were willing to sign undertakings to invest in CU&C, if that was necessary to keep it afloat. The activists pledged the necessary money without flinching. As it turned out, they were never called upon to contribute. Their undertakings, though, were enough to get CU&C's licence renewed by the superintendent of insurance, allowing CU&C to work its way out of its problem.

Since Graham was doing the audits for CU&C and Central, he was also retained by the League. Inevitably, through these three parent organizations, all the individual credit union auditing work flowed to Graham as, one by one, they hit the $300,000 mark. Soon he set out on his own, taking all these clients with him.

Chartered accountant Graham, with his aspiring professionalism, entered upon this credit union scene like a missionary venturing onto some primitive landscape. He was a trace shy, but his manual of acceptable accounting principles, like a bible clutched tightly in hand, gave him strength. His first big shock, akin to coming across a tribe of pagans with needles through their noses, was to discover that a person could be put in charge of a credit union without knowing anything about bookkeeping at all, not to mention accounting principles. CUNA Mutual had produced an accounting journal for start-up credit unions with rudimentary instructions in sequence. If you receive a deposit, the journal instructed, you do this and this, and enter the figure here. And so on. The novice just had to follow, like painting by numbers. Equally amazing, this primitive ritual worked.

Graham's overarching mission was to establish sufficient controls and to tighten procedures. He began to realize, however, that in an indirect way an auditor could also move enterprise forward. Soon, the small credit unions were no longer small and he was putting his mind to how to process transactions efficiently amid rapidly growing volume. Eventually, credit union treasurers, including his friend Don Bentley, began coming to him for technical advice. It amounted to management consulting. He had in fact already been doing it informally for years.

There was something more to his credit union clients than just the numbers, he realized. True, their set of books was much like any other. Nothing in the figures of their balance sheet said, "This is a co-operative." The people who produced the numbers, however, and their reasons for doing it, were different. "It's what goes on up here that makes it a co-operative or doesn't make it a co-operative," Graham, tapping his forehead with his index finger, was fond of saying.

They were a think tank without the name. Dick Monrufet, who ran the League, was the political animal—meeting with his board, working closely with McMaster, going to Victoria, pushing the movement. Monrufet was a raconteur with a sense of history and of the drama and wonder of what was being achieved. Rip Robinson, B.C. Central's general manager, was an instigator, like a magnetic force in an open field—gentlemanly and yet effective. He believed in small people—that is, people without wealth, power and prestige—being able to change things. Bentley was the multi-purpose thinker and also, as VanCity manager, reported from the front lines. He was close to all of them and, with that, in the middle of the time-consuming telephone calls, confabs and meetings that came attached.

Did the credit unions need a change in legislation or regulations? Explain the problem to McMaster, and it was done. Every year, he and Monrufet went to Victoria and knocked on Attorney-General Robert Bonner's door with requests for amendments, and every year Monrufet marvelled at McMaster's finesse. Bonner and Premier W. A. C. Bennett were interested in getting some of the levers of economic power into the province rather than being dealt with as a branch office, and the self-help credit union movement fitted. McMaster, also, was a fellow lawyer and was congenial, helpful and instructive. After a few pleasantries, he would fetch out the latest legislative requirements, place them on Bonner's desk, and explain why they were needed. He always made a good intellectual case. "When you get yourself elected, you had to start learning fast," Bonner recalled, "and he was one of my early teachers."

After a few years, Bonner began to despair. It looked like the routine would go on forever: the 1938 Credit Unions Act had been opened up and operated on more than any other piece of legislation. "We've got to stop meeting like this," Bonner thought. He suggested a new Act that would look after the expanding, bustling credit unions once and for all. McMaster drafted the legislation and Bonner put it through the legislature. The next year, Monrufet and McMaster were at the door requesting another amendment, despite the new Act. The movement was growing so rapidly, the Act kept needing changes.

For Bentley, the relationship with McMaster was crucial. He depended on what McMaster could achieve, to give VanCity the elbow room it was after. One of the things Bentley badly needed was to have his hands freed to do lending. As it was, all loan applications had to be referred to the credit committee, which was stuck with having to go through piles of routine applications. Worse, members had to wait until the committee met in order to get their loans. Not being able to provide members with quick service on loans and mortgages had become a bugbear for VanCity in its competitive world. Lloyd Widdifield was particularly insistent that a change had to be made to what he considered an absurd situation. "What's the point of having a manager if he can't make loans on his own?" Widdifield kept asking.

The new 1961 Credit Unions Act, which McMaster had drafted, gave Bentley the necessary authority, subject to board approval. The board quickly passed on to Bentley a lending limit of $15,000, which was gradually increased as housing prices rose. The Act also allowed for unsecured loans (loans on a person's signature) up to $3,000, with the inspector's approval. The previous limit was a mere $400. Bentley asked the inspector for a $2,000 ceiling, but was granted just $1,000. There was something fusty, anachronistic, comic, about an inspector making small-dollar bargains with VanCity, which had $4.5 million in assets, but Bentley shrugged it off. Even the $1,000 limit was an improvement.

The 1961 legislation also belatedly allowed VanCity to dispense with its supervisory committee, which was no longer needed. VanCity had been audited professionally for a decade.

Simultaneously, Fred Graham, with credit union representatives from a few other provinces like Saskatchewan, was fighting the chartered banks over their charges for clearing cheques. When a VanCity member deposited a cheque, it and others went to B.C. Central, which pooled all such cheques for the B.C. credit union movement. These cheques in turn were forwarded to the Canadian Bank of Commerce, which acted as Central's agent in the clearing system—a system the banks owned and controlled. Credit union organizations in other provinces had the same kind of arrangement. The charges were negotiated with the individual banks. They vied against each other to get the agency business, so rates were reasonable. In their powerful financial aeries, they hadn't paid much attention to credit unions. The agency fees they collected provided some extra petty cash.

By the mid 1950s, the banks still weren't paying much attention to credit unions, but they had at least spotted them, particularly the caisses populaires in Quebec, which collectively had close to $600 million in assets. Credit unions were growing fast. The bankers now got together, cartel style, working through the Canadian Bankers' Association. They decided that with one imperial gesture they would swat credit unions, by increasing the clearance fee by as much as six times. Credit unions could still have access to the clearance system, but at a punitive cost that would render them uncompetitive. In or out, they would be contained. "You must understand," one of the bankers' representatives told Graham, "that we built these particular tracks and if you want to run your train on our tracks you are going to pay us for it."

It looked to Graham as if, for the credit union side, it was a losing game. The power of the banks, however, only made him want to resist all the more. He led negotiations, for the credit union forces, at a showdown meeting with the bankers' association in Montreal. The credit union negotiators had only one advantage: the caisse populaire movement in Quebec, with which they had a close working alliance. The caisses were strong enough on their home turf that they were prepared to circumvent the banks if need be, and they had political muscle as well. The banks backed down. Graham wondered long thereafter what would have happened had they lost this battle. For open-ended community credit unions like VanCity, the setback would have been crippling.

Bentley, meanwhile, was helping Rip Robinson with B.C. Central. Central, in effect, was his second job. He was on the board and for two years was president. That meant one or two meetings a week, often held at the drop of a hat, first thing in the morning, over lunch or after work at the end of the day. Bentley was impelled by the realization that the strength of individual credit unions depended on a strong collective infrastructure.

Once, Central's credit line with the Canadian Bank of Commerce broke down and Bentley, who was president at the time, had to step in and lead an emergency rescue mission. The credit line provided the float for Central's cheque clearing arrangement with the bank (as cheques flowed through, they came out of the credit line) and also loans to Central to pass on to member credit unions. The arrangement was backed by a certain amount of Central liquidity (short-term securities serving as collateral). Rip Robinson had allowed the required ratio to get out of kilter, and the bank had called him on it. The ramifications were ominous, since to cover the gap, Central would have to call on injections from member credit unions, putting them on the spot. If they didn't manage that, Central's credit line fell apart, and with that, not just the network of loans, from the bank to Central to the individual credit unions, but also the credit union system's cheque clearing. The whole structure would collapse.

There was a panic. Bentley and other Central principals, who were on Vancouver Island when the problem surfaced, drove up and down the island, calling on credit unions and collecting whatever bearer bonds and spare cash they could manage. They stored them in a suitcase in the trunk of the car. They joked later about what would have happened had the police stopped them and asked to take a look. Bentley and the suitcase made it to Vancouver on the last ferry that day. It was too late to do anything with the cache, which amounted to $200,000, so he kept it under his bed overnight. Ethel didn't sleep a wink all night, worrying about what might happen. VanCity threw in what it could. There was a great deal of fear in VanCity that, because of the outlay, they wouldn't have enough cash on hand left for operations. Bentley also raised funds from the Saskatchewan credit union movement. The crisis passed.

One central-banking matter particularly preoccupied Bentley. There was nothing to protect a member's money if a credit union went under or to help it out of difficulty. VanCity and other credit unions each had reserves, required by statute. This money was invested in Central. Bentley also had a small extra reserve on the side. The credit union, moreover, had a superb loan-loss record. In 1960, a curious Bentley went through the credit union's entire lending history for all of the thirteen previous years and discovered that, out of $9,772,000 in loans, bad-debt write-offs amounted to only $15,789, or just one-sixth of 1 per cent.

Bentley still wasn't happy. It hardly made much difference what precautions VanCity itself took. Credit unions were fighting for respectability. If one credit union anywhere in the province defaulted, no matter how small and unrepresentative, they would all be badly hurt. A default in one location could even, theoretically, touch off a spiral of withdrawals elsewhere and destroy them. True, such a turn of events was highly improbable and credit unions could freeze withdrawals until everybody calmed down, but that didn't eliminate the danger.

Bentley also knew that he faced a marketing disadvantage because of this gap in the structure. The banks were of such a large size that their stability was taken for granted. VanCity, over and above its reserves, had its members' credit union idealism, or rather the idealism of some of its members. This was powerful as far as it went, but it did not go very far. It stopped short of the wider public. What the movement needed, for Bentley, was a central, autonomous reserve board to back them up, even if only for cosmetic purposes.

Bentley wasn't alone. Farley Dickinson had been toying with the idea for years. Everybody who was anybody in the movement, in fact, had been talking about it, ever since the Saskatchewan credit unions had created a province-wide reserve fund a few years earlier. The League decided to go ahead. Dickinson, McMaster, Bentley and the others worked on legislation for a fund, and the attorney general was ready to bring the bill forward, in early 1958, when lightning struck. A mining company abruptly, without warning, closed down its copper mine at Britannia Beach. Miners wanted to withdraw their shares from the Britannia Credit Union as they left town to find new work. This was impossible, however, since the funds were tied up in loans. Repayment of those loans, in turn, had to be suspended, because the now-unemployed borrowers couldn't possibly meet their commitments. Emergency meetings were held. Credit unions across the province, including VanCity, threw in funds, in the way of share purchases, so that the Britannia members could withdraw their savings. Solidarity aside, they couldn't afford to let Britannia go under. Eventually, as the Britannia accounts were settled, those outside investments were all paid back. Britannia Credit Union, with just a small grant-in-aid, even avoided a loss.

A year after the shock of the Britannia mine closure, the Credit Union Reserve Board of British Columbia was established, according to the enabling legislation. Bentley was appointed to its original board. He had, belatedly, the reserve fund he wanted.

Well before the encounter with the banks about cheque clearing, Bentley, Robinson, Monrufet and others had made a trip to Lévis, Quebec, to look at the Mouvement Desjardins first-hand and establish contact. The Mouvement was more the leader than ever—large almost beyond imagination and far ahead. The visit was a pilgrimage.

For Bentley, the trip to Lévis carried an unexpected excitement. He already knew the Quebec story, but seeing caisse populaire operations close up brought the story to life. He was as proud of what the Mouvement Desjardins had accomplished as if he had been responsible himself. He could see, in how far the caisses had gone, how much further VanCity could travel itself. Other English-speaking credit unionists also made their way to Lévis and were taken by the caisses' progress. The Lévis people, in turn, warmed to this excitement and were encouraged by being accepted and recognized on their own terms. It was out of these meetings that the strong relationship between the credit union movement and the caisses had developed.

One of the Desjardins executives in Lévis was Rosario Tremblay, a chartered accountant by training. Bentley, at one point, talking about VanCity, mentioned the Victoria Drive branch they had opened. Tremblay was taken aback. They debated the issue. Tremblay disagreed profoundly with what VanCity had done. The Desjardins principle was to have a caisse populaire in each parish, based on the local area. "As soon as you branch out, you play the game of a capitalist organization," Tremblay argued. "You move away gradually from co-operative principles based on decentralization." The object of co-operation wasn't to increase business. It was to lift up members to be masters of their own destiny. Branching was contrary to a co-operator's own principles. He began to think that Bentley was perhaps more of a businessman than a co-operator.

Bentley didn't argue back too strenuously. He had long before made up his mind. Vancouver wasn't a collection of parishes. It was a diverse, ever-changing city, where people moved from neighbourhood to neighbourhood. Besides, VanCity, branches or not, hardly counted compared with, say, the many caisses populaires in Montreal or Quebec City, plus the regional federations grouping them, plus the powerful Confédération des caisses populaires above them all. Co-operation took different paths, according to different histories. VanCity had its own history.

CHAPTER 13

VanCity Patriots

ROLF PERRY WAS IN A fighting mood and wasn't going to take backbiting, backward little credit unions any more. A back of the hand to the B.C. Credit Union League as well.

It was 1961. Three small credit unions had filed resolutions for the League's annual convention aimed at stopping credit unions from overlapping other credit unions' territory. The resolutions were aimed not too politely at VanCity. They had been sparked by a motion, at a VanCity annual meeting, that VanCity study the possibility of a branch in the Capitol Hill area in North Burnaby. The motion was defeated, but the idea that there were VanCity members around who actually countenanced the move and, even worse, might be residents of Burnaby (VanCity's charter was limited to Vancouver residents), had some smaller credit unions up in arms. Where was VanCity going to stop, they asked rhetorically? What small but honest credit union would it not force out of existence as it opened branches? Perry was VanCity's delegate to the League convention. He sat down at his typewriter and knocked out a draft statement.

Harold MacLean, the chemist at the Forest Products Lab at UBC, where Perry worked, and a fellow VanCity director, considered him a bit of a Casper Milquetoast. Perry, the administrative officer, was always meekly, obediently covering for his boss. He was short, thin, underweight, pale and sickly—one of those people with troubles. MacLean used to wonder if Perry was going to make it through the day. As it turned out, Perry hung on to a ripe old age. Most of all, when it came to credit union principles, he was a fighter.

He wasn't going to bother defending VanCity's position, he now wrote in his draft statement for the convention. He would just make a few observations, especially for delegates outside the Greater Vancouver area. There was no way of going back to beginnings, he explained. The credit union movement had to change and adapt to changes, or it would cease to exist. VanCity had led the way with change, had been a pioneer. Often, when a business showed a marked success, envy and fear arose in the minds of its competitors, possibly as a measure of excuse for their failure to do equally well. In this case, the critics had concluded falsely that VanCity had managed its success only by poaching on other credit unions' territory. The growth of large credit unions had come through service, and if one put too tight a rein on that progress, the service would falter, those credit unions would decline, and the entire movement would suffer. The presenters of the resolutions seemed to have forgotten that they were all credit unionists together.

Perry then went into some of the details. VanCity had eight thousand members in an area with over half a million people. There was plenty of room for all. Indeed, nearly one hundred credit unions had been established in Vancouver since VanCity was chartered. They could be said to have poached on VanCity's territory, but so what? VanCity didn't care. Should people be denied the benefits of credit union membership because eligibility for a credit union that they didn't want to join prevents them from joining another? Even more foolish, why should a man working in VanCity's office, for example, not be allowed to join because he lives in Burnaby or Richmond, when he could step out the door and be welcomed by any of several banks and loan offices within a block or two?

If that weren't enough to get tongues wagging, Perry, like a defiant heretic, then went on to challenge the common bond. It still had its place, he allowed rhetorically, but if it seriously limited service, the bond was uneconomic and was going to die of inertia and maybe destroy the savings of its members and damage the reputation of every other credit union in the province. Amalgamation of such credit unions with VanCity wasn't a matter of their being "swallowed up" or of somebody stifling them, but of salvaging their credit unionism. The days of the small credit union, which prospered by lending $5 or $10 to members until next pay day, financed by penny deposits, were finished. VanCity had opened its branch office because members had demanded it ...

Perry went on in that vein for several pages. "We in Vancouver City have a job to do and we intend to do it," he concluded, and hoped the delegates would consider the facts of the case.

Perry carried this speech in his briefcase to the convention like a guerrilla fighter carrying a charge of dynamite. He was under orders from the board not to use it unless he had to. As it turned out, the anti-VanCity resolutions did not generate much support on the convention floor, so it never came to open pitched warfare. For the VanCity board, though, which had read and approved the draft, the speech was an apt manifesto. They were fighting on two fronts simultaneously—a rearguard action against snipers and intransigents in the credit union movement behind them, and the chartered banks they could see hulking on the horizon in front of them. They couldn't take on the main battle unless they were allowed to expand. "These banks have branches all over the city on every other corner. That's what we should be doing," Gladu snorted. Bentley was equally intense. Dick Monrufet at the League remembered how pushy Bentley had been when the two of them talked about branching. VanCity was going to expand, however much the common-bond critics barked against it. Their defiance made for a wonderful esprit de corps, where Bentley's quiet but passionate mission and the directors' feelings coalesced. VanCity was different—it had its own soul and culture, although they didn't use those words—and to be part of it was to mark oneself off as belonging to something quite extraordinary.

The one-mile adjacency rule came into play. It was really the VanCity rule. It held that an open-bond credit union could not establish an office within one mile of another credit union. It wasn't a rule at all, in the legal sense, just an understanding, ingeniously dreamed up by Tom Switzer, then the inspector of credit unions, when the rumbling about VanCity's branching ambitions had begun. It allowed VanCity to open branches while placating the rest of the movement.

What most tied VanCity's hands was the limitation in its "common bond" confining it to residents of the city of Vancouver. Given the mobility of people, this was a totally artificial stricture. Members moving to, say, Burnaby could retain their memberships, but VanCity could not establish a branch in Burnaby to serve them conveniently and hang onto them, and add new members to make the branch viable. The board in 1961 tried to extend the bond to include "Greater Vancouver." The attorney general turned them down. He felt obliged to listen to the League, and in the League small credit unions, fearful of VanCity, had voting weight. He struck a compromise. He allowed people who didn't live in Vancouver but who worked there to join VanCity. Not until 1972 did VanCity break free of that restriction.

Meanwhile, VanCity was absorbing smaller credit unions as they fell by the wayside—seventeen of them, by the end of 1965—often salvaging weak loan portfolios in the process. Bentley was pointedly scrupulous about amalgamations. VanCity never approached another credit union with an offer to take it over. It would only respond to credit unions that wanted to join VanCity, either because their common bond was no longer viable (because of the closing of a factory, for example), because their financial position was deteriorating or because VanCity offered much more in the way of services. Bentley worked out a protocol with the League whereby a credit union wanting to amalgamate would be referred to the League first, learn of different possibilities and then freely make up its mind, so that VanCity could not be accused of takeover ambitions. It was accused of them anyway.

No occasion was too small to "stick it" in VanCity's face. One night, Rolf Perry presented a seminar to the local credit union chapter on VanCity's public relations and promotional work, like its educational meetings. Perry thought he was generously sharing VanCity's expertise. Instead of appreciating his gesture, some closed-bond members got their backs up. Promotion, for them, meant reaching out to every Tom, Dick and Harry at large— catering to their personal self-interest without a thought to credit union principles of mutual aid and solidarity. Perry, becoming more of a VanCity patriot every day, emotionally described the scene to his fellow board members at their next meeting. He didn't want them to miss how irretrievably backward some of those closed-bond retrogrades could be.

What grated Perry most was that they ignored how committed VanCity was to the movement. When he wrote that VanCity and the others were all credit unionists together, he did so spontaneously, with conviction. He, Gladu and Payton, even relative newcomers like Widdifield, had been in the trenches. And it wasn't just them. The board from the start, in 1955, had given its young man Bentley carte blanche for outside involvement—using his own judgement as to the amount of time he could spare from the office. The manager of VanCity, as the formal motion spelled out, had a responsibility to other organizations within the co-operative movement. If this meant he needed to be absent for undue amounts of time, well, that could be cleared too, by consultation with the administration committee. The time Bentley spent working with McMaster and Graham on legislation and on the boards of B.C. Central and the Credit Union Reserve Board was the credit union movement's for the taking.

The closed-bond naysayers, at the same time, freely used the money that came from VanCity's size, about which they complained so much. VanCity paid an increasingly large amount of dues to the League coffers, based on a per capita formula. VanCity, however, had only one, unweighted vote at League conventions, so the small, closed-bond credit unions, each also with one vote, could do with VanCity's dues what they chose.

A slow, seemingly endless tug of war was taking place. A yawning cultural gulf had developed between VanCity and the League. VanCity was forging ahead, and the League, out of synch, tied to its disparate membership, could not keep up. Disagreement over the League's dues structure surfaced first. Bentley wanted a dues ceiling for larger credit unions, reflecting educational and legislative services. The other part of the League's activities—field work—hardly benefited the larger credit unions at all. Bentley did not mind the higher dues if he was getting what he needed from the League, but that was the problem. VanCity and other larger credit unions were in direct competition with the banks and trust companies. They needed stepped-up research, communication with members, and advertising of new services—services that members were beginning to assume they should have. This meant hiring some first-class people and using real money. The way the League was set up, however, it couldn't respond.

Bentley and Dick Monrufet, managing the League, used to discuss it over a table at the Co-op Coffee Shop. Monrufet argued his case. Sure, it was true that VanCity was paying a lot of dues and getting little directly in return, but the VanCitys and the Richmond Savings could look after themselves. The little credit unions and the newer ones finding their feet—some with part-time treasurers—were the ones that needed help. Weren't VanCity and the others all a family and a movement together? Either they had a family or they didn't. And this family meant something for all of them. All those little sections of the movement added up. When the League went to Victoria asking for legislative changes—changes that VanCity needed most of all—it could speak for 225,000 members rather than for just VanCity's 8,000 or 9,000. He knew the changes Bentley was after and could see them coming, but not right away.

This only deepened Bentley's frustration. He cringed when Monrufet talked about the credit union family. Monrufet could always corner Bentley with that kind of appeal, because Bentley was a committed co-operator. Monrufet also knew, however, that Bentley could not wait any longer than he had. Bentley answered back just as Monrufet expected. VanCity did not mind making a contribution to the League, but it was contributing too much and badly needed additional resources. Monrufet could protest all he wanted about having to think of the whole movement and "the broader picture." VanCity was a key element of that movement, and its broader picture included the banks and trust companies against which it had to contend.

The tug of war went on for years as the League tried to avoid dealing with the issue. Bentley still got along with Monrufet—they were in the same building—but he no longer expected anything from the League. Widdifield was also in the building, running Co-operative Insurance. He liked Monrufet and considered him a good manager, but he also saw the problem. The League was trapped in the idea of protecting the little common-bond credit unions against the "octopuses." Monrufet was caught in that web. Unable to free himself, he talked vaguely about things having to sort themselves out.

Unrecognized by Monrufet, this was already happening, relentlessly. Bentley had a fallback strategy in play. He had cultivated a direct alliance with other larger credit unions, in a do-it-yourself mini-league. Credit unions with over $500,000 in assets began meeting in chapter. A couple of years later, the gathering became the "Million Dollar Credit Union Treasurers Club" (VanCity was up to $5 million). Stry, Richmond Savings, Vanfed and VanCity treasurers and credit committees held working sessions together. Richmond wanted to open a branch in Steveston and touched base with VanCity to discuss branching and League politics, and to get advice. Richmond's treasurer, Lewis van der Gracht, an ex-furniture salesman, had run the credit union for years from his kitchen table. Richmond was now growing fast, making great strides in market penetration. Van der Gracht lined up with Bentley. Rolf Perry reported that sympathy at League conventions was actually beginning to move towards VanCity.

The League was falling apart. In 1963 and 1964, Westminster Credit Union, South Burnaby, and eight other credit unions pulled out. The reasons were debatable, sometimes niggling, but they disaffiliated anyway. Monrufet attended the 1963 Westminster general meeting that dealt with the issue and blew his stack. It was one of the few times in his life when he lost control. He denounced the manager in front of the two hundred members present and walked out. He was so furious that he could hardly drive home. When he did get home he wondered what he had done, called the hall where the meeting was taking place and proferred an apology. He was still fuming, though. He had put twenty years of work into the movement, only to find someone he considered an opportunistic idiot casually proposing to throw it all away.

Bentley had his own response. He had VanCity announce its intention to stay in the League, but expressed a belief that certain changes were necessary, namely all the things he had been pressing for. A couple of months later, the League's principals attended a VanCity board meeting and generally agreed to VanCity's suggestions. It was too late. Psychologically, VanCity had already left and was making its way in another world, the one with competition from the chartered banks. Bentley was determined that the growing VanCity, with the advantages of its co-operative culture, would not be sideswiped by the banks' superior resources.

He had already plugged one hole—the limitations of the savings account, that is, share deposits—by introducing term deposits, but he had other strategic concerns. He had done an analysis of loans. Consumer loans, especially car loans, were weak. Most members buying new cars arranged their financing through the dealer, using the manufacturer's financial arm. This was an everlasting frustration for Bentley, all the more so because the Bank of Nova Scotia seemed to be making headway there with its Scotia Plan. The chartered banks as a whole had suddenly discovered consumer lending. The biggest threat, however, was in mortgages, which had become VanCity's mainstay. The banks were excluded from residential mortgages except for one minor category, and because of other restrictions in the Bank Act, they had abandoned even that segment of the market. There was a good possibility, though, that they would be given permission to enter the field with all the restrictions removed. When that happened, Bentley thought, the banks would hit VanCity's operations with the same powerful right hook that had stunned them with consumer loans.

VanCity's loan rates, like their savings rates, weren't the problem, Bentley explained to the board. They were competitive. It was the frustrating inability to advertise them effectively, even to VanCity's own members. He remembered a talk by some professor, to credit union delegates in convention, about adapting and facing competition. The talk was interesting enough, but he knew all that. What did it mean in practice? For all such conferences and seminars, credit unions weren't truly aware of the problems ahead and weren't geared to meet them. He had talked to his credit union colleagues about the need for research and for staff training programs. Most of them hadn't paid much attention. He wasn't sure what he had in mind himself.

Meanwhile, at the League, Dick Monrufet's job became increasingly nerve-wracking. Central began intruding into the League's jurisdiction over education and research, even though some League directors were also on the Central board. Central also had an interest in legislative change, which the League had traditionally looked after. Monrufet ended up fighting to defend the League's territory. He was proud of his own people.

He watched his field reps being marginalized. They still served a wide scattering of small credit unions, but more credit unions had become larger and no longer needed them. The share of the League's money going to the field reps was out of proportion to the way the movement had evolved. Monrufet, frustrated, found himself in limbo, in an organization caught between two sets of priorities. It was as if the League had been put in quarantine; he couldn't move forward. Although he wasn't quite ready to admit it to himself, the League's days were numbered.

Central was a Bentley organization. By happenstance, it was acting as a vehicle for large credit unions to break through the impasse where they had not managed with the League. The Central crowd considered Monrufet's people backstreet amateurs compared with their own rising professionalism and modernity. The League was a political organization, with all the loose ends that entailed. Central was a business organization—a central banker, with a treasurer's and accountant's culture—where balance sheets balanced and figures were neat on a page. The condescension of Central's cadres towards the League came naturally. Monrufet chuckled at their pretensions. He fought them, but it was like fighting his way out of a paper bag.

Aj Gill, who was running the Lake View Credit Union in Dawson Creek, was a League director at the time. He and some other young Turks had other ideas. They saw themselves taking on what they called "the establishment group." They began pushing for a merger. "I could see more and more conflict arising between the two organizations," Gill remembered. Having both of them was just inefficient, he thought. Management consultants were brought in. They recommended the two organizations should merge under the Central name to stop the fighting and to eliminate duplication. There were fierce debates. The chief proponents of the merger were among the League activists who saw an amalgamation—combining the social and political thrust of the League with B.C. Central's financial assets—creating a powerful co-operative vehicle. Finally, the merger happened. For Monrufet, tossed back and forth by these changing tides, the meetings and consultations to usher in the combined organization were a painful period.

In retrospect, the griping by Widdifield, Perry and the rest of the VanCity board had been the early signals of the League's eclipse. The League had been a glorious organization—pioneering, bold, principled and imaginative. It had reverberated with the enthusiasm of its activists, who realized they were launched on a great and noble adventure and who could hardly believe their good luck, that they were in the middle of it. It had gradually become a prisoner of its past. By 1969, just thirty years after it had been formed, its time had gone.

CHAPTER 14

The New Managers

RAY EVELLE WALKED DOWN BROADWAY at lunch hour, in the spring of 1956. He wasn't quite twenty years old, but he was already head teller at the Mount Pleasant branch of the Canadian Bank of Commerce, a busy, big-cash commercial branch. One of his customers was a B.C. Central employee who used to pick up bank clearings for something called credit unions. One morning he came in and said, "Would you be interested in making a job change? There's an opening at Vancouver City Savings. You ought to go see Mr. Bentley." Evelle wasn't sure what to make of it. He was earning $144 a month, a fantastic sum. His pay had gone up $24 in the last two years! But what the hell, he figured. He had nothing to lose by simply going to see the man.

The Mr. Bentley that Evelle saw was thirty-six years old. He had glasses and black, curly hair, and was a little pudgy. He was quite friendly. "He could be my father," Evelle thought. "He looks like a father." Evelle was introverted, cautious, pessimistic. He was prepared to find somebody who would hold something back, would perhaps even lie to him or would have a severe authoritarian streak. It would be pointless to change jobs in that case, regardless of what money they were paying, he said to himself. He wouldn't survive in that situation. Mr. Bentley, however, seemed different. Evelle liked him. He got the feeling that working at VanCity would be a nice, soft job—not soft in terms of work but in atmosphere.

Mr. Bentley asked him whether he knew accounting. Evelle knew a lot about working a teller's wicket and a front desk, but there was accounting and there was accounting. He wasn't sure what he was being asked. He tried not to commit himself on the subject. Mr. Bentley said he couldn't give him any more than $200 a month. "Christ," Evelle thought. It would be a huge raise. He wanted the job and pursued it. When Bentley finally called and offered him the VanCity position, he promptly handed in his resignation at the Bank of Commerce.

Bentley did become a father figure—the father that Evelle never had. In a way, it wasn't an accident. Bentley picked people by gut feeling, according to his sense of the person. Experience was important, but there were countless people working at banks who might be hired, and what did an impressive-looking résumé really show? Mostly that the person had kept his or her nose clean, followed the bank's manual, obeyed instructions, maintained the approved mien of banker's superiority and probably forgotten how to think for themselves. Bentley wanted people whose humanity was apparent and who, as a result, could reach members and be reached by them. The humanity might express itself in intellectual spark, in plain friendliness, in exuberance or even in vulnerability. Being maladapted in a bank—not quite fitting in, not having blunted edges, wanting to get out, even quitting and trying something else—wasn't a disqualification, for Bentley. It was just as likely to pique his interest. He knew what it was like to work for a bank.

Evelle was extremely young, a bit brittle and uncertain, untutored but clearly intelligent, despite his hesitation. Something about his vulnerability, and hence humanity and promise, caught Bentley's attention. The kid needed guidance. He would also be amenable to learning. He could be a good employee. Bentley took him on as a development project, to see what he could do with him.

Evelle had endured a rocky childhood. He was adopted into a foster family looking for income and was raised a rigid Roman Catholic. Although he got along with his mother, his father, a much older man, was a drunk and constantly cuffed him across the head, giving him permanent ear damage.

They lived in west Point Grey. Young Evelle did well in school, particularly in math. Schoolwork came easy. He played a lot of pool and was good enough to pick up five or ten bucks an evening playing the rich momma's boys from UBC at the local Thunderbird pool hall. Chess was another passion. He and three of his pals would go to the old Dean's Restaurant after school, order a Coke each, feed the juke box, and play chess for two or three hours.

It was his mother who suggested he go into banking. She thought it was prestigious. Just before he graduated, he wrote a test for Bank of Commerce applicants. The exam was mostly math, and he loved math; he had no trouble getting in. After a while on the job, he had put away some savings, whereupon he punched his father in the nose, left home and stopped going to church. He enjoyed banking. He had never written a cheque in his life. Now he was finding out about cheques, withdrawals, balances and mortgages. Suddenly he was in the real world.

There were just six of them on the VanCity premises, down the hall from B.C. Central, when Evelle signed on: Bentley, Ted Sewell, Alice Willson, a steno-clerk, a "swing person" and Evelle himself. Bentley began systematically to train his recruit. Soon Evelle was doing the accounting and the payroll. Bentley, he thought, was an excellent teacher, spelling things out but not being needlessly repetitive. Evelle grasped the detail quickly. He measured himself by his ability to keep up with Bentley and to mesh with his intelligence. "Surviving under Bentley," was how he thought of it.

He was progressing fast. He even was annoyed when, after he had been at VanCity for a year, the branch on Victoria Drive was opened and Bentley hired an outsider to manage it. "I'm ready for that," he said to himself. He was not quite twenty-one years old. "Big-headed," he described himself later. Bentley suggested that it wasn't that Evelle didn't have the background. He just didn't look old enough. People who were fifty years old were not going to bring their money in and give it to him. Evelle had to admit there was something to Bentley's argument.

Instead, Bentley made him office manager. This meant that when Bentley was preoccupied with other things or wasn't in the main office, Evelle was running the place. His salary was hiked to $280, double what he had been earning at the Bank of Commerce. Bentley was also imperceptibly coaching him in small things, like his appearance, and knocking off his rough edges. Gradually he became de facto branch manager.

Knowledge of lending was the biggest part of what Bentley had to impart. There seemed to be three elements that had to be mastered to be a good lender. The first was how not to make bad loans. The second was to make sure that members whose loan applications were approved understood their obligation and where it fitted into their budget. It was important they be impressed with the need to make their payments on time and not force the credit union to send them a notice, which cost money and time. Bentley, he learned, was straightforward with members.

The third element was what to do when a good loan turned bad because of circumstances—a downturn in the economy or the member's losing a job. That was a different situation. You invited the person in, had a discussion with him or her, tried to straighten out the matter. The cardinal rule was to be fair with people. This was different from being soft because, as always, the money lent to some members had come from other members to which the credit union also had an obligation. It did mean, however, taking changed circumstances into account. One such particular circumstance that bothered Bentley, Evelle noticed, was people being arbitrarily laid off or fired after having given the better part of their lives to a job. Bentley always tried to help out. He had once explained to Evelle that when he had been with the Bank of Nova Scotia, he had watched his accountant get fired because a dishonest employee had stolen money and the accountant hadn't caught it. The accountant had been with the bank for thirty years. The incident was a major reason for Bentley's leaving.

Evelle also learned how extraordinary VanCity's lending practices were. Insurance, trust and loan companies, which did most mortgage lending, generally allowed a debt ratio of 38 to 40 per cent. The borrowers' debt payments, including any car loans or personal loans, and accumulated credit card charges, could not exceed 40 per cent of their income. Theoretically, since they also had to pay for food, heat, clothing and other expenses, they could not afford any more. This meant, for a lot of people, that they could not get a mortgage. VanCity, by contrast, went as high as 60 per cent and occasionally up to 70 per cent. Evelle kept saying to himself they shouldn't be doing it. Yet when one analysed the particulars, it made sense. A person buying a $10,000 house might, for example, make a down payment of $4,000. This provided a safety margin in case the borrower couldn't make payments and VanCity had to repossess and sell the property. With every payment made, moreover, that safety margin gradually increased. The debt-to-asset ratio, then, was more important than the debt-to-income ratio. With only 40 per cent of income left for food and other things, the borrower might be hard-pressed, but a budget could be established to make it work.

Bentley, in this lending strategy, relied on stability. How long had the person been a member? Did he or she have a steady job? These were important relationships. By thinking things through in their own terms, Bentley and his board were able to bypass a conventional banking rule written in stone. Many blue-collar workers as a result—and members were mostly blue-collar workers in those days—managed to buy houses with VanCity mortgages that otherwise would have been out of reach. They never forgot how young Evelle and boss man Bentley gave them a hand up.

Little by little, Evelle absorbed Bentley's credit union culture. He was spending a great deal of time on loans and mortgages. Sometimes he also did collecting, in difficult situations where he had a relationship with the member. He picked up skills in dealing with people—those intangible skills that come only from experience. He enjoyed the members, too, because they knew him as Ray and related to him as somebody who mattered in his own right. He discovered that they didn't care about his age, as long as he knew what he was doing. They would even seek him out for advice on their financial affairs. "There were a lot of members," a teller working under Evelle remarked, "who thought the sun rose and set on Ray."

Evelle was bright, crisp, efficient and high strung, and he moved fast—a live wire, always impatient, bouncing around. It never took him long to get to the counter. He filled out loan applications and made his decisions on them quickly, and stuck with what he had decided. He came in first thing in the morning and was often the last in the branch at night. He didn't resent this. He had been told, when he was at the Canadian Bank of Commerce, that coming in early and leaving late was the way to get ahead and he had taken the advice at face value. He was also given the authority by Bentley to hire and train staff. He had a demanding managerial style—was demanding of himself as well as of those under him. John Iseli, a young recruit hired by Evelle, who went on to become a branch manager, remembered Evelle's piercing eyes staring at him. Until he became familiar with Evelle, he didn't know what to make of it.

Ron Spooner's first job with VanCity—managing the new Victoria Drive branch—seemed, at first glance, a gateway to nowhere. He opened the branch with just himself and a teller. The first month's loans amounted to just $20,000, of which four, totalling $2,350, went to new members. There were only forty-four new members at that point, plus sixty-seven transfers from the main office. This tiny, storefront outpost in the working-class cum lower-middle-class southeast neighbourhood—a seemingly bleak financial backwater—was a far cry from the moneyed splendour of the Royal Bank empire and its cathedrals of commerce, like the main branch at Granville and Hastings, where Spooner had put in more than a decade. Something in that empire, however—its bureaucracy, its measured pace—had been slowly marginalizing him. He seemed always a step behind—a second assistant accountant when the fellow next to him, with whom he had been a junior, was an assistant accountant. He didn't stand out. He had neither the determined, calibrated pushiness nor the unmistakable genius to get ahead quickly in the empire.

Bentley's informality and friendliness, on the other hand, appealed to him, as it had to Evelle. VanCity, moreover, had its possibilities. There would probably be other branches. It looked like fun, expressly because there was so little to start with. The notion that there weren't customers in the operation, only members, and that the members owned the business—that they were, so to speak, the boss—also appealed to him if, for no other reason, than because it was different. It seemed, when one thought of it, a wonderful idea—almost exotic, compared with the order of command at the Royal Bank. "I was surprised and yet, perhaps, not surprised," was all that a colleague could say, when Spooner left the bank. Nobody but Spooner himself knew the courage that it took.

Spooner was as different from Evelle as night from day. He was optimistic, extroverted. He liked to keep track of people. He was a staunch Freemason. Unlike Evelle, too, he had been around a long time. Not very tall, pixiesh with his big ears sticking out, often breaking into a warm, toothy smile, handkerchief in his breast pocket, he talked and lived VanCity. "Mr. Van-City," Lloyd Widdifield called him. His cheerfulness and enthusiasm were buoyed by his sociability. He liked company, and he liked his martinis at lunch.

If Evelle's relationship to Bentley was like that of son to father, Spooner's relationship to him became one of younger brother to older brother, although they were roughly the same age. Spooner came to love the man unabashedly, as a brother might. Bentley gave him an open field and a collegial camaraderie, and uncovered in him an unexpected talent for marketing, on which Bentley increasingly relied. He had hired Spooner in the first place because he sensed in him a promotional flair that would come in handy in the future; he didn't envisage Spooner being a branch manager forever. Spooner discovered, after all those years at the Royal Bank, that he wasn't a Royal Bank person after all. He was a VanCity person—not so odd, since he and Bentley were creating VanCity culture in their own guise as they went along.

For the first time in his life, Spooner was at the heart of an organization. Everybody working at VanCity was. There were so few of them. Although membership was already approaching six thousand when he arrived in

1957, members still retained a family spirit when they came into the branch. Occasionally, after an annual meeting, the board would receive a thank-you note from a member who had won the door prize. It was the kind of small, middle-class gesture—a gesture of personal relationships—that Spooner appreciated. One year, all the door prizes were donated by an anonymous member. That said something, too. Nobody, Spooner laughed, made donations to the Royal Bank.

Spooner began going to CUNA and Credit Union Executive Services (CUES) conferences in the United States, when training and public relations were on the agenda. He, Bentley and Evelle met regularly—just the three of them, until the next branch was added in 1962. They would stay after work, go out for dinner, come back to the office and discuss ideas and put together plans. Bentley made a point of telling them he didn't want all yes men and that they should look at his ideas critically and speak out if they disagreed. It might seem to an outsider that Spooner was just a big fish in a very small pond. For Spooner, however, it wasn't the size of the pond that counted, or the splash he might make, but the freedom he had in it. Small though VanCity was, they were dealing with the same kinds of things that, at the banks, were being decided in remote board rooms in Montreal and Toronto.

Spooner was a soft touch and hence a lousy lender—"a horrendous lousy lender," according to Evelle. Evelle considered Spooner generally incompetent and was vocal about it. The two did not get along. Spooner, with his sociability, would take perhaps an hour with a member, poring over a loan application—something that Evelle would handle in minutes. This grated on Evelle. Spooner, for his part, thought Evelle was a young and pushy upstart who hadn't paid his dues.

After Victoria Drive, Spooner opened the East Hastings branch for Bentley. Art Farnden, a lantern-jawed former manager of the Powell River Credit Union, was hired to replace him at Victoria Drive. Managing the new branches at Victoria Drive and then East Hastings wasn't the most important role Spooner played for Bentley, however. Bentley had talked to him about VanCity's inability to communicate to a larger public or even to know what VanCity's own members were thinking. Spooner became a one-man public relations department, doing the work on the side.

The dilemma Bentley and Spooner faced was obvious. They had used radio spots as part of the advertising mix in opening the Victoria Drive branch. The League did a credit union televison campaign, to which VanCity contributed. Most of VanCity's promotion, however, was grassroots, like schoolbook covers and householder pamphlets. In the fall of 1958, VanCity made an initial foray into sponsoring worthy causes and other public relations. The budget: $250. Milestones, like reaching a certain number of members, were good hooks for promotion. On one International Credit Union Day, members were invited out to look at displays, have fun with guessing contests and enjoy refreshments in the Co-op Coffee

Shop on the third floor of the Credit Union Building. Six hundred people showed up.

All this helped. It wasn't much different in kind, however, from the lawn bowling scorecards George Payton had suggested in 1947. Bentley was frustrated by this, but not sure how to proceed. Promotion wasn't his métier. He fixed on the idea of "research," with its intimations of scientific modernism. "Research," for Bentley, was really a code word for trying to get an objective grip on something he could not quite sort out.

He and Spooner began with membership discussion groups, at an annual meeting, to get better feedback from members. A questionnaire was distributed immediately after the sessions. Staff were asked to keep a daily tally of reasons why new members joined. This gave Bentley, Spooner and the board relatively objective survey information. Two years later, they developed a much more detailed questionnaire, distributed to only a small portion of the membership, selected at random, to get some sense of status and trends within the membership.

New kinds of advertising vehicles were also tried, like the Lougheed Drive-In Theatre and weekly newspapers. A large billboard was mounted on a scaffolding on top of the flat-roofed East Hastings branch. "VANCOUVER CITY SAVINGS, 6 SAVINGS PLANS, UP TO 6% INTEREST," it announced. After some hesitation, Bentley and Spooner also sprang for a series of ads in the *Vancouver Sun* and the *Province*, as an experiment—a weekly insertion for nine weeks.

The trouble was that the budget was woefully limited. In 1963, with East Hastings on line for the whole year, only $2,800 was spent on advertising and only $16,000 for all marketing, promotion and education, including the annual report and convention travel. The overall budget item was still listed as a transfer from undivided earnings into an education reserve, which was then gradually depleted during the year, as if it were some special category removed from the mainstream of operations. "Education reserve" hearkened back to the days of Alphonse Desjardins gathering a few people together in somebody's kitchen to prepare tracts on the credit union idea.

Extra money for mass media advertising nevertheless was hard to justify. There were only three branches, with one, Victoria Drive, still quite small, and the other, East Hastings, just getting on its feet. They weren't generating the extra discretionary income to underwrite major spending. Even if they were, the mass media, for Bentley, had diseconomies of scale. He would pay to reach the whole city, yet there were just those three offices people could go to, which meant that most people in the city still would not become members.

Spooner did the best he could in the circumstances. He did not pay much attention to strategy. He functioned by instinct and happenstance. He liked talking about VanCity. He was a good conversationalist. He would talk to anyone for hours. He kept his eye open for local, low-cost promotional possibilities, like display booths and area events, which fitted the scale of VanCity's operations. An occasional full-page ad on the back of the *B.C. Credit Unionist* tapped into VanCity's own membership and the movement.

Jac Schroeder, the League's education director, had been after Bentley and Spooner to also get VanCity directly involved with its membership. The information forums, where people like Bentley and Bob McMaster discussed specific subjects, had been his idea. He also convinced Bentley to publish a newsletter for distribution to members, describing what VanCity had to offer and how members could manage their financial affairs. He wrote the first issue, after which Spooner took over. The newsletter was called *Our Working Dollars*, later renamed simply *Working Dollars*. It was well designed and typeset, with an eye-catching banner, small cartoon drawings, photographs and graphs. One of its early objectives was to get members and their friends who were borrowing for cars and refrigerators away from finance companies and costly instalment buying, and it worked. Spooner was able to use copies of the publication as part of his external promotions as well. Bentley was sure, now, that if they introduced a new service, like term deposits or personalized cheques, they could at least get through to their members and, through them, by word of mouth, to a wider circle.

Spooner was a skilful propagandist. One of his handouts was about the origin of credit unions and VanCity's beginnings and growth. He enjoyed the telling; the story was so unusual and inspiring. He wrote a piece for the *B.C. Credit Unionist*, with case histories of how VanCity had saved members money, as compared with dealing with other financial institutions and their misleading, exploitive practices. He had something of the populist, credit union true believer about him, with his flair for human interest—The Credit Union Saves!—as if he were one of the pioneers in the early League days of the 1940s. He wanted to get across the idea that VanCity not only had a history, it was making credit union history day to day. As Bentley had anticipated, Spooner knew how to communicate. It had nothing to do with an advertising and marketing background. Spooner didn't have any. It was a spontaneous extension of his own amiability and enjoyment. What Bentley hadn't anticipated was Spooner's writing gift.

The absence of a large pot of money to throw at Vancouver-wide mass media turned out in this way to be a blessing as well as a curse. It forced Bentley and Spooner to think through other ways of reaching their members and the public. Through that, they developed a communications mix with many levels and hence with unexpected potential. It wasn't so much a matter of Bentley liberating Spooner's aptitude as liberating his temperament. Spooner's temperament brought to VanCity a lightness and sparkle that the organization hadn't had before. This fused with Bentley's serious credit union purpose. The results were like a sorcerer's creation of a magical alloy. Young VanCity became at one and the same time exceptionally flexible and both exceptionally strong.

CHAPTER 15

Bentley Takes Stock

IT WAS THE SUMMER OF 1965. Don Bentley had been with VanCity for ten years. He sat in his office thinking of Jerry Voorhis, an idealistic American co-operator and former Democratic congressman from California. Voorhis had come from a well-off but deeply religious Kansas family, and had taken the social message of the Gospels to heart. Ever since his childhood, he had harboured a desire to be poor. "I didn't want as much as I had," he once explained.

Bentley admired Voorhis immensely. "What would Voorhis make of Van-City?" he wondered. Like Voorhis, Bentley was interested in the co-operative project—the inner morality of it. Spending one's life becoming rich and powerful would have been, for Bentley, a waste of time. He sometimes, in these early years, had turned down raises because he was being paid enough to be comfortable and thought that any spare money could be better used to build up VanCity's reserve. At one point, the board forced him to take the raise and hired a consultant to peg Bentley's salary at a competitive level. He also declined to expand his office, which was a small corner space. Whenever VanCity passed a benchmark, like $2 million in assets, the board, which was willing to cover the cost of enlarging his space, used to rib him about it. "Get something bigger for yourself," they'd insist, half in jest by this time because they knew Bentley would refuse. He would do things only when he was good and ready.

The psychic imprint of the depression made Bentley more compassionate in dealing with members. He still remembered what it was like for families to be thrown into disarray by unemployment with no unemployment insurance to fall back on and not much in the way of welfare, either. In 1958 the economy levelled off, and by 1960 some of the same signs had begun to appear. Unemployment rose. Mortgage foreclosures and car and furniture repossessions became commonplace. Bentley bucked the trend. VanCity had always worked with members who were having trouble making payments because of unexpected unemployment or illness. Bentley went to pains to persist with the policy and avoid foreclosures, even though the amount of loans in arrears increased.

On occasion, a member denied a loan or a special arrangement by Ray Evelle would walk into Bentley's office and appeal the decision, much like appealing to Solomon. Sometimes, Bentley granted the loan or dispensation knowing that every time he did so, he was causing a problem for himself. Evelle would have to back off and more or less apologize to the member for something he had thought was right. Bentley was frustrated by these circumstances. He scrupulously tried each time to base his judgement on the merits of the case. If he thought the member was wrong, he would say so. Fairness was the measure: The idea of fairness gave him a workable context to think things through.

Fairness worked both ways. When a member wanted to sidestep a provision, say, redeem a term deposit ahead of time—and members were just becoming familiar with term deposits—Bentley turned thumbs down. It wouldn't be fair to other members. An organization couldn't function that way. He always had in the back of his mind the need for credit unions to maintain financial discipline. If the member persisted, Bentley offered to take the matter to the board. The board always backed him on these items.

The gentleness inherited from his mother also was at work. His sister Ruth remembered an incident when the Bentley boys had done something unspeakably naughty, and their mother, who never raised her voice and never cuffed her kids, made them line up in front her. She then laid them across her knee one after the other, and spanked them with her husband's slipper. The boys howled with laughter, while she cried the whole time. She couldn't stand to hurt them. Don couldn't stand hurting people, either.

Credit union opponents who mistook this gentleness for softness, however, didn't know the man. Underneath his consideration for people was an unremitting determination. He didn't gossip about the conflicts he faced in the movement and kept his feelings close to his chest. He had competence on his side. Incrementally, over time, this competence carried power. He knew what he wanted and ultimately he got it. He had gone into branching, had prevailed over the backbiting at League conventions, had marshalled allies among larger credit unions and had seen a reserve board put in place. He had got the infrastructure and the freedom that he needed.

Whatever the impact of the depression on his thinking, moreover, he realized he was living in a different age, in which even many working-class people were generating savings, buying cars and large appliances as well as houses, and going on holidays. The 1960s were different from the 1950s, not to mention the 1930s. He made the cultural shift in his own mind. People were raising their expectations. He felt a storm of change about to occur. Credit unions, responsive to their members as a first principle, could capture that change. "Credit unions," board member Geoff Hook put it, looking back, "had perfect timing. They were on the scene to begin with and they were with the public at large." Bentley was determined not to lose touch with these demographic shifts. A young and religious Jerry Voorhis, in pre-depression America, might have wanted to be poor, but VanCity's members had aspirations. The trick was to stay true to the co-operative, humanitarian impulse behind the young Voorhis's sentiment—to stay true to

VanCity's slogan, "Where people are more important than money"—while at the same time adapting.

Bentley now saw clearly he was caught between two worlds. In the first was the original credit union spirit of co-operative solidarity. Credit unions provided loans to the "little guy"—people spurned by the banks. He made it a point to remind his branch managers about this. He didn't want them to forget what credit unions were for. Yet he knew that credit unions run just by grassroots idealism were a thing of the past—had known it when he came to VanCity in 1955. Even professionalism wasn't enough. One had to get a grip on the future. VanCity needed to keep in touch with what its membership and the public needed, right down to what tellers might pick up from members from day to day.

Most of the credit union movement, however, was lagging behind. Did his own members understand where he wanted to take the credit union? He had decided the previous year, 1964, to write a short essay in the annual report, to get across his preoccupations. He called it "Casting Shadows," an unusually dark title, especially when VanCity was doing so well. It read much like a sermon. It included the usual words about VanCity's strength being people; Bentley did not want to be misunderstood or to give his traditionalist critics in the movement ammunition. The essay, however, really dealt with change. The notion that the only constant in life was change would later become a cliché in business, but for Bentley, in the 1960s, the reference was futuristic and part of an urgent fight to shift credit union culture.

The essay contained two leading notions. First, "change must be recognized without having to wait for it to be forced on us." VanCity should keep ahead of others and not always be trying to catch up. Open mortgages and lending to women gave him glimpses of the possibilities. Second, VanCity would be "only as successful as its state of planning for the future, both immediate and distant." It was the first time he had mentioned the word "planning" in an annual report.

By the next year's annual report, he had moved another step, with a slightly longer piece called, simply, "Reflections." It was calmer than the previous article. An economic analysis of credit unions in the province had shown that large community credit unions would become dominant. Their size meant greater efficiency, and greater efficiency meant better service to members and more effective competition ... Others, Bentley had realized then, were finally beginning to see what he was after.

Even CUNA in the United States had suddenly wakened up. In the past, it had reflected the aging culture of small, closed-bond credit unions. CUNA officials, influenced in part by what was happening in British Columbia—through a prominent Nanaimo credit unionist, Rod Glen—were now talking about how society was becoming increasingly affluent, mobile, and educated. There would be more younger people spending money and more older people with substantial savings. Instead of "saving" because of fear for the future, employed people would be "investing" with an eye to rate of return, safety and liquidity. Goodbye to the man under the umbrella, sheltering himself with his credit union from life's vicissitudes.

Unsaid, but understood, was that banks and trust companies were now taking an interest in the "little guy" because he wasn't quite so little any more. They were beginning to make themselves more accessible and were even offering inducements to attract deposits. If credit unions didn't meet this competitive challenge, they would lose even their traditional base. This, again, Bentley had long argued. The key, he knew, was convenience—in VanCity's case, more branches. He could now use these movement-wide findings to beat back his critics.

Bentley knew, as well, that as VanCity spread from its working-class toeholds into other areas of the city, it would inevitably change character. He saw no irony in this. The credit union movement was always a mix of people. The whole idea was to bring credit unionism to everybody. He, Bob McMaster, Fred Graham and Rip Robinson were managers or professionals and lived on the west side. Why not more of them in VanCity? The deposits they would bring would make the credit union's lending capability, in its working-class neighbourhoods, all the greater.

Bentley, himself, was thoroughly middle class. Golf, bridge, and scotch and soda were the staples, with double Gibsons (the ones that come in martini glasses) for business lunches. Unlike Voorhis or McMaster, he wasn't a practising Christian. Ethel Bentley was active in the United Church and took the children with her to services on Sunday morning. Don rarely went. His church was the Quilchena Golf and Country Club in Richmond, and his congregation the foursome—himself, Fred Graham, accountant Art Teed and Ben Blockberger, who ran Broadway Printers, the union shop that did a lot of VanCity's printing. Bentley and Graham would golf in the rain, wearing slickers, or in the snow, using orange balls.

Bentley golfed both religiously and intellectually. It served as a catharsis, draining away the accumulated tensions of the week. There was something spiritual about stepping up to the first tee, breathing in the fresh air and surveying the fairway like a god looking out on the universe. Swinging the golf club the right way—a combination of elegance, mechanics, precision and power—itself had an inherent interest.

Bridge was another Bentley diversion. It was Ethel's game—she was a formidable player—but it suited Don's mind, too, and he had a passion for it. The two of them together were a powerhouse. They played regularly every other week—two tables—and sometimes in between, and played the game, engrossed, past midnight, often as late as two in the morning.

Ethel was intent on building a social life for the two of them. Don wasn't a social animal. He saw enough people at work and wanted to relax at home. He always tried to postpone parties when Ethel suggested one, although when she let him know a party was coming up, he would be happy about it and have a good time. Don's mother had told her she was good for Don because she got him to enjoy social things that he would never think he might enjoy. He worked far too hard, Ethel thought, into the evenings and attending meetings. That was the way he was—he loved his job—but they should have a life of their own, too, she felt.

Later, they would become members of the Arbutus Club. Don made the membership part of his salary contract with VanCity. They joined for social reasons, but he also began using it to establish a presence for VanCity in what was upper-middle-class territory. Once they knew him, their picture of VanCity changed. He liked playing the role. Somebody would equate credit unions with a communist plot or otherwise be misinformed. He would lead them on, provoke them and then, when they had got in too far, straighten them out. It brought out the rogue in him. He would call black white just for the fun of it. They wouldn't get angry. They appreciated his grasp of things. Back at VanCity, Bentley would regale his confidants with comic accounts of how he had enlightened his Arbutus Club acquaintances.

He also played bridge at the club. It was another form of argument for him. He loved golf, but he did not have to win at it. Bridge here was different. There was blood on the table. He had to win, particularly if he was playing against doctors, dentists and lawyers—the kind of people who would not likely grace a VanCity door. It was like competing against the banks and added to the enjoyment.

He was still attached to jazz, dixieland and big bands. One of his friends in the neighbourhood was an automobile dealer, Evan Wolfe, who later became a Social Credit provincial minister of finance. The Bentleys had bought their house from the Wolfes. Wolfe was an accomplished piano player—he still played in a big band—and knew the music. Often, after dinner at the Bentleys on a Saturday night, Bentley and Wolfe would listen to a Count Basie LP. They wouldn't talk, just listen, as if in communion.

He was beginning to indulge himself a bit. Liquid lunches with business associates were the fashion and he wasn't above partaking of fashionability, especially if Ron Spooner were part of the company. Spooner acted as instigator. Most evenings, he would come home late. He would stay at the office to finish his work because there were too many interruptions during the day. At home, he had a glass of sherry, read the paper, and only then sat down for dinner. It was a ritual, to quiet his stomach after the tension of work. The doctor had told him he should never put food in it as soon as he got home.

He would bounce ideas and problems off Ethel. She had eight years' experience in the Bank of Montreal and knew about banking. Talking to her about an issue helped him to see it more clearly. She was dynamic, articulate and intelligent, with her own strongly held opinions and not afraid to express them. She was "persuasive in her views," as Fred Graham once remarked, with a mixture of awe and admiration. She was also competent. There was conjecture about how much influence she had. She admitted only to helping Don with decisions by making it easy for him to talk about problems, and he did talk a lot about VanCity at home, baring his feelings and exploring implications. "I wouldn't deem to give him advice," she said. Yet on some matters she did participate in decisions with him. They largely had to do with questions of fairness. Paying women for the job was one of them. Later, she and her daughter Joanne were after him to name a woman branch manager. This wasn't without its irony, since Don, early in their marriage, had asked Ethel not to take an outside job and she had agreed.

He was also working more closely with Laura Smalley, whom he had brought in to operate the Sensitronic accounting machine. Smalley had asked to become involved in other parts of the operation, and Ray Evelle had brought her along. She was opening memberships, interviewing for loans, and helping out on the secretarial side. She had a straightforwardness and outspokenness about her that Bentley liked. The three—Bentley, Smalley and Evelle—became a triumvirate.

He was establishing working links with the city economy, specifically the real estate industry, a key connection for an organization in the mortgage market. "Don made VanCity respectable," younger brother Jack described the process, as if, somehow, it weren't respectable before and links with real estate agents somehow made it so. VanCity became a solid presence among realtors. Bentley, quiet as he was, also had a powerful persona with professionals, like lawyers, because he was somebody in whom morality, social purpose and business acumen came together, an atypical case.

Periodically, something occurred to remind Bentley how much further VanCity and the credit union movement had to go. A new member arrived from Germany with deposits in excess of $28,000 and an illuminating story. On arranging the transfer of her funds, she had been strongly advised by the local Canadian embassy office to use a chartered bank rather than a credit union, which was assumed to be unreliable. Bentley dispatched a letter to the League and CUNA's Canadian office asking them to get in touch with External Affairs and rap a few knuckles.

Such slights and prejudices, however, were now more comic than otherwise. He had no doubt any longer that VanCity had strength and momentum on its side. A levelling off of membership in the early 1960s, caused by the slowdown in the economy, was now behind them. Membership was nearing the ten thousand mark. Assets were increasing 25 per cent per year. Competitive responses like the introduction of term deposits had worked. There were three fully functioning branches, including the main office, with twenty employees. A promotional and member relations department had finally been formed, with Spooner in charge, giving promotion some organizational priority. Radio advertising had been stepped up; it was still slight, but it extended over most of the year and was more than they had used before. Bentley also became chair of the Credit Union Reserve Board. The reserve board now had a full-time manager. The operations of small credit unions had been uneven, with sometimes even a potential default that had to be dealt with. The reserve board, however, had gradually raised standards and wrung out inconsistent procedures, to the point where fees to the board were greater than grants-in-aid and it could build up a contingency reserve of its own.

Bentley's life was changing, becoming more complicated. Not very often, now, but occasionally, older members who knew him and did not have too much to do would ask to see him. They wanted to talk to the big boss, just chew the fat. "Is the loafer in?" one long-time member would ask Laura Smalley. She would poke her head into Bentley's office and ask about it. "Sure, bring him in," Bentley would reply. Smalley would get them some coffee, and the two would chat. While Bentley still spontaneously gave up this time, he noticed, now, that it was cutting into his work.

He had an ambiguous relationship with the labour movement. He did not want VanCity employees to be unionized, but he also wanted to do the right thing by unions. The unionized main branch had decertified in 1962. This had created controversy. Bentley could count on somebody at an annual meeting asking if employees were members of a labour union and what VanCity's position was. There was talk of a possible information picket in front of VanCity's main branch. Bentley thought the two sides had better get together. A high-level meeting took place with a B.C. Federation of Labour representative and the head of IWA Local 217 (they knew that Bert Gladu, who was VanCity president at the time, was an IWA member). The labour delegation wanted VanCity to take the initiative. Gladu and Bentley argued that it was up to the union movement to convince employees to unionize. VanCity would not stand in the way, but it wasn't VanCity's job to do the unions' work for them. VanCity people were getting a good wage. Why, Gladu wondered aloud, didn't the unions go after the banks?

John Anatooshkin, a left-winger, a member of the carpenters' union and chair of their welfare fund, was also involved. Anatooshkin was a long-time and dedicated VanCity member. He believed that credit unions, co-operatives and trade unions should work together. He attended annual meetings faithfully. In 1962, his union picketed a building site where a new Victoria Drive branch was going up and stopped the job. The original contractor was non-union. The VanCity board and Bentley agreed that branch construction should be done by union firms even when, as in this case, VanCity would be leasing the building rather than owning it. The job was completed with union labour.

Anatooshkin, meanwhile, had been waiting impatiently for credit unions to be allowed to accept deposits from labour unions. Bentley had urged the League to press the case with the provincial government. As soon as the attorney general had made the necessary legislative change, in 1965, Anatooshkin withdrew all of the Carpentry Workers' Welfare Plan money and put it into VanCity. He was instrumental in getting the operating engineers and others to shift their deposits, too. They weren't huge deposits, but they were substantial relative to the size of VanCity—by 1967, amounting to 13 per cent of all deposits in the credit union.

Anatooshkin's loyalty to VanCity was great. At one annual meeting, in the Alpen Hall, he, his wife and his two daughters were sitting close to the front. Ted Sewell started making the draws for $5 share certificates, given out as door prizes. One of the winner's was Anatooshkin's older girl. Sewell came over to give her the certificate. "And who is this other little girl?" he asked.

"This is my sister," she replied.

"Oh, well, have one too," Sewell said, handing the second daughter a certificate as well.

The girls remained VanCity members and, in the next generation, their daughters became members, too.

However well Bentley knew Anatooshkin's commitment to credit union-ism, he was wary of having him on the board. When, later, it became known that Anatooshkin was going to run for the board—would, in fact, be part of the slate put forward by the nominating committee—Bentley encouraged Ted Cotter, who worked for cu&c and was well-known in co-operative circles, to put his name up and also get on the slate, to head off Anatooshkin. Enough people were then primed to vote for Cotter that Anatooshkin, who considered himself a close friend of Bentley's, missed being elected. Bentley wanted to keep VanCity free of any direct links with the labour movement, especially with a trade unionist of Anatooshkin's stripe. He was afraid it would set back his attempt to bring the credit union forward to the public at large. He even regretted that credit unions had the name they did. The word "union" confused too many people, who associated credit unions with labour unions. He had begun highlighting the two words "City Savings" in the credit union's name and using it as a shortened version—"VanCity" wasn't adopted until several years later—to help alter that image.

Annual meetings, however, were out of his control. Anyone could raise questions and bring up uncomfortable subjects. Bentley dreaded annual meetings. He was almost sick with trepidation the week before such meet-ings, worrying about what the members would decide and whom they would elect. He had no taste for discussing or arguing things in front of a crowd. Side issues were often in the air, and often he was afraid that the meeting would get out of hand over them and that the feeling of the meeting would be ruined. There were always some members who wanted to sound off or who had a sore head over something. They could be absolutely unreasonable.

Usually the anticipated big fuss petered out. There were ways to control unreasonableness legitimately—through the rules of order—without seem-ing to use a heavy hand. Bentley would still tense up as the meeting date approached. Ethel was always relieved when it was over. "Don needs a rest," she would tell friends. The two of them would take off for a short holiday immediately afterwards, each April. For a week or so, while the holiday lasted, she remembered, life seemed extraordinarily beautiful.

His relationship with staff had the intimacy he liked. He was unauthori-tarian, friendly, egalitarian. When he had to approve a sheaf of loan applications, he did it at a desk in the general office rather than taking the applications back with him into his own office. He was an encourager. He praised good work and avoided making people feel badly if they made a wrong decision. He didn't want to leave a mental scar in the employee's mind.

That spring, 1965, they had held the annual meeting in the Hotel Vancouver, in the main banquet room, instead of in a nondescript hall. Lloyd Widdifield, who was vice-president at the time, claimed to have thought of the idea. He wanted to show Vancouver that VanCity had arrived—that it had substance, that it meant something—and use the event to expand VanCity's presence. Gladu thought Bentley had come up with the idea. Rolf Perry, who had once suggested they give a Cadillac away at an annual meeting, to bring people out, was even more enthusiastic. "This is the year for the Cadillac, by God!" he argued. The others laughed with enjoyment.

The members now crowding into the banquet room in the hotel could hardly contain their excitement. President Bert Gladu, who was chairing the meeting, watched them coming and coming, and coming still. They stood at the back, stood on the sides, pushed in from the entry and sat on the stairs leading up to the stage. Extra chairs were squeezed in. Gladu wondered what would happen if the manager arrived with the fire marshall. Almost 550 members showed up, plus 67 visitors—double the number overall who had attended the previous meeting. Many members had come just from curiosity and pride, to spend a night out on the town in a posh hotel where they, as owners and pioneers-of-a-sort in a co-operative venture, could themselves bask in the accomplishment. Many of them had never been in the hotel. Now they could stride in as if they were taking possession. A few credit union old-timers wondered at the appropriateness of meeting in such an uppity place. Although they were struck by the incongruity of it, even they had to admit to being impressed. If Bentley had ever needed a sign that he was on the right track, he had it now.

Gladu had been a bit nervous the previous year, his first annual meeting as president. This time he felt at ease. He sat behind a long table on the stage. A "Vancouver City Savings Credit Union" banner was draped across the table's entire front, with "City Savings" in large, bold letters and a stylized drawing of the Lions Gate Bridge and West End high rises at one end, symbolizing VanCity's bigtown pride. The door prizes—this time a portable television set, a transistor radio and a camera—were displayed on a small table just to the side. Gladu introduced the others at the head table. There was the outside "parliamentarian," to make rulings on procedure if necessary. There was the vice-president, Lloyd Widdifield. There was Don Bentley. Everyone knew him, pointing him out, or, if they didn't know him, recognized the name.

The introduction of branch managers sent a ripple through the crowd. There were three of them, no less, counting Evelle, and that number, the crowd sensed from the excitement around them, was just the beginning. Gladu also introduced the board members present, sitting at a separate table. He noticed that a woman in the front row had come with her baby, so determined was she to attend. He read the directors' report, using the microphone and the small podium set on the table. Widdifield then reviewed the report, inviting comments. There was the auditor's report. The election of directors followed. Miscellaneous matters of business were cleared up. The floor was then opened to new business. Gladu knew, from previous experience, that two kinds of members would speak up—those with beefs and those with suggestions. He was intent on letting both have their say. All year long the board ran the organization. Now was the time for members to tell them what they wanted done and how they wanted things done.

There were also, now, ghosts in the air—ghosts of an era that had suddenly disappeared into the past almost as soon as it had come to glory. Farley Dickinson, the Stry conductor with the credit union in a briefcase, was gone. People could sleep through the night without being wakened by Dickinson on the phone, with one of his brilliant credit union ideas. Jack Burns, the streetfighter, had also died suddenly, on a visit back to British Columbia. He had gone down debating credit union politics to the last. Bill McIntosh, the first treasurer of that fledgling little credit union with a few members—somebody's bold and bright idea—was gone. Alcohol and emphysema got him in the end.

The following night, the board met in the Sands Hotel. They decided to hold the next annual meeting in the Hotel Vancouver's Pacific Ballroom, accommodating nine hundred people. They also raised Bentley's salary, effective immediately, to the munificent sum of $1,150 a month.

At the annual meeting, a member had suggested that the biggest potential was in the East End and mainly within the trade union movement. VanCity, though, already had two branches in the East End. In November, Widdifield, now president, cut the ribbon for a branch in Kitsilano, in rented premises at West Broadway and Blenheim. It was on the other side of town and, traditionally, for credit unions, the wrong side of town. Some of the directors had been dead set against the move. A foray westward, however, made obvious strategic sense, particularly since there was a good nucleus of members in the area. Bentley had Widdifield on his side and together they had won the doubters over. The Kitsilano branch turned out to be a master stroke. After one year's operations, it looked as if it might become the most successful new location of all.

PART THREE

1965-1974

CHAPTER 16

The Boy from Killarney

WAYNE MCKAY HAD A PROBLEM. He was twenty-three years old, in love, and didn't know what to do about it. He and his girlfriend, Carol Krieger, his sweetheart from Manitoba high-school days, planned to get married. She, however, was in Vancouver, and wanted to tie the knot the next month— May 1, 1965, the same day of the year her parents had been married. He was in Sioux Lookout, on the Canadian National Railways main line in northern Ontario, east of Kenora, working for the Canadian Imperial Bank of Commerce. He had been granted an interregional transfer—an unusual concession by the bank—but it wouldn't go into effect in time. Knowing the Sioux Lookout people were counting on him until then, he couldn't ask for a last-minute change. He had also grown attached to the family he was boarding with and couldn't bear to say goodbye. He did the only thing a romantic, overwrought young man could do in the circumstances. He eloped from both the bank and the boarding house. He packed his bag, threw it out the window into the snow, went around the house, picked it up and caught the train to Winnipeg and beyond.

He and Carol did get married May 1. Wayne then went shopping for work. The fellow interviewing him at VanCity, Ray Evelle, wasn't all that old. Evelle was impressed by McKay's experience and gave him the job. McKay started six days after his wedding. The bank in Sioux Lookout, meanwhile, was frantic. They had assumed the worst. The branch had been the victim of a couple of scandalous defalcations, one spotted by that bright young lad, assistant manager Wayne McKay himself. Now McKay had mysteriously flown the coop. The bank sent in a team of auditors and tore the place apart, but found nothing. They eventually traced him to Vancouver and offered him the position they had arranged. Unfortunately, he felt too awkward about what he had done. Leaving Sioux Lookout had been more than just catching a train. It had been a departure in his mind. He said, no, he didn't want to come back, he would take his chances doing something else even if that something else, as he knew, was working as a teller in a credit union for a mere $225 per month.

Or did it only appear on the surface to be a step backwards? From the moment McKay walked through the door at 96 East Broadway, he felt the place had potential written all over it. The slightly shabby premises did not bother him. He liked the people, particularly Bentley, Smalley and Evelle. Everyone was friendly. There was a different attitude in the branch which, at first, he couldn't quite put his finger on. The fact that members had a vote, and that staff got involved as part of the enterprise, appealed to him. He discovered in VanCity's members what seemed to be a credit union type of person—a kind of denizen he hadn't noticed before.

He also saw an openness he hadn't encountered in the banking system. Anybody working at VanCity could question how something was done and argue the case. McKay was originally horrified at the lack of control and structure that he was used to. Nobody, for example, checked the ledgers to see if the deposits and withdrawals had been posted to the right accounts. Troubled by this, and ambitious to do things properly, he raised the issue with Bentley. Bentley knew all about ledgers from his days in Tisdale. He explained that in the last ten years VanCity had lost about $300 because of incorrect postings, whereas the cost of employing staff for the necessary cross-check would have been a large multiple of that. McKay suddenly felt very small. He learned from this and other conversations with Bentley that if he was going to challenge something, he had to get his facts straight and to look at the costs and benefits. Soon he was focussing that way automatically.

His inquisitive mind had its uses. Two women on staff were deliberately throwing the ledgers out of balance. They would then come in on Monday, their day off, and supposedly look for the problem. They played cards and collected overtime, knowing all along where the differences were. Most tellers didn't have much experience and wouldn't have noticed. McKay, however, began picking up the errors on the ledger cards and forcing corrections ahead of time. Eventually the overtime conspirators gave up.

The Sioux Lookout recruit wasn't expected to stay a teller for long. He began lending, from one of the cubicles in the branch that had been set up to handle the loan demand. When he joined VanCity, there had been a long line of young male employees in front of him. One by one, they moved away or dropped out. Then Ray Evelle, de facto manager of the branch, unexpectedly quit to go into life insurance. Evelle had been with VanCity ten years exactly to the day. He thought his salary wasn't high enough to support his family and the mortgage for a new house he was moving into, which preoccupied him. Underlying that was his feeling that he had come to a dead end. He was bored, restless. He became depressed. The possibility of making a lot more money by selling insurance was a way out. Bentley plugged the hole with the manager from the East Hastings branch, an ex-Toronto Dominion banker, Don Nelson. He then offered McKay Nelson's old job.

The prospect of taking over the East Hastings branch scared McKay. He didn't know the city well. The East End was a tough area, because of racial tensions. It was a polyglot ethnic melting pot, yet McKay spoke only English. There were only three other employees in the branch. Scared or not,

McKay assured Bentley that he wanted the job. His salary doubled. He was twenty-four years old.

Wayne McKay was the compleat egalitarian, an enthusiastic and likeable prairie boy. He grew up in Killarney, a small town southwest of Winnipeg, near the American border. He curled. He played baseball. In his senior years in high school, he also often played hookey—usually to sneak off to the golf course. Hookey or not, he did well in school, vying with another student for top grades. He liked learning and liked competing with his teachers.

For all his enthusiasm about the rites of the young in small-town southern Manitoba in the 1950s, young McKay was also starting to think for himself and assess the world. He wrote a high-school column for the local paper, in which occasionally he took on the school administration—to the amusement of the whole town, although not of the principal, who was a next-door neighbour and a good friend of his father's. Young as he was, or maybe because he was so young, unfairness bothered McKay and he challenged it wherever he saw it.

The family were Baptists. One aspect of this upbringing in particular stuck to him—to be one's brother's keeper, that is, to help others in a jam. The Baptist minister, Audrey Kemp, a single woman, stayed with the McKays. Because of her willingness to help people, she had a large following in town, going beyond the Baptist Church. Later she went to Toronto to work with street children on the Yonge Street strip. Kemp made a lasting impression on McKay's attitude towards women. Watching and listening to her—seeing her stand behind the pulpit—he took it for granted that a woman could do anything.

Southern Manitoba was archly conservative, yet it had a radical, agrarian co-operative tradition. Wayne's parents were members of the Killarney Consumers' Co-op. The farmers in the area helped make the store a major presence. Wayne's father, a contracter, was a committed co-operator. He liked the idea of pooling. He and some other contractors had agreed to buy most of their lumber from the co-op store, which didn't make them too popular with the other lumber yards in town. There was a continuing clash in the town between the co-op and private sector, with some families resenting the business the co-op was taking away from their breadwinners and refusing ever to shop in the co-op store.

McKay, despite his talent, was too much a Killarney boy. He had trouble leaving home. He decided not to go to university, pretending to himself he should be going to work. He took a job as produce manager at the co-op store, until he left in a tiff with his boss over orders to wash the floor on New Year's Eve. The best part of the job had been delivering groceries—where the elderly lady customers would invite him in for tea and a chat. It took him about twice as long to make the rounds. He told the store manager that the public relations value of these visits more than made up for the extra time. He had realized that the ladies were ordering groceries just for his company.

Looking for a job, McKay then joined the local Canadian Bank of Commerce, the only financial institution in town. He learned that banks, those citadels of financial power and respectability, were really made of people, some of whom were struggling with their own demons. The manager was an alcoholic. The staff had to hustle him down the back stairs to keep him away from customers when he was inebriated, which was often. He had a bad eye condition and couldn't drive, which was just as well. McKay ferried him around, to see his relatives or to buy chickens. He became used to taking care of him.

He also learned, by looking at ledger sheets, how much money there was in society, even in a small prairie town. The farmers were prosperous. Others apparently also realized this, because they started a credit union. McKay's manager hated credit unions. He instructed his staff to do everything they could to put the fledgling credit union out of business, including stern phone calls to members who deposited the bank's cheques there.

McKay was assistant accountant, third in command, when he was transferred to Sioux Lookout, a railway town in the middle of nowhere. This was his testing ground, not of banking as most people think of it—working at cash or assessing a loan application, which he had already mastered—but of understanding people and sorting out relationships. That great equalizer of prairie and northern Ontario society—the ability to draw to the four-foot circle—came in handy. Contacts made at the curling rink helped him become part of the town, and soon he was taking business away from the Bank of Montreal and ribbing their people across coffee. One day a hermit bushwhacker, seventy-six years old, surfaced after umpteen years' absence, to have his passbook updated. His ledger card was missing. McKay became sleuth, going through old backing sheets stored in the basement, and discovered a fellow employee had embezzled a chunk of the old man's money. He called the manager, who confronted the wrongdoer. The image of his fellow banker being faced with his misdoing became indelibly imprinted on McKay's memory.

One or two days a week, McKay ran the sub-branch at Hudson, a hamlet just west down the line. Business revolved around the payroll of the Lac Seul Land and Lumber Company, on which the hamlet depended. Hudson was unvarnished frontier. McKay was required to pack a gun and to shoot if necessary to protect the property of the bank. He kept the gun on top of his wicket counter all day long. "Heaven help me if a real robber does come in here," he thought to himself, not knowing what he would have done. He had no experience with guns.

He had, however, taken to the banking business far better than he thought he would. He was a bright prospect. Every year, the bank selected one person from the West and one from the East, and offered to put them through university. They were then fast-tracked. McKay was chosen. He knew it was an honour, but he passed up the opportunity. He realized, in retrospect, it was a stupid thing to do, but something about the immediacy of his work and its human contact—and the curling and girling—kept him from accepting the offer. A decision on a loan might be made by calculation, but a decision about himself was made by feeling, and one of his feelings was to do the opposite of what was expected.

McKay did not have to pack a gun at East Hastings. There weren't rules of any kind like that. Branch 3, as it was now called, was his. He could make of the branch what he wanted. Because the branch was designed by an architect, the layout had a good feeling to it. He liked what he saw.

McKay's openness, with its touch of exuberance and its undertow of genuine caring, was tailor-made for the East End in the late 1960s. His personality was completely at odds with the intimidating, authoritative character of the bank manager, which people in the neighbourhood didn't like—which they felt in a subtle way humiliated by, but had been stuck with. But, then, VanCity's Branch 3 wasn't a bank branch, although it did have money and make loans. McKay, too, being so young, had an unlimited amount of energy. The philosophical idea of credit unions and Bentley's expression of it meshed with his own feelings and impulses. The financial potential of the East End, moreover, was deceptive. The area did not fit the culture of the chartered banks, except as a receptacle for deposits to be used largely elsewhere. For McKay, on the other hand, the East End was a market wide open for lending, particularly mortgage lending. It was a place to put money into. He knew, also, that behind appearances there was saving and striving, which was exactly the place for a credit union to be.

He spontaneously set out to make East Hastings a model branch. Soon he had surrendered most of his spare time. He and his wife Carol spent Saturday afternoons going to weddings, christenings and other happenings on the East Side involving grateful members. On Sundays, after church, they drove around the Lower Mainland, including the Fraser Valley, appraising houses—quite often saving members an appraisal fee. People didn't have an unlimited supply of money, so the fee could be a significant hindrance to buying. He put the touch on developers and appraisers for information. He got to know the real estate market intimately. Members regularly asked him for guidance on buying a house—whether the price was fair, what were the implications of having a septic tank rather than a sewer connection, and so on—and he could tell them what they wanted to know. VanCity also did not require a surveyor's certificate, which made it easier and cheaper to buy a house. The idea was to eliminate as many extra steps and extra niggling costs as possible.

Applications came in from Surrey, Abbotsford—as far away as Chilliwack. Some came from East End members moving into the suburbs. Others came from realtors. McKay was dealing with fifteen realtors, each with a network of contacts. As the branch's reputation grew, the applications through the realtors' contacts flowed in from far afield. McKay realized that the whole Lower Mainland was Branch 3's hinterland. Of VanCity's four branches, his was the furthest east, open to the burgeoning valley.

The East End was a destination point for heavy immigration. Often people who had arrived earlier and were members would bring their relatives to the branch directly from the airport or the train, to deposit their savings, without even first stopping at home for a celebratory drink. McKay watched in amazement as, on more than one occasion, the newcomers opened their shirts and unwrapped money that they had packed in gauze or cloth around their bodies. He built connections through these family relationships, embracing much of the ethnic community. The branch had its own "extended family" in the Italian community, the Chinese community, the Yugoslav community and others in and around the East End. The Chinese and, to a lesser extent, the Italian communities had benevolent associations or family groupings where people could obtain down payments, often financing home purchases 100 per cent. McKay, taking the first 70 per cent, wasn't risking anything and didn't ask a lot of questions about where the other 30 per cent was coming from.

The branch was in the heart of the Italian East Side. It pioneered credit union mortgages on commercial properties—lending to Italian businesses putting up buildings on Commercial Drive. The banks didn't allocate much money to such activity, especially on the East Side. They lent more against business operations, accounts receivable and trade inventory. The people on Commercial Drive either had to borrow money from relatives or go to McKay. At one point, walking up Commercial, he realized that every major development had been underwritten by VanCity.

Even where partners had a bitter falling out and McKay had to disentangle the mess between them, never once did any of them welsh on their commitments. He discovered that people on the East Side always paid their bills. They were good risks, being good savers. They loved VanCity's open mortgage, which allowed them to retire their debt ahead of time. It was particularly popular in the Chinese community, where members invariably retired fifteen-year mortgages in half the time.

McKay also offered progressive mortgages, for people building their own homes. He would advance money for each stage as they went along, so they would only be drawing down money as they needed it. Interest payments were deferred for six months or a year, because while the members were building they were usually also paying rent as well and the double payment would have been too difficult to handle. To keep tabs, the branch paid subcontractors and suppliers directly, so McKay could see where the money had gone.

Insurance companies and other mortgagers hung shy of these progressive mortgages because they were such a nuisance. VanCity and other credit unions in effect paid a slice of each of these mortgages with the extra time of their branch managers. That time in turn usually came out of their weekends. McKay felt that doing the work was part of his role. He and the other VanCity branch managers saw progressive mortgages as a way of getting members, especially young couples, into their first house and building up their equity. It also saved members who were handymen or who had building experience large amounts of money.

McKay poured through millions in these mortgages. Neither he nor any of the other VanCity branch managers ever lost a dime on them. People had their own blood, sweat and tears in these self-built homes, and the last thing they were going to do was to default on payments and lose them. Traditional lenders somehow never understood that. There was also a real sense of duty by members to the credit union, born of appreciation, so that they made their payments regardless of difficulties. They may have tried to borrow money elsewhere and failed, except with finance companies, which charged huge rates of interest. Freeing oneself from the finance company was a great relief. VanCity had cut the interest costs dramatically for such members. They didn't want to make a mess of things now and slip back down again. Family were often involved, as well, and were checking with McKay to make sure commitments were being adhered to. Borrowers didn't want to let them down and have older brothers and sisters, or Mom and Pop, on their case.

Occasionally McKay found himself having to ration mortgages. He would draw up a waiting list. Not for the first time, VanCity found it didn't have enough money to go around, even though deposits were increasing 25 per cent per year. Remarkably, a lot of members were content to wait. They preferred to delay construction and deal with VanCity, whom they knew and trusted from a loyalty built up over several years. Some members didn't have a choice. Banks wouldn't lend to anyone with less than a thousand square feet of floor space, or within a mile of railway tracks, or with a septic tank. They had all kinds of reasons to reject people, it seemed to McKay.

For community events like Hastings Days or Italian Days, or the march-past of the Pacific National Exhibition parade, McKay and his staff, in turns, would be out in a booth on the sidewalk, with hotdogs and lemonade, or frying up hamburgers, selling them at a reasonable price and giving the money to charity, and handing out VanCity leaflets on the side, in the carnival atmosphere. People loved it. It was a conscious attempt at a participatory style, with VanCity front and centre and McKay with a spatula in the middle. Aside from the publicity, the booth reflected VanCity's genuine sense of community. Branch 3 also decorated the branch for these and other occasions, like Halloween. The banks, stodgy, cold and indifferent, watched these shenanigans as if VanCity's people were creatures from another cosmos. Members looked on the branch's Christmas decorations as part of their own celebration. They showered staff with compliments for the service they had provided and brought along chocolates and liquor in abundance. McKay, who didn't drink, took Bentley two dozen bottles of liquor one year, which members had given to him.

At the beginning, VanCity was considered alien by the shopkeepers on the east side Hastings strip. Many of them had a vague conviction that credit unions were on the other side of the political fence and shouldn't be patronized. It was a replay of Killarney, Manitoba. Some merchants were outright nasty, telling McKay they would never deal with a no-good communist organization like VanCity. The fact that he belonged to the chamber of commerce—you couldn't set up shop on the street without being signed up by the chamber—wasn't much help.

McKay discovered, through members who had heard stories from their friends, that some bank managers in the area were surreptitiously smearing VanCity. He checked the stories out and found they were almost always accurate. Some of the bank managers told customers, especially immigrants from Eastern Europe, that VanCity was a communist organization, trying to infiltrate the community. They suggested that somehow it was going to exploit them or, alternatively, that it would take their money, close down and run. They dismissed VanCity as not being "full-service," which was true, and as a place where people couldn't do normal everyday banking, which was very much false.

McKay, making the rounds up and down Hastings, was discouraged but not beaten. He and Carol bought locally—for children's clothing, for example—which helped. Little by little, he won over the local merchants. He carried signature cards in his pocket so that he could open accounts on the spot. Once the merchants had tried VanCity, they were hooked. They saw how friendly the branch was. Soon the whole street was dealing with the branch in one way or another. VanCity also had longer hours and was open Saturday morning, while the banks were still open on weekdays only from 10 A.M. to 3 P.M.

Most of these new members didn't shift whole accounts from their bank, for fear of alienating their bank manager. They would save up cash and bring it directly to VanCity without the bank knowing. The banking environment was punitive and austere. Italian immigrants were used to the banker being a major-domo in their community. They no more wanted to offend the banker than offend a priest. Many ultimately, however, became full-time converts and said goodbye to their bank. The deposit base began to grow. The disparaging fictions about VanCity began to backfire, as word got around about how much VanCity was helping people.

The East Hastings branch grew increasingly more crowded, and McKay added two more employees. The small staff, with their branch growing topsy turvy, worked flat out all the time. On Saturday mornings, the place was jam-packed. On a particularly wild Saturday morning, McKay might take ten or fifteen loan applications. With only six people on staff, including himself, he sometimes couldn't even make it to the bathroom: If he left his office, there would be nobody to take calls. Some of the older members didn't take kindly to the growth. They liked it when there were just a couple of thousand members. McKay shrugged his shoulders amiably at their complaints, kidding them about sending too many of their friends and relatives to VanCity.

Ann Duggan, McKay's assistant, worked the side counter. She spoke Italian. The ledger-keeper was Yugoslav. One of the tellers was Chinese. Duggan, the second-in-command, already knew the ropes and had been making "automatic" loans on her own hook. McKay trained the others to do each others' jobs, partly to raise their qualifications but mostly to enable the branch to make it through the day. The ledger-keeper filled in as teller, the teller might take loan applications and McKay handled assorted cash transactions in his office. He knew that using a ledger-keeper as a teller was taboo—auditors insisted on a separation of functions—but something had to give if they were going to handle the traffic. McKay ordered in pizza or Chinese food at night and took them through the drill.

He was interested in new things, and he was bright, so Bentley assigned him to look after computerization for VanCity. VanCity was a member of a pioneering computer consortium, Central Data Systems (CDS). It was processing VanCity's postings overnight, at a central facility, and sending back the updated accounts in stacks of accordion print-outs. McKay became chair of the users' committee, even helping CDS introduce the service to other credit unions. He did this on top of managing the branch.

Life for McKay became one big, around-the-clock VanCity kaleidoscope. It played havoc with his health. Almost from the first day that he took over the branch, ulcers showed up and became inflamed. The combination of adjusting to the large city, getting married, the death of his mother, becoming a branch manager and trying to please Don Bentley was more than his system could take. He had been drinking a lot of coffee, which was killing him. He swore off coffee. He took Amphogel, a standard antacid medication at the time, used for ulcers. He went on a bland diet, with lots of milk and puddings. Nothing worked. Virtually every morning at five o'clock, routinely like an alarm clock, severe pain jolted him awake. It wouldn't subside until he had vomited and cleared the acid from his stomach. About three hours later, the pain would start to die out, just about the time he had to leave for the branch. Sometimes he tried holding back and beating the pain, only to have to throw up just before going out the door. This went on for more than two years. He was drained physically, but he could still get through his long days. He joked that he had more stamina than brains. He and Bentley used to compare their stomach problems.

Ulcers or not, he was in the habit of working late into the night. He was never a morning person, always a night person. Because the branch had been robbed three times, walking to his car behind the branch late at night carried with it a shadow of drama. He also worked weekends, save for the social outings to members' houses and Sunday morning church. Somebody would drop by the office and say, "Hey, will you come by on Sunday? We're having a roast." He and Carol, when she could make it, would be there. The weddings and christenings were automatic invitations. There was a certain status to having a manager of a financial institution in one's house. The relationship worked both ways. McKay's presence fixed members' loyalty to VanCity like bands of steel.

These were joyful times for McKay. People didn't have a lot of money—he was in a position to know—but they shared whatever small bounty they had. The food sometimes bothered the McKays—Wayne didn't like rabbit and Carol had a hard time with Chinese food, but they went anyway. Even when the glasses were clinked, VanCity wasn't altogether absent. It wasn't that business thoughts intruded; they were more a natural adjunct of the gathering. McKay, by visiting members in their homes, acquired a sure sense of what they were like and of their ability to make commitments—namely, whether VanCity was going to get its money back for loans and mortgages. The members, enjoying McKay's company, often wanted his advice on something financial as well.

Soon members were asking McKay to handle negotiations for them. Usually they involved agreements for sale—those private "mortgage" agreements that had been the common way of buying and selling houses on the East Side. A member holding an agreement for sale, for example, might want to sell it to VanCity and pocket the remaining principal immediately, with VanCity collecting future payments as if it were a mortgage. McKay found himself acting in a quasi-legal capacity with no legal training.

Sometimes he ended up trapped in a Solomon-like dilemma. In one case, a family with a VanCity mortgage wanted to sell their house. McKay knew them well and knew that the house was infested with dry rot. The purchasers, a young couple who were also members, applied to McKay for a mortgage to buy the house. What should he do? He decided he had an obligation to tell the buyers what they would be getting into. He first went to see the vendors to explain his intention. They were furious. Ultimately, however, years later, after they had sold the house to another party and moved on, they agreed that McKay had done the right thing. Angry as they were, moreover, they didn't leave the branch. Whatever else, if they had left Branch 3 they would have had to explain their reason to an uncle or cousin—the kind of accounting, in a tightly knit ethnic community, that nobody relishes.

McKay's five-and-a-half years at East Hastings were the best years of his life. He made lifelong friends. He was able to help a great many people. He saw them buying homes in droves, with VanCity mortgages, and then remodelling or repairing them, again with VanCity money. Then he watched some of them spread out to North Burnaby, in a second wave, also with mortgages from Branch 3. He and the branch grew together. Given a free hand by Bentley, he was able to turn his maverick playfulness to advantage. He had set out, with young ambition, to build a model branch. After a few years, people from other credit unions in the province, and sometimes from outside the province, came to see the branch at work. He had done it.

CHAPTER 17

The Gang

DON BENTLEY AND HIS SMALL band of branch managers were like a gang of amiable anarchists. They were different in age and temperament—not formula bankers cut from the same cookie-cutter mould. Other than adhering to the basic rules that bound them to Bentley, they did things as it suited them. That was the most important rule of all: They had leeway and were supposed to use it. They talked and argued, some more than others. They competed against each other, as if their branches were horses in a race. They revered Bentley, and they produced for him.

They were seven to begin with, in the mid-1960s: Bentley, Ron Spooner, Laura Smalley (Bentley's secretary), Wayne McKay (East Hastings), Don Nelson (who ran the main office), Art Farnden (Victoria Drive), and a young ex-Bank of Montrealer, Monty Lambertus (Kitsilano).

Along with Spooner and McKay, Nelson was the most prominent of the gang under Bentley. All three came from chartered banks, all three came from the Prairies, and all three could not have been more different. McKay and Nelson were particular opposites. McKay was rambunctious, curious about people and their stories, ready to help them beyond his credit union duties and eager for new devices and stratagems. Nelson was a numbers man. He was good with numbers and enjoyed using them. He thought McKay, with his insatiable interest in people and their well-being, was too much of a Mr. Goody Goody. He wasn't like that; he had a certain skeptical caution about the world and about himself.

It wasn't that Nelson was unfriendly or unkind. Outside the office, he was warm and engaging. He did not, however, let people who worked with him, or under him, get close. There was always that reserve which he carried in front of him—the reserve of someone who has seen tough times. Jan Chapman, a later VanCity manager, remembered going to his house after curling and seeing his family enter into his life in a way that she and others in VanCity could not imagine.

What bound members to Nelson was his unvarnished honesty. He would tell the truth even when he had to say difficult things. Members knew this and trusted him. He was grassroots. He had a plain-talk stubbornnness against pretension, even VanCity credit union pretension. He refused to admit, even for the form, that there was any difference between a "customer" in a bank and a "member" in a credit union. You would try to give them the best service either way. He deliberately kept thinking of VanCity's members as customers—a small heresy behind a larger thought, that what counted was a manager's commitment to actual service, not what you called the person who came through the door.

He was also tenacious. He especially knew how to lend money, although he liked to say, wryly, that inflation, which raised the value of houses—the collateral behind mortgages—made good lenders of them all. The original branch at 96 East Broadway, which Nelson ran, flourished. Bigger than the others and well-established, it was by far the largest lender of the four.

Although Nelson was straightforward, he had his own memories. He had grown up poor, very poor, on a farm near Moose Jaw. His father had died when he was four, during the bitterest years of the Great Depression. His mother was left to bring up several children. His first job out of school was in a window factory. After six months, he was laid off. He then applied for a job at the Dominion Bank in Moose Jaw for the same reason that Ray Evelle went into banking: His mother told him that if you got into a bank, you had a job for life. He enjoyed the work, and rose quickly to the position of accountant. Annual wage increases were $75 a year, or about $6 a month. Not having much to start with and not getting much later on, he learned to respect money. He moved around, in what became, through a merger, the Toronto Dominion Bank, to Regina, Winnipeg, Swift Current, back to Winnipeg and then to Vancouver. He thought there were other things that might be more interesting, yet he really liked the bank, its premises, the contacts and the people. Unfortunately, he disagreed with the personnel manager in Vancouver about how pay increases should be allocated—the personnel manager ignored Nelson's recommendations—and they had a parting of the ways.

Nelson and his brother, a mechanic, then decided to go into the service station business, at 41st and Main. It was a leased Texaco station, where they found themselves squeezed by the narrow margins the company allowed on gas and by the company's other controls. They lost their shirts. "The oil companies knew a heck of a lot more about the financial game of service stations than I did," Nelson quipped about that episode.

He had once borrowed $50 from VanCity. A friend of his, a machinist, who was a member, had told him that if he wanted anything he should go down and talk to Mr. Bentley at Vancouver City Savings. Nelson had title to his house and offered that as collateral for the loan. Bentley laughed and said that VanCity trusted him for the $50. The loan was important to Nelson at the time, as loans usually are when they're asked for.

Nelson also knew VanCity from his banking days. The Toronto Dominion Bank branch where he had worked was just across the street at Broadway and Quebec. He applied for a job at VanCity. He had no great co-operative commitment or interest in credit unions. He just needed work. He was taken on.

He had been at VanCity for only a month when Bentley asked him to look after the Victoria Drive branch while Farnden was on holidays. Nelson hardly knew what a credit union was. He realized Bentley might be testing him, to see what he could do. Even then, he thought the assignment a remarkable gesture on Bentley's part. Half a year later, when Spooner was assigned to work full time at advertising and promotion, Nelson was given the East Hastings branch to manage. He was surprised and happy. Then he took over from Evelle at 96 East Broadway. Unemployed just two summers earlier, he was now running VanCity's main office.

Art Farnden was different again: a kind, genial man, with old-fashioned credit union values and nervous about introducing new systems. He was comfortable with the way things were already being done. When the others introduced employee appraisals, Farnden was aghast. He couldn't imagine sitting down with employees and talking to them about their work perform-ance. He was older than the other branch managers and they tended to ignore him. Once Wayne McKay organized a birthday party for him. They took him out to lunch and gave him a gift. He was totally surprised; he never thought the others would do that kind of thing. They were glad they had, because he died not too long after.

Monty Lambertus at West Broadway was the odd man out, never fully accepted by the others. He wasn't much of a team player and didn't seem to share their dedication. Jan Chapman, who worked for him at the Kitsilano branch on West Broadway, found him terribly moody. "Some mornings he would be very friendly," she remembered. "Other mornings, say 'Good morning,' and he would bite your head off. One was always on eggshells with Monty. I had never met anybody like that." The West Broadway branch hadn't blossomed the way it was expected to, but Lambertus remained in place.

The monthly management meetings started right after work, first in the main branch and later moving to the other branches. Either dinner was brought in or the gang would go out to a restaurant afterwards and carry on with the usual libations and free-ranging discussion. The meetings dealt with operational matters, like branch workings and adjusting interest rates, but also went far afield. There were no holds barred. Bentley insisted. He liked ideas and argument. He wanted to bring out people's opinions. The others had no fear of contradicting the boss if they felt it was required. Everybody was fair game. This worked two ways. If one was open to chal-lenge oneself, including challenge from Bentley, one had to think out one's position very carefully. This brought a hidden discipline to what sometimes appeared to be a free-for-all.

They made up policy, rules, and procedures as they went along, since VanCity, with its growth and energy, was continually plunged into new situations, with no formal routines in place. They simply selected whoever's idea was best on a particular issue. Usually, in these cases, the managers, who were in the front lines, prevailed. Alternatively, a manager would bring up a problem he was having in his branch, or relate the success of something he had tried, and they would bat the subject around.

Bentley often had a preconceived idea of what he wanted and then would subject it to dialectical discourse, like Socrates with his students in the courtyard. He would put his proposal forward—about a service charge, for example—and ask for the group's opinions. They might all agree. He would then disagree with them, contradicting his own proposal, citing reasons—trying to stir up controversy, to prod them, to elicit what they really thought. They might then agree with his new position, upon which he would express reservations. They knew he had some figure in mind, although they didn't know which one. Inevitably they would be plunged into argument. This might go on for half an hour. If they all ended up with one figure, but one he didn't like, he would announce a Bentley compromise—the figure he had finally arrived at in his own mind. Usually, because he had an uncanny sense of the market, he proved right.

His managers never resented this exercise because they knew that if they had enough facts on their side, they could change his mind. Notwithstanding that Bentley always had the last say, they nevertheless felt they were part of a collective decision-making process, and that any decision he made was somehow their decision, too.

Some of the most crucial issues were discussed at long, liquid lunches, with just the core group—Bentley, Spooner, Nelson, and McKay. The sessions went on for several hours, sometimes to the end of the afternoon. Bentley had a favourite restaurant near each of his branch managers' neighbourhoods, which he used in rotation.

McKay was a teetotaller. He had decided years earlier that he wasn't a good drinker and that, given his compulsive nature, if he didn't quit he would become an alcoholic. Now, despite his best efforts at insouciance, he watched the martinis and wine go down, at these sessions, like a doctor in a clinic. Spooner was an enthusiastic martini-with-lunch man and had introduced Bentley to the habit. This also vaguely troubled McKay. For Bentley, on the other hand, these lunches were a good moment to relax and let the ideas flow. Bentley had similar long lunches with VanCity's auditor, Walter Dyck, and others, when he wanted to explore broad issues or bring himself up to date. Dyck remembered these well-oiled tête-à-têtes vividly—was struck by what a great talker the sometimes quiet Don Bentley could be.

The managers' meetings involved a growing management group in thinking about what was to come—how Vancouver and its people were changing, and how VanCity was going to respond. Jan Chapman, who came to the process in 1974, as manager of the new Main Street branch, kept reminding herself how much different it was from the Royal Bank, where she had worked before. Bentley really allowed people to be independent thinkers and to put their minds to innovative possibilities. He had created an atmosphere that fostered it. A young organization, she reflected, needed people to be able to gather, talk and genuinely communicate, and to let ideas build. Bentley was fabulous at that, she said. Most managers in an organization would not have had the openness. They would have wanted too much control, would have fallen into the habit of manipulating people. Didn't that come with corporate life?

Most of all, she realized, Bentley loved ideas. He would take the time, when she had an idea, to listen to it and encourage her to develop it. She never heard him say no, that idea won't work. Mike Borch, an outside computer programmer whom Bentley later had contact with, was also struck by how carefully Bentley listened to him, although Borch was quite young. Bentley was a tremendous motivator, Borch thought.

The managers thought of themselves as working for Mr. Bentley as much as for VanCity. That's what they called him — Mr. Bentley. Several times Bentley told Nelson to call him "Don." "No," Nelson replied, "I just can't do that. You were Mr. Bentley when I came here and you'll always be Mr. Bentley." The only one who called him "Don" was young Lambertus. Worse, Lambertus was the most junior of managers. This irked Nelson and Spooner no end. Nelson even raised the matter with Bentley.

"What is this Don business with Monty Lambertus?" he asked.

"It doesn't bother me," Bentley replied. "Why should it bother you?"

"Well, okay, I'll mind my own business then," Nelson answered.

Lambertus's familiarity did bother them, though, because it indirectly called into question their own reverence of the boss. The reverence ran deep, could be emotional. "I never questioned why I was there, what I was doing," McKay remembered. "I really did idolize the man. That was the kind of loyalty that he inspired in me."

Bentley, just by being himself, was slowly creating the VanCity culture. His willingness to bend over backwards to be fair to members made an impact on the others because it was so at odds with the culture of the banks where they had come from. Bentley really was an egalitarian. He had told McKay, when he sent him out to manage the East Hastings branch, to be careful to treat women loan applicants the same way he treated male applicants. This almost casual reminder of principle, in a heavily biased society, wasn't lost on McKay.

They got caught up in Bentley's ramblings about the future. He was a visionary, in their minds. This made working with him exciting. Spooner remembered the early bull sessions much like romantic excursions, with "D. B." presiding. Bentley had a leading vision of a financial supermarket providing services of all kinds to members and, as the group talked about it, they were carried along on the ride.

Bentley's concern about people was also picked up by them. He was able to deflect anger. Irate members might stride to the counter in the main office, ready to chew Bentley to pieces or take VanCity to task. By the time he had talked over the problem with them, they were thanking him.

Members wanted to see him. He had a physical magnetism about him. His accessibility to members made a profound impression, particularly on Nelson, who was with him in the main branch.

What most fed their loyalty, however, was Bentley's readiness to stand behind them and give them a chance. He had a novel arrangement with his managers for making loans. Under the Credit Unions Act, none of them had lending authority. Only the "treasurer"—and, of course, the credit committee and the board—had that power. This was all right for most credit unions, but for one with branches like VanCity, it would have meant poor, slow loan service. Besides, VanCity wouldn't flourish if its people were denied responsibility. Bentley followed his own anarchist code: if a rule didn't make sense and he could safely get around it, he did. He told his managers that as long as they were working for him, they could lend any amount that he could lend (his own limit wasn't all that high). He dropped by every week, after the money had been handed out, and signed off the loans. This went on for years, until the Act was changed.

For the group, this arrangement was a bold gesture of confidence. If Bentley didn't like the loan, he'd still sign it, although he would point out what was wrong with it and expect the same mistake not to happen again. With Spooner, with whom he had a special relationship, but who would lend money to anyone, this was tricky. "Jesus, Ron," he would say to him, "this one's going to be a bad loan, there's no doubt about it." Or sometimes he wouldn't say anything, just make a mental note in the back of his mind. They all knew, however, what was at stake. Bentley once told Nelson good-naturedly that if VanCity's defaults exceeded 1 per cent, he, Nelson, was going to be fired. Except for a few problems, usually on Spooner's part, they had good control of their loans and an effective collection system. VanCity's loan losses continued to be low. On mortgages, the biggest part of the portfolio, they lost nothing at all—had an astonishing perfect record—until the mid-1970s. The clean slate on mortgage losses went back to VanCity's beginnings, to the time it had finally accumulated enough deposits to issue a mortgage in the first place. There were foreclosures, but there was always enough margin for VanCity to recover its outlay.

The leeway for lending was a talisman of almost complete decentralization in the way a branch operated. In many ways, the branches were autonomous units. They hired and trained their own people, on the fly—what little training occurred. There was no such thing as a personnel or human resources department, or even the thought of one. Until the early 1970s, VanCity didn't even pay the same from branch to branch. Only when the branches began transferring people around did it occur to them to have more uniformity and to put some common rules in place. Each branch looked different. The cultural identity of a branch depended on the manager, around whom everything revolved. "If you every need something, go see Mr. Bentley at VanCity." "Ask for Wayne McKay, the manager, and tell him you're a friend of mine."

McKay was the most anarchistic and hence benefited most from Bentley's tolerance. He regularly showed up late for work and for meetings, despite Bentley's remonstrances. He didn't like mornings. He also began a vaguely conceived policy—it was more than a habit—of talking to people as long as they felt the need to talk to him, regardless of his schedule, which played havoc with appointments. Nelson used to set up lunch with McKay and McKay would arrive an hour or an hour and a half late. To cut his losses, Nelson arrived half an hour late himself. He still had to endure a long wait. After a while, he couldn't bring himself to go through the routine again. McKay's tardiness was really a way of setting himself apart, a deliberate non-conformism to show he was different—a challenge to accept him as he was.

Anywhere else, McKay would have been long gone. Although Bentley got after him, he also knew that the strength of individualism was just that—individualism—and that if one insisted on suppressing its idiosyncrasies, one risked destroying its strength. There was no doubt McKay's individualism had strength to it. Bentley pushed only so far and never managed to reform him.

The family of managers competed first of all against each other—branch against autonomous branch, like siblings—rather than against the outside world. Staff reflected this. They didn't spend much time thinking of VanCity. It was their own branch that counted. McKay was particularly energetic. He wanted to beat Lambertus. It irritated him that Lambertus's branch in the well-off west side might catch up to East Hastings when he, McKay, was so much better. It was true, in all this, that they were trying to draw people away from the finance companies and their abusive rates. It was also true that they were attracting many disillusioned bank customers. The banks, however, were only beginning to enter fully into the residential mortgage market, VanCity's niche, following changes to the Bank Act in 1967, and they had a different clientele. VanCity branches, on the other hand, were a direct benchmark for each other.

There was no collective goal, no central plan, other than for each branch, on its own, to expand and make its way. If the branches did that, collectively they were going to prosper. Bentley, always astute, played up the informal competition without ever appearing to do so. It seemed to work.

CHAPTER 18

Central Data Systems
Does it

WAYNE MCKAY IN 1965 HAD just joined VanCity. Don Nelson was feeling his way as manager of the East Hastings branch. The introduction of the Burroughs Sensitronic accounting machine marked the period. The compact technical wonder of the early 1960s that Don Bentley and Fred Graham had been so proud of now stood in the main office like a dinosaur, an old clunker, a piece of big, heavy-duty equipment like a gravel separator or a pile driver, it seemed. It took up lots of space, made lots of noise and kept breaking down.

Even when the machine was working well, it had its limitations. Posting at 96 East Broadway was a day and a half's work, involving two shifts. The ledger keeper had to stick in the ledger card, type in the entry, wait for the machine's arm to go thunk with the imprint, take the card out, stick in another one, and so on, ad infinitum. Each branch had its own version of the machine and had the same problem. So did the banks. People were tied up posting on these machines who otherwise could be serving the public. Because of the machine's slowness, too, this supposedly backup person had become the pacesetter for the branch, controlling the flow. Not that the ledger-keeper enjoyed the role. The work was excruciatingly boring. It was the rare bookkeeping machine operator that stuck it out for long. Bentley and a few others in the hothouse B.C. credit union milieu saw that they were going to have to get off ledger cards, but how and when, they had no idea.

Upstairs at 96 East Broadway, on the third floor, Ted Cotter was musing on a different technological plane. Cotter was assistant general manager of cu&c Health Services. Through a series of jobs, he had fallen into accounting and, from accounting, into data processing. He knew all about running numbers through machines. He supervised cu&c's billing system and payment of claims—endless thousands of pieces of paper going out and coming back in. When he had arrived at cu&c, in 1958, the processing of these transactions was done with punched cards—cards with holes punched in them—which were run through a large, mechanical Remington Rand processing machine. The machine swallowed the cards, read them by pins going through the holes, converted those readings into digits on counters, and printed out the results, doing the necessary adding and subtracting along the way. It accumulated information in a series of wheels. The basic technology had been dreamed up by a nineteenth-century English mathematician, Charles Babbage. In Remington Rand and IBM processing machines, it actually worked.

Cotter, however, now had a computer to play with. It was an IBM 1401, the original IBM medium-sized office mainframe. It still used punch cards, but it sensed them differently. It was capable of reading them at about ten times the speed of the mechnical equipment. Moreover, it was programmable. That is, you could instruct it to lift different bits of information from each card in a stack and total up the findings, or you could ask it to sort information in a different order. Previous computers were also programmable, but in a limited and awkward way. Programming on those machines was done with a wired grid called a plugboard. The operator had to manually change the configuration of wires, by moving the plugs around, and shove the grid back into the machine. Programming the 1401, by contrast, was done with punched cards—clean, simple and broad in its applications. Cotter's boss at CU&C, Joe Corsbie, a long-time co-operator who would later serve on VanCity's board, had wondered whether the machine could be used for credit unions and had put the bug in Cotter's ear.

Cotter soon learned that it could not be done, especially not for chequing accounts, with all their volume. At least, that was what he was told. A researcher at the League had written a thesis on the subject, as part of his work to become a registered industrial accountant. He had concluded it was impossible to move the information back and forth quickly enough to make a computer scheme practical. Cotter mulled this over. He wasn't convinced. He thought of his IBM 1401. It was an exciting machine. It was so different from the mechanical past. "See what I can do," it seemed to say.

Several banks in Canada had already begun computerizing the processing of accounts, overnight—including personal chequing accounts—for branches in major centres like Toronto and Montreal. Cotter didn't realize they had gotten so far, and in any case he did not have access to their technology. He began looking around. He discovered an industrial credit union in the U.S. which was using a 1401, made available by its sponsoring company, Boise Cascade. It used the computer only for share and loan accounts, not for chequing accounts, which was the real problem in British Columbia. American credit unions did not have chequing accounts. Still, the Boise experiment was a start, and Cotter acquired copies of their programs, to use for reference.

Backed by an enthusiastic Corsbie, Cotter then organized a meeting to discuss the possibilities. B.C. credit unions were supposed to be too small to undertake anything so imposing as computerization, but they had one understated advantage: They drew simultaneously on the collective strength of the movement overall. Credit unions in British Columbia were becoming a force in the industry. They were well managed and very profitable, and they were attracting savvy people with banking backgrounds.

Cotter put together a formal proposal on how he thought a data process-ing service bureau, owned by credit unions and co-operatives would work. The meeting was held in May 1966 at the University of British Columbia, with its ambience of scientific knowledge. About twenty-five organizations, most from the Lower Mainland, were represented. Don Bentley was there for VanCity. The presentation bristled with the excitement of new technol-ogy applied. Seven organizations, among them VanCity, decided to go ahead. They each threw in $2,000 seed money and named a representative to form the board of the newly constituted venture. They called it Central Data Systems Limited (CDS). Cotter returned to the third floor at 96 East Broadway with a mission.

Mike Borch worked for Cotter. Only twenty-five years old, a Vernon boy, he was already supervising CU&C's billing and underwriting departments. He had taken to spending a lot of time in the computer room, after hours, watching the operators and helping out. He seemed to have a knack for its mysteries. Cotter noticed this and arranged for Borch to go to the IBM office in Vancouver and take a series of computer courses. When CDS was formed, he asked Borch if he wanted to come along for the ride. Borch became CDS programmer and then ran the computer as well.

Borch now sat down to write the programs that would convert credit union postings to the 1401. He had to write the instructions in a language the computer understood—a series of letters or numbers for each instruc-tion—and send it to the right place in the computer's memory. In order to debug a faulty program he also had to know the different sequences by which the computer, a "binary" machine which chose between zero and one, made up characters to register the instruction. In other words, he had to understand conceptually how the computer worked.

Those were the mechanical aspects. The art of programming was some-thing else—an inspired and inspiring game. Somehow, as Cotter had guessed, Borch had an aptitude for it. There weren't that many program-mers around. Merely to be a programmer was to be at the leading edge of a whole new technology. Programming the system for a new application (really a new package of applications), ordering the sequence, testing it and seeing it work broke new ground each time it was done. It was supposed to work; the technical gods at IBM said it would. When it did, however, it was still a delightful wonder.

Gulf & Fraser Fishermen's Credit Union, one of the seven CDS members, was Borch's guinea pig. Gulf & Fraser had a colourful, folklorish history. It was charter number 35 and hadn't lost its pioneering spirit. Far from being a massive financial institution with countless technical legions, it was just one branch, but that suited the experiment. Borch had Gulf & Fraser's chequing accounts converted and the system running by February 1967. All the rest was administrative housekeeping—setting up the drill with the other CDS members and hiring extra key-punch operators. Chequing accounts were done first, then share accounts. It was just a matter of arranging to handle the volume.

The system was simplicity itself. At close of day, the member credit unions sorted out their accumulated slips by type of account and by deposits and withdrawals. They then ran totals for each category on an ordinary adding machine and attached the tapes as a reference against which the computer processing was to balance. The bundle was dispatched to CDS, arriving around six in the evening. CDS's key-punch operators punched the transactions onto computer cards. The computer operator, for each run-through, fed the 1401 a stack of punched cards containing the relevant program. The transaction cards followed, and all the transactions and new balances, plus general-ledger totals, were printed out on fifteen-inch-wide accordion paper. This arrived back at the credit union before the start of business next morning. A teller, checking to see if a member had sufficient funds for a major withdrawal, had only to thumb through the computer print-out to the right place. The print-out included all previous transactions for the month, so it got bigger and bigger through to month end.

The 1401 also printed the members' monthly statements. Cheques from the clearing system were batched at the credit union, again with an adding machine total as a control, and then passed on to CDS for posting just like withdrawals and deposits. Ledger cards were bypassed. In one form or another, since the days of stone tablets and papyrus, ledger cards had made banking possible. Now they were doomed.

Years later, when the principals had died and the archival record had mysteriously disappeared, different people had different recall about who, at VanCity, first thought of daily interest. Wayne McKay was quite sure it was Bentley, but not absolutely certain. It was the kind of revolutionary idea that Bentley would come up with. Don Nelson thought it was Spooner. So did auditor Walter Dyck and Mike Borch at CDS. Borch worked with Spooner on the project. He could see in his mind's eye Spooner going to Bentley and saying, "I've got this great idea," and Bentley replying, almost without hesitation, "That sounds good. Why don't we try it?" It would have happened just like that, Borch thought. Spooner was a real fly-by-the-seat-of-your-pants guy, and this idea, at first impression, was just crazy. Who else but Spooner would think of it?

Laura Smalley, on the other hand, seemed to recall that Bentley and Spooner had read about the feasability of it in the United States. Ross Montgomery, a later board member, thought one would never know, because Bentley and Spooner wouldn't do anything without talking to each other about it, and the idea would come forward as something from the two of them. Lloyd Widdifield said he himself first came up with the idea, or rather he had got it from the manager of the Port Alberni and District Credit Union who had been a bank manager in Phoenix, Arizona, where the idea was floating around. He had then put the concept to the VanCity board.

Spooner himself, in an extant letter, attributed the origin of the concept vaguely to a bull session in the late 1950s. According to his recollection, it was one of those umpteen ideas that surfaced at the no-holds-barred management meetings, with its brainstorming "What ifs," "Why can't we do this?" and "Why can't we do that?" They wondered aloud why, if VanCity charged interest on loans on a declining basis, it couldn't pay interest on deposits in the same way, on an accumulating basis. Until then, credit unions and banks paid interest according to the minimum quarterly or semi-annual balances. This meant that new and sometimes quite sizable deposits might not generate interest for several months, while the credit union or bank nevertheless was collecting interest on the very same money lent to borrowers. Conceptually, that wasn't right. In fairness to members, VanCity should be paying interest on deposits as they came in.

There was, however, an obvious problem. To implement the idea meant calculating interest daily. That would have been so extraordinarily laborious, as deposits dribbled into the teller's station, that the possibility, in the past, had not arisen. Bentley and Spooner shelved the idea. Now, with CDS, things had changed. Spooner was looking for a promotional idea that would bring the young Kitsilano branch into the black as soon as possible. On one of Bentley's visitations, he brought up daily interest again. They could get their computer consortium CDS to do the daily calculations. Wasn't it, in fact, possible?

Unknown to Spooner, several banks in the western United States in the interim had introduced daily interest, as a way of increasing interest payments that in the United States, for savings accounts, were limited by law to 3 per cent. Or he had blocked mention of it from his mind, for one of those banks was in Phoenix, just as Widdifield later claimed. Spooner thought VanCity would be the first with daily interest. It was nowhere to be seen.

Bentley, Spooner, McKay, Nelson and the others in the small management group met to go over the proposition. They realized that in one place at least, Vancouver, for the handful of credit unions in the computerization venture, the pre-existing banking world would be turned upside down. As they talked, and all this sank in, the anticipation of a daily interest account lifted them up and washed them forward like a tsunami. They were going to take the world by storm. Spooner had visions of members hammering at the door. Nelson, playing the role of a cynic and not afraid to rankle Spooner, took a few shots at it, but was interested in giving it a chance.

Those at the meeting swore themselves to secrecy. They had nothing to fear from the banks, who hadn't the technical capacity and weren't eager to pay depositors more money in any case. They didn't, however, want another credit union to learn about the idea and grab it from them. Spooner was assigned to flesh out the concept and come up with a name for the account. Spooner gave his sidekick Hermann Myers a call. Myers did advertising and other copywriting work for Spooner and would probably have some ideas. Bentley, meanwhile, contacted Ted Cotter and set up a high-powered VanCity-CDS meeting.

Borch remembered the cloak-and-dagger sequence of events vividly. Cotter walked into his office one day and said, "We're having a meeting with VanCity. It's about a new savings account, and if you tell anyone, you're in big trouble." Borch's reaction at the meeting, when he learned what they had in mind, was undiluted delight. All he wanted to do was to write programs—fifteen hours a day, if he could. With the chequing and share account conversions on track, he was becoming, instead, a routine computer operator. The daily-interest assignment gave him a chance to get back to what really gave him a kick. It was an exciting challenge, too. He would be writing a program that created the product—was essential to it—rather than just converting a product that had long existed.

Borch told them it could be done. From the moment he went to work on the program, Spooner began haunting his office, keyed by anticipation. He came up several times a day, asking Borch how he was doing, how he was getting along, what was happening. Borch assured him that at some point he would have a report in his hands. Then, suddenly, it was there—a report on the program, including a test run using the East Hastings branch's chequing account as a proxy. Borch had written the program and run the test in just a few days. Spooner was bubbling with pleasure. He had gotten much more than he expected, and gotten it much faster than he expected.

What Borch hadn't told Spooner was that he and Cotter already knew it would be easy. The program just took 1/365th of the interest rate, times the balance, and accumulated that amount. For VanCity, daily interest was a new-fangled, complicated idea, based on a unique feature. From a computer-programming point of view, it was straightforward and program-efficient. Countless such computer programs would be written, unnoticed, in the future, as the use of computer technology became more common.

Spooner was aware of none of this. For him, young Mike Borch was a genius, an alchemist who had turned the fanciful idea of daily interest into gold. An excited Spooner knew, now, that daily interest was going to happen.

CHAPTER 19

The Lancashire Gentleman

HERMANN MYERS WAS A MIDDLING man with a middling advertising business in a middling office. Yet, like many others who came in contact with VanCity in the Bentley years, he ended up being given something to do and the freedom to do it whereby, unexpectedly, he showed an impressive talent. By the time he left, he had created two masterpieces.

Myers ran a little advertising shop in an office in the old cupola-topped Sun Tower at Pender and Beatty. The building had once been acclaimed as the tallest in the British Empire, but it was now well past its prime, in a decaying fringe on the wrong side of downtown. Myers had two rooms on the third floor—his own large space, and a smaller room where his receptionist-secretary worked. His wife, Elsie, looked after the books. It was a far cry from the glitzy furnishings and ultra-modern atmosphere of the full-service advertising agencies, with their creative directors hustling through the halls, sheets of television-commercial frames in their hands. Myers didn't do anything as snazzy as television and radio commercials. The work he did do, however—pamphlets, posters, and newspaper ads—he had a knack for and was comfortable with, and he made a reasonable living.

Myers had always been interested in art, from the days when he was a small boy in Bolton, Lancashire. As a young man, he had once had a job with a poster-making firm, where he sketched posters and banners. He was never long without a pencil or marker in his hand. Put him down at a Lions Club dinner—he was a dedicated member—and he was as likely as not, when the speaker stood up, to reach into his jacket pocket, pull out a pencil, look around for a cigarette package or paper serviette, and start sketching, with the portrait finished by the time he came away.

He was plagued all his life by bad lungs, the reason why he and Elsie had left industrial England and settled in Vancouver, with its mild climate, in 1947. Hermann—dark, debonair, quiet-spoken—was a fighter though, had a sense of humour and had learned to live with his illness.

As it turned out, he had to be a fighter. It had been difficult getting started in his new country. Life had always been, for Hermann, a matter of moving from one job to another as he and Elsie tried to find their place. At one point, desperate, he tried selling real estate, but his honesty obliged him to point out the faults in a house, and it didn't work out. Eventually he landed a position as a sales manager with a printing firm. At last he had something he wanted to do. His talent now came in handy. He could sit down with customers and sketch what they wanted. They also liked his sense of humour. He lived by his wits, or rather his drawing ability attached to his wits. Business was good.

Unfortunately, the owners of the firm decided to break it up because of union matters. Myers bumped around to a couple of other places. He wasn't too happy with his situation. He had always wanted to start his own business. His wife told him now was the time. He began Hermann Myers and Associates, working out of his basement—not discouraged, although he was now fifty. He called himself a printing and advertising consultant.

One of his brothers, who had come to Canada with him in 1947, had obtained a loan from the Westminster Credit Union to build a house. Myers became interested and joined VanCity in 1957, when the Victoria Drive branch opened. He met Ron Spooner then. Spooner was now, circa 1963-64, managing East Hastings. One thing led to another, and soon Myers was doing work for him and his initial efforts at promotion.

It was the beginning of a proverbial beautiful friendship, and the beginning of something that proved extraordinary for Myers and VanCity both. Myers could do everything that involved print, and VanCity needed everything. He handled VanCity's newspaper ads. He blocked out their forms and letterhead. He produced their pamphlets, which were an important part of VanCity's marketing. He looked after the newsletter *Working Dollars*, starting with the layout, using Spooner's editorial material, and ending with supervision of the labelling and mailing. Posters on the windows of branches were Myers's doing. He laid out and supervised the production of VanCity's increasingly sophisticated annual reports. He was also low cost, which was important for an organization with just a few branches, and he delivered on time.

For Myers, this work was an extension of being alive. For Spooner, meanwhile, Myers was a real find. What bound Spooner to Myers most, though, was Myers's accessibility as a person. He wasn't a cloned organization man, not even an advertising agency man. He was a slightly eccentric Englishman of modest expectations who had found a niche for himself. His skill was collaborative and non-threatening, and he was sensitive. He was able to get inside Spooner's head and come up with ideas. Spooner took to calling him "the Lancashire gentleman." Myers had that combination of dry humour, civility and an affectionate understanding of the human condition that was characteristic of a certain strain in the British lower middle class.

Bob Partridge was a hard-drinking, hard-swearing graphic artist from England who was a service representative at Broadway Printers in this era. Broadway Printers did *Working Dollars* and some other VanCity work. Partridge remembered the moment he first encountered Myers, when two men he hadn't seen before walked up to the mica-topped counter. They looked like something out of a 1920s movie. One was a gaunt, skinny mannequin in a suit—Spooner. The other was a rotund gentleman with a pencil-thin moustache, a beautiful smile and an imminent double chin—Hermann Myers. Myers was nattily dressed, as usual. A photo showing him with Spooner a bit later in this period shows him wearing a fine-check coat, a three-piece suit with the vest sloping down over his stomach, a bow tie crowning the vest and a narrow-brimmed felt hat with a feather in the band, atop his now-white hair. The bow tie, a hat—he wore a hat everywhere— and the little moustache, Myers considered his trademarks.

Something besides business impelled Myers in his work now. He really believed in VanCity. He wouldn't hear a word against it. When any of his friends skeptically, or condescendingly, questioned why he would bother doing his banking at VanCity rather than at a proper bank, Myers rose to its defence. Soon they found themselves listening to a full-blown credit union lecture. Myers didn't quarrel. He had a gentle manner, seldom raising his voice, and only then when he was extremely angry. He accepted the fact that people might disagree with him; he had a keen appreciation of the value of a way of life in which people could disagree with each other civilly. But on this one question he was convinced he was right. He tried to convince people to join wherever he could.

His friends took it in stride. It was just Hermann talking. They knew he liked to talk and to analyze and debate. Sometimes it seemed he would never stop talking, but that was the fun of him. Spooner liked to talk, too. They met often for lunch to bat around VanCity projects. Myers was truly at home at these rendezvous, for he was first of all a visualizer, an ideas man. He was actually incapable of rendering finished graphic art, although he could tell someone else, clearly, exactly what he wanted. He drew roughs, perhaps refined them and then passed them on for production. With VanCity and Spooner he had an open field to laugh, trade humorous asides, take his pencil in hand and contrive. He also had a good rapport with Don Bentley.

The assignment now was daily interest. Bentley and Spooner explained the concept to him—how the advent of computers had made daily interest possible and what the advantages were to members. Bill Wright, VanCity's lawyer, was making things difficult. Since the interest wasn't credited daily, he wouldn't allow them to call the account "Daily Balance Interest." "That was too simple," Spooner commented sardonically. Wright insisted they had to describe it as "interest calculated on the daily closing balance." He wouldn't let them boast that it was a first in North America, either—how could they establish that for sure?—only that it was the first in Canada, and only if Spooner was absolutely certain. Wright had the sneaking suspicion that it had at least been tried somewhere in the United States.

Myers turned the concept over in his mind. He was of the old school— stuck in the 1940s, as one hard-edged young advertising acquaintance put it. His material didn't hit people in the face; it didn't stand up and jump out at them. Myers tried instead to achieve simplicity—an uncluttered presentation. This fitted, since an important part of the credit union culture was to be straightforward and ungimmicky. Myers thought the most central symbolic element in the idea of daily interest was the number 24, after the twenty-four hours in a day on which basis the interest would be calculated. He promised a drawing, although he had no idea what he was going to do. He took the mental image of the number 24 back with him to his office and shut out everything else until he had a sketch on paper.

He came up with the name "Plan 24" for the account, and a logo that was at once simple and uncanny. It was a circle on a short handle, drawn in a medium-sized band, after the image of a clock. It wasn't exactly a clock, however, because the circle didn't close at the bottom, and the band, at that point, incorporated an arrow at its end, suggesting continuous, dynamic flow. Yet it was a clock: the clock went around and, bang, you collected interest every time it did. In the middle of this circle was "PLAN 24" in block capital letters in two lines. Myers cut off the left leg of the A so that it sat in the lap of the L. This allowed him to use the largest letters possible. The logo could now also be taken for a magnifying glass focussing on the two words "PLAN 24." Finally, around the bottom of the circle, Myers added, in small capital letters, "INTEREST COMPUTED EVERY 24 HOURS." The word "computed" suggested the technical wonder of it all—a wondrousness that Myers felt was bound to impress members and the public.

The last VanCity logo that had any impact was the generic credit union "man under the umbrella," concocted by a newspaper artist for CUNA in 1923. It was long gone from VanCity copy. The Plan 24 logo was of a different generation—modern, stylized, visually ambiguous and bold. Such imagery for a new product didn't exist anywhere in financial institutions. One had always used just words. Wayne McKay remembered thinking it remarkable that a small organization like VanCity should even have the logo. Everything the banks, trust companies and credit unions had done in the past in the way of appealing to the public seemed to him, now, primitive and passé.

Myers, too, realized that he had done something exceptional. Passbooks were printed up with the logo. Extra advertising and promotion were put in place—an additional $4,000 worth for the month of June, which was all that Bentley could afford. Borch and Cotter were ready at CDS, only a few scant months after they had begun credit union data processing of any kind, with the Gulf & Fraser chequing account. Myers didn't bill for the logo. Designing it was just another chore covered by his small retainer. On June 1, 1967, Plan 24 was sprung on an unsuspecting Vancouver.

CHAPTER 20

Plan 24 Magic

IT WAS ALMOST AS IF THE launch had never taken place. From Bentley and Spooner to the tellers, the staff knew that Plan 24 was revolutionary. The banks never gave anyone a break. Here was an idea that righted the balance in a dramatic way—that said justice will be done—and that could also play off the image of the chartered banks as arrogant and greedy. Yet as June and then the summer wore on, and then the fall, the Plan 24 assault on the world began to appear like a phoney war, where the battle is engaged, yet there is no sound of cannons, only the occasional rattling of machine guns.

The idea was so new and different that members at first didn't know what to make of it. Some members were out-and-out puzzled, because the plan seemed too good to be true. They were looking for a catch. Bentley reported to the board at the end of the year, seven months into the plan, that it had met with tremendous acceptance and 899 members were using it. Altogether, they had put $1.2 million into the account. This "tremendous acceptance" was a fair start for something ordinary, but for a bold innovation like daily interest, which stuck a finger in the eye of the banks, did it really mean anything? The 899 users were barely 7 per cent of VanCity's own membership. And what did 899 people count for next to a population of 412,000? In Wayne McKay's East Hastings branch, only 83 members had a Plan 24 account at the end of 1967, the worst record of all.

Several non-Vancity credit union managers thought Plan 24 was the dumbest idea ever to hit the system. Paying the extra interest, they muttered, would cut into VanCity's margins and might even do serious damage. They did nothing to hide their negativism. "The credit union system and certainly the banking system thought they were nuts," Mike Borch remembered. "A lot of credit union people thought they were nuts anyway. They didn't like Bentley. He was aggressive. They were intimidated by him." Spooner, who was pushing the account and enjoying it, became a pariah.

A few years earlier, Bentley had introduced something called an Accumulating Investment Deposit, later rejigged and redubbed Futura 50. The way the deposit was legally structured—ending up with its face value instead of beginning with it—a member didn't have to pay taxes on the accumulating interest until the deposit matured. The product had been launched as a bright VanCity innovation. It had gone nowhere. Now VanCity was at it again.

For a brief while, that summer of 1967, it almost looked as if the detractors of Plan 24 were right and the new plan would enter into that same limbo of VanCity ideas that they could safely dismiss as too clever by half.

VanCity members, however, inevitably realized what was being offered them and, excited about the plan, put substantial new deposits into the account. Plan 24 was now at least a modest success. For all that, something was lacking. It was true that VanCity's overall assets increased by an impressive 29 per cent in 1967 and by an average 24 per cent annually in the next few years. Yet VanCity had been growing at roughly that rate before Plan 24 was introduced. Membership was increasing much more slowly, at about 8 per cent per year—important, but not earth-shattering. The not-so-little credit union that could did not have sufficient presence to carry such a revolutionary concept quickly to the public. VanCity had only four branches. Total marketing for the Plan 24 launch was limited. Word of mouth and VanCity staff's explaining the account to existing members were the main vehicles for getting the word out. The minor advertising expenditure seemed risible, but given VanCity's other demands and its relatively small base, the limited expenditure wasn't surprising. Strategically, Plan 24 appeared to be caught in a hopeless and frustrating catch-22.

Bentley was a tumult of mixed, hidden emotions as he reflected on the plan's ambiguous progress. He not only understood the strategic impasse, he had in so many words predicted it. He told the board they would have to spend more on education and promotion, even though the spare cash he had squirrelled away in the "education reserve" for such a contingency was already gone. He had been talking for years about the need to communicate better with members and with the public—had made enemies in the credit union movement with his unhappiness at how slow they were to see the obvious. Now the crunch had come—not, however, because the banks had mounted a charge against VanCity and credit unions, as he had anticipated, but because of VanCity's astonishing momentum.

Overlying these feelings was another set of emotions, also hidden behind his calm exterior. From the inside looking out, he saw VanCity's world opening up, replete with expectation. He had to force himself to restrain his excitement for fear that he would lose perspective. His small gang of branch managers was going full tilt, their branches hopping. The past year, 1967, had been extraordinary, with the largest increase in assets ever—making for a total of $17 million—and a record surplus. Bentley recommended that the dividend on share accounts—the symbolic return for investing in the co-operative enterprise—be ratcheted upwards. Including insurance coverage, it came to ¾ per cent above the rate paid by the banks on their flagship savings accounts—a hefty differential when rates on savings accounts were only in the 4 to 5 per cent range. Bentley thought of raising the dividend even higher—the earnings were there—but as always in financial calculations, he wanted to be on the safe side. As he told the board, he just couldn't visualize another year as good as 1967, forgetting that he had said exactly the same thing about prospects the year before. The ratios in 1968, as it happened, turned out to be almost as good as in 1967, and in 1969 even better, notwithstanding leap-frogging growth.

One could chart in cycles how the momentum had developed. It had begun with the credit union principles of member ownership, self-help and humanity, captured in the slogan, "Where people are more important than money." This was VanCity's 1946 inheritance. It moved from there to an ethic of providing the best service to members and to opening the doors wide to the public. Fighting off restrictions that came from closed-bond credit unions was an essential element. Scale of operation also became important. So did an awareness of change—in people's needs and in the population mix. This led, in turn, to new services and innovations—sometimes called "products"—but always, again, in terms of giving the members something that might be useful.

This latter stage was now approaching critical mass. Open mortgages, mortgages east of Cambie and lending to women on an equal basis were mainstays. Plan 24, with its appeal to everybody who had savings, added an entire dimension all by itself. These plans and services were only available at VanCity or, in part, at other credit unions. "Exclusives," Spooner called them. Promoting them was like running with the wind at one's back. The major chartered banks did not introduce daily interest until 1979, twelve years after the Plan 24 launch. The first bank of any kind to do so, the fringe Unity Bank, did not offer it until 1976, or nine years later. This was an enormous lead time for VanCity.

Less obvious, but with a powerful undertow, Bentley's doctrine of internal free speech had created a culture that was constantly generating and implementing new ideas. Of course, that was the whole purpose of it. Yet Bentley had approached it as an exercise. Theoretically it was a good tack— a way to come up with ideas and check their practicality. It also suited him. He needed the give and take for himself, like nourishment. What he hadn't realized was how good the theory was. Piece by piece, this VanCity culture— it was now identifiable—was revolutionizing retail banking in Vancouver and, by its repercussions, in the rest of British Columbia and beyond. There was a revolution about to happen after all, and daily interest was the spark touching it off.

Plan 24 was like an arranged marriage that, after the artificial hoopla of the wedding, slowly turned into a love affair. Once the members took to the plan, they embraced it avidly, and all past suitors looked pale by comparison. The banks didn't have daily interest. The trust companies didn't have it. VanCity members had it. Even a new member, who perhaps had crossed the street from a bank with a few hundred dollars to try out the account, instantaneously came to feel that the bank was a laggard from another age and credit unions were a bright invention, and wondered why he or she hadn't seen it before, it was so obvious.

Plan 24 also had niche appeal for real estate agents who had dramatically fluctuating amounts of money either in trust or in their own accounts if they were dabbling—sometimes large amounts, where interest on the day-to-day balance was important. They loved the account. Their VanCity membership, in turn, reinforced the link between them and VanCity for mortgage business. By the end of 1970, three-and-a-half years after the launch, there was $7 million in the Plan 24 account, almost a quarter of all members' deposits (including term deposits, shares and the chequing account).

Jack Webster, "The Mouth That Roared," coincidentally helped VanCity out. Webster ruled the airwaves with his morning open line show on CKNW. A friend of his approached him in despair. She was a single mother. To keep herself and her family going, she worked as a cook at Simon Fraser University during the day and ran a parking lot at night. She wanted to borrow $8,500 to buy a house. She went to her bank, not realizing she wouldn't get a loan from them, and predictably was turned down.

Webster knew Don Bentley from a casual meeting and had heard a few good things about VanCity. VanCity was becoming part of the cognoscenti's Vancouver scene—a good thing waiting to be discovered by other people less in the know—and Webster had picked up on it. Bentley was unavailable, so Webster was referred to McKay. McKay interviewed the woman at his branch. As he remembered it, with the benefit of hindsight, he knew from the look in her eyes that she would never miss a payment. He stretched the rules a bit and gave her the loan. When Webster heard the story from her, he put her on the air to tell his listeners what had happened. Until then, when a woman had gone to her bank for a loan and had been rejected, she gave up, unless she had a friend who was a VanCity member and knew of the possibilities. Webster's enthusiastic plug for VanCity changed that. As it turned out, the woman never did miss a payment, although the value of the publicity would have more than covered a loan write-off.

Her story wasn't unusual, even for women with professional and managerial jobs. The banks still hadn't caught on. VanCity's now well-known lending policy became a marker of an organization that was different in kind, modern in spirit, enlightened, freer, bold, egalitarian and open—where people counted and were even shareholders. A pride and cachet went with belonging, for men, too.

A housing development called The Meadows had a parallel impact. Lloyd Widdifield, Bentley and some other board members had been talking about housing for several years. VanCity underwrote mortgages and financed builders. That is, it provided money for others to build houses. Why not do housing themselves? Why not use VanCity's growing financial muscle to extend the co-operative principle beyond mere banking, eliminate a level of profit and provide quality housing to members at the lowest possible cost? It was a natural spinoff of the credit union's financial expertise. It was also, because VanCity wasn't in the housing business, an adventure coloured by the risk of something new, marginal though that risk might be. The membership enthusiastically approved the initiative at the annual meeting in 1967. In a booming Vancouver, which badly needed new affordable housing and where land costs were spiralling—where developers were considered opportunistic profiteers if not outright bandits—it had a built-in social message with a punch.

Bentley and the board tried first to acquire land in Vancouver or Burnaby. In the end, they had to settle for Surrey. Because of high mortgage rates and land costs, they couldn't afford a development for the bottom-income group in society. They aimed instead at lower-middle-income families with average annual earnings of at least $6,000. The development was to consist of 39 two-bedroom and 79 three-bedroom townhouses spread over seven acres, with a swimming pool attached. Prices were $16,000 and $18,000 respectively. Minimum down payments were $2,395 and $2,700. Monthly payments at that level, which covered everything, including cable, maintenance, and taxes, were $150 and $178. Paying rent for something similar, and ending up with no ownership at the end of it, would have cost $220 and upwards. VanCity provided the mortgages. With eligibility for a provincial government second-mortgage program, purchasers could reduce their down payment to $1,000. The townhouses were to be built by Dawson Development Limited, which had put the land together. The company was one of the province's largest contractors and the only one with large-scale townhouse development experience. The overall cost was $2.5 million.

The Meadows was the first development by any credit union in North America designed to provide modern, low-cost housing for members. *Enterprise* magazine, the new magazine of the B.C. credit union movement, described it, in an editorial on Credit Union Day, as a "new area of service," as if condominiums were to become an integral adjunct of what a credit union provided its members. In one striking way it was. VanCity members had the exclusive right for thirty days to buy the townhouses. As it happened, only 40 per cent of the units were bought by members. The message, though—that being a member of VanCity had all kinds of advantages—went as far as word of mouth could carry. So did the imagery that went with it: An organization that had the savvy and the money to take on the developers at their own game must have something to it. The non-members who bought units, meanwhile, were now members, carrying VanCity mortgages. A separate subsidiary, VCS Housing Developments Ltd., had been set up for The Meadows project and others to follow.

Other pieces fell into place. Since 1963, VanCity had been using the name City Savings to identify itself. Vancouver City Savings Credit Union, or even Vancouver City Savings, was considered too long, not snappy enough for the times. While the whole name might appear on a sign, "City Savings" was in much larger letters, standing out. The phone was answered with the greeting "City Savings." There was a "CS" City Savings logo. Then an intruder from Alberta, City Savings and Trust, arrived on the scene with a Vancouver branch, effectively using the same name. Bentley was not amused. The parallel names confused even many of the credit union's members. Some of them started going to the trust company's premises. The doubling of the City Savings name turned out to be a blessing in disguise. A decision was made at the credit union to switch to VanCity. For a while some people thought VanCity was a place that sold vans, but the name quickly established itself. Nobody could remember who first came up with it.

The rotund, bow-tied, gentlemanly Hermann Myers was now asked to devise a logo for the new name. Logos were, after all, supposed to be his department. Myers began with the idea of building blocks—the notion of VanCity, with its loans, mortgages and savings plans providing the where-withal for members to build their future. He also had physical "building blocks" in mind—the construction of houses financed by VanCity mort-gages. VanCity's "cs" logo had building blocks in it, or perhaps buildings—three overlapping squares like a bar graph, atop the thick flattened letters "cs" suggesting a foundation. This logo was heavy and clunkish.

Myers bought some children's blocks and started playing with them on his desk. He tried, among other things, piling them high in individual columns, like skyscrapers. There were going to be a lot of tall buildings in Vancouver, he thought. He had romanticized VanCity in his mind and anticipated it would somehow be part of this new high-rise, big-city urban scene. The idea was to capture the future. Myers began sketching. Rec-tangles going straight up, however, looked flat. There was no feeling to them.

The children's blocks also had some striated sides. These caught Myers's eye. The lines provided a contrast to the solid colours on the blocks' other sides. He tried using this contrast, slanting his three blocks together, pyra-mid fashion, to give them cumulative power and to create the effect of this power rising into the sky. The lines, he realized, played two roles—contrast and upward motion. He had also achieved the uncluttered simplicity he was continually after. Once having done the sketch, he couldn't change it.

Everybody in VanCity had a shot at the logo. The forms looked like sky-scrapers, they said, which were inappropriate for VanCity, which did resi-dential mortgages. Or were they skyscrapers? They could also be described as stylized building blocks. Or could they? Like the Plan 24 logo, this one had just enough visual ambiguity to be nothing other than it own creation, which was the genius of it.

Under the three squat forms, paradoxically rising, Myers then inserted the new name, "VANCITY," in capital letters. Here again appearances were deceiving. The letters "N" and "I" were actually in lower case, although raised up to the same height. The "Y" was also in enlarged lower case, but in a font of its own, with its leg moving horizontally right to left at the bottom of the line. Like a mischievous little boy playing at printing, Myers had drawn in the letters to please the eye. He then did over the whole thing in flaming orange, in a last contrarian flourish. Whatever the misgivings over the skyscraper imagery, Myers had translated into visual form the thrusting energy and modernism he felt whenever he and Spooner talked about where VanCity was going.

Myers was irrepressible. One day he was in the main branch at 96 East Broadway doing his banking business, and happened to get into the wrong line—the one that moved much more slowly than the others. He was furious at the wait and at the disorder, as some people tried changing lines. Still steaming, he had a word with Bentley on the way out. Why not, he said, have a single line and distribute members to the next available teller in turn? Bentley thought it was worth a try and improvised a temporary barrier for the purpose. The more permanent version had built-in desks where members could fill in their deposit or withdrawal slips, or endorse their cheques, while they were waiting. It was the first time, anywhere, as far as anybody knew, that a single-line system was used. Ultimately it became common in credit unions, banks and post offices around the world.

Myers dubbed the system the First-in-Line Teller Service and marketed it like a new kind of account. "Something new has been added at VanCity," the First-in-Line pamphlet announced. "IT'S FAST! Go to the 'First-in-Line' sign ... As soon as you are the first in line go to any teller not attending to another member. IT'S FAIR! You can't get 'stuck' in a slow line—everyone takes their turn. IT'S CONFIDENTIAL! You are the only one at the teller's wicket—no one is behind you. LESS FRUSTRATION! We know you will find this new service time and temper saving."

The arrangement caught members' fancy, made them proud. It was so sensible and obvious and, yet again, only VanCity had it—had, apparently, even thought about it. The innovation wasn't a momentous one in technical terms, but it underscored VanCity's service ethic. That did say something important. It was fun just getting into a First-in-Line line and remarking to one's neighbour in the line how far ahead of the banks VanCity was.

The branch premises were undergoing much more of a transformation than just the First-in-Line arrangement, however. Bentley, with the new logo in hand, set about systematically to rebuild his branches. He had met an architect, Ray Toby, through a common friend, and had suggested to him out of the blue one day that he and his firm, Toby Russell & Buckwell, might want to do some work for VanCity. Toby wasn't sure why Bentley had approached him in particular.

The firm then did The Meadows project. Now Bentley was explaining to him his plan for the branches—new premises altogether for the main office, plus Victoria Drive and Kitsilano. He needed more space and more parking. He also wanted people to recognize VanCity branches, starting with the logo and the new name. He wanted to establish a common look before other branches came on stream, so that each branch in the city would visually help the other. He was after the same physically identifiable atmosphere on the inside, too, with lots of space for members and as much natural light as possible. Toby was further instructed to use good materials, even if they cost more.

After that, Toby was left on his own. Bentley had given him the work, but wasn't prepared to point him in the right direction. Toby was supposed to figure that out himself. There wasn't even a single point of contact with VanCity where he and his juniors could get definitive opinions about particulars. Toby was astonished by this informality and autonomy. He never did quite get used to it.

The architect who did most of the figuring out was Henry Ciccone. Ciccone's father was a longtime VanCity member, and Ciccone was a member himself. For him, VanCity was an institution of the people. He tried to get that across physically in materials and colours. He avoided marble, granite, and similar-looking materials, which were forbidding and cold. He used wood and clay floor tiles instead, which were softer to the eye and friendlier. He wanted to make people feel at home. Flashiness and complication, moreover, would suggest waste and ostentation, whereas simpler materials aesthetically reassured members that their money was being spent wisely. Bentley didn't want temples, Ciccone knew.

The new premises for Victoria Drive and the main branch were both completed in the spring of 1971. The main branch was on Broadway, just west of Oak, in what had been a Safeway store. Bentley loved Safeway stores because they were a good size and, most of all, because they had parking. Two years later, East Hastings was also moved into an old Safeway store, at Kamloops and Hastings.

While this work was being done, Hollyburn Credit Union, Ted Sewell's old credit union in West Vancouver on the North Shore, asked to join VanCity. It became Branch 5, VanCity's first branch outside Vancouver city limits. Because VanCity couldn't be accused, in this case, of encroaching on some other credit union's territory, the merger occurred with little fuss. Some North Shore Credit Union board members showed up at VanCity's annual meeting to protest, but since Hollyburn's members themselves wanted to join VanCity, the protest did not go far. The Hollyburn Credit Union's premises were on a narrow mews off Marine Drive called Little Wall Street. Five months after Hollyburn became a VanCity branch, its modest assets had increased fivefold and it was moved to a new location. Toby Russell & Buckwell looked after that one, too.

The days of tiny, improvised VanCity branches were coming to an end. The main branch now had twenty-six employees. The new premises were large, luminous, stylish and inviting. The exterior was solid, almost massive. On both sides of the northwest corner, at second-storey level, was Hermann Myers' orange VanCity logo blazoned large. Ray Toby hated the logo. His architects went to great trouble creating the right look and ambiance, he argued, and the logo only got in the way.

He also hated signage. He would drop into a branch to take a look around, six or eight months after it was up and running, and there would be all these oversized posters working against the carefully wrought architectural design—posters that in Toby's view were just telling the obvious anyway. "Somewhat Army and Navyish," Ron Spooner admitted, with a mixture of shamefacedness and huckster's pride. Spooner was insistent on the posters. They identified VanCity locations for people hearing about the credit union on radio or reading their flyers, and were a useful reminder for members. Spooner also wanted the VanCity name displayed more boldly on buildings to reinforce the link between the name and the logo. On dark, rainy nights at 1030 West Broadway, where the new main branch was located, the two matched VanCity logos glimmered over the street like a lighthouse.

Spooner was having a bang-up time. Assets were going through the roof, or so it seemed. They had been $4 million in 1960. By 1970 they were $31 million. The more assets, the greater the turnover, and the greater the turnover, the more there was available for advertising. The advertising and promotion budget was incrementally feeding off the growth and feeding it in turn. In 1961, when the board decided to reach out systematically to the public, the promotion budget, including the educational side, was just $6,500, with none of it allocated for media advertising. Booklets, pamphlets and calendars were as far as the money went. By 1970, the budget was $93,000, with $47,000 for advertising proper. Spooner had just enough money now to really tell people about VanCity—his Cinderella—and he relished the expanded possibilities the money gave him.

He expanded sports sponsorship and other local contributions. VanCity also established scholarships, for marketing students in UBC's commerce department. These outlays were an extension of the original community ethos of VanCity. Full-page ads in theatre programs emphasized VanCity's connection to the arts. Spooner also tried television, with spots at least weekly on one channel. Bentley still wondered about the usefulness of these diverse expenditures, because he couldn't measure the returns. He vaguely assumed, however, that what Spooner was doing would have at least some long-term value. Besides, he didn't know how to go about it himself and had adopted a hands-off policy. "Okay, Ron," he would say. "You do it, I don't understand it." He sensed Spooner had a flair for it and gave him as much slack as he dared.

With radio advertising, on the other hand, neither of them had any doubt. It was by far the greatest single part of the budget and, in spring and fall campaigns, they pushed it to saturation levels. These campaigns were combined with a mail drop of *Working Dollars*—60,000 to 70,000 copies a time—and a membership mailing. CKNW was the radio station most often used. It had a singular copywriter named Tony Antonias. Antonias got Spooner and Bentley humming.

Antonias was a native of Port Pirie, near Adelaide, in South Australia. He hadn't heard of credit unions until he came to Canada, and in his early years in town subconsciously avoided writing ads for them. His spontaneous reaction to any mention of them was, "Oh, they're Commies." When the station's sales rep handling VanCity told him the account had reached the size where he should look at it and a meeting with Spooner was set up, Antonias was less than excited. "I'll go and get it over with," he shrugged.

Instead of imagined monsters, he discovered nice, middle-class people. He warmed up to Spooner from the moment they were introduced—odd, he thought, because they were so different in personality. Spooner never seemed to get upset, and if he did, he was smiling while he was upset. Antonias, as he once gaily confessed in Australese, had a short wick, and would fly right off the bloody handle. He also met Bentley and liked him. He liked the delightful and picturesque Hermann Myers, although they did not work together and he had reservations about Myers's advertising instincts. For Antonias, they were the VanCity "family." He was taken by their friendliness.

Spooner seemed to be telling him that he, Antonias, was the doctor, who knew of the mysterious pathologies of radio advertising, and that whatever he said was fine. Spooner was trusting. The more this happened, the greater the challenge. There was no way he was going to let Spooner or VanCity down, Antonias thought to himself. He became protective of them. Mr. Bentley, as he called him, also gave him that trust. VanCity made him feel that he was the key to their future success. He revelled in the psychology of it. He knew he was being stroked, but there was no artifice to it. They really were counting on him and they really did care about succeeding. It became his personal goal to help VanCity succeed in any way he could.

Antonias years earlier had come up with a signature jingle—called a "musical logo" in the trade—for Woodward's Department Stores' famous $1.49 days. He now set out to do the same thing for VanCity, using the three words "Vancouver City Savings." It began running in ads on the eight o'clock news every evening—a major timespot and a major financial commitment. Antonias first did a low-budget version of the logo. When he saw how well it worked, VanCity gave him a larger budget and he had an orchestral version done with top singers.

He had VanCity concentrate their term-deposit advertising in the fall, when Canada Savings Bonds were being advertised. He argued that VanCity might as well ride on the government's coattails. Spooner and Bentley went along, and the strategy worked exceptionally well.

He had a fetish about being truthful with listeners, albeit artfully truthful, and VanCity's credit union philosophy of avoiding the hard sell meshed with this approach. The ads he did for them were product and interest-rate oriented—straight goods—and depended on whatever VanCity needed at the time. Usually it was deposits. "And you can get your money on Saturday" was one of Antonias' favourite Plan 24 pitches, taking a poke at the banks' restricted hours. He quickly realized he had an advantage with his VanCity work: their products really were better than anything else around. They had Plan 24 and their interest rate on term deposits was invariably higher than the rates offered by the banks. He could get his teeth into these differences and play with them. What he remembered most of these copy-writing days for VanCity was how aggressive the credit union was.

As the trust between Spooner and Antonias grew, Spooner did a most unusual thing. He turned over the entire radio budget to Antonias. Antonias did the creative and production work, and then he, rather than Spooner, did the buying on radio stations in the market, depending on what VanCity wanted to achieve. A CKNW employee, in other words, was making the decision for VanCity as to how much of the radio budget CKNW would receive and how much would go to other stations. That there was a conflict of interest didn't bother Antonias. As he saw it, they had trust in him and he had loyalty to them. He often dropped by VanCity, on Saturday mornings on his day off, to find out how well his ads were working. They proved to be potent. Bentley, warm and courteous, never failed to thank him after a campaign or to mention, when they bumped into each other somewhere, how he liked the ads and how they sounded on the air. The bond tightened. Spooner, watching the results of the radio campaigns, could finally enjoy cause and effect.

Bentley, meanwhile, was parrying a major initiative by the banks and the federal government. Ottawa, in 1967, had created the Canada Deposit Insurance Corporation (CDIC) for the banking system—a full-fledged guarantee fund protecting depositors. Bentley was chair of the Credit Union Reserve Board (CURB) all through this period. He and the others on the board did not want to be outflanked by the obvious appeal such a guarantee would have.

CURB offered to become part of the CDIC system. The federal minister of finance, Mitchell Sharp, reflecting the banks' interests, replied that it could not be done, since credit unions and caisses populaires did not accept deposits from the public, only from members, and therefore should not qualify for public insurance. CURB had no choice after that but to go ahead and create a counterbalancing deposit insurance system of its own. Dick Monrufet, at the League, cleared the way with the attorney general in Victoria. CURB had its guarantee fund within a year. It wasn't backed financially by the province, but the legislation gave CURB the extra supervisory powers it needed for the scheme, including the power to take a wobbly credit union under direct supervision and even wind it up.

Bentley wasn't finished yet. He and CURB decided, while they were at it, to outmanoeuvre the banks and Ottawa in turn. CDIC provided coverage up to $20,000 per depositor. CURB, for its own fund, pushed for complete 100 per cent coverage. This meant that the annual assessment for credit unions in the province would have to be doubled, but they were in a fighting mood and agreed. Then, once the fund was established, they undertook a promotion campaign to press the advantage.

The economies of scale that Bentley had talked about from the beginning, in defence of VanCity's open charter, also began to tell. This was the final piece to the puzzle. Every year, VanCity's annual report carried a section on operations. Its core was the expense ratio—how much of every dollar of gross income, mainly from interest on loans, was allocated to salaries, insurance and other costs. The lower the expense ratio, the more that members could receive in interest on their deposits. Bentley's frugality, plus operating efficiencies, computerization and sheer growth had sliced the ratio in half, from 57 cents in 1959 to 29 cents in 1969. This meant interest and dividends to members could be raised. VanCity and other credit unions, moreover, were still the only ones offering open mortgages, which were also insured. They charged a premium up to 1 per cent for that, which widened VanCity's margin and again allowed it to offer more interest. As the 1970s began, VanCity was paying 1 to 1¼ per cent more than the banks on term deposits and almost 2 per cent more on savings accounts (Plan 24 versus the world). The difference with trust companies was smaller but still substantial. Dividends on share accounts represented a 2 to 3 per cent margin over competitors' savings accounts. These higher deposit rates weren't offered only out of generosity to members. They brought in more money to meet the incessant mortgage demand. The potential was explosive.

Plan 24 evolved in this atmosphere of change like fissionable material in a cyclotron. Its percolating expansion quickly created handling problems for CDS. CDS and VanCity hurriedly worked out a transition to punched-paper tape, to take the pressure off the consortium.

   Computer technology was changing on the go. Punched-paper tape was one of its newer developments. Instead of VanCity delivering the bundles of vouchers to CDS, key-punch operators in the branches entered the information from the vouchers directly onto paper tape, using an add-punch machine. The add-punch machine was an adding machine configured to punch tape as well. CDS then fed the tape into another machine, which automatically punched a corresponding stack of cards. The cards were then fed into the computer. It meant that the posting of transactions was moved back into the branches. The add-punch machines, however, were small, quick, inexpensive and relatively quiet. Later, as computer technology moved ahead another step, the data on the punched-paper tape was transposed to a magnetic tape instead of cards, and that would feed the computer. Computers could read magnetic tapes much faster than they could read cards.

   It soon became clear that Plan 24 was more than the sum of its deposits. It was boosting term deposits, especially the one-year term. People who joined VanCity because of the talk and advertising about the daily-interest account discovered the rest of VanCity, including attractive term-deposit rates, which were higher than Plan 24 interest. Soon Nelson, McKay and the other managers were talking to new members about the advantage of shifting more of their savings, perhaps still in banks, to VanCity term deposits instead. Term deposits began to get equal billing in VanCity's advertising. Bentley, drawing up each month's financial statement, followed the Plan 24 and one-year term accounts like a punter watching two favourites in a horse race. Out of the gate, in 1967, the one-year term was ahead. In 1968, Plan 24, finding its feet, pulled in front. It held the lead, but just barely, to the end of 1969. The following year, the one-year term regained the lead and appeared to be widening the gap.

Bentley was still writing the occasional strategic think piece in annual reports. He had changed the format of the reports from a small booklet to the regular letter size, together with a glossy cover. The reports had become increasingly sophisticated and graphically smart, reflecting the internal changes at VanCity. Bentley's language had also changed. He had begun using words like "sociological," "problematic," "divergent," "innovation," "creativity," "redesign" and "urban culture." He was roaming further afield. In one item, in connection with The Meadows housing project, he sketched out a housing policy for the federal government. On another occasion, he talked about the greater role of women in the labour force. Credit unions could adapt more easily than other institutions, he thought, because they were close to people. He explained how the solemn, funereal atmosphere of banks' loan departments was disappearing in favour of a swinging "with it" image and how "courtesy cards" everywhere and for everything were on the horizon (courtesy cards later came to be known as charge cards).

VanCity, Bentley in effect was saying, was adaptable and open enough that it would not be caught unawares. The cultural shift that he had made himself almost a decade earlier was now internalized. Computerization had helped push it along. The shift was much like a butterfly emerging from a chrysalis.

When the new main branch opened in the spring of 1971, Spooner ran full-page advertising features in Vancouver's two daily newspapers. Everything was there now—open mortgages, the other exclusives, the high rates on deposits, First-in-Line, modern premises and, in the text, an evocative account of VanCity itself. "Credit, not sex, rules loans to gals," read one headline in the *Vancouver Sun* version. "Dollars aren't all to VanCity," read another. The added protection to depositors, from the new Provincial Share and Deposit Guarantee Fund, was underscored for readers and reinforced with the fund's seal—looking very much the official seal of approval, especially since it had the word "provincial" in its name, although it wasn't a provincial government guarantee. VanCity was celebrating its twenty-fifth anniversary. The logo designed for the anniversary was used in the advertising features: "25 YEARS SERVING OUR COMMUNITY." "More than 20,000 members ... assets exceeding $35 million ... established 1946 ... 'Owned by the people it serves.' " The fission had occurred. All hell broke loose.

CHAPTER 21

The Takeoff

YOUNG JOHN ISELI COULD NOT get the spectacle of it out of his mind. His little branch at Broadway and Blenheim, on Saturday mornings, was overflowing with people, like a Noah's flood of mankind.

Iseli had shown up at 96 East Broadway in late 1965, in response to a newspaper ad, six months after Wayne McKay arrived. Like McKay, he was from Manitoba, but he was a farm boy, from Swan River, near the Saskatchewan border. His parents, like McKay's, belonged to the co-op store, a large, multi-faceted operation that was dominant in the Swan River area. He began working in the co-op hardware outlet part-time in his last years in high school and stayed with the store afterwards. Soon he was in the "head office," in the accounting department. His parents decided to retire from farming and move to the West Coast. He could have taken over the farm, but the idea didn't appeal to him. He had done enough farm chores, as a boy, for a lifetime, although the work and the discipline, he realized, had been good for him. He went to Vancouver with the family.

He began at 96 East Broadway in the usual way, as a teller. He had done both cash and accounting at the Swan River co-op, so the transition was an easy one. Vancouver was the big adjustment. It was a big, big city. He took pride in going to work every day and doing his job. For a teller, the test was to balance at the end of the day. Others had difficulty, but he never had a problem. Ray Evelle was his initial boss. Iseli did not at first have much interaction with Bentley, but somehow he quickly became aware of Bentley's priorities: serving the member and being fair. The members also made an impression. They understood and believed in the credit union philosophy and took a proprietary interest in the branch.

The office was a fun place to work. Iseli got to know everybody, including the people at the other branches. There weren't that many of them—only twenty-five, all told. Decisions were made quickly, since there was no bureaucracy to refer to. Everybody did everything, and everything was done manually, except for the clanking of the Burroughs posting machine. In a year and a half Iseli was assistant manager. He expected the promotion. He wasn't pushy, but he had done the other things—teller, member service, loans. At almost exactly the four-year mark, when Iseli was just twenty-four years old, Art Farnden's death touched off a shuffle of branch managers, and Bentley handed Iseli the key to the Kitsilano branch, the storefront at Broadway and Blenheim.

The Kitsilano branch, circa 1969, was the last-born in the family. It was always in the shadow of its older, super-achieving siblings, especially the aggressive, ambitious, next-youngest—East Hastings. It was the first on the west side, like a beautiful child in a family of rowdies—a darling baby that had got off to a healthy, clucking start and of which so much was expected. Yet try as it might, and increase deposits in percentage terms as it might, it still was a laggard. It had four years behind it to catch up to East Hastings, but had only half its deposits, just $1.5 million. Boisterous East Hastings, meanwhile, with $3 million in deposits, was shouting for yet more dollars to meet its loan demand. Kitsilano, on operations, was even falling short of its dividend requirement—in effect, it was still losing money.

Iseli knew this and also knew how lucky he was. Although he was in line for the manager's job, had he been in a bank branch in Swan River or Winnipeg, he might have been stuck below manager's level, in agony, for years. He had other things on his mind. Like McKay when he started managing East Hastings, Iseli found himself having to deal with members who couldn't quite believe he was the manager because he was so young. He was constantly having to prove himself. He was also, now, the person accountable for hiring and firing, and for morale. Soon these concerns were superseded by another, inescapable one: how to keep up.

Kitsilano was nothing like the main branch, where Iseli had come from. It was small and homey—the banking equivalent of a slightly down-at-the-heels corner grocery store. There were only four staff altogether, including Iseli. The frontage was no more than eighteen feet. The teller counter at the back had to fit into just part of that length. When Iseli needed to add an extra teller, he put her around the corner, behind the member-service counter on the right. This counter, however, had been built so tight to the desks behind it, against the wall, to allow for more space on the members' side, that when the added teller became pregnant, there wasn't enough room for her to stand there. She had to be taken off cash.

In Iseli's first year, 1970, deposits increased an extraordinary 71 per cent. In the take-off year, 1971, the increase on top of that was another 135 per cent. The same kind of astonishing growth was occurring on the mortgage side, where the value of first mortgages Iseli was putting out quadrupled in 1970 from a small base, and then tripled the following year—a combined 1,200 per cent increase over the two-year span. Like a young sibling rivalling a slightly older one while imitating him, Iseli was repeating McKay's experience. Instead of having an Italian connection, he had a Greek connection. He discovered, too, that if one made an impact on a few members of an ethnic community, the word of mouth travelled fast. Iseli, similarly, would often eyeball mortgage applicants and then stick his neck out, when the paper qualifications didn't altogether support the loan. The two major paper factors were collateral and income. Iseli, like McKay, also took into account saving habits—how much the applicant had saved from even a modest income and a menial job, perhaps as a dishwasher. This was a good proxy for character where character was usually unknown to him.

The impact of the trust Iseli showed members in these cases, working on fierce immigrant pride, reverberated throughout the neighbourhood. He also offered commercial mortgages, or working-capital loans based on home mortgages, for a restaurant, a shop or a service station. He became, in effect, the immigrant's business partner. These relationships, once cemented, often lasted for the borrower's life, through business changes and residential moves to the suburbs.

Word of mouth also spread like wildfire from realtor to realtor. Iseli did not have time to go knocking on real estate brokers' doors. They knocked on his door and rang his telephone off the hook instead. The VanCity first mortgage—the "open mortgage," with no esoteric clauses and no interest penalties—had magnetic drawing power, pulling in realtors from as far away as Surrey and Delta to Iseli's Kitsilano corner shop. In his own area in particular, the west side, property values were escalating quickly. People were anxious to get into the market. Iseli had the west side mortgage market locked up. The VanCity mortgage was called, internally, the "three-year mortgage" because the rate was renegotiated every three years. It seemed at times, to the overworked Iseli, that VanCity on the loan side had just that one product, but what a product it was.

One of the first mortgage's most compelling features, for realtors, was the speed with which VanCity could issue it. Lloyd Widdifield's and Bentley's determination a decade earlier to speed up the loan process was now paying off in exploding multiples. Typically a loan application to a bank, even for a mortgage, went east to Toronto or Montreal and came back in a couple of weeks. Subject to appraisal, Iseli and his people could do it in a day. They had to do it in a day, otherwise the backlog would have become unmanageable. Appraisals, which were farmed out, usually took another day or two, but if the member needed the money quickly, as often happened, Iseli could obtain an appraisal in an hour, put the lawyer on it that afternoon and have the mortgage approved and registered, and the actual money disbursed, in twenty-four hours. The branch kept whole pools of lawyers busy drawing up these mortgages. Sometimes the volume did overtake Iseli and his staff. "Phenomenal," he would say to himself at the end of such a spell, "just phenomenal."

VanCity's ability to issue loans so quickly, because it was a local institution, appealed to people's British Columbia pride and anti-central Canada animus. This pride of localism had to overcome the nagging assumption that distant central Canadian banking power was somehow superior regardless of particulars. With a VanCity open mortgage in one's hand, however, good for a large sum of money that paid for a house that one was going to possess—yes, own title to, live in and build equity upon—that assumption vanished. VanCity seemed now to have a power that the banks didn't have.

On the deposit side, Iseli began tapping into the faculty and administration at the University of British Columbia. The university people had good incomes and were relatively sophisticated. They recognized that Plan 24 and the term deposits were good investment vehicles. The Kitsilano branch was the closest to the university.

So many people were coming into the branch, and it was so small, that there was sometimes no place to put them, even if they were packed so tight they were jostling each other. On a late Friday afternoon or a Saturday morning, the premises looked like a madhouse. The line-up might extend out the door and down the sidewalk—"pouring out the door," Iseli thought of it. Instead of giving up in discomfiture, however, members looked upon the madhouse as confirmation that they were on to a good thing and brought their friends with them the next time. More members required more staff. There was no place to put them. There were some cubbyholes in the back along a narrow hallway, each with just enough room for a desk. Iseli stuck some people in there, for administrative work and posting. Then he stuck a desk in the last place he had—the lunchroom. The back end had the appearance of a slave camp, except that the people there were having such a good time. Starting with four staff people in 1970, including himself, Iseli had packed in eleven by 1972. Partly because he didn't have room for more staff and partly because the branch had become a sizable operation, the expense ratio went from being the highest by far in VanCity to being the lowest, and the branch changed from running a loss to a hefty surplus. It had become clear earlier that a new building was needed. The building went up at Broadway and Waterloo. It was VanCity's pride and joy. When it opened, in 1973, staff expanded from eleven to twenty, like actors popping onto the stage out of trapdoors after waiting patiently through the first act.

The stripling Iseli and the not-much-older but already streetwise McKay saw their branches as having the most in common, so their rivalry was the most intense. They did a lot of good-natured ribbing. If Iseli had a particularly spectacular day, he would telephone McKay the next morning and innocently ask how East Hastings had done, knowing that McKay would play the same game on him whenever he got the chance. Iseli, and later his assistant manager at the new location, Jan Chapman, were constantly on the phone to other branches finding out the latest. CDS provided month-end reports, with aggregate totals for each of the branches. Iseli and Chapman scoured these reports. They would definitely phone if another branch was low that month, to rub it in.

The in-house competition was friendly, a pleasurable indulgence. At the monthly managers' meetings, ideas and experiences were shared freely. There was no hoarding of advantages. Intelligence about what the banks were doing in their respective locations was also shared, in addition to the tracking done by Bentley and head office.

Iseli was certain that his branch had outdone McKay's in this period, the early 1970s. He was right in percentage terms, but not in absolute terms, although Kitsilano was closing the gap. Each branch was growing so fast, it was almost impossible for one branch to overtake another, incredible as its performance seemed to be. In 1973, deposits at Kitsilano almost doubled and Iseli still didn't quite catch East Hastings. East Hastings never quite passed Victoria Drive in deposits. Times were frantic at all the locations. The main branch under Don Nelson, although much larger to begin with, showed similar dramatic rates of gain. Nelson remembered that when they made the move to 1030 West Broadway, the place had exploded. Normal perspective went out the window.

Staff turnover, meanwhile, was atrocious. In the most frenetic year, 1971, the branch managers had started off with 39 employees (excluding themselves), lost 33 in the course of the year and had to hire 53 just to end up with 59. Even allowing for the fact that some people came and went in the same year, so the attrition of incumbent employees wasn't as great as the figures suggested, the turnover added complications. Surprisingly, the majority of those who quit left because they had moved outside their branch's area, not because of the pressure of work or the crowded conditions. Given the turnover, most employees didn't have much experience. Don Nelson recalled how painful the turnover was to handle. He and the others worked overtime in a desperate attempt to get everything done.

Bentley now had an office in the back of the main branch, at its new location. He knew the deposit and loan figures, as they came in, were correct, yet the numbers seemed beyond belief. When he drafted the directors' annual report, he often mentioned how VanCity had reached targets much earlier than predicted. At the end of the 1960s, assets were almost triple the forecast made a decade earlier. Year after year, in his internal manager's reports for the late 1960s, he would comment that the exceptional growth could not possibly be matched the following year. Sometimes he spelled out his reasons: Competition would increase or the economy would slow down. He was pessimistic and conservative, he confessed, and found it hard to convince himself such rates of growth could continue. They always did.

Notwithstanding those lessons in false caution, however, he had hesitated to predict, at the end of 1970, more than 10 to 20 per cent growth for the following year. It turned out to be 89 per cent, then 59 per cent in 1972, and 71 per cent in 1973. Taken together, assets increased more than fivefold over this short and frantic three-year span, from $31 million to $160 million.

Bentley remembered how he, Don Nelson, and a small crowd had stood around an adding machine at 96 East Broadway, it seemed not too long before, watching totals being entered and waiting for the machine to spit out the breakthrough to $10 million in assets. The machine, they discovered, couldn't handle the extra digit. They had all gotten a big laugh out of that—VanCity's growth breaking the machine. Assets for all the branches put together, at that time, were $17 million. Were they really, now, heading towards $200 million? Membership, meanwhile, had reached forty thousand and was still rising quickly. In the one year 1973 alone, it had shot up twelve thousand—almost as many members as VanCity had in total when Plan 24 was launched six years earlier.

Bentley was now increasingly preoccupied with opening new branches. His financial conservatism, which had stopped him from quickly opening branches, had finally caught up with him. Property offers, counter-offers and architects' plans flew through the air. A sixth branch, North Burnaby, further out on Hastings, opened in 1973 and pulled in a remarkable $10 million in deposits in its first eleven months. Two other branches, on Main and on Fraser, opened in 1974. VanCity, through its expansion, had made home purchases possible for innumerable young and modest-income families who otherwise would have been out of luck. The name VanCity had also gained currency, if not yet become common coin. Ron Spooner jokingly pitched a VanCity membership to everyone he had dealings with. Instead of arguing or quizzing him, as they would have done ten years earlier, they spontaneously were taking him up on his offer.

Bentley was deeply pleased. How had they really done it? "Some day," he wrote to the directors with his 1974 manager's report, "a credit union historian may, with these reports as a base, be able to figure out what has made VanCity the thing it is." The manager's reports were a detailed quantitative analysis of every aspect of the operation. They were illuminating and thorough. Bentley realized, however, from what had happened, that they told just part of the story. There was a magic beyond it that figures and analysis couldn't capture.

The same credit union managers who had so derisively dismissed Plan 24 began insistently knocking on the door once they saw VanCity's deposits rising. It became obvious they had to have Plan 24 to keep pace. This was now a well-established pattern: VanCity introduced something amid, often, great skepticism, and then, as the idea proved itself, the others followed. Bentley and board members like Widdifield, Gladu and Perry were VanCity partisans, but they were also dedicated credit unionists. They simply gave the Plan 24 package to their fellow credit unions—logo, marketing materials and all—charging only a nominal fee for putting the package together. As the inquiries continued to come in, VanCity sold the plan to B.C. Central, that is, to credit unions throughout British Columbia, for the original development cost. The price, for "all rights and title," was $2,405. Bentley did not even bother charging for VanCity's brainstorming and meeting time.

Plan 24 also propelled CDS forward. It was the key product in helping Ted Cotter and Mike Borch sell the computer system. A credit union could not have Plan 24 without being on a computer, and CDS was the only system around that had the program. Borch liked to muse about how rich he would be if he had a personal share of the business. The pressure on the two men, from new credit unions as they clamoured to join, was intense, outstripping their ability to manage it. They worked long hours and hired extra people. They bought time on a powerful outside computer, then left CU&C for larger premises and a new computer of their own, then updated their technology—all in attempts to stay on top of the growth. CDS was now serving so many credit unions beyond the original consortium that it was decided B.C. Central should take over responsibility. The system, of which VanCity was a part owner, was passed on to Central at historical cost.

Central also began selling Plan 24 to the credit union movement outside the province. Gradually Hermann Myers's logo made its way across the country, along with the plan. In 1976, nine years after the VanCity launch, the Ontario Credit Union League was promoting Plan 24 to its member credit unions as "the exciting new deposit account" and "a totally new financial service"—an "opportunity to beat your competition to the punch"—which, in Ontario, it was.

Myers received no residuals from this national use of the name and the logo. He hadn't expected any. He had earlier joked about it to Spooner. Spooner arranged a $100 bonus, as a symbolic award. In any case, for Myers the real reward was the adoption of the name and artwork that he had created from his own imagination. It justified everything he had gone through and tried to do and talked about, going back to the days in Bolton, Lancashire, when, as a young man with very bad lungs, he had first tried his hand at sketching posters.

CHAPTER 22

The Status of Woman

IT WAS THE LATE 1950S. Jan Chapman, in the Royal Bank branch at Commercial and Graveley in the East End, was at the bottom of the heap and knew it. She was lower in rank than a teller, which was getting pretty low. They called her a junior. She picked up the manager's laundry. She went downstairs and worked through the rat-ridden boxes, fetching something that needed looking up for a customer. She delivered drafts, a common way merchants paid their bills in those days. She learned how to do clearing—processing cheques that had come into the branch. It was the most tedious job of all. She didn't care. It was a learning process.

She moved up to teller. The young women who worked with her never thought of going beyond that teller line, but she was different. There were young men working as tellers, and they were moving up. She saw no reason why she shouldn't have a promotion as well. She was brighter than most of them. Barely out of high school, she was ambitious and egotistical, just like those boys, and, as it dawned on her later, she was terribly naive.

The naivete came from her upbringing in Burnaby. She went to Catholic schools and was taught by nuns. They culturally sheltered her. She wasn't aware of any kind of discrimination between men and women. Out in the working world, she assumed it was going to be just as easy for a woman to rise to the top of an organization as for a man. True, her mother stayed at home while her father provided the family income, but that pattern did not dampen her expectations. She and her mother were of different generations. It was her father she took after, anyway. He had run sheet metal and scrap metal operations and was operating an auto body repair shop. Some of that penchant for being in business crept into her life. She was a first child and was strong-willed. If she had it in her mind to go a certain way and do a certain thing, that was it. She wanted to go to university but, even more, she wanted to make money and stand on her own feet. She herself was going to do it. The work at the bank was the first job she got.

Her naivete was paradoxically helpful. Otherwise she would have been too discouraged to begin with. It was only a matter of time, however, until this naivete was shattered. She approached her manager and explained that she wanted to do lending and to supervise. She asked him what education or training was necessary and what particular kinds of work in the bank

would help her along. He told her there was no point to it because she was
a girl.

She had a boyfriend who worked for the Canadian Pacific Railway. The
work was erratic because it was a call job, and it was blue-collar as well. A
bank manager would not likely even give him the chance to explain himself.
Nevertheless his credit union, a place called Vancouver City Savings, had
given him a mortgage to buy a house in Coquitlam. Chapman was curious.
She found out what she could about the organization. It was small and there
was probably a chance for women, she thought. She had other questions.
Her private-school Catholic training had left her with a philosophical bent.
She wanted to do something in her life that seemed worthwhile. She set out
to get an idea of the philosophy that lay behind the credit union—not the
abstract idea of member ownership, but what it was like in the here and now.

She decided to find out whether VanCity would do the same thing for
women that it had done for her boyfriend. She went into 96 East Broadway
on her day off one Saturday morning in 1961 and feigned interest in a
mortgage application. She told them she was thinking of buying a house
and cited the cost. She expressly mentioned that she was single. She made
up a job with enough income that she could probably handle the payments.
She was young, too, only twenty-one. They talked it over. In the end, it
seemed in fact that they would be prepared to grant her a mortgage.

That was enough for Chapman. The next Saturday she returned and
asked for a job application. She went the following Saturday and put in
another application. She did that for six Saturdays in a row. Bentley, the
sixth time, called her into his office and they had a long discussion. He
explained how small the operation was—less than $5 million in assets—
and how limited the opportunities were. He seemed to be discouraging her.
"No," she said, "I want the job, I really do want the job." The following
Monday he called her in the evening and asked her how much notice she
would need to give at the bank. What impressed her most was that Bentley
himself had called. She knew he wasn't the president of some huge corporation like a bank, but he still was the organization's manager.

She had grown up in a business world where how much money one made
was the only thing that counted. Bentley and Ray Evelle, while they watched
the bottom line, talked first about philosophy and especially about "members." "What can we do for people in the organization who belong to us?"
was the leading question. Members owned the organization. She was soon
conditioned to think of members in the same way.

It was a small, parochial place, but a good one to work in. There was lots
of office gossip, retailed in the lunchroom on the building's third floor.
There was also a chess board and a continuing cycle of tournaments. There
weren't many chess players better than she was in those days. She even
prevailed over Ray Evelle, the chess-playing graduate of Dean's Restaurant.

Breaking into management was a different matter. She didn't expect to
do it overnight, but she wanted at least to find the path. That was hard.

Here, too, all the routes seem to be closed. She did accounting, but she wasn't allowed to get involved in lending. The branch hired a young man for loans. The three women who might have stepped up to do lending were left sitting at their desks. Women need not apply, she thought. When the East Hastings branch opened in 1962, Chapman wanted the supervisory job. She didn't get it. At least, however, the person who did was a woman and someone who was already with VanCity. That was important to her.

She was married now. She decided—like most women, she thought—that it might be smart to have some children. She quit VanCity to have one child and then, when she was pregnant with the second, went back to work, but at the Bank of Montreal. She thought she would try the larger banks one more time. It wasn't that she was disillusioned with VanCity. She was disillusioned by how the whole system held women back. One just didn't belong to the club. Her idea was to move about from place to place, as if to jostle the system with an elbow here, a toehold there, trying for an advantage. The bank put her to work troubleshooting in branches where they were having difficulty balancing their books. They had taken male students fresh from university and had put them into supervisory and accounting positions, on the way up to management. Without actual experience, many of them made a hash of things. Chapman and the rest of the troubleshooting team went into one branch after another, cleaning up the mess. She saw the irony: a woman blocked from management making up for the inexperience of male management candidates. At least, though, her talent was being used.

She took only a few weeks off to have her second baby. That was something else she had to handle that a man didn't need to worry about. She breastfed her new baby for a few months, as she had her first, using a breast pump. Her mother or sister would stay with her when the children were very young. Then she would hire someone to live in.

Then Bentley called. Chapman had been at the bank for only a few months. He had heard through the grapevine that she was back at work. Had he seen something special in her all the while? He offered her a supervisor job at the small Kitsilano branch.

There was an irony attached to that, too. There were only four employees in the branch. The manager, Monty Lambertus, was one of them. Jan Chapman, the supervisor, would be supervising only two employees. She understood the meaning of title, though. She saw the offer as another door opening for her and jumped at it. She was an opportunist, she liked to think. She had that driving ambition. She bought a house on the west side, near the branch, and went hard at it, which was the only way she knew.

Chapman's forte was accounting and administration, the areas she had managed to work in. Taking charge of accounting was her initial task at Broadway and Blenheim. The branch was converting from the Burroughs posting system to CDS and its computer printouts. Interest was disappearing from where it should have been and showing up in other places. The ledgers were out of balance. Perplexed, Chapman contacted Wayne McKay, who was responsible in VanCity data processing. McKay came over for several evenings and they worked on making the adjustments.

Most people don't like problems and are annoyed by details. Chapman loved them both. She had that kind of mind, always wanting to find out what was going on and putting the particulars right. The CDS problem, moreover, was not just an average, run-of-the-mill problem. It had an inherent attraction because computerization was a totally new thing. No bank branches that she knew of were using computers. Chapman's world, from that moment, became tinged with excitement.

McKay had heard negative stories about Chapman from staff members who had been at the main branch during her earlier sojourn. Chapman was young and shy, then, and careful about what she said, but she always had an opinion and, at informal branch meetings, wasn't afraid to share it. She felt she had nothing to lose. One got ahead by being noticed and by what one did, not by being quiet. She was a strong person. A reputation grew out of that. She was very demanding, it went. She didn't suffer fools gladly. She didn't have a broad enough focus. Sometimes her comments got out of hand, touching on individual performance. Feelings were hurt.

Working with her on the CDS printouts, McKay had discovered a different kind of person. Chapman was good-hearted, well-spoken, a dedicated worker, conscientious about the credit union and had great skills. Chapman, for her part, found herself a soul mate. McKay was always on the lookout for good people for his own branch and invited her to join him, which she did. A bond formed. They became good friends although, as she joked, he was a Baptist and she was in her agnostic phase.

She was a delight for McKay, and the two of them flourished. McKay became her mentor. He was a few years younger and had leapfrogged forward. The irony of it didn't bother Chapman. She recognized it as a fact of life. In an age when women could not attain management as quickly as men, many women were mentored by men younger than they were.

She discovered that he did help people. At one point, she quit to have her third child. She had no choice, since there was no maternity leave. When and if women came back to work after having children, they lost their seniority, including longer holidays. Women had just accepted these practices. Chapman, however, needed to return to work and to return quickly. She was having marital and financial difficulties. She gave McKay a call. He brought her back at the level where she had left off and continued to support her.

For all of Chapman's ambition to join management, McKay found her curiously hesitant. She seemed to consider management a mysterious lore that one had to spend a lifetime learning, whereas McKay knew from experience it was mostly common sense. He kept pushing her, reminding her how capable she was, and pointing to women who were already managing credit unions. Chapman saw things differently. There were no women managers around her. They were in small credit unions out in the hinter-

land. Women did face obstacles. They could not be seen to be too ambitious. Talking to Bentley and Ron Spooner about the possibility of a woman
moving ahead was as far as she thought she could go. She felt she had to be
better armed than a man.

McKay and Bentley had introduced performance reviews. A supervisor in
the branch did a review on Chapman. She received a copy of it, which was
the practice. Her colleague had decided she wouldn't work out in business,
and said so. She didn't handle herself well, he wrote. She didn't handle
people well. The review wasn't an appraisal that allowed for a follow-
through to correct weaknesses. "There was no hope," it said, in effect. "Get
out of this business. You're no good at it." It was the first time in Chapman's
life that she had been cut off at the knees. It was deeply hurtful. She
imagined it would have a powerful limiting influence on her future and
follow her wherever she went, but there was nothing she could do about it.
She carried her copy with her, in her purse, as a marker of the pain she had
to go through and as a goad to succeed despite it. It never did have the
feared influence. The person who wrote it was subsequently let go, and his
opinion carried little weight.

The hurt faded. The branch was a busy intersection of people coming
and going. She met real estate agents and local business people. A social
courtship was taking place between the local powers that be and the branch,
almost a paying of respect, as the branch now was putting out mortgages by
the hundreds. Plan 24 had hit its stride. Everybody, it seemed to Chapman,
was coming through the door. McKay allowed her considerable independence. She felt directly involved in the organization, rather than being a
little cog. Since McKay routinely came in late, Chapman was de facto
manager for part of the day. She savoured these mornings, not only for
themselves, but also for what they said about McKay's confidence in her.
She had begun doing loans before leaving the Kitsilano branch and continued at East Hastings. That gender barrier, at least, was finally down.

She was intent on systematizing the branch's operation. The staff rebelled
against her because she was too controlling. They lodged a complaint with
McKay about her insistence on certain administrative routines. They were a
spirited bunch. Chapman herself thought they were a wonderful group.
Their protest was just something she had to cope with. The two sides talked
it out. They arrived at a trade-off, in which they could work together without
compromising her supervisory role. They were right in some cases, she had
to admit. Looking back, she reflected on how more rigid she had been
when she was younger—wasn't it a general failing of youth?—and she had
to learn how to bend a little. Just as she liked her independence, so did the
staff who worked for her.

The really big fights, however, occurred when a management recruit,
Garry Smith, arrived on the scene. Smith came from the Whalley Savings
Credit Union. McKay had urged him to join VanCity, and he was slotted to
become a branch manager. Although he was very young, Smith had branch

manager experience. This grooming of a man brought in from elsewhere, rather than a woman, was, for Chapman, all too typical.

Smith had a bulldozer streak. The way that Chapman had arranged the microfiches, which stored past records, did not make much sense to him, so one evening—McKay was also on the premises—Smith changed them around. Neither of them asked Chapman about it. The next morning, the staff, trained to use Chapman's system, couldn't figure out what had happened. Chapman was furious. She chewed Smith into little pieces and, when McKay arrived, took after him, too. McKay had to apologize for not consulting her. She didn't hold grudges, but that didn't mean she had to like Smith. She didn't.

There were no overpriced seminars featuring the guru of the week to help them sort themselves out, not even a human resources department with ministrations on how to be supportive. There was just a fallback VanCity solidarity, an ultimate tolerance, where fights, arguments and idiosyncrasies stayed in the family. McKay, Chapman and Smith in the same branch were like three rambunctious tigers in the same lair—not just three tigers, but three workaholic, striving tigers. Being of the same species, although of different temperaments, they all survived.

Shortly after, Chapman was transferred to the main branch at Broadway and Oak to straighten out the accounting. There had been a serious breakdown, full of snarls, and like Red Adair putting out an oil-well fire, she was thrown into the breach. There were long hours into the night as she tracked the problems back to source. They related back to staff doing wrong things without knowing it. There was little training of staff when they came to VanCity and virtually no formal training thereafter. There were only two ways new tellers could understand what they were told—by the grace of God or by osmosis. Chapman set her mind to analysing how staff did things and working out the flaws. She tried to get them to have fun with what were otherwise prosaic tasks—to inject excitement into seeing that things were done right. She began exploring quicker and easier ways tellers could handle their transactions. This was frontier territory, and she was putting her creativity to work.

It was sinking into those around her just how valuable she was. Bentley sent her to the Kitsilano branch, as assistant manager to John Iseli. They were both ambitious and both learning as they went long—learning especially about people in an organization and the pitch of their own emotions. The two of them went at each other. Kitsilano was Iseli's first branch and he wanted to ensure everything was done right. Chapman was the supervisor, was six years older than he was and had her own ideas. Like the people at East Hastings, to whom she had learned to give more room, she did not like a lot of control. She would ask a teller to do something and the teller would say, no, John had told her not to do it. She tried to talk the problem out with Iseli but ran into a stone wall. She was frustrated, angry. She announced that she was quitting.

Bentley intervened. He interviewed them separately, calmed them down. Chapman had to admit that, however angry she was, quitting didn't make sense. Bentley encouraged her to stay. He told her she was a bright lady and had a future with the organization—he said all the right things, she knew. She and Iseli shook hands and subsequently became friends. Chapman thought it was exactly because they had gone head to head with each other.

When they moved to the branch's new building at Broadway and Waterloo and staff doubled, her world opened further. Two supervisors (one for tellers and one for accounting) and two loan officers reported to her, with the rest of the staff in behind them—a far cry from the supervision of just a few tellers, which she and Iseli had wrangled over at the old location. Had it been only two years ago? She was now management proper. It felt good.

The pace at this branch was even more frenetic than at Broadway and Oak. She was also involved in feminist and business organizations and, to a lesser extent, in community activities in the area, where her children were growing up. She had been part of the pioneering, nameless gatherings of women interested in equal rights and equal pay, who later became members of the Status of Women. Her loyalty never wavered. Discriminatory practices in the workplace were never far from her mind. Only retrospectively did Chapman understand how much this involvement with other women was helping her personally. The help was indirect and psychological. The groups talked about changes coming in the business world, where women and feminine views were going to be felt. Chapman, responding to this positivism, broadened her thinking. She started a Toastmistress Club. She joined the Soroptimists, an invitation-only service club for women who were leaders in their field.

She was driven now, compulsive. Her young son Hugh remembered her going to bed at about ten in the evening, with five books spread around the bed for another round of work and inquiry. She was taking courses on banking at Vancouver Community College and UBC, and this was her homework. She herself had little sense of how the hours were apportioned. It wasn't relevant. The work took her away from her children, but they seemed to cope.

The work routine, though, was taking its toll. She had to be all things to her family and to prove she could be in the business place, too. The family paid for it lots of times. Her marriage wasn't working. It was no different, she thought later, from marriages in which the husband devoted all his time to his job. For a marriage to be good, one needed to have a balance, and she did not have a balance in those days. Arranging for child care—making sure she had somebody at home in the afternoon and the kids were safe— was terribly stressful and added to the pressure. Once, not having anyone and picking the children up from school herself, she broke down in tears, sitting in her car.

She amplified her training ideas, working through her supervisors to pass on to tellers the efficiencies she had developed. Because she was a woman, she had thought a lot about cross-training. She pushed the idea with Iseli and Bentley. She knew how boring it was to hand out cash all day or stamp cheques—jobs predominantly done by women—against which a supervisor's enthusiasm and friendliness could go only so far. People doing that kind of work also thought of themselves as having little ability, although many of them had real talent. Chapman began training tellers to work at the counter, to do accounting and, using small loans, to take loan applications. People moved from teller stations to the counter and back. They were intelligent and picked things up quickly.

She pushed the use of computerization beyond posting, into such things as keeping track of term deposit expiry dates, in order to eliminate paper and duplication. She did not, however, want to destroy the comfort her staff had with their work. She organized them into teams, around functions like accounting, to look at each step and piece of paper. They were to cross off anything that wasn't necessary, keeping in mind what the computer system could do. The decentralized team approach put them in charge of the change. Some staff members at first were disquieted by relying on a computer system in that way. Chapman, herself, had no sense of risk at all. She had confidence in the technology. "We're not going back to ledger cards, nah," she once exclaimed. "We could burn them all." The time saved by the elimination of extra steps was not only a good thing in itself, it was also something VanCity had to do, because it was growing so fast. The process had a momentum of its own. The staff, once engaged, continually revitalized their routines in a loop, from the way they did things to the technology and back to themselves.

One day, late in 1973, Bentley asked Chapman into his office. He told her he was going to appoint her to manage a new branch at Main and 26th. She had a moment of vertigo. She wanted it to happen, she expected it to happen, but somehow she never thought it would actually happen. The North Burnaby branch had opened at the beginning of the year and she hadn't got that one, although she thought she had more experience than the man who did. Now it had happened. When Bentley got home that evening, his daughter Joanne, who used to kid him about being a male chauvinist while knowing that he wasn't, announced that he had really arrived. Bentley was pleased, and not just by the compliment. He thought this was the way things should go, too.

There had been another VanCity woman manager earlier, Margaret Skelcher. She had run the small Hollyburn Credit Union and had come with the merger in 1970. She had left the branch after a year. Chapman was the first woman in VanCity to be promoted to the job from within.

She had three months to set up—from deciding on furniture to interviewing and hiring staff. There were no branch operations department and personnel department to look after such tasks or to tell her what to do. It was like starting up her own business. A few days before opening, she moved in all the supplies—every piece of paper they would need. It seemed a mammoth amount. She brought her people in then, too, to sort everything out and decide who would do what. Ron Spooner placed an ad in the local community paper and one in the *Vancouver Sun* and the *Province*. Chapman herself telephoned existing members in the area to let them know that the branch was opening.

Excitement and fearfulness were her first emotions in those three months —feelings, however, she thought common to everybody who received that kind of promotion. Most of all, she was antsy, really antsy. She had worked hard to get there and she couldn't wait to start.

She bought a new suit for the opening—a conservative and authoritative brown, the management fashion of the moment about which, later, she would have a good laugh. She checked to see it had the "pure virgin wool" logo on it—she wanted the real thing. She wore new earrings to match the suit. She had her hair done the evening before. Breakfast at home on D-Day was absolutely normal—everybody shouting and yelling and going off in their various directions. She drove east down King Edward in a bee-line towards Main and 26th Avenue, turning down the alley just before the branch. There was a parking space reserved for the manager, the first reserved space she had ever had. Driving into it this particular morning gave her a kick. She opened the back door of the branch with her own key and routinely turned off the alarm system. It was shortly after eight o'clock. She checked everything out, then walked back and forth for an hour until the branch opened.

There was a large banner over the member-service area and another large banner outside, facing Main Street. The first person to walk through the door was a member from the Kitsilano branch, whom Chapman knew from her days there. Chapman stood and chatted to her for a couple of minutes and then ceremonially transferred her membership—the first transaction. People were encouraged to stop for tea or coffee and a piece of an oversized celebratory cake. There were pencils and pens to give away. Magically, the place became quite busy.

The official opening was at one o'clock. Bentley and Spooner came out, along with several board members. Bentley made a short speech. He talked about the days when VanCity had just one small branch at 96 East Broadway and how loyal members, many without cars, travelled considerable distances to support their credit union. He reminisced about the progress that had been made since, and what a joy it was to have reached the stage where they could open branches to serve people in their own communities. Chapman said a few words about her feelings as a first-time manager in a brand-new branch. Pioneer board member Bert Gladu and his wife Flo cut the ribbon. The crowd applauded. At the end of the day, Chapman brought in pizza and there was a quiet staff party.

It had been a bang-up first day. They had opened more than one hundred accounts. The branch had been established to relieve the pressure on East Hastings, Kitsilano and particularly Oak and Broadway, where crowded conditions had led to considerable member dissatisfaction. It quickly drew members and new people from its perimeter, like a sponge. About one hundred members followed Chapman personally from Kitsilano. This was typical when a manager moved to a new branch. She worked until nine in the evening for two or three months to handle the influx of transfers. She might have hired extra people to carry the load, but that would have put her over budget. She had drawn up the budget herself, and she wasn't going to break it.

She began with just five staff, other than herself. This limited the kinds of things she could do. After the large Kitsilano branch, it took some getting used to. In a few months, however, Bentley asked her to take over the Victoria Drive branch. It had staff and member problems, and needed to be worked back into shape. It was the second-largest of the eight VanCity branches, measured by deposits, and had a staff of twenty. Chapman had to deal with racial strife as well. There had been an inflow of East Indians into the area. There were incidents of pushing and shoving in line-ups, between whites and East Indians, bordering on fist fights, which she had to break up.

Chapman was thirty-four years old when she became manager at Victoria Drive, not as young as some credit union executives, but still fairly young. She remembered when she had come back to VanCity after having her first two children. Her banker acquaintances had told her it was a hick organization that wasn't going any place and would probably falter. Returning to VanCity wasn't a smart move on her part, they said. The banks were more stable. They had always been there. Being so large, they also offered a great number of career positions. Besides, banking had to be international or, if not international, at least country-wide.

She had ignored them and found her niche. There were no women bank managers anywhere in the country when she had begun in banking. There were still only a token number. She herself, on the other hand, was the manager of a large and thriving branch, near the top of her organization. She had learned at the Kitsilano branch that she could challenge "the system"—challenge the way things were done—and introduce innovations. Bentley gave her and others that freedom of action. With computerization and innovative products, VanCity had left the banks behind in a bygone age. The more that VanCity was at the forefront, the more Chapman wanted to move VanCity faster ahead.

Jan Chapman had a passion for getting ahead—for being a success—and VanCity was feeding that passion. Work was excitement. She loved the organization. It wasn't just herself, she knew. VanCity was full of exciting people who were constantly thinking of the future and how it was going to happen. She was part of them now—accepted for what she had to offer. She had wanted that most of all. Now she had it.

CHAPTER 23

Planners of the World

LLOYD WIDDIFIELD SHOULD HAVE BEEN in his element on the board, and in many ways he was. He and Bert Gladu had been president for two-year stints, and Stan Parsons for three years. By 1970, Gladu was into a second cycle. They were the powers among the directors, and these were halcyon days. Widdifield cut the ribbon for the first branch on the west side. Parsons turned the first sod for The Meadows housing project. The camaraderie at meetings was strong. "They were good times and we were a good team," Widdifield remembered. "Everything we accomplished was done by the combined effort of the whole board. Sure, somebody might bring an idea to a meeting and throw it out, but ultimately, if the idea were accepted, we all made it work together." For some other directors who, like Gladu, went back to the early years—Rolf Perry, George Payton, and Harold MacLean—the blossoming of VanCity was even more wonderful to savour. The board had also acquired some young blood: Mike Betts, a sidekick of Stan Parsons at his wholesale plumbing supply firm, and Ross Montgomery, assistant general manager at CU&C. They were both twenty-nine years old when first elected.

Widdifield, however, knew he was different. He was constantly bemused by Stan Parsons. Parsons was the quietest of the triumvirate. He liked to play the backroom politician, helping to get a board consensus. He functioned by jovial sociability. He was a tortured fence-sitter on controversial issues. Bentley would have to push him off the fence. Parsons drove around Vancouver in his work, so he was able frequently to drop by VanCity and say hello to Bentley. Dropping by was what a good salesman like Parsons did, but he was drawn to 96 East Broadway for other reasons. VanCity had become a big part of his life emotionally. Stopping in was like keeping in touch with family.

In Widdifield's two years as president, Parsons had been vice-president. Widdifield never knew whom Parsons was talking to and what he was doing. He thought a president should at least know what his vice-president was up to. He resented Parsons's manoeuvring behind the scenes. He wanted decisions made at the board table, based on critical discussion, but Parsons could not operate that way.

Widdifield, unlike Parsons, had edges. Being in the Credit Union Building and physically close to VanCity's main branch and Bentley's office, he knew everything that was going on. Geoff Hook, who was now CEO of B.C. Central and had served earlier with Widdifield on the VanCity board, thought him strong-willed, a leader and smart. The self-confidence, Hook thought, had something to do with Widdifield's coming from Saskatchewan, like Bentley, where co-operative business was mainstream. Widdifield was also shrewd about lending. Mike Betts, sitting for the first time on the credit committee, remembered Widdifield especially. He was inquisitive about the loan applications. He knew about the financial variables. Betts learned by listening carefully to the questions Widdifield asked.

Widdifield pushed his fellow board members to think of VanCity in more professional ways. When he first joined the board, they met behind the counter in Branch 1, among the desks, and ate Chinese food. Widdifield thought eating take-out was ridiculous. It might be all right for small administration committee meetings, but for board meetings it was shabby. It suggested a two-bit, improvised organization without any substance and expectations. Later, the board met in the Co-op Coffee Shop, upstairs on the third floor. They had to take their dinner out of the oven, where it had been left for them, and serve themselves. That didn't seem right, either. The building, too, was a bit dingy and wasn't air conditioned. In the summer, it was stifling hot. Widdifield felt that directors who weren't paid for their services should at least have a decent place to meet and be able to enjoy a good dinner. When he became president in 1965, he moved dinner and board meetings to the Eldorado Hotel, a large motor hotel several miles away on Kingsway. He was sure this made board meetings more productive. It also added to the members' realization that they were no longer a hole-in-the wall enterprise. Since the Eldorado had a liquor licence as well as air conditioning, the meetings were more comfortable in another way. Stan Parsons, playing the connoisseur, majestically ordered Chateauneuf du Pape for their dinners. They knew they were on the way up, and they were enthusiastic and proud of it. Dessert was taken after the business meeting ended. Bentley and Widdifield, reflecting the new expansiveness, ordered apple pie with a strong blue cheese, plus snifters of Courvoisier cognac.

Widdifield was the most vocal of the directors. He argued freely about issues he thought were important. He had opinions. He would even argue with Bentley, whom—unlike most of his fellow directors—he did not hold in awe. Most of the board, like Stan Parsons and Bert Gladu, were unswerving Bentley supporters. Harold MacLean thought of board meetings with Bentley as a mutual love affair. "Anything that Don wanted to do, we were absolutely 100 per cent in favour of," MacLean laughed. "I don't want to make him out as a god, but he was." Bentley himself once gently chided the directors for not recognizing how important they were. Widdifield, on the other hand, did not consider Bentley a god and never had any doubt that directors had a key role to play. He was a skilful professional manager in his own right. When he was president, he insisted on writing the annual directors' report to the members himself, instead of having Bentley ghost-write it for him. He wasn't malleable like the others. He could get under Bentley's skin.

Widdifield had his own vision of what VanCity could do. The co-operative movement's horizon should be unlimited, he thought. Harold MacLean quit the board in 1972. VanCity was heading towards $100 million in assets. MacLean laughed that making multi-million dollar decisions wasn't for him. He wasn't sure whether he was getting cold feet or whether he was just bored, and he was up to his ears in his work on wood chemistry. For Widdifield, on the other hand, VanCity was just getting started. He believed in One Big Credit Union for the province. The wheat pools, after all, covered whole provinces. He wanted credit unionism to have the muscle of the big banks. He scorned the idea of common bond credit unions, like the parish credit union or the company credit union. Maybe they once had their usefulness, he would admit, but they were behind the times and a limited concept to begin with. He dismissed the common-bond doctrine as "a bunch of garbage."

If Widdifield couldn't have One Big Credit Union, then he wanted at least a VanCity untrammelled. For Widdifield, that meant not only opening branches wherever it was practical for VanCity—and forget the yelping of the rest of the movement—but also pioneering new areas of activity. He was especially interested in land banking and housing. He thought VanCity should go into it in a big way. It was a natural for VanCity, he argued. They were already providing money for housing through mortgages. Why not take the next step—accumulate land, develop it and hire builders—that is, go into the development business? He envisioned VanCity taking on the role of Block Bros., the largest developer in the region at the time, which was banking land for itself. It bothered him that land speculators could rake off such large profits when VanCity, by going into the business, could eliminate that margin and provide housing at a more reasonable cost. VanCity members who funded mortgages were collecting good interest on their deposits, but where was the big slice of profit going? Developers, indirectly through homebuyers and their mortgages, were making fortunes with VanCity members' money.

As Widdifield saw it, the two most important things to a young family were food and lodging. The co-operator stores should be providing food, but they hardly existed in Vancouver. Housing, by contrast, was something VanCity could take charge of. He had instigated a trip by himself and Bentley to Port Moody to look at a condominium that Dawson Development had built—an expedition that ultimately led to The Meadows project. He could see the opportunities come and go—large blocks of land in key areas in Coquitlam and White Rock going for a song, as little as $2,000 an acre. Widdifield was so impressed that in 1970, when Co-operative Insurance reorganized and wanted to bring him back to Regina, he stayed in Vancouver and went into the house construction business, in a small way, himself.

Except for the occasional project, however, he couldn't convince the board to act on the issue. "We're not in the land business," they would say. "But we are in the business of lending money," Widdifield would retort. He constantly brought the subject up. In the face of the board's resistance, he seemed dogmatic about it. He would go through the connections again, explaining the logic of vertical integration and the advantage to members of cheaper housing. It was useless. The problem, Widdifield knew, was Bentley. He couldn't budge Bentley on the subject, and the others simply deferred to him. There wasn't much he could do about it.

Bentley agreed theoretically with Widdifield about housing development, but was half-hearted about it in practice. He was wary about extending VanCity too far into new areas. Some B.C. credit unionists wanted the movement to become involved in launching new retail co-operatives. "Does the Royal Bank sell groceries?" Bentley rhetorically questioned. Widdifield argued that housing, unlike groceries, was directly connected to what VanCity did. That didn't change Bentley's mind. Widdifield had been deeply frustrated by Bentley's conservatism in opening new branches. Now he was faced with what he took to be that same conservatism again.

The one tack left open to him, which he pushed simultaneously, was planning. In doing a plan, one looked at the world, laid out the strategic possibilities, objectively assessed those possibilities, and then explored how one would go about achieving them. If VanCity had a bold long-term strategic plan, housing development could be part of it. Widdifield had always wanted a plan, housing aside. It wasn't that he was a formalist. He thought VanCity could do much more if it had a plan—that without it, it was missing some of the future for the co-operative movement.

The idea of planning wasn't new to the board. They had established a short-lived planning committee in 1960, chaired by Widdifield, which had set out strategic priorities. Bentley's work on the credit union infrastructure, and the board's backing for it, involved lucid strategic thinking. Bentley himself, in his strategic musing in annual reports, had talked about planning.

Widdifield realized, for a start, that VanCity did not even have a statement of principles and objectives—in 1990s planning parlance, a vision statement and a mission statement. Such statements were de rigueur in planning circles. Conceptually, they were the necessary first step in the planning process. Widdifield set out to provide one, borrowing freely from the principles and objectives of Co-operative Insurance. He ended up with a ringing, cogent manifesto of co-operative principles and of VanCity's credit union possibilities.

Widdifield now wanted a real, honest-to-goodness planning process. Bentley dragged his feet. Finally, in 1970, Bentley put together a strategic planning committee to look into long-range issues. "Strategic planning" was the latest thing in managerial circles at the time. It had various subsets, some of them faddish. One of those fads was tapping the expertise of professors in university business schools—or commerce departments, which were business schools without the cachet. Bentley, always interested in what outside experts had to say, was susceptible to the idea. He saw academics as having professional respectability. He had made contact with a UBC finance professor, Whata Winiata, a Maori by origin, and unilaterally invited him to sit on the committee. Winiata in turn brought in a marketing professor, Jim Forbes. Widdifield was the board's representative on the committee. Bentley and VanCity's lawyer, Bill Wright, from Davis & Company, were the committee's other two members.

For Widdifield, the committee was a miscarriage. It only deepened his frustration. It met six times and ended up with a few washed-out academic generalities. Widdifield and the professors came from different worlds. He resented their arrogance. The committee's report talked about the need for "an adaptive type of organization" and "managers and personnel with flexible and analytical minds." It also contained a phrase about ensuring "that fresh, innovative and promising ideas" were forthcoming. As Widdifield wrote in a separate note to the board, VanCity was already an innovative organization. The professors' sermonizing to VanCity about innovation was, to Widdifield, a case of the crow giving singing lessons to the meadowlark.

He was particularly peeved by Forbes. Forbes knew nothing about credit unions. He kept making extraneous arguments, but being skilled in intellectual combat, he could pursue them anyway. Widdifield and Forbes did not get along. The committee members would sit down with an agenda, argue, not accomplish much and then go home. "A good part of the committee's time, and more of Bentley's time," Widdifield sardonically recounted later, "was taken up explaining to the professors what a credit union was." He thought Bentley should at least have consulted with the board about the kind of people he was going to bring in. The professors could not grasp the connection between VanCity and extending the co-operative principle. They didn't have Widdifield's co-operative inheritance. They saw VanCity instead, one-dimensionally, as just another version of a savings and loan association.

Widdifield managed, nevertheless, to push an aggressive resolution on housing through the board. VanCity was to use "all possible means" to provide housing for its members and others. The means included VanCity's housing subsidiary (VCS Housing Developments Ltd.) and partnerships with others. Nothing was barred. Widdifield still, however, did not have a planning process that would bring forward a five-year plan outlining what VanCity was actually going to do. Without that, the resolution was just a statement of intent. The strategic planning committee, for which he had waited so long, had failed him.

The closest he managed to a planning process was a retreat at Lord Jim's, a resort on the Sechelt Peninsula. Bentley had taken a liking to a young research analyst at B.C. Central, Bob Hornal. Hornal had a BA in economics, an MBA, and additional background in organizational psychology. These were ultra-fashionable qualifications. Hornal's ideas bubbled over in every which direction. Bentley found him entertaining.

The planning retreat in some resort hideaway was now a standard, voguish item in the kit bag of aspiring facilitators. Hornal helped to convince Bentley it would be useful. It would improve communication with his board, Hornal said. It would bring backward-looking, amateur board members into the future, he added, with easy technocratic conviction. It would set out Bentley's mandate, and he could get on with his job without getting bogged down in board arguments over small matters, especially arguments from people like Widdifield. Besides, Hornal had already done a session with Richmond Savings, and if Richmond had undertaken a planning session, should number one, VanCity, be left behind?

Widdifield and other board members went up to Lord Jim's with their wives for the planning weekend. The idea was to canvass the future. Insurance, a travel agency and Widdifield's push for housing were some of the possibilities that came up. Most directors thought the session was productive. Widdifield considered it aimless talk and a waste of time, albeit Lord Jim's was a fun place. Nothing definite with a timetable was set down. He thought of the weekend as a gift by Bentley to board members for their endless hours of voluntary participation. It was a holiday excursion. When somebody suggested to him that such sessions were good for loosening up minds, Widdifield riposted, laughing, that it loosened up a lot of tongues, because the booze really flowed.

The marketing professor, Jim Forbes, was also at the retreat. He was now on the board. Bentley had asked him to run. Widdifield, knowing Bentley's shrewdness, wondered if Bentley had brought Forbes in to create some opposition to Widdifield himself, because he was so pushy and Bentley did not like to move fast. Didn't everybody, Widdifield thought, have a Machiavellian streak?

Forbes had no prior interest in the credit union movement. On the contrary, for him the board members' interest in co-operation was one of VanCity's big problems. "They kept trotting out 'helpful hands in many lands' crap," he said, in a reference to the international credit union slogan and logo. "They believed this crap about credit unions and co-operatives, and it simply didn't work." He was corrosive, sarcastic, argumentative and opinionated, used to scornful academic put-downs and repartee. He soon had the board in turmoil.

His specialty was "scientific marketing," based on the collection and analysis of survey data. He grew increasingly frustrated by Bentley's lack of interest in his marketing obsessions. The organic, social nature of enterprise, meanwhile, was lost on him. VanCity was a long way from Alphonse Desjardins's kitchen table, but the co-operative ethos nevertheless continued to give the organization its special connection to its members and lay behind its creativity. This was invisible to Forbes. So was Bentley's shrewd grasp of numbers and what they meant; Forbes didn't know much about banking.

Forbes also found that neither Bentley nor any of the other staff understood modern planning techniques. They were incompetent, in his view. For that matter, he didn't see much of any kind of management. Bentley would not even put business plans down on paper. He didn't know enough to set the numbers down on any issue and lay out the alternatives so that the board could make an informed decision, Forbes contended, and he didn't know how to do it anyway.

The trouble, in Forbes's opinion, was that neither Bentley, McKay (who seemed to have some smarts) nor any of the others on staff had been to university, where they might have picked up planning and management skills. The banks in the past had not been any better, but at least now they were hiring university graduates for management roles. Bentley wasn't following suit because, as Forbes saw it, he would not have known how to handle them.

Meetings became harder and harder for Forbes to tolerate. He didn't bother hiding his growing impatience. He swore freely. "But that's me," he once explained. He had never been the easiest guy to get along with. "I'm not a very good conciliator," he said.

Like a body's immune system rejecting a transplant, the VanCity board slowly rejected Forbes. Directors like Stan Parsons and Bert Gladu did not know what to make of Forbes or how to respond. One board member, however, Lloyd Widdifield, did argue back. They were always arguing. "Holy rows," one director called them. Bentley was usually able to smooth over antagonisms. He hated open discord. It got at his stomach. In this case, he was helpless. Ethel Bentley, noticing the extra pressure the meetings were putting on her husband, thought she would just shoot them all. Widdifield wasn't prepared to let pass Forbes's seeming attitude that VanCity board meetings were beneath him and that all board members should automatically accept his opinions like meek undergraduates. If Bentley and Forbes disagreed, Widdifield made a point of siding with Bentley.

Gradually, over several months, Forbes's impatience and alienation rose to the surface. One meeting descended into a shouting match. All the board members were disagreeing with Forbes once more. He was furious. Laura Smalley was taking minutes. "He's totally out of control," she thought. Stan Parsons, who was president, worked up the nerve to call him on his language. Forbes wasn't interested. He had been to too many of these meetings. He was tired and had other things to do. He walked out and never came back. Nobody ever called him. "They didn't care and I didn't care," he said later.

One thing did survive from the brief, discomfiting appearance on the scene of Forbes, the commerce professor: his and Widdifield's dislike of each other. It was etched in their memories as only intense moments of feeling can be. Ironically, Forbes was Widdifield's one potential ally on the planning issue. They were the only ones interested in a formal planning process, but Widdifield had no way of making a useful connection to Forbes. They were both planners of the world, but their worlds were a galaxy apart.

Widdifield never did get his five-year strategic plan, where a larger role in housing might have been spelled out. Bentley never seemed to get around to it. The rush of ideas—computerization, Plan 24, more advertising, the opening and rebuilding of branches—appeared to do his planning for him, in a form of controlled anarchy. Widdifield talked planning, but actual formal planning was too abstract and artificial for him. It lacked suppleness and flexibility. It was detached, outside his instinctive feeling for the organization and what it had to do. Bentley, Widdifield shrugged, looking back, was one of those managers who simply did not want to be bound to a plan.

The year after Forbes's departure, Widdifield himself left the board. VanCity undertook to build two clusters of detached houses, in Surrey and Burnaby, and sell them to members—twenty-one units in all. Widdifield was one of the potential contractors, and he and Bentley agreed that his presence on the board would be a conflict of interest. He chose to leave.

He was also instrumental in involving VanCity, as a developer, in a sixty-unit project in Port Coquitlam. A forty-three-unit townhouse development at Arbutus and 2nd Avenue in Vancouver was nearing completion. These projects, however, were far from what Widdifield had envisioned, where VanCity would be the leading presence in housing development just as it was in mortgages for that housing. He now realized that it was not going to happen. The missed opportunity continued to bother him.

Widdifield had made his decision to leave in any case. The time involved had become too great. He thought of all the hours he had given to VanCity in the past—two or three meetings a month for all those years. It had been worth it. As he wrote in his resignation letter, they had built together "the finest credit union to be found." They had "led the way in providing cooperative service to members."

He no longer enjoyed the meetings, however. Forbes was out of the way, but the complexion of the board had changed. Sandra Sutherland, a self-contained, hard-edged downtown lawyer, was on the board. Widdifield wasn't anti-feminist, but the camaraderie wasn't what it had been. He didn't know in which way; it was just different. It still hurt him to go. He had been on the credit committee and a director for almost twenty years, and there was too much to remember. In the end, though, despite the hurt, he did not find it tough to leave.

CHAPTER 24

Ron and Don

SOME FRIENDSHIPS TRANSCEND UNDERSTANDING. When one of the two friends is much stronger than the other, the puzzle grows: How did two such disparate people bond in the first place? Ron Spooner and Don Bentley had one of those friendships. Since it was largely a working friendship, it illuminated VanCity as long as the two were both alive.

The more that VanCity grew and the more complex it became, the more disparate the two of them appeared. Bob Partridge, at Broadway Printers, remembered that Spooner always seemed on the edge, as if he were looking over his shoulder. Spooner was hyperactive. When Partridge called on him, Spooner's material, instead of being ready in a file folder, would be all over the place—on the credenza behind him, on his desk, on a shelf. Spooner would frantically be up and down and moving around the whole time, gathering the material together. After a while, one got used to the jitteriness. Lloyd Widdifield once remarked that Spooner wasn't the nervous type. That was just his nature.

Spooner's heavy smoking added to his edginess. Cigarettes and Gibsons were part of his personality. His weaknesses were well-known. He couldn't say no to radio and television airtime salesmen coming in and schmoozing him. One salesman in particular would take him out to lunch and, after two or three double Gibsons, Spooner would make the purchase. This annoyed Tony Antonias, the CKNW copywriting chief, no end. Antonias was in charge of Spooner's radio budget. He would burn the midnight oil looking at the various demographics and Bureau of Broadcast Measurement surveys, and setting up the campaign within budget. He would then make the buy, only to learn later from Spooner that Spooner had bought additional airtime without consulting him. "You can't start fiddling around with the budget once it's set," Antonias recounted, trying to explain the bizarreness of it. "What are you going to do? He'd make ridiculous buys, totally irrelevant to what we were aiming our cannons at."

Antonias would then have to straighten out the mess. "Ron ..." he would begin to say, and before he could go further, Spooner would reply, "Oh, I know, I know. I'm sorry, Tony. It won't happen again." He'd laugh that little laugh of his. His eyes would sparkle and he'd look at Antonias, and Antonias would believe every word he was being told, that it wouldn't in fact happen again. It always did.

One campaign season, Spooner didn't even tell Antonias what he had done, fearing Antonias would blow his stack. At the end of the campaign, Antonias, with Spooner's faithful secretary, Rhona Lythgoe, tallied up the accounts, only to discover they were $5,000 short—an astronomical amount in those days. "Rhona, it can't be!" Antonias exclaimed. Yet, almost as soon as the words were out, he realized what had happened. "Oh, well, that's Ron," Lythgoe would say, which said it all. Spooner had a residual insecurity—he wanted too much to be loved and appreciated—and no imploring or scolding could change him.

According to Wayne McKay, some of the suppliers, like radio-station people, also touched Spooner for small personal loans, up to a few thousand dollars, when Spooner filled in for branch managers, in the late 1960s. Or Spooner would forward a loan application for them with a strong personal recommendation. Several of these loans were dubious, given the raffishness and transience of some of that crowd. B.C. Lions football players also got onto Spooner. Spooner had season tickets to Lions' games and he, Smalley, McKay and Nelson used to go to the Touchdown Club luncheons. Spooner was so engaging that the football crowd liked to chat with him, and when they discovered he could also lend them money he became even more popular. His supplier and football friends, as if by radar, always knew where to find him. Bentley tolerated Spooner's generosity. The financial fall-out was minor. When the branch managers expressed their concerns, Bentley suggested that any write-offs could be chalked up as promotional expenses that Spooner had incurred.

Spooner had never been good with detail, including the detail that goes into a judgement about a loan. None of the managers had wanted Spooner to relieve them during holidays, because he left such a mess of soft loans behind—loans that, for their duration, had to be carefully managed, which took up time. They kidded Spooner about these relief sojourns.

There had been open debates about lending in managers' meetings. Spooner's approach was deliberately not to question the honesty, responsibility or reliability of loan applicants. It was more important to him to take people at face value and to please the member, inasmuch as the lending rules allowed. He trusted people. McKay and Nelson argued that they tried to please members, too, but that one had to be more guarded in lending, and that it was important as well to close off all the administrative details in a loan. Spooner might lend money on a car without doing an ownership search to see if there was a lien outstanding on it.

Behind the conviviality Spooner had a streak of shyness. In crowds, he preferred to stand back a little bit. Ross Montgomery, a young VanCity board member in the early 1970s, noticed that whenever Bentley and Spooner walked into a meeting, Spooner was always a step behind. It was as if Spooner wanted to remain in the shadows and protect his privacy, Montgomery thought.

Spooner was fiercely loyal to Bentley. Bentley was "D. B.," "the chief," the visionary. Spooner was good at sitting at Bentley's elbow, exploring ideas with him and putting Bentley's often inchoate vision into writing—a Boswell to Bentley's Samuel Johnson. Now he began to ride more and more on Bentley's coattails. With the advent of computerization, he had lost his sense of where the organization was going. The comfort with detail that even a lay person needed to have in order to chart the computerized future wasn't Spooner's strong point. When Bentley was away for a few months in 1973-74 for heart-valve surgery, McKay, although much younger than Spooner, filled in as acting general manager. This bruised Spooner. Ethel Bentley, who knew both men well, reflected that Spooner wasn't a heavy-weight—he didn't have the acute intelligence that McKay did. Sometimes Spooner betrayed his sensitivity to hurt. Once, after having lost an argument to Nelson and McKay at a managers' meeting, he stubbornly carried on the argument in *Working Dollars*, which he looked after.

Managers' meetings were held in the evening. Spooner now was not contributing much at these meetings, although he was as spontaneous as ever. McKay, who was a friend, although not close, attributed this to Spooner's drinking, which was becoming heavier. Spooner's wife was concerned. Spooner also became increasingly dependent on his secretary, Rhona Lythgoe, to pick up the ball when he fumbled it and to keep his work organized. Fortunately for him, she knew how to take emergencies in stride. He was also having difficulties with his children. Being inundated with problems made it impossible for him to function at his old intensity. Bentley took the time to listen to him and supported him. Spooner was a great procrastinator. Bentley put up with it. Every time there was an annual meeting, Bentley would keep his fingers crossed that Spooner would reserve the room at the Hotel Vancouver. He always did, but at the last moment.

There was no question, however, of Bentley's moving Spooner aside or even of challenging the hefty "business lunch" vouchers, inflated by liquor charges, which were turning into a big chunk of change. Bentley's response, when McKay, as comptroller, brought this spending to his attention, was that VanCity didn't pay Spooner all that much, and if he was making up for it this way, tax free, he, Bentley, wasn't going to be too upset. Bentley's decision had been made long ago: as long as he was general manager, Ron Spooner in one capacity or another would be an officer of the credit union.

If that was all there was to it, it would have been just another case of a leader, perhaps myopically, protecting a faithful servant out of kindness. Spooner was much more than a faithful servant, however. He was Bentley's alter ego and compatriot. They were buddies. Bentley enjoyed Spooner's company and respected his talent. Spooner's sparkle and his way with words and ideas were embedded in the VanCity character, intertwined with Bentley's own achievement, so that saying goodbye to Spooner would be like saying goodbye to a part of himself, a kind of amputation.

Spooner, Wayne McKay recalled, was gifted, able. He knew how to communicate and to stage events like annual meetings. He could put flash to

ideas. He could write, penning his drafts in a distinctive oversized, rounded
longhand. He had a knack for taking a story and putting emotion into it
with words, fleshing out the bare bones to make them come alive. He had
something that Bentley lacked. For all that it was true that he picked up on
Bentley's thinking, from carefully listening to him—and that was part of his
job—it was also true that in capturing it in writing, expanding on it, and
interpreting it for others, he was giving it an immediacy that it would not
otherwise have had. He was continually trying to conceptualize in a larger
sense what VanCity was doing, providing a vision for others, like Hermann
Myers. He talked big concepts. When the little, marginal organization duly
became expansive and ushered in major innovations, it seemed to Spooner
the most natural thing in the world.

Niceness and amiability were other Spooner traits—expressions, in his
case, of a deeper goodness. Everyone who knew him agreed about that.
Margaret Skelcher, who briefly managed the West Vancouver branch and
felt intimidated by Bentley, was struck, on the other hand, by Spooner's
empathy and compassion. She thought him a great person. He had really
helped her.

He had a terrible taste in clothes—he liked to wear loud checks—but it
suited him. He made tellers and secretaries feel good, because they knew
they could joke with him. Marina Lowe, McKay's secretary, remembered
Spooner once chatting away on the phone to her. He was "long steam," as
she phrased it. "Could you speed it up, Mr. Spooner?" she asked. "I've got
to get some work done here." Spooner laughed. Lowe knew he wasn't the
kind to take offence. Since he handled member relations and complaints,
he got close to members. He had a way with people. If VanCity bungled, he
sometimes visited the member personally to make amends. He sensed, in
his contact with people, that they needed certain things from their financial
institution, after which he did anything he could to provide them, even if it
meant departing from policy. He had fastened like a limpet onto the idea
that VanCity existed for its members.

There were two schools of opinion about the way Bentley and Spooner
worked together. One had it that Bentley was the idea man and Spooner the
publicist who got behind those ideas, sometimes in that role becoming their
driving force and hence appearing more original than he was. The other
saw Spooner as the pixilated, unbankerly, seat-of-the-pants idea man, and
Bentley as the organizational maestro, sorting the wheat from the chaff and
somehow putting the good ideas into effect. This was Mike Borch's view at
Central Data Systems (CDS). He remembered Spooner, jumpy, talking with
clenched fists, which were going up and down like pistons as ideas issued
forth. The ideas people of our world, Borch thought, don't get too concerned with how something is actually going to work, because if you get
bogged down with that, you quickly decide it's not worth thinking about.
Spooner was like that. He was always talking about, "What if we do this,"
"What if we do that" and "How about trying it this way?"

Both schools of opinion were right and wrong at the same time. The truth was that Bentley and Spooner each had their own form of originality, but they were different in kind. Bentley's was reflective, strategic and intellectual. Spooner's was spontaneous and scattered.

Spooner's fragility was a strength as well as a weakness. VanCity operationally, for Bentley, was meetings, numbers, administering, expansion and bright and ambitious branch managers. Spooner was the human condition, like a court jester in a room of solemn advisers. Having Spooner with him reminded Bentley of VanCity's humanity. Getting together with Spooner and Myers on some minor promotional matter—the meeting of an unlikely trio—took Bentley into a countervailing world of sensibilities.

They were getting older. Bentley and Spooner were in their fifties. Myers had passed sixty. Myers was hard of hearing, and because he often missed much of what was said at a meeting, he came across as a bit of a country bumpkin. Spooner, who was so very fond of Myers, would not see him displaced. Bentley himself was at the height of his powers. His organization was muscular, fast-growing and boldly innovative. The heart-valve surgery, to correct a congenital heart defect, however, had slowed him down. He wasn't sure how long he could provide the lead.

As it happened, he didn't have the peace of mind to think about it. He was now faced with a problem that threatened disastrous consequences. The CDS computer system, despite technological updates, was falling short and producing irregularities, with mounting difficulties for VanCity. In 1967, when CDS converted the accounts of VanCity and other consortium members, and the brave new world of computerization was ushered in, the feat seemed dazzling, and it was. By 1973, just six years later, it was clear to Wayne McKay and to Bentley that CDS, for VanCity at least, was already outdated and that measures to get more out of the system would soon reach their limit. VanCity had become too large for CDS to handle and was going to grow larger. Without adequate posting and other processing of information, VanCity's operations would break down. Nor was there any turning back to ledger cards, still being used by the banks.

Unless something else were found or devised, VanCity would explode from its own growth. But what that something else was, nobody knew.

PART FOUR

1970-1975

CHAPTER 25

The Geniuses

ONLY GUS GERMAN SEEMED TO KNOW what he was doing. And if it didn't have to do with computers, he didn't know what he was doing, either.

He was one of two principals, and the technical head, of a small Toronto computer company, Geac. The company had a new contract with Donlands Dairy in Toronto for an order taking and delivery system. German's partner, Bob Isserstedt, who ran the administrative side, had been so anxious to close the contract that he gave Donlands Dairy any extras he could. German, on the other hand, was worried about the pricing. There had to be enough money in the contract to cover the work. His exasperation grew until he finally told Isserstedt, "No more." He found out after the contract was signed, however, that Isserstedt had also thrown in free paper for printouts. He was furious. He did the only thing he could think of: He decided to go paperless with the system and hence eliminate as much paper as possible.

The idea was to have multiple order stations use the same computer. German had picked up a newfangled "multiplex card" from a time-sharing company downstairs in the building. He couldn't remember having paid for it. It was just there, he said. He began to fiddle with it. It appeared that with the card one could "read and write" sixteen terminals at the same time. The trick was to handle the terminals at random and to do it so quickly that each operator felt the computer was serving her instantaneously. German realized that if he could do that, he would not only be saving some paper, he would also be eliminating the need for key-punchers to punch data onto cards, not to mention the computer operator who fed the cards into the computer.

Best of all, he would be providing up-to-date information from second to second, and doing so on CRTs (cathode-ray-tube terminals, like small television sets) rather than teleprinter terminals, which took time to print out their information and required paper. Only a few, large airlines had systems that could do that. There was one slight difference. The airline reservation systems were based on mammoth, multi-million-dollar mainframe installations. The pioneering Air Canada ReserVec II system, using two huge Univac computers, had set the company back $34 million, at a time when a million dollars meant something. German was proposing to do his on-line system with a minicomputer which cost hardly anything and required little space. It was, in the embryonic computer world of the time, just an outrageous idea.

Gus German was different from others. He thought differently. When he was a toddler, he decided to try flying, took off from his high chair and fractured his skull, or at least that was his story. Later, when he was about twelve, he went over on his bicycle and fractured his skull again. He always had a skewed intelligence, and his account of the fractured skulls was a way of laughing about it.

He grew up lower middle class in a pleasant neighbourhood in Willowdale, a suburb of Toronto. He didn't talk until he was three. In school, he had difficulty focussing, with his mind changing subjects rapidly, going off on tangents, racing—a problem that continued to plague him in adulthood. He also had red hair. He got teased a lot. High school was not much different. In most subjects, his performance was woeful. Part of this was due to his rebelliousness, but mostly he couldn't grasp the point of what was being taught and couldn't pay attention. He just didn't get it. In mathematics and science, on the other hand, he did extremely well. He was fascinated by them. He would stay in school after hours and play with the chemistry equipment. At home, he began fooling around with electronics, collecting radio tubes and making amplifiers and other things by looking at books. In his early teens, he repaired radios for friends.

In an incident that was to become legend, German once acquired a transmitting tube and made a little transmitter in his basement, setting it up to broadcast off the upper end of the AM radio band. It was late spring. He went to school with a small transistor radio and bet kids that he could get "Frosty the Snowman" on it. They guffawed. "You're off your rocker," they said. He then picked up the song from a repeat record-player hooked into his transmitter at home. It was his first "miracle."

He flunked grade 12 because he failed English and French. Although he managed to pass these courses on his second try, he was left without the grade 13 equivalents needed to get into university. His mother, however, wasn't to be stopped. Gus was a mathematical whiz, and she managed to get him into the University of Waterloo. The University of Waterloo was just establishing its reputation as the training ground for cadres in new technology like computers, and the young Gus German fitted in. At first, he applied himself and did extremely well. Then life began to fragment. He failed his second year. He had never failed so badly in his life. He discovered bridge and alcohol. He had not drunk at all until then. He became a wild man. He couldn't handle methodical, repetitive tasks and he couldn't spell, but he had always had trouble with those kinds of functions. In one algebra test, he got a zero. He had, in his own words, gone off the deep end. He didn't understand himself, nor what his mind was doing to him—and although he knew that he did not understand, he could not help himself.

He did, however, understand computers—the large and cumbersome mainframes and plugboard machines that were around at the time. Computers focussed him. If he wrote a program, it would either work or not work. The computer didn't call him a dummy because somehow, despite his apparent brilliance, he was having difficulty at ordinary tasks. The first computer he dealt with was the IBM 1620 mainframe at the university. It was in a special room, closed to undergraduates. Somehow he managed to get into the room and make friends with the graduate students. The contact with the machine was addictive. He wanted desperately to know how it worked.

He made himself useful. Despite his academic ups and downs, he became the first employee of the University of Waterloo's Computing Centre and its resident expert. He had an unquenchable curiosity about the giant mechanical secrets lurking in the various machines housed in and around the computer centre. He believed in liberating these secrets, in sharing information in a paradise of unlocked doors. In his case, this meant literally no locked doors. He made master keys. He just needed to see a master key briefly in order to memorize its key sequence. If there was a machine behind a locked door, German went through the door after hours and played around with it. A machine that he had altered, sometimes to the horror of the people using it, was then considered "gussyized." It reached the point that when anything went wrong, German, with his reputation, was blamed for it. He became a character at the university. He had something of the angelic, otherworldy quality of the idiot savant.

The university acquired a new, high-speed research computer, the IBM 7040. Unfortunately the compiler that came with it—a program that translates the code of an end-use program into language the computer, as a machine, understands—required auxiliary tape storage. It was, as a result, painfully cumbersome and slow. German was part of a team of four undergraduates that put together a new and much more efficient compiler. It was called Watfor, after Waterloo and Fortran, the standard compiler language used. Watfor, capable of handling reprogramming tasks quickly, revolutionized computer use. It was five to fifty times faster than other available compilers, making the 7040 accessible to large numbers of people. It was soon picked up by other computing centres across North America. German wasn't the best writer of "code"—he would get too distracted by it. His forte was conceptualization. When the team ran into a roadblock, he had umpteen suggestions for working around it. He ignored the possibility that things were so complicated that they couldn't be done. Complication frustrated him, infuriated him, intrigued and excited him—it was god and the devil at the same time.

German and two other students also solved Archimedes' famous "cattle problem"—a problem that had defeated the best minds in mathematics for over two thousand years. The students solved it on a bet. Archimedes, the Greek mathematician and inventor, had concocted a mathematical problem involving the total number of cows and bulls of various colours on an island. The smallest answer—the smallest combination that worked— was 206,545 digits long. Mathematicians claimed that a computer would never solve it. German and his friends came up with the entire number. An academic paper was written documenting the achievement. Notices about the feat appeared in papers around the world. German had a few minutes of international fame. This impressed him.

Watfor gave the four people who wrote it a reputation. They had suddenly become a valuable commodity and, still students, did work for Northern Electric in Ottawa. Somehow German got his bachelor of science degree. He turned into a fixture at the university. He was, by this time, drinking too much, but still functioning. He may have had an undiagnosed thought disorder. He wasn't dyslexic. The thought disorder explained why he couldn't spell or focus on repetitive tasks. His mind instead raced and jumped around. Working with computers and other technology, as he had discovered, was one of the few things that could integrate his mind. Computer experimenting and taking machinery apart and putting it together again were weapons against his helplessness. The drinking, however, made this battle between focus and disorder more difficult. He had also begun experimenting with amphetamines. He entered into a disordered private world of his own, which, with shorter or longer intervals of clarity, he remained in for twenty-five years.

He was nevertheless on top of the heap, doing more and more consulting work. He married a high-school sweetheart and bought a house. They had a small daughter. One day, driving to Ottawa, his wife went off the road and was killed. German lost control of his drinking. He became suicidal, more or less trying to drink himself to death. Only the realization that he had a small daughter to look after stopped him from doing it. He made a fair amount of money as a consultant—he could do that even in a stupor—but otherwise his life was in disarray. A couple of years later, he remarried. The decision was a hysterical, drunken impulse on his part, he said. He was worried about his daughter.

Much of his consulting was done for data processing people. He was also working on terminal projects, hooking up terminals to large computers and writing languages that could work on these terminals. He was one of the first people to have an intelligent terminal tied remotely to a central computer in this way. IBM had a machine that did it, but the machine was expensive. German had a minicomputer at home. He made it appear to the big computer like the IBM terminal, and using his teletype console, plugged into the big computer from his house.

The minicomputer in his den was a Hewlett Packard—a "loaner" from the company. Minicomputers had been used largely for industrial control and laboratory testing functions. They hardly counted in the computer firmament. As German in the early morning hours monkeyed about with the Hewlett Packard, however, he began to wonder. The Hewlett Packard cost $20,000, compared with at least $2 million for a mainframe, yet it was almost as fast relative to its functions. Although it was much heavier than the small microcomputers of the future, it could be lifted up and taken elsewhere. This startled German, who was in love with mainframes. The trouble with the big machines was their unreliability—they kept breaking down—a defect against which German was helpless. With the less sophisticated mini, he had to do everything for himself. He made mistakes, but the mistakes were his own and he could correct them. The machine was within his control. He paid increasing attention to what it could do and to enhancing his capability on it.

The trend was to invent more and more instructions for the big mainframes, with programming language to match. German instead became interested in doing things in the simplest, most economical way possible. The university, with its latest IBM model, was wedded to its mainframe success. German, on the other hand, was slowly switching his affections. He had come out of his depression. His new wife, Kiki, had got him to cut back his drinking and he was concentrating on making more money. He knew about the innards of equipment. He knew about compiler languages. He knew how to condense programs. He knew about data processing and about terminals. Most of all, he had a machine that in its simplicity and deftness was after his own heart.

The head of the computing centre at the university decided it was time for German to go. German, with his outside consulting work, was hardly ever in Waterloo anyway. He was making $60,000 to $70,000 a year, a huge income at that time, about three times as much as Don Bentley was earning as general manager of VanCity. Afraid he would run out of steam from overwork and be considered a flake, he decided he needed a manager. Management people, in German's view, were different creatures from technocrats like himself. They knew how to hold things together. He put an ad in the papers looking for a president for his own consulting company and conducted a series of bizarre interviews with strangers in a fruitless and doomed attempt to find somebody compatible.

To add to his anguish, Hewlett Packard wanted its "loaner" back, to lease to a customer called Huntington-Rockford. German simply declined to part with it. His contact at Hewlett Packard, however, told him that the Huntington-Rockford people hadn't the faintest idea how to use the machine. He went along to meet them, trying to figure out a way to avoid giving the machine up.

Huntington-Rockford was everything in a company that German detested. Its niche was educational data-processing—timetables and grade reporting. The company name had had been pulled out of the air by one of the original group for the sound of it—solid, respectable and with a hint of technology. Then it went public, exploiting the rage surrounding computer technology. It raked in $500,000 in a share issue. This bounty was quickly dissipated on big furnishings, big cars (a few Lincolns), big-spending sales-men and a leased twin-engined aircraft. In the meantime, the technical potential of that money had been lost. The company had a contract with the Simcoe County Board of Education in Barrie, Ontario, to computerize its thousands of accounts, but the contract was beyond them. Altogether it was true, as German put it, that "these guys did not know their ying yang from a dooey dot."

Huntington-Rockford, however, had two things that interested German. First, its client, Simcoe County, had a real problem. German saw the opportunity of starting a company to develop computer applications for such problems. Second, one of the originators of Huntington-Rockford, a marketing analyst, Bob Isserstedt, fulfilled in every way German's image of what a president should be. He was tall, suave and debonair—every-thing that German wasn't. He wasn't much older than German, but seemed older and more mature. He had the gift of the gab. German had found his long-sought-after managerial counterpart, although how good a manager Isserstedt was, German had no idea.

German agreed to give up the Hewlett Packard if he came attached. In fact, Huntington-Rockford needed German more than they needed the machine. The original scheme was to use the minicomputer to feed the data from Barrie to a shared mainframe in Ottawa, for processing. It didn't take much for German to convince them to handle the whole job with the minicomputer instead. The school board was psychologically prepared to spend $6,000 a month for the Ottawa mainframe arrangement. If German could manage his ground-breaking feat, Huntington-Rockford would have a good chunk of that revenue for itself.

Huntington-Rockford went into receivership before the Simcoe County project was completed. There was no point, however, in stopping the project. Isserstedt and German formed a new company and bought the contract from the receiver for a nominal sum. They were equal share-holders. German liked the idea of a non-public company. He wanted it to make money rather than live off the proceeds of a stock issue. Isserstedt, fishing for a name with a technical ring like Univac, came up with the name Geac, derived from his father-in-law's suggestion of General and Education Computing. Isserstedt was dubbed president.

These were good days for German. There was no money to throw around. All the attention was focussed on the technical task. He had four technical people with him, inherited from Hungtingon-Rockford. He quickly put his inventiveness to work, devising programs to order that not only did the job but also eliminated steps in the process. His boldest move was a money-saving hardware modification, so the computer could drive a low-cost printer. The modification meant that technically the computer was a dif-ferent machine. German had his stepfather, a carpenter, make up a veneer wooden cabinet. He put the machine inside the cabinet and called it the Geac 500. Geac had become a computer manufacturer.

With revenue coming in from Barrie, Isserstedt leased office space on the fifth floor atop a building, a kind of penthouse, on Don Mills Road just north of Eglinton. It overlooked IBM across the way. Then came the Donlands contract and German's idea of creating an online system with the same small machine.

The multiplex circuit board that allowed German to connect multiple terminals to the same computer far from solved all of his problems. The operating system for the Hewlett Packard—the bottom-level program which made the machine usable—was too fragile and limited for the job. Hewlett Packard had devised its minicomputer for industrial uses. Only incidentally did its programmers begin to explore the minicomputer's other possibilities, and they hadn't progressed far.

The operating system had another, virtually prohibitive drawback. Its programming was too complicated, so it took up too much of the computer's memory. This didn't leave enough room for all the things German needed the machine to do. On a large mainframe, a bulky operating system would not have made that much difference, but on the minicomputer, the space simply wasn't there. Most damning, it could drive only one terminal at a time instead of the multiple terminals German had in mind. He would have to write his own drivers, not to mention other peripheral device controllers. The project looked totally impossible to German, yet he sensed, in the recesses of his mind, that it could be done.

His well-honed computer acumen helped him out. He had come across an especially fast editing program for the Hewlett Packard. It was "shareware"—a program created by another user and shared freely. What particularly impressed German was the absence of documentation. Programming code almost always came with elaborate comments describing what each piece of the program did. German had an intense dislike of this documentation because it discouraged improving the program. Changes in the code required laboriously changing the documentation. He himself read the code straight. He could follow the sequence line by line—understand the "algorithms"—without benefit of commentary. He concluded that whoever had done the editing program and left out the documentation was as bright and as quick as he was. "This guy's a genius," German told Isserstedt.

The genius turned out to be a young engineering professor at the University College of North Wales, in an out-of-the-way place called Bangor, on the Irish Sea. Geac brought him to Toronto. His name was Mike Sweet or, as German liked to refer to him, Dr. Sweet, because he was the first Geac employee with a doctorate. Sweet was originally from Bristol. German explained what Geac needed in the way of an operating system. He then gave Sweet three months to write a new one.

Computers, unfortunately, were not Sweet's area of expertise. His special field was control engineering, circuit theory, and motors. He had left out the documentation with his editing program not because he was a scornful computer guru but because he did not know any better. He had no formal computer education. He didn't even know what an operating system was, until German described it for him.

Mike Sweet, German thought, as he watched him, was an odd duck. Given the source of the observation, this was saying a lot. Sweet had a thin, scraggly beard, which he chewed constantly. He had a hole in his mouth with a steel pin, where a tooth had fallen off and hadn't been replaced. He was short and skinny and had long-flowing hair. When he moved to Canada to work with Geac, he bought a chicken farm outside of Toronto and often showed up in the office on Don Mills Road in big gumboots covered with chicken manure.

On a brief expedition to Vancouver—later, on the VanCity project—he showed up early at the premises and couldn't get in. It was only 5:30 A.M. He had flown in from Toronto the night before. He had arisen at Toronto time, 8 A.M., and walked from his hotel in his open-toed sandals, through the deserted streets, to VanCity's address. His feet were wet and hurting, so he took the sandals off. He felt liberated. "It was incredible!" he thought. He went barefoot thereafter. He was introverted. He had the anarchistic, private impulses of a cat. If it was more comfortable for him to conduct a conversation lying on his side instead of sitting up, he lay down without a second thought.

He was extremely impatient. He had written his faster editing program because he could not tolerate waiting for the computer to execute after he punched the keys. The waiting just drove him nuts. He reduced the execution time per instruction down to about two seconds. He had worked out how to do it, without instruction, by first looking into the machine while it was running, and recording the pattern of flashing lights. Sweet's impatience could break out in discussion—impatience with the slowness of minds, impatience with the perverse stubbornness of argument—and erupt like a geyser.

As German suspected would happen, the naive engineer who had tinkered with a Hewlett Packard quickly became a bona fide computer expert. The monster assignment turned out to be no monster at all. At each stage, Sweet would ask German, "How are we going to do this?" German would tell him. He would reply, "Oh, that's how we do it. It's not too difficult." He would then go ahead and do it, learning as he went. He enjoyed it. His creation was, in fact, a tour de force—an operating system that was barebones to the point of being crude, that took little space in memory and that drove up to ten terminals. "Our key scientist," German described him, as if a bailing-wire outfit like Geac could have something called a scientist.

Sweet realized in turn what a master German was. German always had good ideas for dealing with technical problems. He was continually inventive. He knew how to use computers to solve practical problems in the real world. He was good at convincing other people that he was capable of coming up with these solutions, or rather, that what they really wanted was what German was proposing, outlandish as it might at first appear. Most of all, the idea of using the small, cheap machine, and getting it to do big things by stripping down process, was such a revolutionary concept that one could only marvel at its prophet. Gus German, and Gus alone in all of computerdom, had come up with the idea that it could be done and had the broad knowledge of particulars to know that it could in fact be done.

The operating system was only part of the Donlands adventure. The other part was the programs that would actually do the job for the dairy. The senior program writer was Russell Smith. Smith was a University of Waterloo product. Although young, he was an old hand at the work. He had been around in the Huntington-Rockford days. Don Bagshaw, an eighteen-year-old co-op engineering student from the University of Waterloo, also helped out. Bagshaw, in his own words, was a "dead rookie." He had never seen a computer terminal before. The technical people at Geac showed him things he could do right away, then corrected what he had done. In two weeks, he was writing programs.

The idea of the system was synchronicity itself. Donlands Dairy order takers would key in their codes, engaging the relevant computer programs. The programs would put the operating system to work activating disk controllers. The disk controllers, like dancing devils, would pick the relevant bits of information off whirling disks and feed those bits back down to the order takers, pulsating from one operator's line to another. Then, as each order taker finished with a caller, their new information—the customer's order—would be sent in the other direction, up through a disk controller to one of the disks, like a spawning salmon following an intricate river system to a remote uplands creek. At the end of the day, some of this information plus similar information from other spots on the disks would flow down in reverse to the estuary and be printed out as loading and delivery instructions for the drivers the next morning.

Superficially German, in this development work, did not seem to do much of anything, yet he made everything go. Once, while the others were desperately working on specific tasks, German became engrossed in taking apart a television set. Bagshaw could not believe it. German, it turned out, was trying to find out how the cathode-ray tube worked, so he could get better performance out of the terminals. Hewlett Packard's disk controllers were too expensive. German knew a couple of people at the University of Toronto who had a touch for electronics. He had them design and make the controllers for him, moonlighting after their regular work. These were random-access disk mechanisms, by which the computer could pick up bits of information from anywhere on a series of disks, piled up in stacks. German understood the technology so well that he did not hesitate to bypass the conventional manufacturer.

Here, too, German's powers of conceptualization led the way, although he did not write much of the code himself. His attention span was only about ten minutes. From time to time, however, he produced little pieces of code exceptional in their brevity. Sweet referred to them—half in awe, half in jest—as German's "little gems." These were small bits of code that nevertheless did the job they were meant for. The feat was more than a matter of programming artistry. German was trying to create a whole new world, different from the "other world" of the mainframes. Programming style was a key element.

It was like a chess game, Sweet explained. You might be able to check-mate your opponent in twenty moves. German wanted to see if they could do it in three or four. It meant efficiency in the actual operation of the computer. Back in the "other world"—the mainframe world occupied by everybody else—data entry systems were written in a language called Cobol, a "horrendous thing," Sweet described it. The Cobol programs, sitting on top of the operating system, filled a huge space in the computer's memory. For German, this was akin to driving to work in a semitrailer truck full of boulders. It got you there eventually, but was it necessary? The vehicle he was building had just a small engine and four wheels, nothing else, and it still got you there. The configuration German was putting together, Isserstedt realized, was the secret bargain of the computer world. People from the "other world," who thought in Cobol, could no more conceive what Geac was doing than strangers from another planet.

There was another problem. There was no computer language to write what they wanted to write. The only language reasonably close to what they needed, Fortran, wasn't suitable for the small computer. German added ingenious modifications—in effect, created a pidgin Fortran—to do what he wanted it to do.

They all then pitched in to install the system at the dairy itself. They spent two months on the site after that, trying to work out the bugs. They had made the installation far too early. The system went down before it even got up. There were too many new and untried elements. Sweet remembers once prying himself out of bed at three in the morning to handle some emergency. German was working around the clock. The pressure was intense. Finally the system stopped breaking.

They had succeeded against all odds. Donlands Dairy had been in a hopeless situation, attempting to handle its increasing order list and manage its inventory manually. For Donlands, the Geac installation was miraculous. The operators took pride in it. It was an on-line, on-screen, multiple-terminal system, and it had been done with a small, stripped-down machine that, next to the prestigious elephant mainframes, cost virtually nothing at all.

CHAPTER 26

Showdown with Central

WHEN AUDITOR WALTER DYCK THOUGHT of the showdown between Don Bentley and George May, the CEO of B.C. Central Credit Union, he thought of the maxim that where there is a king, everybody wants to kill the king, but where there are two kings, they want to kill each other. May tried to contain Bentley and VanCity's power. Bentley did not want May and Central holding VanCity back, and the more he dealt with May, the greater his distrust of May's motives and behaviour. He came to see May as a threat to the credit union movement. May, in return, saw Bentley threatening Central, which was a threat to himself and what he wanted to achieve. Besides, for May, Central represented the credit union movement—the small and large credit unions together. Bentley, by bucking Central, was fighting the movement. May, moreover, had bold ambitions for Central. In playing out these ambitions, he encroached on VanCity territory. Bentley resisted. May manoeuvred against him. This only deepened Bentley's distaste for Central politics which, in its previous incarnation in the old B.C. Credit Union League, he had never much liked, either. May thrust, Bentley parried and counterthrust. May's weapons were politics and flamboyance. Bentley's weapons were the logic of VanCity and the fierce pride of leading the way. Bentley won.

The most important thing that ever happened to George May was poliomyelitis. He contracted it at a boys' camp one summer when he was a youngster, in the postwar years before anti-polio vaccine was invented. George was one of the lucky ones. He recovered from total paralysis. His right arm, however, was totally disabled. It hung there limp and thin, from muscle deterioration. When he left the hospital, he could hardly walk and was very unbalanced.

The polio was a terrific blow. He was angry and resentful, but he fought back. He became aggressive and hard, and extremely competitive. Sports was his arena. He had height and he had speed: he grew to an even six feet. He was a one-armed baseball pitcher. He was also a strong soccer player. He had no fear of being hurt—nothing could hurt him more than losing the use of his right arm—so he played straight ahead and often hurt others. He wasn't dirty, just fearless.

In high school, in Richmond, where the family was located, he felt he was going to be a leader in whatever field he entered. He was interested in banking. His first job, though, was as assistant to the president of a large trucking and warehousing company. He became president of the Richmond Chamber of Commerce in his mid-twenties, and shortly after was elected Richmond alderman.

He married young. His in-laws were left-wingers and strong proponents of credit unions. On the occasion of their daughter's wedding, they had opened an account for the young couple at Richmond Savings Credit Union and put some starter money in it. His interest in credit unionism began from there. He soon was deeply involved. He became one of the credit union's directors and then president. Richmond Savings was growing like topsy, and his job allowed him the flexibility with his schedule to do both his paying work and his volunteer credit union work. He put in unbelievable hours. The first place he would go to, after work at 5 P.M., was the credit union, where he would stay until midnight, planning on how to move Richmond Savings ahead. He put in weekends there, too.

He also joined the board of the B.C. Credit Union League and became president of that as well. He was a director of B.C. Central. He co-chaired the co-ordinating committee working on the merger of the two organizations. The merger process opened his eyes to the schisms, clefts, crevices and wrinkles in the credit union movement. He discovered the split between the pro-Central forces like Don Bentley, and the pro-league forces opposing him, like Rod Glen, the co-operative firebrand from Nanaimo. It was the "banking" side (Central) versus the "political" side (the League). There were layers upon layers of these divisions and alliances. He tried to play a conciliatory role in bringing the sides together.

He was on the selection committee to find a chief executive officer for the new organization. The acrimonious politics of the merger had sidelined the two incumbents (from the League and the old Central) as possibilities. The committee had difficulty finding somebody suitable. According to May, he had no aspirations for the position. Cynics said that May, as a member of the original selection committee, and a clever, assertive operator to boot, had ways of making things happen. May was named chief executive officer. He was thirty-one years old.

George May had drive and plenty of ideas. He wanted to bring credit unions all across the province—all those small- and medium-sized ones—to the point where they could compete against the banks and provide the same service that VanCity and Richmond Savings members were getting. He wanted to make credit unions a major financial and economic presence in society.

He put in place a new management team—young men with commerce and business administration degrees, who knew the latest in finance and marketing techniques. He talked about management by objectives. The holdovers from the League he gradually sidetracked. Dick Monrufet was one of them. He stayed on for a while as May's deputy, handling the old League side of things. Monrufet, though, was no longer at home. The way May was integrating the two staffs and restructuring the finances was, as Monrufet saw it, a goddamn madhouse, like somebody putting a car into over-drive. May was impatient, autocratic. It was an odd management style, to Monrufet, something totally foreign to him. As far as he was concerned, May was a bully who couldn't face up to his handicap. For May, on the other hand, the laid-back Monrufet simply moved at too slow a pace.

Others, like young Mike Borch at Central Data Systems (CDS), saw May quite differently. Borch liked May, not least because he was so aggressive and combative. That's what was needed at the time in the credit union system, Borch thought. "He promoted a lot of change when there were a lot of old farts in the system who didn't want change," Borch recounted. May was articulate, demanding and a workaholic. If he left a lot of dead bodies behind him in the process, that was the way it was. Even Monrufet had to admit that, given the discord leading to the new organization, there was going to be turmoil. May got along with people that he wanted to get along with.

The May organization plunged forward. The leading objective was to create a uniformity of services in credit unions across the province, so they could be marketed on a collective basis the way that a chartered bank used the mass media to market all its branches. This had implications. To reach that objective, every credit union, for example, would have to provide Plan 24 daily interest. That really meant extending the reach of CDS, now wholly owned by Central.

May launched provincial advertising campaigns boosting credit unions generically. He took an embryonic mortgage-money facility and turned it into an active lender—Central Financial Corporation (CFC). If a small- or medium-sized credit union, or even a larger one, couldn't handle a developer's housing project or other commercial loan, it could refer the borrower to CFC, bring the business into the credit union movement and add presence to their own operation in the process. To finance the expansion of CFC, May and his chief financial officer, Aj Gill, put together a Canadian bond issue, the first credit union bond issue in the country. They also developed a money-management business, re-investing long-term bond money raised cheaply for a 2 or 3 per cent margin—profit that could be used to finance the organization's expanding services.

There were other initiatives. May negotiated regulatory changes whereby government agencies like liquor stores could deposit money in local credit unions. He obtained a similar regulatory change for lawyers' trust accounts. He was a supreme publicist, appearing on open-line shows and giving newspaper interviews, explaining why credit unions were good and the big banks were bad. Later he hired a chief economist for Central, which gave the organization even greater presence.

Central took on an aura unto itself. It became large and influential. It was an exciting time to be in the organization. The cadres were aggressive and enthusiastic. May found himself working hard to hold them back while pushing them at the same time. May was moving the fastest of all. He was on the road constantly, as many as 150 days a year, and his family life broke down. He and his wife separated. He enjoyed parties. He also liked to talk about issues and politics. He was to Central conventions born, because they were parties, issues and politics in one big, blurry mix.

Mike Borch came to the conclusion that May was a visionary much like Bentley—oddly enough, because their personalities were so different. Peter Cook, the chief economist May hired, felt the same way. "Have a conversation with George May," he remembered, "and you were never left in any doubt as to where he wanted to go, and he was very aggressive, and he was going to get where he wanted to go." He drove things. He pushed Central into the big leagues. "Sure he spent lots of money, was flamboyant, spent half his life on airplanes, but that sort of thing did well for the system." It helped that member credit unions, and especially VanCity, were growing so fast, increasing the asset base, and indirectly generating money for Central so that May could spend it. The times were dynamic.

So far, so good, for May, but Bentley was resisting some of things he was doing. Bentley didn't like the liberties May was taking with the CFC. In theory, CFC was supposed to do mortgage lending where small credit unions had neither the capital nor the know-how to handle a big loan. CFC was also, however, lending in Greater Vancouver, VanCity's own market. Sometimes it did it in conjunction with VanCity's credit union competitors, like Richmond Savings and the North Shore Credit Union. In many of these cases, CFC was lending to the individuals buying the housing units themselves— the retail market—in addition to interim development loans.

May pretended that it was all healthy competition and that Bentley should not complain if Central gave a hand-up to Richmond and the North Shore, which were smaller than VanCity. Bentley was openly antagonistic. He didn't mind competition by other credit unions, banks, or insurance companies, regardless of size. However, Central competing against one of its own members, VanCity, and doing it indirectly with VanCity's own money (its mandatory share capital in Central), was wrong in principle, thought Bentley. He proposed a consortium of large credit unions for such projects if, in fact, individually, they couldn't manage them. Central was supposed to be a wholesale facility, serving its credit union members. It had no business being in retail lending. On one occasion, Central put out mortgage money one-quarter per cent below market, undercutting VanCity, which particularly offended Bentley.

There was skirmishing around VanCity's line of credit with Central. In some periods, Central had to cut back on its lines of credit to credit unions, because excess deposit money was scarce. VanCity's line of credit ended up far below what it should have been, based on its share capital in

Central. Bentley had the VanCity board instruct him to seek a line of credit with a bank, with its corollary, that VanCity would shift offsetting reserve deposits to the bank. Central's chief financial officer, Aj Gill, asked for a couple of days' reprieve and, in the upshot, more than doubled VanCity's credit line.

Bentley also negotiated interest rates with May and Gill, on both VanCity's line of credit and its reserve and surplus deposits. He was a tough negotiator. There was more to these superficially technical negotiations than met the eye. The biggest part of Central's operating budget came from its financial margins. The rates that Central paid, accordingly, were reflective of its internal costs, which were subsidizing the smaller credit unions. Bentley had done his own analysis and knew it was costing VanCity money to let Central manage VanCity's surplus funds compared with what VanCity, with its size, could do on its own elsewhere.

The more that Bentley received for VanCity from its Central deposits, on the other hand, the less money Central had to play with for its programs and ambitions. Bentley's toughness, particularly his implicit threat to shift reserve deposits to a bank if he was pushed, was seen by Central as politically motivated aggression—of wanting to keep money out of Central's development programs and to marginalize Central. For Bentley, the key element in the system was the individual credit union. Each one-half per cent off interest rates on VanCity's reserves held it back, and if VanCity was held back, the movement was held back. Besides, VanCity and its members should not be obliged to subsidize Central's bureaucracy.

Once, in a tight money situation, Central set an extra-high interest rate for drawing on a credit line over a certain limit. The break point was far below what VanCity's normal credit line should have been, leaving smaller credit unions unaffected. Bentley did not like VanCity being taken advantage of or its growth slowed down by a Central contrivance. It wasn't that he actually needed a credit draw above the break point. It was the rank discrimination of the arrangement that bothered him. He contacted Gill, and they had a quiet chat. VanCity's readiness to go elsewhere was the ultimate leverage. Gill buckled and reduced the supplementary rate by 3 per cent to a manageable level. Central felt humiliated. Anything that Bentley did was conveniently reinterpreted, through the prism of Central's ambitions, as against the credit union system. Each move or intimation by Bentley was relayed to the Central board, by May or Gill, as the latest event with VanCity. "Bentley was a big guy," Bob Hornal at Central thought of it, "and was making Central grovel a little bit."

The big battle, however, was over VanCity's common bond—what areas VanCity could expand to. May tried to contain Bentley, backed by the animus in the movement against VanCity. Bentley was determined he was not going to be hamstrung. He had patiently worked within the movement for the kind of change he wanted, and he had run out of patience.

It had begun with the idea of one big credit union for the province, in the late 1960s—an idea developed by Aj Gill, then manager of Lake View Credit Union in Dawson Creek. Bentley was one of the idea's original backers. A single, large credit union for the province had its attractions for Bentley. It would have sufficient size to face up to intense future competition by the banks. It would be organized as a branch system, governed by a province-wide representative board, although there would be local advisory boards to develop policy for local differences. All credit union locations, being branches, would carry the same name. The most attractive part of the idea, for Bentley, was that the one single credit union would be able to act quickly. The slow and cumbersome decision-making process of the League, full of political quagmires, would be avoided.

The idea was discussed at the League convention in 1968, in a policy session. It had considerable, although minority, support. The proposal, however, did not get to the floor. Bentley wasn't surprised. It struck him, however, that regional credit unions were an immediate possibility. He envisaged six such regions covering the province. Bentley and Geoff Hook, who was managing Central at the time, toured the province promoting the concept. It went nowhere. Bentley also opened merger talks with the Richmond, Surrey, Westminster and North Shore credit unions, for the Lower Mainland, but those talks broke down—predictably, Bentley thought, although at one point he had detected a faint glimmer of hope. After that, it was just a matter of deciding where VanCity would open its next branch. Bentley would build his regional credit union himself.

He wanted to move into North Burnaby. It would be the first new VanCity branch outside the city of Vancouver (West Vancouver having become part of VanCity through a merger). The one open-bond credit union in that half of the municipality, the North Burnaby Credit Union, was small and had a limited reach. Bentley by this time was arguing openly for the lifting of all restrictions, backed by board member Lloyd Widdifield, who had always wanted to open the gates. First, VanCity's common bond, still restricted to the city of Vancouver and to West Vancouver, had to be changed. The roadblock was the chief inspector of credit unions, George McCulloch, variously described by Widdifield as an idiot, an incompetent, a harmless duck, a hater of VanCity and vindictive. McCulloch was not very sophisticated. Whenever he had a problem, he went to Central to help sort things out, and George May and his cadres explained things to him, Central-style. McCulloch duly refused to change VanCity's bond.

McCulloch was also a pal of Reg Robinson, the manager of the South Burnaby Credit Union. Robinson was a credit union fundamentalist who, among other things, had bitterly opposed chequing accounts. He could barely stand to be in the same room with Bentley. VanCity, for him, represented betrayal—turning credit unions into pale imitations of banks—and Bentley was the false prophet. Robinson marshalled support against the infidel. He was livid over the VanCity move—"up like a bloody skyrocket over that thing," Dick Monrufet recalled.

Bentley and VanCity's board responded to McCulloch's foot-dragging by putting forward an extraordinary resolution to VanCity's annual general meeting in 1972. It would change VanCity's common bond to extend from Powell River on the coast eastward as far as Princeton in the Similkameen, south to the U.S. border, and taking in the Fraser Valley in between. The resolution passed 428 for to 89 against. McCulloch refused to file the resolution and returned VanCity's cheque. His refusal was academic. Bentley had located a site in North Burnaby, signed a lease for it, and was going ahead. Several credit unions sent letters objecting to VanCity's plans. The board decided not to bother even acknowledging them.

The North Burnaby branch opened late in February 1973, like a rogue outlaw. Almost immediately, the inspector sent in a posse to instruct staff only to accept members who either lived or worked in Vancouver or West Vancouver, but his position was untenable and the restriction soon went by the boards. The branch had a dramatic first ten months, running up $10 million in deposits. This was far and above anything done by other VanCity branches in their first year. If it had been a separate credit union, it would have instantaneously ranked as the twenty-sixth largest in the province.

May and Central now had to catch up to get control of the issue. They put forward what they called a "marketplace" approach, which would give members and potential members a choice. Credit unions could reach out to cover all those "whom they can conveniently serve." There was a hitch for VanCity, however. Credit unions would need the approval of the inspector to open an additional branch. The idea was to stop a large credit union, namely VanCity, from moving into a municipality that already had an open bond credit union, at least until that latter credit union covered its entire market with branches first. Bentley rejected this. He would not accept an outsider telling VanCity where it could go, least of all an inspector in Central's pocket.

The battle was intricate, complex and psychological. Hardly a week went by without May talking to Bentley on the phone or otherwise getting together with him. May and Bentley also had lunch about once a month. VanCity was too important to Central for May to ignore. May considered their meetings amicable and, in one sense, he was right. They did not go at each other's throat. They did, however, argue heatedly, disagreeing not only about co-operative philosophy but also about management style. Bentley, intelligent and experienced, would point out something illogical or constricting that Central was doing. May, smart and combative, fighting for Central, would riposte.

May, the more aggressive, would let his emotions show. He'd raise his voice. Bentley, despite his calm manner, would then feel justified in raising his voice himself. May liked to get his own way. If he didn't, he became upset, sometimes losing his temper. Bentley, more calm, would just back off. "I've had enough of this," he would say. "I don't want to have anything more to do with this situation." Then they would get back together later on.

Bentley was coming under increasing attack on the common bond issue. May had a scheme for reducing the number of credit unions in the province from just over two hundred to eighty, with Central as their nucleus and flag-carrier. The Lower Mainland would be neatly apportioned out, eliminating competition. VanCity would be limited to the areas it was already in. May took the argument out to the province.

Part of the argument was that, whatever arrangement was put in place, it should be the democratic decision of the movement together. May played on this theme. The credit union movement was democratic. If Bentley disagreed with what was happening, he should stand up on the convention floor. They could debate the issue back and forth, and the membership would decide. Bentley's failure, May shrugged, was simply that he was totally unsuccessful in being able to convince the majority of credit union delegates of VanCity's position.

May knew he was getting at Bentley's weak spot. Bentley was shy and uncomfortable in convention situations. Large meetings literally scared him. He was no match in that arena for May or Central's president, Rod Glen, who were natural convention performers. Bentley had always felt, anyway, that conventions were not a good vehicle for the dispassionate debate of issues in detail. They were highly charged, political and limited by time—often, expressions of politicking and talk that had occurred before the convention, and May politicked while Bentley was running VanCity in Vancouver.

May also knew that in one way Central conventions were not democratic at all: They did not reflect credit union membership. VanCity, despite the size of its membership, had only one vote. The same was true for the other large credit unions. The Nalley Valley Credit Union, with forty-three members in 1973, had the same vote as VanCity, with forty thousand. In his many arguments with May, Bentley on occasion would become so exasperated that he would lose his temper and threaten to pull out of Central. The refusal of Central to accept proportional voting—the small credit unions blithely holding VanCity hostage—was most often at the root of this threat. Bentley was adamant that the voting system had to change because it was so blatantly unfair.

Rod Glen was particularly outspoken. Glen was leader of the movement in Nanaimo and a major credit union figure continent-wide. He had once been president of CUNA, the American-based organization. He was feisty, political and a renowned orator, able to sway a crowd in minutes. He was also a savvy political operator. Once at a convention, when he needed a delay, he surreptitiously lit the tablecloth at his table with a lighter. In B.C. credit union politics he was "sort of like The Godfather," Aj Gill put it.

Glen argued that if the movement let larger credit unions like VanCity swallow up smaller ones, people would be left in the end with just one big credit union. Bentley, in this view, was not thinking in a co-operative way; he was a destroyer of credit union unity. Glen disagreed with Bentley about everything, almost as a matter of principle. "A big bag of gas," Lloyd Widdifield described him, unimpressed. Widdifield, as it happened, thought one big credit union was the best idea of all.

The feelings against VanCity at B.C. Central conventions by this time had become poisonous. Anti-VanCity delegates would gang up to humiliate VanCity on the convention floor. Ross Montgomery was VanCity's delegate to the B.C. Central convention in 1972. Montgomery met Glen at one of the early social functions and was immediately accused of being part of an organization that was out to destroy small credit unions. Others approached him to let him know that VanCity should be split up and that no credit union should have more than $20 million in assets. Only a handful of delegates, from credit unions like WestCoast Savings, Richmond Savings and Stry, showed any friendliness. The animosity was focussed on Bentley the person, as if he were a demonic figure.

Bentley wasn't at the 1972 convention. He had stopped going. Montgomery tried to convince him to attend. He argued that if unfriendly delegates actually heard what Bentley had to say, they would not be so antagonistic. Bentley shrugged. He had tried that before, going back to the old League days, and had given up. He had always preferred to do things at the personal level. He had swallowed enough of small-minded credit unions with few members casually disregarding VanCity's needs and holding back credit unionism in the name of credit unionism.

Glen disliked Bentley for another reason. Glen had been the leading force behind a supermarket and household supplies co-operative in Nanaimo, the Hub Co-op. He saw credit unions and other co-operative ventures as supporting each other. Bentley had his own co-operative background, but for him a credit union was a credit union. It was up to others to start co-operative ventures, and then the credit union could help them with a loan. That only upset Glen further. He castigated Bentley as a right-winger and an ultra-conservative. May labelled him the same way. VanCity's arguments were parochial and minuscule, May contended, compared with Central's mission of building a movement of tremendous size and influence. VanCity did not want to be "broad community." All Bentley was interested in was taking deposits and lending money.

The May and Glen camp were not the only ones who were critical. There was growing interest in Vancouver in using credit unions for larger social goals, particularly for housing and helping low-income people. Several VanCity members in the labour movement and in the New Democratic Party speculated about making an attempt to take VanCity over. Bentley, for them, seemed to be interested only in size. At the 1973 annual meeting, they made a concerted effort to put their position across. It disturbed Bentley. He handled them badly, showing no flexibility. He saw them as wanting to use VanCity for political purposes. A credit union board, he told May, who talked to him about it, had to be broadly representative and politically non-partisan.

Many of the larger credit unions, like Richmond and WestCoast in Victoria, on the other hand, sided with VanCity. They were becoming suspicious of May's manoeuvring for control and the threat to their autonomy. A motion at the 1974 Central convention to introduce proportional voting almost succeeded.

There was another front to the battle: the Model Bill. The Model Bill was draft legislation prepared by Central for the provincial government, to replace the old Credit Unions Act and give credit unions a greater field of action. Central, in the Model Bill, tried shoring up its position against VanCity. When VanCity's input was ignored, Bentley wrote Central politely that, since there were major points of difference, VanCity would be making its own direct presentation to the attorney general. This set feathers flying.

As long as B.C. Central officially represented the movement, however, it still looked like May had Bentley stymied. Bentley, though, wasn't finished. He retained a separate lawyer to look into the possibilities of VanCity re-incorporating as something other than a credit union, perhaps as a co-operative savings and loan association. It would give him a fallback position. He talked to May about it at one of their lunches, asking him for his views. It was a good way of getting the word out that VanCity would not be trifled with: it was actually prepared to leave the movement if it was hemmed in. This caused further outrage. May warned Bentley that a move like that would invite a takeover by upset members. He nevertheless could not afford to take Bentley's manoeuvre lightly. To Bentley's detractors, it confirmed the worst. Some of them began pushing to take the initiative and kick VanCity out of Central first. May worked hard to keep such resolutions off the convention floor.

Bentley was leading a double life. On the surface, dealing with May and Gill, he was full of sang-froid. Underneath this surface, however, he was intense and churning. He took things to heart; he had strong feelings that sometimes broke through. "Low-level emotion," Gill described it. The battle against Central consumed Bentley. He was getting headaches as well as suffering from his bad stomach, and chewing aspirins for the headaches, which didn't make his stomach any better. He blacked out at a Canucks hockey game he had attended with Ron Spooner and was taken to hospital in an ambulance. The fainting spell was traced to a defective heart valve, and corrective surgery was scheduled. Those closest to him, however— including Gill, who was a longtime friend—were convinced that the pressure from the feud with Central had contributed to the incident. He was constantly fighting against his fatigue—he had been fighting it, he realized, for quite a while. Dick Monrufet used to drop by and say hello. "Dick, I'm so tired," Bentley once told him. "I'm always tired." Ethel Bentley developed a passionate hatred of Central. Don had been so unselfish and done so much for the movement, was such a true co-operator, had continually led the way—had even given the movement Plan 24—and in return they were cheaply maligning him.

Wayne McKay picked up the same signals. Bentley, loosening up after a few drinks at restaurant gab sessions with his lieutenants, would hold forth passionately into the night about the Central menace. Teetotaller McKay didn't know what to make of it. The boss's condemnation seemed too overblown, his description of Central's stupidities too charged, or perhaps Bentley had quaffed one Gibson too many. It seemed, in those moments, that Bentley was pursuing a vendetta against Central. McKay, listening, would think to himself, "Let's give it up and forget Central, they're not that much of a factor, let's just get on with VanCity and not let it eat away at us." When he sat down with Bentley in the cold light of day, however, and Bentley rationally, step by step, analysed the implications of what Central was doing, McKay could not answer back. Bentley, it seemed to him then, was right.

What disturbed Bentley most about the George May model was that it would become hopelessly bureaucratic and beyond the credit unions' control. Once that bureaucracy was built up, credit union members would never get rid of it. It would be extraordinarily expensive. It would not be successful. If a credit union developed its own expertise, those people would speak directly to each other and be focussed on serving the credit union's members. If they were in Central, they would become entities unto themselves, outside a credit union's reach, removed from members and without the edge of responsiveness that VanCity's people had.

The tension between May and Bentley filtered down into the ranks. Wayne McKay found the undertow at the meetings between the two so excruciating that he avoided them whenever he could. He knew that Bentley did not like conflict and, more painful, did not know how to handle conflict. He hated to see the boss in these demeaning situations—actually having to deal with May and Gill, whom he regarded as shysters and scoundrels. McKay, as comptroller, had his own guerrilla war with Central, over particulars in their operating relationship where he felt VanCity was unfairly losing dollars. As far as McKay was concerned, anyone involved with Central was suspect. "He thought Don Bentley could do no wrong," Mike Borch at CDS described it. "If Don Bentley came back from a meeting and said he was pissed off with Central, then Wayne McKay was automatically mad at Central and everybody who worked at Central."

Lloyd Widdifield was particularly scornful of Central. He regarded it as a group of spendthrift parasites who didn't have to be efficient, living off VanCity's and other credit unions' money. As for the politics of the feud, on the other hand, Widdifield was blasé. The current fight was just business as usual, in his mind. Not so for Bentley, though, he thought. The image of Bentley as anti-Central was all wrong. Whatever Bentley had to do for VanCity, he was still loyal to what Central was supposed to stand for. The confrontation really distressed him. Central had been his organization.

In the Central camp, the cadres feared Bentley. He was a credit-union Darth Vader—an outlander with such powers that he cast a shadowy presence on their own office. One of the first things Bob Hornal learned, when he started at Central in 1972, he recalled, was that Bentley was a bad man.

May continued to resent VanCity. He could not stomach its cast of mind. VanCity seemed to think the world revolved around it and that Central was only an adjunct. The credit union movement was much more than a single credit union, he kept arguing. It was national, international. However much he worked at expanding Central, though, and dreamed his dreams, the B.C. credit union world did revolve around VanCity. VanCity's force of example drove the movement. May also read the figures. Although all credit unions were growing fast, with Central able to build on that, VanCity was growing faster. In 1970, when May became chief executive officer of Central, VanCity, measured by assets, represented one-eleventh of the B.C. credit union movement. By 1973, it was one-sixth of the movement and five times as large as it had been at the beginning of the period. VanCity was growing ever more powerful as May watched.

May could have tolerated all this, and the opening of VanCity's North Burnaby branch as well. He had a long journey yet, and there was plenty of time. He would have remained confident, had it not been for Bentley's decision to leave CDS, Central's computer subsidiary. That stung him. Although computer use was in its early days, May knew that the core element in banking was the processing of information and that to be master of that activity was, in a sense, to be at the centre of everything—a Central not occupied with political structure but with the ordering of data. Mastery of data also meant mastery of product. Product wouldn't survive in the oncoming computer age without a computer program to handle it and a computer system to ingest and record its transactions.

May had asked Ted Cotter and Mike Borch to extend CDS service to credit unions across the province as quickly as possible. They converted Kelowna, Penticton and Prince Rupert, and kept on going, expanding phenomenally and holding other credit unions at bay, as they tried to catch up at each stage. It was exhilarating and nightmarish at the same time. The amount of paper being pumped out was mounting crazily; CDS was barely chugging through it every night. Cotter and Borch, exhausted, were working extraordinary hours and were gradually being worn down. Every time they wanted to take a rest, they had more credit unions coming through the door.

To make matters worse, Wayne McKay was constantly on their case. He had never agreed with the decision by the original CDS consortium, including Bentley himself, to hand over the system to Central. He had argued that the members of the consortium would lose the advantage of control. He had understood nevertheless that, after the changeover, CDS would at least restrict itself to the Lower Mainland until the key programs were perfected. CDS's main focus now, however, was extending its reach. "No question," Mike Borch recounted frankly. "It was one of choice." Improvements in

service to VanCity and the other Lower Mainland credit unions, and program enhancements, would have to wait.

The CDS batch system inevitably began to deteriorate. With so many
credit unions patched on, errors cropped up more frequently. Worse, CDS
could not seem to correct them promptly. An operator might accidently
punch in the wrong date or the wrong month, which would throw all the
calculations off. Ledgers didn't balance to the general ledger. Printouts
weren't always arriving at credit unions on time and were sometimes being
sent to wrong locations. At the peak, CDS had three input-output clerks
doing nothing but distributing paper coming in and going out. Inevitably
they wouldn't always put the printouts in the right slot. Silly operating
mistakes, so that work had to be repeated, meant late deliveries. The system
was so stretched and rigid that it looked as if it would fall apart at any
moment.

Borch was unapologetic and defiant. Sure, reports were occasionally late,
but occasionally your television set doesn't work, he said. Sure, there were
some mistakes, but that was par for the course; dealing with mistakes and
refining the process was inherent in the development of new technology. In
any case, the integrity of VanCity's data was never at risk. That was the main
thing. CDS worked well. Nobody left. New credit unions were clamouring to
get in. Many had visited VanCity to see how the system worked. That was the
real measure.

McKay, however, did not relent. Borch was missing the point. VanCity's
volume was doubling and doubling again. Its people could not take the
time to deal with problems or inconvenience caused by the system. McKay's
relationship with Borch and Cotter became unglued. Cotter became emotional under pressure, which didn't help. McKay made remarks to him that
he found difficult to understand, as if McKay had forgotten what he was
really like and had replaced him, in his mind, with another Ted Cotter.
"Somehow," Cotter recounted, "we became non-friends."

Most frustrating for McKay and Bentley was that VanCity had no priority
in CDS to change products or introduce new ones. Its ability to innovate was
put in a straitjacket. McKay had warned about this. In 1970, he had done a
review of computer technology and data processing. He had recommended
staying with CDS, but added that VanCity would have to work hard to
keep CDS from becoming another League or Ted Cotter empire. "Another
League" was Bentley language. It meant an organization captive to politics,
in which VanCity's priorities would be disregarded. This is what happened.
McKay, sitting on a restructured users' committee, was now one of a large
crowd. He couldn't get at the source of problems directly. His opinions and
views ended up diluted by the group. The Lower Mainland credit unions, at
these meetings, fought the credit unions from elsewhere—a war within a
war. CDS tried balancing the demands of the two groups. "VanCity was
never, ever happy with that, ever," Borch said, exasperated. He and McKay
were having running battles.

Bentley, listening to McKay about what was happening, realized that data processing was not just a technical service. It was part and parcel of an organization's freedom of action. VanCity had to regain some measure of control in order to protect its own destiny. Other things also concerned him. CDS might become unionized (it eventually did), in which case a CDS strike would bring VanCity to a halt, although VanCity itself would not be on strike. Moreover, if VanCity ever was forced to break loose from Central, because of Central's politics, it could summarily be kicked out of CDS and be left high and dry.

In August 1973, Bentley and the board decided to make their move. They voted for an in-house computer—a radical departure for a mid-sized organization at that stage of technology. Bentley submitted an offer to Central to buy a copy of the CDS programs at market value—$27,000. May was rattled. He bluntly rejected the offer. They exchanged correspondence on the matter. Bentley's letter was laced with polite irony. If VanCity went ahead, it would be foolish to force it to spend large amounts of money to write computer programs that already existed. Besides, VanCity was the base on which CDS had been built; it had carried the major share of the cost and provided the best part of the expertise on the credit union side. VanCity members had already paid to develop the programs. He himself had been president of CDS, and it was on his recommendation that CDS was turned over to Central at no charge. The loss of VanCity as a client, moreover, would result in only a momentary slowdown in growth for CDS. It would actually help CDS by giving it respite, so it could do the job it wanted to do for the remaining participants. Central, in fact, if it wanted to provide leadership, should expand its role to provide assistance and research for credit unions that, because of their size, wanted to establish their own computer facility.

May understood the ironies. He was being calculating, whereas Bentley, with Plan 24 and CDS, had been generous. There was nothing inherent in data processing, either, that philosophically, as co-operators, required them to stay together. Only six years earlier, they had all been completely separate, with their own ledger cards. He nevertheless still had to resist. He was fixated on the idea of a "centralized data processing facility" that, like a ganglion with its fibres reaching out, would tie every credit union to the centre. He needed it for the image of what he wanted to do with Central. If VanCity left, Richmond and Surrey would not be far behind. WestCoast in Victoria was exploring alternatives. As these parts broke off, albeit just in data processing, his Central would be politically diminished.

His only recourse was to make CDS more adaptable. He formed a management task force to work on CDS. The key strategic objective was a "real-time" on-line system, where transactions would be instantaneously entered into the database and where tellers would have immediate access to the details of an account. This would get rid of the paper. There was a larger reason for the strategy. The banks had begun to pour money into the research and development of such systems. They hadn't made much progress, but if they succeeded, they would leave CDS behind. Cotter realized he had to go to on-line and tried using that to hang onto Bentley. He sent Bentley an outline of the steps he had already taken and invited VanCity to be the pilot credit union, working closely with him. Staff had been hired. Research and specification phases were underway. He expected the real-time service up and running by the end of 1974.

Bentley was also moving. He retained the head of the computer science department at the University of British Columbia, Al Fowler, as a consultant, to give VanCity independent technical expertise. Fowler did an analysis of CDS and deemed them hopelessly behind the times. VanCity, he reported, couldn't expect an on-line system from them. Cotter was furious. Fowler's report was garbage, he said. "Fowler was a man of letters who didn't know anything about the real world," Cotter said. "Those of us in the know had no respect for him or his report. Bentley spent a lot of money hiring somebody who didn't know anything."

Meanwhile, Cotter's on-line development program, despite its impressive facade, was flagging. The technical expert he had hired to lead the CDS team was producing wonderful manuals but not any programming that would actually do something. Time and money were simply being wasted.

May, too, was helpless and frustrated. Data processing was too technical and complex. Management by objectives did not work here. Nothing he had learned about management applied. Perhaps it would be different if he had large amounts of money to throw at the problem, like the banks, but he also knew that data processing was one area where one could expend a lot of money and still not make progress. He wished he could push a button and technically fix the situation. He wondered whether he had the right people for the CDS job, but without a great deal of money, how could he establish the leadership he wanted, and even with money, how could he be sure? So he didn't do anything. It wasn't worth the risk.

In the summer of 1974, VanCity signed a contract with a small Toronto computer company, Geac, to install an in-house, on-line computer system for the credit union. That meant, finally, leaving CDS. Cotter was bitter and angry. He and Bentley had been close. As manager and president of CDS respectively, they had created the computer company together. Cotter treated VanCity's decision to leave as a personal abandonment of himself by Bentley.

May was shaken by the threat to Central's credibility that the move represented. Bruce Higgs was a Central middle manager at the time. It was a power struggle, Higgs described it, simply, and the VanCity decision eroded May's power base. "Certain personnel at Central thought it would lead to the downfall of western civilization," he quipped.

When May was disturbed about something, he went on the offensive. He sent an acrimonious letter to VanCity on the matter, although the decision had already been made. The letter had nasty overtones. It was archly worded and carefully controlled. Nevertheless, in so many words it managed to accuse Bentley of betraying the movement, spinelessness, lack of character and financial folly. It predicted ignominious failure with this "unknown computer company given to phenomenal ... claims." It warned Bentley not to blame CDS if, during the conversion, Geac did not produce.

Despite its careful wording the letter was self-indulgent—a mistake Bentley never would have made. VanCity's decision to leave CDS, on the surface an accounting matter, became a powerful psychic ingredient in the VanCity-Central feud. Bentley always tried to keep emotion out of decision-making. At one point, the VanCity board, enraged by Central, wanted to cut any dealings with it to a minimum, starting with the cancellation of a marketing research project. Bentley talked them out of it. He argued they should continue to use Central on a strictly business basis. Letting feelings interfere with the best business decision for VanCity's members would have been, for Bentley, a capitulation.

May then took a critical misstep. He and Central reopened the common-bond issue after most people thought it had been decided. He issued a circular questioning the very concept of open common bonds. VanCity wasn't named, but it was quite clear whom Central had in mind. The document, circulated to all credit unions, was a last, desperate attempt to stop VanCity. It accused VanCity of wanting to "steal" business from other credit unions. It referred to self-destructive, costly, inter-credit union competition and other evils and dangers. It did not, however, substantiate the charges. May then took a jab at Bentley himself. The reason for the destructive competition, the document said, "appears to be more centred around the individual ambitions of certain key personnel as opposed to having considered the co-operative nature of the movement."

Bentley was angered and hurt by the circular. The document was so unbridled, wild and personal that at first he didn't know what to do with it. He realized it would generate yet more bitterness and misunderstanding among credit unions. He consulted Sandra Sutherland, a new VanCity director who was a lawyer, about strategy. The more he mulled over the document, the more it grated on him. For several days, his fretting immobilized him. Then Sutherland and a few others stepped in to help him formulate a reply. He ended up drafting a closely argued rebuke, which went out over Stan Parsons's signature as president.

May's attack on Bentley only proved Bentley's point. If he stayed with CDS, VanCity would suffer critical damage, and if VanCity was damaged, the whole credit union movement would be set back. The more May had fought the VanCity move, the more he had convinced Bentley how dangerous and ego-driven he and B.C. Central were. May could inveigh against him, but he had his own choices to make.

CHAPTER 27

VanCity Meets GEAC

WAYNE MCKAY WAS IN THE office of the Geac Computer Corporation in Toronto, meeting the company's people. He and his wife, Carol, had spent the weekend being shown the sights of the city by Geac's salesman, Geoff Treseder, and his girlfriend. Now Treseder introduced him to Geac's president, Bob Isserstedt. The two Geac executives began explaining their system to McKay. Geac was a small company, with only twenty-four employees. Its offices were spartan, devoid of pictures and other decorations. There was little furniture. It looked to McKay like the executives were running a tight ship, and this impressed him.

From time to time other people wandered in to say hello. One, Gus German, had a pencil behind his ear. He looked like a carpenter. He was jolly and animated. McKay did not talk to him for long. Isserstedt and Treseder seemed to be trying to shoo him back into his office. Only later that day did McKay learn that German was one of Geac's two owners and its main figure. And only some time after that did he realize that the strategy, on that occasion, was to keep German away and leave the customer in the hands of the more polished, sales-oriented Treseder and Isserstedt. They didn't want to let German loose with the customer for too long. It was a curious incident, but everything about computers, for McKay, was a curiosity.

He hadn't been quite thirty when he became VanCity comptroller in 1971 and set up shop in the basement of the Victoria Drive branch. As comptroller, he sat at the centre of the information flow in VanCity. He felt centuries removed from the years not too long before when he had started out in banking in Killarney and Sioux Lookout. He was part of the dawning computer age. Computers broke the mould of banking as a function of clerks.

He had been chair of the original CDS users' group, spending as much as 60 per cent of his time on computer-related issues, even while managing the East Hastings branch. In VanCity's branches, now, the Burroughs and other accounting machines, with their thump and clunk, were gone. So were the ledger cards. They were just gone, as if some burglar had lifted all of a family's cherished heirlooms. The transition had been a cultural revolution. The absence of ledger cards in the VanCity branch took some getting used to.

McKay, Ted Cotter and Mike Borch at CDS had gone through a lot in the two hectic, intensely productive years when he had chaired the users' group. They were a dedicated bunch. There had been a good spirit among them. It seemed to McKay, when he looked back, that together they had moved mountains to accomplish what they did. The CDS batch system was a wonder.

He had then watched unhappily as the CDS batch system itself became a problem. He admired Ted Cotter and knew, from working closely with him, how conscientious he was. He didn't like getting after Cotter and Borch, but he felt he had no other choice. He had to be aggressive. The amount of paper CDS was going through for VanCity alone was discouraging, and it was relentlessly growing larger and taking more time to pump out. After a while, leaving CDS became inevitable.

The alternatives weren't promising. An on-line system, which would do away with paper, was the most desirable option. The technology of communicating with a database through a telephone line, using a video terminal, already existed and was being used in the scientific community. Business applications, however, were at the infant stage and were few and far between—largely airline reservation systems. All the large computer companies—IBM, Honeywell, NCR and Burroughs—had already been to VanCity with presentations. Their proposed systems were much too expensive—costing in the millions of dollars—and too far off in the future. They had nothing in place to actually look at. Some wanted big money just to do proposals for VanCity. CDS itself made a presentation but, like the others, it could only talk about an on-line system.

The caisses populaires in Quebec, and some of the banks for savings accounts, had so-called "on-line" systems, but they were sorely limited. Because of a shortage of memory, they contained only account balances and other barebones information like names and account numbers. A teller could process a withdrawal against a balance, or enter a deposit, but that was all. The transactions then had to be reprocessed overnight, this time in the main database on magnetic tapes—in a batch format—just like before. The tellers' terminals, too, were simply teletype-style printers, printing the front-end transactions on sheets of paper for passbooks. For other account details, tellers had to go back to the stacks of paper produced overnight.

McKay by this time had been scouting alternatives for over a year, on top of his comptroller duties. He was working himself into the ground, barely able to keep going. He hired a programmer, Mike McMullen, as computer co-ordinator, to give him a hand. Then, one day, Bentley got a call from Moffat Goepel. Goepel, the comptroller at Dairyland, had been on VanCity's board in the early 1960s. His data processing manager had read in a trade journal about an on-line order entry system at Donlands Dairy, and the two of them had gone to see it. It had been installed by a company called Geac. Goepel had asked Geac whether it could do the same for Dairyland, but Geac could not see its way to sending a team to Vancouver without a second, larger customer in hand to make it worthwhile. Goepel knew Bentley was looking for an on-line system, and immediately thought of VanCity.

Nobody had heard of Geac. Fowler did not know the name. Yet the company's Donlands installation sounded interesting. McKay, at Bentley's request, made a short reconnaissance trip to Toronto—the original visit— and then headed back a second time, with McMullen in tow.

On this second trip, McKay fully realized what VanCity had stumbled across. The encounter was full of surprises. What passed for the Geac boardroom had sliding glass doors that gave out onto a boardwalk on the ledge of the roof surrounding the top-floor office. Inside, McKay and McMullen met with Treseder. Outside, two men walked by on the board- walk, pacing, gesticulating and looking as if they might fall off the edge and plunge to their deaths. McKay inquired as to what those people were doing. He was told they were part of Geac's senior management group, having a discussion. McKay recognized Gus German. The other, whom he hadn't met, was Mike Sweet. They appeared and disappeared again, still pacing and talking. This went on for the course of the meeting. McKay found it hard to concentrate. McMullen wondered if it had been staged as part of their introduction to Geac—two gurus on the edge of the roof, eccentric like Albert Einstein. In fact, Sweet, whom German thought of as the wild man from Wales, had blown up over something, and German had taken him for a stroll on the boardwalk to talk things out and calm him down.

McKay was impressed with Bob Isserstedt, but wasn't sure about the other owner—Geac's technical chief, the flakey-looking fat guy, German—who had been out on the roof. He wondered how such a well-turned out and affable businessman like Isserstedt had got stuck with a bumbler like Ger- man in the first place. He managed, however, to spend a little time talking to German, Sweet and the youngster, Don Bagshaw. There was something adventuresome about German that appealed to McKay. German's oddball character, instead of frightening him, matched his own hankering for the unconventional. Other computer companies that he had dealt with had a very professional, buttoned-down style that approached the mundane. Some were condescending. This was the first time he had seen a genuinely creative group, although they were somewhat off the wall. It was clear that Geac had technical brilliance. Looking at the Donlands operation, he found it easy to visualize that where he saw a Donlands order taker there would be a VanCity teller.

He returned to his hotel room in a state of suppressed excitement. He telephoned Bentley and told him they had finally found what they were looking for. The application, McKay said, would take VanCity into the next century. They were the right people, even though they hadn't done any- thing yet for a financial institution. He felt in a state of grace. He had been suddenly rewarded after searching fruitlessly for two years, like searching for the Holy Grail.

German was also elated. This stranger, showing up out of the blue from Vancouver, was an exciting omen. In talking with McKay, he had sensed the size of the problem VanCity was facing. This doubly excited him. A large and seemingly intractable data-processing problem was, for German, like a banquet for a gourmand. He was already beginning to work out in his mind how he would solve it. It would be a cinch, he thought. School boards' data processing was complicated. They had thousands of kids for time-table synchronization, oddities like budget encumbrances, endless inventory itemization, and payrolls with phenomenal complexities. Even Donlands Dairy, with its various products, had inherent complexities. With VanCity, by contrast, the inventory was just money. It didn't seem that hard.

A contract with these people in Vancouver would also bring in much more cash for Geac and give German the freedom to do new things. It would mean more than just the one job. It had the potential of being a stepping stone to the huge banking and trust company market. A breakthrough in that market would be a bonanza for Geac and turn it into a major company. As it was, Geac, despite several contracts, was dead broke and German was close to civil war with his partner Isserstedt. Once, he took after Isserstedt with his fists. He was enraged at the way Isserstedt spent money and negotiated poor deals at the cost of the technical side, which was what really constituted Geac. Some contracts were punishing. One minor installation, providing negligible revenue, required Geac to be on the spot within a few hours of any breakdown, and it was in an out-of-the-way place. Isserstedt had to make an arrangement with the dry cleaner next door to cover such incidents. The dry cleaner was to don white coveralls supplied by Geac, walk over to the installation, and nod his head, meeting the terms of the contract while giving German or another member of his technical team more time to get to the location. With revenue from VanCity, on the other hand, German could take on the world.

Geac was invited to make a presentation. Two other contenders, one a batch processor, had preceded them. German came to Vancouver two days early, to learn more about VanCity and take a look at its branches. He could not stand the pressure of presentations. He did not have the slick skills required. He knew his mind might jump around. He never had anything written down to keep him on track, because he was unable to write things down. He had to resort to speaking off the cuff. The buildup of tension and worry was enormous. He had great difficulty getting to sleep in such situations, although he usually managed to drop off eventually. In order to bolster his courage, he would take a few drinks, or more than a few drinks.

By the night before the presentation to VanCity, he had managed a long head start. Geac, including Isserstedt and Treseder, had invited McKay and McMullen to the hotel bar to chat about the presentation the following day. McMullen had already arrived. Unfortunately, McMullen was sceptical about Geac. German, inebriated, was finding him extraordinarily obstinate. He took a growing dislike to him. At one point, he grabbed McMullen by the shirt and tapped him over the head with an ashtray. It wasn't a hard hit, but it was enough that he noticed. Isserstedt, who knew McKay was on his way, hurried German to his room. He didn't want McKay to see German drunk.

Isserstedt was now worried about the presentation. Having seen German on benders before, he doubted he would get him to the meeting the next morning. McKay's reaction was that German had better be there or they could pack their bags, go back to Toronto, and forget about VanCity. McKay, whose heart was set on Geac, was furious with German. Unfortunately for Isserstedt, there was a large bottle of rye in German's room, which didn't survive the night.

At seven o'clock the next morning, McKay received a call from Treseder saying German wasn't going to make it. McKay repeated his message. Isserstedt, desperate, went to work on German like a member of a pit crew. He pulled him out of bed, got him into the shower, somehow managed to have him shave, and poured him into a suit. German arrived at the meeting in terrible shape. He was wearing his usual plaid outfit, saved for such occasions. The VanCity committee was waiting for him, looking, in German's groggy eyes, like a circle of buzzards. It included McKay, McMullen, consultant Fowler, auditor Walter Dyck, branch managers Jan Chapman and Garry Smith, and John Smith, the accountant from McKay's office. Bentley was out of town.

Isserstedt said a few words. German shuffled forward to make his presentation. He was nervous. There was a chalk board in the room. He picked up a piece of chalk and began talking and drawing, the sweat gathering on his face. "Mad squiggles," he called his sketches. McKay knew that German's vision for the system was so technically novel and forward that it was sometimes hard to grasp the context of what he was saying. His ideas were overwhelming. For this audience, however, German reduced the concept to its essentials so that everybody could understand. Soon he had them captivated. He began with the basics, to clear the air—how many calculations a machine could do in a second, and what that worked out to per teller station. Looked at that way, the feat of creating an on-line system did not seem so forbidding. He explained how the data would flow from tellers in different branches, in turns, through to the central processing unit and from there to the storage disks, and how, also, the data would be pulled up by tellers on their monitors when they were serving members. He sketched out the other elements. His hair, which in younger years had been red, was grey now—had been grey, ironically, since Geac began. His jacket became covered with chalk. He was the proverbial brilliant professor, holding his class in thrall.

Fowler, the high-powered academic, began asking questions. Treseder, who had met Fowler on an earlier visit and argued with him, had warned German about him. Fowler, he said, had claimed that what Geac was proposing just couldn't be done. German hadn't been worried. "I've got him pegged," he had told Treseder. "I know where he's coming from." As soon as Fowler, now sitting in front of him, opened his mouth, German knew that he would not have a problem. At the end of the presentation, totally exhausted, he slumped into a chair.

It had been a bravura performance. The concept German had outlined was so much more enlightened and advanced than anything else the group had heard that there was no contest. Jan Chapman, recounting the event years later, remembered how excited she was. "They were miles ahead," she said. Except for McMullen, there wasn't a person in the room who had any doubt that German could do what he had described. McKay, with a bit of arm-twisting, brought McMullen on side as well. German had little recall of the morning. "Apparently," he said, "I redeemed myself."

McKay had earlier heard reports of German's drinking, but the hotel incident was the first time he had been faced with it up close. He decided, nevertheless, not to tell Bentley about it. He did not want to worry Bentley unnecessarily, especially with Bentley not long out of his heart-valve surgery. He knew there was a risk involved, but, thinking it over, he felt sure he could get German to perform when it mattered. He could not bear the idea of turning Geac aside.

The board then agonized over the proposal. Al Fowler's observations now became important. German was a revelation for Fowler. They met subsequent to the presentation and were soon deep in technical talk. Geac's scheme was as unclassical a proposal as Fowler could imagine. He quickly realized how far ahead of IBM and everybody else German was. "I wasn't in Gus's league at all," he recounted later. "Gus was a much brighter person than I was." His most vivid memory of German was drinking beer with him in his hotel room, talking computers, while German, who wasn't feeling well, kept putting a thermometer in his mouth, trying to decide whether he was sick. Fowler was also impressed by German's practicality. Most good computer scientists were theoretical, but German wanted to take the theory and change the world with it. Whenever Fowler asked German if his system would do something, he invariably found that German was several steps ahead of him.

Fowler never did present the board with a systematic technical analysis of the Geac proposal. He couldn't see the point of trying to second-guess German on technical matters; German knew so much more than he did. His qualified recommendation was based simply on his reading of Gus German and of German's ability to do things. Everything depended on German and Sweet not being run over by a bus. Their proposed system was technologically a quantum leap, and much more modern, too, than anything one could get elsewhere. The key hardware peripherals, like the disk controllers, were also of Geac's devising. Both hardware and software could fail. One would need a tremendous amount of insight to make sure they both worked, but Fowler was quite sure German had that insight. "One just had to put one's faith in a genius such as Gus was," he reflected.

Geac had something else in its favour: its novel financial approach. Geac promised to develop and install the system on its own hook, and then, when it was operating, charge VanCity 50 cents per member per month. No VanCity investment would be required. If Geac failed, it, not VanCity, would take the blow, although VanCity would then have to scramble to find a batch-system replacement. The Geac system would also be extraordinarily cheap for the kind of sophisticated on-line service provided. It would cost no more than CDS's batch system and virtually half of what CDS was projecting for on-line charges. It was the least expensive of the options rather than the most expensive. For five years, Geac would manage the facility. In that period, VanCity would have exclusive credit union rights. Marketing to other credit unions would be through VanCity, with a royalty to VanCity assumed. If Geac, which had a propensity for living dangerously, went bankrupt, the hardware and software in the facility would become VanCity's property, as it would, also, at the end of the five-year contract.

For somebody like German, who wasn't supposed to have a business sense, the assurance this arrangement gave the customer was a brilliant business idea. German knew that Geac, not being an IBM, had to offer such terms in order to make sales. The approach also said much about German's extraordinary confidence in his technical abilities. He hated phoney, pasted-up technological companies. He liked the idea of taking money only when he had actually given the customer what had been promised.

McKay was feisty. "Many in the industry will hope we fall flat on our faces," he wrote in his own report. "I am prepared to face the consequences if Geac bombs out. The easy thing to do is to stay with CDS. However, I don't expect the development to fail. I think we will have a system that is second to none, and the world will beat a path to our door. I will then sit back and thumb my nose at the critics and skeptics."

Whatever the board's thoughts, the decision to go ahead was really Bentley's. "If you are prepared to live just a bit dangerously in the expectation that the gains will be great, then choose Geac," Fowler wrote. Bentley took the leap. "I'm going to bite the bullet," he told Ethel. "I'm going to take a lot of guff about it, but I'm going to do it." The board, which had developed a taste for innovation, backed him. "When I look back," McKay said later, of the board, "that group was a really courageous lot."

Bentley deserved a lot of credit, Fowler thought. Not going with IBM took guts. The contract was ultimately settled in the revolving restaurant on top of the Sheraton Landmark Hotel on Robson Street. The restaurant bill, calculated German, always interested in machinery, cost roughly $100 per revolution.

When VanCity's decision was finally made, McKay and McMullen met with Bentley in his office. "You guys ... " Bentley said, "you'd better be right."

CHAPTER 28

The Secretary

MARINA LOWE, WAYNE MCKAY'S SECRETARY, was terrified. She had just moved into the new head office space along with McKay, above the parking lot at the main branch. Until then, she and comptroller McKay had worked out of a basement office at Victoria Drive. Lowe would now be on the same floor as Laura Smalley, Don Bentley's secretary, and she wondered what she might be in for. It wasn't that Lowe was inept. She was, in fact, a superbly efficient performer. Besides, she worked for McKay, not Smalley. Smalley, however, had a reputation for toughness that went beyond her own doors. Lowe, who was a bit shy, was wary.

As it turned out, Lowe need not have worried. She enjoyed Smalley. They got along well. Smalley, she found, might be tough on the outside, but was soft on the inside. Lowe also found, however, that once Smalley's mind was set on something, she became very determined. Smalley was more than just a tough secretary. She had spunk. She had made herself a presence by her forcefulness, and she had Don Bentley's ear.

Smalley had arrived at VanCity in a roundabout way. She grew up on a farm near St. Paul, Alberta. French was her first language. Northeastern Alberta, where St. Paul was located, was part of the French-Catholic northern belt across Canada, from Ontario to Alberta, where rural Quebecers without prospects at home were encouraged by the church to settle. Her maiden name was La Boucane. She had dropped out of high school before graduating, during the war, and joined the army, working in the motor pool in Red Deer. After the war, she went to business school in Edmonton, through the army's vocational training program. Her first postwar job was in Fort Nelson, but it was too cold. She ended up at the Fishermen's Co-operative Federation in Vancouver, first as a receptionist, then as a key-punch operator, using an IBM key-punch machine. She loved the machine.

Don Bentley had been her boss. When Bentley, in January 1960, learned that she was no longer working, he asked if she would come in to operate the Burroughs electronic accounting machine that was about to be acquired. The machine, for posting on ledger cards, was the latest in banking technology. Smalley needed the money and agreed to help out, but only until the summer, because she wanted the summer off. She stayed for twenty-eight years.

Smalley and the machines she worked with had a rhythmic resonance to them, as if they were part of a single body—her rhythm timed to the workings of the machine. At the end of every month, she stuck the cards for each kind of account into the reader and totalled up the balances. These balances were supposed to agree with aggregate figures in the general ledger (the running balances, from tellers' totals, carried forward from day to day). Uncannily, when Smalley did the posting, they always agreed. If there was a difference, she knew instinctively that one or more of the ledger cards had been missing. She would search the branch looking for the absent cards. She would find them, and they always were the difference.

After a couple of years, she began to ask about doing other things. She wanted to learn about the credit union's operations. Ray Evelle showed her the ropes. He taught her how to open accounts, sell term deposits, and take mortgage and other loan applications. He was still a young kid then and she was almost forty years old, but he was patient. She appreciated his openness and solidarity, and admired his quick mind. They became close friends. The two of them ruled behind the counter at the main branch at Broadway and Quebec. Bentley was there, too, in the partitioned office.

The members at the main branch were the original VanCity people. There were only eight thousand members altogether, at the two existing branches, when Smalley arrived. They were a friendly group. Smalley, like the others working in the branch, did not have to be asked to be friendly in return. They enjoyed what they did. Smalley knew most of the members by name. It helped to have seen the names so often when she had worked with ledger cards on the bookkeeping machine. It was as if she knew them in a more intimate way.

Smalley was a force in the office. She was opinionated and demanding. She had high standards. Young Wayne McKay thought of her as an office sergeant major. He vividly remembered an early run-in he had with her. It was his very first day at VanCity. He had failed to update a member's passbook, because the member hadn't presented it to him. Nobody had told him that he should ask for it. Smalley, who ended up doing the task, came back to where he was and straightened him out. "Who is this?" McKay asked himself. "Why is she yelling at me?" He was a bit alarmed at what he had gotten himself into. Banking was much more respectful.

He decided he would not become negative and critical, but would smother Smalley with kindness. He would demonstrate how capable and efficient he could be. One of Smalley's routines was to look at sample term deposit ledgers to check calculations and to make sure changes of address had been entered for all of a member's term deposits. McKay took extra time to make sure his entries were correct. He tried to keep a step ahead of her. It worked. She became friendly.

Smalley, on the other hand, recalled the incident as a routine matter of instruction. She made the same demands on all new employees in the branch. If she took to them, they were all right. If she didn't—if someone crossed her or upset her—they had better watch out. She could be brutal in her criticism. This caused consternation, particularly among younger employees. Don Nelson, who as manager of the main branch worked alongside her in the late 1960s, vividly remembered her tearing a strip off a young woman one day. "Regimental," he thought. Some days she wouldn't speak to him. It made sense, though, to try to get along with her. If one did, Wayne McKay recalled, one inevitably began to like her. She was fair. She didn't go behind people's backs. She had a concern for people. She had a sense of humour. It was true her officious manner got in the way. One simply had to get behind it.

Jan Chapman, in her early days at the main branch, used to go out to lunch with Smalley occasionally. They had an older woman-younger woman relationship. Smalley gave her good advice about how to get ahead as a woman. They discussed the subject openly, something that wasn't often done. They talked about the workplace. Smalley's image as a sergeant major meant nothing to Chapman, although she knew Smalley could be tough. Chapman assumed that any woman who was in a position to give orders would be stereotyped that way. "She knew herself very well," Chapman remembered. Chapman liked that.

Smalley in this period became Bentley's secretary and secretary to the board. If, working on the month-end statement with Bentley, she wanted something, she would go through the office like a hurricane. Often when Bentley was away from the office, she made decisions for him. She had confidence in her judgement and also knew that he would back her. Wayne McKay discovered that if one wanted to get something particularly important brought to Bentley's attention or have him act on something quickly, it was better to work through Smalley. There was nothing in her position that gave her that clout, but Bentley allowed her the clout, so McKay tried to get her on side for anything he wanted Bentley to do.

She generated hostility and catty talk among women her age in the office, a lot of it pettiness and jealousy, because of her position next to Bentley and her forceful nature. The tension was always there. She had spindly legs, the talk went. She had tattoos (one small tattoo, a dove, on her wrist, which she acquired when she was eighteen, and had regretted ever since). She still thought she was in the army. She was having an affair with Bentley—that was a common rumour. Smalley laughed at the notion. She did not have much time for other women who were vying for Bentley's attention or putting her down.

She did have a relationship with Bentley: They worked closely together and liked each other. People were not used to seeing that kind of close man-woman working camaraderie, which was something more than boss-secretary—or even seeing a boss talking to a woman as if she had brains—so the inference about an affair came freely. Ted Sewell, who dated back another generation, was least able to understand it. He considered Smalley Bentley's greatest challenge. She had taken a fancy to him, Sewell thought;

wished she would go away. "She made life a bit too hard for Don," he put it, in code language. Her presence seemed to overlay everything.

Bentley, however, thought her something special. She had more influence on him than did any of the others. Nobody quite understood what Bentley saw in her. She was a take-charge person. She was supportive. She could deliver bad news to people, which Bentley did not like to do. She was outspoken. She was committed to her work, rarely missing days, although she had children. (She once stayed home sick for three days. Her absence was treated as a news event.) None of that, nevertheless, explained the relationship. What bonded Bentley to her was her vitality and forthrightness. She wasn't sophisticated. She had a direct, untutored humanity—one that he could trust, because it was so direct. Her "Good heavens," or "Ah, that's ridiculous," or "Oh, pffft, give me a break"—phrases picked up in her second language—had real meaning. Bentley listened to her, sought her advice. There was a spark to her. She had a strong intuitive sense. She had created a presence simply by being herself, without benefit of title.

She would stand up to Bentley and tell him he was full of what-have-you. He admired her for that because it was so unlike himself. At managers' meetings, she argued with him or anyone else who didn't share her opinion. At one restaurant meeting, Don Nelson accidentally spilled wine on her dress. The wicked thought entered Wayne McKay's mind that Nelson hadn't made much of an effort to catch the falling bottle, although it was an innocent enough occurrence.

Loan applications that were above branch managers' limits and went to Bentley passed through her hands until Nelson became chief loans officer. She would look them over and offer her opinion on any that caught her attention. In terms of her formal position, the loan applications were none of her business, but she had them in her hand, she was interested and they were the business of the common enterprise. Offering her opinion seemed a natural thing to do and, given her unorthodox relationship to Bentley, it seemed natural to him as well. Once at a board meeting, where she took minutes, she pitched in with a comment. It had come spontaneously. She had thought of herself as part of the circle. This time, though, Bentley gave her a withering look. She realized she had assumed too much.

She and Bentley would have spats—about loans, choosing suppliers or particular employees. "They fought like crazy," it seemed to Wayne McKay. If she were pitching Bentley on a loan application and she liked the member, she would fight for an approval. If she didn't like the member, she might do the opposite. Often Bentley would challenge her, to make her justify her position or, playfully, to create sparks and start an argument, which was his favourite way of exploring an issue.

On one occasion an older woman came into the branch and wanted a small loan. She was in dire need and might not have been able to repay the loan. The application was predictably turned down. Smalley took the woman's application in to Bentley and had a fierce argument with him.

"Isn't this why VanCity was started in the first place?" she lashed out. "People couldn't get loans from the banks and so they pooled some money together and made loans to themselves." Bentley riposted that if VanCity made these kinds of loans, they would go broke. Smalley wasn't satisfied. Bentley was always yakking about "not for profit, not for charity, but for service," she told him, and here was something that might reduce profits a trivial amount and he was holding back. "You preach one philosophy and then you do another." The loan would only be for a couple of hundred dollars. VanCity rarely received such loan applications, where there was nothing behind them, so why not issue the loan this one time? The woman might actually surprise them and repay it ...

Smalley knew that she could get away with taking on Bentley in this way. It wasn't insubordination. If one couldn't express one's feelings and one's thoughts, it would have been, for her, ridiculous. In the end, Bentley, holding fast to the principle that a credit union was not a charity, still denied the loan.

At other times, there would just be flare-ups. Smalley would be so convinced that she was right. She would raise her voice; Bentley would speak quietly but with no less resistance. They were both stubborn. They were close enough to each other that it could happen—a domestic fight not about who should be taking out the garbage or picking up their socks but about an item of VanCity business.

Smalley was protective of him. He would show up tired after a late-night bridge session or some other social engagement. "God, you're not a teenager," she would tell him. "You can't burn the candle at both ends." She blamed Ethel for Don's fatigue. She thought Ethel had him on a social treadmill. Her feelings were intense. "She was a powder keg about to explode," Wayne McKay recalled. Ethel too, however, was also protective of Don and, after the heart surgery, became even more watchful. Ethel Bentley and Laura Smalley were fiercely devoted and loyal to the same man.

There were some issues, however, that Smalley never did discuss with Bentley. One was B.C. Central. She knew he was bothered by the relationship, but how deep the turmoil went, she wasn't sure. Only when he came back tired from a meeting on the issue would he let an offhand remark slip, as if by way of explanation, that Central was trying to tell him what to do or that George May was an empire-builder. There was nothing she could do about that herself, so she said little.

Bentley offered her the management of a branch, the ultimate prize. She declined. "Bentley probably knew she would turn it down," Jan Chapman speculated. "As the organization grew, she didn't have the background or talent to be manager of a branch." Smalley's own explanation was more personal. She had been to all those managers' meetings and listened umpteen times to the talk, she said, and she had watched all the work that managers did at night, taking them away from their families. "I didn't want any part of it," she said. "I didn't think it was worth it." She stayed with Bentley at head office instead.

The application for incorporation, September 28, 1946.

(inset) Evan Roberts, the original promoter of an open-bond community credit union for Vancouver. This shot was taken at an editorial meeting of the B.C. Credit Unionist. Roberts was volunteer business manager of the magazine.

Martha Mackie, VanCity's first member and the woman behind the counter, handling VanCity's business in its start-up years. "You become so interested in the people you meet—their individual problems and hopes," she told the B.C. Credit Unionist, circa 1951.

The Credit Union Building at Broadway and Quebec, a former machine shop, where VanCity operated during its early years, until it was torn down and a new Credit Union Building was erected, in 1954.

The historic beginning of branching—the opening in 1957 of Branch 2, a storefront just off Victoria Drive on East 41st Avenue. Tom Wiltshire, VanCity president; Sally McGinn, teller; Ron Spooner, the branch's manager; Don Bentley, general manager, and George Payton, vice-president; Jim Johnstone, architect.

Laura Smalley, whom Don Bentley hired, in 1960, to operate the Burroughs electronic bookkeeping machine. She later became Bentley's secretary. Smalley, with Bentley and Ray Evelle, were a Branch 1 triumvirate. That's also Smalley at the machine, with a Burrough's salesman looking on.

Ray Evelle, office manager at Branch 1 in the new Credit Union Building, Broadway and Quebec— making loans and running the branch for Don Bentley although only in his early twenties.

Vice-president Lloyd Widdifield addresses an excited overflow crowd of more than 600 people at the annual meeting in 1965, held for the first time in a prestigious hotel (the Hotel Vancouver) rather than a nondescript hall. On Widdifield's left is president Bert Gladu and Don Bentley; on his right, secretary Dorothy Timmons and "parliamentarian" Betsy McDonald.

General manager Don Bentley and Dick Monrufet, managing director of the B.C. Credit Union League—good friends despite Bentley's unhappiness about the League. Shortly after, the pioneering League would merge with B.C. Central Credit Union, disappearing as a separate entity.

(below left) The new Credit Union Building at 96 East Broadway featured VanCity's first modern sign. In the mid-1960s, VanCity was offering term deposits as high as 6 per cent.

(below right) Ron Spooner with his buddy Hermann Myers, whom Spooner affectionately called "the Lancashire gentleman." Myers designed the Plan 24 and VanCity logos.

The "gang" of branch managers, at the 1969 annual meeting. From left to right, Art Farnden (Victoria Drive), Wayne McKay (East Hastings), Monty Lambertus (Kitsilano), Ted Sewell (once VanCity treasurer), Ron Spooner (then doing advertising and promotion), and Don Nelson (main branch at Broadway and Quebec).

Stan Parsons, Bert Gladu and Lloyd Widdifield—the powers on the board in the halcyon days from 1963 to 1975.

(left) Selling young couples on The Meadows, a 118-unit VanCity townhouse development in Surrey, complete with swimming pool. The Meadows was the first development by any credit union in North America designed to provide modern, low-cost housing for members. "Operation Homeowner" it was originally called.

(below) The original storefront Kitsilano branch (Branch 4) at Broadway and Blenheim. It was only eighteen feet wide.

The new Victoria Drive Branch, 1971, the year VanCity's assets almost doubled. Plan 24 (daily interest), term deposits and open mortgages were the rage among VanCity members. The joint is jumping, typical of all VanCity branches in the period.

Are they constructions blocks or high rises? The VanCity logo glimmers over the street at the relocated main branch, at 1030 West Broadway, near Oak. The logo was sketched by Hermann Myers in 1969 after he tried out various patterns with children's building blocks.

CHAPTER 29

Money in, Money out

IT WAS DON BAGSHAW'S FIRST time in an airplane, December 1974. He had
quit mechanical engineering at the University of Waterloo after only two
years. He was exceptionally bright. In his last semester, his computer
science professor took exception to the way he did certain things and
flunked him in programming, insisting Bagshaw did not know how to code.
"Idiot," Bagshaw thought. He was working weekends for Geac at the time
and had become a top-notch programmer. Another course he was taking at
Waterloo went on about rocks, which wasn't Bagshaw's favourite subject. He
lost interest in school and joined Geac for good.

Now, on the way to Vancouver, he was feeling queasy and trying to keep his
meal down. German, sitting beside him, had promised VanCity that the Geac
on-line system would be up and live in six months and that they could have
an interim batch system going in three months. McKay had been dubious,
because Geac was starting from scratch without any applicable programs.
Geac also didn't have any experience with credit unions or banks. According
to the standard computer-industry wisdom, three years would be required to
develop a system like the one VanCity was after. German had nevertheless
assured McKay he would indeed do it in six months. Now Bagshaw was
curious about how they would manage. "It's easy, Don," German told him.
"They just put money in and they take it out."

Russell Smith was also on the plane. Geac's arrival in Vancouver had been
briefly delayed until the new head-office space for VanCity was finished,
with places for a computer room and for Geac to work. McKay did not want
Geac setting up at a separate location. He was intent on keeping a close eye
on what they were doing. He was particularly anxious to keep tabs on
German and keep him sober. He and Bentley had gone to bat for Geac and
now had their reputations on the line.

Geac computer equipment had already been shipped out. The system
was called the Geac 800. Geac's technology was considerably improved over
the original installation at Donlands Dairy. Mike Sweet had rewritten his
operating system. He had also, with German's help, created a new programming language suited to Geac's purposes. It was called OPL, for Our
Programming Language, and had gradually replaced PL/1, which had
come from the mainframe "other world." Writing programming languages

217

required a mind capable of high-level abstraction. Sweet had just that type of mind.

The first task in Vancouver was to procure the computer tapes from CDS and transfer the information to the Geac computer, in order to create a working model and play with the data. CDS was now using magnetic tapes. McKay had been deeply worried that summer, when the contract with Geac was signed, that B.C. Central might block VanCity's access to the tapes, especially given May's hostility. The alternative—entering the accumulated data manually from the printouts—would have been a staggering task. McKay, wary, went to see Ted Cotter about it. Cotter assured him the tapes would be available. McKay left feeling higher than a kite.

The data was now transferred from the CDS tapes to disks and brought up on the screen. How to read the data posed a dilemma. Computer manufacturers, at the time, could not read data from one another's machines, because of their different formats. Conversion was a new technology in itself. Moreover, the formatting of the CDS data, which used a Burroughs machine, was nothing that German had ever seen before. The record layouts, which were supposed to explain the formatting codes, were cryptic and hard to decipher. Worse, the layouts changed from one section of the data to another so that any conversion program would soon stop functioning. German, ever inventive, decided they would write a special add-on program of their own, to get over this obstacle. They called it The Liberator. It allowed them quickly to change the conversion program every time the format of the CDS data changed—and hence quickly to reformat the data for their own use. German joked about writing another program called The Enslaver, which would reverse the process.

For McKay, seeing the information on the screen represented a major breakthrough. For German, Bagshaw and Smith, it was a routine piece of business. VanCity branch managers started coming around to take a gander. They seemed to have great expectations. The Geac crew wrote some demonstration programs, using master-file information (names, addresses and so on), to show how the system would likely work when it was completed. The first demonstration was for McKay. They asked him to key in his name. From that, his name, address, membership number and other personal information came up. Could they tell him which name was most common? They could. It turned out to be Lee, not Smith. Could they identify people by address, McKay then asked them, and they did that for him. No matter what he threw at them, they could bring it up. He was euphoric. He could not fathom how they had arrived at that stage so quickly and how they could so deftly manipulate the data. He had believed in Geac from the moment they had met, but there had been a faint, residual skepticism, which was now erased. He did not know how long they were going to take, but he was now convinced they would succeed.

German and his team then turned to the main task. The demonstration routine might impress VanCity's people, but there wasn't much of anything underneath it. They had to design the way the data would be put together and then write, from scratch, programs that would calculate and enter interest, service charges, expiry dates, roll-overs and the other variables for the different kinds of accounts. The process began with McKay and German discussing how VanCity worked, what was needed, and the best approach. German would then go to Bagshaw and Smith and explain to them what had been decided, and leave them to it. Once the program was done, it would be tried out and, if it seemed to be working, would be tested. Reports would be printed out parallel to the CDS data to see if the two streams of calculations came out the same.

Another test procedure, and a key accounting function, was to balance the overall numbers. The Geac crew never managed to do it. They discovered that the information from CDS was incomplete or inaccurate. This nagged away at German. He and McKay eventually decided that until the Geac system had taken over, the-out-of-bounds limit, for the mismatch in balancing, would be $20,000. Anything less than that and they wouldn't worry.

Each step, also, needed to be recorded for reference. German, with his thought disorder and often in an alcoholic haze, was incapable of writing two sentences at a time. McKay watched German desperately try to do it. The sweat would gather on his face. He would break the lead in his pencil out of frustration, his tongue almost contorted in his mouth. It seemed to German that his brain was faster than his hand; he would lose a thought before he could get it down. "My heart went out to him," McKay remembered. McKay was baffled that somebody with such extraordinary genius could not at least convey a simple message on a piece of paper.

McKay wrote for him, instead. He put down, in layperson's language, all the things they had discussed and how they should work, as reference material whenever German and his programmers got stuck. McKay also had to try to document what Geac was doing, including the documentation of operating instructions for VanCity. He walked around with German, asking him questions and taking usually quite technical notes. German could verbalize reasonably well, although in a scattered way, often veering off on tangents. McKay learned the jargon and the way German's mind moved, and could fill in the blanks well enough. Having been closely associated with CDS, he was also something of an amateur techie. If he finally came to a dead end, he could ask consultant Al Fowler.

German challenged everything VanCity did. VanCity, for example, did not charge interest on past unpaid interest when loans became delinquent, although it was provided for in the contract. McKay felt it would be unconscionable to impose that extra charge on people down on their luck. German, on the other hand, was offended by the inconsistency of not charging interest where interest was due. After a month of arguing, McKay won, and the computer program for delinquent loans left out interest on interest.

Arguing was part of a process by which the Geac crew, talking through each programming task, gradually absorbed VanCity's culture and then began amplifying it with their technical brilliance. They had no idea at the beginning what a credit union was. The more they learned, the more they became attached to its co-operative principles, particularly VanCity's credo of doing the best for its members. The development of the system came to reflect that ethos. This made the system exceptionally useful and adaptable when it went into operation.

The accountant, John Smith, who had come up through the branch system and knew branch operations intimately, played a key role in explaining to German the nitty gritty of transactions. German also read everything about operations that he could put his hands on. At night, after Bentley had gone home, he even sauntered into Bentley's office and read Bentley's mail and other documents, to see what had happened that day. He was still keeping to his "no secrets" doctrine. He went around to Janet Chapman's and Garry Smith's branches to find out what people were doing. He opened accounts at all the banks in town. He would make small transactions at each of these banks, and then, on the spot, ask the tellers everything he could about how they had entered the transactions and where the information was stored.

German, typically by this time, did not do much programming himself. Bagshaw and Smith together did the database layout. Then Bagshaw did the interface with the tellers—the on-line processing by which money would be put into, and taken out of, accounts. He was just twenty-one years old. German was in awe of him. "I couldn't begin to write code like Don," he told McKay. "I wouldn't even try." Russell Smith did the programs for calculating interest and everything else that would happen after the doors closed.

They worked all the time, stopping only to eat and sleeping as little as they could. They needed to finish as quickly as possible in order to generate revenue. They settled into a thirty-hour day—twenty-four hours of work and six hours of sleep—seeing the city at different hours of the day, in a cycle. They would keep at it until they decided they needed a break, perhaps after a couple of weeks, then take two or three days off, like a rest-and-recreation break from a military front.

Bagshaw and Smith shared an apartment in the West End. It was a messy hole in the wall. The office was more pleasant. Psychologically, this was an added inducement to stay at work. As often as not, they slept in the office. Smith would work to the point of exhaustion, refusing to give up, and fall asleep at his terminal. Bagshaw would usually conk out on the floor. Marina Lowe, McKay's secretary, and others in the office, arriving in the morning, often found them asleep, like sculptures in a park. German, in his early thirties, maintained much the same routine, catching a few hours of sleep here and there. Even when he went home, he did not sleep for long. As compensation for the long hours, German bought his programmers steak-and-egg breakfasts, only to become alarmed at the accumulating expense—money that Geac didn't have.

To meet looming deadlines, they worked several days at a stretch, nodding off now and then to revivify themselves. Bagshaw once chose a reclining chair for the purpose. The chair fell over. He kept sleeping without getting out of the chair. Even in these long, multi-day stretches, they had an unusual ability to concentrate and get things done. Mike Sweet, who was in Vancouver only briefly, had the highest powers of concentration of the group. He was able to sit at a monitor for twelve-hour stretches without a bathroom break and without looking up, impervious to the noises around him. If he had to wake himself up, he would run up and down the big, long hallway at the branch in his bare feet. For relaxation, he sat on a desk cross-legged and meditated.

Eventually, in these cycles, Bagshaw and Smith would hit the wall and head off to their apartment to crash. On one celebrated occasion, they crashed a few hours too early. They and German had mounted a special demonstration for the VanCity 1975 annual meeting. Isserstedt had come to town to tell the meeting about the system. His presentation was to be backed with live illustrations on large television monitors. The monitors were connected by telephone lines to the office, where Bagshaw and Smith, listening in on a voice line, manned terminals, ready to go. They fell dead asleep waiting and the demonstration foundered.

Bagshaw, when he slept in the office, took off his cowboy boots. This had repercussions if he hadn't gone home for three or four days. By morning, the place reeked. Marina Lowe remembered showing up for work in the morning and being hit by the smell. Isserstedt, when he was in town once, was so horrified at Bagshaw's lack of attention to his feet that he brought him some foot powder and half a dozen pairs of new socks. Bagshaw's more serious problem, however, was that he wasn't washing his socks. He didn't want to take the time. He put his dirty socks into a plastic bag and, when he ran out of socks, reached into bottom of the bag and pulled out the ones that had dried out. Bagshaw's sister came out to Vancouver for a visit, intending to see the sights. She was so disgusted by the smell and mess in the apartment that she spent a good part of her time cleaning it up instead. Washing socks wasn't the only thing that was deferred. Bagshaw and Smith had bought a clunker to drive from their apartment to VanCity, but it got a flat. They drove on the flat for a week, with people yelling and waving at them, attempting to point out the problem.

They were so wound up, German quipped, that if some alien had arrived from outer space and asked for a pizza, they would probably have given it a pizza without noticing. Months after they had begun work, Smith looked out the office windows facing north and exclaimed, "My God, there are mountains out there."

German was supposed to pick up extra technical help in Vancouver. By his own admission, he was a notoriously poor hirer of people. He had a tendency to hire the weakest, rather than the strongest, because he liked to make people shine. He preferred rough rubies, which he could then polish,

as opposed to proven talent. He also liked people who had a skewed
intelligence or skewed temperament, like Dr. Sweet and himself, and tried
to find a home for them in Geac. Attention disorder was no barrier to entry;
look at himself. Such people were more likely to think differently than
others and to look at computers in new ways, which is what German wanted.
Unfortunately, two of the people he hired in Vancouver didn't do any work
and had to be fired. He even had to fire one of them himself—the only
time he had ever done it, and he felt absolutely terrible about it. He had
chosen the rottenest rubies instead of the roughest, he joked later.

The one person who did prove valuable was an honest-to-goodness local
hippie, Nigel Burnett. Burnett told German that his marks at university had
not been all that good. "That's okay," German answered, "the lower the
better." He was hired. He was then plunked down, without much background, in the intense, rarified, and highly specialized Gus German computer culture. He walked around looking distracted. A very weird guy, German
and McKay thought. Scatterbrained, unkempt. He was German's worst
nightmare—the embodiment of German's fear of what he himself, German, was really like. He drove German to exasperation with his mistakes.
He was, however, enthusiastic, tried hard for acceptance and did real work.
He turned out to be useful in the end, installing the terminals.

German, however, was the grand eccentric. He regularly lost or forgot
things, including his car keys. He was always running around in chaotic
fashion and showing up late. He seemed to be just an overweight, messy guy
who tore things apart and wasted most of his time. His dress habits were a
standard joke. Usually he didn't bother, or didn't think of, tying his shoe-
laces. He wasn't a pretty eater, either. He also didn't smell good, because he
had been drinking. He always, though, had that cherubic, vulnerable innocence about him. McKay thought him a lovable, huggable kind of guy.

McKay and German became close friends. "Wayne was the guy that had
his neck in the sling in this thing," German recounted with laughter,
"and he knew it and I knew it. We were crazy, but we were happy." McKay,
much to German's delight, was a nighthawk, too—showing up late in the
morning and then working seemingly forever, to midnight or two in the
morning, and eating Chinese food with them in the late hours.

German, in conversation with McKay, would often go off on an explora-
tory inquiry, the ideas bursting out of his head. McKay, now having a sense
of the technology, would follow. Before long, they were far afield, discussing
how VanCity might take advantage of the future, and not even Bagshaw,
who occasionally listened in, understood what they were talking about.
Once German and McKay were scheduled to catch a 2 P.M. plane to San
Francisco and Los Angeles, for a computer show and a meeting with the
people who were producing VanCity's terminals. German picked McKay up
first thing in the morning so that they could talk. They drove around the
city, ran out of gas, found gas, got going again, and continued. They missed
the plane and had to catch the next one.

If McKay and German hadn't been good friends, they would have been mortal enemies. They were spending days, nights and often early mornings together, virtually working out of each others' pocket. Church-going McKay even worked most Sundays. He had two young children. His wife, Carol, was resigned to the family not seeing much of him. She befriended German's wife, Kiki. German's daughter by his previous marriage and McKay's daughter were roughly the same age and were able to play together. Later that year, Kiki gave birth to a baby boy.

McKay's strategy was to police German carefully, keeping track of what he did every day to try to keep him on the straight and narrow. McKay knew he could not be with him constantly. All he could do was increase the odds. The idea was to have German working at VanCity as much as possible. As long as he was at VanCity, he was all right. McKay also tried to spend as much off-work time as he could with German. The strategy wasn't totally successful. German, inevitably, would slip away. He might join drinking buddy Moffat Goepel on binges and crawl around the streets of Vancouver.

German's prowling around the branches, looking at how things were done, eventually had to be curtailed. He was causing too much disruption. Often he was tipsy, having had a few drinks for the occasion, because he hated meeting people he didn't know. He had imagined a comic, Dadaesque scenario in which these strangers called him a geek, screamed at him and pointed, "Oh, fat person!" On one occasion, in Jan Chapman's branch on Victoria Drive, Chapman decided that research into VanCity by the genius from Geac could wait. "Let's get him out of here," she told McKay, "he smells to high heaven." It was another event that German later couldn't recall. Chapman was particularly upset because she had supported the choice of Geac. She implored McKay to do something about German's drinking.

The computer-visionary part of German, however, was somehow untrammelled. As long as he did not have to write or do repetitive mental tasks, computers were his safe world—a galaxy open to his mind. Often he did not seem to do anything palpable, yet as long as he was on the scene, everything got done, even things that were thought impossible. Everybody at Geac except German wondered whether they they were crazy in attempting the VanCity project. German, who saw how the parts related to each other, and also knew everything about most of the parts, had a surer sense of the possibilities. The others were carried along by his assurance. He had done it before. He was their guru. "He was tremendously inspirational," remembered Howie Stevenson, an administrator brought in by McKay.

If anyone had a new design or concept, or an intractable problem, the typical procedure was to put the matter to Gus. Sometimes his response was impossible to understand, because it required anterior knowledge or more familiarity with how his mind worked. The only recourse, then, was to ask questions until his technical logic became clear. Bagshaw, of a later incident involving hardware design, described how Sweet had followed German around like a puppy for three days until he finally understood what German had meant by some comment.

If, on the other hand, a task did not require repetitive concentration, or if it was urgent, or elemental, German might do it himself. For the main on-line programming—the teller interface—he produced for Bagshaw a short bit of code fifty lines long. Bagshaw ended up writing around it, but everything he needed to know was in those original few lines German had provided. The concept was there. German also filled in programming cracks. It was typical of German to produce overnight, as if by an after-thought, the essential lines required to make the rest work. Things that were too difficult to explain he would also do himself, although perhaps not until the last moment, driven to it by the despair of circumstance.

He tried to make a cult out of his technical people. He had a theory that technical people needed a perceived evil—a wrong to be righted—to keep them going in what, in one sense, was arid, abstract work. Otherwise they became apathetic and went to seed. They would no longer put in twenty-nine-hour days. They would get the feeling that programs were just stupid, passive little things that sat around computers forever and didn't matter at all. The perceived enemy, in this case, was IBM and the pretentious, puffed-up mainframe otherworld that didn't want to acknowledge that Geac existed. The more they dismissed Geac, the more German loved it. That was enough to get them going. The fun was in beating the odds. Isserstedt and the other Geac whiteshirts were also sometimes the enemy. German tried keeping Isserstedt away from his technical cadres.

Obsessed as usual with simplicity and functionalism, German designed the VanCity system with the tellers in mind. He was particularly scornful of procedural terminology that did not describe simply what was taking place. McKay used words like debit and credit, and then told German that for banks it was backwards: when a bank took a deposit, it owed it to the customer, so it was a debit rather than a credit. German could not believe him. When German went into a bank, he either gave them money or got money. Debit and credit, much less debit and credit backwards, did not come into it.

German also disliked complicated codes. He wanted tellers to have a dialogue with the computer instead of being trained as rats to operate machinery. The tellers, German thought, should have the flexibility to do things in different sequences rather than having to adhere to rigid and abstracted "procedure." The task was to create a "language" that both tellers and the computer understood.

Mike McMullen, McKay's assistant, marginalized otherwise by the Geac work, came up with the one-letter codes that they came to call "teller language." For entering a withdrawal, a teller would merely have to press W instead of a multiple-digit code that had to be memorized or looked up. Plan 24 was P. Accordingly, a withdrawal from Plan 24 would be WP and then the amount, say WP 150.34. D was deposit. C was the chequing account. S stood for shares. The language was extensible, allowing tellers to do complex things that previously had been handled at the side counter. A member making a loan payment, for example, could now go to a teller. A loan payment, in teller language, was simply a deposit like any other money handed in. DL, or deposit to loan, was the instruction. A transaction involving a paycheque, part of which was going to a loan, part to Plan 24 and part to be paid out in cash, could be handled by the teller in a single line.

Each discrete instruction was two letters long. For a new kind of account, tellers had to learn just one extra letter. For German, the logic of this teller language was obvious enough. The language was also technically elegant and efficient, because it required so few characters. For McKay, the banker, on the other hand, it seemed revolutionary.

At the end of the day, the teller would then need only to press a few keys. The computer would list everything that had happened during that day and tell the tellers how much cash they should have. All they would have to do after that would be to count their cash and cheques, and they could go home.

In German's forays into the branches, he also became intrigued by what the people in the back rooms were doing. They weren't tellers, nor were they answering the day's mail, yet they all seemed to be working. He discovered they were trying to correct, or keep under control, the errors that CDS was making or that VanCity itself was making. Countless clerks were putting little red check marks, little blue check marks and little green check marks against figures on a printout in the attempt. The further back an error went, the more difficult it was to unravel and, worse, to adjust everything that had followed. German concluded that mistakes were the biggest problem a financial institution had to deal with.

McKay even confessed to him, under questioning, that sometimes, after several attempts to correct an error, the numbers still didn't balance. In that case, staff just said the hell with it, gave the member the difference and hoped the member would go away. "Is there a gratuity fund for that?" German asked facetiously. "Well," McKay replied, "as a matter of fact there is." German laughed. "The gratuity fund for chaos," he called it.

He and McKay hit on the idea that the only way to fix an error was to go back in the account to the point where the error happened. In order to do that, they had to store all past information on the system. There was another, defensive, motive in storing all past transactions. Geac had no previous experience with financial institutions. With all transactions stored, it would be prepared for any contingency. German committed himself to the data storage program, although it was a hard stand to take technically. It was one more thing that people said could not be done. It would take up too much space on the disks.

German was unfazed. He had already pioneered data compression for previous contracts—coding data to take up less space. Disks were expensive. The possibility of packing extra information onto a disk, by compressing it and using fewer disks, and hence saving Geac money, had popped into his fertile mind. With VanCity he took data compression the extra step. He did some research and settled on something called Huffman encoding. He was one of the first people to use it commercially, although it subsequently became a popular method of compression. The Geac group at VanCity worked hard on the application, making it possible to store many tens of millions of transactions on the system. The data compression also made things go faster, rather than slower, because, while the computer had to compress and uncompress data, it grabbed much more data off the disk in any one sweep. Russell Smith then stumbled on a way of writing a program to automatically calculate the impact of a correction, even if entered far back in somebody's account history with all the variable interest calculations in between.

The terminals for tellers posed another technical challenge. The computer could handle only sixteen telephone lines at a time. Indeed, in the Donlands case, the computer was able to handle only ten lines before it got too busy. At VanCity, German was looking at one hundred terminals. Somehow they had to have several terminals sharing the same line—preferably all the terminals in a branch. Even if they could have used separate lines for each terminal, the extra cost in telephone line charges was worth avoiding.

The trick was to "poll" these several terminals—have the computer continuously ask each in turn if it wanted to communicate, and go ahead if it did. This would happen at such a high speed that tellers would not notice. Terminals needed their own "names," or switches, so they would answer only when polled and not respond all at once. German knew the routine. Unfortunately, the terminals available for the purpose were the usual bulky monsters, unsuitable for a teller's small counter space. German remembered, however, being at a computer show in Atlantic City, years earlier, where he had seen a very small monitor. All the electronics were in a separate small, black box that could be kept underneath the counter. The terminal was being made by a start-up California company called Informer, which had so little money that its exhibit was in the open air, on the boardwalk. It was assembling its terminals in the proverbial workshop in somebody's garage. German thought the monitors were cute little things. He and Bagshaw had later seen them demonstrated in Toronto. Now he ordered them for VanCity. They were small enough to sit on a post up front and to the side of a teller, and could be turned part way around so that members could see the details of their own account. This had never been done before. It was equivalent to showing the members their ledger cards in the old days, except this time it was electronic.

German was still, as a matter of routine, taking apart any new thing he put his hands on and looking at its innards. The Informer monitor was no exception. Inside it, he discovered a brand new chip that had replaced an entire circuit board. The newfangled chip was called a communications adaptor. It occurred to German he could use it in Geac's computers as well.

The computer at Donlands Dairy, for example, spent most of its time trying to identify and grab onto the first pulse of each stream coming at it randomly from terminals. This smart-chip could save it most of that work. The applicable piece of equipment, in the computer, was the multiplexer, which allowed it to deal with more than one line. German had his moon-lighters at the University of Toronto make up a sophisticated multi-layer board with these chips in them—one for every line—and stuck it in the VanCity computer. It worked like a charm. It freed up 80 per cent of the computer's time and allowed the computer to communicate with termi-nals at a very high speed—much faster than before. "A really incredible device," German thought. Handling one hundred terminals at a time on a minicomputer, with what seemed to be instantaneous response, now became possible.

That wasn't all. Minicomputers circa 1975 did not have much memory, which limited everything they did. German's master stroke was to put three of the minicomputers together in a configuration, overcoming this hand-icap. The arrangement distributed the work load. It was still vastly cheaper than an elephant mainframe, while handling large volumes at high speed. The three machines worked in syncopated harmony. The front-end compu-ter pre-digested the input from the terminals, adapting it into quickly usable form for the middle computer. The middle computer ran the pro-grams and processed the data. The back-end computer ran the disk control-ler—the apparatus that handled the disks storing the data. The throughput for all three functions was much faster now. German then, as he had originally envisaged, duplicated the whole configuration, as a back-up. When, eventually, all branches came on stream, response time turned out to be only half a second.

McKay, watching these developments, was under the impression that German and his crew could do anything. They had rigged a terminal on his desk, with a keyboard attached, to acclimatize him to what a teller would be doing. Bagshaw had entered, into the computer itself, a few menus from take-out restaurants in the neighbourhood. McKay's sole technical duty was to bring up one of these menus, find out what everybody wanted, select the items and press a key, which automatically placed the orders. The restau-rants, he believed, had their own terminals and alert system, hooked up by Geac in some ingenious way without, apparently, even a dedicated tele-phone line. It was quite extraordinary. The set-up worked wonderfully, too, because the chop suey or pizza never failed to arrive. What McKay did not know was that the order items were simply being sent to a monitor at the other end of the office, where the Geac people were located, and being phoned in by old technology, namely somebody picking up the telephone, dialling, and talking into it when the restaurant answered.

Bagshaw's database design played a crucial function in how the system worked. CDS had formatted the data by ledger, that is, by kind of account, based on different interest calculations. All Plan 24 accounts were together, and all term deposits were together. It was convenient for CDS to process accounts in this way. German realized, however, that when a member walked into a branch, everything revolved around the member. The member might want to know his or her balances in different accounts, or make transactions involving different accounts. The teller would also find it useful to be able to see the member's various balances and related information. A member with a loan payment that was due, for example, might be reminded of it when making a withdrawal. Bagshaw reformatted all the data accordingly. The computer consequently had much less work to do. It did not have to search in different pockets of the database to pull together information about a member. With one read from the disk, it got it all. This enhanced response time and freed capacity. By contrast, general ledger work—say, totalling up deposits and withdrawals for different kinds of accounts— involved more work for the computer, since it had to search out the separate entries member by member. This, however, along with printing out monthly statements, could be done overnight, when the system was free.

It was an extension, in database design, of VanCity's member-oriented culture, hearkening back to the days when Martha Makovichuk had signed up as book member number 1 in 1946. VanCity and other credit unions already had an advantage over the banks on this score. Bank customers had a different number for each kind of account, which they had to try to recall. A VanCity member had one number, which was easy to remember. Bagshaw's database extended that advantage.

Nigel Burnett was assigned to install the monitors. He had the first ones up, in Branch 1, by February. He drilled a hole through the counter and down, at each teller station, and ran a wire through the hole. Unfortunately, the first time he did it, the hole, and the wire with it, went through the drawers in each station, and the tellers couldn't open them. He had to go back and do it all over again. Occasionally, to finish up, he worked around the tellers on regular days, loping softly around the branch. Some of this work was at floor level. The female tellers thought he could look up their skirts.

Meanwhile the clock was ticking. About two months into the project, it was decided to bypass the interim batch system and go directly on-line. The six months' total time envisaged was now running out. So was Geac's money. Before coming to Vancouver, German, fearing that Geac was about to go under, insisted to Isserstedt they bring in a new partner with financial skills. The new man renegotiated contracts, hoisting revenue. Whatever was gained in Ontario, however, was now being eaten up in Vancouver. Geac could not get revenue from VanCity and turn itself around until the system was working, but could not possibly get the system working without more funds. The dreaded "snowball," as German referred to it—in which the larger that Geac grew, the more it went into debt—was still gathering size.

The tension was constant. On one occasion, German lost control in the newly built computer room. Exasperated with things not getting done, he threw a metal bolt against the floor with such force that it ricocheted off the walls and broke a window. The noise rocked the outer office. McKay and John Smith ran in. German was beet red and beside himself. McKay talked to him for a while, to calm him down.

Another time, when Mike Sweet was in town working on the project, German took Sweet's pencil without asking—not that he needed it to write, since he never wrote anything. Sweet, barefoot, took offence, jumped on top of his desk to make sure he had German's attention, and began yelling at him. German climbed on another desk opposite Sweet and they screamed at each other like two banshees.

Everybody, including McKay, was running a bit scared. Each day was fraught with crisis. If it wasn't news from Toronto that Geac was financially disintegrating or pressure on Vancouver to start earning income, it was a piece of equipment not working or not arriving from Toronto on time, or a program malfunctioning. McKay, who refereed when fights broke out or when German was screaming at young Burnett, was growing weary from the long hours and, sometimes, sleepless nights.

German was simultaneously fighting his own demon, depression. He treated it, as usual, with alcohol. He became depressed regardless. The drinking held him down. He thought, at times, he might be suicidal, but it was difficult to focus and to tell what was happening to himself when he was drunk. He managed, nevertheless, to keep a grip on the project—or perhaps the project kept a grip on him, by powerfully engaging his mind. Working day after day, endlessly, with little sleep, was hypomanic, the opposite of depression.

The difficulties and delays of the work in itself did not depress him, however, angry as he might get. He had underestimated the size of the mountain, but that made climbing the mountain more exciting. He and his techies were propelled by blind enthusiasm. They felt they were going to succeed, so they would just keep going until they did. When German thought of the amount of work involved, it scared him. An intelligent person should never get into such situations. He called it the "hot coals." Nobody sane ever went onto the hot coals. Somehow, though, German and his techies always tricked themselves into it. "Perform or die," said the hot coals. Yet what could be better? When Don Bagshaw looked backed on this frenetic year on the VanCity project, what he remembered most, for all the grind and fatigue, was that it had been lots of fun.

McKay finally had to lend Geac $50,000—VanCity money—to keep it going, and later advanced another $50,000. Now VanCity was financially on the line, effectively underwriting the project. McKay himself was under siege. Word got out about the difficulties, and the gossip increased. Central's hints that VanCity should give up and come back to CDS—that they should recognize they were going to have a disaster on their hands if they persisted—became more blatant. Talk that VanCity was crazy reverberated through credit union circles.

VanCity was in a corner at CDS as well. It was still, necessarily, using CDS but, because it was leaving, service deteriorated even further. Mike Borch, now running CDS, was sympathetic to what VanCity was trying to do, but couldn't bring himself to waste time upgrading VanCity's service when it would shortly be gone and when he had all the other credit unions in the province to look after.

Borch was tormented by his own nightmare. He had replaced Ted Cotter, whose stay at CDS had run its course. He was responsible for supplying Geac with VanCity's tapes and other information. George May had instructed him to co-operate. Borch found himself sitting at his desk muttering, "I have to obey orders," until it sank in. He accepted intellectually that VanCity would be leaving and that he was going to help it, but he was CDS manager and was losing his biggest customer, and if Geac were successful, Richmond and Surrey would leave, too. He was deeply unhappy.

Worse, on looking into CDS's own on-line project, Borch discovered, to his horror, that behind a fine-looking set of documentation there was nothing. Two years on the project had gone by, and he would have to start again. The specially recruited on-line team, consultant and all, had gone nowhere. Bentley, on the other hand, had committed himself to a weird-looking group of hippies with sandals and long hair, and they were actually doing it. Borch did not know about the Donlands Dairy system. He thought, erroneously, that Bentley had committed VanCity to the Geac technology simply on his perception that the Geac people were geniuses. It made Bentley's decision appear even gutsier and more clairvoyant than it was.

Borch, from his talks with German, quickly realized that he was out of his depth. What really upset him was that his own CDS team, who were supposed to be technical experts, were not much better. Half the time they did not know what the Geac people were talking about, either.

Ted Cotter, in one of his last decisions before he and B.C. Central parted company, had replaced the on-line team with an external consultant, Computech. It was the only thing he could do. Computech was highly respected. Borch saw that it was beyond its depth, too. The problem, he belatedly realized, was that there was no computer to do the job. Computech was limited to going through the motions. The Geac people, by contrast, knew hardware as well as software and were building the necessary computer as they went along. Borch also noticed, half in awe, half in horror, that the Geac hippies were not writing anything down. They seemed totally disorganized. Their administrative skills hardly existed. Yet they had mastery at the frontier of computer technology. By comparison, hiring highly qualified, respected programmers, as CDS had done, was like bringing in a bunch of lab technicians to do atomic research. Borch had the sinking feeling that CDS's efforts were doomed, and he slipped slowly into a personal crisis of confidence. The brave new world of computers was no longer his world any more. He was just thirty-five years old, and he had hit the wall.

German and McKay then laid an ambush for IBM. WestCoast Savings in

Victoria had organized a seminar on data processing for credit unions on Vancouver Island, at which IBM was to make a feature presentation. McKay cadged an invitation. The seminar was held in the prestigious Empress Hotel. An IBM representative told the gathering that it would take two to three years and several million dollars from that point to develop the system. He was accompanied by a posse of "blue shirts"—his technical cadres. German started asking embarrassing questions. He claimed it could be done for much less and in a shorter time frame. The IBM spokesman scoffed, upon which McKay invited all those attending to come up to VanCity's room in the hotel to see for themselves.

Most of the credit union people took up McKay's offer, although IBM itself declined. German, with a modem and improvising a telephone line connection, had managed to plug into the VanCity database. He loved lying in wait for people who were slaves to large systems. Garry Smith had been brought along and did a demonstration. Twenty minutes after the IBM presentation, McKay and German had undermined everything that IBM had said.

Shortly after, IBM Canada's president and an entourage came to Vancouver to see what lay behind the Geac project. They apologized for their statements in Victoria and, according to German, asked about negotiating an agreement. German, however, wasn't interested. For McKay, the fact that mighty IBM had made the trek to VanCity was triumph in itself.

McKay ploughed on. He couldn't take any more time to answer the project's critics. Everything ultimately depended on Don Bentley, and Bentley was beyond going back. His support deflected the political pressure away from McKay. Bentley talked enthusiastically about the system to VanCity's tellers. On the surface, he was unexpectedly relaxed about Geac. It was as if, having made the decision to go with Geac and having stared down Central, he had won his war and left the front. He liked German because of German's great curiosity. When he eventually found out that German was reading his mail, he only chuckled. Bagshaw's smelly feet and stories about foot powder he also took with a sense of humour. He became aware, from seeing German in action, that there was some sort of problem. McKay filled him in about the drinking. Not even that shattered his confidence. He told McKay, who was critical of Geac's waywardness, that he had to take into account the kind of work they were doing and the pressure they were under, and not to be too harsh. He encouraged McKay to give them the benefit of the doubt.

He was playing his double game again—calm judgement on the outside, troubled feelings on the inside. Ethel remembered him tossing and turning, wondering if the system was going to work. He wasn't sure what to make of the bare feet and the irregular hours. He wondered sometimes what he had done. German and the others, however, seemed to know what they were up to. If they failed, Bentley thought, he would be eating a lot of crow.

Nevertheless, whether because of his health or as a managerial judgement, he kept himself at a distance from the project. There was something else in Bentley's sympathy for the Geac people, however. They were, in fact, succeeding. He began inviting people up. Others were curious as word got around and asked if they could take a look. Richmond Savings came by and paid Geac a nominal $1,000 to be next in line, after VanCity. Sherwood Credit Union in Regina dropped in. The Royal Bank in Vancouver stopped by. Bentley watched over the demonstrations, radiating pleasure. Central at first stayed away, fighting temptation. Eventually, however, curiosity got the better of it, too, and it accepted an invitation to come up on an open-house day. The feeling at Central that the project was silly and risky was gradually giving way to a feeling of being threatened, as word leaked out that the system might work.

· The Canada Day weekend, 1975, was chosen for the first conversion. McKay selected the main branch for the trial. It was the largest branch by far, but it was also next door to the computer site, upstairs over the parking lot, and handiest to use. July 1 fell on a Tuesday. With the regular closing on Monday, that gave them the better part of four days. They needed to transfer the CDS tapes into the system—not only the current information, which was easy enough, but also the historical records. They calculated that this task in itself would require three full days.

Geac was already past its deadline. It badly needed the money that would come with a start-up. More than that, German felt it needed the catharsis of actually seeing the system at work, even if it wasn't ready. The monitors in Branch 1 by this time had been sitting on the teller counter, like a row of silent sentinels, for more than four months. On Valentine's Day, Geac, via the monitors, had wished all the tellers Happy Valentine's. They loved it. Then there were birthday greetings; then, for Easter, a little bunny with flapping ears. These amusements were beginning to pale.

The tension kept rising. Ray Evelle was managing the branch. He was mentally on edge and lost his composure. McKay sent him away for a week because he was getting in the way. It was "run and run and run" as they headed for the conversion, Bagshaw remembered. Then they worked the four-day weekend non-stop. Bentley was pacing around at home. "I don't think they're going to be ready," he told Ethel. He ran down to the office and came back. "Well, maybe they'll be ready," he told her, and kept pacing.

At six on Wednesday morning, three and a half hours before the branch was scheduled to open, Smith and Bagshaw, drenched with fatigue, realized they had forgotten to hook the loan and term deposit programs into the main system. They wrote the connecting program on the spot, finishing it minutes before the doors opened in the branch downstairs. Members suddenly began arriving. The system seemed to be working well. It was an exciting moment. After a while, Bagshaw and Smith went for a walk. They felt like heroes. When they returned an hour later, everything was in disorder. The system had crashed. Tellers were keying in their transactions, hitting send and nothing was happening. Other glitches had surfaced.

German, who had stayed behind, was in a daze of fatigue and anxiety. He was going down and up the stairs like an automaton—down, to see what was happening in the branch; up, to see if he could put his finger on the problem. Bagshaw and Smith, in a state of controlled panic, went back to their terminals. The extra-long weekend proved to be a curse. That Wednesday was the busiest day in VanCity's history, as members flooded in. German took the system down for an hour to make some quick changes. With all the traffic in the branch, he tried to keep it going after that, but intermittently he had to take it down again. Its response time was slow. The tellers, still coming to grips with the system, desperately kept at it. By early afternoon, German called a halt and asked the tellers to stop using the terminals.

Elizabeth Miller, head teller in the branch, remembered the occasion vividly. "It was a very high day," she said. The tellers were excited, upbeat. Geac had given them all roses. Computers at the time were considered big, weird things that sat behind glass walls and were operated by scientists in white coats, and here they had their own computer terminals in front of them. They weren't just tellers anymore. Marina Lowe, Wayne McKay's secretary, also remembered the electricity in the air that day. "Everybody was so positive, so up for it," she recounted. "It was like, this is it, we were going to blast off."

Miller had everybody that she could working up front. The lineup went out the door and down Broadway. The tellers had little training on the system—only an hour or hour-and-a-half each—but still felt they could do it. It was a challenge. The Geac people were helpful. They stood by so that if a teller was having difficulty, they were on hand. They did errands for the tellers. If somebody's pen ran out of ink, they fetched another one. Bob Isserstedt was there, nicely dressed. "All the girls thought he looked really good," Miller remembered.

The slowness of the system was frustrating, but the tellers persevered, as long as the system was available to them. Some found the going difficult, but there were no flare-ups and no crying. Everybody was working hard together. The members were patient, despite the lineup. It seemed to Miller that it took half a minute to bring up an account, although looking back she thought it might have only been ten or fifteen seconds.

From the tellers' point of view, the system was functioning, notwithstanding the breakdowns and slow response time. The entries for members worked. The recording of the identical data for teller and general-ledger balancing, however, in another computer file, was badly jumbled. The entire day had to be balanced manually. Bentley came through at one point, only to find McKay on his hands and knees on the floor checking out figures. Miller let most of the tellers go home by seven o'clock that evening. She herself stayed until ten-thirty. She wasn't distressed. "I loved the computer system," she said.

By closing time at five o'clock, McKay had decided to pull the plug for the interim. If the branch had tried using the system the next day, they

would have ended up in a hopeless mess. The branch's staff then spent
another two days catching up on the old batch system. McKay, overcome by
fatigue and stress, was deeply upset. He didn't know what to do. Some of
the tellers were also upset. They looked on the abortive launch as a management failure and their own failure, rather than a Geac failure. They
hadn't been well enough prepared, they said. Bentley was horrified by the
problem start, but at the same time undismayed. "They'll do it," he told
his wife.

The system was still too fragile. It had "borked," as German put it. A new
discipline of fear settled on the Geac crew. Before, the VanCity project had
an esoteric quality to it. The frame of reference for Geac was Donlands
Dairy, where programmer Bagshaw could chat to the order takers, because
often there were no customers calling, and where, if something needed to
be fixed, he could send them off on a coffee break. Now, here at VanCity,
relentlessly, the system had to operate continuously in real time.

German, nevertheless, wasn't discouraged. He had expected what had
happened. While it was a horrible feeling to have failed, it wasn't too
horrible. It was like a young prizefighter going into the ring, knowing that
he might end up beaten to a pulp, but, after endless months of training and
sparring, having to do it anyway. German had been after McKay to let them
go up, even though the system might not work too well. Sometimes one had
to get knocked down to get back up again.

He also knew, in the way that only he could know, that despite appearances they had not really failed. Almost everything about the system was
different, from the terminals to the computer architecture. The project had
the complexity and newness of a space launch. Problems were bound to
crop up. They had to see the system operating for themselves in order to
move forward. The Branch 1 trial had demonstrated that, whatever the
problems, the thread of the system did work and they were on the right
track. There were chinks in the programming, but those were the result of
inadequate testing. Problems like that could be fixed.

Consultant Al Fowler, who had dropped by from time to time, was the
least taken aback. Like German, he knew the difficulty of the task the Geac
crew had set themselves. He had told Bentley that he would be the most
surprised person in the world if they met their deadline. Six months was an
incredibly short time, he said. What astonished him was how few problems
there were and especially how fast they had arrived at that point.

For Bagshaw, too, the abortive trial was a turning point. He was more sure
than ever that his faith in German had not been misplaced and that the
pieces fitted together. Over the next two months, the team rewrote the
software and finished pieces that hadn't been done earlier. They also did
much more testing. McKay manoeuvred German into hiring a couple of
young techies whom Al Fowler had found, to beef up the ranks. German was
touchy about new people being brought in when something had gone
wrong, but McKay had done it in such a subtle way that he had hardly

noticed. All the panic had gone. The board also held fast. Stan Parsons, who was president, told McKay he was on the right track and not to let the detractors get to him. McKay decided that the next time they went on-line, they would start with the small Main Street branch. In the smaller setting, they would be able more quickly to identify problems as they came up.

The relaunch went off without a hitch. It was a good thing it did, McKay laughed. Otherwise he would have had to go through those notes he had written and try to make sense of them. The Geac crew, who had stayed up through the night, watched the transactions coming in for about an hour and then went over to the branch. It was eerily quiet. The tellers were routinely going about their work. Bagshaw felt let down by the anti-climactic ordinariness of it all. There was no champagne. It would have been out of place. Bagshaw went home to sleep.

They continued making adjustments for another six weeks and then proceeded to convert the other branches at the rate of one every two weeks. German had to deal with so many little problems on a day-to-day basis—the kind of niggling, post-triumphal housekeeping that drove him wild—that there was no single moment when he sat down and realized the system was in place. The VanCity project was no longer fun. It was time to move on. McKay had put together a transition team to train staff, which worked well. Terminals and keyboards were then rare, leading-edge artifacts. The change, McKay recalled, was like going from the horse and buggy age to the supersonic era in one leap.

The technology performed as promised. The information pulsed in alternating bursts through the telephone lines, back and forth from VanCity's eight branches to the computer. With the compressed data and the other architecture, the accessibility was seemingly instantaneous. No lead time was required. Once the teller entered the appropriate instruction, the information flashed on the screen.

People who came from the banks to work for VanCity—and the banks were primarily where VanCity got its employees—could not at first believe what they saw before them. The system made their life infinitely simpler, compared with what they had been used to. The automatic balancing took tellers about fifteen minutes instead of up to an hour that tellers spent in the banks.

Key-punching was eliminated: another efficiency. The mounds of computer paper that arrived every morning were also gone. Tellers, similarly, no longer had to walk back to those stacks of paper to check somebody's balance. The balance was in front of them on the monitor. The members, to their delight, could even see it for themselves. There were now fifty-five thousand of them. The saving in time, for the tellers, meant not only that members were served more quickly, but also that fewer tellers were required for the same number of members. This meant a delay in the expansion of premises—a long-term saving in premises costs.

Posting to the wrong account was also virtually eliminated. With the old, batch system, some entries would inevitably be posted in the wrong place, no matter how accurate the keypunch operator was. Members also could inadvertently get their account number wrong. When these errors surfaced, somebody would have to go to the time-consuming trouble of correcting them, often having to search out old vouchers. Now the tellers posted the entries as the transactions themselves occurred, with the member's name and account number on the screen. The name and number had to jibe. If they didn't, the teller corrected the mistake on the spot.

The data-processing time bomb was defused. There was no longer the fear that VanCity's expansion would outstrip the data-processing capability available—the nightmarish chaos scenario. The main objective of the on-line system had been to get over this data-processing hump, but all the new things that VanCity wanted to do, and had been indefinitely postponed, also now became possible. Totally new departures, like multi-branch access for members, were foreshadowed in the system. The data, instantaneously updated on a central computer, could be retrieved at all locations.

The system made a powerful impression on members each time they came in, with its startling technology and its reminder, once more, of how far VanCity was ahead of the banks. There was nothing like it anywhere else in the world. Word of mouth and media publicity about the system brought in new members. Media coverage also hearkened back to VanCity's pioneering of daily interest in 1967. The banks still did not have daily interest. A popular picture emerged of a small, local financial institution that was superbly innovative and immensely attractive. People in the industry who had until now ignored VanCity suddenly became aware of it.

Members loved seeing their name, account balance and recent transactions in front of them on the screen. It was like seeing their name in lights. The teller could even go back in time and look at old entries. Because of the system's elegantly simple "alpha" references—for deposits, withdrawals and different accounts—anybody could be trained to use it. With most other systems tried later, such references had to be coded in a complex way, which made the training curve very long. McKay could take kids out of school, with no experience, and train them on the VanCity system in a day. Experienced tellers could adjust quickly. Since the computer did their arithmetic for them, tellers just had to be careful to count the cash properly when they gave it to a member or took it from a member for a deposit.

It was so very easy—money in and money out, just as German had told Bagshaw less than a year earlier. It now seemed a lifetime ago.

CHAPTER 30

End of the Jazz Age

DON BENTLEY WAS WORRIED. VanCity was no longer the organization that it used to be, and Bentley wondered if he had the ability to look after its future.

His heart-valve surgery, he supposed, had been a success. He was still alive. Could one work out an accounting system by which a comptroller could enter into the books the results of a medical procedure? The question made him smile. He didn't need a comptroller to tell him that he had to be careful. He had cut down on his liquid lunches and his drinking. He would say, instead, that he already had an engagement, which was his jocular cover story for going home for lunch and lying down in the den for a fifteen-minute nap.

He wasn't working the hours he had put in before. He was even managing some golf on Wednesdays. He had gotten a bad surprise one day when, sitting in his office in the summer, he had noticed that his left hand was much paler than his right hand. He assumed, in that instant, that something was terribly wrong and that he was going to have a heart attack there and then. The pale left hand, it turned out, was caused by his golfing glove, which he wore on that hand, as compared with the other, which was tanned. That was wonderfully funny. It was just as well he hadn't been involved in overseeing the Geac project. That would have really killed him. He wanted to keep ahead of the times, not just be even with them, and he was no longer sure he could do it.

By custom, VanCity in the past had a spot on B.C. Central's board. John Lucas, a major figure on the board and a VanCity director, had died in the spring, leaving that slot open. Bentley decided to fill it, to keep track of Central from the inside. He had come to the conclusion that it was better to have heartburn knowing what was going on than to have heartburn not knowing. With a little bit of skullduggery among friends, he got himself elected. He and Ethel laughed uproariously about the manoeuvre and its shock effect on George May.

In the fall of 1975, a wayward political incident reminded Bentley just how complicated life could be. An ad hoc community group calling itself the Pender Street Committee was fighting the blockbusting efforts of a small-time developer, in its neighbourhood immediately behind VanCity's East Hastings branch. The lawyer-developer had torn down three low-rent houses, and wanted to demolish some others he owned, for commercial development. The battle had gone to Vancouver City Council. It turned out that the developer in question had bought several of the lots from VanCity, had financed the purchase through a VanCity mortgage and also, as a lawyer, had handled some of VanCity's mortgage work. The lots were across the alley from the branch. They had been acquired at the same time as the purchase of the branch, but Bentley had decided not to undertake a VanCity housing project on them and they were sold off.

The neighborhood committee picketed the branch with signs reading "VanCity Supports Blockbusting." Several of the people being evicted were VanCity members. Their own money, they argued, was being used against them.

What to do with VanCity at large, however, most preoccupied Bentley. Its growth had been phenomenal. In 1955, when he had taken over, VanCity had $1 million in assets. In 1966, before Plan 24, it had reached the $13 million mark. Now, in 1975, it was approaching $300 million in assets. There had been a decline in growth in 1974, although there was still an impressive 23 per cent gain, but VanCity was running well ahead of that again and might boost assets by more than a third in 1975. This wasn't as sensational as the record 89 per cent increase in 1971, but it was on a much larger base.

Bentley had gradually come to understand that whatever the rhetoric, VanCity was no longer just serving its members. It was too large. It had taken on a life of its own. It had to be interested in its own welfare and survival, and not only in the welfare of its members. Where would the people come from to do that new kind of work? He wasn't sure. What kind of organization would VanCity have to become? He wasn't sure, either. Was he the right person to take VanCity through the next phase of its development? He was least sure of that. He did know, however, that his operating style had to change.

He thought about the irony of it—that he had become a prisoner of VanCity's roaring success. He was immensely proud of what they had done and his role in it. VanCity was his baby. He remembered talking to auditor Walter Dyck about the need to redesign the financial statements, because the numbers were becoming too large for the previous small, cramped format. That hadn't been so long ago. He insisted at the same time that the figures not be rounded off to the nearest thousand dollars, a practice that had become fashionable in accounting circles. He did not want members with less than a thousand dollars in VanCity to think their deposits were insignificant. One day VanCity would probably drop the last three digits. Something invaluable about the credit union would then be lost—had already been lost. He regretted that, but organizations do evolve. With fifty-five thousand members in eight branches, tellers would not remember members' numbers and probably not many of their names, either. He would not, however, want to give away any of those members to a bank or otherwise try to recover the past.

What was amazing was not that the organization would now have to change, but how far it had come as it was. He was more determined than ever to defend VanCity's autonomy and the creativity that went with it. Central would never have signed a contract with Geac. Bentley had always felt in his bones the logic of autonomy. Autonomy and co-operation were two sides of the same coin: co-operation meant people freely, in their own way, coming together for a co-operative purpose, not organizational centralism. He remembered going to a national conference of credit union leaders in Winnipeg shortly after he joined VanCity. The participants spent most of their time trying to establish unity. The conference consisted mostly of bitterness and backroom politics. Unity for unity's sake, he had concluded then, was not a sensible thing.

He liked keeping his managerial overheads to a minimum. He had just three lieutenants—McKay, Spooner and Nelson—and among the four of them, they oversaw the organization, all $250 million worth. They had started building up middle management apart from branch managers—a system accountant, a personnel officer, a computer system manager, a trainer for tellers to use the system, someone to handle registered retirement savings plans—but they had been slotted in as the need came up, ad hoc, without any master organizational plan. It wasn't that Bentley tried to run VanCity all by himself, as some people thought. His informal, personal style only made it seem that way. VanCity had become highly personalized as Bentley's organization.

Its creativity still amazed him. In 1975, VanCity had introduced its own RRSP and Registered Home Ownership Savings Plan, designed to be as simple and straightforward as possible. The plans had no commissions, no administrative charges, and no withdrawal restrictions—the first of their kind in the country. They also allowed for quarterly adjustments in interest rates because of interest-rate fluctuations. It was Widdifield, with his insurance background, who had suggested there be no fees. Widdifield was familiar with how life insurance companies had loaded policies with front-end fees and how objectionable and exploitive they could be. He did not have to convince the board. The difference between a VanCity RRSP, which refused to take advantage of people, and the RRSPs offered by the banks and others, delivered a powerful message. The branches were overrun with money. Plans were underway for an insurance department and a real estate department, which would take VanCity even further into the future as a financial supermarket.

Laura Smalley was still with Bentley. Spooner retained his sparkle. Nelson was looking after commercial real estate loans and VanCity's housing projects, as well as supervising branch managers' lending. Bentley had suggested to Nelson that he get a general manager's job somewhere, because he knew how to run a credit union and could be of great help to credit unions who needed assistance. Nelson had responded that he was happy where he was. He appreciated the opportunity to work for Bentley and would stay with VanCity as long as he could.

McKay had somehow seen the genius in those unusual Geac people. McKay was different from others. Bentley had given up trying to figure out why McKay wouldn't get up on time in the morning. Once he was late for a specially arranged trip to Victoria and they had to leave without him, flying at considerable cost instead of taking the ferry, because, after waiting, they were behind schedule. McKay showed up on his own in Victoria hours later. Bentley was upset, but there was no help for it.

Branch managers were given wide latitude. Bentley thought of Ray Evelle in Branch 1. How long would Evelle have survived in the Bank of Commerce, where he started? Would they ever have put him in charge of their main branch if he had left them in mid-stream, as he had VanCity? Bentley had welcomed him back. John Iseli, not quite so young any more, was flourishing in Kitsilano. The intense Jan Chapman, unsure about how far she could go and fighting for her standing, had turned out to be a better resource than even he had anticipated.

Together they were something like a Dixieland jazz band. They had the superficial appearance of anarchy and disorder, but some unwritten, inner discipline held them together. A sideman, say, Spooner, with Plan 24, could pick up the tune and run with it. Then another, like McKay, with the computer project, might step in at the right moment. They had that most valuable of jazz qualities—spontaneity. He, Bentley, looked ahead carefully and watched the numbers but, after that, he left them to it. He could even step off the stage and do something else, or sit down for a while. If one of the players was drinking too much, like Spooner, one tried to say something, but ultimately it was their spirit and inventiveness one thought of. It was a mistake, too, to think of VanCity as organizationally primitive, just as it was a mistake to think of Dixieland as a primitive species of jazz, when real, New Orleans Dixieland was imaginative and finely articulated. In jazz parlance, his people weren't trained "readers," like the bureaucratic chartered banks, they were "rehearsers," who listened to each other. They played hot or cool as they fancied, were all different, came as they were, played all at once, played each in their own way, until you would think they would break apart, yet the freedom they had to be themselves had the opposite effect.

Still, he did have to change because the organization had changed. A metamorphosis was under way. He had felt it ever since he had moved into the new premises upstairs, separate from the branch. In late 1975, he got together with Walter Dyck over lunch and asked him if he would come on board and also do a study on how a new VanCity should be organized. Dyck agreed to join VanCity. Bentley had more or less decided to leave and, in talking to Dyck, was choosing a successor. The next day, he took off to California for a holiday and some golfing.

Bert Gladu had affectionately reminded him to make sure he was back for the annual directors' and managers' dinner, Saturday, December 13. Ron Spooner had set up a special evening at Ming's Cabaret in Chinatown and sent out a humorous notice. Bentley wasn't due back until the following day, but as his holiday wound down, he decided to return a bit early and surprise them at the party. The Pacific Northwest was hit with a snow storm. Bentley, intent on getting back, concentrated on his driving. It was hard going. By the time he and Ethel arrived home, it was already early evening. To get from the car to the house, they had to trudge through deep snow. He had trouble breathing. He was taken to emergency, where he suffered a heart attack and died. The party had begun. Stan Parsons, who was president, was informed of what had happened and met hurriedly with a couple of other directors. They decided not to announce the news that evening, so as not to cut the party short.

The funeral was held in the Canadian Memorial United Church at Burrard and 16th. A huge crowd packed into the church and flowed over onto the street. Golfing partner and original credit union auditor Fred Graham delivered the eulogy. Old credit union brother-in-arms Rip Robinson, who otherwise might have done the eulogy, was too ill. George May and other Central people attended.

Ethel Bentley had asked Evan Wolfe to find a jazz trumpeter for the ceremony. It was, she said, what Don had wanted. Wolfe got in touch with a journeyman, cross-over trumpeter, Donnie Clark, who played with Lance Harrison's Dixieland Band. Bentley liked News Orleans jazz, Wolfe told him. Clark wore his ordinary gig suit for the occasion. Between designated parts of the service, he stood up and played "St. Louis Blues," "Birth of the Blues" and "Basin Street Blues." "It was just like Don to plan his own funeral," architect Ray Toby quipped. Ethel had originally thought of "When The Saints Go Marching In," but could not face it because it was so upbeat. When Clark began playing and she felt the music, she wished she had included it. It would have been triumphant.

When the service was over, Ethel turned to leave. Wayne McKay, thinking she was heading over to where the Central group had been, to rage upon them in her grief, blocked her way. Looking back, he saw that the Central contingent had already slipped out. No reception was announced. Ethel had decided against one. "There was no way I was going to have those Central people back to the house," she explained. "So many people in the credit union movement had made Don's life miserable with their bitching and bickering. They were so two-faced about Don. I knew what they had put him through. I would have spit in their faces." Her friends would drop over to the house anyway. Bentley's ashes were scattered along the fairways at the Quilchena golf course.

Ron Spooner earlier in the year had started an internal newsletter called *TATS*—To Advise The Staff. He wrote an obituary issue. He referred to Bentley as D. B., the way Bentley signed off his memos and the way Spooner had come to refer to him. The use of the initials had an old-fashioned ring to it. Yet, in the article, Spooner captured Bentley with unusual insight and clarity, given his emotions. The obituary was addressed particularly to newer employees who hadn't known Bentley. Spooner was giving Bentley voice, for the people of VanCity, this one last time. It was the only way he knew of saying goodbye to his friend.

Wayne McKay felt the bottom of his world had fallen out. Don Nelson was also badly shaken. He tried joking to himself that if Bentley had been thinking at all, he wouldn't have died on him and left him there. Stan Parsons and the board, shocked and disconcerted, were wondering how they were going to proceed now, on their own. Bert Gladu kept thinking that if he hadn't insisted that Bentley return for the party, Bentley might still be alive. He couldn't bring himself to go over to the house after the funeral. It was too much for him. He thought back to the early days, when a young and bright Don Bentley had started working for them and VanCity was one crowded, proud little branch at Quebec and Broadway. The great jazz age at VanCity had come to an end.

PART FIVE

1976-1984

CHAPTER 31

The Successor

GEOFF HOOK TOOK THE CALL from Stan Parsons at about midnight, in late December 1975. Parsons was still at a VanCity board meeting. Hook had been asked by a couple of directors if he would let his name stand for general manager, and he had agreed. He had been manager of the Credit Union Reserve Board for six years and was ready to move on. He had never been far from VanCity. Parsons wanted to know, now, if he would accept the position. Hook did not hesitate.

He slept only two or three hours that night, his mind racing. He thought of the building job he could do. Don Bentley's heart surgery, Hook knew, had slowed him down. For about a year VanCity had been marking time, in Hook's view—not that it wasn't doing great things, like the Geac project, but it was in strategic limbo. VanCity was becoming a large organization. It needed different management structures and leadership qualities different from Bentley's personalized style.

Hook churned the implications in his mind. VanCity was on the verge of really flourishing. Hook saw himself grabbing a baton from Don in some historic marathon relay race. VanCity's image was good. VanCity had also been lucky, because the banks were so ossified and massive. This gave VanCity a tremendous advantage. It would have the Geac computer system. The kinds of new services it could deliver to members were waiting to be explored. Gus German must indeed have been brilliant, Hook thought. The timing was good, too. Vancouver eastwards to the growing suburbs was starting to show it was ready for VanCity. The fight for the recognition of credit unions—that they were as as reliable and competent as they said they were—had been won.

He wasn't Don Bentley, though, he reminded himself. He was Geoff Hook. He had his own style of management, just as Don had done things his way. He would have to be careful with staff and the board. He could not make the same assumptions about their support that Don could. Don had been there a long time. Hook would have to win his own place. He couldn't buy that place or talk people into giving it to him. He would have to gain their respect day by day...

His mind drifted on.

Arriving at work that morning, he called the chair of the Credit Union

Reserve Board and told him about the job offer. He could hardly wait to get over to VanCity. Officially, he wasn't to start until March 1, but he made an arrangement with the reserve board whereby he worked there every morning and at VanCity afternoons and evenings. He had been a member at Branch 1 for almost twenty years, since 1956. He had always entered the building from the front door on Broadway. Now he came at it through the lane, parked his car at the back, and walked through a back door almost directly onto the third floor. It was the first time it had occurred to him that the building was set into the Fairview Slopes.

He caught the smell of newly laid carpets as he stepped inside. Wayne McKay and Don Nelson greeted him. He knew them fairly well. He saw the computer room and his empty office. He recalled that Don Bentley had worked out of an office at the back of the branch, downstairs, for a couple of years. The "back room," it was called, as if it were a historic site. Hook had often dropped by to chat. The room was windowless; it was like a cave. Hook wondered how Don had tolerated it for so long. It was typical Don Bentley, though.

Hook met the board, most of whom he already knew. It wasn't that he was among strangers. He also quickly visited the branches. He shook hands with the branch managers and staff. He had strong convictions, even at this point, that one should never neglect branches. He had the feeling he was going to like it.

Geoffrey Hook was one of those middle-class Englishmen who, once in Canada and freed from British class-bound society, was thriving, as if he were North American bred in the bone.

His father was a tool-and-die maker in York. He had made aircraft parts during World War II. If Geoff had stayed working with his father, he would have been exempt from military service because the factory was a wartime industry. The young Hook, however, eighteen years old, was looking for adventure. He quit to join the forces. He ended up in the Persian Gulf, attached to the 43rd Indian Infantry Brigade, which was part of the Indian army. His job was to organize convoys in the Iranian port of Bushire, carrying Canadian and American trucks and supplies overland through Tehran to the Soviet Union. He lived in a tent in stifling heat. The logistics were complicated, since ships bringing in the supplies might fall victim to German U-boats. At different times, he had from one hundred to two hundred people working for him. He took naturally to running things; he was a bit of a dominant type.

After being demobilized, Hook spent six months in London. The wartime travelling, however, had given him itchy feet. He decided to go around the world. He made it to Toronto. From there, with some new friends, he headed off in an old Model A Ford to Vancouver by the perilous all-Canadian route. He arrived with no money. He and another fellow in the group got jobs with a gyppo logger in Bamfield, on the west coast of

Vancouver Island. They did choking and then falling. It was dangerous work, without protection. They didn't even wear hard hats. Hook had never seen a power saw before. Once he put an axe into his shoe and lost two weeks' work, and on another occasion he grazed his leg with his power saw. The job meant good money, though, and good food. It was normal to have porridge, eggs and bacon, steak, apple pie and extras all for breakfast, eat like a horse at other meals too, and yet burn it all off. Hook liked the exuberant outdoor physicality of the job and its frontier quality.

At a party in Vancouver, he met a radiological technician, Mary Bancroft, who stopped him in his tracks. After that winter, he decided to stay in Vancouver. He found a job doing bookkeeping for Spencer's Department Store on Hastings Street. It was his first brush with accounting. The following year, he and Mary got married, and a year after that, he joined the B.C. Co-operative Wholesale. He began as the assistant to the accountant. Soon he and Mary had a daughter, and he discovered ambition. He entered a five-year program in the UBC extension department to become a certified general accountant. It meant fifteen to twenty hours of homework a week on top of his job and his travelling for the co-op. He studied weekends for five long years, using his office. It was the only way he could survive in the course. Near the end of this period, he became treasurer of the co-op. It was his first big job.

The B.C. Co-operative Wholesale was a business operating by its wits. Its leading people came from the prairie co-ops, particularly Federated Co-operatives in Saskatoon. They were honest-to-goodness intellectual believers in co-operatives. They had drive, motivation and enthusiasm, and carried others along with them. Hook was in a new world. His family were all conservatives—farmers, teachers and businessmen—although he knew something about co-operatives, since they were widespread in Britain. He picked up the stories of the great co-operative struggles in Canada, like the fight to establish the Saskatchewan Wheat Pool. His boss had been a fieldman for the Pool.

The task at B.C. Co-operative Wholesale was an uphill battle. There weren't that many retail co-operative outlets in the province. When Hook told people that he worked with co-operatives, they didn't know what he was referring to. The wholesale society itself was very small. Its people had to fight tooth and nail to procure supplies—businesses regularly snubbed them—and then had to struggle with cash flow to pay for them. One of Hook's jobs was to juggle the accounts payable, doling out the money to suppliers a bit at a time, because the society had no capital. It always made a little money, but just barely. One year it managed a $30,000 net profit, the members were ecstatic.

While its wholesale operation was modest, the society also ran a division that managed retail co-ops under contract. Many of the co-op stores, while well meaning, were amateurish. The outlets were scattered across the province—Ucluelet, Tofino, Castlegar, Grand Forks, Revelstoke, Terrace,

Prince Rupert, Fort St. John. Most roads to the outlets were unpaved washboard. Coastal flying was by stripped-down float plane. Hook ended up in charge of this side of the operation. Clutching three big briefcases, he would hit the outlying locations, take inventory, give the operations a look-over, offer professional direction and sometimes replace the manager. B.C. Co-operative Wholesale was thin in senior management, so whenever there was a crisis, Hook had to go out and look after it; there was nobody to delegate work to. He was constantly out of town. It was a physically demand-ing routine, but he was young and healthy.

In Vancouver, he took to walking early in the morning. It was the only time he had to himself. Lunchtimes were spent meeting people. In the evenings, the telephone calls began. The co-operative movement was full of politics. Hook threw himself into his work, so that even after he had finished his accounting program his week often extended to seven days. There were meetings on many weekends. People in the movement, he thought sardonically, loved the camaraderie of meetings. Going to a meet-ing on Sunday was their idea of a good time. Hook always showed up because it was part of his job, and he was intent on doing his job well. "If they want us there, we'll be there," was the co-op's working philosophy. He began to feel there wasn't a farmer's institute or small co-operative any-where in the province that he hadn't visited and eaten homemade baking. The co-operative wholesale and the credit union groups did not generally mix, but there were connections there, too. The wholesale's line of credit was with Central. Hook, himself, was on VanCity's board.

One day in late 1964, John Lucas, Central's chair, asked Hook if he could drop by after work at the Biltmore Hotel, the new uptown watering hole at Kingsway and 12th Avenue, a stone's throw from the Credit Union Build-ing. Lucas, at the rendezvous, offered Hook the job as Central's general manager, to succeed Rip Robinson. Hook was in line to take over the wholesale society, but its future was up in the air. His leaving would upset his boss, but the offer from Central made more sense and he took it.

Working in Central's office in the Credit Union Building put him just across the hallway from Bentley, but their relationship went back a decade. The two men had hit it off right away. They both had financial minds. They shared a distaste for politicking and an interest in professionalism. Bentley was always looking for people with a combination of co-operative back-ground and operational experience to join VanCity's board. Hook was a good find.

They became friends. Bentley was on Central's board and had made sure Hook's name came up when they were looking for a new general manager. Hook met the Bentley family, including Don's father. The Bentleys had a certain charm, Hook thought. They had a nice way of speaking and were very smart. They were mavericks, too. They liked to go their own way.

Hook and Bentley had lunch together as often as once a week. They were preoccupied with the overall financial soundness of the movement, particularly how to deal with its inadequate capital base. Hook, when they first met, wasn't yet a golfer. It had been survival to that point—just work, travel and study. Having received his certified general accountant accreditation, however, he took on the sport. He played frequently with Bentley, although, compared with him, Hook was just a hacker. He and his family had moved to a house just two blocks away from the Bentleys. Hook's wife, Mary, and Ethel Bentley played bridge together.

Running Central was an arduous development job, which was exactly what Hook liked. Central had become important as its member credit unions expanded and gained strength. Hook's non-stop work habits, however, were beginning to tire him. He remembered travelling to Ottawa on a cheque-clearing issue and working intensely while he was there, only to come back to a desk piled high with paper.

He also had to deal with the proposed merger with the B.C. Credit Union League. The League's and Central's organizational cultures were polar opposites. League conventions never ceased to amaze Hook. CU&C's convention lasted a day. Central's convention followed the next day, fairly expeditiously, like an annual meeting of a credit union, which it in fact was. Then the League went on for three days after that. There were approximately 250 credit unions in British Columbia in those days, most of them fairly small. Hook had a thesis that many of the people on their boards, whether civil servants or tradesmen, did not have very exciting jobs, whereas serving on a credit union board, just like serving on a municipal council or a school board, allowed them to express their leadership potential. They loved the interaction of conventions.

The delegates would party the prior Sunday night at whatever location the convention might be held. They looked upon the meeting as a big holiday. There might be six hundred delegates. No matter when they went to bed and despite their hangovers, they were on the convention floor, bright-eyed, first thing Monday morning. They were still going at it at dinnertime. Then, after dinner, they sat around in hotel rooms, having a few drinks, and still carried on. The whole week was shop talk, drinking, socializing and arguing night and day, so that even the sleeping seemed to be part of the energetic activity. There were also factions at these conventions, to add a few sparks. The Kootenay faction, for example, reflecting its geographic isolation, would always be fighting tooth and nail over some perceived wrongdoing or injustice.

Hook had a great time at these conventions. As an observer, he could sit back and enjoy them. League politics had nothing to do with him. Dick Monrufet, the League's managing director, had to handle them. Now, with the merger talks, Hook had to deal with them, too. If the League and B.C. Central were going to merge, something had to give. There was a struggle. For all intents and purposes, the League side, with its pushing and pulling and politics, won. If Hook now applied for the position of CEO of the new organization, he would have a fight on his hands. Even if he succeeded, he would be faced with the same discord. He was burned out. The drawn-out merger process had taken away his zest for the job. The League style of politicking wasn't his favourite activity, either, and it would be part of the new Central. He had been going at it day and evening, many weekends, often travelling, for almost twenty years. Suddenly his sense of purpose disintegrated.

Bentley was aware of Hook's unhappiness. One day on the golf course, he asked Hook if he would like to take over the Credit Union Reserve Board, which Bentley chaired. The offer caught Hook at this low moment in his life, and he said okay on the spot. He realized later that he should have taken a month off, gone away on holiday, and then come back and made a decision. There were always things in one's life one could look back on with a little more wisdom.

Hook's job at the reserve board was larger than it appeared on the surface. He tightened up practices in the disparate credit unions across the province and increased board monitoring. He knew it was important work. Yet for all the initiative and skill it required, the board in the end was just a supervisory body. VanCity had what the reserve board didn't have: dynamic action. Hook was the logical person for the VanCity job, too. Even Walter Dyck, who was passed over, thought Hook was the best choice. Wayne McKay had also been considered, but the idea of stepping into Bentley's shoes—of replacing his hero—was beyond him. McKay couldn't see how he could possibly do it.

The irony of it all was that Hook had to follow—and, for him, that meant improve on—the one person everybody had idolized, and someone who had been a friend as well.

CHAPTER 32

The Clash of Cultures

GEOFF HOOK HAD NOT ASSASSINATED Don Bentley, but he had replaced him and been thrown into that same ambivalent, complicated world of cross-currents where the pretender takes over and is met with memories and mixed loyalties. Let oneself get caught in those cross-currents and one was finished. Bentley was in every nook and cranny of the organization. Hook concentrated on implementing the working plan in his head.

He projected an image of the stern accountant. "He sure looks mean and ugly!" Wayne McKay's mother-in-law exclaimed, when she saw Hook's picture for the first time in the *Working Dollars* newsletter. He had a hawkish mien. From the sombre visage in the photo, one could imagine him as some middle villain in a Shakespearean tragedy. Hook felt he had to let people somehow know there would be no more of the old ad hoc atmosphere. He maintained his stern front the same way teachers learn that, in a new school, they should never smile before Christmas.

Hook was a structure freak, Wayne McKay thought. Something in Hook's CGA training or in the stiff-necked accountants' culture said structure was all-important, McKay speculated. Under Bentley, if there was a job to be done, people just did it, without worrying about lines of responsibility. If something was too time-consuming for the person with the assignment, an available body was recruited to help out or someone extra was hired on the fly. Hook started instead with an organizational chart, the first one VanCity had ever had. On the chart were boxes, one for each position. For each position there was a job description, typed out on a sheet of paper kept in a file. People in these jobs would have specific, well-defined responsibilities.

Hook also created "divisions," which grouped managerial activities together so that the lines of reporting would be clear and so that people could see where they fitted into the organization. There was an operations division, which would look after branches and lending, a marketing division for advertising and member relations and an administration division to look after financial controls and the computer system. Underneath the division managers were the middle managers. Laid out in the chart in that way, they made VanCity look like a different organization. It seemed, suddenly, bigger and more powerful.

Bentley had already begun building a middle-management level. Hook set out systematically to plug the gaps in this level so that the organization had greater capability and more specialization. He pencilled in new, empty boxes for managers of branch operations, for security and premises and for investment. He decided he would oversee the operations division himself. The key new boxes to be filled were the two for the remaining division managers.

Hook knew the dangers to stability of coming in and sweeping senior management clean. It wasn't his style, either. He decided nobody would be fired. He could see people were upset and tense. He would take what was there and gradually move forward from that point. It was a delaying action, giving himself time, rather than any surrender of his determination to re-create the organization. He already knew where he was going. As he saw it—and one did not want to speak ill of the dead—Bentley had let the organization grow beyond his ability to manage it. There had been no management structure. Bentley had killed himself because he had been running VanCity out of his hip pocket.

Having rejected the Bentley culture, Hook inevitably saw Bentley's people in a different light. McKay had been a dynamic and innovative branch manager, had been comptroller, had piloted the introduction of two ground-breaking data processing technologies and had run VanCity in Bentley's absence. Hook knew all this but, for what he wanted to do, McKay was an unknown quantity. McKay had no accountant certification and his track record was at VanCity. VanCity was too much of an anomaly—too different from anything else and too much a Bentley organization—for such a track record to stand by itself. Ron Spooner, the force behind daily interest, was seen as even less of a fit—so much so that one of Hook's new people, Frank Coffey, was under the impression that Spooner had been only marginally involved in the innovation. Some outside marketing guy was supposed to have done it all, Coffey thought. In the new management optic, Spooner's intuitiveness seemed simply wild and unpredictable. Spooner and Nelson, like McKay, had no extensive professional training—the kind that ended up with a certification. By inference, VanCity had now outstripped their capabilities. They were products of the Bentley culture, which Hook was trying to replace, and they would naturally be loyal to it.

In the summer, he had made a decision. He hired a comptroller at the regional office of the Canadian Imperial Bank of Commerce, Frank Coffey, to become manager of the administration division—the financial and computer side at VanCity. Coffey replaced McKay. He was a Hook protégé. He had worked under Hook at the B.C. Co-operative Wholesale and later had replaced Hook at the wholesale as comptroller and treasurer.

For the marketing division, Hook brought in the marketing manager at the Bank of British Columbia, Jack Stimson. Ron Spooner was knocked down a notch, to member relations, reporting to Stimson. Hook had thought carefully about Spooner—he had even talked to the board about his decision—and was satisfied it was the right thing to do. Nelson, as chief loans officer, was also slotted at the middle-manager level. McKay was left in limbo. Hook appointed him "special projects manager." It was a way of keeping McKay occupied while Hook decided what to do with him.

Coffey and Stimson, arriving at VanCity, were like ambitious émigrés who had left a settled, old-country life for the frontier. The banks had been good to them by giving them a wide range of experience. Something, however, left them dissatisfied and itching to move on. In Coffey's case, it was the CIBC's politics and closed doors; in Stimson's case, the Bank of British Columbia's impersonality. They both knew that VanCity would be different.

Coffey was a wandering CGA, forever searching for a management function. He did not like being labelled an accountant. He was an in-between man trying to get out. He had the guarded, sardonic, self-deprecatory humour of someone who never quite fitted in.

As a young man, he had decided in one fell swoop to drop university, get married and go into accounting. The object, however, was not to be a bookkeeper. He wasn't a number cruncher, although he did not mind handling numbers. He saw accounting as a way to achieve a prominent business role. At one point in his moving about, in California, he ended up, because he was an accountant, as an internal auditor instead of a member of the management group, as he had expected. The work was too "ticky ticky" for him, he said. He left, to wander again.

At the B.C. Co-operative Wholesale, he simply made himself a planner, because nobody else was doing it. He worked long hours at the job, sometimes as late as midnight, and often weekends as well. He was tall and thin, and a heavy smoker. His energy seemed to come from nowhere. The struggling wholesale society did not take his planning advice, however, so he moved on to the CIBC. There, he finally did do full-bodied planning, as well as overseeing a large department, as comptroller. He became familiar with virtually every aspect of the operation.

He was not a banker, which, paradoxically, only added pleasure to the job. He had none of the traditional fears that the highly autocratic bank had inculcated in its staff. One paid a good deal of attention in the bank to relative position and ranking, both socially and at work, and hence to what one could and could not do. Coffey, not used to these hierarchical relationships, cut across these lines. If he needed to see someone, he saw them. He was able to walk into senior managers' offices at practically any time. The middle ranks could not understand how he got away with it.

The hierarchy, however, did block him. If he was going to rise in the organization, he needed to have a lending background. Otherwise, he would never be accepted as a "banker" in the club sense. If there was a route upwards at all, it was through the comptrollership function at head office in Toronto. He had once, however, opposed Toronto over a plan he considered unworkable, and he had lost that battle. Although he was proven right in the end—perhaps *because* he was proven right in the end— his prospects in Toronto, he thought, were atrocious.

Hook, now, was offering him freedom from politics and hierarchy. Coffey was familiar with VanCity. When he worked for the co-operative wholesale, he had needed a personal loan. There was no chance of getting it at a bank, but through the co-op connection he had heard of VanCity and met Don Bentley. He applied for the loan and got it. Later he ran for the VanCity board and served as a director for a couple of years. He wanted to see how things looked from the other side of the table.

He realized that VanCity was miles ahead of the banking system in meeting people's needs. As Hook talked to him now about the crowds at VanCity, Coffey imagined it bursting at the seams. He understood what Hook meant by potential. He also understood Hook's reference to Van-City's thin management structure and how it needed to be changed. Hook talked about putting together a completely new management team. Coffey had always wondered how Bentley had managed to run an organization of VanCity's size and complexity, and so effectively, with so few people.

Jack Stimson was another emigrant from the banking system. He had come up through the Bank of Montreal in his native Alberta. The culture of the Bank of Montreal, as Stimson experienced it, was "big." The bank had a vastness and influence so massive that it was almost beyond comprehension, to young Stimson's mind.

The bank seemed prepared to do anything to help develop Stimson and his young colleagues, but it did not always know how to respect them. Stimson started night school, working towards a commerce degree through what was called the Bankers' Training Program. Then one day an MBA graduate was placed with him for training. The trainee was paid two and a half times what Stimson was getting. Stimson realized that his night-school work did not mean much in the eyes of the bank.

His Alberta nationalism ultimately got in the way of his moving up the ladder. He had begun to do marketing, specifically branch-location work. The bank decided he should go to Montreal and offered him an attractive promotion. He went to look the city over. It was a different culture, almost a different country, it seemed to him. Stimson had grown up on a ranch. He told his superiors in Calgary that his family and heritage were western and he did not feel comfortable in Montreal. He refused to go. They pretended to understand, but he knew his chances at the bank were limited from that day on, and he let it be known around town that he was available.

Somehow the Bank of British Columbia in Vancouver heard of his situation and made him an offer. Ensconced as marketing manager, he found the bank stillborn. It had no separate identity; its employees lacked spirit. This gave him one advantage, however: he had an open field. He introduced a package account, in which customers paid a modest single fee every month to cover all service charges. Such accounts had taken California by storm, but the large Canadian chartered banks scoffed. Stimson called the proposed new account the Western Account. It took off like a rocket. The name was also used as a slogan for the bank itself—"Canada's Western

Bank." The large banks, seeing the success, quickly brought in their own versions of the account.

Stimson then pioneered a package account for seniors that had no fees at all. For the Bank of British Columbia, this meant foregoing fee revenue, but it pushed up deposits, which the bank could then lend out and use to cover operating costs. It needed those deposits, which, unlike the older banks, it did not yet have.

Stimson was acquiring a reputation in the banking industry for doing things and doing them right. He nevertheless was bothered. He believed in the team concept. Everybody had to be involved. The bank, on the other hand, was hard on people. There were random firings, often based on personal dislike and often, he felt, without regard for individuals or their families. He wondered if there was a smart company that also had a heart and that he could identify with. His own president, incredibly, viewed him much as a consultant rather than as part of a committed team. "I am approving your budget," the man once told Stimson. "Just don't make me look stupid." Stimson still felt that he was on the outside.

Hook, on the other hand, was different. Stimson liked him immediately. He recalled, of their initial meetings, that they both had a high sense of urgency, of "Let's not talk about it, let's do things." The same afternoon that he was offered the job, Stimson called his wife. "I'm going on to VanCity," he told her. "I think I've finally found a company that's got a heart as well as a head. I know what they want from me. I can deliver the goods."

It was clear, now, what Hook's intentions were. Hook, Coffey and Stimson began meeting on Friday afternoons to discuss what changes they might make. McKay was kept on the periphery. Coffey and Stimson accepted Hook's analysis of VanCity without question. They owed their loyalty to him, but, more important, they had been chosen because they fitted his reading of what had to be done. They were immediately caught up in his intensity and his restructuring mission. They were blind to what made the Bentley culture work and downgraded it instinctively.

Coffey was horrified at some of the things he saw. VanCity seemed to be in chaos. Policy and procedure in one branch were not necessarily policy and procedure in the next branch. Coffey thought it a wonder the place wasn't falling apart. Adding to the apprehended chaos was the number of new members walking through the door, despite the limited number of locations. Hook had told him how, looking down from his window during RRSP season, he had seen a line-up extending out the door of the branch and down the sidewalk. He had even seen cars lining up on Broadway, waiting to get into the parking lot. One member brought a stopwatch with him whenever he came in and then told Hook how long he had stood in line. Coffey realized that the potential was even greater than he had imagined. The demand was far in excess of what VanCity's branches and the organization could handle.

Coffey saw lending practices in particular as anarchy in action. There were no guidelines and nothing to follow, it seemed to him. Some of the managers had made a lot of wild loans, he said. Not enough attention was given to ability to repay, and too much reliance was placed on the collateral value of houses and property, which could be undercut by a cyclical fall in prices. The term "debt servicing," which refers to the ability to repay, was unknown in the organization, as far as Coffey could tell. Some managers were softer than others. The philosophy seemed to be to provide people with as much money as they felt they needed. When, a year later, Coffey himself took over branch operations, and hence lending, he became even more uneasy about lending practices.

Where Coffey saw anarchy, Don Nelson, on the other side of the cultural divide, saw orderly operation. Nelson, still chief loans officer, prided himself on keeping lending in good shape and out of trouble, and if it did get into trouble, he wanted to know about it. There were in fact lending guidelines, but they were not spelled out to the last detail in a manual, by which a branch manager largely became an obedient processor of paper. Besides, placing more reliance on collateral and less emphasis on ability to pay was how VanCity had always done business. This allowed families with modest incomes—hence lesser ability to pay according to a rule book—to obtain a VanCity mortgage, if the branch manager felt it would work. The family's income had to be regular, but the branch manager could also take into account the applicant's determination to save in order to make the payments. The propensity to save was especially strong in immigrant communities, and VanCity's managers had considerable experience with them —in Nelson's case, with Portuguese immigrants. That particular experience had been so good that Nelson speculated one could give them a loan and not even worry about their ability to repay.

The autonomy of his branch managers did not bother Nelson, either. Managers were meant to put their experience to work and to use their own judgement. They were also, however, responsible for their loan-loss ratios. Hadn't Bentley himself done it that way? The proof of the matter was in VanCity's performance. Loan-loss ratios were exceptionally low.

Coffey did not see it. He discounted branch managers' experience because most of the branch managers at VanCity were home-grown products. They were not finance people, as he vaguely conceived the term— "finance people" being those who Coffey felt had the necessary prudent judgement. VanCity experience alone was ipso facto deficient.

Hook, and Coffey with him, were convinced that while a more decentralized structure and branch manager autonomy might have worked with just a few branches, and might even pass with the eight branches that VanCity had, it would not work if VanCity were, say, to double the number of branches. Expanding quickly, moreover, was exactly what had to be done in order to capitalize fully on the VanCity name and meet the overflowing demand pressing in around them. This demand was visible and graphic.

Membership had increased 20 per cent in 1975 and was increasing at the
same rate in 1976.

The variations in procedures from branch to branch also struck Hook
and Coffey as an extraordinary anachronism. How could division managers
or middle managers introduce system-wide efficiencies and controls or even
keep things straight in their own heads if one branch did things differently
from another? It also meant that people moving from one branch to
another might have to relearn how they did certain things. One could not
properly train new employees, either, if procedures were not uniform.
Equally astonishing, VanCity did not even have a training program. That
would have to change, too.

More systems uniformity and common training made sense. Computerization was already forcing those changes. Branches were basically the same.
Where should uniformity leave off, however, and individualism begin? The
Bentley culture was fed by individualism. Branches had shared innovations,
but in a less centralized way. A branch manager or supervisor in one branch
could independently introduce a new way of doing things. This would be
talked about at management meetings, and other branches were free to
follow the example. Given the interbranch rivalry, where gaining an edge
was important, good ideas would be picked up and become absorbed. This
allowed maximum creativity at the branch level—what, in a later cycle of
management fads, would be called "empowerment."

Hook and Coffey, however, had other things to think about. They were
making their own difficult transition, trying to come to grips with an
organization that wasn't yet theirs. Bentley had kept the parts together amid
explosive growth, without a centralized structure, but Hook did not have
Bentley's feeling for personal relationships. Nor did he have Bentley's sure
intimacy with members borrowing money and managers lending it to them.
At B.C. Central and at the Credit Union Reserve Board, and earlier as a
VanCity director, he had acquired a detailed knowledge of credit union
operations, but running VanCity was different from thinking about it.
Lending was particularly troublesome for Hook, and also for Coffey, because neither had direct retail lending experience—yet lending was at the
heart of what a credit union did.

Hook instinctively turned to more formal structures and detailed guidelines. He could not have done things Bentley's way even had he wanted to.
The one part of the Bentley legacy he did embrace was VanCity's populist
image, yet his strategy was aimed at transcending the organizational culture
that had created the image.

Still, as Bentley himself had realized, it had to be done. As Hook made his
changes, he found himself much like a stepfather in a new, wary and
sometimes hostile family. There was too much emotion. Hook did not know
how to deal with it. He made the mistake of sharing his analysis that Bentley,
in his last two years, because of his heart surgery, had been incapable of
making decisions. This was hard to take for the Bentley loyalists because it

did not jibe with the Bentley they knew. If Bentley had procrastinated in making certain decisions—decisions involving people—it was because of his compassion rather than any lack of courage. His Geac decision and his stand against Central had shown boldness enough. Hook, they concluded, was intent on obliterating Bentley's name and reputation from the VanCity record books. His exclusion of all of Bentley's people, even McKay, from his inner council, reinforced this impression.

Spooner was particularly upset. Hook thought the transition was going smoothly because nobody had abruptly resigned. Spooner, for example, had stayed with VanCity after Bentley's death. For Spooner, the transition illustrated only Hook's arrogance and ambition. Spooner and Nelson speculated that Hook was going to change things because he did not want people to remember VanCity as something Don Bentley had built; he wanted to show what Geoff Hook had done. They then watched as Hook, whatever his motives, fulfilled their prediction. In explaining something to Hook, Spooner would say, "Oh, well, the chief did it this way," or "The chief wanted it done that way," as if any change would be a transgression. This only confirmed Hook's view that Spooner could not move forward.

Spooner knew he was being marginalized. When Bentley died, the board had not asked him if he was interested in the general manager's position, although it did ask both McKay and Nelson. Spooner was upset that he was not even given the chance to apply. He was deeply offended now by having to report to a newcomer, Stimson, who had taken his job.

The aggressive and well-organized Stimson and the soft, intuitive and effervescent Spooner did not get along. Stimson was not stand-offish. He believed in involving people. He was also straightforward, which for him meant being open and honest with others. He struggled at first with his relationship with Spooner and then just talked to him about it. He asked Spooner what he disliked about the set-up. Stimson ended up saying, "I want to make it happen for you, whatever you want to make happen, but we have a job to do, and I expect you to do that job, as you expect me to do my job. I won't be any harder on you than you are on me. I work for you, but you, too, have got to deliver."

It was meant to get across the idea that they were a team, dependent on each other, and hence to establish a real connection between the two of them. Stimson would have been better off not saying anything. For Spooner, Stimson's talk was just patronizing. Spooner's feelings went much deeper—they were beyond team-building exercises and notions of treating subordinates with dignity. They touched on matters of the soul and of memories intimately connected to the bond that had existed between himself and Bentley and the intangible spirit around them in VanCity. Spooner was even less friendly towards Hook. There was nothing Hook could do that Spooner would agree with.

Ethel Bentley was also upset and angry. Some of Hook's comments about her husband had reached her. The remark that Don was not a good administrator struck her as ridiculous—Don was known exactly for being a good administrator. She remembered bitterly that Don had been instrumental in getting Hook his jobs both at Central and at the reserve board. She ended her friendship with Hook's wife, Mary. She could not stand to be with her after that. There was also some question about the disposition of Don's car, which was a VanCity car. Eventually it was given to Ethel, but the fuss in sorting the matter out caused ill feeling.

She tried supporting Ron Spooner. Hook had apparently explained to Stan Parsons, on the board, that Spooner was an alcoholic. Ethel took exception. Spooner had a drinking problem, she argued, but he wasn't an alcoholic. An alcoholic did not function. At the annual board dinner, to which she was invited, she made a point of sitting next to Parsons and defending Spooner.

Something deeper separated Hook and Ethel Bentley. Hook respected Don Bentley, but unlike Ethel and the Bentley team, he did not revere him. That counted against him.

The board had decided to name the head-office building at 1030 and 1034 West Broadway the "Don Bentley Building." There was a dedication ceremony, but no special effort was made to use the occasion for something larger that would have put the seal on Bentley's contribution. Typically, nobody called the building the Don Bentley Building. It was the main branch, or Branch 1, or the Oak Street branch or head office. The dedicated name wasn't used in VanCity's literature, either. Less than two years later, head office was moved to a large, imposing building at Cambie and 10th Avenue, and the plaque commemorating Bentley, although historically in the right place, went largely unseen and forgotten by both head-office staff and most members.

Staff were unsettled—"antsy," as McKay described it. A sense of trauma hung in the air. Ray Evelle, managing the main branch, was becoming more autocratic. He had been away too long and had not successfully made the adjustment to computerized operations when he returned. The employees in the branch unionized. The Main Street branch also unionized. Hook, to settle down the main branch, offered Evelle, who had once been in insurance, the chance to manage the new VanCity Insurance Services. Evelle at first declined but, thinking better of it, changed his mind. That left the main branch up for grabs. Jan Chapman and John Iseli were the two front runners. McKay lobbied for Chapman and she got the job, much to the dismay of Iseli, who had once been her boss.

Laura Smalley was the next to go. When Hook finally told her he wanted his own secretary, she "let him have it with both barrels," she said. She did not mind being replaced. It was the way that Hook had dealt with Spooner and Nelson that bothered her. Hook was so entirely different from Bentley, Smalley thought. She went to work with Evelle in insurance.

McKay, the one person from the Bentley team who might easily have stepped into the general manager's position, was still in limbo. Hook thought he and McKay had gotten along well from the beginning. McKay felt differently. He was emotionally at sea and wary. He had begun working for Bentley when he was very young. For him, the early days with Hook were stormy. Bentley's daughter had come up to McKay at the funeral and expressed concern that her father's memory would just be erased at VanCity and that they would all forget him quickly. McKay vowed he would not let it happen. He was shaken by Hook's attitude to the Bentley culture. He sided with the family. He was quickly caught in the middle, since Ethel talked to him rather than to Hook. He thought of the two of them as warring factions. He regarded Hook as a stiff Englishman, the kind who went to cricket games, although in fact Hook had little interest in cricket.

McKay's previous workload had exhausted him. He was mentally tired. Because he did not fit in any of Hook's boxes, he was left wondering whether he would be staying or leaving. It took Hook more than a year to decide what to do with McKay. Hook was concerned about the widespread unhappiness among VanCity's staff and asked McKay if he would head up a new human resources division. Hook also was looking ahead to large-scale growth, which would make staff development critical. He thought McKay would shine in the position. McKay was a good listener and soaked things up intuitively. McKay's initial reaction was negative; managing human resources was not what he wanted to do. He had been a branch manager and a comptroller, and could not see himself in a human resources role, which was off to the side and did not rank with operations. He suggested it would be better to have someone more qualified, with a background in the area.

The offer, McKay thought later, was an astute move. Hook was under pressure from the board not to treat McKay shabbily and also not to remove all connection to the Bentley years. If the offer worked out, Hook would look like a genius for making it. If it did not—and McKay was being thrown into an area where he had no expertise—Hook would have an excuse to part company with him.

McKay considered his options. He had never thought of leaving, at least while Bentley was there. He had begun a lifelong affair with VanCity. If he did not accept the offer, the affair was over. He decided to accept the offer. He joined the team, however, only after a fashion. It meant joining outsiders. He held himself back. He wasn't that positive about human resources, and he kept thinking about the past with Bentley and what it had been like.

There were four senior VanCity managers now: Hook, Coffey, Stimson and McKay. Spooner and Nelson were on the rung below, out of the circle, and Smalley was off to the side and out of sight.

CHAPTER 33

The First Stage

GEOFF HOOK WAS AN A-type's A-type. He wanted to get things done. Entering an elevator with an associate, he might unconsciously take the person's elbow to move him into the elevator with more expedition, or he might poke someone in the arm in a conversation to make sure they were listening. There was nothing unfriendly in these gestures, just a kinetic intensity.

The executive management meetings were the crucible for Hook. He had set things up that way, with himself and the division managers on top, the middle managers below them, then the branch managers, the assistant branch managers, the supervisors, the tellers and all the others on the front line below them. The four of them—Hook, Coffey, Stimson and McKay—met on Monday afternoons. Bentley's meetings, which had involved branch managers, had become unwieldy. They were held only monthly and after the branches had closed, at the end of a long day. Hook's management meetings, by contrast, involved the same small executive group, every week at the same time during the day in a meeting room. The meetings were formal, too.

Hook was more outwardly assertive than Bentley. He harnessed himself and his intense energy to VanCity, almost as if it were a physical act. Six- and seven-day weeks were common. He wanted to build a team of managers that functioned together with the same co-ordinated intensity that each of them individually brought to their work. The executive management meetings were critical, because that was when information was shared. VanCity, as Hook saw it, could not continue with a Wayne McKay doing his thing and others doing their things, and perhaps mentioning details as they bumped into each other in a corridor. There had to be better communication. Hook had the division managers talk about their difficulties and challenges, so nobody was caught unaware. If, for example, somebody had to be fired, all the managers knew the prior steps that had been taken to try to resolve the problem and what was coming up. It wasn't enough for Hook to be given the details. Information sharing became an object in itself.

For Hook, competing against the banks and trust companies might not be war, but it was close to it. He took the attitude that if the managers all agreed on something, they could do anything. The fashionable jargon for Hook's approach was "participatory management." Everybody participated, everybody reported. The same participation in decision-making was encouraged at other levels. Divisions had their own management meetings. Branch managers met with the manager of branch operations and frequently with marketing people. Branches individually had their regular meetings. Tellers were not given a chance to outvote their branch manager, but they did have a voice in branch meetings, and if all of them were opposed to something, the branch manager at least would have to think twice before implementing it.

Hook also wanted a high degree of accountability. All the division managers knew their area of responsibility—it was clearly set out in those job descriptions—and they were expected to perform. Bentley had never given much thought to accountability other than to look carefully at the results at the end of each month. There was such extraordinary commitment around him, events were moving so fast and assets growing so quickly, loan-loss ratios were so low—and, besides, inventiveness had its own rules—that the concept of accountability was superfluous. For Hook, however, it was an essential management tool. There was a communal flavour to this management style. One couldn't run one's own show detached. Hook himself was a hands-on manager. He wanted to be close to everything. He vetted all the issues of *Working Dollars*, because they were read by members, and whatever was said in the newsletter would reflect on the organization. He attended branch manager meetings frequently, although they were down at the next level.

Hook's hands-on approach, however, stopped short of making decisions for his division managers. One of his main functions, as he conceived it, was to remove the barriers so that the division managers could do their jobs with the greatest freedom possible. He also saw himself giving them as much support as he could. He spent considerable time with each of them, explaining the relationship.

For Jack Stimson, after the autocratic Bank of Montreal and the uncaring Bank of British Columbia, working with Hook was a revelation. Hook was the best CEO he had ever run into, he thought. Hook actually cared about people. He was sensitive to issues. He always made sure that one measured twice, cut once. The aphorism stuck in Stimson's head. Evaluate twice before making a decision, especially when people are involved. Stimson also—and this was the most enjoyable part of it—had a chance to learn about the entire operation and to appreciate how it looked from the leader's side. Hook gave Stimson a whole new lease on life as a manager.

For Frank Coffey, too, the VanCity environment was a delight to work in. He had learned at the Canadian Imperial Bank of Commerce how to survive in a corporate political system, where everyone was manoeuvring for positional power. He had never liked it. Monday afternoons at VanCity were a world removed. They were a self-contained managers' group at the top of the organization. Each of them had a clearly demarcated area of responsibility. Everything was put on the table. The managers either agreed or disagreed. There was no political gamesmanship to be played.

Wayne McKay was not so delighted; he liked to banter and relax with people. Hook was more formal. There was friction about McKay's schedule. McKay's best hours were from noon to midnight, Hook's from eight in the morning to six in the evening. For Hook, people in a large organization had to be present at the same time, otherwise how could they communicate? It took the better part of two years for Hook to gain McKay's trust.

Hook also established a conventional planning process, in which the divisional managers each drew up their plans for the year, which were then batted around and combined into a one-year business plan and a five-year strategic outline. They used the computer to project future membership and asset levels. This package then went to a two-day retreat attended both by the board and senior management. Hook, who set the agenda and managed the process, was clearly in charge. Lloyd Widdifield, who was no longer on the board, was scornful of Hook. To Widdifield, Hook was just an accountant who, by definition, did not have a creative bone in his body. He had, however, finally introduced the planning process Widdifield had been after for so long.

The plan gave Hook a measure for pursuing accountability. Every month, the management team reviewed performance against the plan. For Hook, the whole point of good management was no surprises. You knew what you wanted to happen, you made it happen and you monitored it constantly to make sure it was happening. If it wasn't happening, it was up to Hook to jump in, question the responsible division managers and find out what the problem was. Detailed quarterly reviews went to the board.

Hook managed the board in the same way. At annual meetings, members rarely heard from the president, but they heard a lot from Geoff Hook. He set the agenda, literally and metaphorically. A full dossier of information and analysis was provided to directors for meetings, setting out the issues and their details. This was a needed improvement, but since it followed Hook's agenda, it reinforced his almost complete control.

Mike Betts, who was vice-president and then president in these years, saw the difference clearly. With Don Bentley, the board, particularly the executive, had been deeply involved. Directors and management were intertwined. Hook replaced this relationship with a more professional management-board relationship, in which a line was drawn between the two and management led the way. Theoretically the board still decided on policy. In practice, since Hook was so dynamic and well-organized, the board followed in management's train.

The Hook structure was like an accordion file. Once in place, it could be expanded virtually at will to accommodate growth or to generate it. The effects developed slowly, because of the transition. The Geac on-line system in Hook's first year, 1976, was new and still had bugs in it to be worked out. VanCity Insurance Services, already being developed, came on stream. The chequing account was transformed into a "Convenience Account," which combined chequing with a line of credit. Monthly income term deposits and income averaging annuities were introduced. The Burnaby branch was moved to larger premises, and the Victoria Drive branch was expanded.

These were minor adjustments. Growth, however, continued to be amazing. Almost 20,000 new members joined that year and, after subtracting the large number who left, net membership had increased by 11,000, to 67,000. Assets increased 26 per cent. The innovations in the Bentley years were still generating momentum, especially Plan 24, although it was nine years old.

Hook and his new team now began introducing new services and opening new branches. They brought in interbranch access, the first anywhere in the country except for the caisses populaires in Quebec. Gus German and Wayne McKay had anticipated the interbranch capability in their brainstorming in the heady days of the Geac project. A member could make a deposit, withdrawal or loan payment at any branch. The on-line system made it possible, since a teller in any branch could bring up any member's account information. It was dubbed "Universal Access."

Universal Access was the real real-time thing, where an entry made at a second branch ran down the telephone line to the computer and was entered in the account just as it would if it were made at the member's home branch. Unlike the caisse system, that entry didn't have to be reprocessed overnight and printed out on paper for the home branch to see. It was already in the main database, retrievable on the screen. Also unlike the technically limited caisse arrangement, all of a member's account information was available at any branch, and not just the last recorded balance. A member could even take out a term deposit or apply for a loan at another branch.

For members who worked and lived in different places, or otherwise were on the go, the novelty and convenience were exciting. Like the on-line system, it was also the kind of modern application of technology that touched the imagination. Again, the banks and trust companies didn't have it. Hook and Stimson pushed that difference as hard as they could. The Bank of Montreal was the first chartered bank to catch up, two years later, in 1979. It had begun work on its on-line system, on which the innovation depended, in 1970 but had become hopelessly bogged down.

Stimson, who had launched the no-fee seniors' package at the Bank of British Columbia, convinced the VanCity team to do the same. They called it the Gold Card Club. It combined a no-charge basic package with reduced charges on other things. To get a march on the banks, they lowered the club's age limit to fifty-five rather than sixty. McKay and Stimson had long arguments about the idea. McKay called it senility savings. For him, a credit union was one for all and all for one. Everybody was a member on an equal basis. Doing favours for some members and not others—when many of the privileged were better-off members—violated McKay's idea of what a credit union was. Stimson argued back that if VanCity did not offer the package, it would gradually lose most of its members in that age group to the banks and, with that, a chunk of its deposit base. Stimson prevailed.

The Hook team also established financial counselling on a permanent basis. Financial advice had begun with Don Bentley and Bob McMaster giving the occasional talk to members about buying a home or managing payments on a loan. These were special events and had died out, but the idea hadn't—it was in the statement of objectives that Lloyd Widdifield had drawn up in 1966. Now financial counselling with an experienced counsellor, by appointment in the branches, was offered as a regular service at no charge—the first time a financial institution had done so. VanCity also began providing free information on legal services from VanCity's lawyers. District meetings were held to review services and to provide information on wills and estates, tax matters and related items.

Hook was trying to have VanCity provide every edge in service. Part of this attitude was ordinary competitive spirit. Mostly it was the VanCity culture inherited from Bentley. Hook freely acknowledged the debt. "Is it in the member's interest?" Bentley had always asked. Hook applied the same test, down to the individual details by which a new product was defined. Even Stimson, who had no prior connection to VanCity or credit unions, was caught up in this ethos. The same measure applied in the ranks. Staff were trained to give members the best return on their deposits. Employees who had come from banks told Hook how much they liked working at VanCity, because this objective was so clear. All they had to worry about was what was good for the member. If they spotted something useful, they could tell the member freely instead of holding back to protect the organization's margin.

This member-service culture was a comparative advantage for VanCity in the same way that natural resources or industrial expertise might be a comparative advantage to countries. Even something as small as handling electricity and telephone bills at no charge was considered important. Low service charges generally were a VanCity trademark. They distinguished VanCity from the banks and provided a constant reminder of the advantage of being a member. Decent parking was also a factor. Bank branches and trust companies did not always have it.

The ongoing reminder to members that the credit union belonged to them added to the advantage. Most members had the feeling that if they were going to trust anyone, they were going to trust VanCity, because they were one of the owners. Member ownership was more than just a rhetorical statement. It had some power, at least implied. Hook found himself fielding calls from members, standing on their rights as owners and lecturing him, often first thing in the morning, on some real or imagined misdeed, or suggesting changes. Hook followed the custom that Bentley had established, of taking these calls himself, until the calls became too time-consuming. He established a hotline for members and assigned an administrative assistant to look after it—to, in effect, act as an ombudsman when a member could not get satisfaction at his or her branch. The calls on the hotline also provided Hook with direct feedback from members.

Hook also introduced six-day service—Monday openings—to half the branches. With the interbranch capability members, no matter what their branch, could get to their money on Monday if necessary. The six-day opening also enabled the crowded branches to handle more volume.

The annual report in 1976 for the first time listed all of VanCity's member services. VanCity was much more, now, than just a share account, a deposit account and loans. Term deposits and RRSPs were there, of course. So were some quite ordinary things like Canada Savings Bonds, and travellers' cheques. Safety deposit boxes were another routine service. Who remembered, not so long ago, when most VanCity branches didn't have them because they didn't even have vaults? There were twenty entries in the report's long vertical column. The list looked impressive. One year later, there were twenty-nine entries.

Hook simultaneously made a foray into downtown, with a branch at Pender and Hornby. It was Hook's first branch opening and the one he would look back on with the most pleasure. A downtown branch had been originally proposed in 1966. Sandra Sutherland, a downtown lawyer who was elected to the board in 1974, had subsequently argued for it. Many people worked in the area and did their banking on the spot, she pointed out. It was extremely handy for them. There were banks and trust companies everywhere. One could drop by at noon hour or after work without losing any time. Some of the people working downtown were VanCity members.

Lloyd Widdifield had opposed the idea. He was afraid it wouldn't work. When one thought of VanCity, one thought of where people lived, where they bought or built houses with VanCity mortgages and borrowed to put furniture and appliances into those houses.

Hook moved John Iseli into the slot from Kitsilano. An air of boldness surrounded the venture. Downtown was a more difficult market than others. The location, on a street corner in an office building, was also expensive—the rent was about twice as much as in other locations. VanCity also would be cheek by jowl with banks and trust companies within a two-block reach. This was quite different from being in a small town, where the credit union could easily stand up to a bank branch. One had to be a little more sophisticated, Hook thought. It was a test. He kept an eye on the new branch.

The dividends from the technological lead and the member-service culture began to compound rapidly. At the end of 1977, with the Pender and Hornby branch just out of the gate and barely showing up in the figures, VanCity's assets had increased a whopping 53 per cent over the previous year, to $522 million—more than half a billion dollars. Net membership increased 21,000, or 31 per cent—almost twice the increase, in number of members, of the year before. This brought the membership total up to 88,000, nearing the 100,000 mark. Hook and his team began talking about "plateaus"—reaching one plateau, taking a deep breath, and then moving up to the next one.

They could see the next plateau in front of them. Three new branches were planned to open hot on the heels of downtown—Broadway at Arbutus in January 1978, Commercial at Kitchener in March, and Kingsway and Joyce in May. It was like firing them out of a gun. Hook's modus operandi was to know at any given time what five new branch locations were wanted, in priority order, based on Stimson's analysis of existing membership and of areas in the city. Locational analysis was one of Stimson's fortés. He began using B.C. Central, whose marketing department was run by a young whiz, George Scott, who was fascinated by surveys and data. Mediocre locations were taboo. Hook wanted only first-class sites. Given the stiff competition for good retail sites, an available location for the top branch priority did not always come up first, so a branch lower down the list might go ahead instead. One had to be patient and be ready to act quickly.

Hook assigned security and premises manager Dave Turnbull to look after building the new branches. Turnbull worked with the architects and turned out to have an unsuspected talent for making good design judgements. The only thing holding Hook back was his capital, especially the retained earnings component, which depended on profits. Hook was a financial conservative. He allowed himself to go only as fast as his financial situation permitted. Once the money was there, though, a new branch came off the shelf.

The enthusiasm on Monday afternoons became infectious. Embryo Communications, the young advertising agency now handling VanCity work, was developing a unique look for VanCity copy. The sharing of information among division managers showed its value. If marketing ran too far ahead, so that operations could not keep pace with growth or the introduction of new services, somebody's back would break. Being aware of each others' workings allowed the managers to maintain balance while moving forward at high speed. This had a catalytic side effect. They realized, as they reported, how much was going on in other divisions and how their success was collectively building.

At the end of his second year, in late 1977, Hook decided to turn over the operations division to Coffey. To replace Coffey in finance and administration, he brought in a B.C. Central cadre, Bruce Higgs. Higgs had both a commerce degree and a CGA designation. Among Hook, Coffey, Stimson and Higgs, there were three CGAs and two commerce degrees. It was a far cry from Bentley's day, when nobody on the premises had a university degree and the only accountants' designation, until close to the end, belonged to the external auditors, Fred Graham and Walter Dyck.

Higgs was from Vancouver's East End. Like Stimson, he was a Bank of Montreal product. Unlike Stimson, he was one of those young whipper-snappers with a university degree already in his pocket, put on the fast track to management. When he joined the bank, in 1967, the Bank Act had just been changed and banks had their powers vastly expanded. Ceilings on interest rates were removed. Marketing and new products, like charge cards, were coming on the scene. This intrigued Higgs. He found his work exciting and fast-moving.

For all that, the bank was a stuffy place. It still had limousines for its top people. The executive floor at the bank's head office in Montreal, where Higgs spent some time, was referred to, respectfully, as "the third floor." Higgs came to work on his first day there wearing a sports jacket and slacks, only to be told that he would not be attending a scheduled meeting on the third floor because he wasn't wearing a suit. "Suit" meant "dark suit." Even a navy blazer and dark slacks were not good enough.

Higgs was contacted in Montreal by a headhunter firm looking for a loan manager for a B.C.-based financial institution. It was B.C. Central. Higgs met them and was impressed. They were not bound by tradition. They had a vision, whereas most bankers he knew only had a job. He made the move back to Vancouver.

He found himself at the centre of a complex eddy of forces. Credit unions had just been discovered by the public, and their growth was staggering. The main protagonists, like Don Bentley at VanCity, Lewis van der Gracht at Richmond and others in different parts of the province, were, as Higgs saw them, entrepreneurs in the true sense. They were building financial institutions. They had ability and they were aggressive. It was exhilarating to be part of that milieu.

He remembered the upbeat camaraderie of those days. He also learned of the VanCity-Central feud. He was in charge of the Central Financial Corporation, Central's mortgage-lending subsidiary, which had been intruding into VanCity's lending market. Now he had Geoff Hook's offer to go to the "other side." He decided to accept it.

Higgs had become frustrated at Central, although his sojourn there had been a good time for him. Central reminded him in one way of head office at the Bank of Montreal. There were layers of bureaucracy to go through— not many, but enough to take away a sense of immediacy. He might design products and services, but implementation was left to individual credit unions. He wanted to be closer to this real action. VanCity, by its strength and creativity, had more magnetism than Central had and pulled him away.

He told George May about his plans. May listened coldly. Higgs's decision touched May personally, because it was also an indirect comment on Central. On the surface, Central still appeared to be a coming power. A new, luxurious head-office building was under construction in the False Creek area beside the Burrard Street Bridge. Below the surface, however, Central was not so powerful. It had been humiliated by VanCity, with VanCity's Geac success and Central's own on-line computer failure. Central Data Systems was just now hooking credit unions up with an on-line system, using a Burroughs computer, and it was struggling; ultimately Central gave up and switched to Geac. Other large credit unions, moreover, were imitating VanCity and going their own way. They now had the assets and the people to do it. Higgs's talk about jumping over the fence to VanCity was one more bitter, unsettling piece of evidence that May's vision of credit union empire might be unravelling just at the moment it was meant to succeed.

"I'm not sure this is the way to go," May riposted. "Central credit unions are going to be the power in the movement in the longer term." Higgs disagreed. There was nothing more to say.

When Higgs arrived for work at VanCity, at 1034 West Broadway, he immediately got a taste of the heady rush of action that he was after. Everyone was piled on top of one another. His own desk was set up in a back hallway, with his chair tight against the wall so that there was enough room in front of it for clearance to the fire exit. McKay and his people in human resources had been moved to another building, but that still did not leave room.

Almost coincidentally, Hook sprang for a new head-office building, at 10th and Cambie. It was four storeys high, in concrete, newly built, with each storey cantilevered and slightly extended over the level beneath it. It stood along the rise of the upper Fairview Slopes like an elegant fortress. For a financial institution, the image was a good one. It was modern without being extreme. It was virtually across from City Hall, the centre of government in Vancouver. People driving up Cambie, one of Vancouver's busiest north-south arteries, could not miss it. Hook was proud of the acquisition. VanCity had a long tradition of frugality, begun in Bentley's day, and although there was nothing spendthrift about the purchase, it was a departure. Hook had moved boldly the moment he heard the building was available, and negotiated the transaction himself. The entire process, including board approval, had taken him only a few weeks. The acquisition cost $5 million. This seemed a hefty price for an organization with just nine branches, albeit extremely productive ones, but it was well below replacement value. The investors had been caught by a downturn in the economy and had run short of cash. Hook had got himself a bargain.

He looked forward to moving in. The building symbolized the effort he had made to build up VanCity's management for a generational advance. He had, however, one more hurdle to cross. He might have his management in place around him, and VanCity might be increasingly successful, but the tellers, accountants, supervisors and managers in the branches were not with him yet.

CHAPTER 34

Riding the Crest

GEOFF HOOK'S VIEW WAS THAT the new people, like himself, Jack Stimson, Frank Coffey and Bruce Higgs, needed to convince existing VanCity employees that they deserved the employees' support. Stimson talked about gaining points with his secretary, Ron Spooner's former secretary, as if the management chart had been turned upside down and bosses ultimately had to answer to subordinates. There was a certain self-indulgent phoniness to the idea, because in the end bosses were bosses, but the basic impulse— that one needed to be deserving—was genuine.

Wayne McKay at the same time had come to realize that Hook was a caring person. Employees still saw Hook as a stern authoritarian. Somehow, McKay calculated, he had to humanize Hook's image. Jan Chapman, now McKay's employee relations officer, came up with the idea of "Meet the CEO" sessions. Chapman had always known of Hook's openness. She had accompanied him on branch visits and was amazed at how easily he talked to staff and at his ability to let himself be vulnerable. He wasn't the kind of person to go drinking with employees or make small talk with them, but he did want to communicate and, she had discovered, he was able to be open with employees even in confrontational circumstances.

The Meet the CEO sessions were held in the morning for two hours. They resembled coffee klatsches. Eight or ten people were chosen for each of the weekly get-togethers. They came from different levels in the branches, providing a cross-section. McKay sat in at first because he did not think much of Hook's interpersonal skills and he could intercede if there was a problem.

There was little in the way of an agenda. The sessions began by people introducing themselves, telling what they did in VanCity and where they came from. Some of their stories, of oppression and hardship escaped, were emotional. Sometimes tears were shed. Working at VanCity, for several of the participants, evoked strong feelings. Hook was moved. He hadn't fully understood the human element in the organization until then. After the introductions, Hook explored any problems the employees had. Then he would say a few things about where VanCity was heading and what needed to be done.

Slowly, word about the sessions got around, and after about a year, participants, instead of just listening to Hook's explanations, began to

contribute ideas. Hook picked up useful intelligence. He became aware of
the high level of commitment and skills within the organization. VanCity
was a much better organization than he had assumed it was when he came
in. He urged Coffey to be more sensitive to staff needs when new services or
procedures were introduced. He wanted more questions asked beforehand
of people in the branches.

He began looking forward to the sessions each week. The participants
had a vital quality to them. They talked without misgivings and, what
seemed wonderful to Hook, they freely revealed something of themselves.
He thought he should get to really know them. He took to memorizing
their names. An organization, he knew, could suddenly fall part and the CEO
wouldn't know why. He wanted to have a gut feeling that it was not going to
happen. He had that feeling now.

McKay also began annual staff-wide forums to introduce major changes
and to get feedback. A key strategic objective was to explain to members
who had money in different places how they could benefit by shifting more
of their deposits and investment activity to VanCity. It was a change in
orientation—more activist, against the grain of traditional credit unionism—and it meant a personal shift for people recruited, in earlier years, as
good caretakers.

The growing staff enthusiasm, combined with the pre-existing momentum and the excitement of new branches, created an irresistible force.
The downtown branch, after its first full year, 1978, had more than
4,000 members. With the interbranch capability, members from other
branches who worked downtown could also use the downtown branch. This
cemented their relationship to VanCity.

The Arbutus, Commercial, and Kingsway and Joyce branches opened as
scheduled. The opening of the Kingsway and Joyce branch was particularly
tumultuous. Many people in the area were members of Branch 1, which,
because of the distance, was getting only about half their business. The rest
was done locally, in bank branches. There was a pent-up demand in the area
for VanCity and its services. The crowd for the opening was so great that
people coming to the branch had to wait just to squeeze into the building.

Four more branches—Marpole, Kerrisdale, one in the Lougheed Mall at
the Burnaby-Coquitlam boundary and another on the ground floor of the
new head-office building—were added in 1979. This brought the total to
sixteen, double the number in 1976. The new branches established in the
public's mind the idea of VanCity as a large organization with a multi-
branch system throughout Vancouver. This fed growth in turn.

The new head-office branch, although it was only six blocks away from
Branch 1, did not fail Hook, either. It drew on the nearby City Hall and the
Vancouver General Hospital. It also took the weight off Branch 1, which,
astonishingly, was still overloaded and whose line-up time was longer than
in other branches. Some members would never leave Branch 1. They had
joined when it was at the original location at Quebec and Broadway, and

had low membership numbers that they would have to give up if they changed branches. Hook's own membership was still there.

Mike Sweet at Geac had developed a new computer, the Geac 8000, which VanCity installed. Unlike the original Geac 800, which was based on the Hewlett-Packard minicomputer, the Geac 8000 was put together by Geac from the bottom up. It gave VanCity a new and expanded on-line capacity.

There was no ceremony when the management team moved into the new head-office building, but Hook was buoyant without benefit of ritual. His management cadres now had office surroundings with a feel of substance and adequate space. They felt the vibrancy of VanCity just by being in the building. Hook looked out the windows of his office on the northeast corner and surveyed, in a sweep, the downtown and then the East End stretching out to Burnaby Mountain. VanCity was taking possession of all of it. Membership that year, 1978, increased another 22,000, passing the 100,000 mark to 110,000. It had doubled in the three years since Hook had taken over. The next year, another 11,000 members were added. Assets hit $700 million, then $840 million in 1979, and in 1980 would pass the $1 billion mark.

The catapulting growth brought out again the usual arguments that VanCity had grown too big to be democratic and responsive to members. Hook had heard the same criticism in Don Bentley's day. He decided to make a list of fifty things in which responsiveness to members was at play, like staff in new branches being properly trained or members with complaints having access to head office. VanCity in each category was one of the top credit unions.

Voting for directors in the branches instead of at annual meetings came out of this exercise. Hook, when he had been with the B.C. Co-operative Wholesale, had studied co-operatives in Europe. Many of them—and there were quite a few big ones—allowed several days or weeks for elections. Hook brought the possibility to the board, and with some trepidation they adopted it. Many credit unions were afraid of the idea, or rather afraid of the unknown. Hook was convinced that if VanCity was going to have 20 or 30 branches and, one could imagine, 200,000 members, it needed to extend the opportunity to vote.

Morale was extraordinarily high. Hook sensed the rising esprit de corps like the quickening of a pulse. The excitement of opening new branches filled the air. There was constant communication up and down the line. Hook's strategy of meetings at every level, extending participation down to tellers, was constantly feeding ideas upwards. When the management team decided on a new departure, they similarly had a way of explaining it to the branches and generating involvement.

Training programs were also in full swing. Every person on VanCity's staff received roughly five days per year of training. This did not sound like much, but it was exceptionally high for the industry. People had to be pulled from their usual duties for that time. A branch might have one or two people off on training at any time. McKay had a mobile staff group who did nothing but fill in for those who were being trained. Because of expansion, new opportunities were continually opening up, and VanCity was giving its people the upgrading to fill those positions. Existing employees had first crack at these jobs. This added to morale. Gradually Hook stopped hiring mostly from outside. He ascribed it to the new training in place, but it was as much his realization, as he became familiar with employees, that they had the required skills and potential after all.

He was intense about getting the job done exactly right. He had hoped to take all the others in the organization with him, and he was succeeding. By the end of the decade, he had depth in staff at every level and in each department. He could mandate a new program, such as a new account, and staff would produce and launch it with a high level of professionalism. There was never any pushing; nobody needed it. The division managers, and their managers below them, were alredy bent on doing things better than anyone else.

Increasingly, also, VanCity was becoming a favoured workplace. Hook and McKay together visited the branches in rotation to give recognition to people. Hook was using organization-wide memos for getting certain messages out, but a memo wasn't the same as going to a branch. He always made the visits, although he was intensely busy and often caught up in emergencies. His organizational structure owed more to democratic centralism than participatory management. The real power was at the centre, and ultimately in Hook's office. He also held sway over his board of directors. However, it was a democratic centralism with such open lines of communication and a participatory, nurturing ethic—"consultative," Coffey called it—that power did seem to be everywhere.

Even something as frivolous as the staff wearing Halloween costumes caught the prevailing spirit. The Halloween costume contest, within each branch, was one of McKay's ideas. He had built it up from a modest beginning until staff, with outrageous costumes, had reached artistic heights. The branches looked like they were celebrating Mardi Gras. Hook never wore a costume. He had to admit he wasn't the type. He made the rounds, however. He liked the fact that staff had grabbed the idea from McKay and made it their own, with no head-office dictum involved. Employees were so at home with their organization and themselves, and with their members, that they could revel in being a Wicked Witch of the West, a Tin Man or a weird apparition while counting out a withdrawal or approving a mortgage.

Coffey remembered those years as an exhilarating time. Hook recalled the euphoria and the elation. The membership was growing every month, every week, every day. Branches were opening. The balance sheet was sound. It was like riding a kayak down endless rapids. Nothing seemed impossible.

CHAPTER 35

The Man
who Knew Typeface

EMBRYO COMMUNICATIONS WAS A SMALL group of graphic artists in Vancouver. There were four partners. They were an advertising agency that wasn't quite a complete advertising agency. One day, what seemed to them a very strange person came to their office. He said his name was Jack Stimson. He was working for a credit union, VanCity, as its newly appointed marketing manager. He was a live wire—very outgoing, very energetic, very straightforward and very blunt.

They had a meeting. Stimson looked at the partners' work and sized them up. The Embryo crowd did not expect to hear back, but Stimson did call and offered them the work. He specifically asked one of them, Chris Bergthorson, to handle the account. He thought the chemistry would be right between them, although, unknown to Stimson, they came from different worlds.

Bergthorson was an anti-establishment spirit. One of the ironies of his career was that much of his finely crafted work was done for establishment companies. He was a member of the Greenpeace expedition that headed out to Amchitka Island in the Aleutians, in an attempt to block a U.S. nuclear bomb test. He was a heart-and-soul environmentalist, although one of his first, and continuing, major clients was a forest company. Saving the old growth rain forest had not yet become an issue. VanCity, on the other hand, fitted his practical idealism easily.

Bergthorson had been drawing ever since his childhood on the prairies. He had finished high school in Dawson Creek. He attended the Vancouver School of Art in the 1950s. In his third year at the school he bought a hundred-year-old platen printing press, which was powered like a treadle sewing machine, with the user pumping a long pedal. Bergthorson was interested in typographic design. He began to do private press work to supplement his income, using large wooden type as a design tool. Sometimes his creations spelled out words, sometimes the letters were used just to form an illustration. He created faces, flowers, automobiles and abstracts with them. He began with invitations. His reputation grew, and eventually he was doing bookmarks, Christmas cards and theatre and coffee-house posters as well.

He was offered a job as a designer at a commercial printer, where he learned the technical side of printing in a highly mechanized, modern lithograph shop. A trip to Europe, marriage and a baby intervened. Back in Vancouver, he needed to make a living. He had already decided he wasn't going to be an artist. He wasn't sure he had the talent for it, but mostly he wasn't driven enough. He established a partnership with an art school acquaintance. They did design work for the Vancouver Art Gallery, including the catalogues, invitations and posters for the famous Arts of the Raven exhibit, the ground-shattering Los Angeles Six show, and a series of other exhibits. The catalogues were works of art in themselves.

Bergthorson, however, was restless. He became a freelance designer. He had several corporate clients now. He ended up sharing space with three other graphic artists, and they eventually formed Embryo Communications. It was at this point that Stimson tracked them down.

The Stimson-Bergthorson relationship proved dynamic from the beginning. Stimson, as Bergthorson remembered him, was so brusque and gung-ho that, by comparison, the other people Bergthorson dealt with seemed to be on Valium. Bergthorson liked it. It was refreshing. Stimson's insistence on good work particulary attracted him. If you wanted to enjoy your work, in Bergthorson's view, you wanted to work with people who were really keen.

Bergthorson had a VanCity mortgage, but he did his banking near the Embryo office in the Yaletown district and did not know much about VanCity. The starting point, for him, was to create a look or an image for VanCity that would establish its identity. Another strategic premise, because of the character of the credit union, was that VanCity ads should be plain-spoken. They should not have a rich, decorative look; they should be straightforward and solid-looking. The language, too, should be simple and straightforward, and not too clever. The object was to communicate quickly and to get across the image of an organization that simply told you what it did, without any guile.

The RRSP season quickly came up. The marketing department, under Stimson, produced a briefing guide—a dossier on the product, the competition, the pricing point, the issues behind the product, the approximate budget available and other information that might be useful. The campaign was to be a large one in VanCity terms, because it included television.

The problem was an obvious one: getting people to buy their RRSPs at VanCity, instead of all the other banks, credit unions, insurance companies and everyone else in the marketplace, when their rates were roughly equivalent to VanCity's and when people were usually most interested in rates. Bergthorson brought in Richard Paluck, a writer who had been a creative director at the J. Walter Thompson agency and who had left samples of his work with Embryo. They inevitably struck on the one essential difference, familiar to everybody at VanCity. Unlike other plans, the VanCity RRSP had no special redemption charges or front-end loads. Paluck came up with the phrase, "No Strings Attached." He just loved the slogan. "It was one of those eureka things," he recounted, "so obvious, so perfect. It was absolutely the right thing."

Paluck went off to write the print copy and television script. He was faced with severe limitations. There was not enough money for expensive television production. Actors were ruled out, to avoid their costs and paying them residuals. Sweeping moves were out because of the expensive equipment required. VanCity could not afford a set, either. Paluck was virtually restricted to a table top. He thought of scissors. He came back with his copy and put on a little performance. "Years ago," he read, "Vancouver City Savings announced a new kind of Registered Retirement Savings Plan, one with no strings attached." Snip. The imaginary scissors cut an imaginary string. "No start-up charges." Snip. Another string was cut. "No close-out fees." Snip. "No commissions." Snip. Bergthorson was captivated.

Stimson and Embryo decided to run the commercial at costly peak hours in high-audience times. This meant that, given the limited budget, there were far fewer insertions, but they wanted everyone to see it. They counted on the strength of the commercial to provide the impact, despite the lesser frequency.

The commercial was riveting. There was something compelling about a large pair of scissors coming into a television screen and, simply, cutting a string. In the print version, the strings were already cut, with the string ends, like a bunch of little worms, at the bottom of the dollar sign. For Bergthorson, this campaign marked the point when the VanCity account came alive.

Bergthorson and Stimson developed a close working relationship. Stimson insisted that Embryo become a full agency and capture all the commissions connected to its VanCity work. He wanted Embryo to become master of the territory. He was demonstrative. When he liked something, he told the Embryo partners. When he had a problem with one of their ideas, he also told them. "What the hell are you trying to do?" he might say. "That's bullshit, Bergthorson, and you know it." Bergthorson never took offence. It was in the nature of the work either to convince Stimson that a concept was on the money or to qualify it and bring it forward so that Stimson could see that it was correct. Stimson, for Bergthorson, was the best of all clients. He was fun to work with. He was accepting of ideas. He wasn't frightened by something that was a little different.

Bergthorson, meanwhile, was searching for the right typeface for the print ads, like an explorer trying to find El Dorado. The first print ad he had done was for Plan 24. He had used a blocky sans-serif typeface—a typeface without the crosslines finishing off the letters. He was unhappy with it. The sans-serif, he thought, was too cold and a bit too industrial for a financial organization. He was well into the second year of his work with VanCity when one of the typesetters he used brought in a relatively new serif typeface called Concorde. It was love at first sight. Concorde had all of the classic, no-nonsense quality of Times Roman, familiar to newspaper readers around the world, but it had a contemporary touch. It was prettier, had personality and warmth—a human look, Bergthorson thought. It had elegance. To Bergthorson's acute graphic sensibility, the typeface fitted VanCity perfectly.

From that point forward, he never used anything else, choosing from Concorde medium, bold, condensed and italic to create the effects he wanted. He put together a communications manual, with Concorde as the corporate typeface, setting out the variations for different uses. The slogan "Owned by the people it serves" had appeared in some of Hermann Myers's old ads. Bergthorson liked it and put it in the manual as part of the VanCity signature.

Embryo also cleaned up Myers's building-blocks logo. It did not have the oomph it could have, they thought. They reduced the number of vertical lines in the blocks. They also made the lines thicker. The logo suddenly was much more solid and had more impact. The reworking was like fixing up an old, ratty piece of furniture by sanding it, sharpening the edges and putting on a new coat of varnish.

For newspaper ads, Bergthorson devised an elemental format that also captured simplicity: an eye-catching, well-spaced, multi-line headline, a concise and straightforward text and the signature VanCity sign-off. The format endured and was still being used in the 1990s, long after Bergthorson had gone.

Bergthorson also decided to scale the height of the ads to just past the centre fold on the page. Newspapers pyramided ads, with the large ones on the bottom and increasingly smaller ones on the top and towards the inside gutter. With the height of the VanCity ad slightly more than half a page, the paper could not put another ad of the same height on top of it. This meant that the VanCity ad, although only half a page high and perhaps two-thirds of a page wide, always dominated. It was the most cost-effective size. It provided much of the impact of a full-page ad while taking up only a third of the space. Print advertising became a much greater part of VanCity's marketing than it had been before.

In 1979, Stimson suddenly left VanCity to become general manager of the Kelowna Community Credit Union. Stimson's replacement was a Royal Banker from Toronto, Eric Hayne. Hayne was friendly and rambunctious. He let Bergthorson educate him in VanCity ways.

Hayne was a son of the Royal Bank. His father had managed various Royal Bank branches in small Alberta towns with names like Cardston, Lacombe, Bellevue and Foremost, and young Eric and the family moved with him. They lived in the proverbial banker's apartment—the suite above the bank reserved for the manager and his family and offered at nominal rent so that the bank's practice of moving them from town to town was not too resented.

He began in the bank as a teller—he called it "toiler"—and ended up in Edmonton. The bank had established an educational program to put selected young employees through university. Hayne was one of the lucky ones and studied commerce at the University of Alberta. He was then moved into business lending in Toronto. He considered going from Alberta into the heart of the Canadian industrial economy a considerable accomplishment. One of the things he learned was how to deal with people's crises. A good banker, he thought, had to at least comprehend what was happening to his customers. He had to share their ups and downs. Otherwise he might as well toss his loan files into a waste basket and leave.

The Royal Bank, like the other chartered banks in the 1970s, discovered marketing. Hayne was charged with the responsibility for marketing in the Metro Toronto division. They were good times. He worked in one of the towers of the Royal Bank Plaza at Bay and Front streets. He was comfortable in this downtown, high-rise, blue-suited environment, and marketing was exciting. Something, however, blocked Hayne's path. He lost his mentor, who had pulled him along. His career goal was to be a senior executive by the time he was forty. His life had revolved around that. He was forty-two now, and he had not made it. He was ranked 176th, he found out, in an organization that employed 23,000 people. That wasn't bad for a boy from Cardston, but with his mentor gone, he did not see himself quickly climbing through the political maze above him.

He had heard of people "hitting the wall" or going through a mid-life crisis. Now he himself had hit it and was going through it. "That's it," he thought to himself. "Life ends." Despite his mid-life anomie, he was still reading his *Globe and Mail* every morning. One day, the executive want ads included an entry by the country's largest credit union, Vancouver City Savings, looking for a marketing manager. Hayne read the details and recognized himself. He wasn't quite sure what a credit union was. He thought it was a near bank, like a trust company. That was close enough. He updated his résumé and fired it off to a Mr. Wayne E. McKay. The call came when he was sitting in his office in the Royal Bank Plaza. "Can you talk?" Mr. McKay wanted to know. "Of course I can talk," Hayne responded. "I've never stopped talking." He joined VanCity that summer.

He could not at first believe what VanCity was doing. It was so much more advanced operationally than what he had known and taken as gospel in Toronto. It had an on-line, real-time computer system. "This is space-age stuff," he laughed in astonishment. VanCity had what he called a "single-account system," which started out with a member number, and after that, all the accounts were displayed. At the Royal Bank, if a customer came in with a savings account passbook, the teller had no idea whether that customer had any other accounts, or an RRSP or a loan.

Hayne spent a good deal of the first six months listening to the people in his department and learning the history of VanCity, especially from McKay. He discovered that lending money in the Vancouver housing market, because of its fluctuations, was quite different from the way it was done in central Canada. He had to make a studied effort to learn of the supremacy of the member, as opposed to the supremacy of the corporation. For a middle-aged, ex-Albertan, central-Canadian banker, it was a rebirth in his thinking. He could see VanCity approaching the $1 billion mark in assets. With the early history of VanCity still a novelty in his mind, the accomplishment struck him as all the more joyful. He was reminded of it every time he ran into former colleagues from the Royal Bank. They never failed to tell him that VanCity was the most aggressive, toughest retail competitor in town. That was nice to hear.

He learned most from Chris Bergthorson. Hayne laughed that he didn't bring a marketing style to VanCity, it was the other way around. Hayne always wanted someone like Lorne Greene, who had fronted for the Bank of British Columbia's Bonanza Account—a strong, likable person who was a "star" and could visually grab people. Bergthorson fought him on that. "VanCity is not a star organization," he told Hayne. "It's not that kind of place. You've got to understand that. People don't come here because they want to be surrounded by stars. The whole thrust of VanCity's product line is to be simple, effective and straightforward, not authoritarian and glamorous." By the time Hayne arrived, Bergthorson, although technically just a supplier to VanCity, had an abiding love for the organization. His early childhood in Saskatchewan was spent going into co-op stores. His relatives were on the boards of co-operatives. VanCity, with its friendly egalitarianism, expressed for him this co-operative élan.

Hayne did not bother underwriting large research projects to measure public feeling because he thought Bergthorson, on his own, was able to articulate it so well. VanCity became a personal challenge for Bergthorson. He was increasingly interested in what lay behind the credit union. "He kept our spirituality," Hayne recounted. Whenever the marketing department people thought too much like a bank, Bergthorson knocked them on the head and reminded them who they were. Hayne wondered later if they had really paid Bergthorson enough for all that he did for VanCity. Bergthorson, for his part, realized that, with VanCity, Embryo had much more freedom than ad agencies usually have. VanCity management, he thought, were much better managers than many people assumed.

The cherubic, slightly pudgy Hayne, meanwhile, was rejuvenated. At the Royal Bank, marketing was taken as an interesting idea, but marketing people had not yet made it to the sanctum sanctorum of top management. In VanCity, he sat at the table. It was more than just form. He had to be there. If one understood by "marketing" the need to serve one's member-owners, VanCity was a marketing-driven organization. At the same time, Hayne needed to be a business person and have an understanding of what everybody in the organization was going through. Hook's collegial style demanded it. This only added to Hayne's zest for the job. He could bring all of his banking experience to bear. He was a whole man again.

The new branches, for whose launch Hayne and his division were responsible, blossomed. Hayne introduced term deposits for as little as $100, for the first time anywhere. They were useful for schoolchildren, with their own accounts, and made good gift items for grandchildren. He introduced the first "plain English" loan agreement, written so that members could easily understand it, with the legal gobbledygook removed. The great coup that year, 1980, however, was a monthly statement that covered all of a member's accounts, including term deposits and RRSPs. The possibility, flowing from the Geac system, had excited Hayne from the moment he walked through the door at 10th and Cambie. It was something VanCity had wanted to do since the computer system was installed. Like First-In-Line, it did not have monetary value, but the convenience to members of being able to look at all their accounts and deposits together on one sheet of paper, and not having to bother with a passbook, had an impact all its own. Members could also more easily decide how best to use their money. Tellers were saved from having to make time-consuming passbook entries, except for older members who did not want to give up the secure feeling of having thepass book in hand.

"My God," Hayne told people about the idea, "we've really got something here. This thing is a blockbuster." He felt VanCity had done so many innovative things that it did not realize the power of what it had. Only because he was coming from the outside, knowing how far away the banks were from anything comparable, did Hayne see the monthly statement's full marketing potential. He insisted that VanCity could market it as a stand-alone product and should "beat on it" for all it was worth.

VanCity and Embryo did a name search among themselves. Embryo came up with the name eventually chosen—the All-In-One Statement. It was simple, it was fully descriptive and, Hayne thought, it had immense marketing power. Bergthorson designed the new statement and also a logo for it, which appeared faintly, diagonally across the face of the statement, like a watermark. A big campaign was launched. "Look what we're doing for our members," the advertising in effect said. "Why don't you join us?"

For the television commercial, Embryo used a milliner's dummy head, with no features. "As if you didn't have enough on your mind, here come all these financial statements," the voice over said. "There's one for your chequing account ..." A hand came down and deposited a statement in a cavity in the top of the head, with part of the statement sticking up. "Another for your savings account ..." The hand dropped in another sheet, and so on, until the head was filled by a messy clutter of these papers. "It's enough to make anyone feel like a dummy," the voice said. Then came the VanCity proposition: "That's why VanCity got it all together for you, the All-In-One Statement, all your money management information in one tidy package. All in all, it's a neat idea." The dummy had appeared again, with a single sheet in front of it. The hand picked the sheet up and dropped it neatly into the cavity. The dummy turned, showing a happy little smile.

Bergthorson and Embryo had done it again.

CHAPTER 36

Builder of Branches

FOR DAVE TURNBULL, IT WAS a baptism by fire. He was responsible for developing the new branch downtown at Pender and Hornby. He had never done anything like it before. He had been a secret service man, not a building developer. He found himself, nevertheless, on the main floor of an imposing downtown office building, putting in a credit union branch.

Clearing the place out was easy enough. Then he had to worry about installing the vault. By law, the concrete walls of the vault had to be at least twelve inches thick and had to be reinforced with three rows of steel bars, each one in a row only four inches from the next. This meant upwards of eighty tons of concrete and thirty tons of rebars. To hold up that weight required a monumental support system. Unfortunately, just where the support was supposed to go, in the basement, was a Chinese restaurant. Turnbull had to negotiate compensation for closing down the restaurant for three months. He ended up, he thought, having to pay a king's ransom.

At the same time, Turnbull found himself at loggerheads with with Henry Ciccone, the architect from Toby Russell & Buckwell. Ciccone, considering himself the expert, was intent on doing things his way. Turnbull was equally determined that he was going to be in charge. It was his job to pull in the inputs of people at VanCity and co-ordinate the branch-building effort. Frank Coffey, he knew, was after a brighter, newer look. Turnbull pointed out to Ciccone that he, Turnbull, was the boss and writing the cheques. He fired the architect and the firm on the spot. Although Turnbull was a novice, Coffey and Geoff Hook backed him. "Go ahead, do what you have to do," Hook told him. Toby Russell Buckwell, to make peace and retain the work, offered Turnbull another architect, Keith Melville, and the relationship began again, from square one.

Then Turnbull discovered that the south end of the floor was sixteen inches higher than the north end, following the slope of the street, so that everything would have to be cut on a bias to keep the teller stations vertical. Why, Turnbull wondered, was he being punished with so many difficulties on his first assignment?

Bringing VanCity branches into the world was the last thing Dave Turnbull had expected to do. He had come to VanCity as a security manager. He had been with the RCMP for twenty-five years, most of it with the secret service. His forte was counter-espionage. Counter-subversion looked after threats from within, purportedly organizations like the Communist Party of Canada. Counter-espionage, Turnbull's work, was concerned with threats from outside, like the KGB and the GRU, the military arm of the Soviet intelligence network. Turnbull's last ten years with counter-espionage were in Vancouver.

He was in charge of a section. It was "tinker, tailor, soldier, spy" stuff, with all its tricks, like doubling agents and planting misinformation, although it wasn't as dramatic as in London or Berlin. Much of the intelligence at stake was economic information belonging to corporations. By 1976, long before perestroika, Staff Sergeant Dave Turnbull's interest in counter-intelligence was waning. He decided to give the outside a whirl. The job at VanCity, as security manager, was much more than he expected. On the day he reported, Frank Coffey, who had hired him, took him in to meet Geoff Hook. Hook was ebullient; he slapped Turnbull on the back and welcomed him to the credit union. They talked a bit about the position, and Hook mentioned, as an aside, that Turnbull was also going to look after premises. This was news to Turnbull, but he didn't mind, since there did not seem to be much to it. A few weeks later, Hook met him in the hall and asked him to look at a property at Kingsway and Joyce that was for sale. Hook told him he was thinking of putting up a branch there. Turnbull sauntered forth, got the price, and reported back.

"What am I supposed to do with this information?" he asked Hook.

Hook looked at him. "Well, what are you going to do about it?" he asked.

"What do you mean, what am I going to do about it?" Turnbull replied, puzzled.

"Well, are we going to buy it?"

Turnbull realized then that when Hook talked premises he was talking new branches and that there was a large role for him in developing those properties. He also realized that Hook was willing to allow him to do things. Coffey, his immediate boss, had the same approach. Coffey had let him know that he would support him if he made an honest decision, even if it went wrong. If he made a mistake by not doing something, on the other hand, Coffey probably wouldn't support him. Turnbull liked that; it had been his own management philosophy. Coffey wanted to know what was going on, but didn't expect Turnbull to clear everything with him. It would be up to Turnbull to decide if something was important enough or touchy enough to mention.

While working on the downtown branch, Turnbull was also developing a common security program for VanCity. How to deal with hold-ups was easy; there were basic dos and don'ts, and the local police came in immediately after the event. Less dramatic issues, like terminations for theft, on the other hand, would have tested Solomon. What was a large enough sin to bring about a termination? If termination was called for, how could one do it in a way that was morally right and not just legal?

He put in Teller Day-Save units—small safes under each teller's cash drawer. They stored the teller's main capital of perhaps $10,000, while the smaller working-cash supply of only $2,000 or $3,000 remained in the cash drawer. It was a predecessor of the cash dispensing machine. There was a time delay in opening the unit—long enough that robbers would not hang around, even if they were able to force a teller to open it at gunpoint. The tellers felt good about the units, because the reduced cash exposure meant their branch was less of an attraction to robbers. Such devices were a new phenomenon. VanCity was the first financial institution in western Canada to install them.

Years later, Turnbull was one of the first to install cash dispensing machines, which took all of the cash away from the teller line. Nobody believed his contention that a teller could get the cash faster by using the machine than by counting it out of the drawer, despite having to walk to the machine and key in. Tests using a pilot machine, however, proved it to be so. Tellers working out of a cash drawer had to count the money three times: once taking it out of the drawer, once in front of themselves, and once for the member. With a machine, tellers did not have to count it all, although in practice they did count it out for the member, as a form of reassurance.

Turnbull was also the first in western Canada to install surveillance cameras in a financial institution. They could help identify and convict not just a robber but also someone passing a bad cheque. Turnbull matched the time of the transaction and the number of the teller station, recorded on the computer, with the time track on the film. The police loved it. Wayne McKay opposed the cameras. He was deeply suspicious of Turnbull and of what seemed to be his police-state tactics.

It had begun with lie detector tests. Turnbull was working on an internal fraud in which he could not get enough evidence to prove or disprove guilt. He had worked with polygraphs extensively when he was with the secret service. He knew their pitfalls and had reservations. They were inadequate for proving guilt; polygraph evidence was not acceptable in court. They could, however, help establish innocence and clear the air.

McKay was not convinced. Employees who declined a polygraph examination were damned by inference. Those who took the examination and were not cleared were also damned by inference. Polygraphs, moreover, were a crude, insensitive way of dealing with suspect employees. A polygraph test could be seen as an attempt to nail an employee to the cross. It was decided, because of McKay's opposition, not to use them.

The surveillance cameras added to McKay's concern. He could see their uses, but they also cast a shadow on a branch. Every member's appearance and every teller's movements were recorded by the camera, visibly spying. Later, staff and members would not even notice the cameras, but at the time they were a conspicuous novelty. Tellers soon realized, however, that the camera could be their best friend. One teller was having a continual shortage problem and was becoming suspect. By looking at a few days' film, Turnbull was able to determine that the problem was another employee who had access to the teller line and was snatching a few dollars out of the teller's drawer.

Slowly tellers began to appreciate that Turnbull was there primarily to help them rather than to harass them. Often he would uncover a stupid mistake that had wrongly incriminated an employee, who had nevertheless become frightened of the consequences. Turnbull needed staff support. The monitoring of internal theft and fraud depended ultimately on branch managers and supervisors bringing irregularities to his attention.

He avoided, whenever he could, calling in the police and having charges laid. Penny-ante theft would not lead to a charge. Usually he suggested to the employee concerned that he or she might want to resign. Human nature was such, he felt, that in most cases having to admit a transgression was sufficient penalty. To take it beyond that, for minor transgressions, would be cruel and unusual punishment.

The potential for serious fraud was in lending, by setting up phoney loans. Turnbull would call in the internal auditors in such cases and then bring in the RCMP's commercial crime squad as soon as possible. Given that wherever there is a lot of money, people may do foolish things, Turnbull was surprised by how little internal fraud there actually was in VanCity.

The philosophical difference between McKay and Turnbull lasted for several years. One day, however, Turnbull got a note from McKay, who was on a business trip to Los Angeles. McKay had come to the conclusion that he had misjudged Turnbull and was writing to make amends.

Most of Turnbull's time was taken up developing new branches. The assignments came at him thick and fast—three to be completed in 1978, four in 1979. He got better and better at it. The process began with Garry Smith, the branch operations manager, and his group. Smith would tell Turnbull how many teller stations they wanted in a branch, how many loans interview booths and how many support staff, and make other suggestions. Then Turnbull and Melville would shoehorn the requirements into the available space, in a configuration that was still user friendly for staff.

Working with the trades came next. Turnbull believed in relationships. He usually hired the same primary contractor and, for work he managed himself, the same electricians. He thought of his trades and subtrades as a trap line on which he depended. He was loyal to them, and they, in turn, developed a loyalty to him. He used union firms wherever possible. This was general VanCity policy, although not spelled out in black and white. Turnbull felt more comfortable with union firms because he could be sure of the quality of the work and he had another line of recourse, the union, if somebody working at the site went bad on him.

It was the small, seemingly insignificant things that Turnbull spent more and more of his time on. For the first few branches, he designed everything, down to the dimensions of individual drawers and how many slots there should be for a cheque drawer. The configuration of a drawer could make or break a branch, as far as staff was concerned—that was what they worked with. Developing a branch had less to do with a building than with allocating square inch by square inch. No space was used more than the branch of a credit union or a bank, and a VanCity branch was used more intensively than the others. Every square inch had to be functional. If it wasn't, Turnbull soon heard about it from staff.

He welcomed the criticism because it helped him improve the next branch. He began involving rank-and-file staff in planning a new branch. They were the ones who lived in that amalgamation of square inches. A plan for a branch went back and forth for a couple of months, being modified and redesigned. Even when Turnbull had done several branches, he would go back and double-check his specifications to make sure they still applied and had not become outdated by changing requirements.

His approach was not to ask what was right about something, but what was wrong with it and how it could be improved. He began making mock-ups of a teller station, when he added changes, so that he could try them out in a dry run first. He learned again what he had already known, that human nature being what it is, people resisted change, even if there was a good reason for it. He thought that if he was effective at all, it was because of his diplomatic ability to bring people around.

He scorned the way banks put their new branches together, particularly the Canadian Imperial Bank of Commerce, where he knew some development people. They would open a branch in a shopping mall, close down a small branch God knows where, and insist that all the dilapidated equipment be moved into the new location. He knew one case where old manual typewriters and rickety chairs were put in a brand-new branch. For Turnbull, this was a terrible sin. The bank worked with a basic branch plan and had the components pre-built, usually in eastern Canada. Sometimes the contractors were also brought in from eastern Canada. If something didn't fit, they forced it. A glitzy branch, shining with terrazzo in a high-profile shopping centre, might look good to the untrained eye. Turnbull disdainfully dismissed the appearance as a facade, behind which there was poor workmanship and a bunch of junk. Since, wherever possible, he had work done locally, Turnbull had control over the quality of components like cabinetry. He had a fondness for workmanlike quality going back to his farm-boy days near Olds, Alberta, where he had grown up.

He began turning his mind to other issues, like the use of natural light in the branches. He realized the older VanCity branches had been built the wrong way. The teller line and the manager's office were usually all on the window side, with the tellers' backs to the window. The members were in the middle, as if funnelled into a locked space. He set about reversing the arrangement, so that when members came into a branch they were in an open area with lots of light and felt more a part of what was happening around them.

He had become a VanCity patriot. There was joy in the learning process and in doing new things. His mother had been a staunch member of the Olds Co-op, and he carried with him that same spirit of co-operative self-reliance. He still had the prairie boy's suspicion of banks and Bay Street and of their distant, aloof decision-making. VanCity's local ownership and its ability to contend appealed to him. He could see the top. It wasn't somebody a few thousand kilometres away in a remote office. Hook was just down the hall, and Coffey was only a couple of doors away. There had been nothing like that in the RCMP, with its long chain of command. Turnbull could talk to people who mattered in his workaday life without having to rely on memos, phone calls or intermediaries. He had the right to express an honest opinion. He mattered.

Hook supported him and helped him. Hook was a father figure. A compliment from Hook meant something. One day, Hook told him that VanCity had hit it lucky when it hired him. Turnbull never forgot.

He knew everybody at VanCity, and everybody knew him. He liked that. He worked in a climate of perpetual excitement. The organization was growing fast and continually breaking new ground. He felt part of something that was bigger than himself. Even meetings carried an undercurrent of expectation. Lunch with his fellow department managers and the division managers at Halloween particularly caught Turnbull's emotions. The sense of fellowship was intense.

The most sweeping emotion came with the opening of a branch. Nothing matched the opening of Branch 13 at Kingsway and Joyce in 1978. The design of the branch had been a difficult juggling act. The two narrow lots VanCity had acquired were too small for the floor area the branch needed. Turnbull and Keith Melville were constrained from adding a second storey by building regulations. They finally managed to get a permit that allowed for a mezzanine. Somehow they squeezed in the required parking, too.

When Turnbull arrived on opening day, he came upon a mob scene. His first reaction was that something serious must have happened, that there must have been a murder on the floor or a spectacular accident. Several of the contractors, representing the trades and subtrades, dropped by for the official ceremony. Architect Melville was there. Turnbull's own construction crew, which did branch maintenance, was also on hand. Geoff Hook slapped Turnbull on the back and thanked him and the others individually for what they had done. A group of them stood around sharing in the glory of the occasion. Turnbull stayed the whole day, letting the pleasure soak in. The place remained jam-packed. Hundreds and hundreds of people kept coming, and coming still. The excitement ricocheted through the building. It seemed to Turnbull that marketing had chosen the best location in the world and that he had built the best branch in the world. He went home thinking of the next branch he was going to build. He was more pumped up than ever.

CHAPTER 37

The Second Life
of Wayne McKay

WAYNE MCKAY, IN THE HUMAN resources department, knew that something had to be done. Staff turnover was atrocious, peaking at 70 per cent a year. He went through the payroll statistics manually to make sure he had not made a mistake. He discovered the average length of service was six months, although many people, after leaving, would return. They would work for a few months and then go elsewhere or go off on a trip. Branches were staffed by extremely young and inexperienced people. McKay realized that he had to broaden the age group and extend the average stay.

The high turnover was endemic in banks, too, although it was slightly worse at VanCity, because VanCity in 1977 did not have an extensive branch network. Employees who moved out to the suburbs in search of lower-cost housing did not want to face rush-hour commuting line-ups or bother with travel. They left VanCity for credit unions closer to home, which were following in VanCity's technological train and replicating its friendly atmosphere. It seemed to McKay that VanCity was feeding other credit unions as quickly as it was ingesting recruits and giving them some credit union experience.

What happened, or did not happen, inside VanCity also took a toll. McKay identified training as the weak link. A single trainer gave a one-day course on VanCity products and on using the computer terminal, and spent a follow-up day with the employee on the job. That was all. After that, people who went on cash for the first time—that is, new tellers—were left to sink or swim. They became better or worse equipped for moving up, or even moving laterally, depending on the luck of the draw—which branch manager and supervisor they ended up with. Potential was lost. Besides, branch managers were not trainers. They were too busy. They gave training some time, but they had other things to do. What training they did provide, moreover, did not stretch employees' abilities and prepare them for change. Staff who were bright and naturally ambitious, and who had considerable background before coming to VanCity, were able to jump in and take hold, but fewer and fewer had the background.

The effect was predictable. Not being equipped to do as good a job as they could, many tellers became frustrated and wondered if they were cut out for the work. They felt they had been left on their own. Often they decided to look around for something that offered a better chance of learning the job, or they just languished and drifted away. Others might want to move up in the organization but did not have the training for it, so they gradually grew unhappy and left.

McKay, pondering this, knew he had no choice but to beef up training. He saw it as more than just bringing people up to speed technically. Training and a high level of functioning would plug people into the organization and raise their commitment, so they would be less likely to wander off. McKay hired a training and development manager, Brian Salvador, to establish a program. Salvador had been a training manager at the Bank of Montreal. Training programs and management development were one thing the Bank of Montreal did have.

Salvador began at VanCity with an empty sheet of paper. It was an unexpected situation for him. He was used to looking at courses that had been designed in Toronto and Montreal. He would receive, for a training course, a leader's guide neatly packaged with handout materials. All he had to do was read the guide and then stand in front of the group and deliver the course. At VanCity, there was nothing at all. He had to decide where he wanted to begin and how to build a program. Rather than being a small cog in a massive wheel, he realized he was actually going to influence the end result.

He also found himself face to face with an intense and aggressive Geoff Hook who, he surmised, had probably never had a training manager in his organization before. He suddenly had to convince this man that some of his ideas were worth thinking about. Hook had quite different notions about the way training should go. The gap was between "hard skills" and "soft skills." Hook wanted tellers and member-service personnel trained in specific tasks so that they would be technically competent. He wanted them up and running on the front line, doing their job.

Salvador, on the other hand, saw the need for something that went beyond mere technical competence. How people managed others, how they related to each other and how they dealt with members was important. There was little or no orientation about the values of the organization and how it worked—nothing about the member-service focus or the fact that the person across the counter was, indeed, a member and therefore owner of the credit union, and what that meant. Yet these same employees were expected to represent the organization to the public. Some managers did a good job of explaining VanCity to new staffers. The problem was with managers who had not been with VanCity long enough to have background knowledge to impart to staff.

Behind this gap between himself and Hook was a larger divide. Hook was obsessed with growth and managing growth—what Salvador called lineal change. He did not seem to appreciate the human side of the organization and the kinds of lateral change that created a climate of cohesiveness. It even showed in his pattern of communication. He had good communication with the top team, who were next to him lineally in the administrative structure, but below that level, nobody knew him or what he stood for, or understood him. (The "Meet the CEO" sessions had yet to begin.) He was just a figurehead.

Salvador had to listen carefully to Hook, who after all was CEO. He struggled with their divergent ideas. He began with an orientation program: a full-day seminar, in a classroom setting, where new people learned about the VanCity culture—who the key players were and what they did, where branches were located and how the computer system worked. The orientation included a slide show about VanCity's history, produced by McKay, and a tour of head office. The idea was to present a common theme to new people. It was driven home to Salvador early that VanCity had a whole raft of new managers, supervisors and staff from a variety of different backgrounds and organizational cultures, each with their own kit bag. Somehow he had to pull them together into what amounted to a new organization.

He also put together an induction package for use by branch supervisors, to ensure that everyone went through a familiarization process. The supervisor was to introduce new people around the office and show them the premises. In many cases—incredibly, to Salvador—this had not been happening. Now, new employees met the manager. They were linked with somebody who would take them for lunch, be their buddy for the first few days, and answer any questions they had about routine things. Somebody also talked to them about employee matters like performance appraisals—when they would occur and what the forms looked like—and salary reviews and increases. They were given instructions about what to do when they were sick.

These were ordinary enough matters, but Salvador knew they were critically important. The most important day of an employee's time in an organization was the first one. If the employee started off on the right foot, the likelihood of success in learning the job was much greater. The strategy was to put to bed as many issues as possible, freeing the employee's mind for getting into the job itself and understanding what it involved.

Salvador hired a second assistant and expanded and upgraded instructional programs. The one-day course focussing on the use of the computer terminal was extended to three days to cover how to deal effectively with members and the member-service culture. He realized that VanCity employees were not like others. Despite the previous lack of orientation and the high turnover, they were unusually committed. The VanCity culture differed in kind from that of the banks. Everyone used the word "family" a lot in those days. There was lots of camaraderie. News about what was going on in the organization travelled fast, too. It was almost impossible to keep information under wraps.

Hook, in the meantime, had changed dramatically. It seemed to Salvador that he had moved 180 degrees in understanding how much VanCity's employees were giving to the organization and hence understanding how important Salvador's and McKay's "soft skill" work was. Hook had become gregarious. Salvador had moved as well. He had come to the job with his own ideas about human resources management. Now he was thinking of VanCity for VanCity. Maybe Hook had been right about the need to concentrate first on technical skills. The gap between the two of them closed.

Salvador felt he now could turn his attention to his deeper interest, the management development side of the organization. The supervisors directly in charge of tellers, member-service and lending—the nitty gritty of a branch—particularly interested him. Many of them had come up through the ranks without any formal training in dealing with co-workers, communicating and motivating. Management development meant shifting their focus from being responsible only for what came across their own desk to being responsible for all those other desks as well.

Management development also appealed to Salvador's professionalism. He was a member of the training and development associations, read the journals, and went to the conferences where trainers from across the continent exchanged ideas and listened to leaders in the field. Two imaginative practitioners were in Vancouver—Mickey McDowell and Steve Marks. They ran courses at UBC in interpersonal communications and in organizational behaviour for the Institute of Canadian Bankers. Salvador had run across them in his Bank of Montreal days. He invited them out to lunch.

As they chatted, McDowell suggested that Salvador might want to take a step backwards. Rather than assuming he knew everything about the organization and putting together a program accordingly, why not conduct a diagnostic exercise first? McDowell had stumbled across just such a diagnostic process when he was completing his doctorate at the United States International University in San Diego. It was the handiwork of an American behavioural guru, Rensis Likert. The diagnostic survey, as described by McDowell, was totally new to Salvador, but it sounded exciting and he agreed. It wasn't just a survey; it was a diagnostic step that identified weaknesses, which could then be worked on.

Salvador took the idea to McKay, and they took it up the line to Hook and the executive committee. Salvador wanted a commitment that regardless of what was found, the organization would deal with it. The survey, Salvador explained, would be only the first step in a much larger program of organizational development.

He got the commitment. That in itself said something positive to Salvador, because there were no apparent problems in the organization at the time. It showed a willingness to always want to do things better. "The Steve and Mickey Show," as it came to be known at VanCity, turned out to be the Mother of All Training Exercises. Because it touched people so personally, nobody who went through it ever forgot.

Steve Marks and Mickey McDowell were an unlikely couple, which is why the Steve and Mickey Show worked so well. Marks was the straight man, McDowell the garrulous entertainer. They could play off each other.

Marks was a professor in the Department of Counselling Psychology, the Faculty of Education, at UBC, and did consulting on the side. McDowell, who also had a doctorate, was a full-time consultant and was soon to become president of a road-paving company. He had been a star amateur hockey player, but he had grown up with a taboo against becoming a hockey bum and opted for an education instead. His interest in business management and the workplace had plunged him into humanistic psychology—an American movement that emphasized people in themselves, leadership, motivation, human performance and organizational behaviour. "Self-actualization" was one of its underlying themes. A later offshoot was the New Age human potential movement.

Rensis Likert, who had developed the survey Marks and McDowell used, was one of the major figures of this humanistic school. Likert had invented the famous Likert Scale, in which a respondent replies to a series of statements by using a scale of possible answers: Strongly Agree (5), Agree (4), Neither Agree nor Disagree (3), Disagree (2) and Strongly Disagree (1). It became a key methodology for attitude surveys and public opinion polls.

Likert's main work, however, was the study of management. He set about to discover how managers who achieved high performance differed from managers who produced only mediocre results. He came up with four systems of management, in order of evolutionary progress: (1) exploitive authoritarian, (2) benevolent authoritarian, (3) consultative management and (4) participative management. Participative management he called System 4. It was much more productive than authoritarian styles of management. Likert eventually identified the four main factors that made participative management work, which he put forward as the Four Factor Theory. They were (1) support, (2) interactive facilitation, or good old-fashioned communication, (3) work facilitation, or giving people the resources and equipment to do the job and (4) goal emphasis.

McDowell had once called on Likert at his retirement home at Kailua, Hawaii. The two became friends. "If you were a leader of a group and could do only one thing," McDowell asked Likert, "what would that one thing be?"

"Be supportive of the group. We know that, it's the number one thing," Likert replied without hesitation.

These ideas underlay the diagnostic survey that Marks and McDowell now distributed to VanCity employees, by which they rated the people above them. Teller supervisors were rated by tellers, branch managers were rated by the assistant manager, supervisors and the branch secretary and so on, to Geoff Hook, who was rated by his division managers. Organizational climate was looked at. "Does this organization have a real interest in the welfare and satisfaction of those who work here?" was one question. "Do you look forward to coming to work each day?" was another. How alert was management to picking up on new ideas? How open was it to new ideas? Was there good co-ordination between units? Did they understand each other? When decisions were made, were persons affected asked for their ideas? Did low-level employees have any influence on what went on?

To ensure that there would be no reluctance in giving forthright answers, people were guaranteed total anonymity. All VanCity employees who managed three or more people received a diagnostic report back from their subordinates in this way, also confidential, showing their strengths and weaknesses.

Salvador had been worried at first about how the information would be used. Frank Coffey and a few others had wanted to get their hands on branch managers' individual ratings, because it was something specific that one could work with in a direct way. Salvador talked long and hard, explaining to them why they could not do it. To get a bad report card could be traumatic. The process depended on trust. Managers and supervisors were assured they would not be fired for whatever came out of the survey. The object was to help them become more effective, not to help some superior assess whether they were good, bad or indifferent. The subjects could share the results with others—say, in asking for help—but, given confidentiality, it was up to them. It was a fine line fraught with risk, but the line held.

Salvador and McKay knew that VanCity was close to Likert's System 4 ideal of participatory management, unlike most large businesses, including banks, which were System 2 organizations (benevolent authoritarian). They did not know how good VanCity really was, however, until the results came in. On a rating scale of 1 to 5, the VanCity profile ran between 3 and 4, significantly higher than others. Team-building, facilitating work and participation in the decision-making process—dependent on leadership skills—had the lowest scores, although they were higher, too.

Salvador and the two consultants then moved on to the next phase. They put together an eight-day training program covering communications and leadership. One of the things the survey had uncovered was that people felt they did not have enough input into dealing with problems they faced daily. The leadership training module, accordingly, focussed on running interactive meetings in which ideas and suggestions could surface. It was essential, Marks and McDowell kept repeating, that when problems and ideas for solving them were put forward, the supervisor or branch manager deal with them immediately. Not only did prompt action get rid of an issue, but employees also realized that they were being listened to and could make a difference.

Every workshop group had a sample of people from different levels of the organization. This egalitarian mix had a lasting impact on raising team spirit. Marks and McDowell were in their element. It was the first time they had a chance to put their ideas, or rather, Likert's ideas, to work on a broad enough scale that they could have a real impact.

Team-building games were played, the most memorable involving Tinker Toys. Simulated meetings were also used, to examine how work-group problems were dealt with. Scenarios were generated by the participants themselves, illustrating the kinds of problems that might occur in a branch. Marks and McDowell wrote them up. One character was Sally Sorefeet, who walked around barefoot in the office. There was Sandy Smelly, who never washed—not the kind of person to deal with members. The most important skill taught to observers was how exactly to tell people about their behaviour. It could be a touchy business. Skills concerned with providing feedback and constructive criticism—what in communications theory was called "constructive openness"—were practised.

The original survey was taken in late 1979. A second measurement survey was taken in late 1981 to see what had happened. The Likert methodology allowed one to do that—take a snapshot, intervene, take another snapshot—but, even then, there were not many occasions when trainers had an opportunity to measure the results of a training intervention so directly.

The prospect, for Salvador, was exciting. He could hardly wait to rip open the envelope. The tension was like the wait at an Academy Awards ceremony. Salvador was sure the organization had moved in that period of time. On the other hand, with the original profile being so good, there wasn't much room to go forward. A nagging thought in the back of his mind kept telling him that the results could go backwards.

As it turned out, the organization had moved almost every one of the marks further up the line, in the year-and-a-half interval. Managerial leadership (team building, work facilitation and goal emphasis) and supervisors being open to ideas had moved the most. These were exactly the areas on which the training program had focussed. Salvador considered it a tribute not so much to the trainers as to the people who had gone through the program and then returned to their work and done something with it, but he also knew that he and the others as trainers had done something powerful.

It had been an exciting time, too, for both Marks and McDowell. They had never worked with an organization like VanCity before, with its exuberant co-operative ethic. McDowell, who was most familiar with the Rensis Likert program, had not seen it used with an organization that was in such good shape to begin with. He was pleasantly surprised at the results. Something else, unplanned, also happened in that interval. The two players in the Steve and Mickey Show became a part of the family, even though they were external consultants. They were invited to Christmas parties and considered bona fide VanCity people. A few years later, the regime changed and interest in Rensis Likert and humanistic psychology faded into the woodwork. The legacy, however, remained.

Wayne McKay, amid all this, was beginning to enjoy himself again. He had no illusions about how he had ended up in human resources. In 1977, when he was shifted, human resources was considered the bottom of the barrel. It hadn't even existed as a section before, in VanCity. He no longer had his old scorecards, either, like growth, volume and profits, by which he could measure what had been achieved. He had hesitated taking the job also because he saw human resources as a dull, pedestrian adjunct to the main business which had been so exciting.

It was now turning out to be the opposite. Because the division was brand new, there were no restrictions on McKay's inventiveness. People's motivation, moreover, was more interesting than scorecards and even computer systems. For someone who, at East Hastings, had dressed up his branch and flipped hamburgers for the marchpast of the Pacific National Exhibition parade, being given the division was like opening the door to his imagination.

He began virtually from scratch. There were only two people at the time, besides himself, who fell into the division. He wasn't a human resources professional, so he decided to run his division by gut feel, starting with training. He set a target of six days training per year for existing employees, an exceptionally high figure, and in the initial years managed to do it. He also tried to give new employees eight to ten days' training in their first year. It was often awkward, since the burgeoning branches were short-staffed, but the division met the target and sometimes exceeded it.

There were no materials on the shelf for these programs, either, and no suitable packages one could buy from others, so Salvador, McKay and sometimes branch help wrote the manuals and training guides themselves. McKay was a human resources naïf, but he knew and understood the work VanCity's people did. The training curriculum was the product of his own invention. So was the sense of history that he imparted. The slide show that he had done allowed him to put his passionate feelings about what VanCity meant into a form that reached every employee and, although Don Bentley was dead, to safeguard the tradition.

It did not occur to McKay to attend courses for trainers, read books in the field, and assiduously follow human resources fashion. He had been used to doing things first and better than others anyway. He took that as a credo. When he went to the Banff School of Advanced Management for a stint, which Geoff Hook had recommended for his senior managers, he had spent most of his time skiing. Listening to conventional management doctrine, for McKay, meant going backwards. When it came to training, Salvador, new personnel manager Larry Wald and a third recruit had training backgrounds. They could feed him their ideas.

One of the first things McKay did was establish an employee benefits committee. It seemed an outlandish concept. Each branch chose a representative on the committee. Head office had two or three. The committee's mandate was to survey the field and come back with recommendations about salary ranges and benefits. Some managers were horrified, claiming it was tantamount to having people set their own pay. They thought the committee would recommend huge raises. The committee members knew, however, that VanCity had only so much money and that their salaries had to be related to what their peers at the banks and other credit unions were making. VanCity's policy was to be 5 per cent better than the competition, in order to attract good people.

Almost every committee recommendation was accepted by senior management. The process generated solidarity. Since the committee was getting its information first-hand, unfiltered, there was no mistrust of management trying to pull the wool over their eyes. The research was also done on VanCity time. The independent information gave employees a feeling of mastery.

Pay equity was another McKay objective, but he had neither the help nor the time to develop the details himself and to sell the many adjustments that needed to be made. He slyly handed the function to the employees' committee—representing the people directly affected. People in the branches, working through their committee representatives, sorted out their relationships to each other and the value of what they did. Then the committee, not McKay and management, wrote the applicable job descriptions, after which they compared jobs to establish pay equity.

Benefits as well as salary came into the calculations. More benefits were added, until VanCity had the most comprehensive range of benefits of any organization in the city. Part-time employees lobbied for more benefits. The pool of part-time people had grown large. Many were former full-time employees with babies. With more branches, they could find a branch closer to home. They were important to branch managers, since they could be scheduled for peak hours. Their benefits increased.

McKay then instituted written performance appraisals. Without the appraisals, managers could play favourites in promotions or could unfairly keep others back. The employee also received a copy of the appraisal. McKay worked hard on the idea. He had never forgotten the time when Bentley had passed him over in hiring a manager for the new Kitsilano branch. He was only twenty-three years old and had been with VanCity for just half a year, but he thought he should have gotten the job. It hurt even more when he had to show the new manager the ropes. There was no performance appraisal assessing McKay's abilities against the field, by which his merit could be recognized.

He also had to devise a fair way of dealing with unproductive employees. Don Bentley, with his deep humanitarianism, had not liked firing people, regardless of the problems they might be causing. Geoff Hook did not accept this approach. VanCity, he argued, could not afford it. Employees failing to do their job not only took away from VanCity, they also could demoralize and drag down a whole branch. He did not advocate mass firings. He did, however, want branch managers to be more honest with their people.

McKay worked on the issue through a committee that included himself and a small, rotating group of branch managers. They decided on a routine, like actors improvising a sketch in a rehearsal room. The manager was to sit down and talk to a problem employee and explain the specific concerns. Employees were to be given six months to bring their performance up to standard or, they were to be told, they were better off finding something else.

The rehearsed scenario helped managers over the psychological hump of being frank with problem employees. Some of the employees managed dramatic turnarounds. Others drifted off of their own accord, not waiting for the boom to be lowered. Not many, but a few, were ultimately fired for non-performance. It took McKay several years to reduce the "problem children" to a manageable field. Altogether, about one hundred people who fell in the non-performance category—equivalent to a quarter of the staff—left or were dismissed for cause in this period.

McKay, at the same time, recruited Jan Chapman, who was managing the main branch, as VanCity's first employee relations officer, to help sort out disputes and work on employees' problems directly. She and McKay looked at cutting-edge programs being written about, including the Japanese model for employee input. Chapman also established counselling for alcoholism and drug use and for other personal problems. Crisis counselling was part of the program. McKay launched a social club that was run by employee representatives and introduced a fitness incentive program, which gave out awards for losing weight, quitting smoking or jogging—the first for credit unions in Canada, and one of the earliest anywhere in the country.

There was now only one unionized branch, Main Street. The main branch at Oak and Broadway, which had certified, decertified and then certified again, had decertified once more. The tension that had led to the second certification had disappeared as employees got to know Geoff Hook. Main Street wanted to decertify, too, but it was encouraged to stay unionized so that unions, several of which kept their money at VanCity, would have a unionized branch to go to.

Something much larger, but less on the surface, was occurring as these steps were being taken. It was triggered by the launching of the on-line system. The Geac system did not just make a teller's work easier, it set off a revolutionary change in the nature of work in VanCity and in the kind of people who were best suited for it. McKay presided over this revolution.

In its original days, VanCity had been as much of a bookkeeping service as it was a member-service organization. Someone had to keep track of all those deposits and withdrawals, loan payments and posting of accounts, and to investigate mistakes. The organization as a result filled up with people who were bookkeepers by temperament, and they tended to stay, too. Even with the Central Data Systems batch system, much of the same kind of work remained. Vouchers (deposit and withdrawal slips) had to be sorted and their data punched onto a tape for processing. Errors had to be painstakingly tracked down to source, and recalculations made.

The Geac system altered the nature of this work dramatically. Once a teller posted an entry into the computer at the moment of handling the transaction, the entry was complete unless the teller had made a mistake. Tellers effectively became their own bookkeepers. This changed the nature of the teller's work, too. Before, tellers did not especially care if they made mistakes. Someone behind them would pick up the mistake. They concentrated on getting through the line-up of members as quickly as they could. Now they needed to control mistakes at the teller station itself. Otherwise, there would be no end of misery. McKay and Salvador had to give them the training for it.

Suddenly, also, a branch had backroom people who were unnecessary. The logical move was to bring them up front to serve members. They weren't equipped to deal with members effectively, however, and were not necessarily personable. McKay and Salvador invented the training to help them adapt, too. Those who could not adapt, McKay shifted to the specialized paperwork that remained, like the filing of cancelled cheques and the statement preparation, done out of head office. Others drifted to other credit unions where backroom functions had not yet been cut back.

With most people in a branch now in the front line, VanCity began changing itself from an order-taking culture to a relationship culture. Tellers and member-service representatives communicated more with members, helping to bring in more of their business. "Cross-selling," it was called. Many members had mortgages with VanCity but had left their deposit business elsewhere. Some members had part of their money in VanCity term deposits or in Plan 24 but did not do anything else through the credit union. VanCity was their second or third financial institution.

These missed chances for business and helping members were not that important when people were flooding through the door and loan officers were frantically writing mortgages. VanCity also had unique products that nobody else could match. McKay knew, however, that these generational advantages would not last. In the summer of 1979, the Royal Bank and the Bank of Montreal, with much fanfare, introduced daily interest—twelve years after VanCity, but they did get there. Soon everybody would be offering similar deposit products, although other VanCity innovations, like the All-In-One Statement, might still be beyond them.

Hook and the executive committee were determined to stay out in front. The cross-selling involved more of a cultural shift than met the eye. Although advertising was widespread, the concept of "selling" in banking was a dirty word. In credit unions it was taboo. A credit union did not sell people anything. A credit union was there to serve. "We were order takers," Salvador described it. "A member came up to the counter and placed his order as if he were in McDonald's and said, 'I want a Big Mac and an order of fries and a chocolate shake.' In the credit union, if I wanted to open a chequing account, the person on the other side of the counter would get out the necessary forms and open the chequing account and that's where the transaction ended."

Paradoxically, the sales skill program put in place for the purpose did not seem to be about selling at all. McKay made sure that VanCity's basic philosophy, that the member always came first, underpinned the program. Employees were to be member advocates, trying to find the best thing for the member—say, moving money to a higher-bearing term deposit—even if it cost the credit union money. Banks did not always want to assume this cost. If VanCity did right by its members, moreover, members would do right by their organization, McKay pointed out. The label "selling" did not quite capture this member-ownership dynamic.

Paradoxically, also, what appeared to be a departure from credit union tradition strengthened it. The new approach provided more of a relationship between the credit union and its members. It was not the original common-bond relationship, where an intimate knowledge of a member's character and situation was crucial for deciding a loan application. It was a relationship revolving largely around a member's savings. Savings and the interest they generated, however, were important to members. VanCity, again, was first off the mark in its market. Only VanCity and other credit unions could do cross-selling properly, since only they could pull up a members' different accounts all at once, on the computer terminal, and see a member's situation whole, without a time-consuming search.

The three sequential shifts—moving people from the backroom up front, more interactive communication among staff and actively engaging members about their needs—represented, for McKay, a final goodbye to the past. Gone was the last cultural trace of ledger cards and eye shades and the sedate, closed banking atmosphere he had first known in the bank in Killarney. This shift had an impact on recruiting philosophy in turn. McKay wanted to find out what made people tick and whether they were outgoing enough. Inward-looking applicants would not be suited to the new culture. Training was aimed at bringing out people's abilities and giving them flexibility.

The key to this flexibility was having a broad understanding of branch operations. McKay wanted people to have that background before moving up to a supervisory position. He arranged a stepped salary system so that people could cross over from one group to another—for example, from tellers to accounting—without taking a financial penalty. Otherwise, people tended to stay in one kind of job. Tellers worked their way up to head teller, then became teller supervisors. The problem was, what did they do after that? Suddenly VanCity needed an administrative supervisor or a loan supervisor, but teller supervisors had no exposure to that side of the operation.

Eventually management passed a regulation that employees had to have experience in at least two functions before moving up to a supervisory capacity. Not everybody liked it. McKay explained to them that VanCity needed to have greater experience in its people, so they would be available for what the organization needed, not exclusively for what they wanted to do. Many staffers who had originally objected later thanked him for the cross-training, especially when they rose to branch manager and saw that they needed that multi-functional understanding.

The cross-training in particular helped women move into managerial positions. Traditionally, in banks, women were tellers and accounting clerks, and hence at the lower end of the scale. People who had a carpet under their desk and a telephone of their own and who could take appointments were largely males and were mostly on the lending side. The promotional route up to management was also on the lending side. McKay was explicitly anti-sexist. He actively encouraged women at VanCity to get lending experience. The converse also held: men were hired as tellers and took their turn on cash. Women were attracted to working at VanCity as a result. The ratio of women to men was even higher at VanCity than it was at the banks, where it was already high, at around 70 per cent.

Ethnic minorities and handicapped people also knocked on the door, because of VanCity's image as an employer that didn't discriminate. McKay had pushed the door open himself. In his early years as manager at East Hastings he had hired a Fijian, James Madhavan, as a teller. He already had a Chinese-Canadian teller and an Italian assistant. Madhavan, however, was very dark-skinned. Several members refused to do business with him and made caustic comments about his presence in the branch. McKay was a sports hound, in fact a lifelong Dodgers fan, and knew the story of Jackie Robinson breaking the colour barrier in professional baseball, first in the minor leagues at Montreal and then with the Brooklyn Dodgers. The Dodgers' general manager, Branch Rickey, had warned Robinson that he would be jeered at and abused, and made him promise not to rise to the racist bait. Although McKay, told of the incident by his father, was just a boy in a prairie town where everyone was white and almost everyone Protestant, the story made a deep impression on him. At the East Hastings branch, he re-enacted this scenario with Madhavan. The two of them worked through difficult situations with members together until Madhavan was fully accepted.

The young McKay had talked to Bentley about these matters, especially about how to handle the Madhavan case. They shared an idealistic prairie egalitarianism. Now all of VanCity's branches were mosaics, as his East Hastings branch had been. A language registry was developed for the system, noting the location of employees who spoke different languages so that they could be called up on the phone to act as interpreters. McKay decided to review it once and counted thirty-five languages.

He was a natural sharer of information and connector to people. The "need to know" was described in every recent textbook on organizational development, but McKay didn't have to read them. He had taken over *TATS* (To Advise The Staff), the internal weekly newsletter, from Ron Spooner. *TATS* was folksy and friendly, with personal notes from the branches, jokes, news about the social club and VanCity's softball teams, quotes and snippets of poetry. McKay, populist-style, wrote the editorial, slipping in pointers, often with a joke as a lead-in, to make contact. Wanting to involve staff in the workplace, he also used *TATS* as a vehicle whereby staff could exchange views. The organization-wide forums were his idea.

He discovered that the job he had wanted the least he was enjoying the most. He had hung on to his habit of starting late whenever he could get away with it. He was a good sounding board. He took the time to listen and would intercede on an employee's behalf. He spent as much time with people as they needed, even though it might back up his schedule or make him late for a meeting, as if defiantly to say that people's worries and problems were more important than the mere arrangements of managers.

He gave rein to his non-conformism. He would refer pejoratively to "suits." He wore suits himself because it was the required costume—he himself had established the dress code at head office—but self-important, deal-making "suits" were another species, to be looked on with mild disdain. Managers who were fixated with numbers and who did not know anything else—representatives of the traditional banking mentality—were "beancounters." They did not realize that the way people were treated and how they identified themselves in their work were the key factors in an enterprise. They were stunted, by definition.

McKay began his baseball collection, which ultimately, along with other sports and non-sports artifacts in his office, reached museum proportions. Eric Hayne remembered arriving in McKay's office for the first time in 1979, when the memorabilia were in the build-up stage. Hayne had a program from a 1947 grapefruit league game between the New York Yankees and the Cleveland Indians that had a Joe DiMaggio autograph on it, and he offered it to McKay. McKay jumped at it.

He chaired the staff-wide forums like an impresario. The forums, held in hotels that had a large enough meeting room, were more than just discussions of strategic direction or celebrations of an achievement. They were ritualistic meetings of the VanCity tribe, grand social events rippling with gaiety and anticipation and the staff's conviction that they were, collectively, the front-runner and like no other. Door prizes were handed out. Satirical entertainment was provided by an in-house cabaret act, dubbed Red Rose and Pity, poking fun at the organization and senior management. McKay was recreating on a larger scale the sociability and family feeling that had existed around his branch on East Hastings. He was in a position, too, in *TATS* and in the training process, to articulate VanCity's values and indulge in light-hearted bank bashing to underscore them. He was the heartbeat of the organization, the grandfather who looked after everybody, Brian Salvador thought.

McKay never did become a Hook man the way he had been a Bentley man. His affection for Hook grew, and he enjoyed working with the other division managers, but he was older, less impressionable now, and had more of his own mind. Dave Turnbull, who was part of the Hook crowd, felt that somehow McKay was keeping his distance from his management peers.

Ironically, although on paper McKay was in the least powerful slot of the division managers, his familiarity with staff and their familiarity with him gave him a grip on the organization that none of the others had.

This sure grip was reflected in his division. Human resources had risen to the top of the barrel. It was the elite division that everybody wanted to model their own divisions on. Ultimately McKay had fifteen people—a full-fledged management and support team that worked together at a high level of sophistication. "There wasn't a great deal of direction or criticism from Wayne," personnel manager Larry Wald remembered. "He brought to the job more his personality and his sensitivity, and I was allowed and encouraged to do my own thing."

The VanCity ambiance that blossomed in this period, with its undercurrent of excitement, was infectious. Every time Chris Bergthorson at Embryo Communications went to VanCity he was struck by how much people liked working there. They were brilliant to work with, he felt. There was a feeling throughout the organization that the VanCity culture was unique and that its employees were part of that uniqueness. They did things not just because it was their job but also because they wanted to do them and move VanCity ahead. Members were attracted to this ambience. McKay had long ago realized that if staff were treated well, they were much more likely to treat members in a friendly way.

This also influenced the way staff listened to each other. Management was inculcated in the importance of active listening. The object was to put oneself in the employee's shoes and then to act on suggestions that had merit. When the employees, in turn, during a training session, were taught about active listening—how to listen to an irate member or one with a particular problem—they already had an inkling of what the concept meant. Banks were notorious for giving customers the runaround if they had problems or requests that did not fit established procedure. VanCity, on the other hand, really did listen. People switching from a bank to VanCity noticed the difference immediately.

Ten years earlier, McKay had preached the gospel of new opportunities on the horizon, but nobody had believed him and many bright lights had drifted away. Now the air at VanCity was full of a sense of opportunity. In 1986, *The Financial Post* published a book called *The 100 Best Companies to Work For in Canada*. VanCity was among the pacesetters. The entry on VanCity noted that its employees had fun and touched on the Halloween costumes and other playfulness. It mentioned the friendliness. It dwelt particularly on the training and on the push to have employees learn as much as they could about everything, so they could seize hold of their chances. The employees were so enthusiastic, the report noted, that they admitted they occasionally sounded "corny." When VanCity asked them to suggest an advertising slogan, the entries sounded like testimonials at an evangelical revival.

McKay, although he was no longer in human resources, handed out copies of the book like a proud papa.

Exile

OF THE BENTLEY ORIGINALS, only Wayne McKay and John Iseli, who took over the new downtown branch, stayed behind. The others moved on or were marginalized. For them, the Hook years hardly counted except as a distorting mirror of what was.

Don Nelson became general manager of the IWA Credit Union. Managing a credit union was the kind of move that Mr. Bentley had suggested he might make—Nelson called him "Mr. Bentley" to the end—but that he had always declined while Bentley was alive.

Jan Chapman, the first woman in VanCity to be named manager, did not stop her striving. She moved on from employee relations to senior management at B.C. Central, in charge of administrative services. Burned out after a few years, she decided to change her lifestyle and became general manager of the Creston and District Credit Union, a small credit union in the West Kootenays, near the American border.

She was doing a lot of personal searching—"getting close to God," as she described it. She had always been searching for God, even in success and even when she was an agnostic. One day, she had an experience with God that took her in a new direction. She began religious studies and, from there, work on a master's degree in theology, with a view to entering the Anglican ministry.

She remembered how much she had loved her days at VanCity. She did actually love them, she said, the passion of work and the excitement of it. She hoped she would bring that same passion to the church.

Ray Evelle, Bentley's 1956 recruit, hung on in VanCity Insurance Services until 1988 when the subsidiary was sold and he was replaced. He was unemployed for the first time in his life. He eventually found another job, in a small credit union, but ended up on stress leave. He realized his credit union career was over.

Laura Smalley, Don Bentley's secretary, retired from VanCity, also in 1988, after twenty-eight years. VanCity threw a farewell party for her. The days when Bentley, Evelle and Smalley ran VanCity from the old main branch at Quebec and Broadway were long gone.

Hermann Myers, who had created the VanCity logo, had been knocked out of action by the time the change of regime occurred. His body had no

more give to it, so he and his wife went to Kentville, Nova Scotia, where their
married daughter and grandchildren lived. Myers ultimately succumbed to
a heart attack. Elsie Myers, his widow, was in the local credit union one day
and there, big as life, was a poster advertising Plan 24 and the logo
Hermann had designed way back when, doodling with a pencil in their
small office in the Sun Tower.

Hermann's pal, Ron Spooner, never could swallow the changeover from
Bentley to Hook and being pushed down the ladder. Myers, visiting from
Nova Scotia, was struck by how bitter Spooner was. Myers tried calming him
down, but there was not much he could say. From the moment Hook had
arrived at the old head office at 1034 West Broadway, Spooner was in exile,
purged from his home and native land, although physically he might still be
on the premises.

Marina Lowe, Wayne McKay's secretary, remembered how sorry she felt
for Spooner. Nobody would even give him the time of day, she thought.
After a couple of years, Spooner had endured enough. He did not like
Geoff Hook. He was given a settlement. He wasn't thrilled with it, but he
wasn't prepared to fight. As far as Spooner was concerned, he had been
forced out.

He and his wife Ruth built a place on Thetis Island in the Gulf Islands.
Hermann and Elsie Myers, in Nova Scotia, travelled to Vancouver every
other year to see him and other friends. Spooner would come into town,
visit with Hermann and Elsie, and then he and Hermann would go off for
a long, long lunch. Spooner and his secretary at VanCity, Rhona Lythgoe,
had given Myers an aboriginal talking stick because Myers liked to talk
so much. So did Spooner. They laughed over that. Theirs, they agreed, was
a wonderful friendship. Then Spooner's wife died. On one of Myers's visits
to Vancouver, Lythgoe told him that Spooner was beginning to go off.
Spooner, in his despair and loneliness, was drinking heavily, recklessly.

He managed to pull himself out of that and was drinking less. His spirit
was up and down. Occasional traces of the original gaiety and sparkle
remained, like a flame in a rainstorm. In 1986, for VanCity's fortieth
anniversary, when Hook was no longer CEO, Spooner and credit union
journalist Clarence Morin put together a special illustrated edition of
Working Dollars chronicling VanCity's history and the origins of the credit
union movement. Wayne McKay had commissioned the work and gotten
Spooner involved. The special issue was entitled "VanCity Pioneers." It
had a photograph of the original charter on the front page and other
photographs of many of the early people, ending with Bentley in 1975 and
long-time board member Bert Gladu. The written chronology continued
through to 1985. It was a scintillating evocation of the past. There was no
picture of Geoff Hook.

Then, as with his buddy Myers, Spooner's heart gave out. The pioneer
edition was his last reminiscence of the VanCity he had known.

CHAPTER 39

The Workaholic

GARRY SMITH WAS A PERFECTIONIST, a workaholic, and a dynamo. He liked to accomplish things. Most of all, he wanted to feel alive, and VanCity gave him that feeling. Geoff Hook had pulled Smith out of Branch 3, which he was managing, to make him his administrative assistant and help with expanding branch operations. Soon Smith was manager of branch operations, reporting to Frank Coffey. Branches were the heart of VanCity. At the time, they were managing a third of a billion dollars. Smith found himself at the centre of this intense activity. Sometimes his impatience got him into trouble. He knew how to laugh, however, and he had an eternal boyishness about him. Hook and Coffey backed him. He was only thirty years old.

Smith was a Surrey boy. His first credit union job was with the local Whalley Savings Credit Union, which soon merged with others to become part of the Fraser Valley Credit Union. Smith was manager of a branch in Chilliwack when he was twenty-one years old, barely out of his teens. He grew restless at its restraints, however. He and some other young musketeers, as they called themselves, figured they knew everything there was to know about the organization, that it could not be run without them and that they should be allowed to do things their way. Otherwise they would go elsewhere, they said.

Smith went to VanCity. He still remembered his interview with Don Bentley at the old head office at 1030 West Broadway. The carpet was dark red. It was a dark branch. VanCity wasn't much then, Smith thought, but at the time it had seemed a big, big credit union, certainly compared with the Fraser Valley outback. VanCity was different in other ways. Bentley, at their meeting, did not ask him any questions about his experience. The two men simply had a nice sit-down chat about nothing in particular. "What did that man learn about me?" Smith wondered, but Bentley hired him.

He became manager of the East Hastings branch when Wayne McKay was moved upwards to become comptroller. Smith's sojourn at East Hastings was the most memorable time of his life. He worked six days a week, fifteen-hours-plus a day, without thinking much about it. He enjoyed his work too much. There was such a good feeling about working with the people at VanCity—"It was just incredible," he remembered—that he wanted to do everything he could to promote the organization. He arrived as early as six in the morning and stayed into the evening, arriving home as late as midnight. He was still living in Surrey, which meant he got up as early as four o'clock to make the trip into Vancouver. Five hours of sleep, sometimes less, was all that he needed. He had maintained almost the same work hours in the Fraser Valley. Because he had committed himself so totally to VanCity, he and his wife were growing apart.

Smith loved the branch. He loved its members. He saw them as a grass-roots kind of people; they put in an honest day's work for an honest day's pay. They believed in common, hard work. They were workaholics, something like himself. Handling their loan applications was easy.

His managerial style was autocratic. He was young and thought he knew everything, and he wanted to conquer the world. He wasn't a great listener, like McKay. He did not have McKay's patience. He had a short attention span, too. Some of his staff took exception to him. He thought they were misreading him. He really did care about them as people. But he wanted things done, and he wanted them done fast and absolutely the right way.

He rarely took holidays. When he did, he took only a week or a week and a half at most, and he seldom left town. This did not help his relationship with his wife, either. He would sneak into the branch at night, like the Scarlet Pimpernel, go through the desks and follow up on the day's events. He wanted to make sure everything was balanced. He also left notes behind congratulating staff members on particular pieces of good work while he was away. He would not eat supper and would be hungry. Once the staff left a brown bag behind for him. He thought it was something to eat. In it was a sanitary napkin. They laughed about this when he got back. They did not like him snooping through their desks and had decided to teach him a lesson.

He had two sons. He did not see much of them. Once he did leave town on holiday, to take them to Disneyland. It was two days driving down, a day at Disneyland, and two days driving back. He did not like himself much for it. He did, though, take them to all their hockey games on the weekends. The family had moved to Delta. Because there were a lot of kids but not much in the way of facilities, games would be scheduled around the clock, including the early morning, sometimes two o'clock or four o'clock. Smith always brought work with him.

Once, with a modernistic house in North Vancouver that proved to be structurally faulty and was condemned, he had to take a $25,000 write-off, a considerable sum of money then. It was the first mortgage loss in VanCity's history. The loss was heart-rending for Smith. He thought he would lose his job because of it, but Bentley was forgiving, as he always was. Smith thought that Bentley in the end was forgiving him for his youthfulness and allowing him to learn from his mistakes. Not all organizations did that, he knew. He bound himself all the closer to VanCity.

He had an infectious laugh and a quick sense of humour. He knew how to joke. As a boy, he had picked up a knack for drawing. He liked copying cartoon characters. He could take an image, make it bigger or smaller, make multiple copies of it, combine it with others, put spin on it. He compared himself to a Xerox machine. At VanCity, he became the resident cartoonist for commemorating special events.

He was in his brown years then. Everything he owned was brown—all his suits, all his ties and all his shoes. His house was brown. The carpet in his house was various shades of brown. All the furniture was brown. He didn't know why, but he had this hunger for the colour. (Brown was, in fact, the fashionable colour for business suits in the period.)

He liked technology and was quick in grasping its intricacies. When Geac developed the on-line system, Smith drafted the format, or template, for displaying member and account information on the screen. He was one of the first VanCity people to learn how to use the system and wrote the procedural manual for staffers.

He was a collector. Hook had brought him into executive meetings, to take minutes. He took pride in the minutes and the way he laid them out. He kept them long after, as he changed offices. He could not bear to throw them away, not so much because they were his minutes as because they contained information. He kept credit union magazines, *TATS* (VanCity's newsletter), everything about the projects he was working on and statistics of all kinds. Eventually a whole wall in his house was dedicated to the collection. It seemed purposeless, but every once in a while somebody would ask him about a past event or statistic and he could help out.

The organizational world of VanCity was changing rapidly. The Hook regime's mystique of formal expertise—of CGAs and commerce degrees—was in the ascendant, and Smith was taken up by it. The cardinal assumption, in the new culture, was the need for sophistication in managing the financial side of the organization. Smith took this as a given. He accepted the idea of McKay being shunted out of finance and administration. McKay did not have an awful lot of educational background, Smith thought, just a lot of practical experience. That was no longer good enough for work that had grown in scope and implication, he reflected. He was already thinking like Hook and Coffey.

When Hook had first suggested to his senior people that they might take a turn at the School of Advanced Management in Banff, none of the divisional managers wanted to risk wasting their time. It was a six-week stint. Smith volunteered—he was the guinea pig. Unlike McKay, who went later, Smith took the exercise to heart. The program, for him, was a proxy for a university education. It covered economics, the sacred discipline of formal business learning. He was supplied with a pile of books two feet high. He read them all. He spent most of his time in Banff studying. One of the things that was stressed at Banff was "adapt or perish." Smith had a plaque in his office with a dinosaur on it and the slogan, in Latin, *Adaptor aut pereo*—under it. He did not intend to perish, like Nelson and Spooner, whose departures he saw as inevitable.

He was in charge of all the operational issues that came up in overseeing branches, including the hiring of managers and organizing managers' meetings, over which he presided. He was a key part of the planning process for new branches, providing input to Dave Turnbull on their design. The excitement of opening new branches, with large crowds showing up, was intense, enthralling for all of them. Smith was pell mell in the middle of this rapid expansion, occupying the key junction between the front lines below him and the division heads and CEO above him.

The strategy was "control." "We've got to control business" was like a mantra, fed in turn by Hook's and Coffey's conviction that, when they had arrived in 1976, business had already grown to the point where an under-managed VanCity was in danger of flying apart. VanCity was still growing at a breathtaking pace; things had to be controlled. There was little thought in the branch system, at this stage, of building business, because business was knocking down the doors. Jack Stimson and marketing, and the cleverness of Chris Bergthorson, by themselves were bringing in the crowds as fast as the system could handle them, and the branches were barely handling them. Implementation of some ideas from the marketing division even had to be postponed to allow operations to catch up. Smith constantly felt the pressure from his boss, Frank Coffey, not to let things get out of hand.

He was a good officer. He asked his managers for detailed quarterly reports, to track operations. He liked reports and statistics. They weren't just little reports, either, but thick compendiums that started out half-an-inch in depth and got thicker. His managers resented having to prepare them. Smith reflected later that perhaps he had made a mistake in asking them to conform to a standard of reporting they did not feel comfortable with. He felt he needed the information, however, as a discussion tool, to sit down with managers in their offices and understand what had happened in the branch. He could not visit each branch constantly to know what was going on from day to day, nor should he. The reports also added discipline. Verbal reporting was too vague.

The reports also fitted the culture of management by numbers, which came naturally to CGAs like Hook and Coffey, with their accounting backgrounds. It wasn't altogether out of place. One had to look at the numbers. Bentley had always looked at the numbers. Smith's objective in the more detailed reports was to compare the last quarter with the previous two or three years to see if any trends were developing. He also used them to follow up on problem areas. He would go through the reports at night and then write memos to the respective managers asking them to look at particular aspects of their operation. He became known for his detailed follow-ups. He felt there had not been enough of that discipline before.

Hiring and sometimes firing added more tension to Smith's life. Van-City's philosophy was to promote people from within, but the growing organization was using up its skills and talent too rapidly. Smith began hiring significant numbers from outside VanCity. Many inside the organization felt threatened by this, but he went ahead anyway. It was no favour to anyone, he felt, to promote people from inside VanCity who weren't ready, only to have to dismiss them six months or a year later.

As it was, too many managers found themselves beyond their capacity. It showed up in a chronic lack of judgement, sometimes in lending practices. Or they wouldn't make the changes mandated by Hook and Coffey that Smith had to implement. There were dismissals. Managerial turnover was high. Smith's decision to fire someone would not happen overnight. Trends would start to develop. There would be discussions back and forth with the employee, intended to help. Ultimately, if questionable situations kept occurring, the point came when something had to be done. Smith would then talk to Coffey. McKay, as human resources manager, and Joan Mac-Millan, the employee relations officer, would also be involved. In every case, they came out of the meeting agreeing with what Smith had to do.

He got the reputation of being hard-nosed. He was the bad guy. Staffers did not see the process behind the scenes. McKay, meanwhile, who had participated in the dismissal decision, was the good guy. The dismissed person, understandably upset, would often come to see McKay the next day and denounce Smith. McKay would sit and listen, cajole, and try to calm. Smith accepted the irony of this with a certain wry pride. He had the dirty side of the job. He was in operations. It was why he was paid what, for him, was a relatively large salary.

He was hit with two court cases. They involved two dismissed managers who had come up through VanCity. This made the dismissals particularly sensitive. The proceedings became a long, drawn-out soap opera, at times verging on Dadaesque. To make matters worse, people who knew their managers at VanCity usually felt a personal relationship to them, and both dismissed managers had loyal followings. They thought VanCity was unfair and focussed their criticism on Smith. A few others who were fired by Smith added their cases to the plaintiff lawyer's VanCity dossier. The *Province* ran a story on the troubles.

Ultimately the two lawsuits failed and Smith was vindicated. He thought later that he might have handled those situations differently. He might not have been so quick to jump at things. He had created a climate in which some managers, if they got into trouble, were afraid to communicate with him, fearing for their jobs. His intense kinetic energy, wanting to implement change, was impossible to avoid. His physical build, with its stocky upper body, added to the impression. He joked later about having been a retrograde manager and having since reformed, but pressures were so great then to move things forward, particularly from his boss Frank Coffey, that he felt he did not have time to act otherwise. The whole organization was under stress and strain. The headlong growth and Hook's and Coffey's enthusiasm impelled him like a prod. He had to keep making decisions quickly. He had been right, he insisted, whatever the fallout.

Meanwhile, new branches were opening. The greater the number of these challenges, the more Smith enjoyed his work, because he could put in his twelve to fifteen hours a day. Managers would kid him about his compulsiveness. He was engrossed with, among other things, how the branches physically appeared to members. Because managers were so busy, he thought he would help out. He had the itch. He also wanted the stickers on the door in a certain place and the posters hung in a certain way. So at midnight, he might stop by a branch on his way home, make sure all the pens worked, rehang all the posters in the branch and scrape off offending decals. Often it was a matter of impulse. He would be driving home in the late hours and he would say to himself, "Why don't I get this one done? Why don't I?" The temptation was irresistible. Many times on weekends he would take his second wife along—he had divorced and remarried—to wash the windows, scrape off old decals and put new decals on properly. He was still the boisterous, boyish loan officer at the Whalley Savings Credit Union.

These escapades added to the Smith legend. One day, employee relations officer Joan MacMillan told him his managers were quite upset by these clandestine entries into the branches. He was surprised. Checking up on his managers was the farthest thing from his mind. He thought of himself as being friendly and helpful. It had never occurred to him, in his exuberance, that his help might be misunderstood and resented. He wrote a humorous memo about his capers, trying to diffuse the situation. It only added to the incipient rebellion. He finally realized how much of a mistake he had made.

Geoff Hook was forgiving. They got along well together. Hook and Coffey stood behind him. They would not make him a fall guy for the incidental ruckus produced by the court cases. He was their man in operations, and they recognized his strong administrative talents, which reflected their own culture. He did "a super job," Coffey thought. Hook felt the same way. Whatever Smith's shenanigans, moroever, morale in the branches was high. There were eight branches when he took over branch operations. There were nineteen when the Hook period ended in 1983. They were all functioning like precision clockwork.

CHAPTER 40

The Allies

LEWIS VAN DER GRACHT WAS known to members of Richmond Savings Credit Union members as "Van." He liked the name. A moniker like that had a friendliness about it. Richmond was a friendly place, still coloured by its rural roots. Van der Gracht was an ex-furniture salesman who had run the credit union ever since it was established in 1948. In the early 1970s it was the second largest credit union in British Columbia, and for the rest of the decade it was in the top four. Van der Gracht had known Don Bentley well and supported him in his battles with B.C. Central. Hook was also fighting Central; van der Gracht was with him, too.

Van der Gracht and Don Bentley had talked regularly about what they were doing. Bentley told him about Plan 24 and explained how it worked. Van der Gracht thought it was a good idea. "We went out to lunch. We yakked away. The next thing we know, we were doing it," he recalled. He couldn't remember paying VanCity anything for the plan. "Not a dime," he said. "There was no such thing as copyright." In fact, there was, but Bentley didn't take advantage of it. The two had that kind of relationship. Van der Gracht, for his part, shared his mortgage innovations with Bentley.

Nor was van der Gracht surprised when VanCity succeeded with its Geac project. Central might badmouth the attempt, but he himself wasn't bothered by the controversy. The whole basis of the credit union movement was, for van der Gracht, doing the unusual, what nobody else had tried before. He researched Geac himself, then got in line right behind VanCity.

He wasn't upset, either, by VanCity's branching, when Bentley opened the Victoria Drive branch in 1957. He thought branches would be nothing but good for credit unions. He intended to open some of his own, and did, in Steveston, not much later, in 1961. He looked upon Bentley as his mentor—picking up on what Bentley was doing and joining together with VanCity to form a common front of larger credit unions, even back in the old League days.

Any animosity that he had, in the swirling world of credit union politics, was directed at Central and its politics, which he knew intimately. VanCity, Richmond and Surrey became known as the Big Three. They saw Central not as a paternal grandfather but as an adversary. It was building an empire that was costly and inefficient, and the large credit unions had to pay for it. Central and its loyalists, in return, deeply mistrusted them.

With Geoff Hook, it was the same battle over again. Hook, like Bentley, fiercely resisted George May's absolutism. Hook did not like May. He considered May ruthless. He did not like where May came from, either— the political, League side of the movement that had taken over Central with the merger. Hook still remembered the sense of fatigue and alienation he felt, as general manager of the old Central, when the merger occurred. Most of all, he didn't like May's ambition to make Central dominant. Hook wanted the power of the movement, which came from ownership, to stay in the community, where members and their credit unions were. That was the real issue: who was going to run the show, Central or the credit unions? Hook and May tangled, with feeling. Aj Gill, Central's chief financial officer, watched them go at it. "It accelerated after Don passed away," Gill said. "There was far more animosity, more conflict. George and Geoff got pretty emotional."

In late 1977, Peter Podovinikoff, the general manager of the Delta Credit Union, took over at Central. May was on his way to Toronto to become CEO of the national credit union organization. The VanCity-Central feud simply continued. Hook was intent on bringing Podovinikoff around. It was absurd, for a start, that VanCity and the other large credit unions had only one vote each at Central, without any weighting. The principle of one member, one vote, Hook argued again, was wrongly applied at the whole-sale level. To genuinely hew to the principle, one should be weighting credit union votes at Central according to the number of individual members each credit union had, passing the principle of one member, one vote through to the next level. Hook and his allies like van der Gracht eventually did get some weighting, but it didn't go very far.

Hook was continually trying to sort out the tension between size and economies of scale, on the one hand, and member-ownership on the other. One needed size to bring members convenience and to compete. He always had thought VanCity should integrate smaller credit unions. "Do we mean business?" he liked to ask. "Are we going to be a real financial service institution and really have a place in the scheme of things? Are we going to be players? Or are we just going to be a little sewing circle or knit-ting group out there? Good, wonderful people, but having no impact on anything?"

Hook, when he was at Central, together with Bentley, had pushed the idea of six large, regional, community credit unions in the province, to be achieved through merger. The idea foundered, but Hook never quite gave up on it. He avoided building branches across the street from other credit unions. He believed in mergers, unity and integration rather than VanCity chasing less powerful credit unions off the street. He kept the idea of a merger alive with groups of his peers, talking over how they would rational-ize operations.

Van der Gracht was part of these discussions. He did not altogether agree with Hook. In the late 1960s he had favoured the idea of one big credit union, but now not just VanCity but also Richmond and others were large enough to have professional cadres of their own, and to contend, he had changed his mind. He saw face-to-face competition as a good thing for the movement. The worst possibility, he thought, was ultimately to have only one credit union in a marketplace. People would feel trapped. They would want to know what the alternative was, even if they never used it. Otherwise they would say to themselves, "I don't want to deal with the bank, I want to deal with a credit union, but there's only one lousy credit union, so now what do I do?" If there were two or three credit unions, on the other hand, they could choose the one they liked the best. They would feel free. They would think much more enthusiastically about credit unions in general and collectively strengthen them all.

Hook almost got his wish for a merger. Van der Gracht and Richmond Savings stumbled when property values tumbled in 1981 and British Columbia was hit badly by recession. Commercial real estate and fishing boat values were decimated, and Richmond Savings had large loan port-folios in both. It was in bad shape. In 1983 it went under supervision by the Credit Union Reserve Board. Van der Gracht retired and was replaced by an aggressive go-getter, Don Tuline. Tuline wasn't sure how far his board or the reserve board would support a rescue operation so, as a fallback, he started talking to Hook about an amalgamation. The negotiations went as far as a written study and tandem board meetings, but when the reserve board backed Tuline's rescue plan, Richmond terminated the talks. The possibility of amalgamation slipped away.

All Hook could do was shrug. He mused about the human condition and people's egos. People did not like to give up their roles, he thought. They loved being on their board. Nobody wants to give up their particular little empire. After a merger there would have been only one board with half the directors gone, so when it came to the gut decision to merge, the Richmond directors had pulled back.

Hook was deeply disappointed. A later, less logical merger with WestCoast Savings in Victoria did not get beyond the speculative stage. Hook tried to be philosophical. He was able at least, now, to concentrate freely on taking VanCity eastward and south, following the suburban mortgage market to offset the deposit-taking in Vancouver. "Think of Richmond and Surrey no longer as potential partners but as competition," he told his people. That was the new strategy: making VanCity most effective on its own, as one group, against all the others.

That still left Central. Its meetings often turned into donnybrooks. Hook felt VanCity wasn't being consulted enough. A lot of Central's money came from VanCity—money that belonged to VanCity's members—and Hook was determined to protect it. He objected to Central not getting consensual agreement from its larger members about the direction it was taking. He particularly objected to Central's adventures in underwriting large real estate developments, which in 1981 and 1982 had skyrocketed, as Central tried to earn more money for itself. It was supposed to be the central banker, not a commercial lender. The Bank of Canada, Hook said, did not get involved in real estate development; neither should Central.

Hook's grievance went deeper, down into Central's financial entrails. Central had no risk capital, other than its share capital and retained earnings. Its money consisted largely of credit union reserves. Those deposits had been made for liquidity purposes, so credit unions could draw on the money quickly if a crisis occurred. The funds, accordingly, should have been invested in something quite liquid and completely without risk, like federal government notes. If, however, some of that money was tied up in real estate assets, which was the case, that portion of the liquidity pool was gone. To exacerbate matters, Central had been lending money to Nelson Skalbania, a controversial wheeler-dealer, once described by the *Toronto Star* as the "master of the quick flip." Skalbania, it was revealed in the press, owed Central $4 million. This news enraged many credit union activists.

Central was also using the financial revenues from liquidity deposits (the interest rate margin it took) for non-financial expenses instead, like the printing shop, a travel agency Central was underwriting, the advertising department and the collections service. These should have been paying their own way or have been fully funded directly by members, instead of being subsidized from another pocket. The extra costs meant dividends "below market" for Central's credit union members. It was a time, too, when the credit unions were running into financial headwinds, from an interest rate squeeze and then a recession, and needed every penny they could get. Central was not cutting back these activities quickly enough. Then, because of the recession, it was hit with loan losses for the very lending to which Hook had always objected. Again, the member credit unions—and, as usual, particularly the larger credit unions like VanCity—ultimately paid the cost.

Because of the voting structure, Hook was handcuffed in trying to change any of this, and it was bothering him. He decided to take countervailing action. He added a few other members to the informal Big Three alliance (VanCity, Richmond and Surrey), until they represented close to half the deposits at Central. They then demanded that Central establish a committee of their CEOs to monitor Central's financial management and provide advice and guidance. The Central board did not like being pushed around. Podovinikoff, however, was not as combative as May and knew he was in a corner. Central buckled. In effect, Hook and his allies on what was called the financial advisory committee constituted a parallel board of directors. Later, VanCity, Surrey, WestCoast and Richmond began exploring the possibility of forming their own central.

"Who owns this Central?" Hook kept saying. "We own you. You do what we tell you. We're not going to do what you tell us." Sandra Sutherland, a lawyer on VanCity's board and chair for two years, hammered Central as a member of its board and at annual conventions. "I was confrontational, contentious," she remembered of those episodes. The smaller credit unions, which feared and disliked VanCity, threw abuse at Hook. Hook did not reply. The abuse came came with the territory. Jack Stimson, arriving in VanCity in 1976 from the Bank of British Columbia, was intrigued by Hook's tribal behaviour. Most credit union people Stimson talked to, and he got to know them quickly, disliked VanCity because it was so big. Hook, on the other hand, made his senior managers consider the sensitivity of other credit unions before they did anything, particularly when it came to locating branches. Stimson laughed at the irony: VanCity was taking so much time to do the best for others, so they would not feel bad, and was getting animosity in return. "What are we doing all this for?" he would ask in his boisterous way. "Let's just go." Hook had ignored him. It was the Bentley fight against Central all over again and, like Bentley, Hook still had a powerful, residual loyalty to the idea of Central and credit unions working together. He had, after all, been Central's CEO for five years. Now even Hook's loyalty had faded.

Behind all the *Sturm und Drang*, Central's imperial ambitions were doomed. Podovinikoff, the Central bureaucracy and their supporters were living an illusion. The voting structure gave them political power within Central but no real power outside it. The large credit unions instinctively kept in touch with each other and shared information. VanCity and Surrey developed automated teller machines together. They had always known they were a different breed. Even Don Tuline, with Kootenay Savings in Trail at the time, was considering the possibility of leaving Central because of its high costs.

Together, against Central, they were like a burgeoning army with an inexhaustible supply of reinforcements. The front pressed in against Central as the balance shifted. "Big fights, an ongoing battle," Lewis van der Gracht remembered. "If ever there was any kind of recrimination and bad feelings, it was not between Richmond Savings and VanCity. It was always between Richmond Savings and Central."

Gradually Hook and his allies weaned Central from commercial lending. Bentley's and Hook's idea of a weak Central and strong multi-branch credit unions won out. George May's notion of an expansive, ambitious Central faded away. Hook, in the process, however, had become tired of Central. The connection had gone cold. On the surface, VanCity and the other large credit unions were still members. Underneath, what was left at Central was a sinking feeling of unity lost, like the losing side in a civil war wondering what went wrong and how to fix it.

CHAPTER 41

Mismatch! Mismatch!

PAUL VOLCKER, THE CHAIR OF THE Federal Reserve Bank in the United States, liked cheap cigars. His favourites were Antonio y Cleopatra Grenadier, which in 1982 cost U.S. $1.20 for a cardboard package of six. They used to cost only 90 cents. That was 33 per cent inflation, Volcker pointed out, by way of moral instruction to those who did not understand the intricacies of monetary policy. In Volcker's mind, this included almost everybody but Volcker himself. Such inflation was not just bad, according to Volcker, it was evil, and he was the battler against it. His strategic assault was to raise interest rates to dampen the economy. According to his doctrine, this was supposed to check inflation. First he raised rates by a few points, and then by a few more, until they were all the way up to 20 per cent.

Volcker never had any doubt that he was right. He was intellectually arrogant and superbly confident, like all good monetarists. He had worked the scheme out in his head. It was internally consistent and therefore theoretically foolproof: that was the test that counted. Few in Washington dared to challenge him, and none succeeded. He was six feet, seven inches tall and weighed 240 pounds. He spoke with authority. He lived in that abstract, theoretical world of economics where, because it was abstract, certitude was possible, and where intellectual arrogance killed questioning and made for credibility.

Volcker had an acolyte in Ottawa, Gerald Bouey, the governor of the Bank of Canada. Bouey shared Volcker's arrogant certitude. He was a small-town Saskatchewan boy who had gone to the Bank of Canada directly from university. The Bank of Canada was a tight, ingrown circle, and Bouey was part of it. The doctrine might be producing havoc in the real world, with economic hardship, but Bouey, calm and articulate, was unshakeable. The press described monetarism as a "new economic religion." Bouey had just that unwavering theological conviction—the conviction of the inventive dogmatist who had cleverly convinced himself of the chosen interpretation and had passed through the wall of doubt to the other side. Volcker's doctrine, instead of eliminating inflation, produced stagflation—high unemployment and rising inflation at the same time. He had created a monster and was resolutely feeding it. The worse things got, the more he tightened the screws. The effect on Canada was particularly devastating.

The overall public debt compounded dramatically: the squeezing of the economy resulted in both less tax revenue and higher social assistance costs. The high interest rates also meant that the government had to pay more to service the debt that already existed. These extra burdens, compounding from year to year, helped create a grave chronic debt problem.

Bouey faithfully followed Volcker's prescription. He had begun in March 1978, when he raised the bank rate from 7.5 per cent to 8 per cent. By the end of 1978, he had it up to 10.75 per cent. The next year it was 14 per cent, and in December 1980 it was 17.26 per cent, the highest ever. Inflation kept rising nevertheless. In August 1981, Bouey raised the rate to 21.07 per cent, its zenith. The prime lending rate at that point was 22 per cent.

For VanCity, each move by Bouey was a nightmare. As the bank rate rose relentlessly, VanCity had to pay out higher and higher interest rates to retain its deposit base. Its loan portfolio, however, consisted mostly of three-year mortgages, which were locked in at lower interest rates. The duration and rates on the deposit side, in other words, did not match the duration and rates on the lending side. This was called a "mismatch." Caught in this mismatch, VanCity's operating margin was gradually being eliminated.

Peter Cook, the chief economist at B.C. Central, watched Paul Volcker with horror. As a member of the clan, he understood what Volcker was trying to do. He did not even hold it against him. The impact of high interest rates on credit unions, though, was devastating. The banks could easily handle the rising rates; most of their loans were demand loans, pegged to the prime rate, which was pegged to the bank rate. They could simply raise the rate they charged. They could at the same time, as a result, pay depositors the higher deposit rate, which had also moved upward in lockstep. Credit unions, on the other hand, with most of their loans in fixed-rate mortgages, could not.

It was an unnerving double bind. If British Columbia's credit unions did pay the higher rates to depositors, they risked running up losses and might even fail. If they did not, and lost their deposit base, their deposits would not cover their loans and they would certainly fail. To make matters worse, Volcker's tight-money doctrine helped plunge the North American economy into a recession at the end of 1979 and through 1980. Caught in the recession, VanCity and other credit unions could not simply leapfrog their way past the problem by growing fast. With their margins squeezed, some credit unions began losing money. Others were struggling. Cook had spotted the threat early and went to work fast. Taking on the mismatch suited his strategic economist's mind.

Cook was from Victoria. He had worked for the Department of Finance in Ottawa, and then for an Ottawa consulting company. He wanted, however, to return to the West Coast. When George May decided that B.C. Central in its expansionist glory should have a chief economist, Cook jumped at the chance.

His initiation at B.C. Central went well. He established an economics intelligence service, telling credit unions through newsletters how they could best structure themselves financially for protection against the vicissitudes of the financial markets. He began making speeches and public pronouncements, and became sought after by newspapers and radio and television stations. He gave B.C. Central and the credit union movement a presence in journalistic and financial circles.

Despite his economist's dogma, he also genuinely believed in credit unions. He had been a member of the civil servants' credit union in Ottawa. He explained his predilection in economist's terms. The banks earned "excess rents" over and above the market, because there were "barriers to entry." Credit unions, on the other hand, could be started by just a few people without much in the way of resources. They passed through those barriers. There was something theoretically liberating for Cook in this idea. Above all, for Cook, nobody in a credit union could take out excess profits for personal gain.

Dealing with the mismatch was, Cook realized, like rounding up the horses after they had bolted through the open barn door, but it was better than losing them altogether. He set out to create a computerized model for matching the terms and interest rates of mortgages to the terms and interest rates of deposits. He had to start from scratch because it had never been done before by anyone, anywhere. The occasion had not arisen. He worked with Chris Dobrzanski, the research director at the Credit Union Reserve Board. They called their schema an "assets-liability model" (loans-deposits model). Trust companies with large mortgage portfolios were in the same position as credit unions. Some ignored the oncoming squeeze and woke up one day to find that their mismatch was so bad, they were going under fast.

Soon Cook was at VanCity (Dobrzanski later would follow him). He was growing increasingly disturbed by B.C. Central's unnecessary spending and its inappropriate use of credit unions' liquidity deposits. Geoff Hook knew this. "Peter, I know you like it at Central," he told him, "and I know you think you're doing a good job, and you are, but how long can you stand the shenanigans there?" That convinced Cook.

He was exactly the man Hook needed in the new monetarist era of chaotic interest rates. VanCity's mismatch problem was huge. It had $300 million of term mortgages funded by demand accounts—which members could withdraw at any time—and short-duration term deposits. The major demand account, Plan 24, was particularly worrisome. The mortgages it funded had been issued when Plan 24 had been paying 6.5 to 7 per cent, leaving a margin for operations. As the bank rate went up and up, however, and the market deposit rate followed, Plan 24 became a dangerous vulnerable point.

Eric Hayne, who had arrived in 1979, remembered their having to make very important decisions very quickly. Hook had built up retained earnings in the prior years, so VanCity could have absorbed a loss. A loss, however, would have set back members' confidence and been a public relations disaster. Hook also wanted enough of a profit to pay dividends on the share account. Dividends were equivalent to interest on a bank's savings account and had not been missed since VanCity's inception. Hook could forestall bleeding on the deposit side by paying higher interest on Plan 24, corresponding to the ever-increasing bank rate, but that would cost dearly. Hook and his management group decided to ride the mismatch out.

Plan 24 had always paid more than the banks' savings accounts. It had been VanCity's pride and glory. The Hook strategy now was not even to meet the market. VanCity would deliberately fall behind what the banks were paying, and risk losing some of its deposit base. It would meet the market, however, for term deposits, a much larger account. That would be costly, but at least term deposits were for a longer term and allowed for greater evening out and better matching.

The ride, which altogether lasted for two and a half years, was much rougher than anticipated. The prime rate jumped an astonishing 6 per cent (from 12 to 18 per cent) in the short three months at the end of 1980 and then continued upwards to its peak of 22 per cent in August 1981. Hook, for all his preparedness, was taken aback. The bank rate was skyrocketing; he wondered fearfully how much worse the impact could be. He had already raised the Plan 24 rate upwards a few notches, despite his intentions, to 8.5 per cent. Since the rate on outstanding mortgages stayed the same, each such raise was a slice out of VanCity's operating margin. There no longer was any "free money." Hook decided not to raise the rate again. It was like the situation in Edgar Allan Poe's story "The Pit and the Pendulum," where the ends of the dungeon were rapidly flattening, forcing the protagonist into the slimy pit in the middle. In the first year of the squeeze, 1979, VanCity's earnings before taxes fell from $6 million to $2 million. The next year, 1980, was slightly better, because there was a recession and interest rates temporarily moderated for six months. Then, in 1981, the squeeze tightened again. At the worst point, the demand deposit rate briefly hit 19 per cent with Plan 24 still at 8.5 per cent, an enormous gap.

It was the one time in VanCity's history when tellers did not actively switch members into more lucrative accounts to their advantage, yet that was a key part of the member-service ethic. The tellers were caught in the cross-fire and wanted instruction. "Let's not beat the drum as much right now," Hook told them. Most members could see for themselves that Plan 24 wasn't paying them as much as term deposits, Hook said.

Hook was hoping for inertia: It takes a while for people to move their money around. Most people don't assiduously compare savings account rates from day to day. Members, however, complained, pointing out that the rate was uncompetitive. Some even said that VanCity was exploiting them and wasn't a good organization. Tellers found that hard to take, but they understood the severity of what VanCity was facing and worked hard to explain the situation. Some members deliberately left money in Plan 24 to help VanCity out, at least in the early stages. VanCity had been good to them, and Plan 24, with its daily interest and higher rate, had symbolized that. Members had gotten used to their money being there. They would not leave large amounts in the account, but with 125,000 members, even small amounts totalled up.

Over the two-year period, 1981 and 1982, the deposit base shrank 9.4 per cent (after inflation), although increasing in inflated dollars. It was not as bad, however, as it might have been. Members moved money out of Plan 24, but sideways into VanCity term deposits. Even the attrition in Plan 24 was smaller than expected, although dramatic just the same—at its lowest point, a 45 per cent decline from its peak. Tellers did not discourage members who wanted to move Plan 24 money into term deposits, but they did not promote the idea, either. Wayne McKay had the uneasy, inescapable feeling that however much one might deny it, VanCity had short-changed its members. Logically, he knew that wasn't really the case, since the organization and the members were one and the same. If VanCity had paid higher rates for Plan 24 deposits, members would have had to forego dividends. And who could have predicted Paul Volcker's monetarist fanaticism, which had led to the mismatch?

Peter Cook arrived at VanCity in 1981 at the worst moment in this squeeze. Hook wanted him to solve the problem—not for the present, which was impossible, but starting from the present. The technical work was complex. Cook had to organize the data in the right form, build a model to simulate the impact of various interest-rate scenarios and then, running through those scenarios, show what adjustments would have to be made, depending on how interest rates moved. It took about a year and a half to wrestle the mismatch to the ground. "The mastermind," Frank Coffey called Cook. The key strategy, on the lending side, was to stop issuing three-year mortgages. VanCity could not fund them any more without running the risk of making the mismatch worse. It offered one-year and six-month mortgages instead. The shorter terms limited the credit union's exposure, but also would help members if interest rates returned to normal. They would not be locked in at high rates for a long period.

The lending side was also thrown out of kilter by the monetarists' folly. It was as if the whole world had gone awry. Most people wanting to buy a house could not afford to do so when interest rates were 15 or 20 per cent, so they weren't taking out mortgages. Those who could were speculating on housing prices continuing to rise in the inflationary spiral. They were desperate to get into the market before prices went up even higher, so they paid the high interest rates. This fed the price spiral in turn, making home-buying impossible for those left behind. Eric Hayne, who had a house built for himself and his family when he arrived in 1979, saw its value double by 1981. The Vancouver housing market had gone crazy.

For houses at the high end of this inflated speculative market, VanCity held back. Its usual ratio for mortgages was 75 per cent of market value. Hook decided that for any remainder over $150,000, only a 50 per cent ratio would be allowed. VanCity lost business as a result, since competitors did not make the same adjustment. Ardent mortgage seekers were not in a mood to listen to a VanCity branch manager's cautionary explanation.

VanCity, in this way, ended up with a low demand for mortgages at both the low end and the high end of the market. In normal times, this would have been disastrous, but these were not normal times. Bruce Higgs invested the unused deposit money in short-term paper like treasury bills, whose rates were continually going up, and made more than in the mortgage market. The inverted-yield curve (short-term rates higher than long-term rates) had produced an inverted world—members who could not borrow, and a credit union that did not have to lend and did not particularly want to.

The pressure was taking its toll on Hook. In 1981, VanCity sold off some of its branch properties and leased them back, in order to show a profit. Hook kept his stress to himself and always appeared enthusiastic, but Peter Cook, who worked closely with him, knew he was worried. What bothered Hook most was that the organization wasn't earning money on a month-to-month basis, and those months kept accumulating. It was his organization, and he was responsible for it.

Then Paul Volcker finally did it. In the second half of 1981, his punitive, ever-increasing bank rate broke the American economy's back and plunged the United States and Canada into the severest recession since the Great Depression of the 1930s. Volcker, with Gerald Bouey in tow, gradually reduced bank rates as the recession deepened. The cost of money to VanCity—what it had to pay for deposits—went down correspondingly, while it was collecting on recent mortgages at the previous, much higher rate. It was a mismatch in reverse, this time favouring VanCity.

This was just as perverse as what had happened before. VanCity now had easy deposit money, while just outside the door, recession was raging. Despite major loan-loss provisions from the recession's fall-out, operating margins in 1982 and 1983 were back up to normal and profits were the highest ever. What Volcker had taken away, he was inadvertently giving back. Hook, Peter Cook and Bruce Higgs knew that it had just been a matter of toughing it out, but the sudden bounty made it seem as if the mismatch had been a surrealistic dream. Volcker was still his supremely self-assured self, and Gerald Bouey was still a model of monetarist rectitude. At least, thought Peter Cook, his assets-liability model would stop them from trapping VanCity again.

CHAPTER 42

ATMs, Goldilocks and Blueface

THE PHOTOGRAPH WAS TAKEN IN the boardroom against a walnut veneer backdrop, with the six of them sitting around the end of the board table. Geoff Hook was at the centre. He had deep saucers under his eyes—lines forming two arcs above his cheekbones—but he was relaxed, with his lips slightly tight and turned up with a sense of the moment. Next to him, on his left, was Bruce Higgs, bearded, stocky, staring comfortably at the camera. Wayne McKay, straight-faced, had put on a bit of weight and had a few lines on his face, but he was still relatively young and energetic. He was just turning forty. Beside him was Peter Cook. Cook had curly hair and wore thin-rimmed glasses, which gave him a bookish mien. He smiled easily. On Hook's immediate right was Frank Coffey. He was slightly stooped, with shadows under his eyes, looking out from under dark eyebrows. His high forehead, bald at the temples, and his hair combed straight back, added to the length of his face. He had a Bassett-hound look. Finally there was Eric Hayne, puffy-cheeked, with a playful smile for the camera.

They were in charge and knew their organization was in front. VanCity had been become quite extraordinary. They were doing it. They had survived the mismatch and were stronger and more sophisticated for having gone through it. They had mastered the new volatility. Morale in the branches was remarkably high, despite the difficulties. Don Tuline, who was then with Kootenay Savings, had dropped by a few VanCity branches for a look and was immediately struck by the spirit of the staff. They had those unmistakable signs of being proud of where they worked and of wanting to come to work each day. Wayne McKay had made working for VanCity fun.

VanCity was a big player now, and it had the other players' attention. Frank Coffey heard through his banking contacts that VanCity had scared away one of the major chartered banks. The bank had dropped an option to move into a Coquitlam shopping mall after discovering that VanCity was opening a branch there. Coffey was astounded. He did not realize until then the true scope of what they had accomplished. He remembered, at the Canadian Imperial Bank of Commerce a decade earlier, having talked to a senior vice-president about the potential of credit unions. The man had laughed at him.

Geoff Hook no longer wondered about his relationship to staff. Peter
Cook, coming from B.C. Central, was taken by how open Hook was. He
could talk to Hook without constraints, even about personal matters. Hook
had also given him complete freedom to do his job. Hook, too, was honest
about where he wanted to take the organization. He let people know. The
interpersonal dynamics at management meetings, Bruce Higgs remembered, were simply terrific. Earlier, when Jack Stimson was still around,
Higgs and Stimson had once gotten into a shouting match. Higgs could not
remember what it had been about, only that it had happened and could
happen without hurting their solidarity. The camaraderie was intense.
Higgs liked the amount of information he was getting from the others.
Participating in those meetings was like eating a good meal. Peter Cook
considered Hook the most enlightened manager he had ever worked for.
"He was a wonderful guy, just a fun guy to be around," Cook said.

Hook, in 1980 and 1981, as the interest squeeze had grown worse and
worse, had been desperately looking for other ways to avoid mismatch.
There was only one other way: variable loans—loans whose interest rate
varied directly with the bank rate. Most bank loans, in the form of operating
lines of credit for businesses, were variable loans. VanCity had no similar
loan portfolio. Hook pressed Frank Coffey to come up with something.
"Geoff was biting my tail," Coffey recalled.

Coffey first went to Alberta to look around. Hook had picked up stories
of the astonishing success Alberta credit unions were having with variable
loans. Alberta had become a paradise for financial institutions. Everyone was fighting to establish a presence in Edmonton and Calgary. Hook
thought it might be a good place to allocate a slice of VanCity's money and
make extra dollars.

Coffey, however, instead of being attracted by the excitement, was re-
pelled. The credit unions were making variable-rate loans to hotels, motels
and resorts, and even to purchase raw land with potential for oil development. That was too risky for Coffey's taste. He knew, too, that from Vancouver, he could not keep track of the wild things going on in Alberta.
Others would have the jump on him in the loan market, capturing the
better risks, and he would be left with the dregs.

He then took a look at operating lines of credit for businesses at home.
He decided against that as well. VanCity did not have the people with the
right experience for that type of lending. It was a different kind of lending,
and it was dominated by the banks. Coffey was driven back to where he had
started: mortgages. Mortgages were what VanCity knew, and variable-rate
lines of credit were what he wanted. Then it dawned on him.

He called the new product Creditline. It combined the two concepts. It
was a sliding line of credit backed by a mortgage on one's equity in a house
or property. It could also be backed by securities, like Canada Savings
Bonds. VanCity already offered a personal line of credit, but it was limited
to a fairly small amount. It was really for overdraft protection, to help

members avoid fees for inadvertent NSF cheques and otherwise allow them to temporarily overdraw their accounts. Creditline, on the other hand, allowed for large lines of credit with which one could take a holiday, buy a boat or a car or make renovations. It was adjusted to the prime rate. Members could draw on their Creditline or pay off the outstanding balance as they saw fit, without penalties. It was tremendously convenient and flexible. If the prime rate shot up, members had the option of holding back on spending and paying what they owed as quickly as possible. Coffey had anticipated $15 million in the portfolio in the first year. Two banking consultants, whom Hook had talked to, thought it would take in $30 million. It managed, in that first year, to hit close to $50 million.

Creditline acted like a shot of adrenalin. Coffey and the senior management team kept putting together similar confections, like pastry cooks with an appetite. The next year, 1982, they introduced "Personaline," a jazzed-up version of the original line of credit, and "Homeprime," a new kind of mortgage in which the rate was variable although the monthly payments stayed the same. Then, in 1983, they launched the "Amazing Prime + 1 Personal Loan Sale." The word "Prime," for prime rate, had a special symbolic ring to it. VanCity was offering to its members the same kind of rate that the banks offered only to favoured business customers. Its personal loan volume doubled. Coffey now had a shelf of variable-rate products that had significant dollars attached.

A personal tax preparation service was next. Eric Hayne insisted on calling it the Rampart Tax Service, with its intimations of strength and security, like the Rock of Gibraltar. It was the last remnant of Hayne's monumentalist Royal Bank mentality. Chris Bergthorson was outraged and fought him on it, but Hayne was adamant. Whatever the name, the service provided members with computer-based tax preparation, another innovative idea for its time. Later the name was changed to VanTax Services.

Bruce Higgs, meanwhile, was working on an automated teller machine (ATM) network for the branches. His job of upgrading the administrative machinery had no glamour, but he had taken to it. He liked nailing things down with manuals and reports. He set out to re-create the accounting system, which he considered antiquated and inadequate for a top financial institution. He wanted up-to-date financial information on every aspect of operations that had a bearing on decision-making. He brought the branches and their information into the planning cycle. He made internal auditing a high priority. People may do foolish things when they're around money, Higgs argued, so internal auditing was doubly important in a financial institution. Higgs was also in charge of VanCity Insurance Services. By buying existing agencies, he had expanded that subsidiary dramatically.

ATMs, however, were an assignment in a class by themselves. They were exotic and futuristic. Several banks had them; the future already existed. Installing ATMs in more locations, however, was a slow process. They were expensive, were crude technically and needed volume to justify themselves.

Customers, moreover, were not in the habit of using the machines, even if they happened to be available. Most people, intimidated by the aura of complicated technology, stuck to live tellers.

VanCity had wanted to introduce ATMs in the late 1970s. Higgs had bought two machines from one of the original manufacturers and turned them over to his computer people. They could not get them to run properly. The expensive development costs were within the banks' massive budgets but beyond VanCity, and no young, brilliant technical genius like Gus German was around to overcome that obstacle. For once, VanCity found itself late in the field.

At this juncture, Higgs and Eric Hayne met an American firebrand named Tom Bass. Bass came out of the data processing department of People's Bank in Seattle. He was running a small ATM development company called The Exchange, in the Seattle area. The Exchange was owned by a mix of small banks and savings and loans (thrifts) that had joined together for economies of scale. When Bass stepped in, it had three employees in a basement. Its "network" consisted of a single, and little-used, pilot machine in a parking lot. That seemed risible, but all of The Exchange members shared the same machine—the first shared ATM any-where—a revolutionary concept that had within it the kernel of great things. Large banks had their own systems, which they kept to themselves.

Bass built up his technical group, updated the switching software and began installing machines in shopping malls and parking lots. Contrary to established banking wisdom, one unit was installed in a bank wall. Nobody believed that customers from one bank would go to another bank to use an ATM, but the customers did make the trip. Because the units were shared and drew on all participants' customers, they could more quickly generate large volumes, making the network economical. Then Bass negotiated a licensing agreement with another firm, Automatic Data Processing, in New Jersey. Soon The Exchange had the first coast-to-coast ATM network in the United States.

Bass was an intense, dedicated visionary. Higgs was continually taken aback by his arrogance. Bass, however, had a lot to be opinionated about. He was continually right. He offered to bet Higgs any amount of money that within five years, the Canadian banks would all link to one another. This was as far-fetched a notion as Higgs could conceive for those inwardly focussed monoliths who were vigorously working on their own proprietary ATM networks. Higgs knew those banks. He bet Bass a lunch on it. Higgs would lose.

Bass had a rare combination of technological awareness and market sense. He was convinced, from his first involvement, that ATMs and the electronic transmission of data were the coming thing. He also knew, from his familiarity with the technology, that proprietary networks developed individually by banks were too costly. This would inexorably drive the banks to share those costs, no matter how big a bank was or how big their managers' egos. Each ATM cost $50,000 to $60,000 installed, and it might be loaded with $40,000 or $50,000 worth of cash. This tied up $100,000 per machine. One needed a lot of transactions to make that investment pay, and most people had yet to even try a machine. ATMs were new and strange, and there weren't that many of them around.

The broader the shared base, on the other hand, the the more transactions would be put through each machine. Bass predicted there would be ATMs in supermarkets, in gas bars, even in 7-Eleven stores. This was the most outrageous, fantastic prediction of all, yet Bass was as certain of it as he was of the sun coming up next morning. "Hmmm," said Higgs. "I don't think so." Bass would be proven right again.

Bass's vision of shared ATM use, nevertheless, was just right for Higgs. Higgs had calculated the development costs, if VanCity were to proceed alone, to be $2 million. With The Exchange, VanCity could get in for $350,000—a lot of money, but a lot less than millions. There were virtually no front-end costs and hardly any technical risk. The Exchange system already functioned. Its people knew what they were doing. To disperse costs further, Higgs succeeded in getting Surrey to join the system. They worked through a jointly owned subsidiary, Pacific Network Services. Subsequently, 10 per cent of Pacific Network Services was sold to a group of four other credit unions and another 25 per cent to the Bank of British Columbia when it came onto The Exchange network.

VanCity's initial connection to The Exchange depended on a then novel concept: using a telephone line that ran into another country and taking advantage of the technology there. This led to another novelty: an international ATM network which VanCity members could use when travelling in the United States. This internationally shared ATM link-up was another first. The opening transaction was conducted on November 7, 1983, in Vancouver's Bayshore Inn. Cash was withdrawn from an account in the Washington Mutual Savings Bank. The event was stage-managed with all the hoopla that Eric Hayne in marketing could muster. A multi-media marketing campaign pushed "Cash To Go 24 Hours A Day." A small, and then rapidly growing, number of VanCity members took to the ATMs and their convenience with gusto. Higgs started with machines in sixteen of nineteen branches and had the remaining branches covered within a year. It was something the banks, with many small-volume branches, hadn't yet managed, although they had a head start.

VanCity members could even access their accounts through The Exchange while on vacation in Hawaii, an extraordinary feat at the time. Higgs, on holiday in Hawaii, tried the link-up himself. He stuck his VanCity card into a machine in a bank at Waikiki Beach in Honolulu, punched in his personal identification number and then entered his request. These steps, later to become routine, were still eerily futuristic for Higgs. The signal went by telephone line to a bank in downtown Honolulu, by satellite to Los Angeles, by telephone line to Clifton, New Jersey, by telephone line from there to Bellevue, Washington—the Seattle suburb where The Exchange headquarters had relocated—and finally, also by telephone line, to Van-City's computer site in Vancouver, where the transaction was authorized. The authorization was then relayed by the same route in reverse. It took about ten seconds. It was, Higgs thought, like using a personal withdrawal slip in a branch that belonged to him alone.

Eric Hayne, in the marketing division, could hardly be contained. He was a teddy bear, softer than his predecessor, Jack Stimson. The intense, bouyant activity at VanCity head office carried him along like a wave. His division was fine-tuned and humming. "Events began to unfold," as he put it, "in a wonderment of accomplishment.

"Chris would say, 'We'll buy a third-page in the forward section of the Sun,'" Hayne reminisced, "and bingo, the wheels started turning, the phone started to ring. Everything we did in those days was so new and innovative and so ready for the market that we had instant acceptance."

The marketing division was like an elite commando unit. VanCity's products had a clear strategic purpose, and it was up to Hayne's division and Embryo Communications to establish a presence for them. The mortgage sale, launched in late 1982, was a typical instance. VanCity, successfully fighting its way out of the mismatch to save its deposit base, had found itself, because mortgage borrowing was down, with too much of that deposit base not lent out. The credit union was floating in money. Liquidity (money readily available) as a percentage of assets approached 25 per cent, far above the 15 per cent VanCity target and even further above the 10 per cent required by the Credit Unions Act. With interest rates rising, that hadn't been a problem. Placing the liquidity in short-term paper, whose rate kept going up, brought a windfall. With interest rates going down, however, in 1982, the opposite was the case. Each excess deposit dollar invested in short-term paper rather than in the mortgage market meant a narrower operating margin and a weaker competitive position—a squeeze of another kind. VanCity desperately needed to get money out to market.

The lower interest rates and the falling Vancouver housing prices brought about by the 1982 recession gave VanCity the strategic opening it needed. Housing was more affordable again. The question was how to exploit it. The divisional managers, at their regular weekly meetings, tried hammering something out. The meetings had a regular feature called "open session blue sky" where any crazy idea could be thrown out and discussed, and might even survive. Somebody said, "Eaton's and Woodwards have sales. Why can't we have one?" Hook thought later it might have been Wayne McKay.

The idea of a "mortgage sale" was radical, which was why, for the group, it had an irresistible appeal. Nobody had ever had one before. Bankers would rather have died than contaminate themselves with anything so crass as a sale, not to mention losing a margin of profit, which the idea of a sale implied. Besides, a mortgage, for the borrower, was a contract for a huge sum of money. Its issuance had always been a solemn occasion. Yet a mortgage sale was exactly what VanCity set out to offer. The concept was to combine an attractive rate of interest, although still at market, with a waiver of legal and appraisal fees, which VanCity would absorb internally. Lawyers were lined up who agreed to participate at a discount.

Bergthorson then took over. He went for power, like a shopkeeper with loud posters. He used big, strong leading type for the words "Mortgage Sale" in the newspaper ad. He bought billboard space. He used the same direct approach on radio. The play of the two words together, "mortgage" and "sale," coming from such different cultures, was magic. The most telling touch, though, was a red sales tag, with jagged edges like a notary seal, carrying the interest rate, with the "Mortgage Sale!" headline slightly overlapping it. "I'll be darned," Hayne remembered. "People beat down the door." VanCity moved $60 million out the door in four weeks. Staff were writing mortgages day in and day out. The next spring, a similar sale pumped out $100 million in mortgages. Years later, long after Hayne had left VanCity, he would still be telling people in the trade about VanCity's mortgage sales and be met with incredulity at their success.

The talk at West 10th then shifted to taking the advertising one step further, from creating new products to setting VanCity itself apart from the banks and trust companies. Staff in the marketing division talked it over with Bergthorson. They identified specific themes like ownership in the community and the branches' personal touch. There was still widespread disenchantment with the impersonality and unresponsiveness of the banks. The VanCity strategy was to capitalize on that unhappiness, beginning with an awareness commercial on television.

Bergthorson took the strategy to one of the writers he used, Tom Baird. Baird came back with a commercial reinventing the history of money handling. It went back to the "cave man" days, with a couple sitting around a fire, chewing meat off bones and grunting about their finances. "Shortly after people invented money, they needed a place to put it," the script went, "so they invented the bank. When the banks got too big, people realized it was time for a money place that belonged to them, so they invented VanCity." The scenario ended inside a modern VanCity branch.

Bergthorson liked the premise, but not the idea of cave people. It made the transition to the contemporary VanCity too great a leap. Also, hiring actors and putting them through various costume changes would be complicated and expensive. He got in touch with a Vancouver animator, Al Sens. Sens thought he could spike the story with a bit of charm and whimsicality. The cartoon characters he came up with still looked "cavemanish," as in the original script. Bergthorson sent Sens back for another try. Bergthorson was, as usual, driven by the search for simplicity and minimalism. He told Sens he did not want characters with a strong physical presence. He wanted just nice little people moving through time.

Sens came up with a portfolio of twenty characters ranging from cutesy to rustic cave dwellers, drawn on bits of paper. In the middle of the pile was an illustration of a little male character and a little woman standing beside him. Bergthorson was struck by the quality of the drawing. The characters were soft and presentable. Sens, playing around with the drawing, had intuitively put yellow hair on the woman. Then he had picked up a light blue, because it looked good with the golden yellow, and had used it to colour the man's hair. He didn't like the blue hair so he had kept going, filling in the face. The man had a bulbous nose, two little pin eyes and pin eyelashes up near the narrow top of his head. A few bits of hair sprouted off the crown. His jaw was big, round and pendulous. Down in this jaw was a little smile. The woman had the same face, without the blue colour, but with a froth of golden curls. Their bodies were dumpy. They had short, thin legs and arms, and little round stubs for fingers.

Their names, as they came to be known, were Blueface and Goldilocks. Originally they were referred to as Ma and Pa. They were a straightforward little couple, whom others could warm to. The story involved, among other things, a cartoon Parthenon-like temple, a Temple of Mammon, representing the banks, with Blueface and Goldilocks looking on. When the script said, "When the banks got too big," the temple rounded out into a pig, which got larger and larger, becoming boar-like, looming over the characters, until it exploded beyond the frame. A smiling Blueface and Goldilocks reappear, safely sheltered under the VanCity logo. The logo comes down beside them. Bouquets of green dollars signs hover around. The slogan "Where Money Works for People" appeared above the logo, in black.

Blueface and Goldilocks became staples in VanCity advertising. One imagined they had discovered the way to the good life. They had VanCity RRSPs. They had a VanCity mortgage—one of those new, variable-rate Homeprime mortgages, no less. They had a flexible line of credit at VanCity. Unsophisticated though they might appear, they used the ATMs that VanCity had installed for their convenience. They liked being VanCity members and sometimes, from the sheer pride of it, they held up a big orange placard, the kind tacked onto a stick, that said "VanCity" and had those three skyscrapers or building blocks or whatever they were stuck up over the name. Lots of people knew Blueface and Goldilocks, and those who didn't know them had at least seen them around.

CHAPTER 43

Coffey Hunkers Down

WHEN GEOFF HOOK SUGGESTED TO Frank Coffey in 1977 that Coffey might take over the operations division, Coffey's private reaction was, "Great, I love it." He didn't know whether he could do it or not, although he didn't tell Hook that. But he sure would give the job a try.

On the organizational chart, the change was a horizontal move, but Coffey knew it was much more than that. It put him in the centre of VanCity—in charge of branch operations, the tellers and supervisors and managers, the deposits and loans, member service and the handling of new products. Hook was not only showing confidence in him, but was also recognizing that he, Coffey, had that special ability to manage an enterprise. He had been working for that chance ever since he had quit university as a young man and gone into the CGA program.

At the Canadian Imperial Bank of Commerce, he had not been a member of the bankers' club. He did not necessarily want to be. The CIBC culture was Toronto culture. He had looked upon their stuffy rituals with a mixture of anthropologist's curiosity and maverick's scorn. Now, at VanCity, he was truly on the inside. It was an organization, too, that he really belonged to, culturally. He still did not have the one credential required by the old bankers' club—direct lending experience—but he knew a lot about lending and what kind of controls were required. His work for the CIBC in British Columbia, drawing up the operational assessments of its many branches, had taken him into the smallest details of operation, including reviews of loan portfolios. He knew the business, he was sure.

Coffey was tall, narrow-shouldered and thin. He was six foot, four inches tall but weighed only 180 pounds. He was a chain smoker. Head office people used to kid him about having smoke coming out both of his ears. He was gruff and seemingly austere. Dave Turnbull noticed that staff in the branches were almost terrified of him, because of his mien and and imposing height and the dark shadows under his eyes. Those who had frequent contact with him, however, discovered a different person. He was surprisingly sensitive and was interesting to work with. A dry, worldly wise sense of humour peeked out from behind the exterior. Turnbull, who reported to Coffey, liked to discuss problems with him. Coffey was intelligent, asked contrary questions, explored side issues and usually gave good advice.

Turnbull felt he was working with Coffey rather than for him. There was no hint of pretension or pulling rank on Coffey's part.

Coffey had decided to get his personal life under control, which meant getting his hours of work under control. He had four children at home. He made up his mind to knock off work around six o'clock. This made for a long day by other people's standards, but was far shorter than the fourteen-hour days he had put in at the B.C. Co-operative Wholesale. Only occasionally, if something had to be dealt with immediately, would he stay through into the evening. He approached his lifestyle choices like a business planning decision, allocating how much time he was prepared to devote to work at his age and how much he would spend elsewhere.

The dynamics of getting things done—this was VanCity, for Coffey. He felt that organizationally the senior group within VanCity was really trying to go in one direction. It was an extraordinary feeling. It had been different at the bank. Perhaps, he thought, it was because, at the bank, they were only a regional unit and did not have much control over where they were going. At VanCity, on the other hand, he and the others in the group were it. If they wanted something to be achieved, it was up to them to conceive the strategy, develop it and make it go.

They had begun with putting together an organization that would have the ability to grow. Being in charge of this growth, at least his side of it, was, for Coffey, absorbing. He groaned to himself every time he went to a meeting because he had so many of them. By the time he met with the people above him and the people below him, and sometimes people on the same level, there wasn't time much left in a day. They were straightforward business meetings. They weren't a joy, but they weren't a trial, either. This was the business, he realized. This was what he did.

The planning process, on the other hand, was a trial. It was like doing dishes or washing clothes. It also took a lot of effort. He didn't like icky-picky details. He knew, however, from the standpoint of results, how effective planning was. The planning process always began with the mission statement. Coffey took it to heart. The statement didn't say much. It consisted of generalities, one might even say platitudes. Going through the ritual of returning to the statement, however, acted as a bond, a common frame of reference, which was something Coffey could respond to.

The job was fun. Watching his middle managers, like Dave Turnbull and Garry Smith, master detail and take action was part of the delight. Small steps, like security cameras and cash dispensers in the branches, were important. So was using designated law firms close to branches for mortgage work, one of Geoff Hook's ideas. The arrangement was more convenient for members. It also gave VanCity leverage over the fees that were charged and over the quality and speed of the work, since Coffey decided which two law firms per branch would receive the coveted business. When Coffey twisted arms to get reduced legal fees for mortgage sales, the lawyers did not have much choice other than to co-operate.

He and his division began to develop standards of operation—the number of teller transactions per employee, for example. Coffey did not consider himself a numbers person, but here the numbers, used for productivity analysis, came in handy. He could see from them which branches were doing better than others and in what way, and then chase down the reasons for that difference. With those findings in hand, he could gradually force through the system a better way of doing things. "Manipulation," he laughingly called it.

One of the better ways of doing things was making sure all teller stations were operating when long line-ups developed, even if, on rare occasions, the manager had to step in and work cash. Members usually would put up with waiting in line; Hook and Coffey were amazed at their patience. When there were big line-ups and some teller stations were closed, however, members were very annoyed. Their discontent showed up in membership surveys, which were a key instrument for membership feedback and input. There were lots of problems getting the operational adjustment done. Perhaps senior people in a branch thought teller work was too demeaning for them. Coffey didn't care. It had to happen.

Some things, he knew, he couldn't make happen. VanCity didn't have the computer infrastructure to handle Chargex (the Visa card) or Master Charge (now MasterCard). The banks would do it for VanCity, but they also wanted to manage the credit and collect the interest on overdue accounts. This, as Coffey quipped, "was like giving my wife to the custody of the brothel keeper down the street." Eric Hayne was insistent they get something. Not having a credit card, on the other hand, was a marketing weakness. That left American Express Gold Card, which allowed VanCity to handle the credit side within its regular structure. The Gold Card wasn't universally accepted and also had a fee, unlike the other two at the time. Coffey estimated the card was doing only 60 per cent of its job. He wasn't going to waste his time fretting about it, however.

He was on an evolutionary curve. At first, as a young CGA, he had been technically oriented. When he got his certificate, he put it on the wall and said to himself that all he had to do was apply that knowledge. He gradually learned that his work wasn't that simple. It was people who made the operation go. The first thing he had to do was to make sure his people were with him.

He began to change consciously, as if he were doing a study of himself. One way to get people on side was to browbeat them or whip them. Coffey preferred instead to bring people together, talk to them, get their input, use it where it made sense, explain what he was trying to do and demonstrate what was effective. He had done Creditline that way. He could have put most of it together himself in a week. Instead, he headed up a development team that included line-operating people down to loan officers. It took several months to develop the product, but he got what he was after: acceptance and enthusiasm for it at the line level when it went on stream.

He wasn't as much of a people person as Wayne McKay, he knew, but he had moved a good way across the spectrum. He took pride in his openness and ability to change.

He had developed an antipathy to regimentation. Bruce Higgs had pushed for a voluminous procedures manual, so that internal auditors would have standards against which to measure whether things were being done properly. Coffey acknowledged that the auditors did need some kind of standards, but he had mixed feelings about what Higgs was trying to do. At the CIBC there were twenty-six sets of books, as he recalled, making up one operating manual, and another five sets for personnel. "Every time you wanted to blow your nose you had to go to the book to find out how to do it," he said. He was dead-set against imposing that kind of regimented structure on VanCity. He forgot that he and Hook had contributed to regimentation by putting in place standardized lending and branch procedures when they first moved in. For Coffey, however, that was simply putting the house in order.

His relationship with Higgs was cool, but for Coffey that wasn't a problem. He wasn't close to anyone in the management group. That wasn't the nature of the relationship. Higgs wanted products introduced quickly. The banks, Higgs argued, were closing the gap with VanCity. Coffey resisted. He had four hundred staff to train for any innovation. He could not do that overnight. The branch managers were already under pressure with other priorities. He wasn't going to throw staff into new things they didn't know how to handle. He had become aware of how important trust and fairness were to an organization. He had found that most people wanted to do their job well. You had to let them do it. If you over-managed them, you bent them out of shape.

He kept his feelings to himself. He wasn't expecting a lot of recognition. A success like Creditline was, for Coffey, just part of the job. He had thought all along it would work. Nor did Hook pat him on the back. According to Coffey, Hook wasn't demonstrative. Hook was, in fact, a great back-slapper and encourager of the troops; with Coffey, however, it did not seem quite right. Branch openings were also lost on him, although branches were in his division's bailiwick. He did not get involved in the speechmaking and presentations. "It's a milestone, sure it is," he said. "But what are you going to do about it? So you've done it, it's there. We knew what we wanted when we went into the thing. We had the process set up to achieve the end objective once the decision was made to go. From that point on, you crank the handle and out comes another one."

The personal feelings were there, nevertheless, and growing deeper. He had never seen a better organization. The commitment and unity of purpose went right down to the tellers. This was unusual, in Coffey's experience. He was deeply committed. It wasn't that he was wedded to co-operative philosophy. He didn't think he was, although he allowed that it could provide an effective structure for doing business. VanCity, however, had become a part of him. He had grappled with its purpose. He deliberately stayed away from his peers in other credit unions. He wasn't interested. There was too much gossip and political turmoil in credit union land. The only thing he wanted to put his mind to was how VanCity might do the best it could.

Without any warning, it seemed, amidst Coffey's exhilaration, VanCity's commercial real estate lending was in trouble and Coffey was under siege.It was a long and detailed story, the irony of which surrounded him like choking gas. It began with his original chief loans officer, Don Nelson, the Bentley holdover. Coffey and Nelson never did mesh. When Nelson presented loan applications from developers to the credit committee—a management committee—Coffey did not know whether to feel comfortable with them or not. He did not have the background. Neither did Hook or the others on the committee. Coffey kept looking for an analysis of the structure of the loans, to help him out. Such an analysis would show whether a loan was market-competitive or, on the other hand, overly generous. Nelson, who relied on his experience, did not seem to have that expertise. Coffey realized that one way or the other he had to get it.

He had another problem: moving overflow deposit money, from the opening of new branches, out into the loan market. Everything depended on it. The homebuyers' mortgage market, however, was not absorbing all of the new deposit money. Coffey, Hook and the others talked about it at length. One possibility was regular commercial lending. This was what the banks did. Coffey could have hired the necessary expertise for it, but VanCity would have been starting from scratch in a tough sector. The other possibility was commercial real estate lending. VanCity had already been doing this in a small way, since Don Bentley's day—interim construction lending and mortgages for apartment buildings, townhouse developments and retail properties.

Nelson's voluntary departure was therefore a godsend for Coffey. He had not known what to do with him. In Coffey's book, one did not just fire somebody who had been in the organization for a long time. Now, with Nelson gone, he was free to hire a replacement who did have the kind of experience Coffey was after. He did a regular candidate search. Bill Thame, who had trust company experience in Toronto, was the successful applicant. Thame was Coffey's man and Coffey defended him to the end.

The management group also decided that if interesting proposals came from out of town, it would consider them. It might at first seem anomalous that a community credit union would make loans outside its territory, but the liquidity overhang—too much deposit money not lent out—was weakening VanCity and hence hurting its members. For Hook, it only made sense to attack it in the best way possible. Besides, VanCity had always lent money outside its own territory when it had the capital, issuing mortgages for homes in Surrey and Delta even though they were well beyond the coverage of VanCity's small branch network.

Commercial real estate lending also had a business advantage. It offered a wider margin. It wasn't a large differential. Commercial lending was a market like any other, and bank competition held down the return. The higher rate of interest charged on these loans, moreover, had to cover the risk—paying for greater loan losses. There were, however, lucrative fees for putting these loans in place. These fees were in addition to the interest charged on the loan itself. As VanCity's operating margin, beginning in 1979, was squeezed by its mismatch, the extra earnings and the fees from this lending became increasingly attractive.

Thame's mandate was to expand this part of the loan portfolio. Some of the larger deals included a highrise in Victoria and another one in Burnaby. Under a subsidized provincial housing initiative, VanCity also financed a Fort St. John condominium project and several other projects that local credit unions were not large enough to undertake. The largest commercial loans went to a Lower Mainland developer, Olma Bros. Most of the other commercial loans were of moderate size.

Neither Coffey nor Hook, however, had counted on Paul Volcker, smoking his cheap cigars in Washington. According to Coffey, the loans to Olma Bros. were secured by "equity" in a shopping centre on Kennedy Heights in Surrey, on 120th Street, one of the municipality's main shopping areas. The shopping mall was stable and well-established, perhaps the best strip shopping facility on the street. This collateral depended on the income stream, for the income stream determined how much the shopping centre was worth. Subtract, from that evaluation, the debt that Olma Bros. still owed on the property, and one had their "equity"—the collateral for the loans. There was plenty of such equity with a good margin of safety, Coffey argued. When Volcker hiked interest rates, however, and Gerald Bouey in Ottawa followed, ultimately pushing up Canadian rates all the way to 22 per cent, the equity was wiped out. The interest rates ate up all the income. They also knocked off some of the shopping centre's tenants, who no longer could handle their own debt. Others fell behind on their rent payments. This hurt income further. The shopping centre by this time had a negative cash flow and was non-viable. Coffey could not repossess it and sell it without losing badly.

Worse, VanCity was in second position rather than first. The original lender, who had provided the mortgage for the shopping centre itself, had first call on whatever might have been salvaged. Much worse, VanCity had become involved with Olma Bros. to a much greater extent than it had intended. One of its loans was for a large parcel of raw land in Ladner, a part of Delta municipality. Financing the acquisition of raw land was the riskiest kind of lending, so the loan ratio would be low, usually around 50 per cent. The credit committee had turned Olma Bros. down when it had been first approached about financing. Later, however, it agreed to provide short-term financing while the developers completed other financial arrangements. Those other financial arrangements never came about. VanCity was stuck with the loan.

It should not have happened, Coffey freely admitted later. "It was like being in the deep end of a swimming pool," Coffey remembered. "What the hell do you do? That's the kind of feeling you had. You know you're there and the best thing you can do is just work like stink to get yourself out of it." He hired some extra "arms and legs." One was a point man with a background in the sector and considerable hard-knock experience. The other was a property administrator. Together, they took over the Olma account from Thame. The point man effectively became a co-manager of the collateral property and the Olmas' various projects. The Olmas also came in weekly to Coffey's office to review their position. There were ultimatums and deadlines, some of them met, others not.

Paul Volcker wasn't through with Frank Coffey yet, however. When his high-interest-rate policy finally broke the American economy's back and plunged the United States and Canada into severe recession, commercial property values in western Canada and the western United States tumbled. Shopping centres and shopping strips in suburban areas were particularly hard-hit, some dramatically falling in value in a few months—seemingly overnight to the banks, trust companies and credit unions that had lent money against those assets. Commercial mortgages that had a wide margin of safety were suddenly underwater. The recession also destroyed earning prospects so that developers could not service their loans. Many went bankrupt or simply gave up. Ultimately two banks in Alberta, the Northland Bank of Canada and the Canadian Commercial Bank, were knocked out. The better part of the Alberta credit union movement went into supervision, supported by the provincial government. In the western United States, banks began falling out of the sky.

Coffey's commercial loan portfolio was also shaken. Several of the loans were underwater, among them, now, the one to the Olma Bros. for the raw land in Ladner as well as the primary Olma loan. The recession waylaid the oil and gas industry in northeastern British Columbia. Everything in Fort St. John stopped in its tracks. The VanCity-financed Fort St. John condominium project, half built, had to be boarded up.

For Coffey, the period was traumatic. He had established procedures and made loans, and suddenly that carefully constructed world was falling apart. He found it difficult to come to grips with the changing situation. He never lost sight, however, of the need to act. "You can throw up your hands in despair," he explained later, "but that isn't going to accomplish anything." He told himself that he and VanCity weren't isolated. The horror was common to everybody. The mess wasn't something that he had gone out and made all by himself.

He was in the habit of reviewing the entire delinquent portfolio every month. With individual members who had gotten into trouble, he had VanCity bend over backwards to help as much as it could. Commercial real estate lending, on the other hand, was cold-blooded. There was no tender emotion to it. There were two ways of being hardnosed, though, Coffey knew. One was to take one's lumps there and then, eat one's losses and quickly reinvest whatever fraction one had managed to recover. The other was a managerial approach, trying to work the debt through to a satisfactory conclusion. One recognized one's potential loss on the books in the meantime. One forfeited the interim earnings that would have resulted from a quick salvage. One also risked seeing the loan deteriorate even further. One stood to gain in the end, however, if one produced a well-managed result, by not losing one's shirt. Credit unions generally had taken the latter approach. So did Coffey this time, almost defiantly, despite the pressure.

Coffey and Higgs tangled on the issue. Higgs had become critical of Coffey's commercial lending approach and had asked Hook about taking over the program. The disagreement over delinquent loans was another stage of the argument. Higgs wanted Coffey to close the shop on some of the loans that had gone sour and get out quickly with what he could. "I've come to the end of the line on this one," he would exclaim, exasperated. "Let's go in and really kick butt." Coffey would want to massage the loan a little further. Higgs was aggressive and outspoken and had a clear idea of what should be done, particularly since he had credit experience. Coffey was quieter, but no less convinced of his position. Their arguments became testy.

Then, in 1983, Bob Williams, a former New Democratic Party cabinet minister, joined the board. He opened an attack on the commercial loan portfolio in particular. Williams charged that Olma Bros. had also borrowed from VanCity under other names and entities and that the connections had been missed by management. The total exposure to Olma Bros., as Williams remembered it, was $12 million. This wasn't much in the world of high finance and wasn't even much in terms of VanCity's overall lending, in the $850 million range. The $12 million exposure, however, was to a single borrower and therefore dangerous, Williams argued, when VanCity's own equity was only $35 million and its entire operation was anchored on that equity. He called it "shocking" and "rank amateur stuff."

Only Coffey fully appreciated the irony of events. He had set a control structure in place that had not existed before, in order to avoid mistakes. It included an analysis of the income stream of commercial properties, on which the value of those properties depended. General lending principles were devised and adopted to avoid high risk. VanCity had decided, in these guidelines, to stay away from restaurants, motels and hotels, and properties that were designed for single use only, like gas stations. A gas station, with huge tanks underground, could not easily be converted to other functions. Net income from a property had to have a safety margin over and above what was required to make payments on any loan. Coffey also set up an internal appraisal group, led by a specialist in commercial appraisals, to give VanCity independent expertise and corroborate the figures coming in from outside appraisers. There were checks at the credit committee level, too. He had put this structure in place out of a compelling professionalism. Yet, somehow, Vancity had got in too far with Olma Bros. That was putting a totally different, negative, colouration on what he had done.

He had also gone to pains not to relax standards on the Fort St. John loan and other loans under the government program, telling the developers they would have to live with VanCity's stiffer requirements. It was easy enough to argue, with hindsight, that had VanCity been a Fort St. John credit union and not a Vancouver credit union, it would have been more aware of the cyclical nature of the Fort St. John economy. Fort St. John, however, was no different from the many other B.C. communities where VanCity had lent money under the program and where the projects had worked out. Who, even in Fort St. John, could have predicted such a severe recession and its effect on the northeast? VanCity had not even lost money in any of those years, amidst the worst collapse of property values in recent memory. As for the exposure to Olma Bros., credit unions had never measured a loan or group of loans against their equity capital, but against total loans and total assets.

Coffey told himself this, rationalized and reminded himself that in lending there were also rough spots, yet that did not eliminate the problem loans and the unsettling Olma situation. He could not get them off his mind. His health was deteriorating, although he claimed he felt fine. With his tall, thin body, he looked more haggard than ever. He was up to more than two packages of cigarettes a day. The shadows under his eyes had turned into deep black lines, like anti-glare ointment under the eyes of a football player.

He was often away sick. At one board meeting, he lost sense of time constraints. The meeting had begun at eight that evening, after a dinner with drinks. Coffey had fifteen minutes to report on an update of the credit department. He went on for what seemed to Wayne McKay to be an hour or more, by which time most of the room had long lost interest. Coffey felt he had to get the whole story out. Fellow division managers tried to shut him up. It was disheartening because, by droning on, he only undercut the board's confidence in him. Hook did not have the heart to interfere and was caught up in the question of the loans himself.

Aside from the delinquent loans, Coffey had to deal with the bizarre legal actions being pursued by the two fired branch managers. His emotions were caught up in the ongoing tension. Then, the new board member, Bob Williams, was "chomping on my rear all the time," as Coffey put it. "It doesn't sort of increase your peace of mind at all," he laughed.

The sharpest irony, Coffey knew, was that lending was the real test in the business. All he could do was hunker down and work his way out.

CHAPTER 44

The President

SANDRA SUTHERLAND WAS NINE YEARS OLD when she handled her first credit union transactions. Her father, Bob, a taxi driver, ran a small common bond credit union called Vantax out of the family house in Kitsilano. It was for fellow cab owners and drivers. It had about 160 members at the time, 1953. Frequently, when she answered the front door, someone would hand her money for deposit to an account. Even at that age, she was well-trained to offer these depositors a receipt, but often they weren't interested. They would just give her their name. In her earliest memory of it, sometimes she did not hear the person's name clearly or it wasn't given at all. The man just handed her what seemed a pile of money and walked away. She was terribly concerned. She and her father would have to work out who it was.

She "assisted" her father with the books. It was a ploy on his part, to teach her how to count and add and to familiarize her with some basic business procedures. In later years, when the Vantax Credit Union grew a bit larger and moved out of the house, she helped him to balance the books every month. Her mother, Lucille, was also active. She established the Western Canadian Credit Union Foundation, or Westcu, the first credit union charitable arm in the world, devoted mostly to young people and education.

Sandra went to League conventions with her parents. They always went to conventions. It was exciting. The convention sites were full of people, and there was a lot of debate. Young as she was, she began to develop a sense of the issues. The interaction of credit unions with each other and with B.C. Central intrigued her. Credit unions were a part of her growing up and learning, like a church or a social club for other children.

English Bay was near home, and she liked walking down to the water, sitting there and looking out, to gain perspective on life. Her passions in Kitsilano High School were poetry and physics. She thought she was going to be a physicist and enrolled in sciences at UBC. She was only sixteen and was overwhelmed by the large classes. She switched to commerce and law, and got degrees in both. She articled at Campney & Murphy, one of the prestigious downtown law firms, and became a partner three years after being admitted to the bar, an exceptionally rapid rise.

She was a member of VanCity as well as of Vantax and often went to annual meetings. The election of directors still took place at those meetings. At the 1973 VanCity gathering, she ended up sitting with a group of people she called the "4th Avenue Crowd." They were "1960s people," as she described them. They were community-interested and anti-establishment. They were making a concentrated attempt to elect directors. They wanted to use VanCity's financial wherewithal for social purposes and talked freely of their objectives. Sutherland was shocked. They had an attitude, she thought, typical of that crowd, that insurance companies, corporations and governments were just bags of money that one could take and use for good purposes. This was extraordinary naivete, in her view. Credit unions were small people's money, middle people's money—their neighbours', their friends', their own families' money—and had to be protected. Other organizations, in her view, engaged social values. A credit union was its own purpose—financially serving its members.

The challengers were actually a group called the West Broadway Citizens' Committee. They were fighting developers who were destroying existing housing stock in Kitsilano and replacing it with expensive condominiums. The committee was particularly concerned with rental housing, including the impact of speculators on rent levels. A pair of notorious housing speculators, they had discovered, was being financed by VanCity mortgage money. VanCity, to their mind, had lost its sense of social purpose. It should, instead, be using some of its mortgage money to build more appropriate housing, working with other groups in society. Any suggestion that they were fiscally irresponsible, one of the group said later, was totally unfounded.

Sutherland, however, could not relate to them or to their questioning what "service to members" really should include. She was even more appalled when the election took place. One woman in the group came close to being elected. Sutherland's parents and others, after the meeting, said the contender had nearly succeeded because she was young and female, which was the kind of person a credit union crowd would want to vote for. Sutherland herself was young and female. She had grown up in the system and was a lawyer. The group milling about talked about her running the next time, to cut the intruders off at the pass.

Ever since Sutherland could remember, only those nominated by the nominating committee managed to get elected. Her name was put up the following year, but the nominating committee failed to support her. She decided to run anyway. It was 1974. She was nominated by Joe Corsbie, longtime manager of CU&C and an old credit union hand. There had never been a woman on the board. She did not expect to win—she just wanted to establish her name for the next election—but she was elected overwhelmingly.

Sutherland had always been involved in the movement. Participating in something her family had created, and then watching it grow, was like building a home or a garden. It was in her blood, she thought. Credit unions issues intrigued her lawyer's mind—questions like the need for new technology, how much deposit insurance was required, what services a credit union needed to offer in order to survive, whether members actually needed a particular new service and if it was fair. The movement was on its own, broaching questions never asked before and having to think things through and decide. Now, on the board of VanCity, the scope for applying her mind to these issues was many times greater.

She enjoyed herself enormously. She was knee deep in things she had grown up with and knew about. Although she was young—not quite thirty at the time—and was the first woman on the board, she felt comfortable. It wasn't as though she had been elected to the board of a ballbearing company. Life was serendipity, she thought. But for the accident of that one annual meeting, she would have never thought of running for the board.

She saw herself on a continuous journey of discovery. It was her first real experience working with a group of people to achieve a specified set of goals. That was good for her, too. She had always liked working things out for herself. Now she had to learn about co-operation and the contribution that others could make. It was a good period in her life, she remembered.

She gained acceptance quickly. She took on the board's nemesis, Professor Forbes, about several of his suggestions. She thought them impractical. She had no hesitation in letting him know. Accustomed to dealing with words, she was able to counter Forbes's argumentative manoeuvres. This comforted other board members. She doubted Forbes was offended by her strong words. He was clever, academic and worldly. Immersed in the issues, she would not have noticed agitation on his face in any case.

It took a long time, on the other hand, for her to gain Don Bentley's trust. She found it difficult to know him. She admired him greatly. He was an appealing character, she remembered. His intelligence and astuteness responded to her own analytic bent, but he was more subtle and reticent than she was. Gradually she established rapport with him. Then, suddenly, he was gone.

It was Bentley's ability both to deal with people and to conceptualize that intrigued Sutherland. The combination was unusual. She asked him questions, at board meetings, that only a lawyer would ask. She also kept raising policy issues. The questioning surprised Bentley because board meetings, for him, were for dealing with business. He did not confront her, however. Even when she realized that he preferred to talk about policy matters in a casual, less formal atmosphere, she continued to ask questions, to get them on the table, and he continued to respond. He was bemused by the presence of new intellectual energy that she embodied, and he began to think of ways he could harness her ability and put it to use.

Her first assignment was computers: the idea of VanCity having its own system, which ultimately led to Geac. Bentley effectively made her a board committee of one on the subject. She had always been interested in computers, although they were a novelty then. She had learned Fortran in university. She, Bentley and consultant Al Fowler inched their way forward. She pushed for the Geac proposal when the board came to decide.

At Bentley's request, she also negotiated the contract—without a fee, because she was a director. She insisted on a royalty agreement, because both parties would be involved co-operatively in developing the system and VanCity should receive something for subsequent applications. She also negotiated a lease-to-buy option. She would not take advantage of a struggling Geac, but as a lawyer and director she had to look to VanCity's interest. Gus German thought she was the worst terror in the world—the most aggressive, most demanding, most unreasonable person he had ever met. For Sutherland, on the other hand, the negotiations were just more lawyer's work. Fellow director Mike Betts remembered how impressive she was. If she had looked at something and said yes to it, especially when there were legal implications, Betts felt it was okay for him to vote yes as well.

She became involved in Central politics, as VanCity's delegate to the Central convention. It bothered her that VanCity had been alienated from the system and that the situation had deteriorated so badly. She was young and idealistic, and did not see why things could not be changed. Bentley was not eager to have her speak from the floor. He felt that this would only generate adverse comment and make the situation worse. He repeated again his preference for sitting down with people individually, away from the convention arena. That, however, wasn't Sutherland's style. She was far better at speaking out on the convention floor.

The situation at the convention, she discovered when she arrived, was even worse than she thought. George May and his entourage were pushing the provincial government's idea of a provincially owned trust company, with credit unions acting as agents. May wanted carte blanche to negotiate an arrangement. Sutherland, suspicious of the idea, rose and moved an amendment that a special general meeting be called before any commitment was made. Immediately, someone from a small credit union seconded her motion. The mood of the room indicated support for the amendment. The officers backed off. Bentley was surprised that Sutherland had been accepted on the floor as a spokesperson for the movement. He began to rethink his position.

He encouraged her to run for Central's board, which she did after he died. When word of the possibility reached Central, George May took her out to lunch. Out of the blue he suggested to her that since her law firm acted for one of the three banks that Central used, she would be in a conflict of interest. She hadn't yet made up her mind about running. May's suggestion made it up for her. She did not like being coerced, and if May was afraid of having her on the board, it was probably a good idea to be on it, she thought. She was elected. She started participating in debates on the convention floor and in credit union seminars. People were suspicious, but she kept talking and slowly they began to understand that while VanCity was its own boss, it cared about the movement.

She had grown fond of Bentley. She did not have the same sense of warmth with Geoff Hook, but she wasn't critical of Hook, either. Hook, it seemed to her, dealt with issues and things, not with people, and she herself dealt more with concepts and ideas than with people. She did not find him cold and calculating, the way some others did. She had no trouble adjusting to his more structured meetings and his formality. The change had to come, she thought. Meetings were longer, and policy and planning were discussed in them. This suited Sutherland.

The transition involved more than just Hook's taking charge. Everything was changing. The time was over when people belonged to a credit union because they believed in the concept or because it was the only place where they could get what they needed. People had less loyalty. It was another era. Nor did Hook appear to have a vision, other than growth. For Sutherland, growth was no evil, but it was not a goal, either. VanCity grew because of what it offered its members.

She could feel the role of board members changing. Hook was reluctant to take advantage of the particular strengths of individual board members. It did not fit into his professionalization of VanCity. Board members were volunteers; they were not expected, in the new culture, to do the development work of a growing and complex organization. There were strong management cadres for that now. Instead of developing policy through board committees, Hook did it with his management team and brought the proposals forward. The new policy for commercial loans came to the board this way. Hook regretted that there wasn't a directors' institute or some facility like the co-operative college in Saskatchewan, where newly elected directors without credit union or business background could learn about their role. Hook wasn't being patronizing. He wanted directors to have more insight into the respective functions of the board and of management.

The board, in this culture, resembled the passive boards of large corporations. Hook did not ignore his directors. He kept them well-informed and involved in the formal decision-making, so that they understood what was happening and accepted their share of responsibility. He liked to say that he never closed a deal, even a rental agreement, without the board's approval. That was as far as it went, however.

In 1981, Sutherland became VanCity president (the next year the title was changed to "chairman"), the first time the post was filled by a woman. She was intense, thin, curious, prepared to argue, opinionated and strong-willed. She was a heavy smoker, which seemed to add to her intensity. She sat at the end of the boardroom table so that the smoke could drift into the corner. She seemed to Mike Betts, who was an admirer, always to have her legal hat on. She loved analyzing, making observations, digging into issues, using her intellect. She encouraged it in others. She didn't like watching board members sit quietly through a meeting, too shy and reluctant to speak, or too modest or simply not participating. She tried drawing them out. She wasn't a political animal. She did not work out a consensus or marshal allies in the backrooms, like Stan Parsons, who was low-key and very political. She couldn't be bothered, and didn't approve, either. She made her points across the boardroom table. Analysing and debating were her way of life.

For Geoff Hook, the board camaraderie was good. It was a camaraderie among people who had known each other for years, in some cases going back to the 1950s. Hook found it easy to work with them. Bert Gladu was still on the board, until he dropped out in 1980, after twenty-eight continuous years. Stan Parsons was there. Ian Strang, a philosophical co-operator from Dairyland, the milk producers' co-operative, was there. His links to Hook were particularly close. Don Campbell was another old co-operative hand on the board whom Hook had long known.

The youngest in the group was Mike Betts. Betts was a Stan Parsons recruit. The two men worked at the same plumbing supply house and had become good friends despite their age difference. Betts had had an account at a Canadian Bank of Commerce branch in North Burnaby since childhood. Something the bank did upset him, however, and Parsons suggested he join VanCity. Betts had always thought credit unions had to do with labour unions. At Parsons's suggestion, he dropped into the East Hastings branch to see Wayne McKay. He liked McKay immediately. He was amazed at how different McKay was from the cold people in the bank. Little by little, he moved his money over.

There was a friendly, communal spirit among the membership in those days, Betts remembered. Members attending annual meetings were ardent credit unionists who often talked about the picnic days, or they were old-time people whom VanCity had looked after when they couldn't get a loan anywhere else. Credit committee meetings had a kitchen-table feel about them.

At his first board meetings, the young Betts was in awe. He recalled how comfortable everyone was with one another. The dedication and loyalty were intense. He became an enthusiastic believer in the movement. He liked the idea of people helping one another and of keeping their money at home to lend to local people. He began to regard the banks with scorn.

In 1978, preceding Sutherland, Betts became president for two years. He felt truly on the inside of things. It was a good time to be in the chair. He cut the ribbon for the opening of the Joyce and Kingsway branch. VanCity was considered a leading innovator in credit union circles across the country. He felt a part of the success, that he had done his bit.

The board members were roughly of an age, except Betts and Sutherland, and somehow Betts seemed to be of the same age, too. Wayne McKay, looking on, thought of them as a right-wing old-boys network. They were slowly becoming less effective, McKay thought. They more or less did what Hook said. Hook, meanwhile, saw them quite differently. The group went back together in time and were unified in a common cause. What was wrong with that? They were a good board, Hook felt. They knew credit unions and understood where he was going.

Sutherland did not fit into this club. She might agree with Hook on substantive issues, but Hook could not get comfortable with her. She was twenty years younger than he was. That twenty years was dramatically different from similar age gaps in other times, especially with young professional women now on the rise. Their two intensities didn't match. The mix could be volatile, and volatility was the last thing Hook wanted.

He was always trying to make sure, unofficially if possible, that his board would come to a consensus and that factionalism would not develop. He wanted board meetings to proceed smoothly. With Sutherland around, he could not depend on it. She had a sharp tongue and quite a temper, when she got going. She wasn't the easiest person for Hook to work with. It was hard to be just friends with her. It was ironic, Hook thought, that with Sutherland's strong philosophical attachment to credit unionism, she seemed to be hanging on to ideas that were twenty years old in business terms and that needed to be updated, whereas he, while so much older, was so far ahead of her.

Sutherland also understood the relationship. She was like an intimate but simultaneously distant and private spouse, who kept something to herself and had her own unassailable mastery. She was not nearly so uncomfortable with Hook as he was with her. She knew that, for Hook, she was too unpredictable. Not understanding her vision of credit unionism, he never knew at what point she might disagree or question what he was doing. He worried about what she might say or do. He wasn't accustomed to board members who were independent like her. They had different views of accountability. Quarrels about that subject were really quarrels about who was running the place, the board or management. Nobody defined it that way, but that was the essence of it. They wound up in discussions, trying to work things out. They always managed, Sutherland thought.

Hook gradually got to know her. The combination of Sutherland and another smart, determined female director, Catherine Robertson, however, unsettled him.

Robertson was a farm girl from Cut Knife, Saskatchewan, west of North Battleford. Her father was a founding member of the Saskatchewan Wheat Pool, and her brother was to become president of the local credit union. The concept of co-operatives, including retail stores and livestock pools, was part of her upbringing.

She grew up country style, attending a twelve-pupil rural school for her first five grades. She discovered that she needed only four or five hours' sleep, which added to the time she had to learn things. After high school, she earned a degree in political science and English at the University of Saskatchewan, and then received a journalism degree from Carleton University in Ottawa. She married a law student and worked for the *Western Producer*, the newspaper of the Saskatchewan Wheat Pool. After moving to Vancouver, she accidentally began doing public relations work. One of her sojourns was at B.C. Central. Then she established her own firm. A few years later, she received a call from a VanCity board member who was on the nominating committee. Was she interested in running for the board? She was already a VanCity member. At the 1978 annual meeting, she was elected.

She was struck by how the others on the board seemed to know what they were talking about and by the gap she would have to cover. She spent a year listening, trying to figure out what made a financial institution tick. She took her responsibility seriously. She noticed that the one question that continually surfaced around the boardroom table was what impact a proposal would have on members. This impressed her.

She was only the second woman on the board, but she did not consider herself a pioneer. Almost everywhere she went in business she was the only woman. She had become used to it. One gender issue did bother her, however. While most of VanCity's employees were women, most branch managers were men and head office was top-heavy with males. The organization had not reached down and nurtured female managers. She once asked why VanCity had no male tellers. The management group looked at her aghast, as if a man would ever want to work as a teller. She had calculated that if she could get some men on the front line, it would be easier to convince management that more women should be in managerial roles. The imbalance continued to irritate her.

She began to assert herself. Soon she and Sutherland were jousting with each other. It seemed to Mike Betts, watching them, that meetings were becoming less businesslike, less structured, more emotional and full of individual sparring—of Sutherland and Robertson trying to score points. Betts joked that whoever sat between them was dodging bullets all night. If one said a teacup was white, the other would say it was grey. Sutherland, the more verbally agile of the two, regularly cut Robertson into ribbons. Robertson argued back. Betts remembered himself, Hook and the others sitting back like astonished spectators, as if saying to themselves, "Oh, gosh!" An interesting pair, Betts thought. They were two powerful women who had a strong dislike for each other.

For the dismayed Betts, the clash of personalities was getting in the way. For Doreen Coen, a female board member who had been elected a year after Robertson, the Sutherland-Robertson rivalry seemed to be an ordinary part of how the board worked. Coen was a self-described oddball—odd, because she wasn't part of the Hooks, Parsons, Betts and Strang circle, "the clique," she called it.

Coen was Hook's age, a child of the depression. She did not talk much at board meetings. She let others lead. She did her homework, though, and voted by her own lights. She considered herself a renegade. She didn't care "boom bugger all," she said, about Sutherland and Robertson going at each other. They were businesswomen on the rise, trying perhaps to make a name for themselves. If it was more obvious than with the men, it did not matter to her.

A fourth woman, Colleen Bourke, then joined the board. Bourke had been a radio broadcaster and communications director. She was initially prompted to run by the statement of a bank president that there were no women on his board because there were no qualified women available. She wanted VanCity to respond in creative ways to the economic crunch that was hitting people in the early 1980s.

She quickly realized she was not going to make much progress. She could not get her suggestions across. She did not have the argumentative strength for it. She often wasn't sure of what she wanted. Hook and his circle on the board, she thought, were insular, introverted and defensive. They were, as she saw it, manning the VanCity lifeboat while ignoring those sometimes desperate members who were floating off into the sea. They were arch-conservatives. They did not seem to care who lost their home and livelihood. Hook kept saying that it was necessary, because of the times, for VanCity to be fiscally more prudent than usual. Bourke had no wish to endanger the credit union. She wanted only some mild risk-taking, to give people more leeway. It was exactly in such difficult times, she felt, that a credit union should be a little more daring in helping members as individuals. "I thought the good ship VanCity had a social responsibility," she recalled, "and they, the board at the time, limited themselves to fiscal responsibility."

When Bourke attended her first board meeting, she had taken with her a letter from a member who had failed to keep up his mortgage payments and was being foreclosed. He had gone through a personal tragic turn and was close to a nervous breakdown. He was an aboriginal who had opened his house to his extended family and the situation had gotten away from him. He did, however, have a good job with the federal government, and Bourke, who knew of him from her radio days, did not think he was irresponsible. Prior to the meeting, she had told Hook his name, so Hook could provide the board with context.

She failed to get the matter on the agenda. Hook accepted the letter, but dismissed the complainant with a knowledgeable air. Management knew this particular member well, he said. He had insulted a branch manager. The inference was that he was a troublemaker. The letter did not circulate to the board, although Bourke tried forcing the issue.

The usual procedure was to leave individual cases to managers. One had to trust their judgement. That's what they were hired for. The rebuff at the board meeting, however, stuck in Bourke's mind. She could not forget the insensitivity of it. It seemed to typify the attitude of the board's majority. They lived inside a shell, where criticism could not get at them. Critics were simply people who were out to get them and destroy the credit union. Any suggestion that was new or different would simply not be accepted. Bourke became more and more disenchanted, regarding the board as a cipher for the executive committee—Hook, Sutherland and Strang—and buddies Parsons and Betts.

Hook and Frank Coffey saw a reverse image. For them, Bourke was the problem. Hook could not understand what she was getting at. He could not decipher her motivation or why she was on the board. She was always complaining but would never be specific. Coffey remembered meetings at which people grilled Bourke as to what she was looking for or what approaches she was objecting to, but she wouldn't answer. This eventually got under Hook's skin. He began ignoring her, which only made the relationship worse. She and Hook, or she and the management group, as Coffey put it inelegantly, "got along like cat and dog."

The sense of commonality among board and management was crumbling. Coffey thought the organization was being truncated. The board and management were going in different directions. Real communication—the open meeting of minds that had added to the exhilaration of the first few years—had broken down. Sutherland and Robertson were "liberated women," Coffey said. They were "hungry for dominance, hungry for power, both of them."

The troubles had begun, he reflected, when Sutherland had first become president. She and Hook clearly were not getting along. Coffey had run into a senior corporate executive, at a social event, whose company had hired Sutherland. They referred to her as the "Dragon Lady." Coffey laughed; he thought it was an apt description. He admitted later it might be a description of which Sutherland was proud. She was forthright and would not be pushed around. That, however, was exactly his point. Hook did not like having an overseer. Sutherland's toughness meant friction.

Sutherland thought there was a good balance between a strong board and a strong management. Coffey thought the board had become weak. It was a matter of perception. The fractious directors did not realize that they had one hell of a fine organization, Coffey reflected. VanCity was doing things that were being talked about across the country and sometimes further afield. Hook and McKay had made VanCity into an exceptional employer. Hook had been a master builder. Why couldn't they see it? Coffey thought management was in fact trying to do what the board wanted. That was the reason for the planning process and the annual retreat, so the board would have a chance to participate and alter the direction put forward by the management group.

Robertson and Bourke, however, continued to be unhappy. They had a younger way of looking at things. Robertson became more combative. Whatever was bothering them—and the others weren't sure—was producing acrimony.

The 1982 planning retreat was held in the Laurel Point Inn in Victoria. Robertson, as usual, wore her oversized glasses, which helped give her presence. She wasn't a weak director. She and Hook were at each other's throats. There was no donnybrook, only Robertson's persistent criticism about how the credit union generally was being managed. Peter Cook remembered the retreat as a particularly nasty session. It was an accumulation of things, he thought. The impact of the interest-rate mismatch was being felt. Net membership had levelled off in 1980 at 125,000 and, in 1981, had slid back ever so slightly. The membership was more than double what Hook had inherited in 1976, just six years earlier, and the decline in 1981 was hardly perceptible, but it was a decline nevertheless, the first since 1961. The operating margin was the lowest ever in percentage terms. Assets in constant dollars had fallen for the first time in VanCity's history.

One could explain away this attrition. It wasn't Geoff Hook's fault that Paul Volcker had been born. VanCity at least had come through the mismatch unscathed. Robertson, however, with Bourke behind her, had broader issues in mind. VanCity was on the wrong track, they argued. It wasn't doing what credit unions were supposed to be doing. It was becoming more like a bank. It was losing its connection to the community. There were no innovative or creative solutions coming from management to deal with VanCity's problems.

Hook did not like those aspersions. He did not like the way his board critics were crossing over into what he considered management's turf. They seemed to want him to be a secretary or an assistant to the board, instead of a chief officer exercising his full authority as set forth in the job description. Robertson's negativism about management was puzzling, frustrating. It did not leave him any room. He fought back. Peter Cook remembered walking out at the end of the session with Eric Hayne. Spouses were invited to these retreats, and Cook's wife happened to be passing by. She immediately commented on their flushed faces. The day had not been fun.

Wayne McKay, also looking on, thought that Hook and Coffey had stopped growing in their jobs. They could not pick up on the new political signals coming at them, that sheer growth was not enough and that women might not only be directors but also would actually want to govern. There were five women on the board now, and only four men. Hook, who had so skilfully set the agenda and controlled his boards, no longer could. The older element on the board were suddenly passé, irrelevant. Next to Sutherland and Robertson, with their hard-edged intelligence, the earlier generation of directors seemed ineffectual.

After the April 1983 annual meeting, the new board met to select officers for the year. As usual, in this ritual, the board members had dinner together, this time at the Vancouver Lawn Tennis Club. Newly elected board member Bob Williams was there, an antagonistic presence. Robertson was elected chair.

CHAPTER 45

The Intruder

THE "ACTION SLATE" TOOK OVER VanCity like a guerrilla force coming down
from the hills. By the 1986 annual meeting, its members had every seat
on the board, except for Catherine Robertson's, and she would go the
following year. Most of them were members of the New Democratic Party.
They had made an organized effort, using party name lists, to get elected.
Critics referred to their "political machine." They had injected party politics, or so it seemed, into an arena in which party politics were supposed to
be taboo.

Many of VanCity's older members were dismayed and angry. For them,
credit unionism was a movement that crossed political party lines. Credit
union pioneers had hewed to the principle that party politics should be
kept at a distance. People came together in a credit union for a specific
purpose, co-operative banking. The logic of the idea was compelling and it
worked wonderfully. Interfere with this logic by overlaying it with another
idea and one demeaned it. Now these intruders from the Action Slate had
become involved in VanCity for their own political purposes.

Bert Gladu, although he backed the NDP and had supported its predecessor, the CCF, felt betrayed. "The Action Slate spoiled the credit union
way of doing things," he said. Lloyd Widdifield, who had also grown up
a CCFer, derisively dismissed the slate. "These goddamn NDPers come
in now and take over the credit union and make like, 'Oh, look at what
we've done.'" Where were these Johnny-Come-Latelys when VanCity was
struggling, he asked rhetorically, forgetting that new people were always
replacing older ones. Ethel Bentley, Don Bentley's widow, was scathing
about what she considered the slate's opportunism—using VanCity, which
was now large and represented real financial power, and where being a
director conferred status, as a political springboard.

They were angriest about former NDP provincial cabinet minister, Bob
Williams. Williams was elected to the VanCity board in 1983 and then had
led the takeover. He was a favourite bogeyman of the Social Credit Party.
They painted him as a wild and doctrinaire left-winger and then pointed at
him in order to scare voters away from the NDP. They dubbed him a "wild
man" and a "knee-jerk leftist." The media swallowed the imagery. Having
built Williams up in this way, Social Credit feared him all the more.

349

What they feared most, however, was his intelligence and scorn. When he sat in opposition in the legislature, he was relentless in his attacks on the Social Credit government and its friends. He was tough and extremely partisan. Worse, for the government side, he was knowledgeable—a resource expert in a province where the government was in bed with the forest companies. Then, when the NDP defeated Social Credit and Williams became a cabinet minister, he proved extremely able. This made the animus against him, by his political opponents, all the greater.

He was, however, much different and more complex than the image his enemies had concocted. Many people in the province identified closely with him, and many of those, in the Vancouver area, were VanCity members.

Bob Williams's mother was Mauritian French. Her family had settled in Vancouver at the beginning of the century. She was only sixteen and unmarried when he was born, in 1933, in the worst time of the depression. She was in a Salvation Army home for unwed mothers until the end of her pregnancy. The baby was to have been adopted; having a child out of wedlock wasn't done openly because of the deep social stigma. Young and besieged as she was, however, she had made up her mind that the adoption was not going to occur, and she escaped from the home with her baby in her arms. She decided she was going to have a life with him.

She later married. Williams's stepfather was a carpenter. His mother worked as a seamstress in a sweatshop on Water Street. They lived beside a little creek at 20th and Nanaimo, a tributary of Still Creek. The neighbourhood was full of wonder. A city garbage fill was nearby, and Williams, as a small child, used to go out with a Ukrainian junkyard picker who lived across the street and spend his days working the dump with him. They would climb through to the railway cut that went through Grandview and watch the CNR steam engines go by. The area was almost all white—largely Anglo-Saxon working class, although overlaid with the first immigrant waves, especially Italian.

For three years, during the war, the family lived at Okanagan Landing, while his stepfather was in the army camp in Vernon. He hated the Okanagan because he loved Vancouver so much—or he would not adjust to the new circumstances—so he was sent back to Vancouver for the summers. He spent them with his maternal grandmother, who had a squatter's cabin at Dollarton, on the north side of Burrard Inlet across from the city. He rowed around in an old rowboat. It was a child's Vancouver utopia.

Young Williams had a taste for learning. His parents played a game about his age and got him into school a year early. He was bright and enjoyed the world of the mind. He went to the legendary Britannia High School, where a whole generation of east-enders made their way academically. His English and history teachers had a strong impact on him. School, for Williams, was the narrow bridge by which a working-class boy reached other elements in society.

He had a keen aesthetic sensibility. He loved art and thought of becoming a commercial artist. He liked drama. He was a boy scout. Most of his non-school time, however, was spent working. He ran a corner grocery store on Sundays, which allowed the storekeeper to take a day off. Weekday afternoons and evenings, he worked as a stockboy at Woolworth's. There was little time to hang out with his peers, and he wasn't much of an athlete.

He knew what it was like to be poor. At one point, after the war, during a severe housing shortage, his family lived in the back of a store. There were five of them. The place had no windows and just a toilet and sink, without bathing facilities. Often his stepfather was unemployed because the need for carpentry work was up and down. Williams did not consider his life burdensome, however. His family's poverty was a given. There were advantages to having to make his own way, he thought later. He had no regrets.

In Grade 12, he started taking a mild interest in politics. A friend in his school dragged him out to some CCF meetings. He remembered, on one miserable, rainy Vancouver winter night, going to the CCF Hall near Kingsway and Joyce to hear Colin Cameron, a doughty CCF campaigner and former member of the provincial legislature, from Vancouver Island. This man in a trench coat and old Stetson hat came out of the rain, talked to a handful of people, was quite brilliant and then wandered off alone into the night. Williams was impressed.

His history teacher was conservative. Williams remembered finding a big CCF poster and tucking it into the rolled-up world atlas at school. When the teacher yanked it down, it said "Vote CCF" and featured a mug shot of the candidate. Williams's stepfather was a union man, and both parents were CCF supporters.

He had made contact with his natural father and gotten to know his natural grandfather, William Pritchard. Pritchard was a socialist legend—one of the eight labour leaders charged with seditious conspiracy in the 1919 Winnipeg General Strike. Williams listened to his grandfather's sometimes hair-raising stories about labour organizing in the early days. His favourite story was of Pritchard and his fellow political prisoners in Stony Mountain Penitentiary arguing about politics. The jailer, after listening to the discussion, leaned over and exclaimed, "To think you're in here on conspiracy and you can't agree on one goddamn thing!"

Bob Williams was gifted in two ways. He had an active, exploring mind, and he was an outsider in Vancouver society. Being an outsider, he could let his mind run free, devise new ways and challenge old ways. His intelligence and creativity carried him along like an independent force, no matter what obstacles pushed him from one track to another.

His first job after graduation was in the sewer department of Vancouver City Hall, as a draftsman, drawing profiles of sewers in the city. He was able to joke later, as a young politician, that he didn't start at the bottom, he started even lower. He realized, working for the city, that if he really wanted a future, he needed to go to university. He hadn't thought of university before. He ended up with a master's degree in community and regional planning from UBC.

He was a bright light. At the age of twenty-six, he became the first director of planning for Delta municipality. Carpetbagging developers were buying land there and carving it up, looking to make their fortunes. Williams stood up against the worst of their grasping. He saved some key areas, including shoreline, for parks and public walkways and rolled back some of the farmland subdivisions from residential zoning to agricultural land, a move of great foresight. He had his own ideas about how far the privileges of land ownership should be allowed to go. These were too hardnosed for a changing council, which became dominated by friends of the developers. He was fired.

The dismissal could not stop his active mind. He was on unemployment insurance for only a week before he had set up a consulting firm. The firm did work throughout British Columbia and in the U.S. Northwest. He was president of the Community Planning Association, which was part of a movement advancing the then revolutionary idea that cities belonged to the people living in them. He had always, as an East End kid, been interested in Vancouver civic politics. The west side was favoured with parks and upgraded streets, while the east side was mistreated or ignored. In planning school, he grew even more offended at this double standard. He had purchased an old house on Wall Street, an underrated area deep in the East End. He decided to run for city council, which was dominated by the euphemistically named Non-Partisan Association (NPA), a right-wing, pro-developer organization that had been formed to keep the CCF out of City Hall and had dominated Vancouver politics ever since.

He pulled together a group of friends from his boy scout days and from the NDP, where he had become active. They spent $900 on the campaign. All he had to do was to catch up to the one person trailing on the NPA slate. In the last week, the NPA tried to raise a scare over Williams actually being an NDPer. It failed and he was elected. He had done what many people thought impossible—established a left-wing presence on council. It began a long reform tradition that revolutionized Vancouver city politics.

City council was a wonderful experience for the young politician. He had a visionary, neighbourhood sense of what a livable city should be like. He led the way for the rehabilitation of Kitsilano, which was in decline. He succeeded in getting a motion through council to change the charter so that non-property-owners would have the franchise, correcting a profound wrong. He made speeches about transforming the Fairview Slopes and False Creek into rich, mixed-used areas with housing, and phasing out the sawmills and beehive burners. Everyone else on council thought he was mad. The mayor, an opinionated right-winger, considered him a communist, pure and simple. Williams played a key role in saving the east-end Strathcona neighbourhood from destruction by a freeway.

He was approached to run for the NDP provincially in Vancouver East. He was intrigued. He would have liked to stay longer at City Hall, but ended up agreeing to run. He had no trouble winning in the next election in what was a safe NDP seat.

He had found civic politics immensely enjoyable. He liked winning on issues that he thought were important and liked, too, the collegial process that made it possible. He had learned how to develop coalitions on specific issues, so he could make progress, despite being the lone left-winger on council. The provincial legislature, on the other hand, with its rigid partisanship, resulted in culture shock. For two years, Williams did not play much of a role. He sat quietly and watched.

He learned at the feet of the master, the Social Credit premier, W. A. C. Bennett. Bennett attempted to victimize the NDP by baiting, provoking and labelling them. Williams did not intend to be victimized and began striking back. "Bennett contaminated many of us," he recounted. Williams got the reputation of being a radical. It was part of Bennett's cleverness in putting labels on his opponents, Williams said, but if Bennett meant that Williams was a streetfighter and he was tough, it was accurate.

In the 1972 election, the NDP, much to everyone's surprise, swept the province. It was an extraordinary government—spontaneous, creative, civilized and far-seeing. Because Bennett had a bare-bones civil service, there were few resistant officials to tell them what they could not do, and even fewer to get in their way. They were not beholden to private interests, either. "There were a zillion things," Williams remembered. "We were going a mile a minute." It was an immensely productive and stimulating time.

Williams was a power in cabinet. The power came from his talent and creativity. He was minister of lands, forests and water resources, but his major vehicle was the cabinet environmental land use committee. It functioned as an environment ministry and an economic development ministry combined—an economic powerhouse.

Williams was close to most of the other cabinet ministers. There was a buoyant camaraderie among them. The shared experience was deep and intense. Williams, more than any of the others, was a great builder, in everything from land and resource management to the creation of Robson Square in downtown Vancouver. Bennett, who had built roads and hydro dams, had been a crude builder. Williams was a modern, sophisticated, multi-talented builder, sensitive to communities and place, history, and form and function.

The media hit the NDP hard. That was a part of the cabinet's shared experience, too. The media were always anti-NDP, but the cabinet group had not anticipated the unreasonableness of the hostility. It was, Williams thought, like the return of the Ku Klux Klan. He reflected later that had he not been so young, it was unlikely he could have handled the pressure and emotional trauma. One had to be very strong.

To his friends, he was shy and gentle. He had an air of vulnerability and awkwardness that came from his shyness, and he had deep loyalties. To his political enemies, however, he was scornful, quick to judge, mean, self-righteous and fiercely combative. Even friends knew they could not argue with him lightly. He was intense and impatient. Since he was brighter than most people, his impatience showed. He took things seriously. "What I like about you," a friend once told him, "is that you're born anew every day, because you're shocked again and again."

Something much deeper than specific cases, however, rankled Williams. The local elites and the media, which had so much influence over public opinion, regarded socialists as illegitimate, even if they did win an election. The snobbery of those elites was based on mediocrity and pretence, Williams knew. Their power was buttressed by ideology and larded with opportunism and incompetence. Yet there they were, the old, pretentious, phony downtown Vancouver crowd and the newspapers that had served them so fawningly, and they would not recognize that the NDP had merit, no matter how well it governed. There was nothing he could do about it, either.

In three years, it was all over and the NDP were out of power. Williams took a break from the legislature. With his wife and another partner, he bought a hotel in Port Moody and turned it into the country music palace of the suburbs. The venture was an inspired gamble that paid off. After two years, he shifted to the Railway Club, an old, walk-up downtown drinking spot. Soon the Railway Club was legendary as a stop for young musicians and as a locale for the artistic left scene in the city. It was the first place k.d. lang played outside of Alberta.

Williams's image in the media underwent a slow process of revisionism. He was a successful businessman, some people now wrote. One newspaper columnist later described him as that rarest of all creatures, "a genuine free-enterpriser." For all of Williams's successes in life, however, he had "a chip on his shoulder the size of a Sitka spruce," the columnist added. The columnist could not understand it. Anyone on the left side of the political fence in the province, on the other hand, understood it instinctively. Chris Bergthorson, the Embryo Communications creative spark, remembered thinking how much respect he had for Williams. Williams had been true to their common ideals and he had a bold mind. He had defended the province's resources against its cynical corporate predators. Most of all, he had not backed off and had not conformed, even though he had been vilified. Now here was VanCity, a community resource, becoming captive, Williams thought, to just that smug, right-wing elitism that he so abhorred.

It was something else to be shocked about.

CHAPTER 46

The Action Slate

BOB WILLIAMS CALLED GEOFF HOOK'S office and asked for a meeting. It was 1983, and he had just been elected to the VanCity board. A democratic financial institution like VanCity, he thought, provided an exciting opportunity for social change. For several years he had kicked around the idea of running for the board, but that was as far as he had taken it. Then he began hearing disquieting reports. Some disgruntled members had come to him, because of his high profile. He had also talked to Colleen Bourke, who had quit the board in frustration. Memories lingered of the little Pender Street Committee many years before, with its protestations that VanCity was financing blockbusters, that it had lost touch with its community roots, that it had a mania for bigness and that it was trying in every way possible to become more like the banks and other financial institutions. Williams was worried in particular about some VanCity commercial lending he had heard about. He decided to run with two friends, both women, as a slate. One was his former town-planning partner, a Red Tory. The other was a Liberal. Of the three, he was the only one elected.

Now he was asking for an appointment as a director. The secretary informed him that Mr. Hook did not meet with individual board members.

"You'd better tell Mr. Hook that I'm insisting on meeting him," Williams told her. Hook ultimately did agree to meet. He was friendly and back-slapping as usual.

"Anything you want to know, I'm here to help you," he told Williams.

"Well, that's great, Geoff," Williams replied. "I'm particularly interested in interconnected loans to a real estate outfit by the name of Olma Bros. I have a stack of information about these major loans."

Hook did not like the confrontational tone that Williams was taking. He had been bruised by Williams's election campaign. The campaign was mild as far as politics went, but it was much more political than anything Hook had experienced. He had never been involved in politics in his life. He had just been on the receiving end of Williams's attacks for three weeks. He was also defensive about those particular loans, which had given Coffey and himself so much trouble. He wasn't sure what Williams was after, but he did know of Williams' reputation. He told Williams he could not get into specific discussions of that kind with an individual board member.

Their relationship, if it had any chance at all, foundered at that moment. Williams had seen evasion like this before, in the legislature. He raised his voice. He was going to get to the bottom of the loans, he told Hook. Hook stiffened. He was not going to be bullied. He shouted back. The clamour of their voices reverberated across the outer office. Hook, later, could not remember the shouting. It would be rare for him to shout, he said. He prided himself on his self-control. Self-control was necessary when one was managing. One never had the luxury of indulging one's feelings. Williams, however, he ruefully allowed, was not someone who stimulated just mild emotions. "Yeah, there could have been raised voices," he said, "there could have been."

Williams, as it happened, already had a copy of the files. He had been given them by people from within Olma Bros. who had a falling out with the company. The documents, as he described them, showed a series of extra loans, interconnected to Olma Bros. but under different names, that made VanCity's aggregate exposure to the group greater than had been realized and well beyond what Williams thought any one exposure should have been. He brought up the matter of the loans at the next board meeting. The board was flabbergasted at the kind of information he produced.

Frank Coffey was brought in to explain the loan portfolio. Williams confronted him. Coffey wanted to say he had not granted the loans carelessly or on his own. They had been done as an organizational initiative, with careful due process and following a policy approved by the board. He wanted to explain, further, how they had gotten in so deep with Olma Bros. despite the checks in place. It should not have happened, but measures had been taken to manage the exposure. He also wanted to discuss the rationale of the commercial loan policy to show that it was much better than it looked. VanCity had weathered the commercial real estate crash better than had most other financial institutions.

Instead, Coffey clammed up. He, Hook and the others had talked a lot about Williams when they realized he was about to show up on their doorstep. He was in awe of Williams and a little afraid. It froze him. His not answering only enraged Williams further, which made it more impossible for Coffey to speak up.

The board's administration committee was assigned to look into the loans. Coffey and his staff prepared a large binder on them for Williams. Hook was intent on demonstrating that everything in the loan process was done properly, particularly that there was no improper collusion between VanCity and the borrowers. There were meetings with Coffey and subsequent confrontations with Hook. "It was outright war, and there was no way he was going to win," Williams said. Hook brought in Bill Wright from Davis & Company, VanCity's regular lawyer, for board meetings. "A security blanket for Hook and company," Williams thought, which only cost the organization another series of fees. Then Williams looked into the out-of-town loans, particularly the one in Fort St. John, which was in difficulty.

He began methodically, rigorously, hammering away. He was convinced that if he did not clean up the commercial loan portfolio, VanCity risked going under and the whole credit union would be lost. It was the relatively large exposure with one or two groups of loans that most troubled him.

He could see the impression he was making on the other board members — they might think him a left-wing political monster. He didn't care. "I intended right from the beginning to be the skunk in the petunia patch, and I was," he said. He felt strongly about what had happened, and business was business, not a Sunday school picnic. These guys in VanCity were blowing millions, he felt, and it was members' money. They had not been prudent lenders. He should be tough with them.

He noticed, as he went along, that other board members began to share his concern. They were not an entrenched enemy camp. Doreen Coen was glad to see Williams on the board. She had relied on management's judgement, because in the past it had been very good. During discussions about commercial lending, she had sat and listened. She began to think, now, that the board had accepted too much without questioning. Williams, with his clout, provided balance. Catherine Robertson, who was chair, was also glad to see Williams go after Hook and force him, inch by inch, to share real decision-making with the board. She gave Williams the opportunity to press his case. He was pleased and surprised.

Hook's relationship with Robertson continued to be difficult. He had asked Peter Cook to attend board meetings with him. He was simply not going to go to a board meeting again unless he had somebody else from management with him as support.

Coffey was caught in the middle. Robertson thought highly of Coffey. He had not just wrung his hands about the commercial loan problem but had put a strategy in place to manage it. She did nothing, however, to protect him. "Once Bob got going," she said, "there was no way of stopping him." She did not want to stop him.

Peter Cook, a Hook loyalist, thought Hook had not pulled the rope in quickly enough on Coffey, because of their friendship. Had he done so, the problem with commercial lending would not have escalated to the point it had. Coffey saw things differently. After all, the large loans were approved by the management credit committee, of which Hook was also a member. He, Coffey, was a fall guy. He realized this was an implicit criticism of Hook, but that was the way it was. He handled it by just locking it away. He did not talk to Hook about it. "Don't dwell on it," he told himself. "It's nothing that's going to get you anywhere."

Williams was most aggressive and garrulous, however, with Hook. He considered Hook a classic bureaucrat who liked being a big wheel among the hoi polloi. This was Williams's worst insult. He kept up the attack until the end. Hook had given notice the previous year that he was resigning. His final board meeting was the planning session in the spring of 1984. He had not been simply a caretaker that final year. He had led in the preparation of the business plan and had been as heavily involved as the day he joined VanCity. Williams, at the meeting, was furious again with whatever Hook put forward. He blew up and tore into Hook like a bareknuckle fighter finally knocking out his opponent with the six or seventh uppercut. It was over then, Williams remembered. "My God," Hook told someone on the way out, "even on my very last day, my very last minute, this guy is not letting go."

"He was an easy mark," Williams thought.

Williams by this time had close allies on the board. He and some others had formed an Action Slate to take over VanCity. The principal figures were David Levi, Darlene Marzari and Tim Louis. Levi was an oddity—a social democrat who was a stockbroker. Marzari was a former member of Vancouver city council, as part of a liberal reform movement called TEAM, The Electors' Action Movement, which had followed in Williams's wake at council. Louis, a lawyer who used a wheelchair, was a member of another civic organization, COPE, the Committee of Progressive Electors, which was to the left of the NDP.

Levi had run in board elections twice before, in 1982 and 1983. The first time, he had come within a few hundred votes of winning. The second time, he, Louis and a third candidate had run coincidentally with Williams's group and had split the left-wing vote. Only Williams managed to get elected.

Levi had had his own fight with the previous VanCity board. In 1982, he had used some of the space allotted to candidates' biographies in *Working Dollars* to briefly say what direction he thought VanCity should take. VanCity responded that he could not make political statements in his submission, as the rules referred to biographical information. He was startled. The restriction seemed bizarre, given that an election was involved. His first inclination was to withdraw and avoid a messy procedural struggle. His wife, however, was a first-year law student and was developing a taste for legal combat. She was indignant at this limitation of her husband's free speech and wanted to fight.

They ultimately threatened to apply for an injunction, which would cost them little money but would generate a mountain of publicity. Levi and VanCity's lawyer, Bill Wright, from Davis & Company, debated the issue over the phone, with Levi from time to time talking to his "legal counsel," namely his law-student wife, standing beside him, who told him what to say. It struck him as comic and wonderful that they were negotiating with a partner at prestigious Davis & Company, from their kitchen and that they might win. The VanCity board did back off.

The next year, the board tried to contain the scope of the campaign. The nomination papers included a pledge not to hand out leaflets and not to put ads in newspapers. Levi filed his papers but refused to sign the covenant. VanCity could not stop him from standing on a public sidewalk, he said. The VanCity board then changed its requirement, prohibiting only the handing out of leaflets on VanCity property. Levi signed. The Levi, Tim Louis and Bob Williams groups all had people handing out leaflets in front of branches that year, during election week. It was chaos. Some board members complained that the leaflet distributors were unruly and were impeding members' uninterrupted entry into the branches. A rule was established that leaflet distributors had to be at least ten feet away from the front door. At the head-office branch, Tim Louis, sitting in a wheelchair on public property, found himself screened by staff people who had been sent down from upstairs to maintain order. Since the staff stood in front of him, members walking along the sidewalk into the door could not see him. Commissionaires were also used to ensure leafleters didn't enter the branches. An all-candidates forum on the community cable channel, on the other hand, allowed candidates wider exposure.

The Action Slate met in living rooms and church basements. It was agreed that Williams would choose one candidate for the forthcoming 1984 election (his own term had another two years to run). He picked Marzari. Levi and Louis would be the other two candidates, for the three available spots (of a total of nine directors). From their work during the two previous years, the group already had a following among the large number of New Democrats and union people who belonged to VanCity. The candidates did the run of local union and NDP meetings, making their pitch. One supporter, a concerned VanCity member, remembered spending a couple of evenings telephoning people who were members or supporters of the NDP and, if they were also VanCity members, encouraging them to vote for the Action Slate candidates. Tim Louis had his own network in COPE and the disability community.

The slate had a coherently worked out policy. They attacked VanCity's out-of-town lending. A credit union should be putting money back into the community it serves, they argued. The delinquency rate for out-of-town loans was two to three times higher than it was for loans in the Greater Vancouver area, Williams said, to drive the point home. The slate brought up the unusually large loans that B.C. Central had made to deal maker Nelson Skalbania. They realized that these were Central loans, not VanCity ones, but cited them as the kind of transactions they were against. Hook explained to them that VanCity did not deal with Skalbania, nor was he a member, nor did they want him to be a member. The name Skalbania was raised in the campaign anyway, and Hook could only shrug. Was VanCity lending to flippers? Since it lent to most people who had good collateral, regardless of their investment motives, the charge couldn't be answered.

Talk also surfaced of a loan outside the country, for an offshore hotel project in the Cayman Islands. There had been such a loan, but it was based on a property in Vancouver. The Action Slate argued that, whatever the collateral, the object of lending should be local—putting money back into the community it came from.

The slate also attacked VanCity's membership in the Fraser Institute, a doctrinaire right-wing lobby group and think tank financed by large corporations. Peter Cook, Hook's right-hand man and strategic planner, had wanted to get on the institute's mailing list, but could not do so without joining. No endorsement had been intended, he said. The action, nevertheless, was highly provocative. It was taken as a sign of how right wing and out of touch with members VanCity was.

Levi and Marzari were elected, along with incumbent Catherine Robertson. Hook left VanCity as he had planned and was replaced by Larry Bell, who had been provincial deputy minister of finance. The next year, Louis and two other Action Slate candidates were elected, which gave the slate six out of nine directors, and control.

Sandra Sutherland was particularly bitter. The kind of people who had frightened her into running for the board in 1974 had now actually taken over. She was angriest, though, at the NDP machine politics they had used to get in. Some Social Crediters had suggested to her, and she believed it to be true, that the slate had used party machinery for the purpose, specifically the constituency office in Vancouver East. The Social Crediters then offered her their own "machine." She declined. She said it was wrong to inject party politics into the credit union, which could do it serious harm. That was her point. Credit unions had to live with all political parties. She resented enormously what the Action Slate had done.

Other members complained that by campaigning as the slate had done, a small organized group had hijacked the credit union. Only a tiny percentage of the 130,000 members actually cast ballots. This left VanCity wide open to a raid by anyone who, with a political organization, could marshal a turnout of a few thousand votes.

Levi disagreed with these protestations. If a credit union were small and elected its directors at a meeting, then members got a real chance to know the candidates. Organizing a campaign would not be necessary. With a branch system, however, and voting in the branches, members ordinarily were not able to meet the candidates. As a result, it was the responsibility of candidates to make themselves known as broadly as possible and to explain what they stood for. Otherwise, members would vote in ignorance.

In fact, what had happened in the old days, Levi argued, was that hardly anybody bothered voting at all. The key element had been the nominating committee, by which the board perpetuated itself. The Action Slate was not the first slate in VanCity's history, he said. The nominating committee's slate was. The committee and its slate were old friends and had been for a number of years. They had their own contacts and networks, and were not beyond reminding members they knew to get out to the branch and vote. Members of the Action Slate, at least, were frank about themselves. They were social democrats. True, they canvassed their friends in the NDP, but the appeal was based on their common philosophy of credit unionism. VanCity should not become a bank. It should be a community-run operation.

Once in control of the board, the Action Slate set out to make it easier for candidates to communicate with members, so that any member, with some initiative, could make his or her way as a candidate. Large posterboards at each branch, with the candidates' basic election material, had already been introduced. The slate established a formal schedule that indicated when particular candidates would be available at various branches to talk to interested members. This brought candidates off the street and into the branches. The nominating committee no longer made recommendations. Its sole job was to administer the process and put forward the names of all contenders.

Williams and Sutherland clashed. He regarded her as an overrated lightweight who had been elevated in the business world because of gender politics. She hadn't noticed VanCity's exposure on the commercial loans. She was an upright stick with a rubber stamp on the bottom, he thought, who might argue with Hook but always agreed with him in the end. Sutherland, on the other hand, regarded Williams as a bully who needed to be resisted. She was reduced to tears at one meeting, but she was tough, too. Once Williams, jousting with her, stood up in the heat of argument. Wayne McKay, in the room, thought Williams was about to attack her physically. On another occasion, Williams pursued Sutherland as she went down the stairs, after the meeting had ended, jabbing at her verbally.

It was her lack of passion about what had happened that bothered Williams most. The issue demanded indignation, he felt. It was the only way of getting at the truth and protecting VanCity. Sutherland and her crowd should have hung their heads in shame. For Sutherland, Williams was looking at everything from a preconceived viewpoint and making outrageous allegations. She was in fact disturbed by the interconnected loans and the large exposure VanCity had ended up with, but she thought Williams's view of VanCity as a whole was wildly out of context.

She stayed on the board for another year instead of resigning, to deal with some outstanding matters, although it meant sharing responsibility for decisions made by a slate she opposed. Then, in 1985, she left. She might have been re-elected if she had remained and run again, but she saw no point to it. Doreen Coen and Mike Betts declined to run when their terms expired. The Action Slate, Coen said, eliminated any chance of an unorganized individual like herself getting on the board. Betts was bitter and cynical about the machine politics of the Williams takeover and deeply upset by Williams's board tactics. "Politically, I just didn't like the way he operated," one longtime board member said. "His style was attacking people all the time. I've just washed my hands of the whole darn thing. All of us just said, 'The hell with it.' "

Another incident preyed on Betts's mind. He, Stan Parsons, Geoff Hook and auditor Walter Dyck had bought units in a condominium tax-shelter project. The participation of a CEO, two senior board members, and their organization's auditor in the same tax-shelter scheme did not strike them as unusual. Nor did it occur to them that it might look wrong. Their closeness was part of the credit union culture. Fred Graham, and then Dyck—the credit union auditors—had been as much partners, consultants and mentors for the movement as they were auditors. Moreover, VanCity was not involved in the tax-shelter development in which they had invested.

Subsequently, however, the developer arranged a loan with VanCity that applied in part to the property. This put Parsons and Betts in an undeclared conflict of interest. They hadn't, however, been aware of the connection. Their failure to disclose it was an inadvertent technical omission at most, but someone had alerted the media to it. On leaving a VanCity board meeting, Parsons was suddenly faced with a television camera and transformed into a director guilty of wrongdoing. He was unnerved and humiliated. Betts was so angry at what had happened that even a decade later, he was adamantly tight-lipped about it, refusing even to describe what had occurred. Hook had declared his interest prior to the loan but had not alerted the other two. They felt betrayed.

The incident ate away at Parsons. He resigned as chair. Unlike Betts, however, he ran again for the board when his term expired, in 1986. He did so, even though he wasn't feeling well and knew he might lose. The attitude of the new board hurt him most and brought out his determination to hang on and not simply let the old board die. His daughter Norma worked for VanCity. "He was a battler," she said, "not a bow-down, put-your-tail-between-your-legs person. VanCity had been his life for so many years, he was willing to continue." He was defeated by the Action Slate. It was as if, he felt, his twenty-eight years on the board and his earlier years working on committees had not counted. It broke his heart, Mike Betts thought. His physical trouble was diagnosed as cancer. Then he was gone. VanCity established a scholarship to keep his name alive.

That left Catherine Robertson from the previous board. She had served nine years and was ready to move on, so she declined to run again. Then there were none.

Hook gradually put Bob Williams in perspective. When Williams first came on the scene, Hook had not known how to respond. He was too close to VanCity and too emotionally involved. From the start, Williams had acted like a cabinet minister calling for his deputy. Hook took offence. He was used to being treated as an equal by his board. He had spent a lifetime in the credit union and co-operative movement and thought he was entitled to that courtesy. He was not going to get it. Not being confrontational, he did not know how to respond to Williams's confrontational style, either. The two men did not have a relationship; there was no way one could develop. Hook began talking more to Wayne McKay to get a sense of what these new people were about and how he might deal with them.

His accustomed relationship with the board—as a dynamic CEO and a supportive, relatively passive board, which was typical at the time—made it difficult for Hook to adjust. He could see with hindsight that board members, and not just management, should have been involved in the credit committee, as they had in the early days. Then the board would have more fully understood the rationale of what had been done and the steps that had been taken.

Hook could not understand why he had been attacked so vigorously. He wondered if it might be something personal, but he could not understand that, either. He could take criticism for the out-of-town lending. With hindsight, he would not make those kinds of loans again, although he was prepared to defend the policy in the circumstances. He wanted, however, to be judged on the overall results. He had taken the credit union from $270 million in assets to $1.27 billion and from eight branches to nineteen by the end of 1983. Staff had more than doubled. There had been revolutionary change in retail financial institutions, with banks moving into mortgage markets and both banks and trust companies catching up to credit unions in their retail operations. On top of that, VanCity had endured the worst recession in fifty years.

It was obvious to Hook that Williams underestimated the severity of that recession. Williams had no sense of the pressures and difficulties Hook had faced amid the recession's turbulence—weak loan markets, excess liquidity, the mismatch, and the real estate crash. Williams, he thought, should have looked around. Richmond Savings had been put under supervision in 1983. Surrey, WestCoast Savings and First Pacific, also in Victoria, showed losses and were subsequently put under supervision. Those were the four next-largest credit unions in the province, all going under supervision at different times because of their inability to cope with the unusual turn of events. VanCity, on the other hand, paid its loan losses out of revenue and never missed a dividend; its commercial lending had been more restrained. Total commercial loans were never in excess of 10 per cent of assets, and personal lending had not been neglected. The credit union's assets—its mortgages and loans—were solid. Its membership, which had grown so dramatically until the recession hit, was rising again. There were record profits in 1983. Morale and the performance of staff were superb. Yet Williams had kept coming at him like a battering ram.

There was another irony for Hook. He and Frank Coffey, who was jettisoned by Hook's successor, Larry Bell, became leading troubleshooters for credit unions that *had* failed. Hook chaired a cabinet task force in Alberta to provide a framework for a new credit union structure. The whole system there had been shaken and had needed government support. Then he ran the Surrey Credit Union until it was ready to leave supervision. Coffey headed up the actual rebuilding work in Alberta and later looked after the reorganization of WestCoast Savings.

Hook kept turning over these variables in his mind. He was baffled. He did not fully grasp that behind the arguments on both sides was something much deeper: the feeling that, beyond members' sharing the services VanCity had to offer, VanCity culturally was not open to the idea of community. The VanCity of Geoff Hook and Sandra Sutherland had over-looked this. The making of out-of-town loans, while it had a practical rationale, reflected this cultural difference. Trying to justify the loans financially missed the point.

The rapid changing of the guard had taken Hook by surprise. He realized the irony of it: it had happened after he and the old board had introduced voting in the branches. He admitted to feelings of ownership. He couldn't help himself, he explained. Dealing with those feelings was tough. Once you give up something and the next group takes over, you're out. From that day on, you don't have any say in it. Not that his group were the only ones that could run VanCity, he said years later, looking back. The Action Slate was doing a good job, too. He was satisfied that they were trying to do the best they could for VanCity.

When he left, the board of directors did not give him a farewell dinner, or anything else, as a gesture of thanks. "Nothing," he said. He felt badly about that. Every board of directors had the prerogative to say, "You had your turn at the wheel, now it's our turn." They could, though, have had a little class about it, Hook thought.

The staff, however, did give him a party, at the Hotel Vancouver. It was Wayne McKay's idea and a complete surprise to Hook. Several hundred staffers came out. They put on skits, offered testimonials and made presentations. Every staff group participated, from the social club upwards. They had come to have a great love for the man—the same Geoff Hook whom, as the stern accountant, they had not much liked at all, but who had become an open and energetic builder of enterprise.

Dave Turnbull, who had built the new branches for Hook, was there. "The love that was poured out to that man on that occasion was fantastic," he remembered. Turnbull had been shocked at what had happened to Hook, although later he realized such things were inevitable in an organization. Brian Salvador, the trainer who subsequently became head of personnel, was also there. Salvador's favourite memory of VanCity was just that evening. Hook, who had originally been seen by the organization as an isolated, lonely individual, was now much loved and admired. VanCity was a collective effort, Salvador reflected, but Hook had been the main driving force.

Hook was deeply moved. So were the staffers, who had come en masse to say goodbye. They were unhappy about the intruders from the Action Slate. They did not know what to expect from them and what the slate might do to the organization. They were wary of the slate's political motives. For that one evening, however, they and Geoff Hook, and not the Action Slate, were VanCity, and they were Geoff Hook's VanCity body and soul.

PART SIX

1984-1988

CHAPTER 47

The Cyclone

LARRY BELL HAD A SPECIAL book that he sometimes left lying around for visitors. It was entitled *Everything I Learned As Deputy Minister of Finance*, and the author was Bell himself. A visitor, waiting for Bell to get off the phone, would inevitably pick up the book and begin leafing through it. The pages were empty. The book had been given to Bell as a gift when he left the Ministry of Finance. Displaying it was his sly, self-deprecating joke.

Many VanCity staffers were of the opinion that Bell had not learned much about credit unions, either, when, prior to that, he had been CEO at VanCity. He had swept through like a cyclone, uprooting and changing things—a cyclone that lasted for three years. They were exhausted by him and resented the way his changes tossed them to and fro. Others thought that Bell brought to VanCity exactly what it needed at that point—a good shaking up. They liked his high energy, impatience, spontaneity and readiness to do new things quickly, because they themselves were energetic and impatient. They could take him as he was and respond to him.

He had a puckish, playful look, which belied his intensity. He was an economist. He had been research director for the United Way in Vancouver and then had gone to Victoria to work for the provincial government, where he quickly made his way up the ranks. He was deputy minister of finance when Bill Bennett's Social Credit government launched a highly controversial restraint program clamping down on public spending. Bell gained a reputation as a hard-nosed administrator, although at one point, manning a welfare office during a government employees' strike, he was moved to tears by the stories of hardship. He still believed in the necessity of the restraint program.

He saw himself becoming a caretaker in the job, whereas he was a doer by nature. When a headhunter came along with the possibility of the VanCity position, Bell decided to give it a try. Bob Williams and VanCity chair Catherine Robertson favoured him. Williams wasn't concerned that Bell had served under a Social Credit government. Bell had also worked for a provincial NDP government, and his United Way sojourn suggested he had some community sensibility. Bell got the job.

Two things particularly intrigued Bell. One was money being spent, and not being spent. The restraint period was fascinating and intense for Bell.

Government expenditures were far outrunning income; the province was caught in a severe recession. Expectations were too high. Bell provided his political boss with mechanisms for tightening up spending. The original model for the kind of governing he was after wasn't, as it happened, a right-wing administration, but the early left-wing CCF governments in Saskatchewan. He attributed their skills to their being prairie Baptists—turning a penny over to make sure it was real and, having determined that it was, making sure they got full value for it.

The other thing that intrigued Bell was how systems worked. Nobody, for example, had ever evaluated how much various procedures cost his ministry in comparison with the risk of modifying the procedures. He discovered that a sizable percentage of the cheques the department issued were for less than $25, but that it cost the department an average of $27 to process the voucher for payment—after the voucher had made its way through the originating department and picked up several signatures of approval along the way. Why not give those other departments their own accounts to a certain limit and let them cut those small cheques? Why not expand petty cash? There might be some petty theft as a result, but it would be nowhere near the cost of processing that would be saved.

Bell changed the way the government managed its cash. He implemented a system whereby all the government accounts were "swept" overnight for free cash balances that were either not earning interest or earning very little. This money would be consolidated and invested. The money desk in Bell's department became a sophisticated cash management system in which payments were made electronically.

He had a calculated phobia against paper. Once, at the Department of Finance, he had gone into his offices on a weekend and piled all the papers from people's desks on top of their chairs. When his managers showed up on Monday morning, Bell told them they had to get their work organized so that so much paper wasn't left on their desks again. A lot of that paper, in Bell's opinion, represented a waste of time and energy.

He was a member of WestCoast Credit Union in Victoria. He had joined it for the same reason people joined VanCity—for its service and the fact that it was a local institution oriented to its community. When Bell arrived at VanCity, he quickly noticed how different it was from other organizations he had experience with. It had exceptionally high morale. It had been extraordinarily successful in its marketing. What appealed to him most, however, was its quest for continuous improvement.

Pushing efficiencies forward, however, wasn't easy in a membership organization. One had to balance business viability against membership interests. Bell learned about that fast. One well-known elderly member posed a particular challenge. He was spending a great deal of time in the branch. The consensus was that he was lonely and was manufacturing things to complain about so that he could legitimately go into a branch and talk to the tellers, who were young and pleasant. Periodically, however, even the best-disciplined teller would lose patience with him and go on to serve other members. He would then become crabby and rude. He also wrote letters to the CEO about his grievances and grumbled at annual meetings.

Bell invited him up to his office. He told the member that people could not use VanCity as a hobby. VanCity existed to provide service to its members at large. Bell added that over the last couple of years this member had probably cost VanCity $10,000 with his shenanigans. Bell then told him what his own time was worth, in dollars per minute. He gave the member fifteen minutes of free time, after which the member would have to pay. At the end, Bell handed him $25 from his own pocket, instructed him to go down to his local senior citizen's centre, join up, make some friends and return to the VanCity branch only when he needed to. The man went off shaking his head.

That was an easy situation. Implementing fees for transferring money from one account to another and for other transactions and services was not so easy. VanCity had managed to defer or hold down most of those fees because of growth and efficiencies. As banks eventually caught up, however, those advantages were eliminated. The banks now had an advantage. Because they could use fees to offset costs, they could offer people higher interest rates for term deposits and other accounts. This meant they could eat into VanCity's deposit base, while members would still use VanCity's cheaper transaction services, which had to be financed out of VanCity's operations. It would be a downhill slope after that.

Bell argued that transactions should recover their own costs. They were in effect a separate business, different from deposit-taking and lending. There was no reason why they should be subsidized by the other two activities. Bell also wanted to use fees as a deterrent, to stop people from over-utilizing services. He called what the banks had done "unbundling." VanCity, he maintained, had to follow their lead, difficult as that might be.

Bob Williams, David Levi and Darlene Marzari—the Action Slate board members—were faced with a dilemma. Fees were something the rapacious chartered banks charged. The logic of Bell's argument, however, was inescapable, and the new fees and increases for existing ones were implemented. Some members were deeply upset. They did not like paying for something they had not paid for before. More importantly, the new fees and increases conflicted with their cultural assumption of what a member-owned credit union was. The board set the level of fees at 90 per cent of the banks' fees, in order to maintain at least a symbolic difference. Slowly members became used to the charges and made the cultural shift.

The use of ATMs was another cultural shift. Bell loved the ATMs. He used to joke about getting them to do everything except say Merry Christmas, so that members would come into the branch just once a year, at Christmas time, to exchange greetings, and VanCity could reduce the cost of cleaning and waxing its floors. Some members were intimidated by the ATMs. Others had philosophical misgivings, because the concept of credit union membership meant, for them, collegiality and personal interaction. Bell considered the debate a generational conflict, between those members with a social idea of membership and a newer generation that considered VanCity primarily as a provider of services, no matter what the mode.

The target was to get the number of withdrawals on the ATMs up to 35 per cent of all withdrawals. "That was just going to be heaven," Bell recalled. He had people work the line-ups in busy times at the branches, taking members out of the lines and over to the ATMs, to show them how they worked. "I'm too old to learn," some would say, or "I don't know anything about this," or, bluntly, "I want a teller."

One weekend, two of the ATMs broke down. VanCity had a trouble line. It was flooded with calls. "Some of the calls," Bell joked later, "were quite frank." The members, caught short on the weekend, were furious. Bell realized, then, that VanCity's introduction of ATMs had turned the corner. Members no longer thought of rushing in on Friday afternoon or Saturday morning to pick up cash, or even thought of VanCity as having limited hours. The change had taken about two years. Bell's focus shifted to keeping the machines up and running without breakdowns.

He still had an obsession about getting rid of paper. He had made some personnel changes. Frank Coffey was out the door. Bell had also removed Garry Smith as manager of branch operations. The board had given Bell an earful about Smith's difficulties with certain managers. Smith was dismayed by the turn of events. Bell, however, then made him manager of administrative services and productivity management. It was a high-flown title for someone who was supposed to make operations more efficient. The appointment proved inspired. Smith, with help from Bell, worked his way through everything VanCity did, systematically improving productivity.

Anything that could be automated and wasn't made Bell unhappy. The debiting of a VanCity account, for a mortgage payment, was done automatically. On the other hand, if a member was drawing on an account at a bank or trust company, postdated cheques were used. That was done manually and was time-consuming work. Why not automate these outside transactions as well, electronically, the way his government money desk in Victoria had operated? One could thereby eliminate the postdated cheques altogether. VanCity, accordingly, had members fill out an application in the branch, authorizing such automatic withdrawals. The transactions would be triggered by a time clock in a personal computer, which was linked by modem to the B.C. Central computer, and through that to the clearing system. "Electronic transfer," it was called. It later became commonplace.

Bell had another bright idea. If a member overdrew an account, for whatever reason, the overdraft set off a costly administrative sequence. Somebody had to call the member and explain what had happened and see that the overdraft was cleared away or, if money was available in another account, transfer the money manually. The other alternative was to return the cheque NSF, with all the cost and inconvenience that involved. Bell wanted these overdrafts to be taken care of automatically. The VanCity team installed a computer program that they called, internally, Get Money. If a member was overdrawn in one account, the computer searched the other accounts overnight to see if money was available and made the necessary transfer.

Bell wasn't after efficiency just for efficiency's sake. For all his inventiveness, his other expenses were up markedly and he still had some inherited commercial loan losses to write off. His operating margin was being squeezed. He wanted to turn a dollar to help his margin. He discovered that VanCity had thirty thousand dormant accounts and spotted a possibility for extra fee income. Some of these accounts had no current address, so it was difficult to get in touch with the member. One trial attempt to re-establish contact proved so ineffective that it wasn't worth the trouble. Bell decided that for any dormant account less than $500, VanCity would charge an annual $25 administration fee. He raised $600,000 in one year, that way.

There seemed to be no end to ways of saving money, if only one's mind was turned to it. Bell challenged everything, questioned everything. On one occasion, a decision was made to change the deposit slip and there was a delay in implementation. Bell wanted to know the reason. He was told the lawyers were reviewing the deposit slip because it represented a legal contract. Bell was flabbergasted. He didn't doubt that it was a contract of sorts, but the real question, in Bell's mind, was whether it had ever been a problem. A lawyer's spending more than a few minutes of time on it was a misallocation of resources.

Garry Smith, meanwhile, was creating an administrative support centre, centralizing all the paperwork that could possibly be taken out of the branches. This killed several birds with one stone. Staff would not be working at desks while members waited impatiently in line—always bad karma in a branch. Employees doing necessary paperwork, similarly, would not be interrupted because members were waiting. The work could also be streamlined. Smith estimated that productivity could be improved by 25 to 30 per cent. His leading precept, nevertheless, was that the branch remained in charge because the branch served the member. Cheque clearing was an example. It was now handled by the administrative support centre. If, however, there wasn't enough money in an account to meet payment on a cheque, it was up to the branch to decide whether the cheque would be sent back NSF or whether the overdraft would be carried. The support centre, in a sense, was a part of the branch, except in a different location.

Pushing for efficiencies was just a small part of Bell's intense personal application. He wanted to make things move to the point of being frenetic. He had a much different management style from that of Geoff Hook, who had been a methodical planner. Bell was always agitating. "Larry was the kind of person," Garry Smith remembered, "who would say, 'Don't tell me why it can't be done, just do it.' He wanted to do an awful lot of new things that nobody had even thought about before." Nor did Bell ask a lot of questions or worry an issue to death. Smith liked that, since it was the way he preferred to work as well.

Bob Quart, who ran VanCity's trust services division, also was struck by Bell's impatience. "What Larry wanted was simple," Quart explained. "He wanted more profits, he wanted this place to shake, and he wanted things to happen quickly, like, really quickly." Quart had a good relationship with Bell and thought he was a great guy, but found reporting to him frustrating. He often had difficulty understanding what Bell wanted him to do. Bell would call him in and explain something, perhaps talking for as long as half an hour, but Quart still would not be sure of what Bell was trying to tell him. The same thing happened to other managers. Bell's ability to theorize and conceptualize ran ahead of his ability to communicate.

Quart would then ask somebody else in the office, who had just talked to Bell, "Did you get it?" They would confess to being baffled, too. Bell, however, did not have time to fill them in. He was already on to something else. "He was so driven," Quart recalled, "I'd never seen a person in my life who was as driven as Larry Bell was." If a manager leaving an ideas meeting with Bell was lucky, Peter Cook was in his office. Cook, with his strategic planning background, picked up on Bell's language better than most and acted as interpreter. Wayne McKay, close to Bell, also acted as a middleman.

Bell never relaxed. He worked all the time. He was compulsive. He went through VanCity like a whirligig, throwing off, with his intense energy, ideas for major innovations and changes as he spun around. He was always looking around for a bigger challenge. Otherwise he got edgy.

He introduced the practice of lending to small businesses. It was a board initiative—part of Bob Williams' idea of getting VanCity involved in economic development—but it also meshed with Bell's own thinking about VanCity as a complete British Columbia regional financial institution. A friend of Bruce Higgs from the Bank of Montreal was in town from Toronto and was meeting Higgs for dinner. He had business lending experience and was interested. Bell dropped by the restaurant to meet him and virtually hired him on the spot. The new business lending program quickly led to a leasing spin-off.

The board also wanted a program aimed at the development of grassroots local business. Bell established the Seed Capital Program, managed by a project officer reporting directly to Bell himself. The program involved start-up loans to people with interesting ideas which appeared to have a likelihood of success.

Bell also opened a "branch of the future," in North Vancouver. It was a kind of financial mini-mall, located on the opposite side of a parking lot from a huge, new supermarket. The building housed not only the VanCity branch but also a VanCity Insurance Services outlet, a travel agency associated with VanCity, a satellite office of a prominent North Vancouver law firm and a chartered accountant. VanCity members could arrange a mortgage, have the legal work done, take out insurance, and put together a holiday to celebrate, all in one stop.

There was much more to the branch of the future than that, however. The object was to change the very face of retail banking. Except for two express tellers, the teller stations and member-service counters were replaced by open desks where members could sit down in comfortable chairs. The idea was to eliminate the barrier, albeit just a counter, between staff and member, and destroy forever the last vestige of the bank mystique, in which the financial institution was separate and above, and the customer entered in like a supplicant.

Most everything the member wanted could be done at one of these desks. Instead of being tellers, the staff were generalists, trained for all functions and called "member service representatives." New technology was involved, too. The loan officer, rather than filling out a loan application by hand, could produce the form and make entries electronically, thanks to a satellite computer in the branch, and then print out the finished version for a signature—the first step on the way to a utopia of a paperless branch.

Members also had available to them a computer terminal of their own where they could make loan calculations or, with an ATM card, print out information about their accounts. It was called a Member Activated Terminal, or MAT for short. Bell saw it as a harbinger of a bold futuristic age, just around the corner, when VanCity would provide electronic access for members from their own homes.

Bell kept going. The American Express Gold Card was replaced with a Visa card, with its greater acceptance and recognition. A telephone service, trust services and a mutual fund were all launched within a couple of years.

Bell had developed a taste for high finance when he was deputy minister in Victoria and had a number of contacts internationally. This gave him another idea. He decided to raise $50 million extra for loans by floating a mortgage-backed debenture in Europe. Why not, he asked himself, borrow in world markets, lend the extra money to VanCity members, and thereby increase the size of VanCity and improve earnings? Borrowing in international bond markets was a long way philosophically from the concept of members pooling their deposits to help each other out, but Bell was undeterred. There was a leakage of people's savings out of the country through retirement funds invested in foreign stocks and bonds. He would simply be reversing the flow.

VanCity was short on long-term deposits, too. Members were uncertain which way interest rates were going and were shying away from five-year term deposits. This meant, in turn, that VanCity was unable to offer five-year mortgages since, after the mismatch scare, it was carefully matching mortgage durations against deposit durations. If Bell could float a long-term issue, then he could also fill the product gap—five-year mortgages—on the lending side.

Bell succeeded in doing it. The CMHC-backed mortgages were "securitized"—put into a bundle—and in effect sold to the European investors. VanCity managed the mortgages and made its margin on them as usual. The real coup was the Standard & Poors bond rating that had to be secured, to establish VanCity's credit rating for the issue. It was "AAA," the highest the New York rating agency provided and the first time it had been granted, for a "structured finance instrument," to a non-U.S. private institution. After that, selling the issue was easy.

Bell also began pushing for new, day-to-day products for members. He had his eye on Canada Trust, which was in a major expansion phase. It was opening new branches—targetting VanCity locations, Bell claimed. In one case, it showed up right across the street. Canada Trust was aggressively introducing new products and aggressively pricing them, pitching for the most profitable customers—people with substantial savings. It was also advertising heavily. Bell, at VanCity, could see the impact of this campaign. A VanCity member might ask for a large draft made out to Canada Trust. The push by Canada Trust was like handwriting on the wall. Bell was determined to bring VanCity up to the standard of its competitors.

He had a particular problem, however. VanCity had a commitment to provide a high level of service. This included services to lower-income members whose low-balance accounts could not possibly pay for the services and whom Canada Trust was only too willing to leave to the credit union. At the same time, Bell had to stop the most profitable accounts from being taken away. This was where the new products came in: keeping up with what was happening on the other side of the street. Bell followed fashion. He wasn't particularly concerned with how long the product would last. He just did not want to be left behind. It was like being in the retail men's-wear business when red ties were the thing, he explained. You knew the fad was only going to last for a couple of months, but if people kept coming into the store and asking for red ties and you didn't have them, they went across the street to Canada Trust Fashions to get them.

The one new product that, years later, he remembered introducing was the U.S. dollar account. There were others that had real substance, like the chequing-savings account, or the Visa card, or the Ethical Growth Fund (the mutual fund). The U.S. dollar account, however—superficial, trendy, ephemeral and speculative—particularly stuck in Bell's mind as a token of how he was not prepared to be sideswiped by Canada Trust or anyone else. He thought of banks, and even Canada Trust, as ponderous ocean liners that had difficulty changing course, whereas VanCity was a speedboat that should be able to zip in and around those big ocean liners at will.

As if the gods were out to foil him, his strategic dynamic generated an even bigger problem. Every time a manual inefficiency was automated out of existence and every time a new product was introduced, it took up computer space. So did growth. In 1978, Geoff Hook had replaced the original Geac 800, based on the Hewlett Packard mini, with the Geac 8000.

Designed by Mike Sweet and built entirely by Geac, the 8000 was an enormous improvement. That second-generation Geac computer, however, was now running out of room. Bell also needed more flexibility in his software. Without it, he could not program a new product quickly, and if he could not do it quickly, he would be outmaneouvred. Plan 24 had a twelve-year lead time over the banks, but everyone was computerized now, and a new product's afterlife, as something unique in the marketplace, was becoming shorter every day. To keep an advantage, or even defend oneself, one had to add other new products constantly. Bell decided to update his computer software as well.

He was off on reconnaissance missions across the continent, too. Under Bell, senior management, for the first time in VanCity's history, got to travel. Seeing up front how others conducted their business was a Bell modus operandi. He was used to making trips to New York, Zurich and other financial centres, and used to dealing in much bigger dollars than he had to handle with VanCity. The $50 million Euro-issue was handled by an invest-ment-dealer friend from Lehman Brothers in New York whom Bell knew from his days as deputy minister of finance. Excursions to New York and visits to Standard & Poors, the ratings agency, were like guided tours led by the master dealer Bell, who knew the territory. Bell loved the mental challenge of dealing with the sharp, slick and specialized investment dealers on Wall Street. McKay and Smith sat in on some of those meetings, held in beautifully appointed boardrooms. They had trouble following the esoteric Wall Street financial language. They were awed and dazzled, feeling very much the country bumpkins in Manhattan. It didn't occur to them that what they were doing in Vancouver had more substance than the financial paper-shuffling in New York.

In one instance, Bell, McKay, Smith and a couple of others spent a week flying across the United States in an IBM Lear jet, at IBM's expense, to look at computer installations. Bell, through his many contacts, had arranged the excursion. It was, thought Smith, who loved technology, probably the most exciting time in his life. Bell was a high-tech buff, too, and liked to see solutions. New York, Boston, California, Texas—everywhere they went, a limousine was waiting to take them to one of the best hotels in the area. They dropped by to visit IBM itself. They went to see Ross Perot's shop, Electronic Data Systems, in Dallas. It was an eye-opener: Everyone there had short hair, as if they had just been discharged from the army, and they all talked the same strange way. VanCity did not buy IBM that time. There were visits to American banks, too, on these occasions.

Going on a junket with Bell meant work all the time, limousine or not. The VanCity party worked on the plane; they worked on weekends, whether they were in New York or San Francisco. If nothing was scheduled on a Saturday night, Bell held a planning session. McKay remembered being so weary at times that he felt unable to move, but there was nothing he could say, because Bell was driving himself even harder. David Levi, chair of the board, accompanied Bell to London, England, for the launch of the Euro-issue. The plane arrived at two in the afternoon, Bell had scheduled meetings from four until eight.The next day there were meetings every half hour or hour around the city until eight that night. That was typical. Levi had a hard time keeping awake.

When the schedule was delayed, on these trips, Bell could hardly be contained. Once, on Long Island, on the way to see a company that was trying to sell VanCity a computer product, the limousine driver hired by the company lost his way. Bell was steaming. He wanted to get out there and then, but the driver wouldn't let him because he had instructions to make sure they arrived. The VanCity group finally hopped out at a red light, which fortunately wasn't that far from their destination. Meetings that slowed Bell down drove him to distraction. The directors had struck several board committees in which they asked for information, criticized management and pushed their own ideas. Bell would become antsy during these meetings. He couldn't sit through them. He sent Wayne McKay to most of them instead.

Don Bentley, general manager, 1955–75.

Wayne McKay, vice-president of marketing and member services, leading the charge for the 1989 Terry Fox Run. On his right is the inimitable Fat Cat, the Junior Account mascot.

Bob Quart, who arrived at VanCity by happenstance after a trust company career and, as he said, was in the right place at the right time—CEO from 1988 to the present.

The new, environmentally innovative head office building at Terminal and Quebec, not all that far from the Dominion Building on Hastings, where VanCity first came into the world.

James LaBonte

CHAPTER 48

Strawberry Tarts

WAYNE MCKAY WAS FLOURISHING. Eric Hayne, manager of the marketing division, had left to join the fledgling Northland Bank in Calgary. McKay became manager of the marketing and member services division, which combined branch operations and Hayne's marketing division. In a sense, McKay ran VanCity.

Larry Bell, who, unlike Geoff Hook, had known virtually nothing about credit union operations, depended on McKay to make things happen. McKay regained the leeway to make operational decisions that he had enjoyed under Don Bentley a decade before. Dave Turnbull, the premises manager, who hadn't known McKay in the Bentley years, saw a metamorphosis take place with McKay. Turnbull wasn't sure exactly what had changed, or how it had happened, but McKay seemed to come out of a shell.

How it had happened wasn't, in fact, a mystery. Bell's frenetic personal style, with its reliance on intuition and spontaneity, allowed McKay to be himself again. Bell once proposed to start executive meetings at eight o'clock in the morning, because to start them any later was to waste half the day. McKay and Bob Quart, who also was not a morning person, joked about the idea and delayed as long as they could, but eventually they had to capitulate. For the first eight o'clock meeting, McKay sneaked in ahead of time. When the others arrived in the boardroom for the meeting, McKay was in a sleeping bag on the boardroom table, dressed in his pyjamas. He knew Bell had a sense of humour. The pyjama incident became part of the mythology of the organization. One young female employee, who had seen McKay furtively slipping into the boardroom in his pyjamas, thought he had lost his mind.

Bell, more than even Bentley, realized what McKay was capable of doing and let him do it. McKay, in response, worked harder for Bell than he had in his entire life. He added another twenty hours to his week but loved doing it because, he said, Bell's heart was in the right place. Bell's honesty of emotion particularly appealed to McKay. He was the kind of guy, McKay recalled, who could go to a play and cry unashamedly, with tears streaming down his cheeks. Bell's impulsiveness, which alienated many others, only increased McKay's affection for him, because it was so open.

Bell continued Hook's coffee klatsches with staff. Often he would get carried away: He would make wild promises with impossible deadlines, which ended up on McKay's desk, with just a longhand note mentioning what had been decided. Or McKay would read about these plans in the minutes, if minutes were kept at that particular meeting. "Oh, no," McKay would say to himself, "what has Larry promised to do now?"

Bell, with his impulsiveness, was an inconsistent recruiter. He did not want to take the time to go through a proper search and assessment. If employees did not work out, they could always be fired and replaced. "Don't hire anybody, Larry. Let us take care of that for you," McKay once told him. Bell dismissed people the same way. When he felt someone wasn't playing on his team, he just didn't want them around. He fired his human resources division manager and moved out Bruce Higgs, manager of the treasury and business services division, at the same time, but without any replacements. He asked McKay to look after both those areas until he could sort things out. McKay at one time had eighteen management people reporting to him.

McKay changed the branch structure, dividing it into two "districts," each with its own manager—John Iseli and Larry Wald respectively. Each of the districts was a mix of branches. McKay wanted more internal competition, and this structure encouraged the two districts to vie against each other. A friendly rivalry built up between them, with competitions, impromptu challenges and humorous wagers on the side. There were twenty branches now, too many for one branch operations manager to handle.

McKay had never liked the Frank Coffey-Garry Smith style of branch operations, so he changed that, too. They were control freaks, he thought, funnelling too many loan applications into head office and not giving branch managers much discretion for the loans that did fall within their limits. The Hook regime did not want to lose a dime, McKay felt, which meant they were too careful in the loans they allowed. The criteria for lending were too narrow. VanCity was not taking any risks with the ordinary member and hence was not helping many people that it should have been helping. Coffey and Smith, McKay also felt, had been more likely to hire a technician than a true branch manager, because a technician best served the purpose of running a tight ship.

McKay loosened up the ship. One of the first things he did was raise the branch managers' lending limits from $75,000 or $100,000, depending on the manager, to as high as $150,000. This more closely reflected property values. It also improved service. With the previous low limit, too many loans had been referred upwards, which slowed loan approvals and was inefficient. The outside competition was sharper, too, and VanCity was losing advantage. The object was to put responsibility back into the branches where, in McKay's view, it belonged and where it had been in his days as a branch manager under Bentley. Loan limits were raised for loan officers, too, so that they could make more decisions without referring them to the manager. This pushed power further down within the branch itself.

McKay was also faced with the realization that the basic products VanCity offered—mortgages, personal loans, term deposits, daily interest, lines of credit—had already been invented. New products were often just variations of the old. Bell was insistent on making the most of what VanCity was bringing forward—in other words, actively selling it—and the best place to begin, he and McKay decided, was with existing members. "Internal marketing," McKay called it. There was, however, no budget for it. McKay was supposed to figure out a way of doing it himself.

McKay, pondering the task, decided to tackle it through the staff instead, by improving their morale and getting them to think positively about selling. He had read about a New York restaurant that had told its waiters to sell strawberries for dessert, in order to increase sales, and sales had doubled. He devised a slogan for it at VanCity: "Think Strawberries." He was already writing the editorial for *TATS* and could throw in the message there. He also added a new back page called "The Hype Report," by Sheer Hype. He was verging on the outlandish. He now decided to write a "Strawberry Memo" as well, later dubbed *Strawberry Tarts*—To Advise and Reassure The Staff, or *TARTS*, for short, as distinct from *TATS*, which was merely To Advise The Staff. It was printed on one side of a sheet of paper. Two copies went out, with the overnight bag, to each branch, where they were posted. *TARTS* could be a few paragraphs or something longer, or just a one-liner. McKay might write about a baseball game, a place he was visiting on holiday, his wife's soft heart or a bit of VanCity history. It was whimsical at times, uplifting at others. Occasionally McKay provided a folksy sermon on some aspect of operations and member service. The memo gave him a personal link to branch employees.

Outside, Chris Bergthorson and his people at Embryo Communications were building on the soft image of Goldilocks and Blueface. Larry Bell became heavily involved in advertising. He liked the way that VanCity had generated a profile for itself. Marketing was more fun than being deputy minister of finance. Bell wanted Bergthorson to reach out demographically and make VanCity's image more all-inclusive. Embryo came up with a new slogan, "You Belong With Us." It expressed in an open, public way what the staff felt about VanCity and its members, and hence about people at large. Embryo also produced a new jingle: "Working on dreams, working together, we're part of a family that keeps getting better. At VanCity, you're one of the family. You belong with us." It did a large You Belong With Us campaign. In the 1984 annual report, a picture of a yuppified couple in front of their townhouse, holding flowers and a bag of groceries, caught the tone. Embryo also created a friendly, fat cat, as a mascot for a youth account, which it dubbed the Fat Cat Account.

Katharine Gallagher, McKay's advertising and promotion manager, then pushed VanCity into sponsorship. She had a cultural side to her and wanted

McKay to help sponsor arts organizations. McKay was skeptical and resisted, but he did put some money into the Vancouver Chamber Choir and other cultural activities. He was amazed at how quickly VanCity started to get a payback. The whole cultural community became aware of VanCity, because the different parts of it talked to each other. They were an upscale crowd, too, with considerable deposit money. Being a sports fanatic, McKay decided to try the same thing with sports. He began with kids' baseball and soccer teams and ended up sponsoring a Senior A Men's fastball team, the VanCity Magicians. He loved softball. He used the Magicians as VanCity's roving ambassadors.

He tried to keep VanCity's sponsorship at a community level as much as possible, in contrast to the sponsorship of high-profile events, whose main function was to have the sponsor's name splashed across the television screen. He turned down offers from breweries and cigarette companies for joint sponsorship, even though the dollars would have been useful. Several of the arts sponsorships involved programs for school children. He wanted the sponsorship to have a genuine community feeling to it. The board, at the same time, established a donations policy, committing 1 per cent of net earnings to community programs, over and above the sponsorship.

This new dimension began filtering sideways into the organization. Soon the social club became involved in charity fund-raising activities, starting with the Terry Fox Run. The staff commitment became not so much a charitable gesture as part of the organization's fabric. The annual report carried a "Community Involvement" section. McKay appointed a manager of community relations.

McKay was unbound and, in *TARTS*, irreverent. He openly scorned "suits" and "bean-counters," although he wore suits himself. He appeared to want to do the opposite of what bankers did in order to push VanCity's difference deeper into the organization. He wrote *TARTS* for daily circulation without interruption, never missing a deadline, although he had to steal, sometimes, when his imagination abandoned him. His routine was unusual. He talked to people and went to meetings during the day, did his administrative work after everybody else had gone home, and bashed out *TARTS* late at night or on weekends.

His most anti-bank, anti-suit gesture was his office. It was crammed full of baseball and hockey memorabilia and gewgaws. McKay was originally a Brooklyn Dodgers fan. There was also a strawberry corner. "The Shrine," he called it. From the moment McKay had begun his "Think Strawberries" campaign, people had been giving him strawberry mementoes—everything imaginable with a strawberry on it or shaped like a strawberry, from a carrying case to dolls to salt and pepper shakers. The pièce de résistance was a large Snoopy telephone on his desk. McKay was having fun.

CHAPTER 49

Teleservice

LARRY WALD, ONE OF WAYNE MCKAY'S two district managers, was mowing his lawn in Port Coquitlam. He did his best thinking when he mowed the lawn. The noise of the lawnmower meant that nobody was likely to interrupt him. There were no telephones ringing, and people weren't coming to see him. He was mulling over a new possibility at VanCity. A lot had happened since he had left the Bank of Montreal in 1975 and went to work for B.C. Central and then VanCity.

He had grown up in the area—across the CPR tracks in Coquitlam, until the mid-1950s, when it was still very much in the country. He was a big, strong baseball player, and later traded baseball stories with McKay. He joined the local branch of Bank of Montreal a week after graduating from high school. The bank manager was king then. Whatever he said was the way it was. The bank opened its doors at ten o'clock and closed them at three, and if a customer did not make it, well, he or she would just have to try another day. There was no rate negotiation and little apparent competition. The "big five" banks had things the way they wanted them. Staff were treated with the same authority. Six months into Wald's banking career, he received a call telling him he was going to Enderby, in the Okanagan, where he was to report in six days. He went. Being single helped. You did what you were told, and so, for that matter, did the customer.

When he went to Central as a director of education and, later, to VanCity, as personnel manager, Wald discovered a different culture. He had hesitated to leave the bank when Central approached him. The first time he heard the phrase "the credit union movement," it sounded to him like a military or political force rather than a financial institution. He struggled with the term. He drove past several VanCity branches to try to get a better idea of what lay behind this movement. The branches could use a paint job, he thought. He sensed a lack of professionalism. What really caught his attention, however, were all the people in the branches. He wondered where they had come from. Once he drove down Hastings, past Branch 3, and saw people lined up not to the door, but outside the door and down the sidewalk. It took him three months to feel comfortable enough to make the move to Central, but that line-up ultimately convinced him.

Central was exciting. These were the heady days, with CEO George May, full of energy, riding the rambunctious Central tiger. People called Wald and his peers at Central the "young rebels," although Wald considered himself a conformist. VanCity, too, was full of surprises. He was taken by its informal, friendly approach. On his first day there, McKay, his boss, as was his habit, did not arrive until halfway through the morning. Wald was struck that there should be so much acceptance of people that the system would permit it. It was the single biggest lesson he learned at VanCity, he thought, and it had come in his first two hours.

He was thankful for this ambiance. He began paying more attention to people and sensitivities. Within the VanCity family, the human resources division was a family of its own. Its staff met formally at least once a week. Discussions often went off-topic into a whole range of philosophical and personal matters. This made the group more harmonious, Wald realized, because its members better understood the larger issues surrounding what they were doing as well as each others' motivations. There was genuine personal caring and empathy with each other. They thought they were the best human resources team in the world.

Now, mowing the lawn, a district manager of branch operations with a zest for competing, he had something else on his mind. His wife was working. He was working. If they had wanted to purchase appliances, or look at a deal for a car, or drop in at an open house, and wanted to see if they could line up a loan to purchase any one of these things, they wouldn't be able to talk to each other about it until the evening. The next day they would go their separate ways. They had no chance until Saturday morning to get into the VanCity branch together. There had to be a better way of delivering VanCity's services. Why not, he thought, a night-loan service, where people busy at work, like himself and his wife, could phone in weekday evenings and arrange a loan?

Larry Bell, in one of his impetuous moments after a coffee meeting, had given a couple of assistant managers in Wald's district $2,500 extra marketing money. Wald was frustrated because he himself had attempted time and again to get more resources. Now he told Bell that if he really wanted to do something, he should give Wald another $2,500 to introduce the night-loan service he had been mulling over. He would start with just one branch, on a trial basis. If it did not work out, not much would be lost. Bell, having casually been so generous in the other case, gave Wald the money.

Wald went to see Ellie Manaigre, the manager of his home branch in Coquitlam. Manaigre, he knew, was the kind of person who welcomed change. She agreed to give "Nightloan" a shot. She found two loan officers willing to alternate on a late shift until eight o'clock on weeknights. The service was an instant success. It was primarily informational; it did not approve loans, but it did give members a sense of whether they would qualify. It could also get the application process rolling. Members spontaneously began calling in for rates on deposits and other matters. Wald extended the service to Branch 19 in Delta.

The logical next step was to allow all members to participate. John Iseli asked Shirley Grindeland, the manager of Branch 8, downstairs in the head-office building, if her branch could be used. It had some backroom space available and, because of the branch's central location, members from all of the outlying areas could call in without a long-distance charge. Grindeland had another idea. Instead of just doing loans at night, they should look into other things they could do for members by telephone.

A committee was struck, including Grindeland and Iseli, her district manager. As they knocked the idea around, they began to see how startling the possibilities really were. One could use the telephone line to do real work beyond the first stage of a loan. One could, for example, transfer money from one account to another. There was no reason, either, why one could not offer the service during the day. It would save many members the trouble of going to a branch.

It would also take at least some work out of the branches, ultimately producing savings in premises costs. Foot traffic in the branches was horrendous; it was difficult to get parking lots big enough or find premises large enough to handle it. Wayne McKay had been trying to find a way of offloading some of that traffic. The expanded Nightloan service quite by chance gave him that possibility. When McKay and Gus German, back in 1975, had built the database around membership numbers, they had speculated about a future in which members, with terminals in their homes, would access their accounts via telephone lines. The new telephone service did not go quite that far—it required a VanCity intermediary—but it had within it a touch of the future.

Canada Trust's hours on weekdays were 8 A.M. to 8 P.M., so those hours were chosen for the new service, to head off that particular competition. Saturday hours were set at 8 A.M. to 4 P.M., also ending three hours later than VanCity branch closing time. Four full-time staff and one part-time teller were recruited for the job. Four telephone lines and phone sets were set up, run through a basic, off-the-shelf PBX telephone switching unit. On July 8, 1985, using an ordinary telephone number, VanCity's new and, as it turned out, radical TeleService began.

Shirley Grindeland watched the TeleService operation under her charge with a tremor of anticipation. It was different and new, and she liked new things that leapt over the threshold of routine—she had liked new things ever since, as a young woman in Calgary, she had bolted the Royal Bank for a small local trust company, because the manager there would give her more responsibility. Unlike many others, she wasn't bothered by Larry Bell's flurry of changes at VanCity, either. The upheaval, she thought, was good. One had to ask questions and be flexible in order to survive.

More than that, the new TeleService was a system-wide operation. It went much beyond merely managing a branch, and that interested Grindeland. Once one had managed two or three branches, Grindeland thought, the basics of the work were much the same. She had become frustrated and restless as a branch manager. She had never set up a new branch, but TeleService was her own.

The volume surprised her from the beginning—six thousand calls per month. In three months, the unit was receiving up to ten thousand calls and had to add two extra lines. The TeleService crew set up mortgages and personal loans, gave out account balances, made address changes, transferred funds, and sold products and services. As part of a general effort to promote personal loans, Grindeland made contact with several car dealerships. Their business managers would phone in for car loans for their customers, and TeleService would approve them and turn them around. The operation was bustling. The equipment, however, was basic, and Grindeland had no idea how many calls were being placed. The calls would back up. She was spending more and more time responding to complaints from members trying to call in and finding the line busy. The number of calls for balance inquiries and transactions, rather than for arranging loans, was suprisingly high. Grindeland needed a more sophisticated switching system that would allow her to monitor the flow of calls and give her some measure of how fast members were being served.

She had already visited some call centres in eastern Canada and had attended a telemarketing conference in Atlanta. Telemarketing, with its connotation of a bank of operators calling up people, uninvited, to sell them something, was a misnomer for what TeleService did, but it was the generic word used. It was a relatively new phenomenon, whose technology was still developing. The applications in banking were few and marginal. The cs Co-op—the civil service credit union in Ottawa—had long provided telephone service through its branches, but that was similar to what VanCity was now doing. The closest approximation in credit unions of what Grindeland wanted occurred in the Pentagon Federal Credit Union and the Navy Federal Credit Union, both in the suburbs of Washington, D.C., which Larry Bell had looked at. They used a military satellite for teleservice. Bell, on his visit, had heard a corporal in Frankfurt arrange a car loan. Another call had come in from an army base in Okinawa.

The most impressive display was the American Express telephone centre in Salt Lake City. Bell, McKay, Iseli, Smith and computer consultant Bob Leighton, who had taken over VanCity's computer operation, listened to calls from people from around the world who had lost their traveller's cheques and from banks, merchants and hotels suspicious of people trying to cash them. The operators, through a number trace, could pull up information that told them where the traveller's cheques were originally issued. The operators traded other information with the fraud department. The VanCity contingent also listened in to a series of conversations that began with somebody trying to cash a traveller's cheque in a bank in Athens, Greece, and ended with the police coming to the branch and arresting the person for fraud. The feat brought home to them vividly what they already knew—that one could execute transactions with people anywhere in the world, once one got beyond the concept of paper and signatures.

On that trip Bell, excited by the potential, decided to hold a planning session in their rented car, while they were driving down a freeway south of Los Angeles, and then continued the session later in a Los Angeles hotel. Some financial institution, the VanCity contingent knew, was going to do a telephone service right, and when it did, it was going to be remarkably successful. They explored how far they could push the concept. Why not, they asked themselves, use the TeleService number for all the branches as well as for TeleService, resulting in just one central phone number? That way, the branches, or at least many of them, could dispense with their own separate equipment and a receptionist. Since all membership calls would go through the one number, moreover, anything that could be handled by TeleService would be taken care of without inconveniencing a branch. Branch staff could concentrate on their street traffic. The rudimentary TeleService operation had already cut down the cost per transaction for VanCity. Maximizing TeleService use, through the one-number entryway, would reduce this cost dramatically.

B.C. Tel was given the contract. Work began in the fall of 1986, with Grindeland closely involved. She now enjoyed the title of "Manager, Tele-service" and reported directly to Wayne McKay. "They actually looked to telecommunications as being critical to the success of their operation," Mike Wadden, B.C. Tel's sales manager, remembered thinking, since it was so unusual at the time. What VanCity wanted, in fact, was so new for the volume required that B.C. Tel had to devise a completely different switching system. The main switch would be located in VanCity's office, rather than VanCity using a B.C. Tel master switch.

TeleService itself was moved upstairs to head office, on the second floor, and became a self-standing operation. Use of the central number for TeleService began in the spring. By July 1, 1987, Canada Day, all the branches were tied in for downstream calls. Grindeland invited the B.C. Tel people over, and champagne corks popped. Roses appeared on the desks of the TeleService operators. The network prefix given to VanCity was 877. The number for TeleService was 877-7000. It was an easy number to remember. "One name, one number," was the slogan Chris Bergthorson and his people at Embryo came up with. All that was required from members was to have a code name entered in VanCity's database when they were in the branch—a member identity code for use over the telephone. Bergthorson wondered later if any of them had realized at the beginning how good the idea was. It seemed to him an amazing service, fantastic, light years ahead, making life so easy for people. It became a product in itself, showing up blazoned on billboards. "If you're busy and you can't get to your branch, all you have to do is pick up your phone ..."

A few months later, the final, obvious step was taken—authorizing the purchase of term deposits, including RRSPs, over the telephone. It was the definitive break with the past. The issuing of term deposits had involved certificates and signatures, with all of the ritual and seriousness that went with paper, stamp, and seal—and all of the time it took, waiting in line at a branch, particularly at RRSP time. Now it could be done by phone, and electronically at VanCity's end. A mortgage set up by TeleService still, ultimately, required the member's signature and other documentation, like a proof of income. Other than that, one could do virtually anything through TeleService, except deposit or withdraw cash itself.

On its very first advertised day, after the Canada Day long weekend, the new TeleService was so overloaded with calls that there were long waits and not all of the calls got through. VanCity had badly underestimated the number of calls it would get and hence the number of lines required. When more lines were added, however, the system worked expeditiously. In its first full year, 1988, TeleService averaged 75,500 calls a month, or close to a million calls for the year, compared with 10,000 calls a month for the old number and separate branch connections. An average day clocked upwards of 3,100 calls.

With the new automatic call-distribution equipment, Grindeland could now see how fast members were being served. The target was to respond to 90 per cent of the calls in any one day within sixty seconds. Knowing the number of calls coming in on different days and in different time periods, Grindeland could shift lunch hours or coffee breaks or put on extra part-time staff to meet the objective.

McKay had decided from the beginning to give the new TeleService its own pride of place. He was insistent that the premises not be a bucket-shop hole-in-the-wall, with its operators reflecting poor facilities. McKay wanted a happy climate, with windows for natural light. The teller positions were rated a little higher than similar positions in a branch, so going to TeleService was seen as a step up and attracted experienced people. There was musing about the alienation of the work, since there was no direct personal contact with members, but that turned out not to be a problem. Some people were more efficient and confident of themselves on the telephone than they were working in a branch. They preferred TeleService work.

Loan officers were a key part of the service. Unlike their counterparts in a branch, TeleService loan officers did not have the benefit of body language or facial expression to help make a judgement about a loan applicant. In lending, however, considerable emphasis was placed on members' credit ratings and how long they had been members. Grindeland defended the lending acumen of her department. She argued that not having an applicant in front of the loan officer was in some ways better. One would not be prejudiced by a person's looks. Setting up loans by telephone was neither better nor worse than handling a loan application in a branch, she maintained. It was only a different way.

About 20 per cent of loans and mortgages for all of VanCity came to be handled by TeleService. Despite an accelerating membership, staff in branches did not need to be increased, since TeleService and ATMs drained off branch traffic.

What most surprised Grindeland was that the heaviest period of use was from 9:30 to 11:30 A.M. Members called from their offices or other places of work. They regarded TeleService not as an after-hours add-on, although the extra hours were convenient, but as a regular part of their credit union. "Branch 18 (Coquitlam) and Branch 19 (Delta) got married and had a child," Larry Wald quipped, thinking back to the original Nightloan experiment.

Years passed, and more years. TeleService's marketing value seemed inexhaustible. The moment that marketing ran ads in the newspaper or bought radio time, and mentioned the 877-7000 number, calls started coming in. "The greatest, most unique marketing feature in the industry," Larry Wald thought.

It wasn't until late 1992, seven years after TeleService began in the back of Branch 8, that the first of VanCity's major competitors, Canada Trust, started an equivalent service.

TeleService's appearance in the world was not so dramatic as the advent of Plan 24, but in its own powerful way it was just as revolutionary.

CHAPTER 50

"I'm Going to Survive Conversion"

JUDY GORRIE, AN ENERGETIC YOUNG woman and a mother, was a VanCity quality assurance officer. Although a VanCity employee, she was attached to Geac, at its location in the Lake City industrial estate in Burnaby. Her job was to make sure that computer programs did for VanCity tellers what they were supposed to do. She was an ex-teller, but not a technical person. She tested new programs, representing users, and also passed on reports of bugs in existing programs so that fixes would be done. Every time a programmer rewrote or added a program, Gorrie or the assistant she had hired, Margo Spencer, would bang the heck out of it, trying all kinds of possibilities to see if it might fail.

She was naturally exuberant and could identify with tellers. She remembered her first VanCity branch, East Hastings, where the tellers all went out together every Friday night and partied it up, dragging themselves to work the following morning. She committed herself to anything she did, because she wanted to do things well. She was open with her emotions. She was also flexible and quick, skilfully picking her way through changed circumstances by touch and feel. Otherwise she would not have been able to function. Every day, sometimes every hour, her job changed without warning. She was always in what she called firefighting mode. Somebody from a branch might call in and say, "This isn't working, I need it fixed now." Nobody warned her, however, just how flexible and able to withstand punishment she would have to be, when, one innocent weekend, in November 1985, VanCity converted its computer system and technological chaos descended.

Everyone at VanCity knew that something had to be done with the computer system. The computer was running out of room. The response time was slowing down, although otherwise the on-line system continued to work fairly well. Gorrie could imagine it grinding to a halt. Whatever could be easily removed from the Geac mainframe had already been removed. Dormant accounts were handled on a personal computer.

Even more critical was the weakness in capability of the software. The VanCity system had been continuously developed from the original software. Each time VanCity introduced a new product or new feature, a computer program was written for it and patched into the system. The software had now reached the point where VanCity was patching what had been patched before. Great care had to be taken not to rip out the original patch in the process. This was becoming progressively more difficult to do. For Larry Bell, the lack of flexibility was maddening. He needed programs up and working quickly, for new products and also for new service charges.

Bell also wanted to move away from Geac towards a more standardized hardware environment, where he would have options both for hardware and software. He had been looking at other banking systems across North America to see what he could find. He put out a request for proposal. The most attractive proposal, however, came from Geac itself. Gus German, the genius behind the creation of Geac, had been marginalized within his own company, but his original concept had been so insightful that nothing came close to it for functionality.

Geac recommended that VanCity switch to its most recent software release, GFS, which stood for Geac Financial System. GFS did not need separate programs to be patched on for changes in a product. It allowed VanCity itself to enter different instructions inside a generic program—say, change an account type so that interest would be calculated in a different way. This provided some of the flexibility that Bell was after.

The other part of the proposal suggested replacing the Geac 8000 hardware with the Geac 9000 range. The Geac 9000 was another one of Mike Sweet's brilliant creations. It was theoretically unlimited in size. Because of its open-ended design, one could keep adding as many processors as one wanted, increasing capacity. For Geac, it seemed the logical way to do what VanCity wanted.

Bell, however, balked. The 9000 wasn't well-established and therefore posed a certain risk. GFS, moreover, was already being used on 8000s elsewhere. Geac's sales staff, meanwhile, when asked point blank if the 8000 was an alternative, agreed that it was, at least as a temporary step. A decision was made to go with dual 8000s—linking the two 8000 machines that VanCity already had.

There were just a few problems. The GFS software, with all its bells and whistles, wasn't nearly as small and efficient as the version it would be replacing. If the 9000 was deemed too experimental, the dual-8000 arrangement wasn't absolutely guaranteed either, especially to handle the processing load for an organization with VanCity's volume. Geac had fudged on this. This unstated risk was like a time bomb ticking away unseen in a closet. VanCity, moreover, decided that it wanted the generic GFS to look and function like the old VanCity system. Modification would save VanCity a lot of retraining. More important, VanCity, which was ahead of other credit unions, had unique features to its products, which the generic GFS couldn't accommodate. That capacity needed to be built in. Even if all of the modifications weren't necessary, they would be nice to have. Somebody later counted 128 of them in all. This meant a double conversion in one—increasing the odds that something might go wrong.

Bell himself was acting manager of the management information and systems division, which was responsible for the computer operation. Bruce Higgs agreed to manage the conversion for him. Higgs had overseen data processing under Geoff Hook and, although he wasn't a techie, he understood technical issues. Geac was to look after the programming. VanCity's own technical staff was to deliver the specifications to Geac and do the testing. Computer consultant Bob Leighton, who knew Bell and had done other work for VanCity, was at the same time to develop a new reporting system for the general ledger—providing data analysis for management— using a second-hand IBM that VanCity had acquired. The IBM, theoretically, would also take some of the load off the Geac machines.

It was spring, 1985. Bell set the Remembrance Day long weekend in November—Remembrance Day that year fell on a Monday—as the deadline. He did not want to wait for the next long-weekend opportunity, which was Easter of the following year. He had too much to do too quickly, and he was assured the deadline could be met. VanCity, he had concluded, would otherwise become hamstrung.

As work on the conversion began at the Geac premises at Lake City, Judy Gorrie—at the bottom of the order of command, far from VanCity head office but doing some of the actual work—had an early feeling of foreboding. She was testing the new software and running into problems. She would take the problem to a programmer. "I don't know," he would shrug. "I don't know where to begin to look. I don't know anything about it." The programmers were as unfamiliar with GFS as she was. While she was testing the software, they were upstairs taking courses to learn about it.

The sinking feeling that began when Gorrie started testing never went away. GFS had new features different from the old system. Gorrie had none of the details of how those new features worked, because the documentation was inadequate. It was too late, however, to develop a more complete book of documentation or a test plan to match. She mentioned the problem to her managers, but nothing came of it. Their attitude seemed to be, "Just do the best you can." She might have refused to go on until the documentation she needed was available, but there was too much pressure and, as she ruefully remembered, she did not know any better.

It turned out later there were a couple of Geac people in the vicinity who knew the GFS software intimately, but they were not assigned to her. She and her team did research on their own to try to understand the new software, by simply trying it out to see what it would do. They were flying by the seat of their pants.

Gorrie and Margo Spencer had been given a dozen people to do the testing. They had divided into two sections. Spencer's team was to test the conversion programs that would take the existing database and convert it to the new system. Gorrie's team was to look after testing the new software on samples of the new database that Spencer provided. Each of the two elements would be constantly upgraded. The intent was that at some point, when sufficient refinements were made, both sides would be frozen. This was a logical division of labour. Because neither Gorrie nor Spencer, however, were able to ascertain ahead of time exactly what they were converting to, the moving environment between the two of them moved endlessly, change following change back and forth, as they tried to understand how the software worked.

Then, in the middle of the testing, someone decided to move the programmers and the quality assurance teams across town, from Burnaby to 1034 West Broadway, above the parking lot at Branch 1. By the time they had done that, equipment and all, two weeks had been lost. With Geac's organization, VanCity's organization and Leighton's organization tumbled together, moreover, nobody seemed to know who was in charge. Gorrie recalled that there were so many chiefs, that if you asked any ten people who was in command, you would probably get ten different answers. The conversion run-up had become so messy that everyone was afraid to make a decision.

The Geac programmers also felt the process was out of control. Many of the programs weren't producing the results they had expected. The programmers were putting in long hours. After a week or two without enough time off, productivity was bound to drop and stupid mistakes made. The closer to deadline, the more the panic, the longer the hours, the less sleep and the likelier it was that things would go wrong. The programmers, run ragged, fell further and further behind schedule.

"We were just peons, just little machines," Gorrie remembered. "Management treated the programmers like garbage, and we weren't far behind." The sensitivity to employees, which was so much part of the VanCity culture, had broken down amid the stress and confusion. Morale among the exhausted programmers was appalling. Somebody had T-shirts printed up with the slogan, "I'm going to survive Conversion." The only thing that kept them going was the feeling that come November 11, it would all be over.

Occasionally Gorrie's VanCity bosses would come by and ask her and the others how things were going. "Terrible," they would say. "Nothing works. We're not ready."

"Well, our chief executive officer is coming in today, so don't say anything," was the response.

Bell then would come in and also ask about progress.

"Oh, not bad," they would reply. "We've got some kinks to work out."

"I'm sure you people will do it," Bell would encourage them.

Gorrie and Spencer were working until two or three in the morning, seven days a week. That should have been Bell's first clue, Gorrie said. Something had to be wrong; it wasn't normal for people to work like that. Instead, she thought, they were considered just a bunch of dedicated people who liked putting in those long hours. She wasn't sure that Bell even knew what they were going through.

They kept making changes—sometimes brand-new modifications—almost to the moment conversion occurred, so that the software would work properly. As a result, their two streams never completely met. There just wasn't the time. There was also supposed to have been a complete systems test—a dry run, going through the whole conversion from beginning to end, instead of just testing in pieces—and then a night or two of testing with a day's normal processing. Ideally, one did that two months before installation and then kept testing after that. Again, there wasn't the time.

Higgs was aggressively pushing them to meet the deadline. Vic Blamey was project manager on behalf of VanCity. He remembered feeling highly pessimistic about their readiness. The technical managers were all apprehensive. They pointed out to Higgs things that were still problematic. Vince Van Damm, the Geac project manager, however, thought that the problems weren't critical; he was ready to sign off. Blamey concurred. In the intense push to make the deadline, they had been inculcated with the necessity of not being late. "There were outside forces saying it had to be done," Blamey explained later. "We felt we were at a point of no return." "Panic and fear," was how someone else described it.

Only the consultant Bob Leighton opposed going ahead, or that was what he claimed; none of the others later could remember. There were so many meetings, blurred into each other in a pressure-cooker atmosphere, and judgements one way or the other were all a matter of degree. Besides, Leighton was preoccupied with the IBM project and didn't know anything about the Geac system, so his view would have been discounted in any case. Techies held all sorts of opinions. There was no certainty in such situations. Bell and Higgs, weighing all the views and keeping in mind the difficulties for VanCity that would result from a postponement, decided to go ahead.

Because there wasn't the capacity to convert all of the database at once, the conversion weekend had within it the tension of putting together a fission bomb. The operators had to break the database into pieces, take the pieces away, convert them, bring them back and glue them together again. Since the procedure was so fragile, it was done twice in parallel, with one team working at Broadway and Oak and the other at Geac's location in Burnaby, to increase the likelihood that, at the end, they would still have a database they could use.

The night before the system went back on line, at the end of the conversion weekend, Gorrie and Spencer sat in the hallway. Gorrie was in tears. Loans and term deposits had not done the same thing twice in testing. "They'll never work," she said, "never." The tears had come often, from sheer stress and exhaustion. Gorrie and Spencer would break down in the office and then, realizing that this wasn't appropriate behaviour, would head out to the hall, the stairs or the parking lot until they recovered their composure.

The first working day after the conversion went reasonably well. The response time was slow, but everything seemed to work. The second floor at 1034 West Broadway was quiet. The odd phone call came in, then quite a few more, but they were manageable. After the overnight processing, the general ledgers balanced against the membership ledgers, so that looked good, too. One of Gorrie's colleagues, however, noticed that Plan 24 in one branch had increased overnight by almost a million dollars, which was wildly out of proportion to the branch's portfolio. Since the change had happened after closing, it would have been generated by the computer system rather than by an actual deposit. The anomaly was traced to an interest payment on a small, rolling thirty-day term deposit, for which the interest should have been minor. Just as Gorrie had predicted, term deposits weren't working.

The second day was reasonable, too, although the system came up late, at about ten in the morning rather than eight o'clock, because the overnight had taken longer than it should have. Gradually, however, similar errors began popping up everywhere. Loans had gone awry. "Loans were just garbage," Gorrie recounted. By the third and fourth days, it was apparent that an increasing number of subsidiary details had been converted incorrectly on the database. The balance of an account might have been correct, but transactions that were supposed to be automatically triggered, such as interest calculations, were coming out wrong. Each day, as more calculations were triggered, the situation got progressively worse. Only a small minority of members' accounts were affected, but the system's integrity was compromised. Money was also being assigned to the wrong general ledger accounts. Tracking down the cause took an extraordinary amount of time.

Gorrie and Spencer were answering inquiries from the branches on the phone. Soon they were overwhelmed, and Garry Smith organized a hotline team to handle the increasing flood of calls. There were a dozen people on the team, inserted into spaces along one side of the computer department area like corks plugged into a barrel. Unfortunately, they had no training in the new software and could not answer many of the questions. They ended up being receptionists for Gorrie and Spencer, who remained caught in the maelstrom. The two women also had to test new software as the programmers worked furiously to fix the bugs in the system. They did it on the fly. "Fix this," they would tell the programmers, then get back a new piece of program with the fix in it, run it through a quick quality assurance test, "boom, boom, boom, okay, yeah, fine" and then throw it onto the live system.

Somebody, seeing the chaos, had gone out and bought them tall spikes fixed in little weighted stands. The spikes were to hold the messages that piled up on their desks. Gorrie's spike was soon full to the top with memos—messages to which she hadn't been able to respond. The branches called back, furious. They had members screaming, they said, and they couldn't deal with them because they weren't hearing back.

The slow response time also was playing havoc with the tellers. Generally the delay was less than a minute, but with the member waiting, the line-up getting worse and some members becoming angry, it seemed an eternity. Occasionally the delay would be even longer. If a member had several transactions, even simple ones, the waiting time was compounded. VanCity was a volume operation, pushing through a high volume of transactions. Even a slight increase in computer response time meant trouble. The line-ups in the branches quicky became horrendous.

The delayed response time, or the unavailability of the system, also meant that ATM transactions backed up, like a sewer system backing up into kitchen sinks. ATM transactions went through The Exchange in Bellevue, but they were unable to proceed from there to VanCity, so they were stored in Bellevue until the system became available. Members using the ATMs were not able to see their balances because they could not get the computer to look at them. Their vain attempts to get through on the ATMs only added to the electronic morass.

Sometimes the on-line system was so slow that tellers gave up on it, letting their vouchers pile up and hoping for a break later in the day to do the posting. Meanwhile, the overnight processing, with its calculations of inter-est, maturities, loan payments, and the clearing of cheques, was taking progressively longer as the problems compounded. The ATM backlog had to be cleared, too. Then there was the desperate tracing of errors, software rewrites and posting of corrections to term deposits and loans, day and night. Two kinds of programs needed to be written: one to fix the problem and one to fix all the accounts that had been contaminated by the problem. If the corrections weren't made, the overnight processing would compound the errors, pushing computer services even further into a hole.

The overnight consequently ate into the next day's processing time. On Thursday, the third day, the computer wasn't available to tellers at all during the morning. On Friday, the system didn't come up in the branches at all.

The next Monday it was unavailable again, when the branches opened, despite the weekend for the overnight to catch up. It was down again for a couple of other days that week. On one occasion, tellers were offered a window at seven-thirty the next morning, barring unforeseen hazards, to work off some of their backlog. They all showed up, but the unforeseen hazards had occurred and the tellers sat on their hands, frustrated, waiting until their branches opened and they could at least do something.

Panic started to set in at head office. It looked like the transaction backlog would grow so large that the system would not have the capacity to clear it and, worse, that errors from the faulty conversion would build up beyond the point of no return. VanCity would implode. Larry Bell was aghast. So was Bruce Higgs, who felt that he had let VanCity down. There was a brief debate about going back to the old system, but that was ruled out as impossible. Bell also knew, now, that people were working around the clock and fixes were being made constantly. At one point he thought he had only a couple of days left before he would have to close VanCity down.

Peter Cook, then VanCity's manager of planning and administration, also felt time was running out. The financial information was not sufficiently secure. VanCity had a system failure on its hands, and it knew neither what the problem was nor whether it could be fixed. The system was breaking down at too many points. One could try ferreting out errors in the database morass, but, Cook was convinced, unless the breakdown was soon contained, VanCity would be out of business.

If, on the other hand, Bell closed VanCity's doors to rehabilitate its data, the rumours surrounding the closure could be combustible and touch off a run of withdrawals when operations began again. Bell, although used to stress, was suffering. It was far worse than anything he had gone through before. "I paced that floor," he remembered," and I thought and I thought and I thought and I said, 'You can't do it. You just can't do it. You can't shut a financial institution down. You can't.'"

Shutting down would not have helped much anyway, because there wasn't enough information about what was wrong to guarantee that if the doors were closed for five days, everything would work well after that. The system, too, was producing new fissures as time went on.

Bell took action. He called in consultant Bob Leighton, with whom he had a personal connection, and asked him to take over. "I had to have somebody who would tell me to go to hell if I was wrong," Bell recalled. "I didn't want polite answers. I wanted to know what was going on. I knew he would do that for me."

Leighton agreed to step in, but only if the organizational division between Geac and VanCity was wound up and it was clear he had responsibility. Bell forthwith fired Geac as VanCity's programming contractor. He wrote out a one-page contract formally turning all computer operations over to Bob Leighton & Associates. He called together the Geac programmers and VanCity's own technical people. "All of you here who wish to carry on working, this man is in charge," he told them, pointing to Leighton. "If you don't want to work for him, leave right now. I've got a crisis on my hands and I don't want any discussion. I don't want to have any debate. If you think you've been hard done by, get a lawyer and we'll solve it somehow, but I'm not debating it right now." Most of them decided to stay.

Bell also apologized personally for the debacle and for the long hours they were putting in. It had become clear to him, he said, that running a computer department was not the same as running a credit union, that it was completely different. He wasn't getting much sleep. He went around to the branches, but had somebody else drive his car; he had too many things on his mind to drive safely. "We just had to hang in there," he said. We just had to beat it. So that was my job. I had to say, 'Look, keep bailing the ship, folks. We're just doing everything we can, and there's no choice. We've just got to keep bailing.'"

From the moment the crisis hit, a computer services war-room meeting was held every morning to exchange information and provide a status report. All parts of the organization were represented. The meeting room would be packed with up to twenty people. The meetings were emotional and intense. Hot words were exchanged and voices were often angry, on edge.

The spectre of a possible scare story in the press added to the tension. Although members knew there was a serious problem with the system, a newspaper headline would be calamitous. Members might start pulling their money out willy-nilly because of a fear that VanCity was out of control—and, to senior managers like Peter Cook and Wayne McKay, VanCity *was* out of control.

Tellers, with their accumulated pieces of paper, had to try catching up on the system in odd hours or evenings and on weekends. Usually Leighton would get the system up in the branches by two o'clock in the afternoon. If it was a good overnight, he might manage it by ten in the morning. He found himself in a Catch-22 situation. The branches would beg him to keep the system available at least until eight in the evening so that they could keep staff in and do late posting. If, however, he didn't start the overnight processing earlier, he would be late the next day. Sometimes he was forced to close that early evening window. He was trying to get as much overnight time as he could, and Wayne McKay, for the branches, was trying to get as much branch time as he could. A communications letter was organized to tell people what was being done. Leighton, himself, was getting only a couple of hours' sleep every night. Operators would call him at all hours of the night, asking for instructions.

When he took over, Leighton didn't know anything about Geac's machines or its GFS software, but he did know about computers. He had some software developed that could monitor programs that were running on the overnight and see what was taking up so much processing time. In the meantime, he had to find some way of cutting back the overnight so that the branches would be able to use the the system during the day. He decided that instead of trying to catch up on the ATM backlog each night, he would let those transactions accumulate at The Exchange facility in Bellevue right through to the weekend.

Unfortunately, having cut Bellevue off from Vancouver in this manner, he had no way of comparing how much money members were withdrawing daily with what they had in their accounts. He could restrict members to a single, limited withdrawal to stop those with little money in their accounts, but that would mean that people who had substantial funds would be blocked, too. He lifted the limit. This left the system wide open. Leighton trusted that most members would police themselves. They wouldn't know what VanCity was doing behind the scenes in any case. There would, as well, always be a final record. One member got away with $60,000 and fled town. Some teenagers discovered they could withdraw money they didn't have but weren't sure what would happen if they took too much, so their raiding of the defenceless ATMs was done in relatively small amounts. VanCity lost $75,000 to fraud in this way. For Leighton, it was simply the cost of doing business in the circumstances.

The cold-storage of ATM transactions still, however, did not remedy the situation. The Geac programmers were using too much of the computer's overnight time to rewrite their programs. One such program was something called NXPD, which stood for "next processing date." Leighton didn't know what it was and wanted to stop running it, again to free up processing time. He asked the Geac programmers about it, but was given evasive answers. The programmers merely said they had to do some fixes on it. He finally cornered Geac's project manager, Vince Van Damm, on the subject. Van Damm confessed that they couldn't operate without NXPD, which was the way the Geac software flagged the next loan-payment due date, or the date when a term deposit rolled over and paid interest, and executed the transaction. According to Leighton, the Geac group hadn't converted it at all. Apparently, they had written the programs for the conversion, but the programs hadn't worked. Geac's programmers thought they would be able to make the installation on the run, the week after conversion, but that hadn't worked out, either. Gorrie and Spencer, who had done the conversion testing, knew nothing about NXPD.

Leighton blew up. He realized instantly that even if he kept the processing going, accounts wouldn't be correctly up to date and ultimately risked becoming corrupted, compounding all the other errors the system was producing. He got rid of Van Damm. Leighton was learning about Geac on the go. He later reminisced that he couldn't have given Bell very good advice in the first couple of weeks—Bell wouldn't have known how bad it was—because he, Leighton, didn't know how bad it was. Now they knew.

Leighton had to drop everything else now and find extra processing time to fix NXPD quickly. He decided to cut cheque clearing, in addition to the ATM backlog, out of the overnight, saving it for the weekend, too. This threw administrative systems, which did the cheque clearing, into turmoil, because they couldn't process NSF cheques on time. Leighton also cut out people in the accounting department who were putting together journal records using the system. "Everybody was angry as hell," he remembered.

By the third week in December, Bell again found himself considering the possibility of closing VanCity's doors. Leighton remembered sitting with him, looking at the snow on the North Shore mountains and wondering if VanCity was going to survive. The debate, at the morning war-room meeting, went back and forth. Leighton convinced Bell to wait until after Christmas; the holidays might give them time to recoup some ground.

When the NXPD failure surfaced, Leighton had brought in Richard Wafer, Geac's regional development manager for British Columbia, to provide the Geac expertise he needed. Wafer knew intimately how the Geac system operated. He went to work with the programmers. They were packed along one wall, their desks crammed side by side against each other. Three managers worked out of a small office meant for one desk. The scene reminded Wafer of pictures of New York sweatshops in the 1920s— crowded, with people working long hours and exhausted all the time. There was surprisingly little absenteeism. The programmers, he realized, had already been destroyed by fatigue by the time the conversion date had come along. Leighton was calmly trying to hold them together. People would come into his office in despair. "We've had it," they would say. We can't carry on any more. That's the end of it." He would say, "Oh no, we've got to carry on. There's a lot more yet."

Judy Gorrie, meanwhile, would come home at two o'clock in the morning, sleep for four hours, get up, shower and go back to work before her family woke up. She went for days without seeing her son and husband. Her husband sometimes phoned her to ask if she had come home the previous night. "When are we going to see you?" he would ask. He could not understand why it went on that way, day after day. Ultimately he accused her of having an affair. "Look, I'm exhausted, I've got circles under my eyes," she said. "Do I really look like I'm fooling around with somebody else?"

"Well, this is stupid," he replied. "They can't do this to you."

She and her husband talked it out. Once over that hurdle, they were all right.

Staff who lived in the outlying suburbs brought sleeping bags and pillows to work. Several of them were put up at a nearby hotel. Gorrie often had to leave her car at VanCity and take a cab home, with VanCity picking up the tab, because she was too tired to drive. There were times when she did drive herself home, knowing that she should not be at the wheel.

Nobody was sure, even at this stage, where all the problems lay. However, Gorrie and the programmers knew some of the faults that came up had been fixed prior to conversion. Speculation arose that the software that had been plugged in was not the final tested version; somebody had loaded the wrong tape. There was no way of proving or disproving the theory, but it was the kind of error likely to happen when a group of exhausted people, pushed to the limit and panic-stricken, were putting a complex system together. The heart-sinking possibility that such a slip had been made, however, was shrugged off, since so much else was wrong at the same time. There was no point in tying oneself up in speculation. The root cause, everyone knew, was that too much had been tried in too short a time.

Several VanCity staff members quit. Two broke down under the stress. Many disgruntled members closed their accounts and went elsewhere. Unfortunately for those members, when they tried to close their accounts, the database often wasn't accessible to establish their balance and enable them to get their money out. This made them all the angrier.

The VanCity Christmas party rolled around. The computer people, suffering mental fatigue, decided to go to the party and kick up their heels. It would be the first real break for Judy Gorrie since the summer. The computer people joked about wearing dark glasses, false noses and trench coats, as a gag, so that they wouldn't be recognized. They ultimately decided, no, they would just go as they were and have a good time.

It was, Gorrie later thought, sardonically, a mistake. Six or seven of them walked in as a group. They were met by a loud scattering of boos. As she remembered the event, people came up to them and said, "Who the hell do you think you are? Why are you partying it up when you should be trying to get us out of the mess we're in? You have a helluva nerve." The odd person said, "So glad to see you, you people really deserve a break," but comments like this were few and far between. Management generally was gracious. The bitterness came from "little Janey Teller," as Gorrie put it acerbically. However, a couple of branch managers also were abusive to Gorrie. They seemed not to have an inkling of the effort the computer people were making to clean things up. "Four months slaving like a dog, giving blood, sweat and tears to this place, and to be treated like this," Gorrie thought. "How badly do I need this job?" Yet an underlying loyalty to VanCity, together with her own stubborn pride, kept her working.

They did make up ground over the holidays and had the NXPD file working by the end of the month. The danger of having to close passed, although VanCity was still in crisis. Bob Leighton had also discovered that a good deal of the GFS was either poorly written or redundant. He remembered in particular a code to handle French, which VanCity didn't need. The machines were running through routines that were useless, so Leighton began stripping back the GFS. He estimated that ultimately 40 per cent of the processing was pared away.

The situation the tellers faced in dealing with members was only slightly less desperate than before, even with the system available. A teller could chat about the weather, ask about the children, and trade stories about holidays for just so long, while waiting for the computer to respond. After that, blind patience set in, with the member staring at the teller, the teller staring at the screen and the others members waiting in the queue. Tellers might let a member leave before the computer responded, trusting that the response would appear and they could close off the transaction while doing the preliminary work with the next person in line. Some members, when they couldn't get their balances, became suspicious. Tellers were constantly pleading for members' patience. Occasionally a frustrated or suspicious member would rage openly.

The administrative systems people under Garry Smith were even more tightly squeezed, because cheque clearing, pushed back in the queue, still wasn't meeting its daily deadlines. Smith had agreed that the branches had to come first, because they dealt with members and were more important, but the delays for his people seemed interminable. At one point, his staff badly demoralized, he went over to computer services and let loose, yelling that they had better do something and do it right now so that his people could get their work done. There was open animosity against the computer people. "It was us and them," Smith said. "It was almost like the computer services area didn't belong to this organization anymore. They were disowned." Even Peter Cook, the usually calm chief financial officer, at one point couldn't restrain his anger and began shouting at Richard Wafer, who was directing the programmers.

The computer crew were, however, slowly getting the software under control and getting better at the overnight processing, like a cast of actors who had gone through enough rehearsals to manage a credible run-through. By the end of January, almost three months after conversion, they had turned the corner, although they would still occasionally keep the branches from coming up for an hour or two in the morning. Wafer at this stage took charge of operations for Leighton.

For Richard Wafer, life at work was scary, the system was so stretched. It was like being in a horror movie in which one never knew what malignant beast might suddenly crash in through a window. Wafer carried a pager. There was hardly a period of more than a few hours when he wasn't in touch with operations. There were times when he managed a full night's sleep, but not many. Even at this stage, he rarely saw a smile at the daily strategy meetings. He would desperately attempt to keep the discussion logical, but all the staff were under pressure, whether they were tellers being pushed by supervisors as lineups grew, or accounting people who did not have the necessary numbers before them. Priorities were set each Monday morning, but every once in a while, regardless, someone would come screaming into Wafer's office and insist that a fix be done right away.

The overnight processing would not have been so nightmarish had Leighton had access to other Geac machines for the programmers to use, which would have reduced the demand on VanCity's own system. He had been trying to procure more time from Geac but was never given enough. Bell threatened to sue Geac for $6 million for the fiasco, in particular for the NXPD failure. As part of the settlement, VanCity acquired four additional 8000s that had just become available—one to add to operations and three for a back-up site. Everyone could now see, with hindsight, that the three-unit configuration was the only way that the 8000s could manage the job, given that development programming and inserting the fixes had to be done at the same time.

Wafer was ingenious at maximizing the programmers' use of the system's time. He and his programmers worked out ways of doing different processing tasks in parallel or in lockstep instead of in sequence. This required meticulous, synchronized timing. Wafer produced a multi-level flow chart for the purpose and put his team through the drill every day so that everyone understood where their task fitted in. Wafer also managed to modify cheque clearing so that it could continue on-line during branch hours. The process was called drip-feeding. The concept had been around before conversion but hadn't tested satisfactorily. It worked like an intravenous feed to an ambulant hospital patient. The batch data would be fed into the system in a thin stream until the on-line volume from the branches became too great, and the drip-feeding would have to be cut off until the branches closed.

Sometimes, during the day, the computer would also inexplicably stop functioning. An account that had been converted with inconsistent data would confuse the computer, and it would try to do something again and again, not letting anyone else into the system. Technicians would have to jump in and figure out what was wrong. Occasionally, when that happened, they would get a "broken record"—lose the chain of data—and would painfully have to recreate it.

Wafer's team also were doing reconstruction work, running fixer programs through the database and finding accounts that needed repair. "Draining swamps," Margo Spencer called it. Most of this work was done on weekends, but some was also done on the live database during weekdays. This high-pressure juggling of time and the pumping through of fixes continued month after month. "It seemed like an eternity," Larry Wald remembered. At the branch level, nothing appeared to have changed. The response time was still slow, the lineups still huge, and the overtime hours still long. Frustration, anger and disappointment ate away endlessly at the tellers' minds. Week after week and month after month, the tellers told members—whom they had told a week ago and a month ago—that things were going to get better, and they never did.

Wayne McKay, head of branch operations, and Larry Wald and John Iseli, the two district managers, were caught in the middle like emissaries daily crossing the lines in a civil war, trying to keep emotions down. Wald remembered trying to create an air of realistic optimism. He would go into a branch after the morning update and be reassuring and encouraging, while he knew, in his heart of hearts, that things were not going to get any better for a while. He had to at least put on an acceptable front, for the staff if not for the managers, so that they felt they were going to come out of the black hole one day.

It took six months, until the spring of 1986, before Leighton, Wafer and their team had the system in good shape. Operationally, however, they were barely making it through the daily overnight on time. The system was functioning at maximum capability, so any additional problem meant that it would not be available when the branches opened. Wald remembered a contretemps with Leighton over delayed preparations for a new branch as late as August, nine months after conversion.

Wafer spent the next year streamlining the operation so that there was a little more recovery time when a problem surfaced and so they could get through each night without heroic effort. Errors made by the conversion kept sporadically appearing, like abandoned landmines exploding in a war-torn country finally at peace. In 1990, with computer operations back in-house and Wafer running the shop, VanCity finally converted to the Geac 9000. Some 1985 mistakes remained in the database, yet to be discovered. They were carried through the subsequent conversion as well. "We never cleaned them up totally," Gorrie said.

The post-mortems were personal, bitter and contradictory, overladen by the trauma that the whole organization had suffered. Gorrie put the blame on Bruce Higgs and the layer of management below him. She felt she could not blame Bell because nobody had been honest with him. Higgs should have told Bell to "stop right now," even if he got fired for doing so. Gorrie admitted, however, that Higgs was not a techie and himself depended on the information he received. Her own bosses, who did know where the project was, had been too wimpy, she said. They weren't aggressive enough with Higgs. She was angry at all of them.

For Richard Wafer, the conversion had been flawed from the start, in its very conception. The dual 8000s weren't adequate, and the project wasn't given enough time. "Somebody should have stood up at the beginning and said this quite simply isn't possible, and nobody did," he said.

Leighton at first considered Bruce Higgs responsible, for Higgs was clearly in charge. It was, however, Leighton thought, a difficult point. Larry Bell was the new man; Higgs was trying to please him and didn't want to come in late and fail on the job. Geac in turn did not want to admit that it couldn't meet the deadline, because Higgs had been so adamant. Higgs, unfortunately, did not have the technical capability to understand what he was forcing people to do. Then there was the VanCity culture, with its people wanting to have their own unique processing system—hence all the modifications, most of which, in Leighton's view, they could have done without. The greatest responsibility, he thought, lay with Geac's project director, Vince Van Damm, who had assured Higgs that the conversion could go ahead, when especially the NXPD file hadn't been ready.

Larry Bell reflected Leighton's view. He had not been aware of the risk that had been taken. Later Bell asked himself if he, as CEO, had done sufficient due diligence to verify the adequacy of the planning and testing. That was really the question, he thought.

Van Damm, himself, was tight-lipped about what had happened.

The conversion poisoned the relationship between Bell and Higgs. Shortly after, there was a parting of the ways, and Higgs left VanCity. Bell said it was because Higgs was conservative. Bell's own style wasn't quite as conservative as was expected in a financial institution, and the fit between them turned out not to be as good as it might have been. Higgs, for his part, said he had been nervous about the conversion time frame. He increasingly saw Bell as autocratic. The rushed implementation of the conversion was just another example of Bell's weakness, for Higgs. Higgs had been bruised by the conversion failure. The two no longer could get along. Higgs too, in his anguish over the episode, assigned responsibility to Leighton. Leighton was a friend of Larry Bell's and had Bell's ear and so, in Higgs' mind, was somehow the real force behind what had happened.

It was, in the end, more than a matter of misjudgement, or even of Bell's formal responsibility as CEO. Bell had created an atmosphere in which the pace was always forced. A project manager or division manager, faced with the drum-beating message from the top that the task had to be done by Remembrance Day weekend, was not likely to talk back, nor was anyone else.

The conversion crisis left behind strong feelings, etched forever in residual memory. "I will never forget those weeks," Bell recounted. Whenever he thought of them, he was attacked by a wave of nausea, like a malarial fever coming back. He understood more deeply than before how important people were. He marvelled at what they had gone through. If the staff had not seen themselves as part of the organization, Bell thought, the credit union would not have survived a week.

Without the loyalty of members, too, Wayne McKay reflected, VanCity would have never made it and would simply no longer be around. VanCity had built up goodwill with them over so many years. While the members might not have liked the long waits, the credit union obviously had a big problem on its hands, so they decided that the right thing to do was to stand by it.

Judy Gorrie compartmentalized those months, in her mind, as "the past," as different from the VanCity for which she had an abiding affection. She was bitter about those events and bitter, too, for having let herself be used as a doormat, for working ridiculous hours and rarely getting a thank you from people in other parts of the organization.

Richard Wafer, later, unable to recall the details of all the errors the system had made, joked, "Thank God I can't remember. It's wiped from my mind." When he managed the switchover from the Geac 8000 to the Geac 9000 in 1990, he was not allowed to use the word "conversion." He was obliged to refer to it as an "upgrade." A subsequent, major conversion was done in 1992. It went without event. Wafer's biggest difficulty then was not a technical one. It was convincing others that a conversion could work, because there were still enough people around who remembered 1985.

They referred to themselves as "85ers." "I think I'd just like to exorcise the thing," Wafer laughed in 1992. "It's all over. It's like the Americans talk about Vietnam. I've done '85 and I don't want to ever do it again."

CHAPTER 51

Young Man,
Will Innovate

"I WAS BORN SOMETIME BETWEEN *Bonanza* and *Wayne and Shuster*," David Levi liked to joke. They were two of the popular Sunday evening television programs in the 1950s, when Levi appeared in the world. Later, Lorne Greene, the star of *Bonanza*, would shill for the Bank of British Columbia in television commercials, and not long after that, a credit union of all things, VanCity, would almost succeed in taking over the bank. The chair of the credit union was a young, barefoot, bearded boy with cheek, David Levi. He had always been interested in trying new things and learning about them, and if one had the chance to take over a bank, why not do it?

Levi grew up socialist, Zionist and democratic, in a family milieu that freed the imagination. His father, a social worker and parole officer, was to become minister of human resources in an NDP provincial government. His mother, Gloria, was a storefront social activist in the East End. When Levi turned thirteen, he began going to Camp Miriam, a Habonim (Labour Zionist) summer camp on Gabriola Island in the Gulf Islands. One learned about Israel at the camp. Its focus was on the kibbutz and the socialist, co-operative ethic of the kibbutz movement. Levi became attached to the kibbutz philosophy and ended up, when he was sixteen years old, on the organization's North American board, made up of teenagers like himself. At University Hill High School in Point Grey—an experimental school within the public school system—he was a radical and rabble rouser and belonged to a students' rights group. He edited the school paper, where he railed against the system. His marks were good, but halfway through Grade 12, he left school from boredom. He was going to a Habonim board meeting in New York. He left a letter with a friend to give to his parents, letting them know he wasn't coming back and neglecting to give them an address where they might track him down. He had $50 in his pocket.

His picaresque adventures were just beginning. He was bright and curious, and interested in the world. He worked as a shipper in a small shoe factory in the Montreal garment district. He made it to Israel and a kibbutz, where he learned all about egg production. Back in Vancouver, he became a family worker for the Browndale Care Society, which operated homes for

404

disturbed children and adolescents. Then he became a special services worker in North Vancouver, helping families in crisis. He did another stint in Israel, on a kibbutz, this time as a dairyman. Back in British Columbia, through a series of coincidences, he became captain of a small gillnet troller, fishing off the coast. Having earned enough money, he travelled through the southern United States and then caught a plane to Hawaii, en route to Australia. Somebody there got him a job as a handyman with a condominium complex, on the north end of the island of Maui. He became manager, then got a real estate licence and ended up selling the complex. He made a lot of money in Maui.

He had a business mentor there, a retired U.S. Army and Pentagon veteran. The older man talked to Levi about the difference between real estate and stocks and generated an interest in Levi in the stock market. Levi at that point picked up a book that changed his life— *The Unseen Revolution*, by Peter Drucker, a famous American management guru. Its subtitle was, "How pension fund socialism came to America." His thesis in the book was that by the year 2000, workers would own the means of production through their pension funds. Drucker argued, among other things, that while employees might own companies in this way, they should not control them. This intrigued Levi. He realized there could be another side to the same coin: workers could indeed control those companies.

Saul Alinsky, a well-known radical American activist, was another seminal influence on Levi. Alinsky was famous for his ingenious, unorthodox approaches to applying pressure for change particularly on behalf of the poor. On the opposite side of the ideological fence from Drucker, he had written books entitled *Rules for Radicals* and *Reveille for Radicals*. What intrigued Levi most about Alinsky was that in Alinsky's last few years, before he died in 1972, he had come to the conclusion that real power lay in amassing middle-class and institutional shareholdings in corporate America. Using those shareholdings, one could take resolutions to the floor of annual meetings and agitate for corporate responsibility.

There were two possibilities for improving the lot of working people, Levi thought, and for applying the maximum leverage to change the powers that be. One was through politics, but that was far too dicey. Besides, he wasn't ready for a political career. The other option, illuminated in different ways by Drucker and Alinsky, was through share ownership. Levi pondered the idea. He decided it would be a good time to enter the brokerage community and get some hands-on experience. His long-term goal was to work with labour unions and invest their funds.

He returned to Vancouver and took the securities course and also courses in economics and commerce at Simon Fraser University. He was offered a position by a national brokerage house but chose instead a firm whose head office was in British Columbia, where eventually he could be more than just a broker. He worked closely with an experienced fellow-broker who ran a high-quality "investment grade" business that did not rely on the daily fluctuations in the market. The older colleague stopped Levi from doing anything silly. Levi developed the same kind of business—managing investment portfolios for his clients. He saw offering advice, rather than buying and selling stock, as his primary function.

Levi turned out to be good at what he did. He snuck into the top ten brokers in his firm after a couple of years. He was an oddity: a child of socialism who was a stockbroker. He had no cultural block against it, however, nor any ideological block. He was attracted by the economic power that one might capture through it. Besides, he said, he had no cultural block against anything. He would try something just for the novelty of it.

He was now a successful stockbroker. In Maui and working in the kibbutzim in Israel, he had learned about pricing, markets, operating costs, bookkeeping and financial decision-making, and had taken several extension courses to add to his skills. Running for the board of VanCity, another co-operative—one of those economic powers that could be shaped into a real force—seemed a natural thing to do.

Levi had joined VanCity when he was sixteen, at Branch 4 in Kitsilano. It was a political decision on his part, motivated by his parents, because VanCity was a co-operative. He remembered that when he went to the counter, happy, smiling people came up to him. Being interested in everything in those days, he also remembered the material VanCity sent to him regularly—annual reports and *Working Dollars*—which he did not get from anywhere else.

The only time Levi had ever been a customer of a bank was when he had worked one winter in Ottawa as an executive assistant to an NDP member of Parliament. He opened an account at a downtown branch of the Canadian Imperial Bank of Commerce because it was just a block away from his office. He was stunned by the long line-ups and limited hours of operation. Most of all, he was taken aback by the attitude of the tellers. The difference, he thought, was that when people took their money to a credit union, it was still their money, but when they took it to a bank, it seemed, it became the bank's money. This was new to him. His sojourn as a CIBC customer lasted all of two visits. He was so annoyed and angry with his experience, that he raised the subject with his wife and they decided to move their account to the nearest credit union, although it was much farther away and less convenient. The staff there were genuinely friendly. If Levi hadn't been a credit union member for life when he arrived in Ottawa, he was shortly after.

David Levi had always taken a boyish enjoyment in facing new situations. His skirmishes with the VanCity board over procedure when he first ran for election, were, for him, comic rather than tragic. His threatening them with a writ for limiting his freedom of speech he thought of as "one of those Saul Alinsky moments"—an ingenious activist manoeuvre to be savoured.

His first board meeting was the routine one at which the chair and vice-chair were chosen, followed by a friendly dinner and get-together, at which new board members were made part of the family. Levi got the cold shoulder from the long-time board members. "If there was ice in this world," he quipped, it was all located in that room." On his way out, VanCity lawyer Bill Wright took him aside and said, "You have a billion dollars of the members' money in your hands. You're going to find this a more sobering responsibility than just being a candidate in a position to criticize. I think you're a very intelligent individual and can apply yourself to the interest of the members."

Levi was astonished at the presumption. He walked out thinking, "What a schmuck!"

"It was just lucky that I was only twenty-nine," he recounted, "and too stupid to respond."

He later had a preliminary meeting with Geoff Hook. It was a cold meeting because the relationships between all of them on the two sides, at that point, were cold. One of his first assignments, as a director, was negotiating with B.C. Central. That wasn't any better. "The animosity between VanCity and the rest of the system was palpable when you walked into a room," he remembered.

None of this fazed him. He had too open and eager a disposition. His situation on the board improved rapidly. He and fellow Action Slate members Bob Williams and Darlene Marzari did not get together in advance of board meetings. They just showed up and were immediately plunged into questions about the operation. Almost from the first day, votes were not an issue. The board's work in common seemed to generate consensus.

Levi joined the audit committee and the board's newly established financial policy committee. He was learning. The financial policy committee returned to the board active control of lending policy and of the review of large loans—a throwback to the board's original credit committee. Levi found working through the non-performing commercial real estate loans to be a horrendous task. He became convinced more than ever that those loans had put Vancity in jeopardy. Digging into the details, nevertheless, was intriguing, because of the sheer complication of it. Shortly after, the board put in place a formal policy to measure large loans against the risk they represented to the capital base (members' share equity plus retained earnings), in order to forestall the development of any threat to the credit union.

Levi saw the old board as tired. Several of its members, he thought, had just been there too long. Everything was generated by management, with the board reviewing proposals and handing them back. As he and Williams in particular, however, began tackling management's presentations and asking for more information, the other board members became increasingly interested. The dynamics changed.

Levi and Williams were temperamental opposites. Williams was shy, intense, partisan and freely scornful and mistrustful of the enemy. He regarded Levi as young, green and undeserving just as the others did. Levi was less partisan, more easygoing and forgiving. He had a high regard for Sandra Sutherland—whom Williams had caustically dismissed—despite their not seeing eye to eye on many things. He regarded Sutherland as one of the toughest, brightest, most committed people he knew. He was articulate and energetic. Shirley Chan, who joined the board later, remembered being dazzled by Levi—he was so young and so intelligent.

By the fall of his first year, Levi felt that the board was working well together. He tried to ignore the feelings under the surface. The older directors were losing a bit of their hard edge towards the newcomers. When Stan Parsons suddenly resigned as chair in early 1985, Levi, although the youngest by far of the directors at the time—he was only thirty—was unanimously elected to replace him. He was the one person with whom everybody on the board could feel comfortable. He joked that he was either the most liked or the least hated, and that one would never be able to tell from what went on around the boardroom table.

He was immersed by this time in the final showdown between VanCity and Central. It had begun with the very first regular VanCity board meeting he had attended. The board had passed a resolution authorizing participation, with the Richmond, Surrey, and WestCoast credit unions, in a study on pulling out of Central. Larry Bell was CEO by this time, but the genesis of the resolution lay with Geoff Hook and the previous board. Levi was puzzled. He asked a lot of questions but didn't get a lot of answers. "You're new here, just take our word for it, we're leaving Central, period," the other directors seemed to be saying. Levi remembered being struck by how strangely vociferous they were.

Levi, however, young and idealistic, wanted to keep VanCity in the movement. There was a growing feeling in some of the other larger credit unions, particularly among management, that they had outgrown the credit union ideal and that operating within the regulatory framework of a credit union was too restrictive. Surrey even called its members "customers," a sinful practice in credit union terms, and later would issue non-voting shares on the Toronto Stock Exchange—shares representing ownership of the credit union, although not control. Levi and the Action Slate, on the other hand, had a philosophical commitment to the democratic idealism of the movement. They had become involved in order to bring VanCity back to the community and its roots. They calculated that by remaining in Central and keeping the other large credit unions inside the family, too, they could, at least indirectly, influence the whole movement in the same way. Levi asked the board if he could go to Central and see what he could do. "They just looked at me like a young pup," he recalled, "and said 'you're wasting your time, but if you want to bang your head against the wall, feel free.'"

He entered into a seemingly endless series of meetings with Central and its key players. "I'm just a kid," he laughed, as he described the anomaly of it. The encounter began with several Central people verbally tearing into him. He didn't understand what was happening. Gradually he realized that no matter how lightly he tiptoed into the room, he would be screamed at.

The participants sat around in a circle many layers deep. Levi brought Larry Bell along with him. Somehow Bell would work himself around the circle so that Levi could see him. Whenever Levi wanted to be sure he was moving in the right direction, he would look up at Bell. Bell would think about the issue for a moment and shake or nod his head. The idea was to be in a family discussion, but it quickly became clear that they were in fact negotiating. Since the unlikely Levi carried a big stick—the possibility of VanCity and other large credit unions leaving Central—the talk came down to finding out what VanCity was prepared to live with.

In the end, Levi and the negotiators for the other large credit unions walked away with everything they wanted. They were granted proportional voting rights based on the number of members in the credit union, which gave VanCity 17 per cent of the votes at Central meetings. Central was to stop all commercial lending, except to its own credit union and co-operative members. The financial margin from reserves and other deposits would not be used by Central management to subsidize non-financial services, which were to be self-supporting, either through dues or on a fee-for-service basis. VanCity, Levi had explained, would not mind paying its share of collective Central programs, like lobbying or the development of products for the whole system, but it wanted a chance to vote on them. Finally, Central would scale back the level of capital contributions it had originally been after.

The proposed pact was known as the Nanoose Accord, after Nanoose Bay, north of Nanaimo, where the Central board had hammered it out in the summer of 1984. Levi made an impassioned plea to the VanCity board to accept the deal. The older directors, Levi laughed, although they now had everything they had been after all those years, hated the deal. They voted against it. It was as if, having waited so long, it was bitter fruit and no longer mattered. Three new Action Slate directors, on the other hand, just elected, knew nothing about the twenty-five-year feud that had split the movement and weren't about to approve anything so drastic as leaving Central. They and the three other Action Slate directors carried the day. Ratification of the Nanoose Accord by Central's member credit unions was the equivalent, in the movement, to a Middle East peace pact between the children of Ishmael and the children of Isaac.

It had taken Levi the better part of a year. He was getting to know Larry Bell. He appreciated Bell's mentoring, high energy and skill in getting along with a pro-active board he might not always agree with. Unlike Williams, Levi had no illusions about Bell's political inclinations. He took it for granted that Bell was a right-winger. This, however, was no problem for Levi. The two of them met every week in Bell's office. They would fly their crazy ideas by each other and then talk about what they could do practically.

The Action Slate now had a majority on the board. Between Bell's manic energy and Williams' and Levi's own push to do things, the changes and innovations followed on each other faster and faster. Levi remembered that the VanCity employees' heads were just spinning, so much was going on. The organization was flying. The "big fun time," he called it.

Bell was having trouble getting the credit rating for the Euro-issue. VanCity was a small player in New York terms, so the process had slowed down, after a year of preparation. The delay was impairing VanCity's ability to lend. Bell decided to take Levi with him to New York, to speed things up. Levi's role was to help inject a sense of urgency into the process by his presence.

The idea struck Levi as comical, especially since he was only thirty-one years old. Standard & Poors, it was explained, however, was an old china-tea-set crowd. Prestige meant a lot to them. They would be impressed by who showed up. Bell, Levi and their agent from Shearson Lehman were scheduled to meet with Standard & Poors's North American president. When they arrived, the Shearson Lehman man introduced them. "This is Larry Bell, CEO of VanCity Savings," he said, "and this is the chairman, David Levi." The Standard & Poors officer did a doubletake. "Excuse me," he said, "I'll have to go and get our chairman." He disappeared and ten minutes later walked in with Standard & Poors's international chair, re-establishing equality.

Levi followed instructions. His job was to listen confidently while his minion, the mere CEO, did the talking. From time to time he was to interject gravely and paternalistically with comments like "We need to get this moving along" and "We've been working hard on this application." Standard & Poors's chair, meanwhile, had not been involved before. Now that he was engaged in the matter, it became his own and so it had to be pursued. The credit rating cleared in a couple of months. "Boom, we were done," Levi laughed.

He was growing into the role. In media interviews, he liked portraying the banks as sitting in fear of the dynamic VanCity. "They hate us," he once told the *Globe and Mail.* "We are the competition in this city. I would say they're petrified." The reporter felt obliged to point out that Levi was overstating the case, but he quoted Levi anyway, and the patter conveyed the spirit of a rambunctious, bold giant killer against whom no bank was too big.

One late afternoon in 1985, at Levi and Bell's regular weekly brainstorming session, the question of mutual funds came up. Mutual funds meant investing in stock markets—the kind of financial game-playing that would have appalled the early credit union pioneers. Both the board and management favoured a mutual fund. Levi himself was a stockbroker. Management felt that with the changing banking system, where banks were free to get into other areas, VanCity had to provide additional, competing products, one of which was mutual funds. Don Bentley had first raised the idea of VanCity providing mutual funds back in 1965, when they were still a minor phenomenon. The board now, led by Levi and a new director, Steve Waddell, a former freelance journalist, wanted a fund with ethical criteria.

This was Saul Alinsky strategy, based on the belief that money is not neutral in its impact on the community and that one should take social criteria, not just financial criteria, into account in making investment decisions. Levi and Bell argued the issue. Bell worked hard at talking Levi out of it. It wasn't that Bell was unethical; he just didn't think there was a market for it. "Fringy," he called it. They would be catering to 1 per cent of the population when it was the 99 per cent they had to rely on. He was nervous about the label that would be put on it.

Bell was reflecting the times. There was no such creature as an ethical mutual fund in Canada, although several did exist in the United States. Corporate ethics were not a major issue in Canada. Wild financial games, associated in particular with mergers and acquisitions, were taking over centre stage on Wall Street. Next to that hard, glitzy, fashionable, seemingly ultra-modern world and its Bay Street derivative, Levi appeared to be a naive do-gooder.

Bell also came up with several theoretical studies showing that ethical investing would end up with lower results. The premise was that if one limited the number of stocks one could choose from, one would come up with fewer winners. Levi rejected the argument. For all the theoretical extrapolations on the issue, he pointed out, there were no factual studies showing the predicted negative effect. The only thing that counted was which stocks one actually chose for one's fund. With a larger universe, one could just as easily choose extra bad ones as extra good ones.

Bell proposed that VanCity offer two funds, one a standard fund for members who preferred it and the other for members who wanted the ethics. Levi joked that, dummy as he was, he could see through that. It was obvious where the marketing and sales resources would go. He insisted that VanCity would have only one fund and that it was going to be an ethical fund. They had done a survey of members with $5,000 or more in RRSPs, showing that 22 per cent would be likely to invest in an equity mutual fund. When the ethical criteria were added, another 12 per cent would be likely to consider it, while almost all of those originally inclined were still favourable. Investment intentions aside, two-thirds of those surveyed liked the idea of an ethical fund.

The board gave the go-ahead. Bell brought in Bob Quart, the manager of the trust services division, to create the fund. Quart had experience in starting mutual funds and obtaining regulatory approval, in a previous life at Montreal Trust. Unlike Bell, he thought the idea was fundamentally good. There were more than a hundred Canadian-equity mutual funds in the country. Strictly from a marketing perspective, having one with a unique angle to it was a benefit. He had also seen the marketing research showing it would work well.

Management brought forward a long list of possible names for the fund, including the "Purer Than Thou Fund," but none of the proposals hit the mark. Levi had learned, from naming other things in the past, to focus on basic function. He suggested "Ethical Growth Fund." That was it. Everyone agreed it was right.

Establishing the criteria—the ethical screens—wasn't so easy. An ad hoc committee of directors worked on them. Quart sat in. The committee members began shouting out their favourite screens, like commodity traders yelling in a commodity exchange. Somebody said "nuclear energy," and Levi wrote that on the blackboard. Someone else said "South Africa," and that went up. Quart watched in amazement as item after item went up on the blackboard. At the end, they had thirty criteria. "They're out of their minds," Quart muttered to himself. There were so many screens that the committee members had narrowed the field almost to the point where, given the amorality of corporate business, they couldn't buy anything.

Fortunately for Quart, Levi also knew that they had to cut back the number of screens. The committee decided that, in order to establish credibility, only black and white criteria would be accepted. They wanted to be absolutely sure they could follow through. They began, on that basis, taking off items one at a time. Environmental criteria were dropped, because deciding how dirty a company had to be before it was too dirty was a grey area. On the other hand, if a company earned just 1 per cent of its revenue from weapons production or had one employee in South Africa, it was out. It was in danger of becoming the "Somewhat Ethical Fund," someone quipped as another screen was removed.

Ultimately the committee boiled the list down to five criteria. For inclusion in the fund, the company had to have (1) a Canadian head office, (2) progressive industrial relations (no union busting or discrimination), (3) operations only in countries with racial equality, (4) no normal involvement in supplying the military and (5) in the case of energy companies and utilities, major sources of revenue that were non-nuclear. A Vancouver investment firm, Connor, Clark & Lunn, was chosen to manage the fund. Quart had recommended they use such an external investment house instead of managing the fund internally, because the fund would not be big enough by itself to enable VanCity to hire the best people.

The last element to be patched in was the fees. Mutual funds were all "front-end load" in those days, and the average commission rate was 9 per cent. The board rejected this as plain gouging. It set the commission at 3 per cent for members who bought fund units through VanCity, and a maximum of 5 per cent for purchases made through brokers. This policy probably cost the fund some sales at brokerage offices, but it set the tone.

Quart surprised everyone by having the prospectus drawn up and filed and the launch ready to go in just a couple of months, by early 1986, catching the end of the RRSP season. Management estimated the fund would take in $3 million in the first year. Levi predicted $10 million. A reception was held for brokers and the media in a downtown hotel—the requisite dog-and-pony show. Bell, by this time, was beginning to enjoy the prospect. The symbol of the Ethical Growth Fund was a dove. VanCity handed out dove pins for the occasion. Long after leaving VanCity, Bell still had his dove pin.

It was the first socially conscious fund in Canada and caught the public's imagination. "Investments with a conscience" became its advertising slogan. Because of some national media coverage and the flood of inquiries that came with it, Levi and Quart then decided quickly to take the fund national, which they did late that October, in Toronto. They had set up the fund to operate through brokerage firms as well as through VanCity branches with just such an opportunity in mind.

A few brokers expressed incredulity that one could mix investment practices and social criteria. On the other hand, social groups, like some churches that were invited, said it was about time. Unexpectedly, the media coverage exploded. Levi and Quart could not believe the amount of attention their little fund was generating. "Thousands and thousands of pages of print, free print around the world, radio interviews around the world," it seemed to Quart. CBC television's business show did a feature on Levi and the fund. General-audience radio shows, like CBC's *Morningside*, as well as business shows, broadcast items. On one of them, Levi debated a well-known financial commentator who said the fund would never fly, would get mediocre results. If people believed in ethics, they should go to church. The argument went back and forth. Levi had heard these criticisms many times before, and played off them like an entertainer. Later, the same commentator publicly ate crow and became a backer of the fund. Quart, who was from Quebec City and whose first language was French, did interviews with the French-language media. A reporter from *La Presse* told him that everybody was referring to the VanCity fund as the Granola Fund. The moniker became a badge of honour. The *Globe and Mail*'s glossy *Report on Business Magazine* did a feature story on VanCity as a whole, with Levi and Bob Williams featured.

The fund raised $10 million in its first twelve months, just as Levi had predicted. It did much more than establish the market niche that was anticipated. It was new, different and pioneering and powerfully enhanced VanCity's image. The publicity surrounding it gave VanCity a national presence. It also made VanCity an even greater force in British Columbia. Once the media began working on stories on the Granola Fund angle, they discovered the rest of the credit union, like the Euro-issue and the attempted takeover of the Bank of British Columbia, which also happened in 1986. The *Financial Post*'s book on the one hundred best companies to work for, with VanCity among the leaders, came out that year, too. All this had spin-offs, bringing business to Vancity outside of the mutual fund itself.

The fringe image that Bell had worried about had not materialized. Bell, Quart, Levi and the others happily soaked up the publicity. They had a unique and tremendously successful product. The success also said something to them about the continuing inventiveness of the organization. It was a link, for them, to the bright VanCity innovations of the past that they knew about but had not lived through. In 1987 Ethical Growth Fund assets rose to $18 million and, in the next year, to $24 million.

With the fund established, Levi and the board then began applying its activist potential. Out of four hundred companies that investment manager Connor, Clark & Lunn followed for investment purposes, about seventy fell afoul of the ethical screen. A letter went out letting them know why they were excluded and asking them what plans they had to change.

In the summer of 1987, with the market in a long and record ascent, Bell and Quart met with Connor, Clark & Lunn for a regular review. They were feeling risk averse. They thought the market might be losing its steam. They were not trying for clairvoyance; they simply wanted to be a little conservative. The main objective, in their minds, was to build a respectable track record, not to shoot for the sky. They went to cash. That fall, the market took a dive and the Ethical Growth Fund looked inspired. It was 72 per cent cashed out the day the crash occurred. Two days after that, the fund started buying back in, at bargain prices. For its first three-year and five-year periods, it was one of the top-performing Canadian equity funds, sustained by that decision.

Subsequently the screen was broadened to cover environmental issues and to exclude tobacco companies. Levi was satisfied that the fund's reputation for applying ethical standards was good enough that it could now move into what he called the "grey screen," where pressure could be applied for degrees of compliance. The fund did not necessarily sell off its shareholdings when a company was retrogade in, say, taking steps to reduce its environmental impact. Levi instead asked environmentalists whether they wanted the fund to be active as a shareholder, writing letters and being their voice at annual shareholder meetings. Almost always they chose that option.

Levi discovered two financial advantages to ethical screens. Because they required extra research into companies, the investment manager sometimes came across financial problems that had not been revealed by the normal financial analysis. Second, violating the screens would often catch up with a company. A polluter, for example, would sooner or later be called to task by government and forced to make large clean-up expenditures. Investors who held stocks in the company would take a beating, but the Ethical Growth Fund would emerge unscathed.

Saul Alinsky, Levi thought, would have been proud.

CHAPTER 52

The Bank Caper

DAVID LEVI AND LARRY BELL approached 1500 West Georgia in Vancouver. The office tower was at the western end of the street, towards Stanley Park, physically removed and distant in ambience from the city's central financial district around the matrix of West Hastings and Howe streets, further east. A long, low waterfall sliced across the plaza. In its cold, modernistic isolation, it looked like a piece of earth art that some eccentric outdoor artist had stuck in a desert. Atop the office tower, like an aerie, were the sprawling offices of Edgar Kaiser Jr., with their broad entrance way and pictures of massive coal trucks. Kaiser, an American scion of the industrialist Kaiser family, was a local business legend and the person Levi and Bell had come to see.

Kaiser was well-known for having charmed the British Columbia Resources Investment Corporation (BCRIC) into buying control of Kaiser Resources, the owner of coal mines in the East Kootenay. He had done it near the top of the market cycle and with a 70 per cent takeover bonus thrown in. BCRIC, which had been created by a privatization of provincially owned companies, never recovered from the purchase. The gregarious Kaiser, meanwhile, with his share of the proceeds, became a financier, doing money-market placements and venture-capital investments.

In 1984, Kaiser pulled off another coup—one that, unlike the slick coal sale, made him a business hero. Because of the 1981-82 recession, which had hit the West particularly hard, the Bank of British Columbia was in trouble. The bank wasn't just an ordinary financial institution. It was the outcome of British Columbians' long-standing historical grievance against the older banks controlled in Toronto and Montreal. Many of its customers had begun using the bank as a result of their regional patriotism. Kaiser, in the role of a western regionalist, stepped in. He became chair of the bank and set about to rescue it with his effervescent energy. He threw in $6 million of his own money, dramatically demonstrating his confidence in the bank, as part of a successful recapitalization campaign.

Levi did not know why he and Bell were there. Despite the bank's continuing difficulties, all the media commentators were certain it would survive. Levi had simply received a call from Bell that Kaiser would like to see them and had gone along to find out what Kaiser had in mind. He took it for granted, though, that Bell and Kaiser between them had something in the hopper.

Levi had met Kaiser before, at a small dinner rendezvous on another matter. Kaiser had impressed him as bright, interesting and open. They had talked, among other things, about the banking scene. It became clear to Levi that Kaiser, who had been chair of the Bank of British Columbia for just a few months, did not understand just how unique a business banking was.

Kaiser now received his guests with a kaleidoscopic description of his own private operations and the impressive dollar figure they were turning over. It seemed to Levi that he was puffing up the scale of his activities, as if it weren't enough to be seen to be big; one had to portray oneself as a financial superman. Then the party proceeded into the boardroom, which was very large, with a large table. "It killed me," Levi laughed, "because it must have seated fifty people and this was a guy who ran the whole operation himself." At the end of the table were white marker boards. Bell sat on one side, Levi on the other. Kaiser was quickly up and selling. He talked about the Bank of British Columbia, its marketplace and where its branches were, and then about VanCity and its operations. He outlined the dynamics of what would happen if the two were combined. The bank was strong on the small-business side. VanCity was strong on the retail side and was also advanced technically. The efficiencies of a merger were apparent. Together they would become the largest financial institution in the province.

What form this new institution would take was ill-defined. It could either be a regular commercial bank like the Bank of British Columbia, or it could become a co-operative bank in which members could buy and sell shares, although each member would have some. Levi had a hard time seizing exactly what Kaiser had in mind. The proposal had an ethereal quality. Levi was left with the impression, however, that over time the organization would lose its relationship to the membership. Who would do what in the new organization, on the other hand, was well laid out in the scenario. According to Levi's account, he, Levi, was to be the chair, Bell the CEO and Kaiser the president. It was a long presentation. Finally, with a flourish, Kaiser ended up. "So what do you think?" he asked Levi.

Levi stopped for a minute to collect his thoughts. "I don't know what the hell I'm doing here with these people," he said to himself. Kaiser had no idea what it was like to work with the board of VanCity. Besides, VanCity was a membership-driven organization.

Levi looked up and said, "Edgar, I can only see this working one way, and that's if we take you over."

Kaiser's face fell. "Well, I just don't see that as a possibility," he replied. "We're doing just fine."

The conversation ended. In just a few minutes, Bell and Levi hit the street. Kaiser, back in his office, was miffed. Definitely a question of ego, he thought of Levi's attitude. Bell, too, was disconcerted. He had hopes for a combined, larger organization—a regional bank that would break through the restrictions imposed by the credit union system. He wasn't wedded philosophically to credit unionism. VanCity was big as credit unions went, but small compared with the banks in the rest of the country. A merger would make VanCity, or whatever the new organization was called, a force that could stand up to the chartered banks and also have an international face. Maybe it could be a mutual bank, like one he knew in Washington State, Bell thought. Levi conceded that the merger made economic sense, but VanCity was a membership organization and there was no way, he told Bell, that the membership and the board would agree to surrender that. It ran against the grain of everything the board believed in.

It seemed the matter was dead. By the fall of 1986, however, the bank was in touch with Bell again. Several major loans had gone sideways. Sooner or later, the loans would have to be posted as non-performing, the bank would show a loss, it would not be able to declare a dividend on its preferred shares and, from these accumulated woes, it would suffer a fatal crisis of confidence. The shareholders, unfortunately, had already poured in extra share capital for the first rescue and could not be looked to again. The Northland Bank and the Canadian Commercial Bank had gone belly up not too long earlier, in Alberta, which added a mood of foreboding.

The major Canadian banks weren't a good bet as possible purchasers because their branch distribution networks were almost identical to the Bank of British Columbia. A sale to any one of them would mean that most of the bank's branches and its head office would simply be wound up. In despair, the bank approached the Hongkong and Shanghai Banking Corporation, but it had other plans at the time. Somebody then thought of VanCity again. There didn't seem to be any other alternative. Kaiser, who was still chair of the bank, turned the matter over to the president, Dale Parker.

Both sides met furtively one Sunday evening in the bank's boardroom to discuss the possibilities. Parker, a traditional banker, knew Bell slightly but hadn't met Levi before. He found Levi to be smug. It wasn't that Levi was arrogant, or talked down to people, or pretended he was in the driver's seat, or showed anything other than respect. It was Levi's confidence that bothered Parker. They decided VanCity would go ahead with due diligence. A VanCity team was formed to go through everything about the bank, from its operating costs (which proved extremely high) to its investment portfolio and especially its loan portfolio. The VanCity people were spending most of their days and evenings at the bank's offices, sneaking in and out by a side door to try to avoid detection by the media.

Bell was excited. It seemed that VanCity could take over the Bank of British Columbia after all, an ironic outcome given that the bank was twice VanCity's size. VanCity did not have capital of its own for the acquisition, but it had ingenuity. Bell negotiated an arrangement with the provincial government whereby it would supply the equity capital necessary, in the form of subordinated debentures. VanCity would pay the government interest at market rates, so there would be no subsidy. The debenture would be secured by the Bank of British Columbia's underlying assets. The VanCity plan was to roll the bank's assets into a trust company, which ultimately would be absorbed by VanCity. At all times, the holding would be controlled by the VanCity membership through its board.

The examination of the bank's loan portfolio now went down another layer. The pressure had become intense. Of a loan portfolio of $2.6 billion dollars, the VanCity team turned up $600 million that did not meet the usual standards. The idea was to put that $600 million into a special loan pool, separately incorporated, to be managed on behalf of the Canada Deposit Insurance Corporation (CDIC). VanCity would assume responsibility for the other loans and any losses they might incur.

Of the segregated low-quality loan pool, the VanCity team estimated they might have to write off an outside maximum of $400 million, and then only if they foreclosed all the loans and sold off the assets at fire-sale prices. The bank's shareholders equity of $200 million would cover the first slice. The CDIC would cover the next $200 million slice, if necessary. The VanCity team at the same time, however, thought they could manage their way out of the whole segregated loan pool so that the CDIC would also be off the hook, and even the shareholders might get a slice back.

The bulk of the loan portfolio and the physical plant were something else. Combining them with VanCity was, as Kaiser had originally indicated, an almost perfect fit, since the bank had branches in Chinatown and other places in the Lower Mainland where VanCity did not yet have a presence. There was little overlap. Wayne McKay, along with Bell, assumed VanCity would keep the branches elsewhere, too, in places like Victoria and Kelowna—in every major community in the province—although the Alberta branches would be sold off. "I used to just go crazy when I marked all those locations on the map and saw the kind of retail network that we had," McKay recalled. "We could dominate retail banking in British Columbia for a long time to come." McKay's excitement built as Bell's enthusiasm ricocheted off him.

Bell and the VanCity group were also motivated by strong feelings about the province and how banks had dealt with British Columbia in the past. Who would own the bank would not make much difference in good times. In poor, recessionary times, on the other hand, regional ownership was crucial. If the decisions were made in Toronto or New York or Hong Kong, B.C. businesses dealing with the bank might risk having their lines of credit abruptly withdrawn.

Bell was ebullient. "If you ever get a chance to buy a bank," he told Peter Cook gaily, "you should take it. You don't get many opportunities." Levi was equally upbeat. He was planning to run for the board of B.C. Central the following spring. "If we go ahead with this," he joked to Bell, "there is no way I'll ever get onto the Central board." All that was necessary was approval by Ottawa. A meeting was arranged to nail that approval down.

Before the meeting occurred, someone leaked the story to the media. The story caused caused a sensation. A daring and agile VanCity—a grass-roots credit union locally owned by its members—was actually going to take over a bank. It was the lead story in the *Vancouver Sun*. Trading was halted in Bank of British Columbia shares. The CBC reported that the deal might be closed as early as the following week. Levi was deeply upset by the leak, because the publicity, showing to others that at least VanCity was seriously interested in a purchase, risked putting the bank into play before the sale was concluded. Levi was convinced that the leak had come from Ottawa.

The meeting took place two days later, on Sunday morning, at the Delta River Inn, near the airport. Bell and Peter Cook, along with downtown lawyer Frank Murphy, were there for VanCity. Murphy was a partner in the prestigious legal factory of Farris Vaughan Wills & Murphy. The other four parties—the bank, the CDIC, the federal Department of Finance and the province—were also represented. They sat around a rectangular table. Cook's job was to present a set of pro forma financial statements showing that VanCity could manage the acquisition. He was optimistic but also tense, although he had once been a consultant in Ottawa and had worked for the federal government. Too much was at stake, he later explained. After his presentation, there were few questions, which gave him the uneasy feeling that Ottawa was just going through the motions. He nevertheless was upbeat. Vancity, he thought, had made a good case, and it had a news release about concluding the purchase ready to go. However, there was no deal that day or even the indication of one.

All during the week, the media coverage, including feature coverage about VanCity, continued. The news also caused a sensation among other credit unions in the province. The small credit unions saw the takeover as dread VanCity on an imperial march. They already considered VanCity too large to be a bona fide credit union. Large regional credit unions located where there were Bank of British Columbia branches saw VanCity, with the acquisition, as entering into direct competition with themselves. VanCity, in this view, was going to form a mega-credit union that would put them all out of business.

Pride was wrapped up in the credit unions' anger, too. The ambition of the other larger credit unions in the Lower Mainland had always been to close the gap between themselves and VanCity. They had grown rapidly, but unfortunately VanCity had grown even faster. Now VanCity, not through ordinary striving but through a bank takeover, would stretch that already large gap by multiples.

Bill Vander Zalm, a colourful Social Crediter, had just become premier, after defeating the NDP in an emotion-fraught election. Bell and Levi dealt with the new minister of finance, Mel Couvelier, and a few deputy ministers. They were supportive, and Vander Zalm had left it up to them. Alerted by the news leak, however, credit union opponents of the VanCity takeover began to get to Couvelier, with protestations of how VanCity's inordinate strength would destabilize the movement.

There was also a right-left political split involved. Many credit union directors, especially in the Fraser Valley, were right-wingers seething at the prospect of what a left-wing board at VanCity was about to do. The historical irony, too, was more than they could bear. The idea of a British Columbia bank originally came from legendary Social Credit premier W. A. C. Bennett, who envisioned the province owning 25 per cent of the bank and holding effective control. Eventually the bank was launched as a totally private venture but still closely identified with Bennett, and hence with the right-wing Social Credit ethos and Social Crediters' sense of British Columbia as God-given free-enterprise country. VanCity, with the hated ex-NDP cabinet minister Bob Williams, of all people, was now about to swallow up Bennett's dream. "It was a seething cauldron," Couvelier recalled. "It wasn't any sweetness and light with credit unions marching together arm in arm."

Bell, however, had his own leverage. He had been a deputy minister of finance under Social Credit. He had also been intensely interested in Vander Zalm's successful leadership race and later met with Vander Zalm to provide policy advice.

Meanwhile, Stanley Hartt, the federal deputy minister of finance, had quietly arrived in Vancouver, much like a school inspector from the metropolis come to inspect the local country school. Hartt was a lawyer from Montreal. He was bright, energetic and, as a journalist admirer thought of him, "annoyingly self-confident." One of the things Hartt was intensely self-confident about, and a task in which he revelled, was redesigning the country's financial institutions.

He had adopted the view of his officials in the Department of Finance, who shared his central Canadian culture, that regional financial institutions were to be avoided. They had a vague master plan in their heads. Regional institutions would be absorbed by the big banks. A few large American banks would come into the country and provide them with competition. Except for Quebec, where the Mouvement Desjardins was too big to be ignored, credit unions were not even thought of. Ottawa had been traumatized by the Northland Bank and Canadian Commercial Bank failures in Alberta. The Commercial Bank's demise had been particularly embarrassing because Ottawa had been involved in an expensive bailout and the bank had failed anyway. The government in addition had then decided to compensate the uninsured depositors at both banks, at a cost of several hundreds of millions of dollars. Cabinet ministers had taken flack for the decision. If a regional bank was to fail, Hartt wanted the remains folded into a larger, national or international bank, which could weather a regional recession and not come back a second time.

While Levi and Bell were waiting for a response from the CDIC and Ottawa—and thinking themselves almost there—Hartt, behind the scenes, was negotiating a takeover with the the the Hongkong and Shanghai Banking Corporation, which had previously rejected the Bank of British Columbia's overtures. Hartt had called in extra troops from Ottawa, had set up shop in Vancouver and was meeting with corporation representatives in board-rooms, lawyers' offices and hotel rooms across town, including one session when he had gone to bed and was brought back at 2:30 in the morning to help the parties work through a roadblock. VanCity had never been a possibility in his mind. Frantically trying to close a deal with the banking corporation, he was offering them money to take over the bank.

The CDIC, while this was going on, kept putting VanCity off. Whenever Bell and Peter Cook made inquiries, they were told that some details still had to be worked out. "They're screwing B.C. again," Bell told Levi. Within a week, they came to the conclusion that Ottawa was not levelling with them. Then word got back to them about what Hartt was doing. Bell and Levi were furious, since the VanCity proposal would not cost Ottawa money and the VanCity offer would mean that ownership would remain in Canada.

They decided the battle now was political and they would have to fight it in the political sphere. They commissioned a survey of Bank of British Columbia customers, which they publicized, showing that 90 per cent of the bank's depositors would stay with the bank if it was bought by VanCity, but only 40 per cent would stay if a foreign-based bank acquired control.

When the news of the VanCity takeover offer had broken, Levi had received a call from Bill Neville, the chair of Public Affairs International (PAI), who was in town, and they met for lunch. PAI was the leading lobby shop in Ottawa and Neville the trade's most prestigious practitioner. Neville had been Joe Clark's chief of staff during Clark's brief period as prime minister, and was a key adviser to Brian Mulroney in his successful 1984 election campaign. He tried to sell Levi his lobbying services, explain-ing how these and other connections worked—in effect, how Mulroney's Ottawa worked—and the kind of thing that would come to pass without PAI's help.

Levi listened carefully but did not act on Neville's offer. Neville's scenario seemed too fanciful. Levi saw VanCity doing Ottawa a favour by taking over the bank without Ottawa having to bail it out. There was no competition, either, at that time, since the Hongkong and Shanghai Bank had consis-tently refused to get involved. The CEO of its Canadian subsidiary, the Hongkong Bank of Canada, had said Hongkong and Shanghai's interest in the Bank of British Columbia had peaked a long time ago. It seemed that the choice was either approve the VanCity offer or wind up the bank and take a serious hit. Now events were unfolding not as they should, but as Neville had more or less predicted. Levi in retrospect concluded that not retaining Neville was a strategic mistake, especially since the Tories were so lobby-driven. VanCity really did need an insider on its side. "I guess I was just too dumb and too naive to figure out what I should have done," he shrugged.

VanCity's support in Victoria, meanwhile, was falling apart. Bell, Levi and others at VanCity compared notes from day to day on whom they had talked to and what they had heard. The anti-VanCity lobbying in Victoria, by other credit unions, appeared to be taking effect. Many businesses with accounts at the bank were alarmed that New Democrats would have control over those files and also weighed in. "Victoria was just a mess after that," Levi said. What really undermined VanCity's position in Victoria, however, were the ministrations by Hartt and his officials that regional financial institutions in the West had been a failure and that one had to be careful—that credit unions had done well because they had concentrated on residential mortgages, but business lending was quite different. Couvelier seemed to agree with Hartt's position. Any inclination he may have had to take on Ottawa politically over the issue disappeared with that conceptual surrender. "I'm telling you," Couvelier explained later, "that a 'B.C. first' argument was just not on in 1986."

In ordinary circumstances, the Bank of Canada would already have acted to close the bank down. Bell had no doubt now that Ottawa was using VanCity's offer to keep the bank's doors open until Ottawa, in the back rooms, could negotiate something with the Hongkong and Shanghai Bank. Each time McKay talked to Bell, he saw Bell's enthusiasm and stamina waning. Bell was clearly becoming discouraged. It slowly dawned on McKay and the rest of the team, watching Bell, that Ottawa was not going to allow their deal to happen.

Central was holding its semi-annual convention at this time. Levi was a delegate and made sure he attended, to explain the VanCity proposal. "It was just like a hurricane," he remembered. He stood alone at one microphone as irate credit unionists lined up at the other two and began pummelling him with waves of angry questions. The attack on Levi continued for two hours, until everyone was too mentally exhausted to go on any longer. Unlike VanCity's management, who wanted to keep all of the bank's branches, Levi had always had in mind talking to the other credit unions about them, but he couldn't say anything publicly for fear of scuttling the deal, which was based on VanCity's taking all of the bank. He had to let them know later, quietly, at the back of the convention room, of VanCity's plans to eventually sell the Interior branches. They shook hands and drifted away. The convention subsequently passed a motion that if VanCity took over the bank, Central would be involved as well, as if putting such a motion on the books could make it so.

Unknown to those at the convention, the VanCity takeover possibility had already petered out. Bell and Levi decided to pull the plug, but Ottawa asked them to keep their proposal alive. Hartt, to that point, according to Levi's sources, had offered the Hongkong and Shanghai Bank $50 million and then $100 million to take over the bank, and he had been rejected. Faced with time pressures, Hartt upped the ante to $200 million in order to close the deal. The money was to come from the CDIC. The $200 million was tax-free, too. It was deposited to the Hongkong and Shanghai Bank in the Bahamas for the purpose. The auditor general subsequently described the tax forfeit as a potential $100 million tax gift to the banking corporation. He called it an odious tax dodge. A Hongkong and Shanghai official responded, simply, that the tax exemption was an integral part of the agreement, without which the deal would not have been accepted.

For the Hongkong and Shanghai Banking Corporation, the largesse was bountiful. In the end, they took $63.5 million of the $200 million to actually buy the bank—the low price reflecting loan losses already recorded. This left them not just owning the bank and its valuable loan portfolio—using somebody else's money—but with $136.5 million, also gratis, for additional loan loss contingencies that, however, they would probably only marginally incur.

Bell, Levi and the others at VanCity were amazed at what Ottawa had done. The federal government, through the CDIC—albeit funded by bank and trust company premiums—had paid a foreign bank $200 million tax-free to take an entire Canadian bank with good assets, whereas VanCity, which was Canadian and British Columbian, would have done it likely without any cost to the CDIC at all.

The conventional view in banking circles was that Ottawa, politically, did not have a choice. It could not afford another embarrassing failure if an economic downturn occurred in the province, and Hongkong and Shanghai was also guaranteeing the bank's deposits on its own, so the CDIC wouldn't be liable. VanCity did not have deep enough pockets. It had low earnings and was taking on another asset twice its size.

Bell, Levi, Cook and the rest of VanCity bitterly disagreed. VanCity, in their view, had been used and betrayed. Bell didn't know whether to be more upset with Ottawa or Victoria. Levi was particularly angry at the role played by Stanley Hartt. It offended Levi that central Canadian paranoia should have been directed at VanCity and other British Columbia credit unions rather than at the banks and trust companies and their culture, where the string of embarrassing and costly failures had occurred.

He talked about VanCity being caught in a turf war between Ottawa and the provinces. The VanCity option might have been less costly and better for the province, but it meant creating a regional force in British Columbia that was not under Ottawa's control. Ottawa did not like the caisses populaires and their close identification with Quebec nationalism, and it wasn't going to give credit unions elsewhere a break, either. They would rather give away $200 million, Levi said. "The feds simply did not want to turn banking assets over to a provincial institution," he told a Canadian Press reporter in an interview. "It's that petty."

Although its takeover bid failed, VanCity came out of the affair well. It could have been painted as the little credit union that was over its head and blew it. The image that surfaced, instead, was of a significant and sophisticated force, able to handle the most imaginative of escapades. Wayne McKay presented Dale Parker and his people at the bank with a big cake, as a way of saying "No hard feelings," and a picture of that event was in the papers. VanCity members felt good about the daring takeover attempt. That it had been sabotaged by Ottawa lent a heroic quality to it.

A year later, testifying before the House of Commons public accounts committee, Hartt and the CDIC, defending their actions, casually dismissed the VanCity offer, arguing that the only alternative to the $200 million gift was to liquidate the bank. The national media reflected this central Canadian wisdom. One rhapsodic account, in *Saturday Night* magazine, described in glowing terms how Hartt had put together "an incredibly complex deal that saved CDIC about $500 million in payments to depositors."

As it happened, and as VanCity had predicted, the bank's soft loans were successfully managed, so that the Hongkong and Shanghai Banking Corporation was able to pocket the largesse as well as pocketing the bank free of charge. "Certainly a tremendous deal in restrospect," admitted Dale Parker, who had given way to the arrangement. Later, Stanley Hartt left government and, in 1991, he became a director of the Hongkong Bank of Canada, the new name for the Bank of British Columbia. "Who could be better qualified?" someone joked. It was, said Peter Cook, the final nail in the coffin.

CHAPTER 53

The CEO Departs

ALL WAS NOT GOING WELL. Innovations like the Ethical Growth Fund were major successes—TeleService was genuinely revolutionary—but Larry Bell's impulsivness was creating fault lines. His forcing of change at too fast a pace was causing consternation among the staff who were implementing the changes. Too many new products were introduced for the staff to cope with. It took time to build the communication bridges to handle new products, and there was never enough of it. The nightmarish computer conversion had left behind raw feelings and mental exhaustion.

The experiments at the branch of the future, in North Vancouver, had not panned out as expected, either. Having members sit down in a comfortable chair, at an open desk, for ordinary transactions, lent itself to chatting back and forth with the member service representatives, who were trying to be friendly. Transaction time took a terrible beating. The branch had to revert to teller stations, with some sit-down positions at the side. The automated loan-application system also foundered. The idea was a good one, but it was a step ahead of the technology available.

Bell had also, as a lesson in controlling expenses, put a moratorium on improving premises. They were now beginning to show wear and tear, degrading VanCity's physical presence, which had been so important to its growth. Bell seemed to have no feeling for the value members put on the look of their branch premises and for the problem he was creating. He recounted later that he had applied the moratorium exactly because of its sensitivity, to make a point. At the same time, however, in mocking counterpoint, other, larger costs at VanCity were escalating out of control, especially computer costs, which doubled in one year, following hefty earlier increases. These leapfrogging costs were unsustainable.

"There was always an element out of control," Peter Cook recalled, "because Bell had everybody running around doing different things all the time. He wanted lots of action around. As long as there were lots of new things coming along, he appeared to be happy." If rapid change produced crises, that was, for Bell, simply the nature of change. Bell was a crisis manager, Wayne McKay laughed. A joke had been going around the office that if there wasn't a crisis, Bell had to invent one so that he could manage it.

Cook, who worked closely with Bell, did not know quite what to make of the turmoil Bell was creating. Bell, he concluded, was brilliant at prioritizing the things that had to be done—brilliant at strategic thinking—but woeful in follow-through and dealing with people. He was good at running a series of projects, but not very good at running a business. For a business, one had to worry about how all the aspects interconnected and keep an eye on them.

The worst cases were business lending and the Seed Capital Program. Willy Young, the manager Bell had hired for business lending, had created a large bureaucracy occupying the fourth floor at head office. It became a separate business services division, centralized, bigger than other head-office departments—a rapidly growing empire, David Levi remembered thinking. The division had to create a book of business quickly in order to absorb its costs. Young began making relatively large loans. He was hired to do small business lending, but, like most bankers, he hated small loans.

Starting from zero, however, his crew was left feeding off the bottom of the market. The better accounts were already handled by others who had been in the game for a long time. The margins Young was earning were not justified by the risks he was taking, and it gradually began to show as some of the loans went awry. Young, moreover, was culturally a misfit in VanCity. For him and his cadres, commercial lending was at the top; retail lending was a nether region. If you were a good retail lender, you did not stay there. You went into the commercial side, where the real action was. This attitude generated resentment in the branches. Branch managers and loan officers hated the pretensions of this new, high-cost head-office bureaucracy, who were paid top salaries and pushed their weight around despite being the new boys in school.

There was more to the antagonism than just feelings. VanCity had a group of about seven thousand small businesses in place. Many of them had conducted their affairs with VanCity on the basis of a handshake or a name. If they wanted a $5,000 line of credit, they simply came into the branch and signed a note for it. They perhaps had been dealing with VanCity for decades and also had their personal accounts there. Suddenly, to fit the requirements of the business services division, they had to produce business and marketing plans and other information. They resented this. Often they did not have the expertise to produce the information or the money to buy the expertise. The branch managers, at the same time, lost much of their authority on these loans.

"It was like a war between two camps," Wayne McKay recalled. Bell regularly called in Young and McKay, who was in charge of the branch system, to huddle over the constant disputes and argue cases. Young and his people, McKay thought, did not understand VanCity and how its strength had grown out of the retail system and individual members. McKay found himself fighting for the VanCity he loved. Within senior management, he felt he was close to losing this battle. Young's patter about large business lending appealed to Bell's ambitions for the organization. The board did not seem to fully understand what was taking place. It was discouraging for McKay.

The Seed Capital Program, involving a much smaller, experimental portfolio, also was not working well. It was aimed at people with good ideas who did not necessarily have business experience, and it was supposed to break even. The program, however, was too experimental—there was no backlog of experience to work with—and it had too high a risk. Director Tim Louis, a storefront lawyer with strong grassroots sympathies, considered the program an unmitigated disaster. Almost every loan that he could recall ended up not succeeding. A committee of the board approved the loans, but on the basis of recommendations made by management. Bell himself had the program reporting to him. Louis wondered how committed senior management were to the program to begin with, given that it was a board project and that failure could be used to demonstrate that it could not be done.

Bell, meanwhile, had other things on the go and could not stop to look back. He was concerned about VanCity's weak earnings. One year, according to Peter Cook, he and his treasury manager, Chris Dobrzanski, had saved VanCity from showing a loss by making positioning and trading gains on the treasury desk. Another year, the stratagem of charging fees on dormant accounts had propped up the operating statement. They all knew, though, that eventually the bag of tricks would empty out. Bell, at this stage, was also losing interest in VanCity and perhaps, Wayne McKay thought, losing heart, too. It seemed, to McKay, that Bell had already decided he wanted to do other things, to take on larger tasks that had more of a strategic challenge. Then, suddenly, in the middle of all the turmoil he had created, Bell was gone. He became chair and CEO of B.C. Hydro and was no longer CEO of VanCity. It was almost as if he had departed by magic in an instant. He had been at VanCity for three years.

Bell left scattered litter across the VanCity landscape—costs running too fast ahead, business loans going soft, an uncomfortably thin profit margin, one division at odds with another. The weak profits meant that retained earnings were not being built up quickly, and that would limit for years what VanCity could do in the future. Bell, by rushing ahead so fast, ended up forcing VanCity to go slower.

Yet McKay and Peter Cook, the two divisional managers most attached to VanCity and its membership culture, would not condemn him. "He was the right man for the time," McKay said. Cook, appalled at the way costs had gotten out of hand and at how morale had suffered from so much forced change, nevertheless thought that, on balance, Bell had been useful. He had taught people at VanCity to think strategically. The Euro-issue was inspired. Bell's push for transaction fees had been strategically critical. Although VanCity wasn't making much money, it was strong in other ways. Strength lay not just in people but also in public image—"the value of the franchise"—and Bell had enhanced the VanCity franchise. VanCity was no longer a small player. Joy Leach, a fund-raiser at Simon Fraser University who had joined the board in 1985, laughed that "Larry Bell shakes all trees really hard. That's his method of revitalizing an organization. But then, of course, you can't stay."

Bell himself knew that he had left things incomplete—that having taken a series of initiatives, it was time to clean up. He wasn't disturbed by the failed experiments. He saw them as part of the dynamics of development, like economist Joseph Schumpeter's idea of creative destruction. "Negative results in a scientific experiment are as useful as positive results," Bell said. The business lending initiative had shown that a solid market for VanCity wasn't there, but to know that, one had to test the market first. Even the failed Seed Capital Program had been worth trying in order to learn from the experience, in Bell's view. Nor had it totally failed; it had strategic meaning. Just attempting it had created a beneficial persona for the organization—that VanCity was trying to serve the community—and members would see that.

As for the whirlwind of new products, Bell knew there was a little discomfort when tellers had to answer questions while not being quite sure of the answers, but that had to be balanced against actually having the product and its usefulness to members. "Some people don't like change," he argued matter-of-factly. "Change makes people uncomfortable."

He was someone who carefully shielded his own feelings, but VanCity had gotten behind the shield. There had always been a sense of fun when he was working at VanCity. He found later, elsewhere, that he could never recapture it. In addition, for all Bell's intensity and action, VanCity changed Larry Bell more than Larry Bell changed VanCity. He learned that although people and strategy were both necessary, people were more important than strategy. The way that staff participated in the organization, even to the point of recommending their own salary and benefits, Bell found extraordinary. McKay and others had slowly coaxed him into realizing the value of taking time with people, explaining and asking questions, even if it appeared to slow down the process. What had burned the lesson most deeply into his mind was the way staff had responded during the conversion crisis. If they had not identified so strongly with the organization, he would have been helpless.

It was like ancient China civilizing the successful Mongol invader who had become emperor. VanCity made Bell more of a whole man, and he knew it.

CHAPTER 54

Misfit

BOB WILLIAMS WAS WORRIED AND UNHAPPY. The public impression of VanCity might have been that of a daring innovator, which was true. Its run at taking over the Bank of British Columbia added to the image. Yet so much was going wrong at the same time that he knew VanCity was in difficulty. He was still, in his own mind, trying to make VanCity work.

His relationship with the departed Larry Bell had turned rocky. Bell's consorting with Bill Vander Zalm and the Social Credit movers and shakers rankled Williams deeply. Vander Zalm was the political enemy. David Levi had told Williams that Bell was a right-winger, but Williams had not believed him. It wasn't just Bell's political coming out of the closet that bothered Williams, however. It seemed to Williams that the Bell sojourn had been a period of fudging, without a good planning process that dug into basics and had orderly substance. Williams would have gotten the board behind him and moved to fire Bell, had Bell not left.

The board now decided to change tack, in an attempt to come to grips with this incipient anomie. It had diligently gone through a formal hiring process, retaining the headhunters Caldwell Partners to search out candidates for the CEO job. Joy Leach was chair at the time. She wanted an outsider for CEO in order to help the board get a financial grip on the organization. Dennis Lunney, a corporate banker, ended up on the shortlist and was hired. He was running the Bank of Montreal Leasing Corporation in Toronto. He had an MBA and had an understanding of finance; he said the right things. He was extremely tall, which gave him an air of authority. Because he was removed culturally from VanCity, the board thought he would bring some rigour and hard-nosed commercial sense to the organization. The board was exercising reverse discipline: deliberately not indulging itself in credit union sentimentality.

Peter Cook, the chief financial officer, who had also applied for the job, was incensed. He had been an applicant, too, in 1984, when Bell was hired. He could not understand how the board could have hired someone with Lunney's background. The rest of the staff were wary. Bell had kept making changes, often without much notice and sometimes without much explanation, until it seemed that changes were being made for change's sake. After three years, the staff had adapted to him. Now they were faced with even an odder choice. Lunney had relatively little experience of the retail side of banking.

Part of Wayne McKay's job was to convince staff that this was the best thing for VanCity. His heart wasn't in it. He had gone with a few others to a welcoming dinner with Lunney, before Lunney came on stream, and was confounded. Lunney seemed aloof, arrogant, and not a good communicator. "Bad mistake," McKay thought. He could not imagine how the board was possibly going to get along with Lunney. Not long after Lunney finally arrived from Toronto, in the summer of 1987, some of the board members themselves had a sinking feeling about what they had done. It was like being trapped, during one's honeymoon, by a gnawing uneasiness that one had chosen badly and realizing that all one could do was to see how things might develop. "He seemed to be just shellshocked," Bob Williams remembered. "He saw disaster around every corner." There was a legitimate concern about earnings, but Lunney went much further. He approached the liquidity problem—the availability of cash to meet an emergency—as if VanCity were in imminent danger of going under. He constantly talked of having to consolidate in order to set the problem right. He repeated this negative analysis often enough that the board, if not totally alarmed, at least agreed to go along. Lunney, after all, was supposed to know about finance. Shirley Chan, who had just joined the board that spring, remembered being shocked at how unhealthy VanCity's financial situation was.

"The liquidity crisis was more manufactured than real," Wayne McKay maintained. The decline in liquidity, in his view, wasn't because members were withdrawing deposits, which would have been unhealthy, but because the economy was thriving and VanCity was doing a bang-up lending business. Liquidity, for B.C. credit unions, always moved in cycles, and it was simply a matter of understanding those patterns and managing accordingly. There were several ways of making up extra liquidity. One could draw on B.C. Central, which could in turn draw on the national credit union organization. One could, if necessary, raise lending rates or lending ratios, thereby cutting lending and increasing deposits on hand. The normal repayment on mortgages would quickly fill any liquidity gap. One could also sell a package of mortgages. Lunney, not familiar with the rhythms of VanCity retail lending, started getting rid of VanCity activities.

He sold out the leasing business. He closed down business lending. He also pulled VanCity out of commercial real estate lending—an area where it had expertise and had been lending successfully since Don Bentley's day. The Seed Capital Program was cancelled. There was talk about closing branches and firing people in order to cut back operations.

Joy Leach, the one board member to whom Lunney confided, described his stay at VanCity as a case of somebody from a Bank of Montreal tower not being able to see the runway, which was close to the ground. "Literally in the large banks you really don't see the ground," Leach said. "At VanCity you see it all the time. Dennis found it very unnerving, because he always thought we were going to land too quickly. He knew how to fly a plane, but not how to land it." VanCity was small compared with the banks, but complex and vibrant, and one had to be close to the operation.

Lunney himself could not get comfortable at VanCity. He wondered what kind of organization he had fallen into. He was shocked by the credit union culture, where ordinary members, even the crankiest, could stand up at an annual meeting and sound off. Management meetings were constrained. Leach, who liked Lunney, thought he hadn't been welcomed by senior staff. "It was very difficult to build natural allies in a hostile environment," she said. Senior managers like McKay and Garry Smith, on the other hand, found Lunney to be, in their view, a cause of the hostile environment. Lunney came from the ultra-conservative Bank of Montreal. VanCity wasn't the traditional bureaucratic, hierarchical banking organization based on fear. Since VanCity people weren't traditional bankers, Lunney was at first unable to appreciate how good the people around him were.

The management team had always shared information and experiences with each other. Lunney's coldness threw them off. People began to withdraw and not express their views, and certainly not share their feelings with him. Garry Smith remembered it was the first time he had felt threatened personally by the arrival of a new CEO. He understood the fear that others had told him about, when the CEO had previously changed. When Lunney walked around head office, people put their heads down because they did not want to talk to him. Smith had his own simple strategy. He tried not to be near Lunney at all. "It worked," Smith laughed. He assumed Lunney had been brought in by the board to clean house and get rid of senior management. There was nothing specific to indicate that was what he had in mind, but there seemed to be no other explanation for his behaviour.

Lunney had brought in an old Bank of Montreal friend from Toronto, as a consultant, who went around asking questions. Because Lunney talked about VanCity being full of sacred cows and about the need to get rid of them, his consultant friend appeared ominous. "It was a very uncomfortable feeling," Bob Quart recalled. "You didn't know what was going to happen the next day, who was going to get blamed for what, who was going to lose their job."

Lunney, isolated, also brought in some young, university-trained analysts and put them in a lock-up for two weeks to come up with a refocussing strategy. Wayne McKay scoffed that this "think tank" of Lunney's spent their days tumbling numbers and pointing out to everybody what was wrong with VanCity, without knowing as much as they might have about the strengths of the organization. Chris Catliff, a management trainee in the group, recounted that senior managers like McKay did not have a sense of urgency about VanCity's weak financial situation and that the only way to establish that sense of urgency was to go around them. The manoeuvre, however, only destroyed what little cohesion was left. Lunney wanted to reorganize management to get around the split. McKay offered to resign to make it easy for him. Peter Cook had never accepted Lunney. According to McKay, Lunney got to the point of firing Cook, but could not follow through. He asked McKay to do it for him, and McKay refused.

Lunney appeared to be equally uncomfortable with his visits to branches. One of his early visits, escorted by McKay, was to a new Langley branch that had not yet opened. He wondered aloud why VanCity, which he thought was overextended, was building that branch. By the time McKay got back to head office, there were already two people waiting to tell him about the negative reaction Lunney had produced in Langley. Word of the Langley episode had spread throughout the system.

Lunney had no notion, either, of how to deal with VanCity's lay board. He saw them as having political aims. The Seed Capital Program, in particular, he saw as a case of a board of directors forcing management to put questionable loans on the books. At branch manager meetings and elsewhere, he freely offered his comments about what he thought of the board. He and David Levi in particular did not get along. "Six months of hysteria," Levi would later describe Lunney's sojourn. Lunney, after just a couple of months, it seemed to McKay, had decided that he could not survive at VanCity with its member-elected board and that he really did not want to be there.

It was one of those irretrievable situations—the longer it went on, the more nightmarish it became. Every year there was an anniversary dinner for people who had completed fifteen years at VanCity. It was a time for camaraderie, for a little motivation and particularly for saying thank you. The group waited interminably at the restaurant for Lunney and the chair, Joy Leach, to show up. By the time they arrived, they were almost an hour late. They proferred an excuse for being so tardy. "The tension in the air was just unreal," John Iseli remembered. Lunney did not say "Hi" to anybody or shake anybody's hand. He gave the impression of being too busy chatting to Leach to talk to any of the people who were being honoured. Finally, the meal arrived. Afterwards, Lunney said a few words, of no moment. He had already left a sour taste in everyone's mouth, and they departed angry and demoralized. Bringing Dennis Lunney to VanCity, Chris Bergthorson at Embryo Communications quipped, was like trying to convince Margaret Thatcher that she should be involved in the co-operative movement.

Bob Williams to this point had left the chair to others. Now, although he was also busy as a member of the provincial legislature, he wanted to step in. He became chair after the annual meeting in 1988. He was a careful planner, but impatient intellectually, and was preoccupied with getting a grip on VanCity's floundering. At one planning session, he tore apart a planning document prepared by Bob Leighton. Leighton, replacing Peter Cook, had been put in charge of drawing up the plan. It was long on description, including an inventory of equipment, but hadn't gotten as far as offering any strategic prescription. "Bob was furious going into the planning retreat," Wayne McKay remembered, of Williams. "I could see the smoke rising." At the session, Williams slammed the planning book on the table and launched into a tirade, dismissing the plan as total garbage. There was stunned silence. Everyone was afraid of the legendary Williams temper. "Other than that, Bob, what do you think of the plan?" Tim Louis quipped.

"No one who was there could forget it," George Scott, from marketing, recalled. Most of the senior managers considered Williams's criticism justi- fied, at least intellectually. Williams, himself, felt the responsibility for VanCity on his own shoulders. He was being pushed by his pride, too.

At board meetings, under aggressive questioning, Lunney wasn't inclined to be forthcoming. The strategic document he had commissioned, pre- pared by his young business administration honchos, was set aside. Lunney wanted to lay off 20 per cent of VanCity's staff in implementing it, and the board balked. It was prepared to do what was necessary, but, if there were to be cuts, wanted a more humane approach. Once, at an unhappy board meeting, he walked out during a break and had to be coaxed back in. According to the story that circulated in the office, he thought the rest of management should have walked out with him, too. By this time, the spring of 1988, less than a year after he had come to VanCity, his days at 10th and Cambie were numbered.

There was tension everywhere. Everyone was on edge; the negativity was getting to people. Tim Louis had been trying for months to get support to remove Lunney. The other directors now finally agreed to go ahead. Even Joy Leach, who had been Lunney's patron on the board, knew that hiring him had been a mistake, because of the bad cultural fit.

It was an intense period for Williams. He had inherited what he called "all the heavy-duty stuff"—in particular, doing something with Lunney and finding a successor. Largely because of the business lending, the loan loss provision for the prior year, 1987, was $6 million, even higher than the 1983 loan loss provision under Geoff Hook, at the bottom of the economic cycle in 1983.

Profits were abysmally low. Williams was looking at a situation far dif- ferent from the one he had imagined for VanCity when he first ran for the board in 1983.

He had already spoken to the vice-president of trust services, Bob Quart, about becoming CEO. Quart had applied for the job the previous time and had made a strong impression. He had been vice-president of Montreal Trust's branch operations at one time, so he knew the retail side. He had done a good job launching the Ethical Growth Fund. He had been around VanCity long enough to get a sense of its credit union values. He had a coherent plan for fixing VanCity.

Williams told him that the board was going to fire Lunney and did not plan on doing a search. Quart accepted Williams's offer. He had been appointed, though, only as acting CEO, pending confirmation later. The

Canada Day weekend intervened. Quart went to his place on Salt Spring Island to chop wood. When he got back to Vancouver, he told Williams that there was a huge job to do and he could not do it in an acting capacity. The board would have to have faith in him.

Williams, knowing a decision had to be made, went along with Quart's assessment. He could only hope they had got it right this time.

PART SEVEN

1988-1996

CHAPTER 55

The Quiet Man

A CREDIT UNION, PARTICULARLY ONE governed by left-wingers, was the last place Bob Quart thought he'd find himself. He had been a trust company executive. He hewed to elemental, conventional business principles. He prided himself on his knowledge of the trust company function, in which, in his mind at least, the customer's deposits or the late customer's estate were sacrosanct. He seemed a typical conservative. He did not pretend to be a jack-of-all-CEO-trades, like Larry Bell. He described himself as a professional working in financial institutions. That was what he did. Yet, oddly, as the new CEO at VanCity, Quart never felt more at home.

It was the relationship among people at VanCity that gave him that feeling. He had always been motivated by relationships. His sojourn in charge of branch operations for Montreal Trust had been almost entirely a matter of maintaining relationships and communicating. When he became VanCity CEO, the staff didn't know him. He distributed a basket of strawberries to every employee, in line with Wayne McKay's strawberry theme. Quart was the jellybean man—jellybeans were associated with the RRSP season, in VanCity horseplay—but strawberries, he laughed, were year round. It was something he wanted to do, as a way of letting everyone know he was with them.

His business-management posture was misleading. He had an egalitarian, democratic streak to him, although it was tinged with a hint of a stiff back that would resist if pushed too far. He tried to remove the natural fear that rank-and-file employees had of a CEO. He didn't see himself as being scary. He liked to describe himself as just an ordinary guy—another spoke in the wheel—who had fallen into the CEO position. When he visited branches, he talked mostly to staff rather than to branch managers, because that was where he thought the real answers were.

His friendliness, however, did not mask his willingness to make decisions. He had self-assurance. He knew where he was going. On Quart's second day on the job as CEO, Bob Williams took him to meet the president of the Credit Union Deposit Insurance Corporation. The president told Quart that unless VanCity improved its financial position, he would put it under supervision when its next annual report appeared.

"That was probably the biggest boost I ever got," Quart remembered. He knew how serious VanCity's situation was, yet he had not had time to establish any natural authority. He used the supervisor's threat to rally management and the board around the major changes he wanted to make. He argued the case forcefully. It was no longer time to put things off, he said—no longer time to wait and see what might happen in the next few months. He got their support. They went to work together, cutting back on everything they could possibly manage, shedding some functions altogether and slowly rebuilding others, in an attempt to bring the credit union back to strength.

Bob Quart's most vivid memory of his childhood was when he was three and a half years old. It was 1945. He, his mother and his paternal grandparents crossed the river from Quebec City, where they lived, to Lévis, to intercept one of the endless flow of troop trains moving up the St. Lawrence River towards Montreal and points west. His father, whom he had never seen, was returning home from the war. He remembered his mother, just like in the movies, running up to his father one coach ahead while Quart's grandmother held him back, and jumping into his arms.

They were a close-knit family. He spent a lot of time as a youngster with his grandparents on both sides. His mother was French-Canadian, so French was the language he learned. On his father's return, he was totally immersed in English. By the time he started school, he was perfectly bilingual.

His paternal grandmother, Josie Quart, was active politically in the federal Conservative party, which was unusual in those days for a Quebec resident. Most Quebecers were Liberals. She later became a senator, appointed by John Diefenbaker, after the Progressive Conservative landslide in 1958. Young Quart became political by association. He enjoyed meeting the people and listening to their stories. Once he drove John and Olive Diefenbaker around the Gaspé, as Diefenbaker campaigned from church hall to church hall. Quart was only seventeen years old, had just gotten his licence and was prepared to do anything in order to drive a car.

Quart studied commerce at the University of Ottawa. He loved economics and got good marks without having to study. His first job on graduating was with London Life in that most conservative of towns, London, Ontario, selling group insurance. He talked to corporate treasurers and company presidents. The job gave him confidence and taught him patience. Insurance was, he thought, probably the most difficult thing in the world to sell, because one was talking about death, which people did not want to hear about. Insurance people did not have a good reputation, either. He was nevertheless effective. Because of his work on pension plans, Montreal Trust spotted him and lured him away. He became a pension trust officer. He was now in the "fiduciary business"—holding other people's money in trust.

He was only thirty-two when Montreal Trust sent him out to manage its main branch in Vancouver. This was supposed to be a two-year stint, after which, being bilingual, Quart would return to Montreal and take a larger role in the organization. He aimed at being president of the organization on its one-hundredth anniversary in 1989. He hadn't counted on British Columbia. British Columbia changed his life.

He arrived in late 1975, when the western economy was about to boom. He had a heyday. Vancouver became the largest mortgage producer and the fastest-growing branch in the Montreal Trust system. Quart was one of a new breed in trust company managers. Montreal Trust was fusty, ultra-conservative and tightly controlled. Quart forced change on the system, upstream in the hierarchy, from Vancouver. Montreal Trust would not issue a mortgage for a home with a septic tank. A good part of fast-growing Surrey, prime mortgage territory, consisted of homes with septic tanks. Quart had the company limitation removed. Montreal Trust would not do land-development loans, either. Quart did them in Vancouver. "It was a real fight," he recalled, "but I had the energy to fight in those days."

A lot of his fighting with head office had to do with a credit union, VanCity. VanCity had open mortgages and no-strings-attached RRSPs and was getting the lion's share of business. Quart complained to Montreal Trust that he could not compete against them, since Montreal Trust was not supplying him with the products he needed. His bosses never did give him the products. A group of them came out to take a look for themselves. They were in disbelief. They told Quart to leave VanCity alone. VanCity was not going to be around very long if it continued with what it was doing, Quart's bosses told him. "They're just going to blow their brains out," they said.

After five years, he was called back to Montreal. He loved the West Coast, but he had made a commitment to his wife, Louise, who was from Quebec City, to return when the time came. All of her family were in Quebec. What he did not realize was how much his wife had also fallen in love with British Columbia. One evening, sitting in their living room in Montreal, they asked themselves, "What are we doing here?" Quart had the possibility of managing a large family trust, for a Montreal Trust client, out of Vancouver. He now took the job, although it meant saying goodbye to an established financial institution.

His new job took him into a different, fascinating world. Acting on instructions to buy a ranch, he purchased British Columbia's famous Stump Lake Ranch. He applied his due diligence skills to the purchase. He was a trust officer in ranchland, and a tough bargainer, too. He even went on a few cattle drives with the cowboys. Differences of opinion between the generations in the family, however, finally made his job impossible. He began looking around for something he could do on his own.

He conceived the idea of a trust company owned in British Columbia that would provide real trust services—act as trustee of savings plans, execute wills, and serve as a transfer agent—functions that were done largely by trust companies owned elsewhere. He thought he could bring in customers by trading on localism. He identified potential partners, from connections he had built up over the years, but those possibilities fell through. In the end, he approached Larry Bell at VanCity. The VanCity board liked his plan but did not want to share ownership with outsiders. Quart agreed to start up a trust service inside VanCity instead.

On the surface, it seemed an odd arrangement. Quart, brought up a Conservative and from the conservative side of Canadian business, would be consorting with a credit union whose board was dominated by known left-wingers. Quart, however, aside from knowing VanCity as a Montreal Trust competitor, was a VanCity member. He had joined in 1982 to take advantage of its innovative mortgage sale, in which legal fees and other costs had been paid. He had wanted the money to build a house on his Salt Spring Island property. The promotional flair of the mortgage sale had stuck in his mind, and he had been impressed with the way VanCity had dealt with him personally. VanCity, moreover, had 145,000 members and nineteen branches, so it had a strong distribution system in place. It was genuinely interested in providing fiduciary services. Besides, Quart was unemployed.

He had not realized until then how much was involved in providing a trust service. Without systems and experienced trust staff in place, everything had to be created. It was the toughest job of his life. At the one-year mark, there were just four people in the division, excluding secretaries. Gradually, however, the trust services division began to take shape.

Quart discovered that no one in VanCity understood what being a trustee meant. Management looked on a trust service as a marginal sideline. Whatever they might think, Quart, with the fiduciary business imprinted in his brain, saw trust services as a flourishing part of the future. He conceived of VanCity as a repository of the funds of retired people. He could become emotional talking about his responsibility to depositors. RRSPs and RRIFs (registered retired income funds) were part of his bailiwick. The manager of financial services, Bob Saunders, an energetic, folksy chartered accountant, was also enthusiastic. Saunders had established VanCity retirement counselling as a full-time service, replacing the part-time counselling provided by a group of retirees. Quart and Saunders now saw how much more important it could be. Saunders and his counselling assistants moved out of the RRSP department to set up their own specialized retirement counselling department. Quart also created self-directed RRSPs for VanCity.

He wanted to make trust services accessible, populist. He introduced an executors' course, in which members could learn how to execute wills on their own and save themselves money. It did not work out. The first thing people did in such cases was go to the lawyers, and the lawyers quickly took over. Members ended up paying much more than they should. Quart's counter-strategy was to build up a "will bank," in which VanCity itself was appointed the executor. He priced the service so that people with small estates could continue to use VanCity. The will bank began to grow quickly. With this connection made, members, as they grew older, and finding it difficult to keep track of their affairs, began asking the trust services division if it would act as investment manager for them. Quart also began bidding for "salary leave plans," by which teachers financed sabbaticals. The Ethical Growth Fund came on stream. VanTax, the income tax service, reported to Quart. Trust services, seemingly out of nothing and with nebulous prospects—was there really anything substantial to them, anyway?—was now a respectable division in its own right.

Bob Quart was a relative newcomer from the nether region of trust services, but his appointment as VanCity's CEO in 1988 nevertheless came as a relief to Wayne McKay, Garry Smith and the others on the third floor. Quart wasn't, after all, a total outsider. Even Peter Cook, who was passed over, could come to terms with it. Quart reflected on how he happened to be in the right place at the right time because, coming after Dennis Lunney, it wasn't too hard to be liked. When he set out to execute his plan, he already had the co-operation he needed.

His first objective was quickly to reduce expenses by paring back everything he could. The Surrey-Langley branch—the one that Lunney had been quizzical about—had opened the previous year with a full staff complement, but there were fewer than four hundred members using it. Quart cut back the staff from nineteen to eight. He reduced some six-day branches to five-day-a-week operations where there was another six-day branch within convenient travelling distance. He knew this did not improve service, but it gave him a chance to reorganize financially and begin again.

He sold VanCity Insurance Services to its employees. It was a tough decision—not in his own mind, because he saw clearly the rationale, but in its impact, because it meant a loss of face for the organization. He was jettisoning a key element of the VanCity financial supermarket. Quart, however, considered the insurance subsidiary a managerial failure. It had reported, over its history, to too many people, including himself—to senior managers who were not insurance people and did not necessarily understand the business. It depended, for efficiencies, on volume, but only 15 per cent of VanCity members used it, so the expected synergy wasn't there. Most of all, the subsidiary was losing money, when one included head office and other overhead costs.

It was a good occasion for Quart to put his negotiating skills to use. He grasped implications easily. He set up the sale so that VanCity was protected on all sides. The VanCity name would stay. The change would not even be noticed by members. The new, separately owned company would also pay rent for its space. Quart, moreover, would be able to reinvest the proceeds of the sale and earn substantial interest income on it. These factors would turn a loss into an appreciable annual gain. VanCity, too, would have the first right of refusal if the new owners ever wanted to sell, which gave it the option to return to insurance later.

Quart also closed down VanTax, the tax preparation service. He got rid of

Willy Young, the vice-president in charge of business lending, and cleaned out the department, leaving just the bare minimum to look after the existing portfolio. Paper, telephone and travel costs were reduced. Dinner for the long quarterly board meetings, which had been catered, was replaced with sandwiches or take-out food, hearkening back to the board meetings of the early 1960s. The change was mostly symbolic, but it made a point. Quart also began unloading properties that had been acquired when commercial loans had fallen through.

In just a few weeks, VanCity had put in place measures to reduce operating expenses 10 per cent, shoring up its weak earnings. Quart was impressed by how committed his senior people were to what he had asked them to do. Oddly, for Quart, he was more or less implementing the strategy Lunney had put forward in the spring. "I didn't have to reinvent a lot of wheels," he said.

The difference lay not in the plan on paper but in the approach. Quart saw everything he did as a team exercise. He avoided laying off large numbers of people—an element in Lunney's plan that the board could not accept. In the branch system, only four people lost their positions after relocation. Most of the cuts were at head office, in business lending. Quart didn't have to be convinced on that issue. He felt, as the board did, that when people lost their work, human tragedy resulted.

Almost as quickly as he had cut back, he began rebuilding. He wanted badly to renovate the branches. They were deteriorating, it seemed to him, and morale was inevitably affected. Dave Turnbull, who had built branches for Geoff Hook, was still around and redid the branches with an altogether different look, abandoning the dark, earthy tones and square corners for rounded lines and colours like very light pink, burgundy and greys. He tried to soften the look to reflect what he considered the evolution in VanCity's philosophy.

Quart also hired someone to do commercial real estate and interim construction loans, which Lunney had inexplicably wound up. Real estate projects, especially those involving residential units, were something Van-City knew a lot about, and they earned substantial fees. Construction loans for condominiums or townhouses also led to VanCity mortgages for buyers of the units later on.

Quart was always trying to cement relationships. He began with branch visits, including breakfasts with employees. Staff forums were re-created. Quart found that even if the news wasn't good, staff would accept it if it was logical and if they were kept informed. At the forums, he would outline the problems VanCity faced. Each table would work out potential solutions and report back. As his plans began to bite, he shifted the accent to award nights, with stories of successes. The building of lines of communication was reminiscent of the Geoff Hook years.

Dave Turnbull, who spanned the managerial shifts and was unapologetically a Hook man, could feel the difference. The credit union philosophy at VanCity, Turnbull thought, had taken a severe beating when Bell and

Lunney came along. What he had missed in those years was the intimacy of people accepting each other and working together. Quart was bringing that back. The culture of trust that McKay had created was strong enough that the organization could still respond, almost as if nothing had intervened.

Innovations already underway helped out. TeleService—One Name, One Number—hit full stride in 1988, fielding 906,000 calls and reducing cost per transaction. VAST—VanCity Automated System Technology—was introduced the same year. VAST was Bob Leighton's scheme of having a computer in each branch that bit by bit would move the daytime load away from the central computer. The scheme had been expensive and wasn't fully implemented, but one function in particular did work out. VAST eliminated the need for members to fill out deposit and withdrawal slips.

The teller, the reasoning went, had to key in the transaction details anyway. Why make the member painstakingly, and unnecessarily, write out the same details first? With VAST, tellers each had a small printer at their teller station. They slipped a blank transaction form into the printer. The transaction data they entered into the computer was formatted so that, at the press of a key, it was printed out neatly on the form. All the member had to do was sign.

The "itemized transaction receipt," as it was called, was an innovation so obvious and elegant in its conception, and yet so unexpected, that members couldn't help noticing. It was, in that sense, much like First-in-Line, the idea dreamed up by jaunty Hermann Myers in 1971. It made it painful ever to switch back to a bank or trust company and have to go through the tiresome process of filling out deposit and withdrawal slips again. VAST's lead time proved enormous. Not until 1995 did any establishment competitor—it was Canada Trust—duplicate VAST.

Quart's plan worked. In 1987, earnings before taxes but after membership dividends were only $1.9 million. In 1988, they inched up to $2.9 million, excluding extraordinary items. In 1989, the equivalent figure was $8 million, and in 1990, $8.8 million. Membership at the end of that year hit 179,000. As retained earnings piled up, more became possible. Quart started looking ahead.

For all that Quart's approach resembled Geoff Hook's, it differed in one crucial aspect. Hook had run VanCity as a managerial enterprise with a compliant board completely wedded to his purpose. When directors were elected who did not fit his managerial culture, Hook did not know what to make of them. Quart had a board both with its own ideas and a much different background. It was also strong enough, at least with Williams and Levi, that Quart's success depended on his recognizing their power. This did not bother him. They were, after all, the board. He accepted their governance.

CHAPTER 56

Return to Community

BOB WILLIAMS LIKED TO REFER to Bob Quart as a Tory from Quebec. It was an opportunistic way of saying, "Look, yeah, we're running this place as directors, but we're running it as a business, not as a political organization." Quart thought the description "Tory from Quebec" was taking liberties, although he definitely was not a member of the NDP. He did not belong to any political party. He did, however, understand Williams's intent. He had helped sell himself to the board as someone whose presence could assure the public that the board was putting its responsibilities as directors ahead of politics.

"Tory from Quebec" was also an expression of tolerance on Williams's part. Williams had, in fact, several conservative friends. They weren't the unvarnished "free enterprise over everything" Social Credit kind, but Red Tories, or at least those who had a sense of society and sharing. Quart was close enough. His Quebec City anglophone roots made him open to cultural differences and sensitive to the role of social traditions. Quart, Williams noticed, was also able to deal readily with a wide range of people. He could maintain his equilibrium in arguments. He had more patience than most, certainly more than Williams himself.

Williams was spending up to half his time on VanCity matters, working intensively with Quart to change the organization. The two men got to know each other's strengths and weaknesses. It was one of those intricate relationships, like an arranged marriage, that worked because there were no romantic illusions and because everybody, including all the relatives, knew that it had to work. The relationship depended on flexibility and, as in all such cases, a matter-of-fact respect—including, in this instance, a respect for each other's territory.

After Williams and David Levi, Tim Louis, of the Action Slate directors, had been around the longest. He had first run for the board in 1982 and been elected in 1985. Community activism was second nature to Louis. His involvement grew out of his own battle to win services for the physically disabled. He was born with spinal muscular atrophy. He had a small, frail body, had severely limited ability with his hands and had been in a wheelchair all his life. His disability, however, was for him simply a practical matter of having to do things differently.

Louis was a lawyer. He had built up his own practice from a tiny window-less office to a substantial firm, Tim Louis & Co. Louis had a well-developed political philosophy. He did not support the free enterprise system and freely said so. He disliked its over-emphasis on materialism and competition. One of his mentors was Harry Rankin, a locally famous left-wing Vancouver city councillor, with whom Louis had articled. Louis had a deep admiration for the Committee of Progressive Electors (COPE), the left-wing civic party that Rankin had formed. He had even let his NDP membership lapse to become active in COPE.

Shirley Chan joined the board in 1987. She had been executive assistant and chief of staff to the mayor of Vancouver, Mike Harcourt. She was best known, though, as a spokesperson for the grassroots campaign to block a freeway through Chinatown, which also would have levelled the Strathcona neighbourhood in East Vancouver where she had grown up. Chan was very young then, still an undergraduate at the new Simon Fraser University. Afterwards, she did work in community organizing and social planning, and acquired a master's degree in environmental studies. When she joined Harcourt at City Hall in the early 1980s, she asked the people around her where she should do her banking. Harcourt and the others were members of VanCity. They talked about what a credit union was. The concept made sense to her, and Branch 8 was nearby so she became a member.

Others in the Action Slate group came from the same political stream. Steve Waddell was communications officer for the Health Sciences Association, a public-sector union. Jim Woodward was project manager of a co-operative housing society. Paul Gill was business manager of an International Brotherhood of Electrical Workers local and later moved into real estate sales.

Franca Zumpano was the odd person out. She wasn't political and she had worked for VanCity. She was, however, a determined woman, and one of the things she was determined to do was to get on the VanCity board.

Zumpano was an east-ender who had grown up near the Pacific National Exhibition grounds. As a female teenager in an over-protective immigrant family, she had stubbornly asserted her independence. Her school counsellor told her that she should think of getting a secretarial job, which impelled her all the more to go to university. She majored in education and was looking for part-time work to help herself financially. While door-knocking on East Hastings, she walked into Branch 3, where Wayne McKay was manager, and kept calling back until McKay decided to take a chance on her. The work there grew. She did everything, including becoming a loans officer. She put in extra hours. For the rest of her life, it remained the most memorable and satisfying place she had ever worked. She was honoured as a person; what she said really mattered. They were a group of eight people in the branch, getting the job done together, and they took care of each other.

After Zumpano became an elementary school teacher, she kept in touch with her VanCity friends. She watched them move up through the blossoming organization, and she was envious. They were in senior management, extremely successful, and she was "just a lowly teacher," she laughed. It seemed the only way that she could still be a part of VanCity was to be on the board. She wanted to run with the Action Slate, but Bob Williams kept putting her off. She ran once against them, although she liked what the slate was doing. Finally, they made room for her and she was elected.

The Action Slate had just become the majority, in 1985, when Louis joined the board. He imagined the boardroom as an austere, intimidating place with some magical power, but it was just an ordinary room with a table and chairs. He found it exciting to be part of the high-level discussions. He watched Levi and Williams, who were both capable of implementing an agenda. He hadn't been exposed to that kind of decision-making before. He joked that directors should be charged a fee for sitting on the board, it was so instructional.

The difference between Williams and Levi, around the boardroom table, Louis noticed, was like night and day. Levi, Louis thought, was "like oil that enables the machinery to run smoothly." He had greater interpersonal skills. He was far better as a mediator between board and management. There was less stress and conflict when he was chair. Williams, on the other hand, intimidated new directors, partly by his bearing and partly by his reputation. Chan remembered being afraid to open her mouth for fear that Williams might jump on her. Zumpano felt the same way.

Coro Strandberg, a young social worker, wasn't so cautious. She was recruited by the Action Slate in 1988, because of her interest in community economic development. One of her first sessions with the board was the annual planning retreat, held at the Yellow Point Lodge near Ladysmith on Vancouver Island. Williams chaired the meeting. At the end of the first day, they had the usual freewheeling "blue sky" session, in which anyone could throw out adventurous ideas. Strandberg asked about philanthropy. It was the wrong word, for Williams, with its intimations of dependence and of paternalism by the wealthy. He berated her. Nobody came to her rescue. She sat through it as stoically as she could, but afterwards went into the bathroom and cried.

When she came out, she saw Williams walking down one of the paths at the retreat. She followed him and grabbed his arm. "Bob, I need to tell you how best to work with me," she began. She explained how he should be more encouraging and should try to elicit her point of view. He apologized. This warmth on his part was in character, too. Chan realized that while Williams might be tough and difficult with some people, he was gentle, supportive and warm to others who needed that approach from him.

These others to whom one extended warmth did not, for Williams, necessarily include management. He could be "just unbelievable, brutally wicked," Louis remembered of some of Williams's more memorable cut-and-thrust forays against management. He might scold them or dress them down for lack of creativity, or progress, or vigour. "It's a hard thing to describe," Louis reflected. "He has such an incredibly bright mind. He'll read the same report I will, and to me, it will be an uneventful housekeeping item. He'll see all these things in there that should be this way and that way, and after you hear him, you think to yourself, 'Well, of course he's right,' and 'Why didn't I see all that?'"

It was hard to suppress one's feelings about Williams one way or the other. Richard Wafer was vice-president of computer services. He didn't mind the board pushing management, but Williams's "ranting and raving," with its implications of incompetence, he regarded as insulting and unprofessional. He didn't think it was done maliciously. It arose, it seemed to him, from strongly held beliefs and the feeling that it was simply the way to make things happen. Wafer had no problems with the objectives, but the tactics he disliked. "We did some ugly things that we didn't need to do," he once told the board, at the end of a planning session.

Wayne McKay was also alienated by Williams's attack style. He considered it counter-productive and demoralizing for staff. What bothered him most was the chilling effect it was having. Some people in management were afraid to stick out their necks in disagreement for fear that Williams would cut off their heads. The board said it did not want "yes men," but that's what Williams had produced, McKay thought. He blamed Quart for not protecting his people in order to maintain his relationship with Williams.

What actually transpired between board and management, or among those on the board, depended on the eye of the beholder. Tim Louis was unsympathetic to McKay's complaint. The job of the board, he thought, was to prod and challenge management to strive harder, and if Williams was doing it with feeling, all the better for VanCity's performance in the end. Besides, management were very well paid. They were at the top of the socio-economic ladder. To be challenged or even scolded a bit once a month wasn't a terrible burden.

Whatever the effect, it came with Williams's force of character. Steve Waddell, who was on the board in the late 1980s, chuckled over the challenge Williams presented. "He respects people who bark back," Waddell recounted. "What you've got to do is bark back on Bob, and then you can have a discussion that sometimes you could never have if you just tried to ignore him or were intimidated by him."

The board shared a deep sense of collegiality around re-establishing community values in the credit union, and Williams was in the centre of it. He was a mentor by example. "He knew what to ask for and how to ask for it, to make sure he got it" Steve Waddell recalled. "That was something we had to learn. Bob influenced a lot of us, to stand up and be aggressive about our positions, which included taking him on, too, when he disagreed with you."

It was more than strength of presence. Williams was a rare original thinker and also knew how to keep focus. Wendy Holm, an agro-economist and consultant, joined the board in 1990 and became a Williams fan. Holm had run independently and had managed to dislodge one of the Action Slate candidates. She was impressed by the warmth of the board. The Action Slate members also never brought up politics at the table, which would have caused a problem for her. The dynamics between boards and managements were fraught with perils, yet this group, it seemed to Holm, was managing that interface well and leading affirmatively.

Williams, it was clear to Holm, had undertaken that leadership. "You have to understand the intense dynamics of such relationships, where management tries to manipulate and subvert the positions of the board," she said. "If it's all sweetness and light, somebody's asleep at the switch." In the branches, Williams was gracious with people, but when talking to the CEO and vice-presidents, why not speak directly? Holm, an ex-New Yorker, had fewer problems with Williams' style than most. She was particularly struck by how Williams was able to bring big-vision thinking down to a concrete level. "Should people be living under bridges in a city like Vancouver?" Williams might ask, and want to do something about it and have feelings about it.

Williams himself was unrepentant. He also took stands on principle. Once the board was discussing whom to nominate as a director for B.C. Central, to represent Central's largest shareholder, VanCity. Steve Waddell's name came up. Waddell was gay and, as he put it, "quite out." He told the board they should take into account that his sexual orientation would inevitably be an issue with some people at Central. Williams would have none of it. That would be unacceptable, he said, with intensity. Whomever VanCity put forward would be the one who sat on Central's board and would be heeded.

It was Steve Waddell who had coined the phrase "Action Slate." The members of the group couldn't figure out what to call themselves, so Waddell simply stuck it on the letterhead.

The group was eclectic and, for Waddell, extraordinarily creative. Outsiders may have painted them as a clutch of New Democrats or left-wingers, but they were as various as humanity. That was a key Action Slate idea: to have the board reflect different constituencies. One just had to look around the boardroom table, Waddell thought.

Management saw the Action Slate members as neophytes. That was the big challenge, in their minds. Some had business experience. They did not, however, know banking. They had to gain those skills while pushing the envelope—the community perspective, accountability to members, the "co-operative tradition," as Waddell thought of it.

Everyone remembered the tension with staff. "We wanted to get things done quickly, and we saw wonderful ways that VanCity could spread its goodwill and investment in the community," Shirley Chan described it. "Then management would say, well, this will have an impact on our staff, it will have an impact on our branches, it will mean this much money, it's going to cost, here are the problems, these are the risks." All the negatives. There was always the feeling that management was trying to stop them from achieving their objectives because it wasn't what a banker would do.

The Action Slate board members ended up having separate forums of their own. They wanted to discuss issues frankly, and sometimes the discomfort around the boardroom table, with management sitting in, overcame freewheeling debate. Waddell was part of these meetings before he joined the board. The meeetings were one of the reasons why the board pursued the Ethical Growth Fund so vigorously. Levi had brought the idea to the caucus and they had identified it early as something they could do in the short term, despite staff resistance and moaning about financial implications. "We sounded to management just like, I guess, a bunch of kooks, wanting to have things done for social reasons," Waddell said.

Waddell was particularly interested in greater membership participation. He pushed for creating district structures and devolving at least some of the powers of the board. The board, however, found the idea too unwieldy. It tried branch councils instead, at two test branches, but since they were only advisory, interest could not be sustained and the experiment was dropped. A "Meet the Directors" picnic was also tried. So were director "Open Houses" at several branches. None of these devices, tacked on to the organization, accomplished what Waddell was after.

Just as frustrating was the attempt at more community investment. For a credit union, that meant more creative lending and broadening access to credit. Initiatives like the Ethical Growth Fund were nice, but, in the end, implementing this central idea about lending was what really counted, if the Action Slate's effort to change the culture of VanCity was to have meaning. The failure of the Seed Capital Program, however, had set back the whole concept.

It had, though, not been forgotten. Joy Leach, when she was chair, had suggested a foundation for the grassroots community economic development they had all talked about. Leach had a background in foundation work. Bob Quart latched onto the idea as a way of marrying his own and the board's objectives. If the separate program lost money because it was experimental and risky, or simply because it was building community in difficult circumstances, the financial integrity of the credit union itself would not be affected. That was the key, for Quart. The losses would be booked to the separate fund, and that fund would have to live within its means. VanCity's basic operation, Quart argued further, was essential to everything the board was trying to do. Unless VanCity was earning more income, the board's community goals could not be met.

Williams himself knew that VanCity's profit margin was far less than it should have been, and how that was holding the board back. He became more demanding. He asked that VanCity's performance be compared, in reports, not just to other credit unions but also to the banks and trust companies. He kept pushing for higher performance targets. He also wanted more branching eastward. The Action Slate, in its attack on the Geoff Hook regime, had originally argued that additional branches in Vancouver were more valuable than branches in the suburbs. Suburban branches were removed from the dense, urban Vancouver community to which a locally responsive VanCity should be committed. Williams, however, quickly realized what Hook had always known—that the savings took place in the city, and the borrowing in the suburbs, and it was only logical to match the two.

He had been after VanCity to catch up in the Fraser Valley, where a lag had developed. Quart felt the same way. Over the next several years, Quart opened branches in White Rock, Richmond, three different areas of Surrey (in addition to the first Surrey branch already in place) and Maple Ridge, penetrating the valley on the north side of the Fraser River. The Richmond branch, which generated large volumes almost instantaneously, was at a high-traffic intersection not far from Richmond Savings' main branch. Both flourished together. Richmond Savings had previously invaded Vancouver with a downtown branch. The old, bitter credit union battles to ward off VanCity and maintain exclusivity in one's territory were now forgotten history. Maple Ridge picked up many traditional VanCity members who had moved into the valley and were waiting for a VanCity branch to arrive. A Chinatown location was the only infill branch.

Richmond Savings had made a decision to favour members with signifi-cant deposits. These members were more profitable and they weren't simply piggybacking on the credit union's services. The VanCity board looked at the Richmond strategy, but worked from a different premise and went in an opposite direction. It insisted on maintaining service for poorer members with little money. Plan 24, instead of being phased out as had been planned, was used for the purpose. There were no chequing privileges with the account, but no fees, either. Members with restricted incomes who could not afford to pay fees still had a place to deposit cheques and could withdraw money at the branch or at a VanCity ATM without charge.

The interaction at planning sessions was difficult. Everybody on the board had something to say, had an interest, wanted something checked out. Management was the same. Planning sessions were legendary for burning out facilitators. Even when facilitators were briefed on what to watch out for, they were unable to keep the session on the rails. "Things don't evolve in what you would think of as a normal corporate way," Linda Crompton, vice-president of human resources, quipped.

Little by little, the two sides began to understand each other. VanCity's improving financial position helped. In 1989, the annual meeting approved the creation of the VanCity Community Foundation. The original endow-ment formula was two-sevenths of the membership dividend, which would have been, for that first year, a few hundred thousand dollars. Quart proposed instead a separate $1 million for the first allotment, which, he said, was not much. A lesser endowment would not generate enough revenue for the foundation to do anything. The board was surprised and pleased.

Williams was like a lion in winter. While agreeing to Quart's strategy for the basic operation, he took the community side as his own, as if by right. For some time he had in his mind the idea of creating a real estate arm with a social conscience. Beyond that was his own conviction, from his background in city planning, that VanCity could be more creative than others in producing good design and livability, and could use developments to strengthen social growth in neighbourhoods as well.

He pursued the idea privately with the other board members. He contacted a former Manitoba NDP cabinet minister, Wilson Parasiuk, who had extensive planning and development experience, to run the agency. He then spelled out the project for Quart, including the hiring of Parasiuk, and simply gave him no choice. Quart, however, drove his own bargain. He wasn't enamoured of providing equity up front, which could be lost without repayment. Everything else in VanCity was subject to financial discipline, and he wanted some discipline here, too, to protect VanCity's position, especially since the players were so close to the board. VanCity itself wasn't flush with capital, either. Quart agreed to provide the agency with money, but only as a loan and at market rates. "There was give and take on both sides," Quart said. "The reality there is Mr. Quart," Williams shrugged. "Pretty conservative."

The board called the new venture VanCity Enterprises. It would be a wholly owned VanCity subsidiary. Its first significant project was the redevelopment of Branch 3 at Kamloops and Hastings, in Williams's old neighbourhood in the East End. It was done in conjunction with a non-profit housing society, Entre Nous Femmes. The new building had social housing for single mothers on two floors above the branch, and for elderly women on another. There were also three units for people with physical disabilities. The senior women were available for babysitting for the mothers downstairs; that mix had been one of the ideas behind the project. The second floor had a courtyard with a playground, above the street. The units for people with disabilities overlooked the courtyard so that they could watch the kids playing. Staff in the branch, instead of giving Christmas presents to one another, gave presents to the kids upstairs. The building developed into a kind of community in itself. It won awards across the country and a prestigious American award. It was financially successful. Most of all, for Williams, it was an investment in neighbourhood building. It wasn't only in Kitsilano, the recherché west side area, he argued, where one could build apartments above shops on the street.

An EnviroFund for local environmental initiatives and a community-oriented corporate donations policy were also established. The newly created VanCity Community Foundation had some initial grassroots lending and technical assistance underway. These initiatives were small in themselves, but they slowly began to create the community colouration that Williams was after.

In the 1990 annual report, Williams sounded almost defiant about VanCity's local community purpose. VanCity wasn't like the national and international banks and trust companies, he said. VanCity's profits, instead of being put into offshore investments, stayed where they were generated. "After all," Williams wrote, "not only is this our place of business, it is our home."

CHAPTER 57

Den Mother Gone

WAYNE MCKAY WAS IN Lions Gate Hospital in North Vancouver when Larry Bell, exiting VanCity for B.C. Hydro, came to see him. McKay had undergone major gall bladder surgery and was about to be released. Bell was desperate. Dennis Lunney had just been appointed the new CEO and the announcement was forthcoming. Bell had helped the board make the selection but was fearful of the repercussions, particularly from Peter Cook and Bob Quart, who also had been candidates. Lunney's appointment would be provocative enough as it was. Bell wanted McKay to go to work as soon as he left hospital, smooth things out and keep the fort intact for a few months until Lunney arrived. Because of complications from the surgery, McKay was not feeling well, but he nevertheless gave Bell his promise. He showed up at VanCity the morning after his release, knowing that he was in no condition for it and should not have come.

He ended up effectively running the credit union during the waiting period. It wasn't a new role for him. He had first done it in 1973, when Don Bentley had been in hospital for heart surgery. What was odd about the the arrangement was that McKay, who to his people was the best qualified of them all to become CEO and who was immensely popular with staff, did not apply for the job. Nor had he in 1984, when Bell took over, nor in 1976 after Bentley had died, albeit he was still quite young then and disconcerted by Bentley's death.

Jan Chapman, whom McKay had mentored as a branch manager and who was now a theology student, wasn't surprised. "Wayne thought you got a position because of all the good things that you did," she said, "but you also have to grasp for the ring. You can't just wait until somebody hands you something for what you did. You have to make a move." McKay would never do that. He would go all out for others, but not for himself. He saw VanCity as a living and breathing whole, and himself as just part of it.

McKay claimed he had never wanted the job. He did not want to be in the limelight, he said. He didn't know if his nerves could handle the daily exposure and the annual meetings. He wasn't the right kind of person politically and socially for the job. He was just interested in working. He joked about how, given the way he dug himself into his work, being CEO would have probably killed him, and he preferred not to die quite that young.

He had found himself, as a result, in the difficult position of knowing more about operations and having a much surer connection to VanCity's people than his boss did, so that he might be seen as a threat. He was certain Geoff Hook had seen him that way. With Hook, he held himself back a notch. Only Larry Bell was completely open with him, he felt, and only then was he able to give everything of himself.

With the Action Slate board, he felt even less right for the CEO position. He got along well with them, but they thought differently than he did— they didn't have his sense of VanCity's relationship to its public. He feared they would say or do something that fitted their view of the world but would alienate members. He saw politics becoming a major factor in the way they would take VanCity forward, and he didn't want to deal with the directors in those terms.

The Lunney appointment, moreover, had disenchanted him with the way the board chose a CEO and how it saw the CEO's role. It was making its choices for reasons other than ability, he thought. He had begun, then, considering something other than VanCity—he had, in fact, been thinking about it vaguely since 1985.

He was weary. With so many roles in one job—handling both marketing and branch operations—his hours were as extended as ever. It wasn't so much the physical wear and tear, however, as the fact of increasingly finding himself alone on one side of an issue at management meetings, with all the others on the other side. He was always looking for ways to give members a break. It was harder for him to get things done that he felt should be done.

He still had his old playfulness and zest for bright ideas. He liked the Fat Cat account for kids, with its striped-cat mascot that showed up in parades and elsewhere, its Fat Cat watches and other paraphernalia. He knew from marketing research that if you could capture kids in their early years, most of them would be with you for life. The early Fat Cat campaigns tripled the number of junior accounts at VanCity, from six thousand to more than eighteen thousand.

His overloaded desk became a bottleneck. Some people thought the job was getting away from him. He disagreed. They were critical of his spending so much time, at his level, with individual members, but if members wanted to talk to him—and they knew where he was at head office and came right up to see him—he wasn't going to turn them away.

After the Dennis Lunney debacle, he saw the CEO job in a different light. He realized he could do it. Compared with Lunney, he had more than his share of social and diplomatic skills. "Wayne," his wife Carol once exclaimed defiantly, "would have made a great CEO." The political tinge of the board still bothered him, but the directors had turned out to be not as bad as he had anticipated. Had he had another chance, he might have changed his mind about the job. Now, however, it was too late. There were two times in his life when his feelings had betrayed him, he laughed. The first was in Sioux Lookout, when he had turned down the CIBC's offer to send him to university. The second was never applying for the CEO job at VanCity.

Ending his love affair with VanCity was not an easy thing for McKay to do. It took him five years to get the courage to say goodbye, which he did in 1990, after twenty-five years. He was nervous and fretful that he might miss VanCity so much that he would be at odds with himself. He set up a small consulting firm, Wayne McKay and Associates, with Dan Lenarduzzi, whom he had hired to do community relations for him at VanCity. He did a mix of credit union consulting, sports marketing and anything else that caught his fancy. Working with other, smaller credit unions in the province, using his VanCity experience and seeing tangible results, confirmed for him his own feelings about just how good VanCity was.

For a while he was in touch, by phone, with his former colleagues' ups and downs with the board, feeling almost as if he were still there. As the management-board relationship improved, he was more hopeful. Quart and his senior management team were, however, culturally different from McKay and his VanCity past. Their edges were rounded off. They did not have the idiosyncratic characters of the previous managerial generations— no anarchistic Ron Spooner, no haggard Frank Coffey, no driving Geoff Hook, no bizarre genius Gus German in the wings. McKay, still attributing such differences to the impact of the Action Slate board, thought collectively of the new style as "bland" and "plastic."

His fears of being lost without VanCity weren't realized. He was working long hours, as always, and enjoying himself. In 1992, he missed VanCity's annual meeting for the first time in twenty-six years. He was no longer interested. A year after leaving he had called on Bob Quart on a VanCity errand. There were jokes about Quart, the jellybean man, as different from McKay, the strawberry man. There were smiles and greetings up and down the hall from staffers glad to see him again, and expressions of dismay at his not having dropped by more often. These were expressions of genuine warmth, as McKay knew. Yet he also knew, from small things in his relationship with Quart since his departure, which he nevertheless noticed and felt, that he did not belong as he once had. Amid the conviviality he betrayed a shadow of discomfort—an urge to escape. VanCity was quite visibly no longer his world.

CHAPTER 58

Exploring the Frontier

EVEN AS A CHILD, LINDA CROMPTON had explored the edges. She was what she called "a major reader." By the time she was ten years old, she had read a good sampling of the classics. She loved Dickens. She had to take two runs at Victor Hugo's *Les Misérables*, but she eventually got through it. Her parents would kick her out of the house, force her to go outside and do other things. Otherwise she would be endlessly engrossed in a book.

By the age of seventeen, in Langley in the Fraser Valley, she already had a year of college under her belt. She wanted to attend the University of British Columbia. She was a young seventeen, however, and didn't have much experience in the big city. Her father wanted her to take another year at the local college. They argued about it. She decided that if she could not go to university, she would get a job instead.

She set off for downtown Vancouver, visiting every business and asking if it was hiring. Later, she wondered where she had gotten the nerve and the confidence. An insurance company on Pender Street was looking for a filing clerk-receptionist. That first job led to another, in insurance, and then on to the fledgling Insurance Corporation of British Columbia, the publicly owned automobile insurance company. Crompton was one of the first people it hired. Originally she did not even have a desk. She begged, borrowed and bought her own supplies. She began as a receptionist in the human resources division, but the title was misleading. She did everything. The rush of events in the instant creation of the large corporation was chaotic and energizing. The corporation hired about fifteen hundred people in its first year. Crompton developed some screening tools, then became an interviewer and kept moving. After seven years, she was a supervisor of operations and was familiar with all aspects of human resources. It had been enormously exciting. Everything was fluid, open, changing. The people that human resources had attracted and put together became the new organization.

She had married in the interim and left work to have a baby. She then became manager of staffing and employee development at the Vancouver General Hospital. The hospital had an in-house bank, but the employees were brusque and the atmosphere was unaccomodating. Crompton grumbled about it one day to a colleague, who was a member of VanCity. The colleague suggested that Crompton join the credit union. VanCity's head-office branch was close by. The atmosphere was positive and friendly, she was told. Crompton dropped by to see for herself and was convinced.

She was a member during the ill-fated 1985 conversion. When she ran over to the branch to do something, she had only a short period of time. She should have been frustrated by the long line-ups, yet for some reason, although the delays were inconvenient, they were tolerable. She concluded it was because of the staff. Their friendliness kept members loyal.

She quit her job to finish a university degree that she had begun in her spare time. When she was ready to return to work, in 1987, there was a place open at VanCity—manager of personnel services. Crompton applied for the position. As part of the interview process, she was taken through head office. The ambience was just like that of the branch downstairs. It did not take Crompton long to decide she wanted the job, and she got it. Shortly after her arrival, the head of human resources left VanCity because of personality clashes. Crompton was asked to take over. She became de facto manager of the division (later she would be named a vice-president).

It was her first position as head of a department. She was enthusiastic but also a little nervous. VanCity's people, however, she discovered, supported each other. There were no murmurs echoing, "I bet you can't do it." That gave her confidence. She also knew the organization had a reputation for being receptive to new ideas. She was sufficiently young, only thirty-four, that she had plenty of ideas of her own. VanCity had only recently been named one of the country's best employers. Far from discouraging Crompton, as if nothing were left to do, this forwardness seemed to open the way. "Everything is possible, all things can happen," she felt.

Not long after, two women in her department came to see her. They asked to share a job as part-timers instead of putting in a full week, as they were doing. They wanted more personal time. Crompton vaguely remembered a reference to an experimental idea called job-sharing. It wasn't technically complicated, she realized, it was socially complicated—a problem of communication and understanding. The two people in this instance handled recruiting and personnel problems for various divisions in the organization. A task that arose would not necessarily end before the job changed hands for the week.

Crompton consulted other human resources workers. Some of her peers had heard of job-sharing, but no one knew how it worked or where mechanisms for it were in place. Crompton and her people sat down and discussed how they would go about it. They decided there had to be an overlap. It was the only way that each of the participants could bring the other up to speed on a case. The overlap, of a day or even half a day, would mean an extra cost, but not to have gone ahead would have meant, for VanCity, losing two long-term employees with their experience and knowledge. It would be much more expensive to recruit and train new people, Crompton argued. The program worked and became a model for others.

Another idea, return-to-work, concerned women who had left to have a child and never came back. VanCity had lost considerable talent among female staff for that reason. It had been assumed the biggest problem was the worry that they had fallen behind and would have difficulty catching up. Studies in Britain, however, had discovered that the largest factor was the womens' feeling of isolation from the organization they had worked for. They were no longer part of something. Crompton had been through it herself, when she had her own baby, and recognized the syndrome. She set out to pioneer a program that would keep people connected.

Those who registered for the program continued to receive in-house newsletters. They were invited to social club events. To keep them current, so they would not have too much of a learning curve when they came back, they were asked to do two work stints of two weeks each during the year. Slowly, employees began to take advantage of the program. One of them, as it happened, was a man. He was in the marketing department and wanted to go back to university to finish his degree. Years later he would still refer to the program, and the liberty it gave him, as something that made a lasting difference to his life. It would take a lot for somebody like that ever to leave VanCity, Crompton thought.

She consciously went about correcting the gender imbalance in management ranks, insisting that there always be women candidates for management positions. The policy was to create a population in the organization that was consistent from bottom to top. At some point one had to step in and make it happen, she felt; otherwise the change would be too slow.

She found herself rescuing community relations, known then as "Community and Corporate Affairs" and reporting ultimately to the CEO. Dennis Lunney, in his downsizing mission, wanted to get rid of it. He thought it simply unnecessary. Crompton argued back. It was the main formal link with the community, she said. If VanCity lost that connection, all the goodwill that Wayne McKay had built up would be lost. "That would be insanity," she thought.

"Well, what are we going to do with it?" Lunney grumbled. "I don't want it reporting here anymore, because it's an illogical fit and I don't have time to supervise it."

"Fine," replied Crompton, "I'll take it. Put it in human resources."

In her off time, she had begun working on a masters degree in political economy at UBC. She was increasingly skeptical of traditional economic theory and was exploring alternatives, particularly those that took the environment into account. She decided to do her thesis on the World Bank's lending practices. The World Bank, in theory, alleviated world poverty by financing projects in Third World countries. In reality, many of its megaprojects were having negative social and environmental impacts. It was much easier for the bank, though, to move out large sums of money in megaproject loans. Managing a plethora of smaller loans, for projects on a local scale, would be much more time-consuming and the outcome not so predictable; hence it did not lend itself so easily to number-crunching.

Her thesis work changed Crompton. She began to question how decisions were made and to think of social responsibility. Her interest in environmental issues was sharpened. She had implemented a pioneering paper-recycling and waste reduction-program but wanted VanCity to become involved on the environmental front much more seriously, beginning with an environmental audit.

She knew such a commitment would at first seem highly unconventional. VanCity, after all, was a financial institution, not a resource company in which the connection between operations and the environment was obvious. Money wasn't neutral, however, she had come to realize. Banks were not just providers of capital. Money was actually used for something, and that something could affect society beyond mere transactions. Even a supplier who turned a profit on a VanCity account made choices that touched the environment, like the kind of paper the supplier provided.

The rest of senior management did not quite know what to make of Crompton's enthusiasm. All they could see was an added expense. Quart supported Crompton, but he, too, was mystified as to where she was going. Environmental audits, soon to become old hat, were unknown. Crompton tried putting her plans into context. VanCity prided itself on being a leading organization, responsive to the public, and the environment was a huge issue that people cared about. Not to address it was to make a mockery of what VanCity said it represented.

She hired two recent graduates of the Faculty of Environmental Studies at York University in Toronto. The ecological mission grew on the organization. An EnviroFund was created, to be financed by a 10 per cent check-off of income from Visa card transactions, for major grants to environmental projects. Internal environmental standards were established, including everything from phasing out styrofoam cups to establishing environmental purchasing policies—among them, moving completely to chlorine-free paper. Later, branches began doing their own environmental audits, and many of them even started worm composters. An environmental screen was added to the Ethical Growth Fund. VanCity became the first Canadian signatory to the CERES Principles (formerly the Valdez Principles) on environmentally responsible economies.

In order to become a CERES signatory, one had to have a senior executive responsible for the environment. Crompton had taken the idea to Bob Quart.

"Well, how are we going to do that?" Quart asked. "You're the vice-president of human resources." "Yeah," she replied, "vice-president of human resources and the environment." Quart went along.

Crompton, meanwhile, was becoming more involved in reshaping community relations. VanCity's sponsorship to that point had two functions—marketing and community awareness. It was strong on sports and also had traditional arts elements. The board committee that approved major donations, however, wanted to refocus on community issues. Crompton also downplayed the marketing objective. She changed the name of the community relations department to community development and brought in an ATM officer, Adine Day, to run it. Day had a degree in the history of western art and came from an environmentally aware family. She had joined Van-City as a teller to pay off her student loans, and had decided to stay. Connecting with Crompton proved serendipitous for them both.

Crompton had an instinct for knowing what the board was looking for. She shared its values. Community initiatives were now clearly aimed at social and ecological change. The board restructured its community donations by what were called "affinity groups" or "focus areas"—areas like the environment, children, women's expression, social and ecological change, violence prevention, co-operative issues, community economic development, land stewardship, and First Nations.

Crompton, on Day's recommendation, targeted the sponsorship programs, which she controlled, to the same areas, to reinforce people's sense of what VanCity was trying to do. She wanted to deepen the relationship between VanCity and its members, and tying VanCity to innovative, grassroots community projects with which they could identify, and even get excited about, was one way of doing it. VanCity's scholarship programs were reconfigured in the same way, for students interested in such fields as women's studies and environmental studies. A high-profile $4,000 VanCity Book Prize was established for the best B.C. book pertaining to women's issues.

Crompton had a good rapport with the rest of the senior management group. Their support came, she thought, from VanCity's general commitment to people. Day, who considered the management group a bunch of conservative bankers, by the nature of what they did, admired her boss unreservedly. "She was a real catalyst for change," Day thought. "Presence was needed at the senior level. Otherwise community development would just be lost."

Day's focus became progressively more grassroots, activist and developmental. Rather than focussing on the funding of specific events that had a public profile or that would get VanCity's name in a program—sponsorship as marketing—her allocations went to smaller, developmental groups that would not otherwise likely get grants. At "philanthropy luncheons" with her peers, she couldn't connect. She remembered sitting on a panel with counterparts from Chevron and Molson's and wondering what she was doing there. Their kind of sponsorship was relentlessly tied to marketing. Day refused to do a marketing analysis of her work. Marketing could do that analysis if they wanted, but she wouldn't.

It was a learning process both for Crompton and for Quart—a learning most of all about tolerance, because engaging community issues inevitably meant controversy around the edges. One grant was given to a group called Women In View, which produced an annual festival. The festival that year included a performance art show entitled "Man on the Moon, Women on the Pill." For publicity, the show distributed a postcard with a photo re-enactment of The Last Supper, except portraying women, all of whom were bare-breasted. It was, for VanCity, Crompton remembered thinking, extremely problematic. Many people were offended by it. It was one of the few such instances that shook Quart. "Now tell me again," he asked Crompton, "why did we fund this group?" They agreed on a position: This was the arts, and VanCity did not want to become a censor. Quart, the banker, Crompton laughed with appreciation, had stood by artistic principle.

Crompton and Day soon realized they were going to achieve only so much from head office. They set out to raise awareness about social justice and environmental issues within VanCity itself. They developed a branch network, in which each branch nominated a community liaison representative, who was to develop a strategic plan for community development for the branch. Artifacts of the programs, like leaflets and bulletin-board displays, became a natural part of the branch scene. The relationship between VanCity and grant recipients varied from handing out a cheque to helping a group write up a business plan around an idea. Where possible, a tie-in was made to a branch. Staff volunteers might get involved. Ultimately, the name "Corporate Sponsorship Program" was changed to "Community Partnership Program," to reflect the close, developmental working relationship between VanCity's people and the grassroots community groups assisted by the program.

Even the annual staff fund-raiser changed character. For several years, staff had raised money for the Terry Fox fund for cancer research. The last time it was done, they had generated a remarkable $120,000. When Day asked them how they felt about it, however, most talked about doing something different the next time. They knew their money was going to cancer research, but they wanted their fund-raising to be for local projects so that they could see the change in their community. Day developed a staff committee to do a project search. The first project they chose was Catalyst House, a safe house for teenage women prostitutes in which they could be secure, take training to recover their self-esteem and enter the regular workforce. Subsequent projects had the same, locally rooted character.

It had not occurred to Crompton and the board, when they changed the focus of donations and sponsorship, that they were planting the seeds of a quiet organizational revolution. As Crompton proceeded, however, the ethic became internalized. "It wasn't so much a structural change," Adine Day said. "It was almost like an energy change, a different focus."

Policy development now automatically took into consideration the social and environmental impact of decisions. The training program for new staff and management explored those issues. The annual report changed. It now, in addition to the conventional financial measures, held VanCity accountable for affordable housing initiatives (VanCity Enterprises), community economic development lending (VanCity Community Foundation), community animation at large (the sponsorship and donations programs), environmental impact and the quality of the workplace—social and environmental audits as well as the financial audit.

Once begun, the initiatives mushroomed by force of imagination. Crompton and the board had tapped into the social inclination in people that in business operations usually is suppressed. Crompton came up with the idea of advisory councils to help identify member needs in particular areas. The first was a women's advisory council. It quickly focussed on single mothers who were caught in pink-collar jobs and wanted to borrow money. Such women could not meet the standard lending ratios.

The new advisory council saw the women's predicament not as a prohibitive lending obstacle for VanCity, but as a systemic bias in the lending ratios, which had been framed without taking the women's circumstances into account. A single mother, for example, might not be able to scrape together a downpayment for an apartment, but was nevertheless paying a high rent and would have the ability to make payments on a mortgage. VanCity, in those terms, wasn't lending equitably at all. Crompton set up an appeal process to review women's loan applications that were rejected, and about 10 per cent of them ended up being approved. This appeal mechanism wasn't, at first, popular with branch managers, but it sent a signal to them that lending equitably to women sometimes required a different kind of thinking. With lenders sensitized, the special appeal process was discontinued; any member could still formally appeal a loan decision.

A day-care financing plan was established, at prime minus ½ per cent, to give non-profit daycare operations a boost. A youth advisory council was also formed, after the board asked for the development of a youth account. These councils, based on particular circumstances, established at least in a small way the wider membership participation that the board had attempted, and failed to manage, with the branch councils.

The new community outreach began to do the same for the branches themselves: offset the impact of VanCity's size and re-establish community roots. In an ad hoc manner, the board and Crompton had ended up fashioning the beginnings of a future kind of business organization. It had been done, finally, by taking the operating structure as it was and focussing instead on the underlying spirit of community behind credit unions.

For Crompton, the openness around her, including the acceptance by her sometimes quizzical management peers, had been exhilarating. Ideas developed in an anarchic way. They might start with the executive group or layers down within VanCity. They would ping-pong across the organization. Small work groups would be formed to do more research. An idea would make its way from there to the board level. There might be a struggle, because the participants were not passive. There were only a handful of people in her division working on community programs, but Crompton encouraged and pushed them, and their work had resonance. She remembered being conscious of a tremendous capacity for ideas within the organization and of how this fed her own intensity.

It seemed to the board, too, that its community purpose was gradually becoming part of management's culture as well. Management saw it through the other end of the telescope: that the need to recognize constraints had gradually become part of the board's culture.

George Scott, who became vice-president of marketing and planning at the end of 1990, had watched this evolution at close range. Scott was tall, unassuming and introspective. He had gone to B.C. Central directly after finishing a commerce degree at university, and was the first to do modern-style marketing research for B.C. credit unions, including surveys for Van-City. He had come to VanCity in 1979. For Scott, management's relationship to the board was like night and day to what it had been. There had been movement on both sides of the table. Most of the board's ideas were good, Scott thought, and they had a clear idea of where they wanted to take VanCity, but those ideas had to be corralled. They required development before they were workable. The big constraint was simply the calendar.

Scott shared the board's social commitment. He might have needed to be pushed, but he had a predisposition to support what they were trying to do. He believed in it philosophically, and he believed it worked operationally as well. He was, after all, a credit union person; he had never worked else-where. VanCity's commitment to improve the quality of life was, for Scott, the 1990s embodiment of the original credit union philosophy. Others, like Peter Cook and Richard Wafer, felt the same way. VanCity's community orientation, Cook argued, had long preceded the appearance of the Action Slate. It had come from Don Bentley and been passed on by Wayne McKay. VanCity, they all knew—one absorbed it by working there—was different from the others.

Quart also took pride in the new activity. Directors began to notice how he worked hard to implement what they wanted, even if he was, and always would be, a conservative and didn't believe as deeply in the direction they were taking. Tim Louis had succeeded Bob Williams as chair in the early 1990s and had come to know Quart. Quart, he said, "had an apparently highly developed ethical value system." Louis was taken by his decency. Working with Quart, he said, had shifted his world view from a belief that there were two groups of people in society: black hats, who voted right-wing and believed in free enterprise, and white hats. Quart, for all his conserva-tism, wasn't a black hat.

In 1993, Crompton took a year off to get a master's of business admin-istration degree and returned to VanCity in a different capacity. In a conver-sation, she heard about the women's advisory council. She was intrigued and asked if she could become a member. The others laughed. "I guess you can become a member," one of them said coyly, "since you established the council." In the tumult of so much happening, Crompton had forgotten all about it.

CHAPTER 59

Gathering Steam

WHAT RICHARD WAFER, VICE-PRESIDENT of information systems, liked most about working at VanCity was being allowed to do his job. Competence was recognized, Wafer thought. Bob Quart trusted him to do his job well. That was important to Wafer, not for the trust in itself but because it meant he could be truly effective. That group feeling, Wafer reflected—that everybody was in this together—had been part of VanCity for as long as he had known the organization. Different CEOs might try imposing other working patterns on the organization, but the group feeling always won out.

Bob Quart fitted this group ethic. Bob Williams remarked that Quart didn't really assert himself in his first few years. He gave people space and hesitated to intrude on their reporting. Even later, he did not report to the board much, leaving individual vice-presidents to speak for themselves. Gradually the organization began to show the underlying strength it had.

In 1990, the possibility of acquiring a trust company, Citizens Trust, came up, and Quart acted on it. The idea of a trust company acquisition had first surfaced in planning sessions back in Geoff Hook's day, but the options were limited. A strategic premise was involved. The Lower Mainland population was projected to grow dramatically through to the turn of the century, and outside deposit money would have to be found for VanCity to underwrite the increasing number of mortgages. That meant having a federally regulated bank or trust company that could pick up deposits elsewhere. Quart knew the pattern. In his Montreal Trust days, he had used Ontario and Quebec deposit money to underwrite mortgages in British Columbia.

Citizens Trust, although small, had what VanCity needed. It consisted of five branches in the Lower Mainland and one in Calgary. More importantly, it was already licensed for western Canada, and a licence for Ontario, to connect it to that deposit market, could be procured. There were other strategic advantages to the purchase. The population was aging, and the baby boom, as it grew older, would add to the wave. An older population meant larger savings. Somebody was going to manage that wealth. Larger savings also meant the need for more deposit insurance. The maximum for VanCity's provincial credit union deposit insurance was $100,000 per member. Citizens Trust deposits were insured federally for up to $60,000.

Between the two organizations a VanCity member could be covered for $160,000 without having to resort to a bank. Citizens Trust was also a major foreign exchange dealer, enabling VanCity to offer foreign currencies conveniently to its members.

Quart wasn't fazed by suggestions that buying Citizens Trust was inappropriate for a credit union. Many other co-operatives had subsidiaries. The purpose, after all, was to make the co-operative a stronger, more balanced organization. The philosophical question wasn't an issue for the board, either.

Quart gave Peter Cook the job of running the newly acquired company. For Cook, it was like moving from a highly developed civilization into a primitive one. Citizens Trust was less skilled, with less depth and with little understanding of where it fitted into the community. It was also a lacklustre performer. Cook's first priority was to make it financially productive. He aggressively increased the asset base to better absorb overhead costs; several of its branches had been too small and weren't paying their own way. He relocated some branches as leases expired. Because of VanCity's backing, he was able to convince the regulators to increase the company's gearing ratio—how much it could accept in deposits for every dollar of equity capital. He worked on the mismatch between assets and liabilities, which was structured for rising interest rates in an era of falling interest rates. VanCity, Cook thought, was probably the best in the country at managing mismatches. In two years, he made Citizens Trust one of the most profitable trust companies in the country, as measured by return on equity.

The takeover by VanCity reversed the stereotype. A credit union had the know-how, discipline and depth to whip a traditional financial institution into shape. It seemed an odd turnabout, but nobody at VanCity was surprised.

Quart and the board, simultaneously, looked at ways of injecting more equity capital into VanCity in order to expand more quickly. A shortage of equity capital had always been a strategic predicament for credit unions. The limit of expansion for a financial institution hinges by a large multiple on its share capital and retained earnings. A bank can simply issue more shares and let investors trade them for whatever capital gain they might pocket along the way. A credit union, by contrast, is dependent on members putting more money into their share account, with no speculative capital gain and no extra voting power.

VanCity, by a membership vote at one of its annual meetings, had raised its minimum share requirement from $25 to $50. Some members argued that it would discourage people from joining, particularly low-income people, but the $50, with inflation, was worth less than the original $25 share requirement. The adjustment was a reminder, too, that a credit union was a co-operative enterprise to which members committed themselves consciously with an investment, albeit, for most people, a nominal one.

The increase, though, did not go far in solving VanCity's capitalization problem. Surrey Metro Savings met the difficulty by simulating a bank. It issued non-voting shares, to be traded on the Toronto Stock Exchange. This took it one step away from credit union philosophy. The VanCity board found that repugnant. Instead VanCity issued what it called "investment shares," to members alone. The new shares' rate of return was pegged at 1 per cent or more above a corresponding Government of Canada bond yield, reflecting the fact the shares were not backed by deposit insurance. The intention was to raise $10 million over a four-month period. Enthusiastic members snapped up the issue, pouring in $17 million in ten days after which the offer had to be shut down. "We were almost in disbelief," Quart remembered. Nobody thought the membership would have such a capacity to bring capital to the organization.

Managing VanCity now was more and more a matter of managing burgeoning complexity; for Quart, it consisted of managing the people who were managing complexity. VanCity treasury guru Chris Dobrzanski had for several years been using "derivative" financial instruments, like futures, options and swaps, for a hedging program against variations in the interest rate. The object was to balance the short-term mismatch. Deciding how much to close the mismatch was an arcane exercise by which VanCity could come out ahead or behind, and also make trading gains, depending on the way interest rates went. Dobrzanski was a master at coming out ahead. He was an enigma—taciturn, not a good communicator, often working better alone, but principled, committed. David Levi was amazed that Dobrzanski was still with VanCity. Levi, in the investment business himself, thought Dobrzanski could be earning four times as much working at any brokerage firm in the city. He had jokingly threatened Larry Bell with murder if he took Dobrzanski with him to B.C. Hydro.

Quart also wanted to beef up his management data. An advanced cost-accounting system was developed to measure the profitability of branches. Branch profitability had always been looked at, going back to Don Bentley working with an adding machine and a pencil. This system, however, involved sophisticated "transfer pricing," by which branches were "charged" for the funds and head-office services they used. The system was then extended to measure the profitability of products. It produced some surprises. Bill payments had a much higher cost than had been thought. Such analytic data suggested its own changes. If submitting the physical bills collected at a branch was costly, then it made sense to look at ways of doing it electronically. "We became much more disciplined," Quart remembered. "We really understood our business much better."

Bob Saunders's retirement services department was generating increasing business. Saunders had made VanCity a major presence in retirement counselling. This was unusual for a financial institution; the other major participants were a few financial counselling and annuity firms. VanCity's financial seminars, in the fall and the RRSP season, had become a fixture in the city. The seminars were accessible; they had a common touch to them.

Sometimes members would apologize to Saunders for having only modest savings and not being an important account for him. Saunders dismissed this. He and his department made a point of taking the same time and care with everyone, regardless of their assets. He liked to say that those with the least savings were the most important clients, since every dollar meant that much more to them and they valued his advice the most. Saunders had an unusual arrangement with VanCity. He and his people were paid on an incentive basis, without a salary, and looked after a good part of their expenses. Retirement services was virtually a business unto itself.

Technology was shifting the ways in which members did business with VanCity. Quart created a new operating sector, sales, and put Larry Wald in charge. "Sales" went beyond branches and beyond marketing. It consisted of selling outside the branch—outside a physical building which, with its sign out front and its counters inside, was what a credit union or bank had always represented. Wald instead had six mobile mortgage development managers working out of their cars and two business-development managers doing much the same with the Chinese and Indo-Canadian communities, but with mostly deposit business in mind.

Although nominally connected to particular branches, Wald's mobile development people communicated with cellular telephones and home fax machines. They might put a deal together at seven in the evening or on a Sunday mid-afternoon if that was required. They cultivated relationships with realtors not through a branch office but on the road.

Wald was an enthusiast. Such "service delivery options," as he called them, and others like ATMs, TeleService and automated service lines, were, he was convinced, the key to the 1990s. More than a change in mechanics was involved. A cultural premise lay behind the shift. When Wald, as a young man, had joined the Bank of Montreal, the range of products was controlled by the banker. Consumers wiped their feet when they entered the door, took off their hats, and said, "Yes, sir" and "No, sir." The financial services business now was member-driven. This was different even from the VanCity past, Wald thought, responsive as it may have been. That, in Wald's mind, could be best described, by comparison, as only "member-influenced."

The results here were surprising, too, underlining how significant the shift was. The six mortgage-development managers were generating more than a fifth of all VanCity residential mortgages, in dollar terms, and the percentage generated by this section would continue to rise, to a third. TeleService, also functioning outside the branch system, now reported to Wald. It also handled about a fifth of VanCity's residential mortgage business. Wald had tried to change TeleService from what he called an administrative component to a sales component. Staffers were given extensive sales training and feedback on how they were doing in comparison with the rest of VanCity. He felt that, strong as the service was, it had just now, in the early 1990s, achieved its real potential. He was frustrated that, although members themselves knew TeleService, it had not taken over the entire market. It was so exceptional and such a powerful advantage that Wald wanted VanCity somehow to tell everyone in the world about it. He knew it wouldn't be long before TeleService had imitators.

Quart, meanwhile, had heard about an energetic Los Angeles psychiatrist, Marty Cohen, who, together with a management consultant, Edward Brown, had developed a novel training program for financial institutions. It was based on medical diagnostic techniques; Cohen referred to bank employees becoming "financial physicians." "Techno-motivational" programs, he called the approach. The object was to create a pro-active sales culture and, with it, "personal relationship banking." Cohen had resuscitated an ailing bank in Seattle, and Quart took a management team down to Seattle to find out how it had happened. After meeting with Cohen on a later trip, he decided to adopt the program.

The idea of staff being more pro-active with members and "selling" what was available wasn't new to VanCity. The taboo against it had been broken in Geoff Hook's day. Cohen took this one step further. His training program convinced VanCity staffers that it was financial malpractice not to suggest to members financial services that would solve their problems, in much the same way that it would be medical malpractice for a doctor not to properly help a patient by listening carefully and proferring a diagnosis. In order to be of greatest help, similarly, one had to have a good diagnostic ear and draw the member out.

VanCity offered so many services that if a member volunteered information, there quite likely would be something coming back from the member representative. If, for example, a member mentioned going on holidays, did the member have travel insurance, extra health insurance, travellers' cheques, a will? Not to give members the opportunity to think about things they may have overlooked in the hustle-bustle of life would be to fail them.

The possibility that such a program might turn VanCity into a pack of hucksters never came up. VanCity staffers innately protected members from services and products that they really didn't want or wouldn't find of value. It was part of VanCity's underlying culture—Don Bentley's saying, "Always be fair to members." Besides, all the staff knew it wasn't in VanCity's interest to push unwanted products on members. It would destroy the relationship with the member in the long run.

Quart, thinking the Cohen-Brown program a much bigger jump for VanCity than it was, expected to lose up to 25 per cent of staff because of it. He decided to go ahead nevertheless. The loss of staff didn't happen. He remembered reflecting, watching this outcome, that he had a staff that was young and flexible enough to change, and what a powerful strategic advantage that was.

Quart was looking ahead to the new world of banking—not just ATMs, an automated service line or direct payment using one's VanCity card, which were already behind him, but also cash cards and the spectre of the electronic cashless society. He had VanCity become a full voting member of Visa Canada, rather than, as an associate member, having to buy the service through one of the chartered banks. It gave him access to the table. He had set himself the goal that VanCity would not be left on the other side of the door when decisions were made on how the evolving payment system would work.

VanCity's relationship to Visa Canada had been an up-and-down affair. When the credit union issued its first Visa card in 1985, it had made the card available in combination with VanCity's own card, so the same piece of plastic could be used at an ATM and as a credit card. Chris Bergthorson at Embryo Communications dubbed it the "Visa Sandwich." Visa Canada (then the Canadian Bank Card Association) did not like its card being referred to as a sandwich and berated Bergthorson, which did not, however, dissuade him from using the concept. Nobody else in Canada had offered the double function, and the marketing team at VanCity was particularly proud of it. A few years later, however, Visa Canada decided it made more sense from a marketing point of view to have both cards and killed the reissuance of the Sandwich. Working second-hand through a supplier, in this case the CIBC, had its constraints, too. VanCity was left with an uncompetitive card, with which it couldn't control pricing or product development, and with no willingness on the part of the supplier to allow VanCity to have the best product in the market. The acquisition of full member status in Visa Canada was a step to repatriate control, for that and anything else in the payment system that followed.

The composition of the staff was changing. In 1986, before Linda Crompton had joined VanCity, male branch managers outnumbered female branch managers four to one. By 1992, their numbers were equal. In 1988, when Quart became CEO, Crompton was the only female senior executive. By 1994, more than a third of senior executives were women, and two of them were in high-profile operations slots, including Crompton, who succeeded Cook as CEO of Citizens Trust. An equity co-ordinator was hired to formalize VanCity's commitment to diversity and equity in hiring. Human resources began paying special attention to encouraging First Nations applicants. Over 90 per cent of management openings were being filled internally. The decade-old pioneering Fitness Incentive Program had been replaced with a more holistic Living Well project in which everything from eating a nutritious breakfast to donating blood, meditating, volunteering in the community or composting kitchen waste counted for points. More than ever, working at VanCity meant something; it was desirous and even had status.

Under the impact of each of these incremental steps, income continued to climb. Earnings after the members' share dividend but before taxes, which had been $8.8 million in 1990, hit the $30 million range by 1992. The dividend was boosted by these results. In one exceptional outlay, 1991, it was set at 21 per cent per equity share. The increased profits also meant larger contributions to the VanCity Community Foundation endowment fund, the community partnership programs and donations. In 1994, they reached 5.2 per cent of earnings after taxes. With these improved results, Quart could also turn to other things. He moved VanCity back into business lending, hoping this time to do it right by starting small and building up the portfolio naturally. Then VanCity repurchased VanCity Insurance Services, which it had sold off in 1988.

Quart had added a senior vice-president. When Linda Crompton left human resources to do her MBA, Quart, as a condition, asked her to find a replacement who was as good or better than she was. Crompton introduced Quart to Tazeem Nathoo, senior human resources manager at B.C. Hydro. Nathoo came over to VanCity. Soon Quart had moved her, putting her in charge of operations, including the branch system. He had always thought of VanCity as an organization of people and hence considered the head of human resources a key figure. Special skills in the financial industry, he conjectured, were no longer, perhaps, as important as skills in motivating and involving people. Moving Nathoo to operations took the thought one stage further.

A hard-nosed stubborn South African, Jeremy Hooper, who had been controller, was also, now, a senior vice-president. Hooper was a carry-over from the brief Lunney period. Quart used him as the house contrarian. Hooper challenged everything until he fully understood it. He also knew how to do due diligence work; he negotiated the repurchase of VanCity Insurance and was involved in the acquisition of Citizens Trust. Most of all, though, Hooper, stubbornly pushing for changes, brought a financial and reporting discipline to the organization, that Quart was after, by second nature.

Quart by this time had eleven vice-presidents under wing, aside from the presidents of the wholly owned subsidiaries (Citizens Trust, VanCity Enterprises, and VanCity Insurance Services) and the director of the arm's-length VanCity Community Foundation. Middle management had the same depth. When Quart set out to build a new head-office building for VanCity, further east just off Main Street, he was able to draw on the people at VanCity Enterprises. A new generation of branch managers, people who had first been hired in the late 1970s, had come into their own, with the same competitive enthusiasm as earlier ones. Most of the branches, as well, were now running six days a week. It was as if the organization were just gathering steam.

Quart wondered how long he could hold on to his senior management. His executives, he had argued to the board, were underpaid relative to the marketplace, but the board had refused to accomodate him. "They're not as overpaid as the others, no," board member Tim Louis commented tartly about the complaint. The board had allowed Quart to implement a bonus system based on profitability but, to Quart, while the bonuses were essential, they still didn't solve his problem. He was the one who had the responsibility of keeping the organization together, he said, and he had to have the best minds for it.

Quart wasn't concerned about his own income. He wondered, though, whether the board recognized just how tough senior management's work was, and how tough the business was. The commitment required of him, he thought, went far beyond what he would do in another organization. "You have to perform magic," he once said in a revealing moment. "You have to take a whole bunch of conflicting ideologies and make them work together."

Quart knew, though, too, that something other than money tied competent people to VanCity. That particular something—the deeply felt camaraderie of the place—had returned. It really had never left, but had just been masked by the turmoil of the mid-1980s. Garry Smith, running what was now called technology services, had joined VanCity in 1971. He had stayed, he said, because he loved the organization. It was the best organization in the world to work for. Although he had been in credit unions for more than twenty-five years, he wasn't preoccupied with credit union philosophy. He would operate the same way if he were at a trust company or a bank. However, there was an atmosphere at VanCity—the way people worked with each other—that just didn't exist elsewhere. Occasionally, on the street, Smith would meet ex-VanCity hands who had gone to another organization, and they would say exactly the same thing. Some who had left in the past had come back. Whatever it was in the organization, it had a way of holding people tight.

CHAPTER 60

The Aficionado

WHEN RICHARD WAFER JOINED VANCITY in January 1989 to become vice-president of information services and bring computer services back in-house, he was flabbergasted. He had left Bob Leighton and Associates, which had operated the system for VanCity, a year and a half earlier. What surprised him was that the patchwork arrangement that he had put in place to pull VanCity out of the 1985 conversion fiasco was still being used, just as he had left it. The overloaded Geac 8000 configuration had not been replaced by the open-ended Geac 9000. The operators were still cutting up and gluing back the database every night, according to the hieroglyphic flow chart he had devised. The system was a disaster waiting to happen because eventually, by the law of averages, someone was going to slip up. It was a miracle, Wafer thought, that some horrible calamity hadn't already befallen them. He managed to convince the board that he knew what he was doing and that they should put up $1.5 million to move to the Geac 9000. Luckily for Quart and the board, he did know what he was doing.

Wafer was a technical person who had a sense of people. He came from Ripon, a little cathedral town in Yorkshire. He was briefly a mathematics and physics teacher. He got into computer work by a quirk of fate when he applied for a computer job, for the fun of it, to go along with a girlfriend who was applying. He was hired, although she wasn't. Later, in Canada, he worked for CDS, the computer subidiary of B.C. Central, but it was his time at Geac, which followed, that he remembered fondly—its exciting, get-things-done atmosphere and dedicated people who believed strongly in what they were doing.

Now, back at VanCity, he was faced with a dilemma. The computer staff did not have a broad enough background to handle any major problems in the system. If a misadventure occurred, he would be helpless. He initiated a program of cross-training and transfer of skills. "I threw them up in the air and put them all down some place other than where they started off," he said. Meanwhile, he developed a long-term system design and an implementation path. By early 1990, he was ready to install the new Geac 9000 machine. Preparation for the conversion had been underway for several months. The conversion date itself was set for mid-March, after the RRSP season.

Two weeks before the conversion date, on the last day of the RRSP season, the busiest day of the year—after the division had succeeded in hanging on for that long interim period—the disaster that Wafer had worried about happened. An operator spotted a small error and, in correcting it, had a mental lapse. The resulting fault in itself was minor, but it was malignant, and it progressively corrupted membership files throughout the next day. None of the regular recovery tools would work. The fallout was worse than Wafer had predicted, since recorded transactions had been erased. To reconstruct the database, Wafer turned to the backup tapes from the previous night, but, to his horror, some of them proved unreadable. It took Wafer and his division six weeks of twelve-hour shifts to painstakingly straighten out the database and produce the necessary verifications for auditing purposes. Later, one of the board members called Wafer up and chided him sardonically for having to prove his point so insistently.

It was the second and last of the VanCity computer disasters, an aftershock from 1985. The belated conversion went well. Everything around Wafer, however, was in flux. Geac had sold its banking development arm to the Saskatchewan co-operative movement, which turned it into a consortium called Co-operators Data Service Ltd., or CDSL. Although based in Regina, the development office still operated out of Burnaby. VanCity had its own customized software. CDSL, however, benefiting from the input of all its users, had produced a new software system, RFS—Retail Financial System—which was more advanced. Times had changed, too. Long lead-times in new products had disappeared. If VanCity came up with something new, the other credit unions would have it in a month. Everybody now had the same products, like daily interest or open mortgages. The delivery of the service rather than the service itself would differentiate VanCity from the others in the future.

Wafer decided that instead of duplicating CDSL's effort, VanCity should become part of it. He led VanCity through a third conversion, this time to RFS. Conversions were no longer so scary. He wasn't willing, though, to surrender all autonomy. He arranged to have some VanCity people work side by side with CDSL's cadres so that VanCity would retain its own capability.

He had particularly wanted RFS for its automated loan origination system, which VanCity had attempted a technical generation earlier. The loan-origination software was ingenious. It customized the loan application, led the loans officer through the process step by step, calculated debt service ratios, produced borrowing alternatives, brought up the applicant's credit rating and created the hard copy of the application on a laser printer. Wafer thought that, fully utilized, the system would cut the interview time by half.

He was part of a powerful Lower Mainland technological community hitting its stride, a development which had begun with VanCity's original Geac contract in 1974. Prologic Computer Corporation in Richmond, which licensed software to a constellation of credit unions, including Richmond

Savings, was a spin-off launched by former Geac people. CDSL was Geac under another name. Cue Datawest, the successor to the original CDS, was the outgrowth of a Geac installation. This advanced regional capability was unseen by most people but very much present. It was umbilically linked to the B.C. credit union movement and its creativity; the banks' computer work was done far away, in remote central Canada. Wafer, the computer aficionado whose personal history was interwoven with this technological current, was now finding fulfilment in his VanCity work. He was as far out on the leading edge as he could reach without being on the bleeding edge, which is where one would end up if one went out too far. The future opened up in front of him, stage by stage, onto the technical horizon.

That horizon included what he called the Member Service System, which would not only print out deposit and withdrawal slips automatically, as VanCity already did, but would automate other front-end functions, like opening new accounts, printing starter cheques and issuing member cards. This and the existing loan-origination system would also be the initial elements of a "distributed system," in which supplementary information about members would be kept locally in branches and be available to terminals in other branches in a "wide area network," without benefit of a mainframe.

Wafer also envisaged using the loan-origination system to allow members to apply for a loan without benefit of a staffer at all. It would happen in the branch through what in the jargon was being described as a "self-service terminal" or a "member-activated device." Members, without bothering with an appointment, would run through the automated loan-origination sequence on their own, enter the finished application and be on their way. The computer would notify a loans officer, who would then call, either approving the application or asking the member to come in because of problems.

The strategic objective was to automate all cash transactions, and a loan was another, albeit multi-factor, cash transaction. This drew up the spectre of a soulless, metallic and plastic, robotic branch consisting of serried terminals and ATMs. Wafer had seen such a branch—an experimental Royal Bank outlet in Burlington, Ontario. Its banking hall consisted of walls of machines, including a coin-counting machine, and looked a bit like an amusement arcade. Only at the back was there a traditional group of tellers, if one really had to see a teller.

Wafer knew this wasn't right for him. He didn't want his technology to discourage members from talking to branch staff. New devices, he thought, should always be options for the member and not primary to VanCity's purpose. He saw extended automation, like ATMs and an automated tele-phone service, as freeing branch staff from the simple high-volume trans-actions for tasks in which the member needed more contact, reinforcing the relationship rather than weakening it. Automation, nevertheless, was wonderful to Wafer, irresistible. Besides, new ways were part of the house tradition. "Our members expect us to be innovative and we don't want to disappoint them," he once wrote in a commentary on VanCity for *Credit Union Technology*, a magazine published in New York.

In 1990, he brought VanCity's 24-Hour Service Line (the automated telephone service) on stream. Some U.S. banks had introduced an embryonic automated service in the early 1980s, but the application had been slow to spread. At VanCity, it had a useful side-effect. By siphoning off routine calls about account and rate information, it took the pressure off TeleService, allowing it to improve its already fast response times. TeleService and the 24-Hour Service Line together were an ideal combination.

Wafer wasn't the only one doing new technology. Garry Smith, who ran technology services, was imaging documents on optical disks, which would get rid of storage rooms of files. It was the first step in going paperless. It would also improve productivity, because the documents so stored would be easily retrievable, via desktop terminals. The next step, yet to come, would be to record transactions directly onto the imaging system without printing a paper copy first. The member would "sign" a loan application by writing on the computer screen or on a pad, or with a thumbprint, and the signature would be stored that way, electronically. Smith was having a late love affair with technology.

Wafer from the first had been determined that VanCity would continue to lead the trend in technology or, alternatively, would be able to react to changes quickly, and to do that he was just as determined to protect the people who would do it for him. He had seen enough of computer staff having their personal lives disrupted. He set up a rotation system so that people took turns being on call; with the cross-training he had done, they could each handle many areas. He refused to set an absolute date for conversions, whereby his team might be forced to go ahead without being fully ready and without enough sleep. Wafer didn't believe in computerdom's compulsive zeitgeist of working all the time. He had a cheerful, wry sense of humour that provided computer work with human relief.

He realized from where he stood in the organization not only how VanCity was different but also how much it depended on his division. In most organizations, he would be somewhere down the line, perhaps reporting to the chief financial officer. At VanCity, he was a member of the executive committee, involved in all stages of planning. It couldn't be any other way, he thought, given the pace of technological change. He considered it a compliment to Quart that Quart had recognized that.

Quart was also willing to spend money on leading technology, relatively small as VanCity was. Quart knew that it wasn't so much putting up risk money as making a mainstream investment in a necessity of business, at least if VanCity were to continue to be a leader. The crucial factor wasn't money but the capability of Wafer and his people.

Home video banking was a mythic technological quest. It had long been talked about, but always as a futuristic venture. Wafer and Quart were in San

Antonio, Texas, at a Bank Administration Institute meeting attended by executives from the financial services industry around the world, when the subject came up again. Quart was inspired. "How far away is it?" he asked Wafer. "A long way away if we do it like everybody else, but I can do it quicker," Wafer replied. They decided, on the spot, to be the first in Canada with a home video service.

Most technological projections for home banking involved the personal computer. Wafer and VanCity opted instead to build the service on the most commonly used device in the home, the television set. People were used to their television remote-control device. The object was to adapt to that technology, making the service the most accessible and the most user-friendly. Cable companies did not have the necessary interactive infrastructure. Wafer instead got together with B.C. Tel, and they jointly came up with a concept, creating their own standard because no other standard existed. For the prototype, he contracted with a programming group that knew nothing about banking but everything about video games. Wafer wanted the service to have an easy "game feel" to it.

In the spring of 1994, a senior Royal Bank executive made an announcement about the introduction of a Royal Bank automated telephone service the next year. He went on to add that ultimately he could foresee this access being available through personal computers and television. A month after his announcement, VanCity staged a media event and made its own announcement: Teleview, its video home service, was fully operational and was about to be tested with "live" participants. "We announced his tomorrow today," Quart joked. He had clipped the newspaper report of the Royal Bank statement and joked about framing it.

The rollout for VanCity's 213,000 members was the summer of 1995, and the service was renamed VanCity Direct. It included both television and personal computer access. Shortly after, VanCity Direct Business, for business members, came on stream. As far as Wafer knew, it was the first television-based home banking system in the world that used an ordinary telephone line.

VanCity Direct opened the way to applying for loans while sitting at home or simply ordering up a loan after prequalifying. Even more so than the telephone service line, it moved the locus of making transactions away from the branch, since one could actually see one's own account on a home screen. The very concept of a branch was changing under the impact. Plans were launched for a mini-branch inside the Save-on-Foods supermarket in Metrotown in Burnaby. It would be Branch 35. A full-service VanCity branch averaged five thousand square feet. This one, providing many of the services, would occupy only five hundred square feet and be open seven days a week.

Technology, it seemed to Wafer, was making traditional retail banking almost irrelevant, and there was more to come: smart cards. Quart pushed Wafer on that one, too. A smart card, with its chip, was essentially a computer on a card. It could store cash. As Wafer envisaged it, members, after having their paycheque deposited directly, could stick their smart card in a device attached to a computer at home and withdraw money onto the card as they needed it. They could even do the opposite: collect their paycheque on the card and transfer money from it to their account electronically. They could buy things on-line and have the cost directly debited from the card. They could, in a sense, conduct their entire lives outside the credit union, not even bothering with the ATM on the branch's wall.

In late 1995, VanCity launched the first Canadian market trial of the Visa Cash smart card, which was designed to eliminate the need for small change—the initial step to the larger application. Then there was Internet banking. Wafer had already started work on it; it would be ready once security and privacy issues were settled, almost as if it were just another humdrum technical chore.

Wafer felt that the VanCity he worked for was becoming more complex and technocratic. Running the business was qualitatively different from what it had been before, when Wayne McKay could keep his fingers on everything. Just from sheer physical size, with more than 1,200 employees, it was difficult to be in touch with employees at the "sharp end," especially in branch operations. There was always a danger of becoming overly bureaucratic, like a bank; one had to be vigilant against it. One of the things that made VanCity what it was, Wafer felt, was its desire to do something wild and crazy, and that sense of adventure and experiment had to be protected. What saved them at head office was their collegiality. The participatory attitude they brought to the job wasn't much different from that of previous generations, Wafer thought.

The new technology, though, had its own impetus. The stronger it became, the more important it was to strengthen VanCity's social character and its connection to members. Wafer was a credit union enthusiast. When he talked about VanCity's future, he was like a circus performer with one foot on each of two horses—technical leadership and community—and hoping the two horses would continue to run together.

CHAPTER 61

Foundations

CORO STRANDBERG WASN'T INVOLVED IN counselling or family therapy like most social workers. She was a director of a seniors' agency in New Westminster. Her major study area, when she did her master's degree, was unemployment. While working on that topic, she happened on the concept of community economic development and set out to become an expert. The key premise of the concept, as she saw it, was to organize communities so that people locally had more control of their economic future. Later, she was involved with a group of women working on community economic development strategies for women, in particular, trying to set up a community loan fund. When she was invited to run for the VanCity board, she called up people in this circle—her peers and mentors—for advice. They were critical of VanCity, which they regarded as establishment. They cautioned her about VanCity's mainstream nature but thought she could help in bringing their group's values to the organization.

Strandberg had previously attended some VanCity accountability sessions, which were open forums for members. The members, speaking at microphones on the floor, demonstrated a real passion for the credit union, but also a deep unhappiness. They didn't know what they wanted VanCity to do, but they knew they wanted it to have a larger role. Strandberg's own network of people had long talked about credit unions taking leadership in financing locally owned and controlled development projects.

The notion of establishing a VanCity foundation, originally Joy Leach's idea, was in the air when Strandberg joined the board. David Levi in particular was mulling it over. Levi had never accepted the outright junking of the Seed Capital Program. He refused to have its basic premise simply dismissed and buried. He was especially interested in lending to non-profit organizations. A co-operative health clinic, the Mid-Main Community Health Centre, had been financed by the Seed Capital Program. Levi wanted to make sure that whatever new vehicle the board chose for community development could do the same thing.

He sought out a lawyer specializing in charities, Blake Bromley, and invited him to lunch to discuss the issue. Bromley told him he thought it was possible and that a foundation was just right for it. Canadian foundations invested their money passively, with a view simply to generating revenue and then distributing it. Several U.S. foundations, however, used some of their their endowment actively, as a community investment vehicle— as loans under another name. "Program-related investments," they were called. Why not do the same at VanCity? It was a bit unusual, and VanCity would be breaking new ground in Canada, but Bromley recommended going ahead. There was another advantage to this mechanism. Even an organization that did not have charitable tax registration, and hence could not receive a grant from a foundation, could receive help in this way. A foundation could even make a no-interest investment, justifying it in terms of "community return."

Levi and Strandberg tossed the notion around. They dubbed it Seed Capital II. Levi had become convinced that what he wanted VanCity to do needed to be taken outside VanCity proper, as it was currently operated. Traditional management tools for lending, not to mention management's cast of mind, simply did not apply to non-profit organizations. Strandberg had energy and interest and took over the leadership of the foundation idea from Leach, who had left the board. Strandberg began with research on existing community development examples—management wasn't doing it— and wrote down some criteria, trying to give the idea some practical focus. She then put together a board-management session to canvass what a foundation would look like.

The two sides, Strandberg recalled, spoke different languages. The board used community language, while management had more traditional ideas of charitable giving. Management also saw the foundation as a vehicle for members to leave money behind. Strandberg nevertheless was surprised by how much common ground there was and how much room she was given to lead the way, young as she was and new to the board. David Levi pushed the financing of non-profit enterprise. Bob Williams wanted a housing element. Community economic development at large was a component. Everyone agreed that helping economically marginalized people get on their feet, either with technical assistance or with the creation of new work, should be an objective. Strandberg drew up a mission statement for the embryonic VanCity Community Foundation and shopped it around. "I'm playing a community development role within my own credit union," she thought. She was elated when, later, Bob Quart suggested they put $1 million into the foundation for a start. The new VanCity agency seemed to be off and running, and she was its first chair.

The summer the VanCity Community Foundation was incorporated, in 1989, Strandberg flew to Chicago to attend a conference celebrating twenty-five years of community economic work in the United States. From her research, she knew the history of the work done in the United States. Now, suddenly, she was meeting the people she had read about. They represented a variety of organizations: community loan funds, community development credit unions, community development corporations and company-endowed foundations with huge assets, like the Ford Foundation.

They were helping poor people develop resources, create work and procure housing, all in a democratic, community-based way.

Strandberg dropped by the South Shore Bank in Chicago and visited some tenement housing it had helped rehabilitate. The bank was established in 1973 by a liberal democrat businessman and activist, Ronald Grzywinski, in partnership with a small group of investors and community organizations. The new organization had set out to revive the decaying neighbourhood where it was located. The group had since created a for-profit real estate development company and a non-profit community development company to work closely with the bank. Much of the financing involved housing, particularly the purchase and refurbishing of apartment buildings by local people, but the bank also provided loans for starting up or expanding small-scale businesses. Two characteristics marked its lending. It was willing to make loans based on character as much as on collateral, in a market that other banks shied away from, yet through a variety of means it had managed to keep its loan loss-ratio down. It also took pains to work with borrowers, often teaching them the business. By 1989, it had financed the renovation of seven thousand rental housing units in its lower-income area.

The South Shore wasn't the only dramatic example of community development. The Grameen Bank, on the other side of the world in Bangladesh, was also becoming fashionable in community economic development circles. The Grameen Bank lent mostly to women, whom it sought out in villages and persuaded that a small bit of cash, perhaps to buy a sewing machine or rice that could be husked and sold, could change their lives. Its loans were very small; "micro-lending" was the term for them. The bank had grown to serve close to two million customers, lending more than $1 million a day to the least creditworthy peasants. What made it revolutionary was the way it controlled defaults: It used peer pressure. Borrowers worked in groups of five, and no one received a new loan if any of them were behind in payments. As a result of this "peer-assisted lending," the bank had a 98 per cent loan recovery rate and consistently was in the black. "Poor women are better credit risks than rich men," economics professor Mohammed Yunus, the bank's founder, quipped.

All this activity summoned up the ethos of the early credit union movement. Strandberg returned from Chicago elated. She too, like Levi, began to see the advantages of a separate foundation. If the foundation were at arm's-length from VanCity, it was also at arm's-length from management. She and her VanCity board colleagues, when they set up the foundation's board, had a freer hand in shaping the organization and what it did—they could pilot ideas that would have been difficult to sell internally in VanCity itself.

The foundation board hired Robyn Allan, a senior economist at B.C. Central, as director. Allan had deep-rooted social beliefs about the economy. The primary resource of an economic system was people, Allan thought. Most people, given education and the tools or credit they needed, as well as an encouraging environment, were capable of creating their own well-being. This was the opposite of the notion of charity, in which the less-advantaged would be left with the thin, trickle-down leftovers of others.

Allan coined a slogan for the organization: "An investment in the human spirit." She tried making the foundation's outlook as free-spirited and imaginative as possible. The foundation helped establish a seniors' store in the downtown east side. It gave a grant to the Picasso Cafe, a restaurant that employed and trained former street youth. It assisted in the launching of Women Futures, a women's loan guarantee fund. The endowment was used to refinance the Mid-Main clinic. A later, similar allocation was made for a Chinese Mennonite seniors' housing project.

Allan became known for her high energy and intensity. Think-tank sessions were held, bringing people from outside VanCity to the credit union's boardroom. Contact was made with community groups. Guest speakers were brought in. All the programs the foundation assisted were businesses with a social mandate. The recipients and the foundation worked together on how to manage the merging of the social and financial goals in each case—in traditional business terms, a merging of contradictions. This was unexplored territory. In Canada, unlike the United States, there weren't many examples to follow.

Here, Strandberg's criteria came into play. The VanCity Community Foundation did not want to create dependency; it wanted to finance on the basis of a business plan. Key elements would be mentoring and connecting the community ventures to expertise, including VanCity volunteers. "Brokering expertise," it was called. Strandberg remembered this experimental period as a time of blossoming.

She was doing more reading and thinking about the subject, roughly categorized as "corporate social responsibility." She discovered a whole stream of business thought—found largely in academic literature, but nevertheless there—on business as a vehicle for social responsibility. There were organizations in the field, with names like Business for Social Responsibility and the World Business Academy, with well-known corporate members like Levi Strauss and Polaroid. A leading example was The Body Shop, with its dynamic, iconoclastic CEO, Anita Roddick. Corporate social responsibility was a movement emerging in the business world, unseen by most, which made the its discovery all the more exciting. The best part of it, for Strandberg, was that it touched her world, too.

She began marshalling arguments, including those framed in traditional business language. Even if VanCity were not a credit union, she maintained, it should operate with social values. There was a marketing case for it. The more that a business established strong social and community contacts, and the more this was reflected in the organization's culture, the more appropriate its products and services would be.

Strandberg's own vision of it, however, was much more profound, inspired by the literature: integrating social values holistically into a business organization. Proponents of the idea, including Strandberg, saw it as a paradigm shift—the next stage in the evolution of the business form that had begun in the nineteenth century with widespread incorporations. It meant a higher order of business and its role in the community, and for that higher order, a credit union was the most apt business organization of all.

Back on the ground, however, in the foundation's own operations, Strandberg found herself hobbled. The director, Robyn Allan, had left prematurely for a senior provincial government position. A capital campaign that Allan was trying to put together, aimed at raising $10 million, stalled. It was difficult in any case for the foundation of one business organization like VanCity to raise funds from other business organizations.

If running the foundation were only a matter of pushing grants out the door, this would not have been so important. The VanCity board, however, had chosen a slower, developmental model for the foundation, as distinct from simple aid, which, once spent, might not leave anything behind. This meant technical assistance, training, skills transfer, help to put deals together and other support, as well as providing funds—and that meant staff, and staff cost money, and for that there wasn't very much money at all. The minimum endowment for the foundation to be effective, according to specialists in the field, was $5 million to $10 million. The projects underwritten had been interesting enough, and the foundation had cut its teeth handling them, but the hopes for it being a dynamic catalyst of community econonomic change seemed, now, vastly overblown. The foundation was floundering. Strandberg went through six difficult months trying to keep it on track. She was uneasy and upset.

Into this tight corner stepped David Driscoll, hired as executive director in the spring of 1992. "Driscoll," as Strandberg described him, "was a renaissance kind of person." He grew up in Calder, a tough railroad neighbourhood in north Edmonton. His father worked for the CNR and was a union member. There was a strong anti-authoritarian disposition in the family, Driscoll remembered. He completed a master's degree in sociology at Simon Fraser University. His intellectual guru was Thorstein Veblen, the biting, turn-of-the-century American social critic and author of *The Theory of the Leisure Class*, a classic study mocking wealth and power.

Driscoll since had worked at everything from carpentry to being vice-principal of Douglas College, a local community college. When he was thirty-eight years old, in 1983, he became mayor of suburban Port Moody, where he lived. He stayed in the position for ten years, until he quit because of his VanCity work. He was creative and innovative. Port Moody became a model municipality for recycling. Driscoll tried to get people to see municipal government as simply community work and stewardship on behalf of friends and neighbours.

Driscoll believed deeply in the developmental model as different from the aid model, in helping the disadvantaged—economic empowerment rather than mere charity. He had been long familiar with the catch phrases of the approach, now become banal: "A hand up, not a handout," and "Give people fish and they will eat, teach people how to fish and they will eat forever." It was a matter of trusting the strengths, energy and inner resources of people, he thought, for they lived with their situation from day to day. That still left the question, however, of how Driscoll was going to manage at the foundation. With its overheads, and at the rate he expected the endowment to increase, the foundation would not be able to make any grants for five years—an intolerable irony and all the harder to swallow given the large expectations.

Driscoll decided that, at least at the beginning, he would be the only employee except for some part-time contract help, which meant both handling the administrative side and working in the field. He also changed the structure of the foundation. A typical foundation was hierarchical. Community groups made applications to the program director. The program director reviewed the applications, summarized them and made recommendations to the board. The board made its determination and sent it back down, and ultimately some grants would be made. Along the way, there might be requests for more information and more meetings. In Driscoll's experience, this long, drawn-out procedure exhausted the community groups in the process of getting their money. Given that the foundation was making grants in the lowly $3,000 to $5,000 range, this routine did not make sense to him, nor was it conceptually appropriate. "If we believe in community economic development," he argued, "we believe that these community groups have abilities and a sense of purpose and we should work with them hand-in-hand."

He was grumbling about this one day to a friend, who then told him of an unorthodox California foundation he had heard about. It had begun with five businessmen who wanted to do good works in their spare time. They each chose a project they believed in. Their relationship to the community groups they were helping, however, was reciprocal rather than hierarchical. They invited a representative from each of the groups to sit with them on their board, and they sat on the boards of the respective community groups in turn.

That was all Driscoll needed to hear. He proposed that the VanCity Community Foundation do much the same. Thereafter, "statutory" board members (looking after the pro forma legal requirements) and "community" board members (representatives from the community "partners") sat around the same table together. This intertwined arrangement validated community, Driscoll liked to say. It told the community groups that the foundation valued them as equals and that they were capable of achieving their objectives. They and the foundation were in a joint venture together.

Instead of a long drawn-out application procedure, Driscoll did an initial front-end assessment quickly, working mostly by telephone and getting a prompt "no" out to those with whom the foundation would likely not be working. With the others, he announced that he was prepared to spend some time developing a relationship. This usually did lead to a grant or other help, approved by the board. There was, of course, a condition. The group had to be committed to a structural change that would continue beyond the foundation's help, so that it would be able to sustain itself afterwards. In exchange, the foundation would make a commitment to work with the group over a three-to-five-year period.

Driscoll began, on that basis, to expand the foundation's activities. He used a hollow rubber chicken to demonstrate. "HEN," he called it. The "H" stood for housing initiatives, the "E" for employment initiatives, and the "N" for non-profit enterprise. In it, he stuffed filler representing loans, grants and technical systems. "This chicken is now much more nourishing," he would say. It was a silly routine, he knew, but it stuck in people's minds and gave the foundation a focus on three targeted areas.

The partnership programs multiplied. One of them, ASTEP, an acronym for Auto Service Training Employment Project, provided a six-month preapprenticeship course for young people coming out of foster care and group homes. PACE, or Prostitution Alternatives, Counselling and Education, was to provide a home base and services for youths and women in the sex trade who wanted out but faced job barriers. The Planned Lifetime Advocacy Network (PLAN), an organization trying to make provision for mentally disabled children after their parents died, was given some support. Programs like these involved only small annual grants, but they connected the recipient organizations to the foundation and to VanCity's expertise through volunteers.

Driscoll's relationship with Strandberg was fractious. She was passionate about the foundation and protective of it—"ferocious," Driscoll described her attitude. He knew she had held the organization together when it had no executive director. He also knew, from experience, the buffetting she must have taken from the VanCity board, since the foundation had seemed in that interlude to be stumbling. Now, however, he felt, she was intruding in his work, often trying to make decisions for him. He found her disruptive, untoward. Strandberg, however, wasn't prepared to stand back. She and her board colleagues, distraught by the hiatus in the foundation's development, had come to the conclusion that there had to be more oversight and accountability. That meant a well-defined plan with documented objectives that could be monitored. It was a battle of two strong wills, Strandberg recalled. Gradually they sorted themselves out.

Of all of the ideas for the foundation, the one that had the most credit union resonance was the Community Loan Fund. The two earlier loans, for the health clinic and seniors' housing, had used the endowment, but for relatively traditional purposes. The peer-assisted lending model, however, had generated interest in helping struggling individuals, as well. The Hebrew Assistance Association of Vancouver, which dated back to 1915, was another model. It operated a revolving fund that provided interest-free micro-loans to individuals.

Something called "heart loans," provided inside VanCity itself, also surfaced. Branch managers, it turned out, were making occasional small loans
to members in distress who wouldn't qualify under normal criteria. They
simply felt right doing it. One branch manager, Jay Tuason, would draw
a big heart on the back of the loan application she had just approved.
It wasn't a question of making bad loans, but of managing loans with
members who might have difficulty paying them back. Nobody knew how
frequently the loans were made, but an audit was ruled out so that branch
managers would not be made to feel uneasy about them. "Heart loans"
were left to the managers' discretion.

This discovery added to the sense that the foundation could do micro-
lending of its own, outside of traditional lending criteria. Driscoll put the
concept together, again using the endowment. The Community Loan Fund
was born. Its loans were to take character into account. "Character is
collateral," said an early piece of Community Loan Fund literature. The
fund's loans, like the earlier conventional ones, would be repaid and
recycled. They would be small in size and made to individuals and groups
who otherwise could not get credit.

Early loans went to a cookbook publisher, a leather crafter and a
chocolatier-mouldmaker team. Driscoll talked about "neighbour to neighbour" lending. One loan provided working capital to a container depot
operation in the downtown east side, United We Can, to handle empties
collected by dumpster divers and keep the handling fees in the community,
as well as to create a few jobs.

Developing self-reliance was one of the fund's stated objectives. The idea
of self-reliance could be played out at both ends of the political spectrum,
Driscoll knew. One connotation of the idea was right-wing, fashionable and
nasty: People should have to get their own jobs or otherwise pull themselves
up by the bootstraps; if they didn't, well, they deserved to sink out of sight.
"Go fix yourself," said this approach. The self-reliance Driscoll was after, by
contrast, was a community process by which borrowers were given not only a
financial boost but also support from the people around them. They were
expected in turn to contribute to the community by mentoring those who
would follow later. A record of community involvement was consequently a
useful qualification for borrowers under the program, in addition to the
required business plan and references.

The young foundation, as it evolved, was becoming part of VanCity itself.
Some VanCity staffers were volunteering in foundation-related activities,
like sitting on the boards of recipient organizations. A VanCity employee
and her family set up a family trust to be administered by the foundation.
The foundation also came in handy as an agent for the annual staff fund-
raiser. With the high-profit years of the early 1990s, VanCity's allocations to
the foundation's endowment were substantial, pushing the endowment
towards the $5 million mark, increasing income in turn and giving Driscoll
a little more leeway.

Strandberg was finally at peace with the foundation and stepped down as chair. She was pleased with what it had achieved, although far from requited. It seemed to her that only round one had been completed. One aspect frustrated and troubled her. The Community Loan Fund, she thought, had created a model of individual entrepreneurship, with self-improvement at its core. That might be fine in itself, but she had wanted the fund to invest in more community, collective, co-operative activity, which she believed was the basis of the credit union's work. In an age when people were so attuned to individual action, it was all the more important that such initiatives be undertaken by this one foundation at least.

The foundation, nevertheless, now had a strategic path. The organization and its partners had also proven themselves innovative. The projects expressed, too, the spirit of what Strandberg had been after. "From a values point of view," she reflected, "every one of these projects was a profound thing." It made her laugh to say so—the words sounded so pretentious, but that was the way she felt.

The same culture was cropping up elsewhere in the organization, feeding back from the foundation and VanCity Enterprises as they established their presence. VanCity Enterprises continued to show a flair for innovation. For Chris Catliff, the young business analyst who had taken over the management of the subsidiary, it was a fascinating, all-consuming business. To get projects underway, one brought together non-profit groups, donators of land, housing advocates and consultants, municipal government, provincial government departments, Central Mortgage and Housing Corporation (for a federal loan guarantee), architects and contractors. "You have so many balls in the air," he reflected. "You go along with some people, then they fall apart and you grab another group to work with. You have to know what's going on with all the groups, so you do all the community functions, a lot of city council meetings, other meetings that go on in the background. You mingle with the housing consultants doing the work. It's amazing what goes on." He thought of it as a political process more than anything else.

VanCity Enterprises, in one novel undertaking, had even found a way to give low-income people equity in their housing, despite high land prices. It had underwritten an apartment development on the west side in which four units were sold at below-market prices, for low-income single parents. The ingenuity lay in what would follow. The buyers, as they paid off their mortgages, would own their units and could sell them, but only at a below-market price in turn, so there would be no taking advantage of the lower entry price and so the units would continue to be available to those with lower incomes.

Bob Williams, who had created VanCity Enterprises, felt that it needed to be quite large to achieve its potential. Catliff saw it differently. He promoted the notion of an award-winning, caring developer undertaking pilot projects that nobody else would take on. Bob Quart was on Catliff's side. Williams had wonderful ideas, Quart allowed, but their scale was too great.

"At the end of the day, I'm here to protect depositors," he said. Neither Quart nor Williams knew how much of an old disagreement it was—shades of an exasperated Lloyd Widdifield, seeing large and wonderful housing possibilities for VanCity, but unable to make headway with a stubborn, financially conservative Don Bentley.

For Catliff, VanCity Enterprises projects involved intense management and, because of their complexity, seemed to take forever to put together. As each of them was completed, however, something exceptional in terms of design, affordability or livability had been done. The projects worked, Catliff realized, only because VanCity's name was associated with them. Other people put up money because they trusted VanCity not to exploit them. Enterprises could bring expertise and its own capital to a non-profit group and make a project happen. VanCity staff themselves chose an Enterprises project for one of their annual fundraisers—a Coast Foundation residence for the mentally ill.

Other aspects of the credit union's social role were maturing. The board's community donations program was now underwriting more than fifty projects a year. The "corporate social role" was a separate category in the planning process. At one of those planning sessions, a representative of the Vermont National Bank made a presentation about a socially responsible fund at the bank. Inspired by the example, VanCity launched its equivalent, the Community Investment Deposit, in 1993. It was a special term deposit paying 1 per cent less interest than the usual VanCity rate and providing loans at 1 per cent lower interest in turn. Its object was to underwrite community betterment initiatives, starting with affordable housing and environmental work. An advisory council was formed to recommend projects. Unlike other deposit products in Canada, the Community Investment Deposit let VanCity members know exactly where their money was being invested.

It seemed unrealistic to expect members to invest money at a below-market rate of interest, but after a few years the account held almost $5 million, with $1 million of that out in development loans to housing and environmental projects. Most of the deposits were small—the average was only $2,000—but in aggregate, the money had piled up. Depositors were doing something with their money that they were happy about.

The Community Investment Deposit wasn't a new idea at VanCity. Bob McMaster, VanCity's original lawyer, had come up with the concept in 1968 and called it the Social Development Term Deposit. Low-cost and low-rental housing were the possibilities he had thought of. A questionnaire was sent out to members, many of whom responded favourably, so the board decided to go ahead. When a meeting was held to make sure potential depositors understood the plan, however, only McMaster, his wife, and McMaster's legal sidekick Bill Wright showed up. The proposed account was dropped "for lack of interest." Now, twenty-five years later, it had been reincarnated.

The "heart loans" weren't new at VanCity, either. They hearkened back to similar dispensations the credit committee used to hand out in the late 1940s, at the rate of one such loan per meeting. "Boy Scout loans," they were called then.

Pieter Van Gils, a socially minded free spirit who had worked briefly for the VanCity Community Foundation, was introducing another kind of lending. Van Gils had become a one-person community economic development department. The heart loans and the foundation's Community Loan Fund had started him thinking. There were a lot of people who had been thrown out of work or were otherwise unemployed, who might want to start up a micro-enterprise, but who had little or no collateral for a loan and also fell beyond the ambit of the loan fund. Van Gils began sketching out a lending idea that might help them. He dismissed peer-assisted lending. The group pressure that made it work, in Bangladesh or elsewhere, was difficult or impossible to replicate in a metropolis, he thought. He came up with something quite different—"self-reliance loans."

Unlike the Community Loan Fund, self-reliance loans were issued by loan staff in the branches. The loan limit was set at $15,000, three times the limit for the Community Loan Fund. The loans were available for expanding a business and not just for an initial self-development stage. They were, in effect, the next step up. Interest was prime plus 4 per cent, to cover the risk, but the rate wasn't all that important to borrowers, since the loans weren't large and borrowers could take five years to retire them. What they most badly needed was access to credit.

The self-reliance loans were the true successor to the failed Seed Capital Program. Van Gils lived with the fall-out of that program. The Seed Capital lending had been targeted at beginners with a bright idea, so while borrowers might have completed a business course to qualify, they were all novices. The self-reliance loans allowed for a mix of borrowers, some of whom might have long experience and even equity of their own. This made prospects better. Van Gils nevertheless treaded carefully. There was no advertising or mailouts for the program. Van Gils did not want to create false expectations. VanCity simply made the loans available and waited for people to come into the branch by word of mouth or chance inquiry. Van Gils calculated that the branches needed to have $500,000 in the portfolio before he and the others would be able to make a judgement on how well the program was doing.

It was the manner in which the loans were made, though, that Van Gils knew was truly significant. They were done within the branch system, not in some attached agency. They were based primarily on character and credit history rather than cash flow and collateral, like other loans. References by other people in the business community, proclaiming faith in the applicant's ability, were useful for an applicant. The self-reliance loans were character lending in the classic sense, just as had been envisaged by Alphonse Desjardins when he held his initial organizing meetings for a caisse populaire in Lévis.

Van Gils, who had a philosophical turn of mind, understood the connection. He talked about paying close attention to the fundamentals of co-operatives and trying to apply those principles fifty years after VanCity's inception. VanCity, in niches within its $4 billion financial structure, was recreating its original self.

In April 1995, a dinner was held in the Raintree Restaurant, in Vancouver's West End, to honour Bob Williams. Williams had been on the board for four three-year terms—the maximum continuous tenure allowed—and a gathering for someone so prominent wasn't surprising. It was an intimate affair, with just board members and senior management present.

Nobody roasted Williams. The problem, quipped Chris Catliff, was that Williams was now chair of VanCity Enterprises and none of them were sure that he was actually leaving and might not be back. Williams, apprised of being so intimidating, could only shrug philosophically. He didn't understand that, he said.

There were pleasant speeches by management and by the outgoing VanCity chair, Shirley Chan. Bob Quart spoke of Williams's humanity, his concern for ordinary people and of some things the two of them had done together. The warmest speech came from Wendy Holm. Serving on the board with Williams, she said, was like taking a master's degree in governance.

Williams hid his feelings. Linda Crompton, now president of Citizens Trust, and who, among senior management, had most furthered Williams's objectives, thought Williams was genuinely touched and hurt about having to go. VanCity had been a big part of his life.

Underneath the surface, the same split about how to deal with Williams was still very much alive. There was a widespread feeling that Williams had done himself damage and hurt his effectiveness by his bluntness. On the other hand, with his originality and forcefulness he gave something to VanCity that nobody else could have. Steve Waddell, who had left the board to become director of a community economic program in Boston, wondered whether the board would have been successful without Williams. He doubted it. This was a widespread feeling, too, particularly on the board side—that Williams was the key player in changing the face of VanCity and revitalizing it, and that without his strength, the change would not have happened.

In any case, they all realized, like it or not, that was the way Williams was.

CHAPTER 62

The Future World

GUESTS ARRIVED IN ANTIQUE CARS, a 1947 antique bus, a bicycle caval-cade and aboard the SkyTrain. They were greeted by two lion dances making their way from VanCity's nearby Chinatown branch. Charter members Martha Mackie and Bill Ramsell were there. So were provincial premier Mike Harcourt, other political dignitaries, VanCity chair Francesca Zumpano and CEO Bob Quart. The occasion was the opening of the new head-office building at Terminal and Quebec, just east of Main, at the head of False Creek. The date was November 1995.

The distinctively designed, pillared building, faced with glass, was twelve storeys high. It straddled the SkyTrain, whose Main Street/Science World station was immediately next door. Every possible environmental and energy-saving feature had been included in the building. Underneath the SkyTrain tracks, beside the building, an alternative transportation centre and a bicycle repair and rental shop were about to be installed. The two projects were the work of Better Environmentally Sound Transportation, a non-profit society that VanCity had consulted and that it was helping with, among other things, a loan from the Community Investment Deposit. The building's location, with its access to SkyTrain, also was an environmental statement. A day-care centre was available next door in the Citygate complex.

Bob Quart, at the opening, made sure to point out that the building wasn't alongside the large bank towers of downtown Vancouver. Real estate agents were baffled that VanCity had preferred, instead, to build in a formerly decaying neighbourhood outside the downtown core, but Quart and the board wanted deliberately to be elsewhere and had other things in mind. The building was more accessible eastward, in a gateway position. By coincidence, it wasn't far from the Dominion Bank Building on Hastings, where VanCity, under the B.C. Credit Union League umbrella, had come into the world. The streetcar that Martha Mackie had taken to work each morning had passed right by, on Main Street.

With the head-office move, Branch 1 at Broadway and Oak was closed and relocated in a much smaller space in the new building. Most of the members in the old Branch 1 had long since moved to other parts of the Lower Mainland and would use branches there. A great deal had changed since 1971, when the gala opening at Broadway and Oak had touched off

Plan 24 magic and astonished Don Bentley. As head-office employees now settled into their new quarters, they faced a world that was much more competitive, one in which the banks and trust companies were trying hard to be friendly and were almost VanCity's technological equal—a world where retail banking itself was undergoing watershed change.

For George Scott, in marketing and planning, VanCity and the credit union movement were facing a world almost unrecognizable from that of the past. Providing access to credit for the "small guy" and being able to get a fair return on a small amount of money were the big issues for credit unions in the 1940s and 1950s. All that had since gone away. The credit unions' not-for-profit ethos, however, still applied. The role that arose from that ethos, trying to improve life in the community, was going to grow. The social safety net was weakening. More and more people were being marginalized in the economy, without work or left to their own devices. This opened up fertile ground for VanCity to act as a catalyst and provide solutions. VanCity's community economic development work was a beginning. VanCity was also looking at actively helping out home-based businesses, a growing phenomenon.

VanCity would have to manage its costs in routine transactions, Scott also thought. It would have to make it more appealing for members to handle those on their own. Branches were not going to close, but they would be doing different things in the future. Information would become a leading product. If, for example, a nineteen-year-old came in for a car loan, the member representative should be able to give that member budget help, also information on how best to pick a car and information for that person's other objectives, say, a start-up micro-business sometime in the future. Members should intuitively be looking to VanCity as a source of information. With technology, there wouldn't be much "product" in routine transactions anymore. They would be a "commodity" that everybody would be providing at slimmer and slimmer margins. The relationship of VanCity to its members—what it could offer on top of transactions—would be the key.

Wayne McKay, doing consulting work for smaller credit unions, had his eye on the banks. He saw credit unions banding together to take advantage of economies of scale and to be able to compete with the bank monsters. They had no choice, McKay thought. Consumers more and more didn't care whether they were dealing with a credit union or a bank, as long as they got the service they wanted. That was sad but it was the reality, he argued. Indeed, all credit unions in the province should merge together. He wished it didn't have to happen—he liked those individual operations—but there was no help for it. The credit union movement couldn't afford to have a hundred CEOs and a hundred boards and senior managements much longer. There could be local advisory boards to set policies for local communities. B.C. Central and its overhead costs would disappear in such a restructuring.

This was the idea of "One Big Credit Union," from the late 1960s, all over again. Where VanCity fitted into this, McKay wasn't sure. VanCity was a hybrid. It already had some economies of scale, but could use more. Whatever the structure, the system needed VanCity in order to be workable.

Bob Quart saw a world full of competitive challenges, but that was normal. "We're threatened every day," he said, "threatened by people that have big pockets." Canadians said they hated the banks but they did business with them, he explained. The banks dominated the market. Research showed they were among the most trusted companies in the country. At least, though, the habit of hating banks allowed VanCity to make a difference, by being more personable and more caring.

Quart wanted to send out a wake-up call to the credit union movement. He sounded like Don Bentley thirty-five years earlier. He was concerned that most credit unionists didn't see the looming threat of bank power, as the banks swallowed trust and brokerage companies and began moving into insurance. "We're very complacent," he said. "We cannot rely on local identities to be our success of the future. A lot of people believe because we're local and have democratic principles, our future is assured. I don't buy that."

He wanted credit unions to be able to take greater advantage of what they had: their relationship with members. Linda Crompton remembered attending a conference at which she had registered as CEO of Citizens Trust. One of the bankers had stood up in the proceedings and observed, "I can say this because there are no credit unions here. Credit unions have what we want, carrying enormous value in their membership connection. Luckily for us, they don't know what they're sitting on." Quart did know what he was sitting on.

The array of services would also have to change, Quart thought. With the population growing older, VanCity culturally needed to shift its focus from mortgages to retirement counselling, tax counselling and trust services. In fifteen years, wealth management would be VanCity's business, Quart felt. It was important to be in that business rather than let competitors have it. Business lending would also become a more important part of VanCity, especially with more people working at home.

VanCity, in Quart's mind, was well-positioned to take all of this on. The smaller a credit union was, though, the smaller the chance that it would be able to cope. Yet if credit unions did get together, they could become a formidable force. Quart wasn't sure how this was going to happen, given how divided the credit union movement seemed to be. The very suggestion raised prickly political questions about territory. He wasn't thinking so much of mergers as of strategic alliances. Some arrangement had to be found in which all credit unions provided the same range of services and shared a powerful, common presence with the public. This was a profound matter, Quart reflected. He felt himself politically hamstrung. "You talk about it as much as you can," he said. "I think we're going to have some nasty surprises. Unfortunately that's usually the way things work. Somebody has to rattle your cage."

Whatever the size of the large banks, VanCity was irrepressible, enthusiastic. Richard Wafer was buoyant. Over the last six or seven years, the people at VanCity had quietly built an organization financially strong on its feet and they were leaders in pioneering a social role. It was true that they had to constantly assess their market and stay ahead technologically, but they had always done that. Wafer was pleased with the new lending experiments, in which character was taken into account, as different from the the the banks, with their restrictive checklists. VanCity might even take equity positions in cases, instead of being just a lender. "We can weather any storms thrown at us," Wafer said. "Members will be well looked after."

For Larry Wald, in charge of non-branch sales, size and a full array of services were obviously going to be requirements in going against the big guns down the street, but it was even more important to retain the family feeling internally at VanCity despite its burgeoning expansion. This was becoming tougher and tougher to do. Wald, since his days as personnel manager, had always been fascinated with what made VanCity tick. "Why we are as competitive as we are, and supportive as we are, and participative as we are, is quite frankly a mystery," he said. Hiring practices, which had emphasized communicative skills, had contributed. Looking to each other as people rather than as technicians was another part of it, Wald thought. Wayne McKay had obviously been a factor, not only in himself but in the people he had attracted to the group. The organization seemed to have a will of its own, so strong that it could override even the intrusion of a contrary force like Dennis Lunney. For Wald, though, that only begged the question of how it had come about. Whatever the seed that had been planted somewhere back in time, the challenge was never to lose the awareness of what made VanCity different.

In 1996 David Levi, like Bob Williams before him, retired from the board after four consecutive terms, but he was still the same bright, boyish enthusiast who had come to the board, full of curiosity, in 1984. He disagreed with many on staff who feared that the march of banking technology might undermine VanCity's strength. The high-tech world had been a boon to smaller organizations like VanCity, Levi said, rather than a threat. Technology had allowed them to provide as much or more service than the banks. It had always been VanCity's success. New technology, combined with the personal touch of being a community organization, foreshadowed a huge role for VanCity, he argued.

Even when members rarely went into their branch, the branch connection was still there. They belonged to VanCity in the first place because they liked the community feeling of it, its localness and the service level. VanCity's highest penetration rates were in neighbourhoods as diverse as West Vancouver, Kitsilano, First and Commercial, and Burnaby. VanCity was a reflection of Vancouver itself. It was the human richness and variety of the people of the region—its urban vibrancy—that made VanCity so strong and different even from other credit unions.

Predictions of apocalyptic change were also off the mark, Levi thought. Residential mortgages would long be a major activity. The key for the board, in the future, was to make sure that VanCity did not become an elitist organization.

For agro-economist and consultant Wendy Holm, belonging to VanCity meant never having to say you're sorry. Everyone needed a chequing account, or a savings account or a mortgage. Being a member of VanCity meant having those and other services, with nothing missing, while at the same time helping the rest of the community. Every single transaction one enters into has ethics, she maintained. Where do the profits of that transaction end up? At VanCity, they stayed at home, were applied ethically and made one's community a better place in which to live.

Larry Bell, now CEO of Shato Holdings, a private holding company that among other things owned the White Spot restaurant chain, waxed strategically as ever about VanCity. There were two forces at play in our society, Bell thought. One was the supranational organizations like NAFTA, the World Trade Organization, multinational corporations and the global financial players moving funds around the world. They eroded nation states. Even the Canadian chartered banks, which had been national icons of a sort, weren't national any longer. They had gone North American and, from their point of view, they had to go that way.

People's natural defence, in the face of all this, was to pull back, Bell continued. They might, in another era, have looked to the nation state, but it had lost much of its relevance. They perceived the province as more important than they had in the past. Local institutions became more important to them, too. They wanted something they could touch and feel an affinity to, that they could control and that gave them a sense of participation. Organizations like VanCity, Richmond Savings and Surrey Metro Savings were going to have a bigger market share, Bell was convinced. "People are just going to want the comfort of dealing with something that's in their community and part of it," Bell said.

For Bob Williams, VanCity was at a major crossroads, and it worried him as much as anything with which he had been involved. He was thinking of a management proposal for virtual banking, if not by VanCity itself, then by Citizens Trust; the trust company, federally chartered, could roam far afield. There were already models for it in the United States and Great Britain, and they were successful. Virtual banking was all done by telephone, with only field offices to manage its mortgages and loans. By stripping overhead down to this minimum, it gained an edge in pricing. It would also require significant capital. Williams was concerned that such an investment would detract from what VanCity might otherwise be able to do. "I always felt that if we really worked on our regional niche and the broader community social responsibility, then to some extent the business would look after itself," he said. He wondered, glumly, if that might be a bit naive.

One area where he thought VanCity could play a major role was in the redevelopment of the old industrial parts of the city on both sides of the new head office, through VanCity Enterprises. He envisaged creating whole new neighbourhoods, reflecting a range of community interests. He was particularly encouraged by the possibilities in housing in which the very poor could have some equity.

He was more and more convinced, too, that, given the tenor of the times, VanCity should think of a quasi-governmental role for itself. He talked about the foundation's support for the Planned Lifetime Advocacy Network (PLAN), founded by a group of older parents who wanted to guarantee the future quality of life for their adult children with mental disabilities. Because of PLAN's connection to VanCity, VanCity Trust Services began assisting the parents with estate planning, the creation of discretionary trusts and the appointment of trustees and executors. The deposits that came in for trust purposes quickly amounted to a fair chunk of money. With the estate and trust services flowing from it as well, this represented a new niche business. "The buzz of family and friends is very significant," Williams described it. "We're playing a whole new role."

Joy Leach, who had been chair in 1987, was convinced that VanCity's strong public profile, especially its connection to community, would underpin its future. Her children would never go to banks, she said. She had heard the same kind of comments from others. "People will always be looking to put their money in an institution that's loyal to its place," she said. The reason that VanCity was so strong, she thought, was that members really did feel a part of it. People actually loved the institution. She realized that others might laugh at her for saying so—might dismiss her perception as fanciful—but she nevertheless thought it was true.

Peter Cook, who had retired as CEO of Citizens Trust, thought VanCity had a bright future. It was, for Cook, a matter of basics. The co-operative form of organization was an extremely effective and efficient way to deliver services to people. It was a better form than the joint-stock corporation, like a bank, because it forced everybody concerned to focus on service delivery instead of the profit motive. That paid tremendous dividends. The crucial problem for co-operatives was to find sufficient capital on which the rest of the operation rested, and VanCity seemed to have solved that one.

Cook admitted that the banks had done their market research and were saying things in their advertising that people wanted to hear. Could they, though, really perform the way a credit union could? He didn't think so. The banks would never be able to get around the fact that credit unions were local and had members. The banks talked a good story, but they didn't deliver the same story in the branches, where it counted, the way that credit unions did.

If there were a serious challenge for VanCity, Cook thought, it was in lending. The mortgage market was filling up. About 70 per cent of credit union assets were in mortgages, but that number would progressively slip downwards. VanCity would have to find something to make up the difference.

In the next couple of decades, the new financial needs would come from people moving to home-based businesses and creating their own jobs. VanCity would have to find a way of supporting them, just as it had supported the baby-boomers with mortgages and the baby-boomers' parents with personal loans. Such lending would require a wholesale change in the way VanCity operated. It would move VanCity back into character lending. It would be more intensive, with different techniques of making judgements. For Cook, though, it had to be done. If VanCity failed to capture that future, he thought, it might well survive, but it wouldn't be the force it had been.

Coro Strandberg, although no longer chair of the VanCity Community Foundation, was still caught up with its potential. She envisaged VanCity exporting the model. "Look at the way we've integrated social values," she wanted to say to the world. She had seen so much hope and passion in the people the foundation had worked with. If anything best symbolized VanCity's future, she thought, it was that kindling of the human spirit.

Dick Monrufet, the Stry Credit Union and B.C. Credit Union League hand, going back in time, was almost eighty years old when VanCity's new head office at Terminal and Quebec opened its doors. Monrufet and his wife, Betty, another veteran credit union partisan, were living at Mill Bay, on Vancouver Island.

"Credit unions are here to stay," he said. "They're going to be throwing a lot of weight around." He thought that credit unions and banks would go head to head for a while. It was true, he allowed, that credit unions were a different animal from what they had been in their early days, and now in many ways resembled banks. Even with their size, though, credit unions were different. They still had social significance. There was hope that they would retain the common touch. They had, after all, pioneered credit in Canada for the average citizen, and that legacy, so profound, would always endure.

You could use VanCity as an example, he said. "I take my hat off to them," he explained. "They might be the largest credit union in the country, but they've done a tremendous job keeping the grassroots approach, with their community work. The board of directors is just tremendous. It's impressive. They did better than I ever dreamed that they would."

At the beginning of 1996, in announcing the dividend and patronage refunds for the previous year, VanCity issued a little leaflet for members, entitled "A Shared Success." It included a few paragraphs about the dividend and rebates and also a short account of recent innovations, like new branches and VanCity Direct. One section dealt with how VanCity had shared its success with the community. "In a world of increasing social and environmental distress," it said, "our goal is to celebrate and encourage equality, generosity and positive change."

It appeared they had indeed done it, and much else.

The VanCity building blocks continued to rise into the sky.

Index